Developing dBASE IV™ Applications

Programming with the dBASE® Template Language

Developing dBASE IV™ *Applications*

Programming with the dBASE® Template Language

Tony Lima

Addison-Wesley Publishing Company, Inc.

Reading, Massachusetts   Menlo Park, California   New York
Don Mills, Ontario   Wokingham, England   Amsterdam   Bonn
Sydney   Singapore   Tokyo   Madrid   San Juan

Library of Congress Cataloging-in-Publication Data
Lima, Tony.
   Developing dBASE IV Applications: Programming with the dBASE
   Template Language / Tony Lima
      p.   cm.
   Includes index.
   ISBN 0-201-19798-7
   1. Database management. 2. dBASE IV (Computer program)
   I.Title
   QA76.9.D3L562 1989
   005.75'65--dc20   89-15187
                                                          CIP

Cover design by Doliber Skeffington
Set in 11-point Times Roman by Context, Inc., San Diego, CA

ISBN 0-201-19798-7
ABCDEFGHIJ-AL-89
First printing, October 1989

Contents

Preface   ix

Part I   Building Blocks   1

          Chapter 1   Introduction: Let dBASE IV Do the Work   3
                      What is the Template Language?   3
                      A Programming Cookbook   4
                      Specific Templates and dBASE IV Activities 5
                      What About QBE?   8
                      Objects: dBASE IV and Templates   8
                      Putting the Pieces Together   13
                      Conclusion   14

          Chapter 2   Views and Query By Example   17
                      Select, Project, Inner Joins, and Outer Joins 18
                      Calculated Fields and Summary Operators   30
                      Grouping, Sorting, and Summary Operators   37
                      LIKE and SOUNDS LIKE Queries   43
                      Update Queries   47
                      Conclusion   51

          Chapter 3   An Overview of Templates   53
                      Elements of a Template Program   53
                      BUILTIN.DEF   64
                      Conclusion   64

          Chapter 4   Screen Forms and Templates   65
                      What Must a Template Do?   66
                      A Simple Data Entry Screen   66
                      Creating the Format File   82

Adding Multiuser Code   89
@ . . . SAY . . . GETs Processing   90
The New Format File   99
Conclusion   103
Appendix A: Substituting for Default GEN Files   104
Appendix B: FORM.COD   105
Appendix C: Constants File FORM.DEF   115

Chapter 5   Labels and Templates   119
What Does a Label Template Do?   119
A Simple Label Setup   120
The Label Template Code   128
Label Printing Code   137
Output User-defined Functions   144
Conclusion   158
Appendix: LABEL.COD   159

Chapter 6   The Report Generator   179
What Does a Report Template Do?   179
The Report Template Code   190
Procedures and Functions   205
Conclusion   210
Appendix: REPORT.COD   211

Part II   Building and Documenting Applications   255

Chapter 7   Quick Applications   257
A Quick Application   258
Comments and Fixes   261
Recommended Changes   262
Conclusion   273
Appendix A: QUICKAPP.COD   274
Appendix B: CUSTOMER.PRG   292
Appendix C: New CUSTOMER.PRG   304

Chapter 8   The Applications Generator   319
The Applications Generator Templates   320
Fixing Two Major Problems   320
Leave Out Code You Don't Need   328
A Sample Application   332
Conclusion   354

	Appendix A: CUSTAPP.PRG	355
	Appendix B: KEYSET.PRG	369
	Appendix C: CUSTABAR.PRG	371
	Appendix D: Applications Generator Template	377
Chapter 9	**Documenting Your Applications**	**433**
	Using the Documentation Template	434
	Conclusion	441
	Appendix: CUSTAPP.DOC	442
Part III	**Special Template Language Features**	**449**
Chapter 10	**A Special Template: FORMBROW.GEN**	**451**
	Using FORMBROW	452
	And the Result Is . . .	456
	A Brief Look at FORMBROW.COD	460
	Conclusion	472
	Appendix A: CUSTINV.SCX	473
	Appendix B: CUSTINV.QBE	474
	Appendix C: CUSTINV.PRG	475
Chapter 11	**The Template Compiler and Debugger**	**487**
	Debugging Strategy	487
	Step 1: Compile Your Program	488
	Step 2: Using the Debugger	489
	Compiler and Debugger Option Switches	497
	Conclusion	499
	The Future	**501**
Appendix	**Template Language Operators, Commands, and Functions**	**503**
	Index	**519**

Preface

"Develop applications without programming." For years, database products have held out the promise of this nirvana to programmers. And certainly progress has been made. Those who remember dBASE II and other CP/M products constantly rejoice at the power and scope of tools available today.

dBASE IV introduces a powerful new tool to the market: the template language. It offers what developers have dreamed of for years — a programmable program generator. Once you have programmed a template, all the dBASE IV code produced from that point on will reflect the way you have programmed the template. Everyone who routinely writes dBASE programs should know something about the template language. At a bare minimum, you should know how to make minor changes to the existing dBASE IV templates — adding, deleting, or modifying to suit your particular style and preferences.

This book is for anyone who is tired of writing the same type of dBASE program over and over again, which was exactly my situation when I first saw the template language in January 1988. Since then, I've followed its development with intense interest. The template language has now sufficiently advanced to the point that there is little reason to ever write much dBASE code by hand again.

About This Book

This is not a book on the theory of template languages, 3GLs versus 4GLs, or CASE tools in general. It's much closer in spirit to *The Joy of Cooking* than to Kernighan and Ritchie's magnum opus on the C language. We're going to be concerned with understanding the templates shipped with the dBASE IV Developer's Edition, seeing how they work, and making changes to them that (in some cases) are essential to making them useful. We'll explore all the files in depth, pointing out where changes should be made and the exact command syntax to use. Along the way, other changes will be suggested that you might want to use on your own.

If you want to know more about the dBASE IV template language but have trouble wading through syntactical or theoretical descriptions of a language, this book is for you. If you just want to improve the current dBASE IV templates, you'll find some of the routines in here essential. I've tried to keep explanations clear and concise. Frankly, the template language manual included with dBASE IV is inadequate for understanding how to use the language. That's why I wrote this book — so you won't have to go through what I did learning how to use the templates.

The first six chapters introduce the template language and walk through the three basic objects: screen forms, reports, and labels. Through an extensive series of examples, the relationship between the dBASE IV programs and the templates is explained in a way you can easily understand.

Part II shifts gears to a certain extent, concerning itself more with how to use elements of the applications generator and somewhat less with the template programs themselves. Chapter 7 covers the quick application generator and recommends numerous changes that make the quick application useful. Chapter 8 covers the overall applications generator, but focuses largely on producing an application and looking at the different functions available; however, a few changes to the applications generator templates are suggested. Finally, Chapter 9 examines the dBASE IV documentation generator and shows how to use it to document your finished applications.

Part III shifts gears once again. Chapter 10 looks at a special template, FORMBROW.GEN, that allows browsing data from three different databases. Many of the techniques used in that template are unique and do not appear in others. Chapter 11 covers the template compiler and debugger. Options, commands, and functions are discussed. Several batch files are suggested to ease the painful process of debugging template programs.

The Appendix to the book contains a complete list of template language operators, commands, and functions, with concise explanations of each.

Using This Book

In a number of places, the code is simply too long to fit on a single line without shrinking the type to an unreadable size. Therefore, I have broken the line. You'll be able to recognize this because there will be no line number on the continuation. When this happens, you can assume the line without a number is supposed to be continued at the end of the previous line.

Other Recommended Reading

For a complete reference book on the template language, find *The Template Programming Language* by Dan Aspenwall and Gary Carter (Tate Publishing, 1989). Aspenwall and Carter designed the template language. I would like to thank them for providing me with an advance copy of the manuscript for that fine reference work. Naturally, the dBASE IV template language and applications generator manuals are also required reading.

However, none of those works concerns itself with *using* the template language or, especially, with getting the most out of the templates shipped with dBASE IV itself. That's what this book is for.

And Thanks to . . .

This book would never have been written without the support of many people. Dan Aspenwall, Gary Carter, and Kirk Nason of Ashton-Tate were kind enough to respond to my questions in a timely manner. Without them, there would certainly be more inaccuracies in this book than is the case.

My editor, Julie Stillman, encouraged me throughout this effort, put up with numerous delays and changes in the outline, and finally got the book to production. She gets a gold star for heroism under fire. Of course, without my terrific agents Michael Larsen and Elizabeth Pomada, I would never have met Julie and this book would never have been.

A special note of thanks to Kevin Strehlo and Jim Fawcette of *DBMS* magazine, who commissioned an article comparing four dBASE template languages for an early edition of that magazine. This stimulated my interest and gave me an opportunity to compare dBASE IV with others in the field.

As always, thanks go to my wife, Gloria Gale, who saw me through some very bad times while this book was being written. This book is dedicated to her and to my parents, Ed and Hazel Lima.

Tony Lima

Part I

Building Blocks

Part I deals with the building blocks of an application: queries, screen forms, labels, and reports. I call these objects building blocks because they make up the foundation of every application. dBASE IV will work best if you create each of the pieces of your application first, then use the applications generator to pull them together and document them.

Following an overview of the activities and objects that can be manipulated by the template language, this section covers the code Query By Example produces; examines the parts of a template program; then moves on to the templates for screen forms, labels, and reports. When you have completed Part I, you will understand how the template language works with dBASE IV objects to generate program code; what kind of code QBE generates and how to modify it for more efficient execution; how each of the other three templates processes its respective object; and how to modify the standard dBASE IV templates to improve their performance and make them generate code the way you want it written.

Chapter 1

Introduction: Let dBASE IV Do the Work

The purpose of this book is to show you how to develop applications in dBASE IV while writing only a minimum of dBASE IV program code. Instead of concentrating on mundane code, you will learn to make good use of the screen objects, such as screen forms and reports, and to change the existing templates to generate dBASE IV code written to your specifications. If that sounds impossible, read on. You're in for some very pleasant surprises.

Always remember this: If you write a line of code in one dBASE IV program, you'll probably write a line of code like it in every other program you ever produce; if you write a line of code in the template language, dBASE will automatically write that line of dBASE IV code for you in all your future programs. The key to productive, efficient programming is to understand when to change the templates and when to actually write the dBASE code itself. Philosophically, that's what this book is all about.

What is the Template Language?

The template language is a programmable program generator. Templates process various dBASE IV objects and produce program code from them. A template program contains the code that specifies the type of object to be processed, the "selectors" that will be used in the processing, and the commands to produce the appropriate code.

dBASE IV objects consist of the special format files it produces. These include screen forms (.SCR), reports (.FRM), labels (.LBL), applications

(.APP), light-bar menus (.BAR), pop-up menus (.POP), and a variety of pick list objects. Screen forms, reports, and labels have specific code generators: FORM.GEN, REPORT.GEN, and LABEL.GEN. When working with the applications generator, on the other hand, you can specify the template you want to use before the code is generated.

The concept of "selectors" is crucial to understanding the template language. Selectors are the elements contained in each object that pass information to the template. For example, there are selectors that return the name of the current database or view, the multiple index tag, the name of any index files used, the name of the file being processed, and so on. The trick of writing templates is to become familiar with the selectors used in each object, learn what information they contain, and see how to use the information to produce the dBASE code you want to use.

One important class of selectors is database fields, calculated fields, and memory variables. The control structure FOREACH FIELD_ELEMENT processes fields sequentially and produces the appropriate output. For a field in a screen form, the loop must process all the clauses for @ . . . SAY . . . GET commands, including picture functions and templates (not to be confused with processing templates), validation and message clauses, and so on. For a field in a report, on the other hand, the template must process print styles, print locations, and other field attributes used in reports. The dBASE IV templates include code that keeps them from processing a report object with the screen form template (for example).

Templates must be compiled before dBASE IV can use them. The template compiler is included with the Developer's Edition, as well as source code files for all templates.

A Programming Cookbook

This book is probably best described as a "cookbook." This is not a book about the theory of template languages, programming theory, or any related esoteric subject. Instead, its objective is to show you how to fine-tune the templates shipped with the Developer's Edition to produce the kind of program code you want. In other words, you're going to learn how to make dBASE IV produce programs written in your style. If you have labored for hours over mundane (but complex!) report programs, you can rejoice — dBASE IV frees you from the shackles of writing dull code one line at a time and lets you concentrate your programming efforts where they belong: on the complicated, tricky modules.

To develop application programs efficiently in dBASE IV, the trick is to let dBASE IV write most of the actual code for you. Let's face it — much of the code used in dBASE programs is basically off-the-shelf stuff. Most of us who have been around dBASE since the beginning have developed libraries of special-purpose modules; we drop the ones we need into an application, tweak them in a few places, and go on to writing the difficult, intricate parts of the code. One reason for the popularity of program libraries like Tom Rettig's Library (Tom Rettig Associates, Beverly Hills, CA) is to avoid reinventing the wheel.

dBASE IV takes this idea a step farther with the template language, a programmable program generator. Different templates are used to convert screen forms, reports, labels, and even entire applications from the applications generator into dBASE IV code. But the most exciting thing about the template language is that those who own the Developer's Edition of dBASE IV receive as part of that package the complete source code for all those templates (and a few others), the template compiler, and the template interpreter for debugging runtime errors.

Lately, CASE (Computer-Assisted Software Engineering) tools have been accorded much attention by the press. Magazines as varied as *Business Week* and *PC Week* regularly devote space to this subject. The gist of these articles is that proper use of CASE tools is the only hope for improving programmer productivity. The dBASE IV template language is a CASE tool, and a pretty good one at that, so read on and see how you can use it to quickly produce finished applications.

The template files I'll discuss are the most current available as of April 1989. There has been at least one upgrade to the REPORT.GEN module; it's available for downloading from the Ashton-Tate bulletin board, along with any other altered COD or GEN files. If you're not a BBS afficionado, call the Ashton-Tate main phone number and ask for information on any upgrades to the dBASE IV templates. I'll try to concentrate on tweaks in areas likely not to have been changed. Nevertheless, if the line numbers in your COD template source code files don't match those in the listings in this book, rely on the code itself. One major advantage of using templates is they can easily be changed and distributed, so minor errors can be corrected fairly painlessly.

Specific Templates and dBASE IV Activities

This chapter is a preview of what you will be learning about the activities and objects manipulated by the template language. The activities processed by the

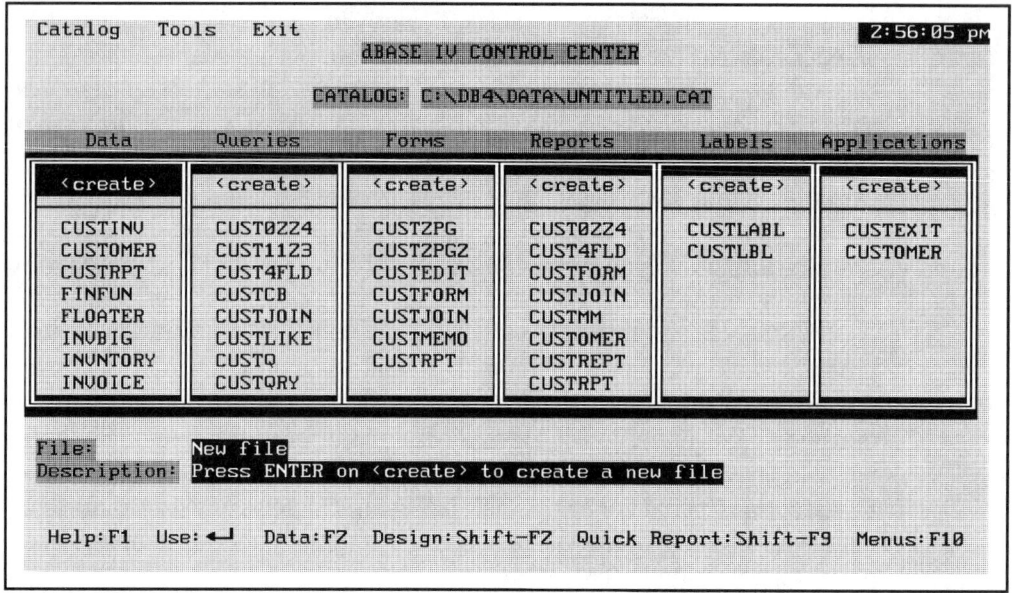

Figure 1-1   The dBASE IV Control Center

template language include creating and modifying screen forms, reports, labels, and applications — see the column headers in the Control Center (Figure 1-1).

Creating a screen is the simplest dBASE IV activity, and the program (FMT file) produced for most screen forms is much shorter than that generated for mailing labels. Screen forms are processed by the template file FORM.GEN, which is a compiled version of FORM.COD and FORM.DEF, the form selectors definition file. (All template programs automatically access BUILTIN.DEF, the general-purpose selectors definition file.) If you have read *Inside dBASE IV*, my previous book, you are already somewhat familiar with FORM.COD and may even have customized it, using my example, to produce personalized headers on the FMT file. The more ambitious among you may have gone on to customize report and label files as well. (On the other hand, if you are not familiar with selectors, COD and DEF files, and so on, don't worry — these will all be explained in this book.)

The second-easiest activity is creating mailing labels (which will also give you a good introduction to the report generator). You'll see how to fine-tune the label generator to automatically include some useful functions in the label code. After looking at the the FORM files, you'll take a look at the files LABEL.GEN, LABEL.COD, and LABEL.DEF.

Creating reports is a little tricky because dBASE IV supports three basic report formats: column, form, and mailmerge. When we look at RE-PORT.COD and REPORT.DEF, you'll see how to strip out one or two of the options for faster code generation. For example, if you only want to generate column reports and to do it quickly, you can remove the extraneous material in REPORT.COD that handles things like word wrap and other mailmerge features. Recompile REPORT.COD (after making a backup, or recompile it under a different name), and your report program code will generate much more efficiently.

Finally, dBASE IV has a powerful applications generator, which is the most difficult of the activities to understand. There are two applications generator programs, quick and general-purpose, which use two different sets of templates. QUICKAPP.GEN, COD, and DEF are used by the so-called quick applications generator. This module lets you generate an instant program that performs most of the standard database operations using your predefined screen form, report, and mailing label definitions. In twenty minutes, you can produce an application that will let you add, delete, edit, and browse data; perform indexed or unindexed searches for specific records; use your screen form; print a report or mailing labels; and do all this with the database, index, report, label, and screen form files you have defined previously. We'll look at QUICKAPP.COD and the selector definitions file it uses, APPLCTN.DEF. This DEF file is also used by the general-purpose applications generator.

MENU.GEN is the more general applications-generator program. It is made up of the main program, AS_MENU.COD, and includes the twenty-nine other files that begin with AS_ or AD_ .

There are two additional templates included with the Developer's Edition: DOCUMENT.GEN and FORMBROW.GEN. The source code for DOCU-MENT.GEN is in the file DS_DOC.COD, which calls the eleven COD files whose names begin with DD_ and the four whose names begin with DS_ . FORMBROW.COD is more conventionally named but might be installed in the sample tables directory rather than with the rest of the COD files. Look for FORMBROW.GEN in the samples directory or on the sample tables disk, too.

Finally, there are twenty-two general-purpose files used in MENU.GEN. These begin with the characters AD_ and can handle the usual database operations such as append, browse, import, index, and pack. We'll see how to include these templates in your custom template programs to make even template programming fairly easy.

What About QBE?

One major omission from the list of templates is Query By Example (QBE). Sadly, there are no templates for this important component of dBASE IV. Instead, on-screen queries are turned into code internally and then written to disk in files that appear to be straight ASCII but in fact contain many special control characters. When appropriate, we'll let QBE write the code for certain parts of programs. Moving data for certain fields from one database to another, inner and outer joins, and simple multitable data queries are most efficiently handled with QBE. However, for some activities, such as posting numeric values in one database to a field in another, the QBE-generated code is not efficient, in that it does not take full advantage of dBASE IV commands. We'll look at this problem and see how to solve it.

Objects: dBASE IV and Templates

To understand how dBASE IV interacts with the template language, you have to know the difference between dBASE objects and template objects. You probably know something about most of the dBASE objects: fields, memory variables, calculated fields, hidden fields, literals (pure text), and predefined fields. (If you don't understand these terms, read my book *Inside dBASE IV.*) dBASE is a database language, so most of its objects are data-oriented.

In addition to dBASE IV objects, there is a well-defined set of template design objects. You are undoubtedly familiar with three of these objects: the special format files that produce screen forms (SCR), reports (FRM), and labels (LBL). dBASE IV adds other objects to this list, mainly objects produced by the applications generator. Table 1-1 shows a complete list of dBASE IV design objects and where they come from. Table 1-2 lists the major file types, the column in the Control Center where each is created or modified, the extensions used for the special format file, a program code file if one is generated, and the compiled version of the program file.

Many, Many Files

If you've worked with dBASE IV, you know it produces a lot of files. For every design object, three files are generated: the design object file, the source code file, and the compiled version of the source code file. Having a big, fast hard disk with lots of free space is almost a requirement for generating dBASE IV applications.

Table 1-1   dBASE IV Design Objects

Object	*File Extension*
Application definition	APP
Screen form definition	SCR
Report form definition	FRM
Label definition	LBL
Pop-up menu definition	POP
Light-bar menu definition	BAR
File pick list	FIL
Structure (field) pick list	STR
Value (record) pick list	VAL
Batch process (copy, append from)	BCH (not BAT)

Source: Adapted from Table 1-1, *dBASE IV Template Language Manual*. (Ashton-Tate, Torrance, CA, 1988) Copyright © 1988, Ashton-Tate Corporation. All rights reserved. Reprinted by permission.

Table 1-2   dBASE IV Files and Extensions

File Type	*Control Center Column*	*Design*	*Code*	*Compiled*
		File Extensions		
Database	Data	DBF		
View query	Queries	QBE		QBO
Update query	Queries	UPD		UPO[a]
Screen Form	Forms	SCR	FMT	FMO
Report	Report	FRM	FRG	FRO
Label	Label	LBL	LBG	LBO
Program	Applications		PRG	DBO
dBASE/SQL program	Applications		PRS	DBO
Applications generator	Applications	APP	PRG	DBO

[a]When an update query is executed, the compiled file has the extension DBO. To use the query from QBE, rename the file so it has the extension UPO.

Source: Adapted from Table 2-1, *dBASE IV Template Language Manual*, p. 12–5. (Ashton-Tate, Torrance, CA, 1988) Copyright © 1988, Ashton-Tate Corporation. All rights reserved. Reprinted by permission.

If you're asking yourself why you should go to all the trouble of producing three different versions of what is essentially the same design object (design object, source code, and compiled), the answer is straightforward. Suppose you want to generate new code using a different template but leave the original design object unchanged. All you have to do is give the correct commands to switch templates, then run the original design object through the new template. The new code produced will reflect the commands in the new template. You can produce different versions of an entire application simply by switching templates — for example, different versions for network and single-user modes. See the example in Chapter 4 in which FORM.COD is modified to generate multiuser code.

The Application Definition File

One file stands out in Table 1-1: the application definition (APP) file. This file is the starting point of code generation for the application. It stores basic information, including the name of the application, your name and copyright information, the name of the main menu program, and information about the opening screen, including a copyright notice. (The opening screen is called a "splash screen.")

Figure 1-2 shows the basic application definition screen, and Figure 1-3 shows a typical splash screen.

Once the application definition file has been set up, it points to a main menu. Menus can be light-bar, pop-up, or conventional pick-a-number batch style. You can combine light-bar and pop-up menus into what has come to be called a "light-bar pull-down" menu system similar to that used by dBASE IV itself. The menu selections refer to other application design objects such as screen format files, reports, other menus, and batch processes. When code generation begins with the application definition file, all other objects are automatically generated as well. But the really nice thing is that you don't have to regenerate the entire program tree every time you change a design object; just regenerate the code for that object, and the rest of the system will handle it nicely.

Pick Lists

dBASE IV supports three types of pick lists: file, structure, and value. A file pick list allows the user to select from a list of files displayed in a pop-up window. You (the developer) must specify the file skeleton using DOS

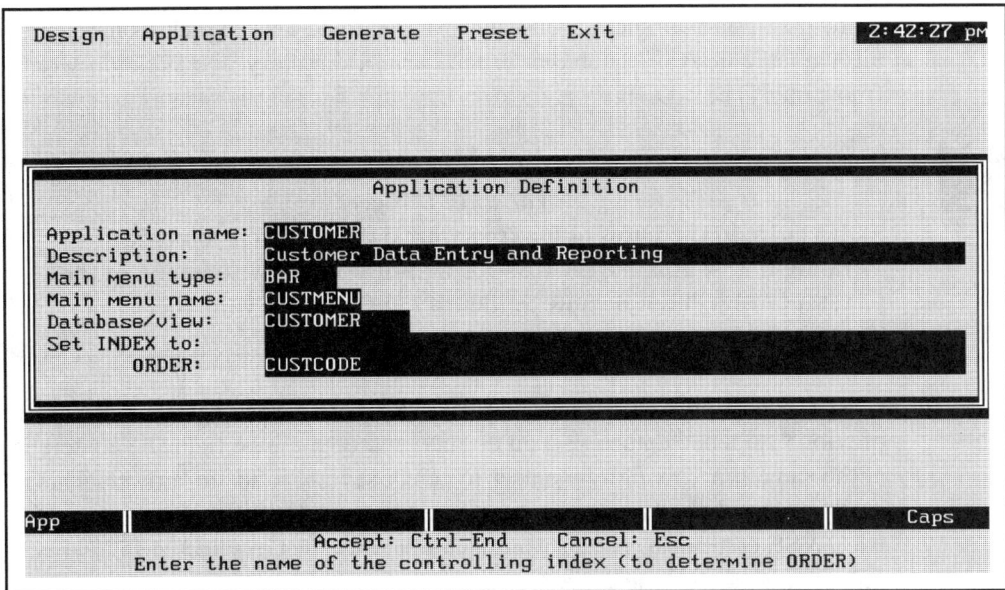

Figure 1-2 Application Definition Screen

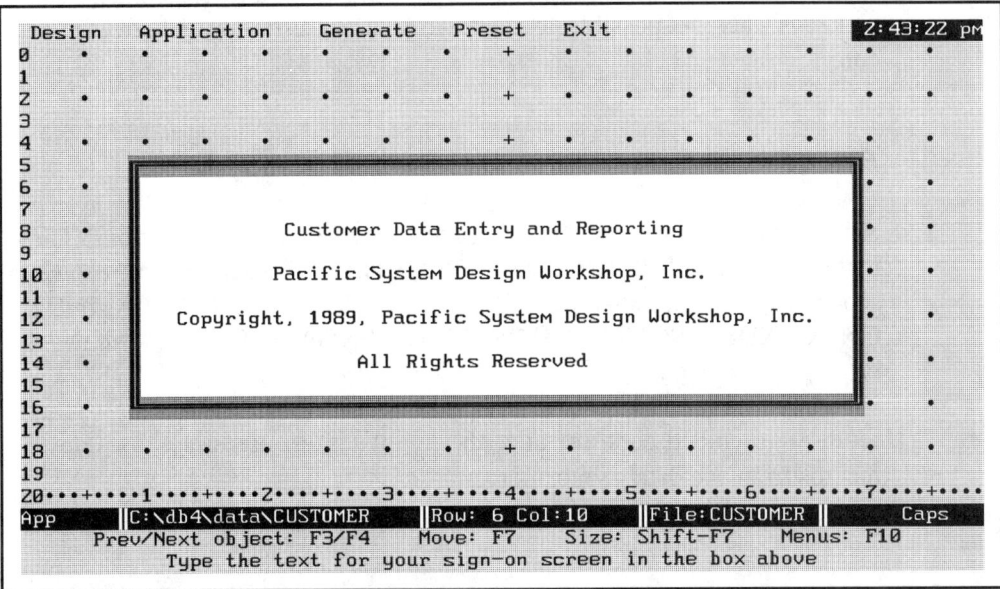

Figure 1-3 A Typical Splash Screen

wildcards. For example, if you want the user to be able to pick from a list of all available dBASE databases in the current directory, the skeleton would (most likely) be *.DBF.

> ### Warning! Danger!
> **If you're in the habit of making your own file extensions, stop doing it now and use the dBASE defaults. Otherwise, many of the templates will not be able to identify and process your file.**

A structure pick list allows the user to select a field (or fields) from a previously opened database. You might want to let all the fields be on-screen at the same time, to allow the user to select several fields to browse. This is easily accomplished using a structure pick list and the FIELDS clause of the BROWSE command. If you want to mark some of the selected fields read-only, that's easily done as well.

Finally, a value pick list allows the user to select one or more records from a single field in a previously opened database.

Most users prefer pick list selection because it's easier than typing in values. This is especially true when one must continually worry about accurate typing, something many of us aren't very good at. I recommend using pick lists wherever possible, to cut down on user frustration and errors in data entry.

Batch Processes

A batch process includes most file, record, and indexing operations. These include COPY FILE, APPEND FROM, COPY TO (with a FOR clause, a scope, and other options), REPLACE, DELETE, RECALL, PACK, INDEX ON, REINDEX, SORT TO, IMPORT, and EXPORT. Figure 1-4 shows the batch process menu.

Note, however, that there is no option to copy records to an array. You'll see how to embed code (or alter the templates) to use arrays for copying records from one database to another.

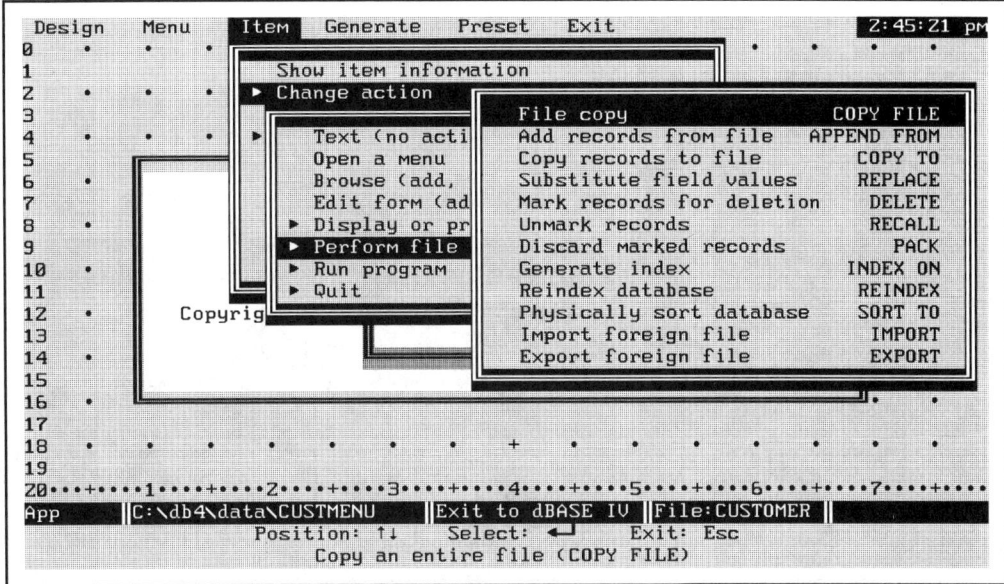

Figure 1-4   Batch Process Menu

Putting the Pieces Together

All these files and processes can get a little confusing. Figure 1-5 shows a sample application that uses a light-bar pull-down menu system. Users can add data; browse data; select records, fields, or files from pick lists; print reports and labels; and exit to either dBASE IV or DOS. The point is to understand where each special file type fits into the system. Note that the three BCH files could actually be incorporated into CUSTPOP1.POP as individual menu activities. Instead, they're separate parts of the application, meaning they can be modified independently of the pop-up menu program. Note also that CUSTFORM.SCR is used throughout the system for all data screens, even though it is not explicitly referenced. Instead, custom screen form names are entered when the activity (add data, edit, and so on) is specified.

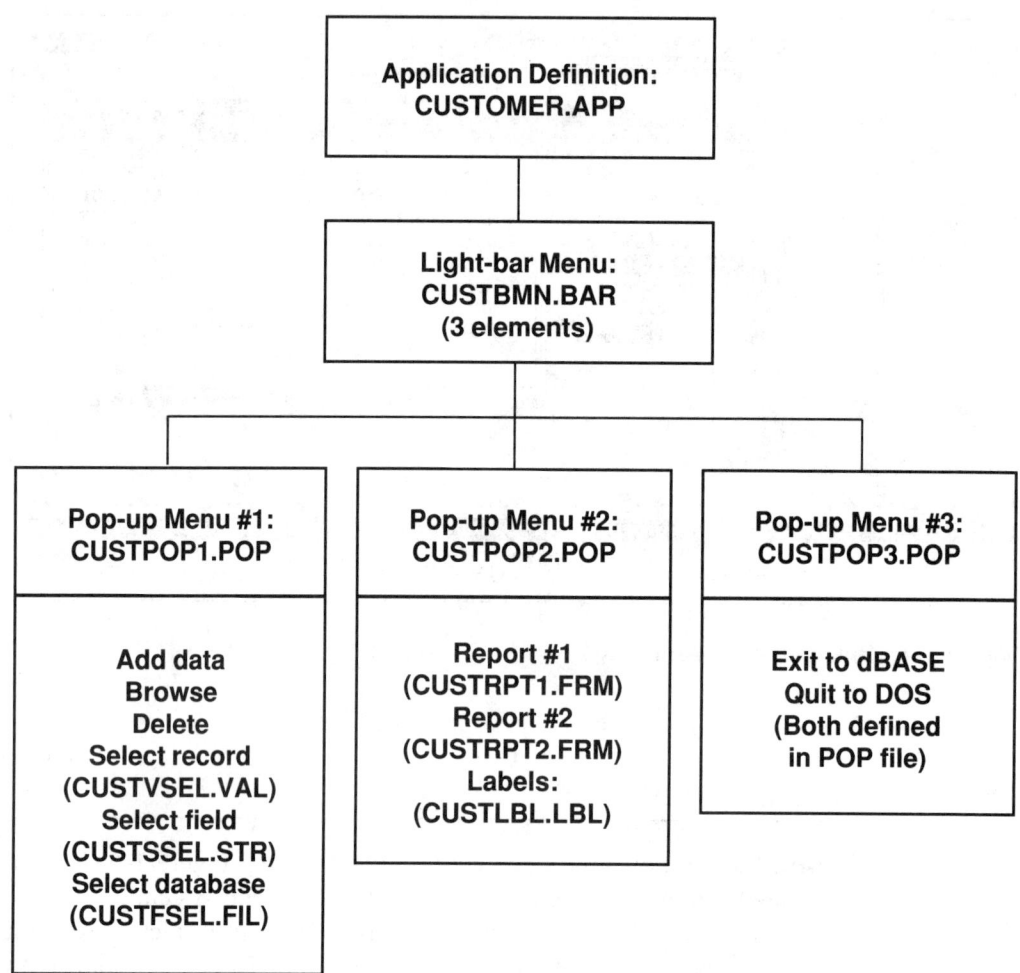

Figure 1-5   How the Design Objects Interact

Conclusion

This chapter has previewed the basic dBASE activities and the objects associated with them. Activities are the basic CREATE/MODIFY options, including screen forms, reports, labels, and applications. Objects are fields, memory variables, calculated fields, hidden fields, literals, and predefined fields.

We also looked at the template design objects: applications; screen forms, reports, and labels; light-bar and pop-up menus; file, structure, and value pick lists; and batch processes.

An important omission from the list of template design objects is Query By Example. In the next chapter, you'll see how to work with QBE and use the code it produces even if you don't want to use the SET VIEW TO command.

Chapter 2

Views and Query By Example

As we saw in Chapter 1, Query By Example is not handled at all by the template language. Instead, QBE files are produced directly by dBASE IV. These files contain control codes, so you can't just use your program editor on them. However, the program code is included in these files as straight ASCII text. Thus, the QBE files combine the characteristics of special format files, such as FRM and SCR files, with those of the program code files, such as FRG and FMT files.

There are two basic types of dBASE IV queries, distinguished by what each does and the file extension assigned to it. *Ordinary queries* display data, link files, select fields, and filter records (the relational select and project operators) and are stored in files with the extension QBE; another feature that distinguishes these files is that the result of running such a query is the creation of a View. *Update queries* actually change data in a database in one of four ways: REPLACE, APPEND, DELETE, or RECALL. Update queries are stored in files with the extension UPD. They do not create any sort of View. Note that compiling a file with the extension QBE produces another file with the extension QBO. However, when an update query file (UPD) is executed, the compiled file will have the extension DBO. For consistency when working with the Catalog files, either copy or rename the file so that it has the extension UPO.

Select, Project, Inner Joins, and Outer Joins

Queries serve three principal functions. First, they let you easily perform the relational operations select (pick records according to some criterion) and project (pick a set of fields from the database). Second, they allow easy linking of tables, including inner and outer joins and handling one-to-many relations. Third, they allow data to be moved from one database to another. The important thing about QBE is that it's easy to use and writes the code for you.

For the relational select, project, and join operations, the result of a query is a View — a combination of fields and records that meet the specified selection criteria. In dBASE IV, a View is created and maintained on the fly without writing a new database to disk. Only if you select the option "Save view as a database file" from the QBE menu will the View actually be written as a disk file. Otherwise, using the commands SET FIELDS, SET RELATION, and SET FILTER, the records and fields in the View are built and maintained in real time.

Select and Project

The easiest operations in QBE are select and project. If you choose "create" from the Queries column of the Control Center menu with a database open, all fields from that database are automatically placed in the View. That's handy if you want all or even most of the fields included. The easiest way to remove a field from the View is to move the cursor to the field in the example form and press F5. If you want to remove all fields from the view, move the cursor to the far left column of the example form (under the name of the database) and press F5. If you're working with a multidatabase View, pressing F5 with the cursor in the database name column of an example form will first add all the fields in that form to the View. Press F5 again to remove all of them, leaving only fields from the remaining example forms in the View.

One other thing — fields appear in the View in the order in which they're added from the database(s), so you can easily shuffle the order of fields. In fact, the easiest way to reorder the fields in a database is to simply create a View that has the fields displayed in the sequence you want!

Now that you're an expert on shuffling fields, let's see how to get some useful work done.

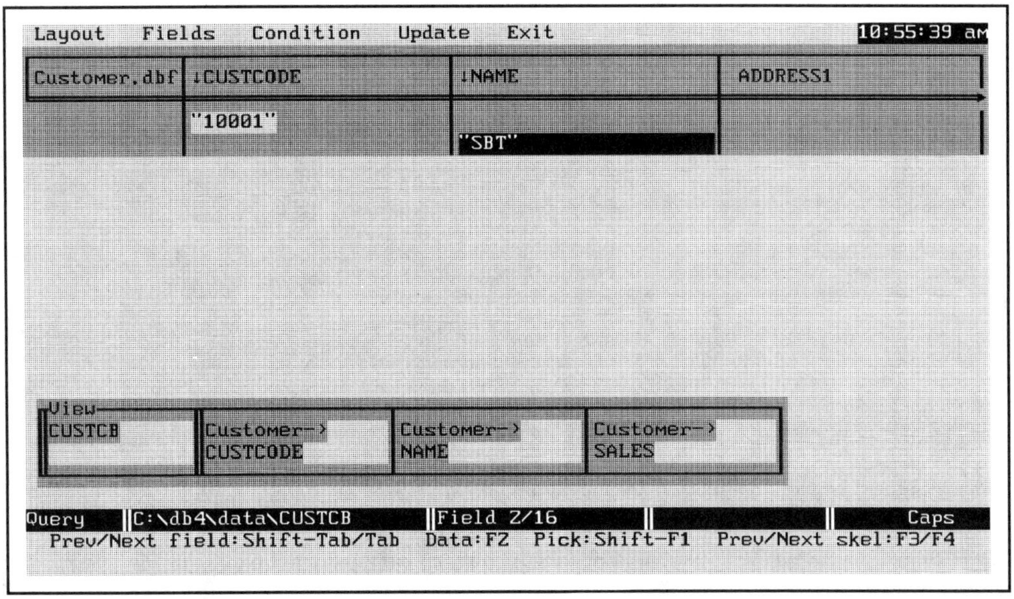

Figure 2-1   Typical OR Query

First, let's do a simple OR query with three fields selected, and see how dBASE IV translates it into code. Figure 2-1 shows how to set up a typical OR query using the CUSTOMER database.

Example 2-1 shows the resulting QBE code. Figure 2-2 is a screen showing the control characters. (This screen was produced using the Norton Utilities NU program.)

Example 2-1   QBE Code for the OR Query

```
* dBASE IV .QBE file
SET FIELDS TO
SELECT 1
USE CUSTOMER.DBF AGAIN
SET EXACT ON
SET FILTER TO ((A->CUSTCODE="10001") .OR. (A->NAME="SBT"))
GO TOP
SET FIELDS TO A->CUSTCODE,A->NAME,A->SALES
```

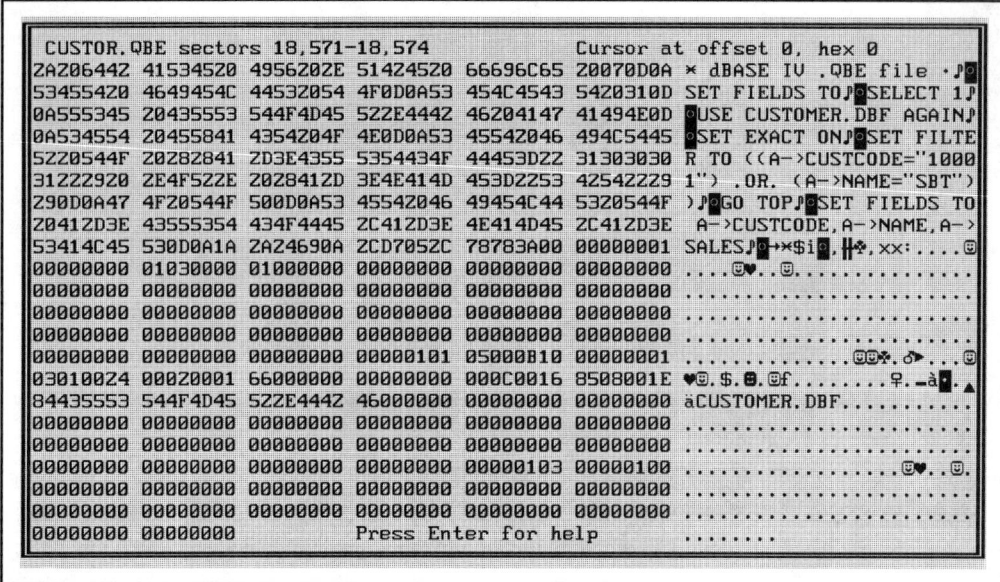

Figure 2-2   QBE File with Control Characters

Note how simple the query code in Example 2-1 is. CUSTOMER.DBF is opened in work area 1, EXACT is set ON, and a filter is set that implements the OR query. The last step is to use SET FIELDS TO to pick only the fields to be included in the View.

The only trick is the keyword AGAIN in the USE command. This allows the same database to be opened in different work areas. Thus dBASE IV can, for example, do a self-join — that is, join the database with itself.

Warning! Danger!
Do not attempt to change data in a database, when the database is opened in two or more work areas, with the AGAIN clause. According to Ashton-Tate, this can cause damage to the multiple index files and possibly data loss.

The control characters shown in Figure 2-2 are important. We'll deal with them in the next section.

Queries using AND instead of OR are simple. Just put the examples on the same line of the example form instead of on different lines. Naturally, this translates into the AND operator in the SET FILTER TO statement.

Using QBE Queries in an Application Program   There are two ways to use the QBE query in a program. The easiest is to give the command SET VIEW TO <QBE file name> .QBE. The QBE file must be the one produced by dBASE IV QBE itself, with no editing done by you.

On the other hand, if you want to make changes to QBE files, there are times when it's faster and more efficient to directly edit the file. The best example of this is a query that produces inefficient code. We'll see later in this chapter that many REPLACE queries fall into this category. In such a case, copy the QBE file to another file with the extension PRG. Edit out all the control characters, and change any commands you want altered. Then, either include the PRG file as a procedure in the program where you want to set the View, or just DO the new PRG file. In either case, be sure to put a RETURN at the end of the PRG file.

Joins, Inner and Outer

Let's start with some basic definitions. The easiest way to understand the difference between an inner join and an outer join is with an example. Suppose you have two databases, CUSTOMER and INVOICE. This is a one-to-many relation — at least, hopefully it is! A conventional one-to-many join using the EVERY keyword, as shown in Figure 2-3, is an *inner join.*

However, suppose there are some customers who have no invoices. They will be omitted from the query results, as shown in Figure 2-4.

Including records from CUSTOMER that have no matching keys in IN-VOICE is called an *outer join.* dBASE IV handles outer joins simply by putting the keyword EVERY in the CUSTOMER example form (the "one") rather than in INVOICE (the "many"). Figure 2-5 shows the setup for an outer join, and Figure 2-6 shows the results.

With that as background, let's take a look at the code that produces inner and outer joins, shown in Examples 2-2 and 2-3.

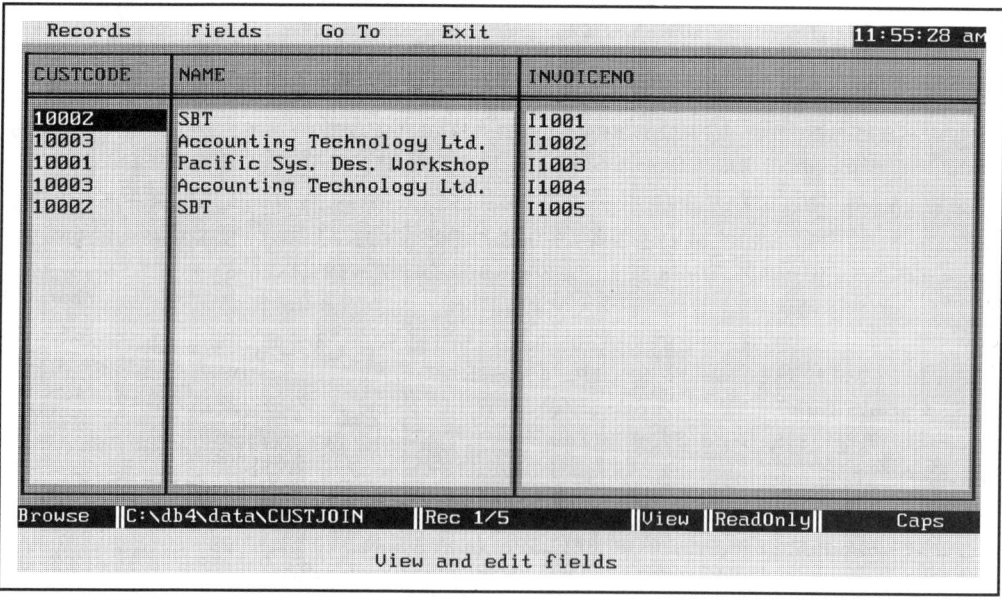

Figure 2-3   Inner Join Using QBE

Figure 2-4   Inner Join Results

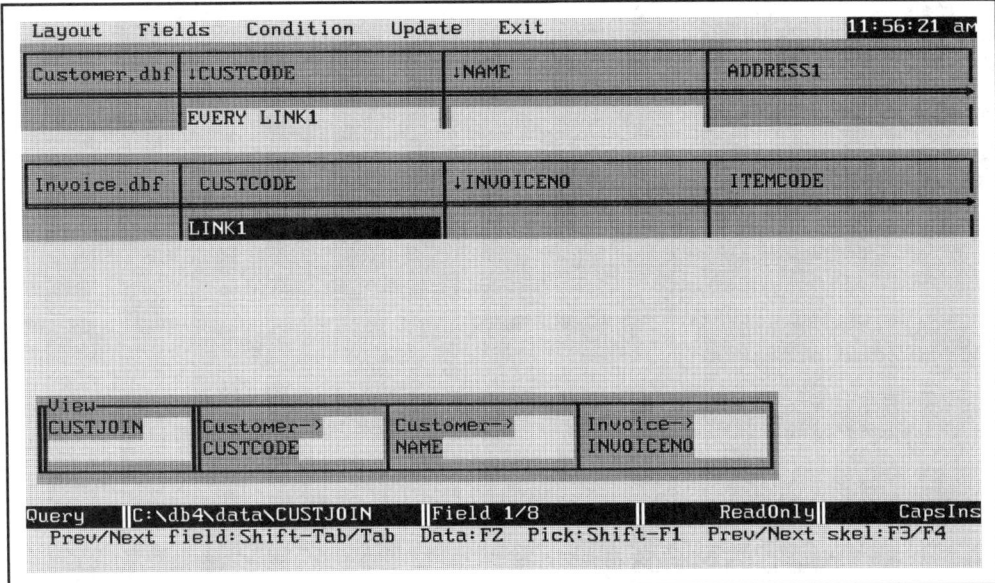

Figure 2-5   QBE Setup for Outer Join

```
  Records      Fields     Go To     Exit                   11:57:09 am
 CUSTCODE    NAME                          INVOICENO

 10001       Pacific Sys. Des. Workshop    I1003
 10002       SBT                           I1001
 10002       SBT                           I1005
 10003       Accounting Technology Ltd.    I1002
 10003       Accounting Technology Ltd.    I1004
 10004       New Customer







 Browse    C:\db4\data\CUSTJOIN     Rec 1/4        View  ReadOnly        Ins
                         View and edit fields
```

Figure 2-6   Outer Join Results

Example 2-2   Inner-Join QBE Code

```
* dBASE IV .QBE file
SET FIELDS TO
SELECT 2
USE INVOICE.DBF AGAIN NOUPDATE
USE CUSTOMER.DBF AGAIN NOUPDATE IN 1 ORDER CUSTCODE
SET EXACT ON
SET FILTER TO
SET RELATION TO B->CUSTCODE INTO A
SET SKIP TO A
GO TOP
SET FIELDS TO A->CUSTCODE,A->NAME,B->INVOICENO
```

Example 2-3   Outer-Join QBE Code

```
* dBASE IV .QBE file
SET FIELDS TO
SELECT 1
USE CUSTOMER.DBF AGAIN NOUPDATE
USE INVOICE.DBF AGAIN NOUPDATE IN 2 ORDER CUSTCODE
SET EXACT ON
SET FILTER TO
SET RELATION TO A->CUSTCODE INTO B
SET SKIP TO B
GO TOP
SET FIELDS TO A->CUSTCODE,A->NAME,B->INVOICENO
```

There are two basic differences between inner and outer joins. First, the inner join sets the relation from INVOICE into CUSTOMER; the outer join sets the relation in the opposite direction. Second, the inner join uses SET SKIP TO A (CUSTOMER); the outer uses SET SKIP TO B (INVOICE). When the relation is set from INVOICE into CUSTOMER, and SKIP is set to CUSTOMER, the pointer is moved through all records in CUSTOMER that match the CUSTCODE in INVOICE. When there is no CUSTCODE for a particular customer in INVOICE, the CUSTOMER record with that CUSTCODE is not included in the View. Only those CUSTCODE values actually present in INVOICE are written to the View. This is the essence of an inner join.

The outer join, on the other hand, works the opposite way. When the relation is set from CUSTOMER into INVOICE, and SKIP is set to IN-VOICE, the CUSTCODE values in CUSTOMER determine when records are written to the View. Even if there is no matching CUSTCODE in INVOICE, the record will still be written.

To understand this a little better, consider what would happen in the inner join example if there were "orphan" records in INVOICE — (invoice records that have a CUSTCODE with no match in CUSTOMER): the orphan records would be included in the View. What we have been calling an "inner join" is only an inner join from the viewpoint of CUSTOMER. From the viewpoint of INVOICE, it is an outer join. The difference between inner and outer joins depends crucially on which database is designated as the parent and which as the child. That, of course, is defined by the SET RELATION TO command. Consider SET RELATION FROM A INTO B. This is an outer join for database A and an inner join for database B. Reverse the relation, and you reverse the type of join.

Many-to-Many Relations

dBASE IV also handles many-to-many relations very well. For example, suppose there are several customers with the same CUSTCODE. This makes the relation between CUSTOMER and INVOICE many-to-many: there will be many records in each database matching many in the other database. Fortunately, this is the conventional link for dBASE IV databases. Figure 2-7 shows the basic setup for linking two databases, and Figure 2-8 shows the resulting View.

Let's look at the code produced by this QBE file. Example 2-4 shows the program produced from the QBE setup shown in Figure 2-7.

Example 2-4   Many-to-Many Join Program Code

```
* dBASE IV .QBE file
SET FIELDS TO
SELECT 1
USE CUSTOMER.DBF AGAIN NOUPDATE
USE INVOICE.DBF AGAIN NOUPDATE IN 2 ORDER CUSTCODE
```

(continued)

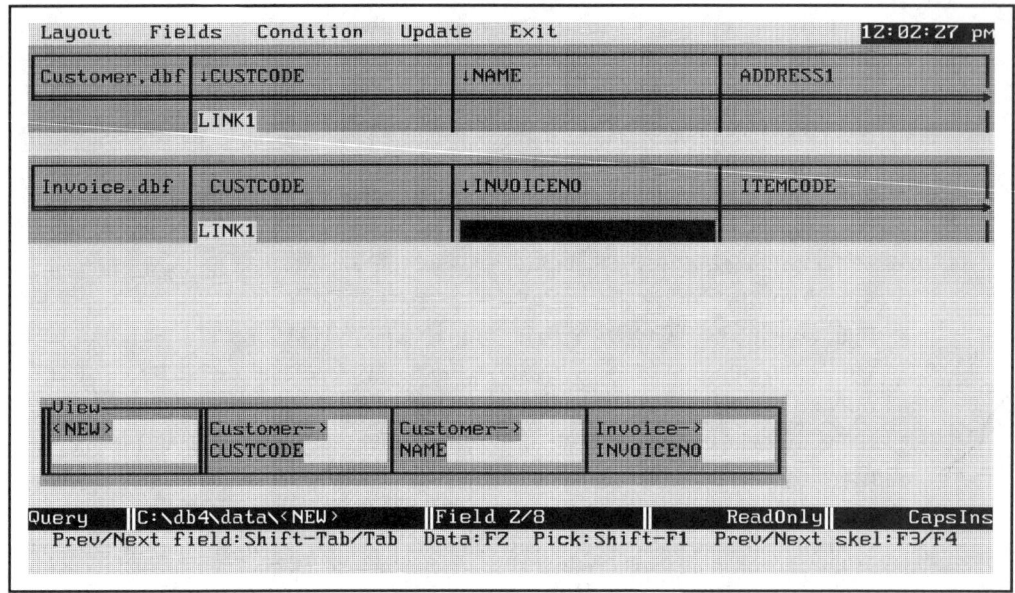

Figure 2-7   Many-to-Many Join in QBE

Figure 2-8   Many-to-Many Join Results

```
SET EXACT ON
SET FILTER TO FOUND(2)
SET RELATION TO A->CUSTCODE INTO B
SET SKIP TO B
GO TOP
SET FIELDS TO A->CUSTCODE,A->NAME,B->INVOICENO
```

The only difference between this code and the previous two examples is the SET FILTER TO FOUND(2) command. Remember, the FOUND() function returns a logical true if a match has been found for a LOCATE, SEEK, or FIND command, and a false otherwise. This is a clever use of the fact that FOUND() can include a work area different from the one currently SELECT-ed in dBASE IV. Here, the relation is first set from CUSTOMER (work area 1) into INVOICE (work area 2). If there is no matching CUSTCODE in INVOICE for the current one in CUSTOMER, the value of FOUND() in the INVOICE work area (FOUND(2)) will be false. When FOUND(2) returns a false, the record in CUSTOMER is FILTERed out of the resulting View.

 Hint: *Interested programmers might consider using this technique with SET NEAR ON, and the LIKE() and DIFFERENCE() functions, to allow different types of approximate matching with an indexed search. I suspect you'll never have to use LOCATE again!*

A Complex Query: Select, Project, and an Inner Join

Let's see how all this fits together in a query that combines selection, projection, and an inner join. Figure 2-9 shows the QBE setup, and Figure 2-10 shows the results.

Now let's look at the code generated by this query. Example 2-5 shows the QBE file. As you might expect, this is a combination of SET FILTER TO, SET RELATION TO, SET SKIP TO, and SET FIELDS TO.

Example 2-5 QBE Code for Complex Query

```
* dBASE IV .QBE file
SET FIELDS TO
SELECT 2
```

(continued)

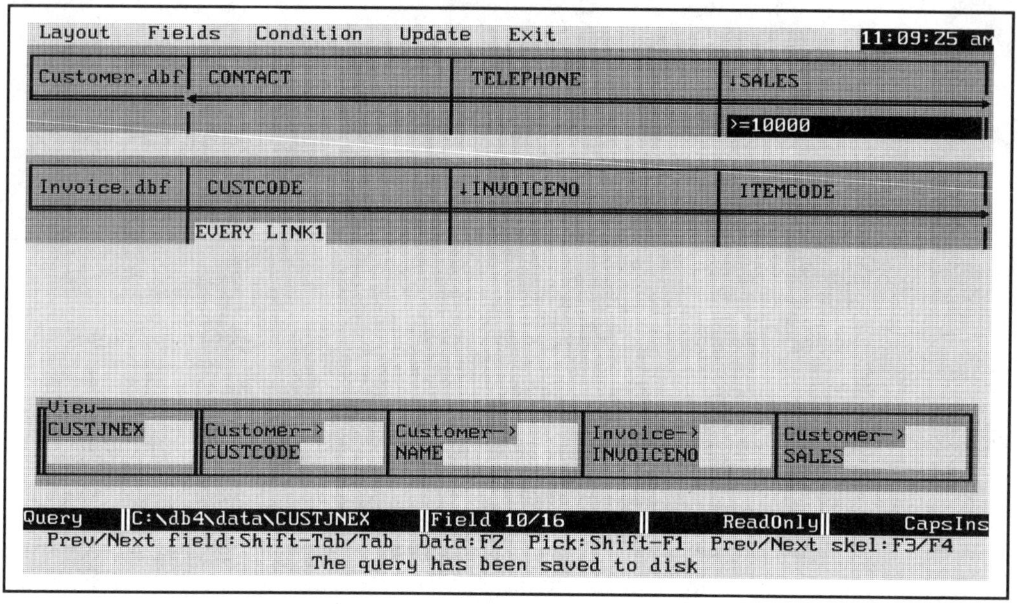

```
 Layout    Fields    Condition    Update    Exit                11:09:25 am
┌─────────────┬──────────────────────┬─────────────────┬──────────────────────┐
│Customer.dbf │ CONTACT              │ TELEPHONE       │ ↓SALES               │
│             ├──────────────────────┼─────────────────┼──────────────────────┤
│             │                      │                 │ >=10000              │
└─────────────┴──────────────────────┴─────────────────┴──────────────────────┘

┌─────────────┬──────────────────────┬─────────────────┬──────────────────────┐
│Invoice.dbf  │ CUSTCODE             │ ↓INVOICENO      │ ITEMCODE             │
│             ├──────────────────────┼─────────────────┼──────────────────────┤
│             │ EVERY LINK1          │                 │                      │
└─────────────┴──────────────────────┴─────────────────┴──────────────────────┘


┌─View──────────────────────────────────────────────────────────────────────────┐
│CUSTJNEX     Customer─>     Customer─>     Invoice─>      Customer─>            │
│             CUSTCODE       NAME           INVOICENO      SALES                 │
└───────────────────────────────────────────────────────────────────────────────┘
 Query    ║C:\db4\data\CUSTJNEX    ║Field 10/16    ║        ReadOnly║    CapsIns
    Prev/Next field:Shift-Tab/Tab    Data:F2  Pick:Shift-F1   Prev/Next skel:F3/F4
                       The query has been saved to disk
```

Figure 2-9   Complex QBE Query

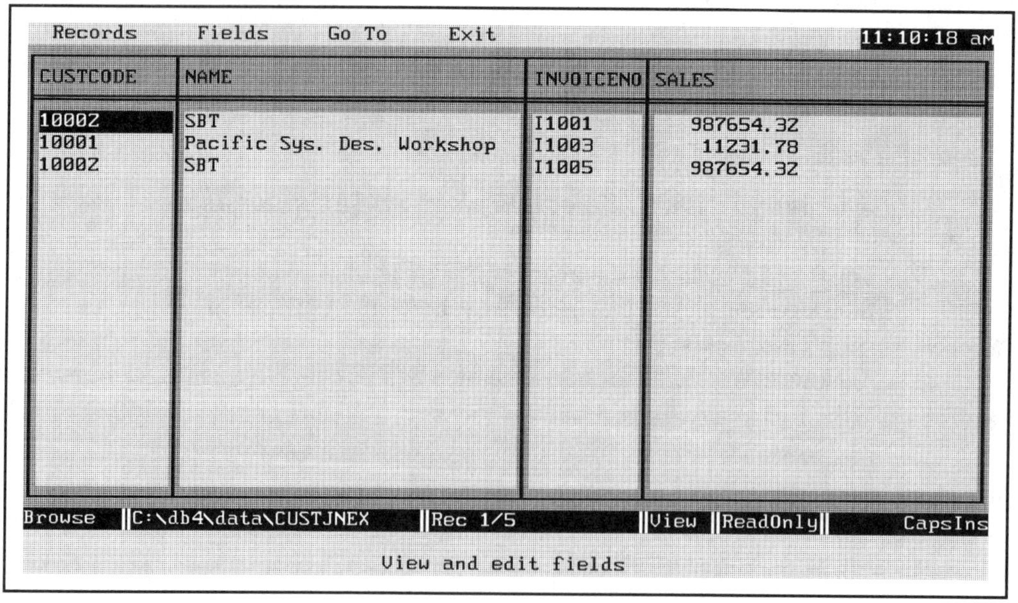

```
 Records      Fields      Go To      Exit                      11:10:18 am
┌────────────┬───────────────────────────────┬───────────┬─────────────────────┐
│CUSTCODE    │ NAME                          │INVOICENO  │SALES                │
├────────────┼───────────────────────────────┼───────────┼─────────────────────┤
│10002       │SBT                            │I1001      │ 987654.32           │
│10001       │Pacific Sys. Des. Workshop     │I1003      │  11231.78           │
│10002       │SBT                            │I1005      │ 987654.32           │
│            │                               │           │                     │
│            │                               │           │                     │
│            │                               │           │                     │
│            │                               │           │                     │
│            │                               │           │                     │
│            │                               │           │                     │
│            │                               │           │                     │
│            │                               │           │                     │
│            │                               │           │                     │
│            │                               │           │                     │
└────────────┴───────────────────────────────┴───────────┴─────────────────────┘
 Browse   ║C:\db4\data\CUSTJNEX       ║Rec 1/5     ║View ║ReadOnly║    CapsIns
                            View and edit fields
```

Figure 2-10   Results of Complex QBE Query

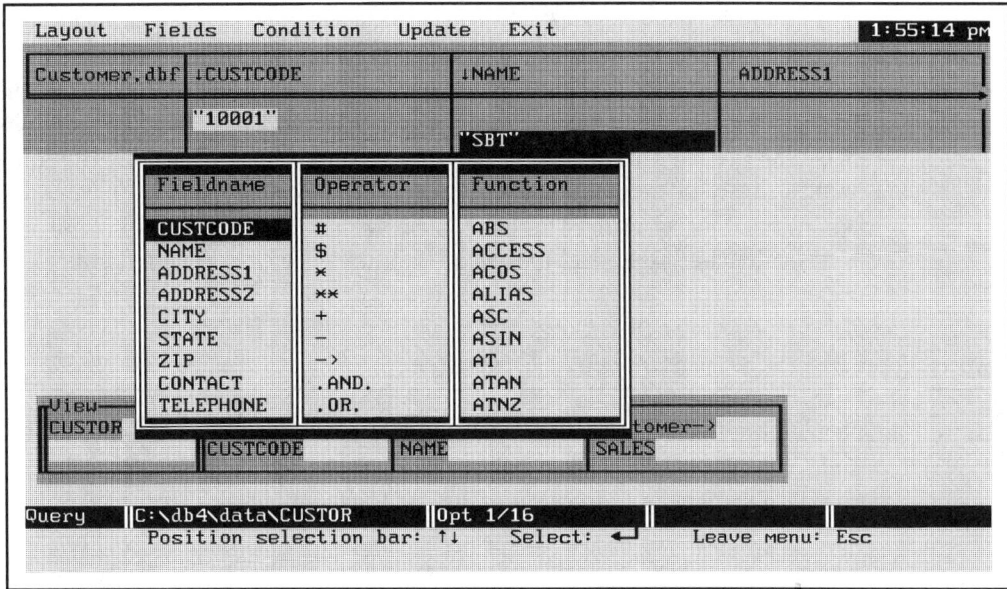

Figure 2-11   Field Pick List for QBE

```
USE INVOICE.DBF AGAIN NOUPDATE
USE CUSTOMER.DBF AGAIN NOUPDATE IN 1 ORDER CUSTCODE
SET EXACT ON
SET FILTER TO ((A->SALES>=10000))
SET RELATION TO B->CUSTCODE INTO A
SET SKIP TO A
GO TOP
SET FIELDS TO A->CUSTCODE,A->NAME,B->INVOICENO,A->SALES
```

Using a Pick List to Build Conditions

There are many comparison operators and functions in dBASE IV. Most of them can be used in examples in QBE. If you have trouble remembering the exact spelling of a function, simply press Shift-F1 with the cursor in a field in an example form. Figure 2-11 shows the top part of the three-column pick list. You can set up query examples without ever typing a function or comparison operator, using this list.

For example, instead of typing >=10000 in the example shown in Figure 2-9, you could place the cursor in the SALES example field, press Shift-F1, and select the >= operator from the second column. (You still have to type in 10000.)

You can use any dBASE IV function or operator in an example as long as it makes sense for the data type of that field. These functions, however, are mainly useful for working with calculated fields in queries. Let's see how to create a calculated field, and look at a few things you can do with them.

Calculated Fields and Summary Operators

Calculated fields are very useful for analysis done on the fly and for creating a field when you don't really want it included in the database itself. For example, a calculated field useful in mailing list applications is:

```
TRIM(CITY) + ", " + STATE + "  " + ZIP.
```

Suppose you name this calculated field "CSZ." Let's look at an example of how dBASE IV handles this calculated field operation. Remember — once a calculated field is included in a View, it is available for screen forms, reports, labels, and the applications generator. (However, it is available to screen forms on a read-only basis.)

First, select "Create calculated field" from the Fields menu. Next, assign a name to the calculated field (if you don't assign a name now, you'll be prompted to do so when you add the calculated field to the View). Select "Edit field name" from the Fields menu, and type in the name you want (in this example, "CSZ"). You'll see an = sign after the field name. Be sure the cursor is on the line below the calculated field's name, and type in the expression for the calculation. Or you can use the field/operator/function pick list to build the expression. Figure 2-12 shows the expression for the calculated field CSZ. (Press the Zoom key, F9, to see the full expression. Press F9 again to return to the QBE screen.)

Next, place the fields in the View. If you want to see the results of the calculated field, be sure you put it in the View! Figure 2-13 shows the completed QBE screen.

Now, let's take a look at the results. Press F2 and you'll see something like Figure 2-14.

One of the best things about calculated fields is that you can use a QBE example with them. Figure 2-15 shows an example with the calculated field we've been working with; Figure 2-16 shows the results of this new query.

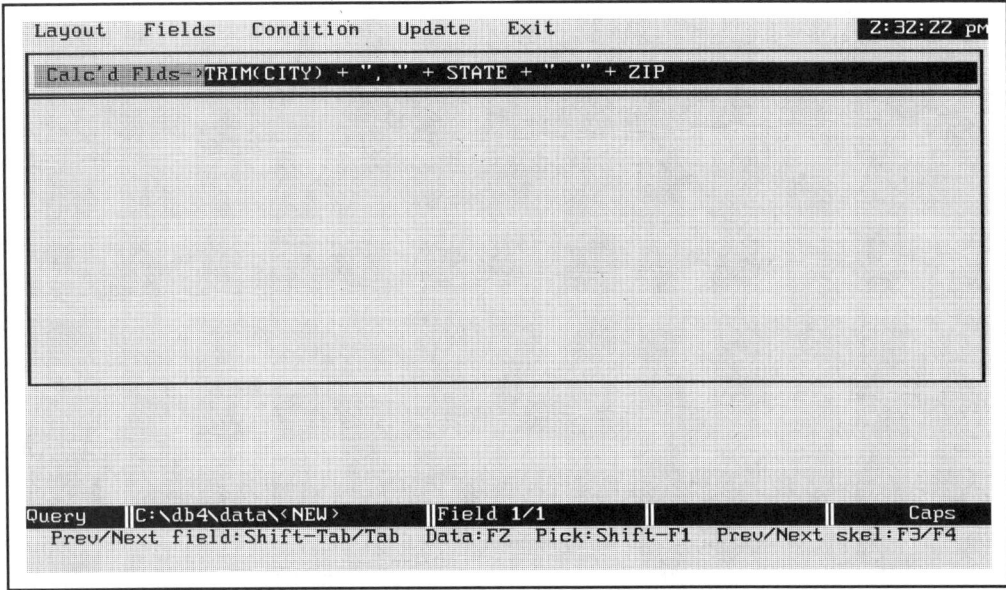

Figure 2-12 Calculated Field

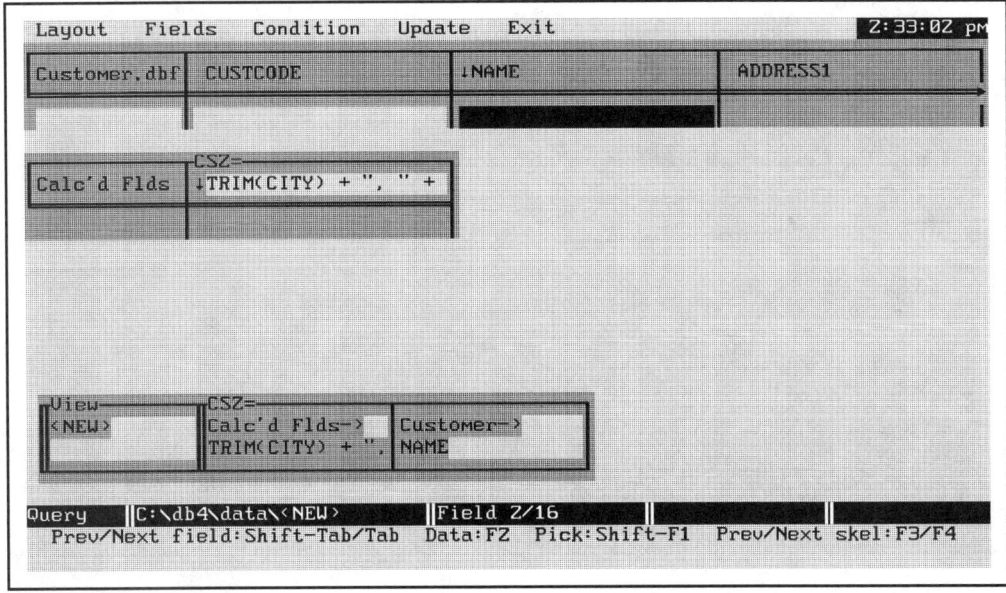

Figure 2-13 QBE Screen with Calculated Field

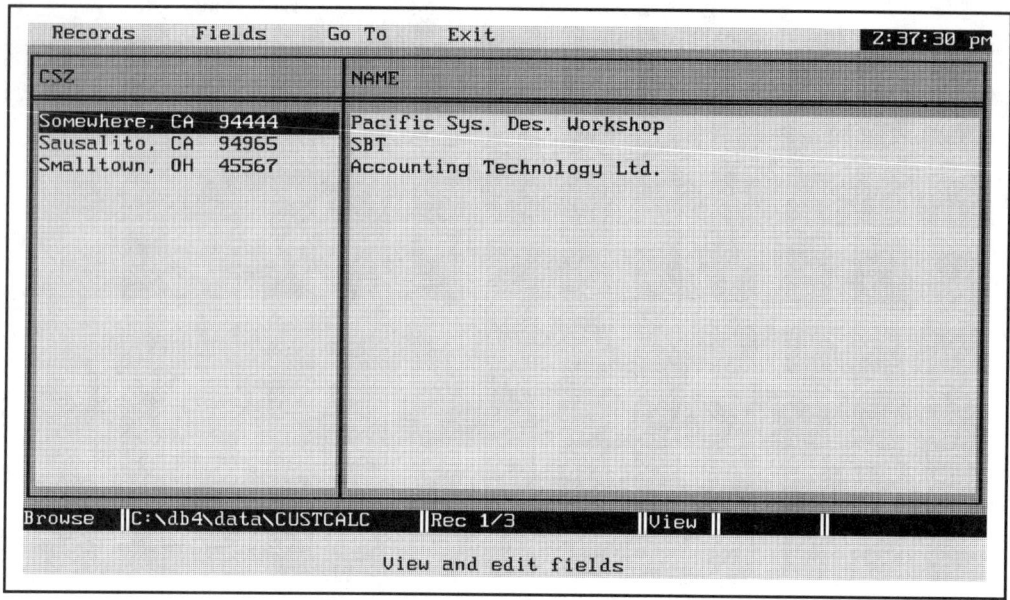

Figure 2-14   QBE Results with Calculated Field

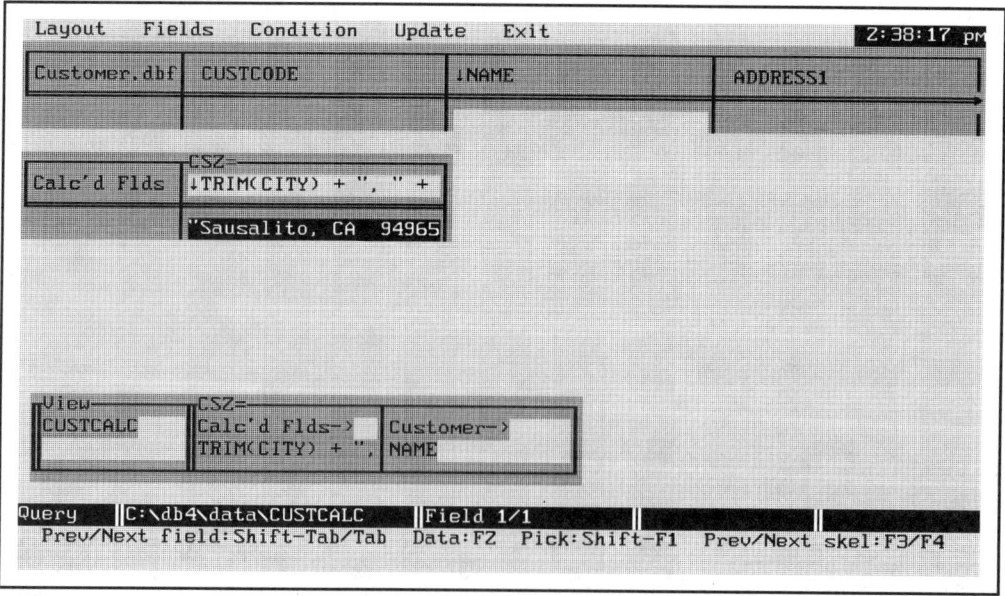

Figure 2-15   Calculated Field with Example

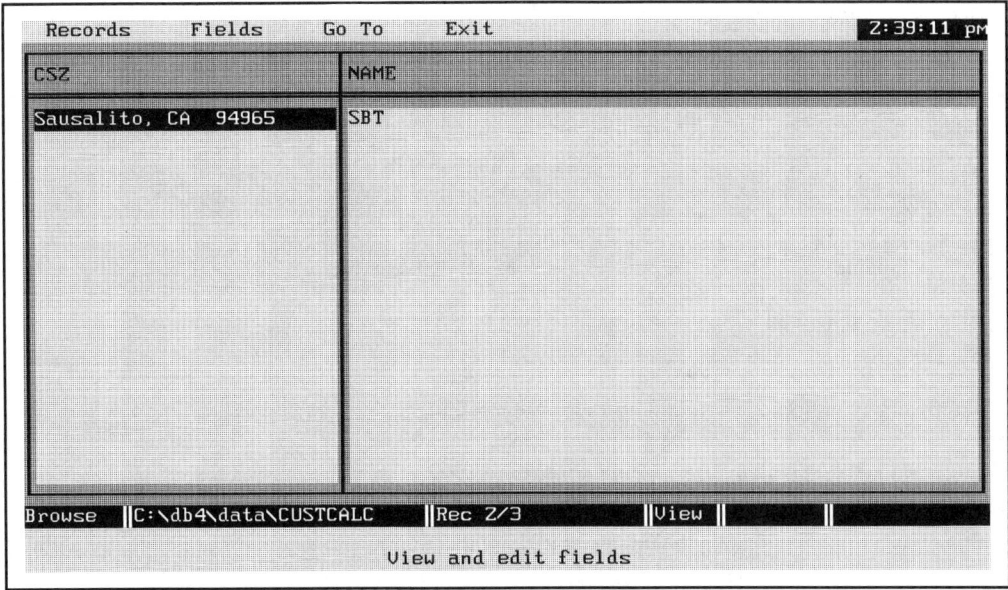

Figure 2-16   Data from QBE with Calculated Field and Example

How does dBASE IV handle this with code? Example 2-6 shows the code generated by the query in Figure 2-15.

Example 2-6   Code for Calculated Field with Example

```
* dBASE IV .QBE file
SET FIELDS TO
SELECT 1
USE CUSTOMER.DBF AGAIN
SET EXACT ON
SET FILTER TO (((TRIM(A->CITY) + ", " + A->STATE + "   " + A->ZIP)=;
"Sausalito, CA  94965"))
GO TOP
SET FIELDS TO CSZ=(TRIM(A->CITY) + ", " + A->STATE + "   "
  + A->ZIP),A->;
NAME
```

Table 2-1   Summary Operators for QBE

Field Type	*Summary Operators Allowed*
Numeric	AVG, SUM, MIN, MAX, COUNT
Floating Point	AVG, SUM, MIN, MAX, COUNT
Character	MIN, MAX, COUNT
Date	MIN, MAX, COUNT
Logical	COUNT

No summary operators are available for memo type fields.

Source: Table 7-2, *Using the dBASE IV Menu System*, p. 7-13. (Ashton-Tate, Torrance, CA, 1988)

Note several new features of dBASE IV. First, you can include an expression for a calculated field in the SET FIELDS TO command. Second, expressions can also be included in SET FILTER TO. Thus, the code generated is not at all complicated.

Using calculated fields with Views in dBASE IV makes life much easier. Those who are in the habit of including such fields as part of the database structure can considerably reduce the disk space required by DBF files by incorporating the calculated field into a View and using the View to produce read-only screen forms, reports, labels, and even applications.

Summary Operators

A summary operator is a short word or abbreviation that can be used to quickly summarize data from a query. Table 2-1 shows the summary operators for the different field types.

Let's see how summary operators translate into dBASE IV code. Figure 2-17 shows an example asking for the average of sales for all customers in the CUSTOMER table. Data will be reported only for the field on which the summary is being done, so that's the only field you should bother including in the View. Figure 2-18 shows the result of this calculation, and Example 2-7 shows the code generated by this query.

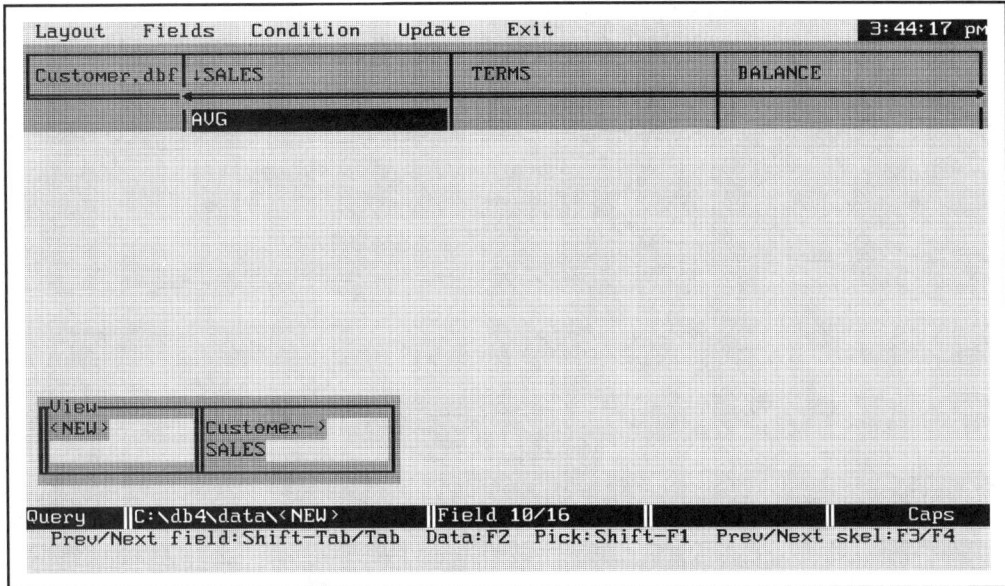

Figure 2-17 QBE Query Averaging Sales

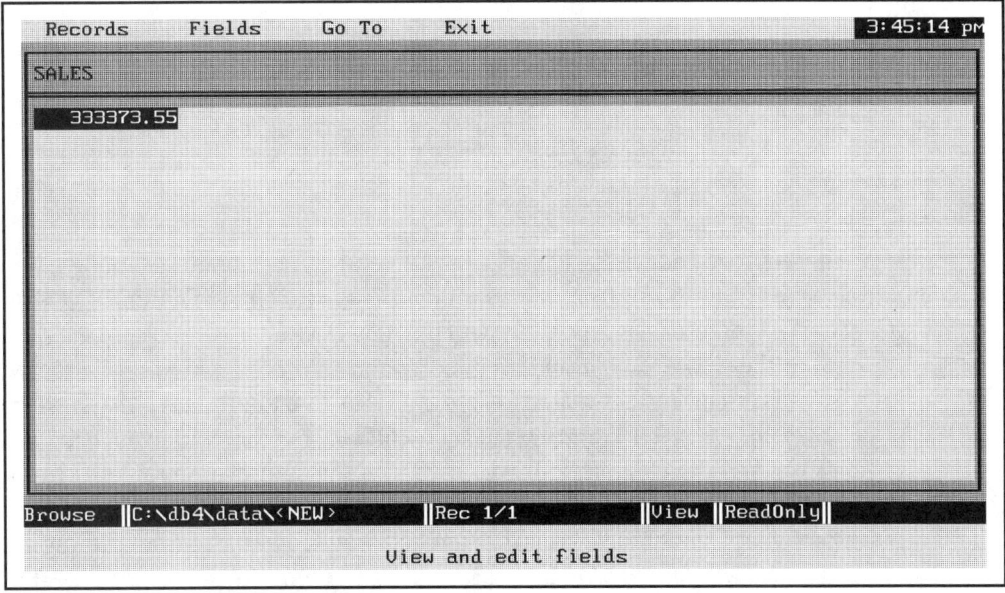

Figure 2-18 Data from QBE Averaging Sales

Example 2-7   Code Generated by Average Query

```
* dBASE IV .QBE file
SET FIELDS TO
SELECT 1
USE CUSTOMER.DBF AGAIN
SET EXACT ON
SET FILTER TO
SET FIELDS TO A->SALES
CALCULATE AVG(SALES) TO QBE___B3
QBE___SAFE = SET("SAFETY")
QBE___CATA = SET("CATALOG")
SET SAFETY OFF
SET CATALOG OFF
QBE___13 = STR(RAND(-1)*100000000,8)
COPY STRU TO &QBE___13
SET FIELDS TO
USE &QBE___13
APPEND BLANK
REPLACE SALES WITH QBE___B3
USE &QBE___13 NOSAVE NOUPDATE
SET SAFETY &QBE___SAFE
SET CATALOG &QBE___CATA
SET FIELDS TO SALES
GO TOP
```

Although the code in Example 2-7 is longer than in previous examples, it's not very difficult. The first new command is CALCULATE AVG(SALES) TO QBE___B3. This is an option with the new CALCULATE command that averages the SALES field and then stores the results to a memory variable QBE___B3. The next two lines use the SET() function to save the current values of SET SAFETY and SET CATALOG to memory variables, because the safety and the catalog both will be SET OFF to prevent problems from possible name conflicts. Turning off the catalog prevents the temporary database that's about to be created from being added to the current catalog.

The memory variable QBE___13 is actually going to be the name of the temporary database where the results of the average will be stored. The expression that defines its value, STR(RAND(-1)*100000000,8), generates a random eight-digit number. The RAND() function is the random-number function. In best numerical fashion, RAND(-1) uses the current value of the system clock to generate the number, reducing the number of duplicate file names. Therefore, the database name will be nearly completely random.

 Hint: You will undoubtedly see files with names that are eight digits followed by an extension showing up in your data directories. These files are created in much the same way as QBE___13. They are temporary files, so you should delete them now and then to cut down on disk clutter. You may also redirect them to a DOS directory by adding the command SET TMP = <directory name> to your AUTOEXEC.BAT file as an alternative to deletion.

Because the file has SET FIELDS TO A->SALES, the COPY STRUCTURE TO &QBE___13 command will copy only the SALES field, together with its length and decimals. After that, the query merely appends a blank record and replaces the field with its value from the memory variable created with the CALCULATE command. The command USE &QBE___13 NOSAVE NOUPDATE is clear except for the NOSAVE clause, which is not documented in the dBASE IV manual. This clause merely means that the file is to be erased once it is closed. NOUPDATE, of course, means the database is read-only.

Grouping, Sorting, and Summary Operators

Suppose you don't want the overall results of a summary operator. There is an easy way to produce summaries by groups. Just type *"Group by"* (without the quotation marks) in the field of the example form you want to use as the basis for the grouping.

QBE also lets you sort on any field using ascending and descending sorts with either ASCII or dictionary sorts. ASCII sorts use the ASCII values of different characters as the basis for the sort. A dictionary sort ignores upper- and lowercase letters. This is important because in the ASCII table all lowercase letters have values 32 units higher than their uppercase equivalents. Thus an ASCII sort always places all uppercase characters before any lowercase character in the same position in the string. For sorts by numeric field, ASCII and dictionary sorts produce the same results. For example, to produce average sales by state, with the averages sorted in descending order, you could use either an ASCII or a dictionary sort.

Figure 2-19 shows the phrase "AVG, Dsc1" in the SALES field of the query example form. This is a command to average sales and sort the results in descending ASCII order. The number 1 at the end means this is the first sort

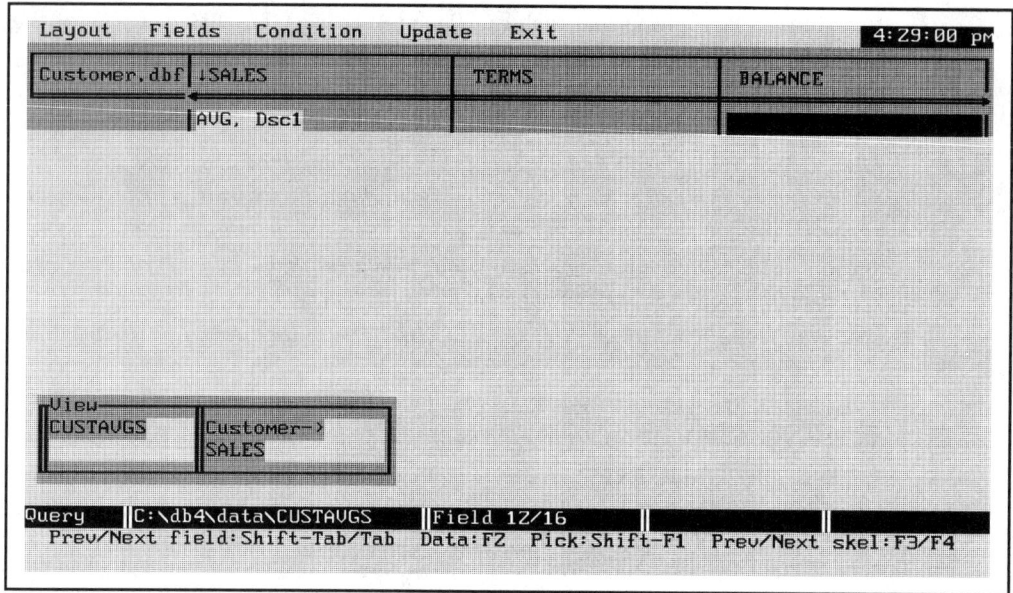

Figure 2-19   Average Summary Operator with Descending Sort

field. You can sort on multiple fields by incrementing the number in the example.

Figure 2-20 shows the phrase "Group by" in the STATE field. Pressing F2, the results shown in Figure 2-21 appear.

Let's look at the code that produces this somewhat complicated result. Example 2-8 contains the listing of the QBE file.

Example 2-8   QBE Code for Average Sorted Grouped Query (Line numbers added for convenience)

```
1 * dBASE IV .QBE file
2 SET FIELDS TO
3 SELECT 1
4 USE CUSTOMER.DBF AGAIN
5 SET EXACT ON
6 SET FILTER TO
7 GO TOP
8 QBE___SAFE = SET("SAFETY")
```

(continued)

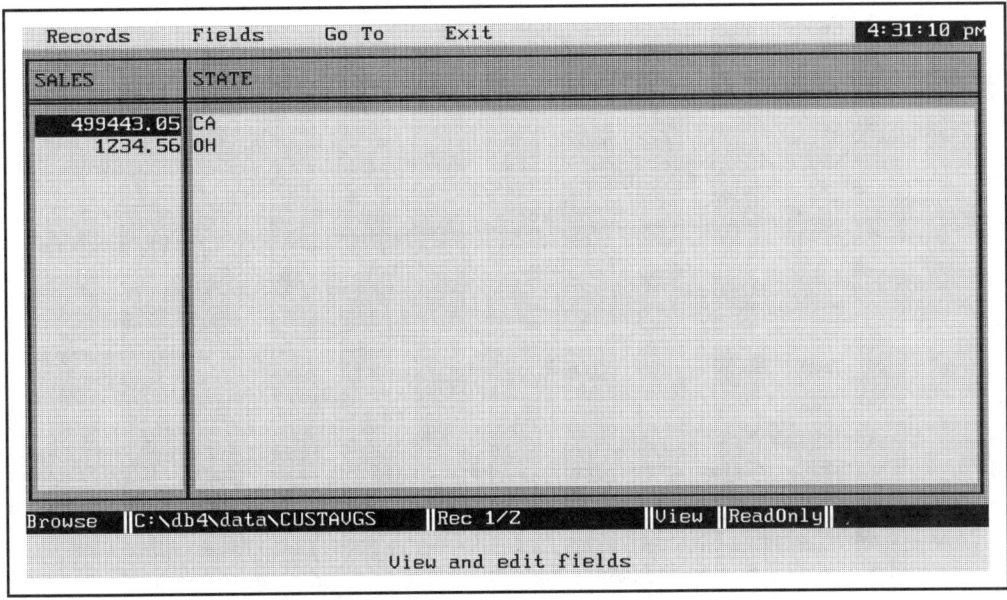

Figure 2-20 Group by State

Figure 2-21 Results of Average Sorted Grouped Query

```
 9 QBE___CATA = SET("CATALOG")
10 SET SAFETY OFF
11 SET CATALOG OFF
12 IF RECCOUNT() > 1
13 QBE___15 = STR(RAND(-1)*100000000,8)
14 SORT TO &QBE___15 ON STATE
15 USE &QBE___15 NOSAVE NOUPDATE
16 ENDIF
17 SET FIELDS TO A->SALES,A->STATE
18 QBE___14 = STR(RAND(-1)*100000000,8)
19 COPY STRU TO &QBE___14
20 SET FIELDS TO
21 GO TOP
22 SELECT 9
23 USE &QBE___14
24 SELECT 1
25 QBE___B4 = STATE
26 QBE___C3 = 0
27 QBE___C5 = 0
28 DO WHILE .NOT. EOF()
29 IF .NOT. (QBE___B4 = STATE)
30 SELECT 9
31 APPEND BLANK
32 REPLACE STATE WITH QBE___B4,SALES WITH QBE___C3/QBE___C5
33 SELECT 1
34 QBE___B4 = STATE
35 QBE___C3 = 0
36 QBE___C5 = 0
37 ENDIF
38 QBE___C3 = QBE___C3 + SALES
39 QBE___C5 = QBE___C5 + 1
40 SKIP
41 ENDDO
42 SELECT 9
43 APPEND BLANK
44 REPLACE STATE WITH QBE___B4,SALES WITH QBE___C3/QBE___C5
45 USE
46 SELECT 1
47 USE &QBE___14 NOSAVE NOUPDATE
```

(continued)

```
48 SET SAFETY &QBE___SAFE
49 SET CATALOG &QBE___CATA
50 SET FIELDS TO SALES,STATE
51 QBE___SAFE = SET("SAFETY")
52 QBE___CATA = SET("CATALOG")
53 SET SAFETY OFF
54 SET CATALOG OFF
55 GO TOP
56 IF RECCOUNT() > 1
57 QBE___12 = STR(RAND(-1)*100000000,8)
58 SORT TO &QBE___12 ON SALES/D
59 USE &QBE___12 NOSAVE NOUPDATE
60 ENDIF
61 SET SAFETY &QBE___SAFE
62 SET CATALOG &QBE___CATA
63 SET FIELDS TO
64 SET FIELDS TO SALES,STATE
65 GO TOP
```

You're familiar with most of what's going on here. At line 13, the variable QBE___15 is defined using the same random-number technique we saw in Example 2-7; the value of this variable is used as the database name for the first sort. The CUSTOMER database is sorted ON STATE in line 14 to this new database. Line 15 opens this database using the NOSAVE and NOUPDATE clauses (see Example 2-7). Line 17 picks the fields SALES and STATE. A new random variable, QBE___14, is defined on line 18, and the SALES and STATE fields are copied to its value as a DBF file on line 19. This database is opened in work area 9 on lines 22 and 23. The value of the STATE field from the database &QBE___15 is stored to the variable QBE___B4 on line 25. Two additional variables, QBE___C3 and QBE___C4, are initialized on lines 26 and 27. Line 28 moves the pointer through the &QBE___15 database. Line 29 checks to see if the value of the STATE field has changed; if so, lines 30–32 add a blank record to &QBE___14 and replace the STATE field with the value from &QBE___15 and the SALES field with average sales. At lines 38–39, QBE___C3 stores the sum of SALES for each state, and QBE___C4 counts the number of occurrences. Finally, the database is sorted again to another database &QBE___12, and the results are displayed.

Note that the structure

```
DO WHILE .NOT. EOF() ... SKIP ... ENDDO
```

is inefficient. It would be faster to use a

```
SCAN ... ENDSCAN
```

construct instead. Using indexes instead of the sort would also be more efficient.

The Unique and First Operators

If you only want to see the first occurrence of each value or to include unique values in summary operators, just put the keyword UNIQUE after the operator. For example, if you want to know how many different customers have invoices in the INVOICE database, just put CNT UNIQUE in the CUSTCODE field of the example form. You can also use the word UNIQUE alone to exclude from the View records that have duplicate values for a specific field.

When you are linking tables, if you want to include only the first occurrence of the linking field, type the keyword FIRST in front of the linking example in the table from which you want the first record taken. For example, suppose you're linking CUSTOMER and INVOICE. If you only want to see the first invoice for each customer, just put the word FIRST in front of the linking example LINK1 in the CUSTCODE field of the INVOICE example form. (Don't put the word EVERY there, too, as that will confuse dBASE IV incredibly!)

Using Indexes

The Fields menu includes an "Include indexes" option. dBASE IV automatically uses any available indexes that will speed up queries. If you select the "Include indexes" option, two things happen. First, any single-field indexes in the MDX file will be noted with a # sign in front of the field name in the example form. More importantly, compound indexes, such as SUBSTR(TELEPHONE,2,3), will be added to the example form at the end. You can then work with these just as if they were fields in the database! This can be very useful. If you have a compound index available that contains some

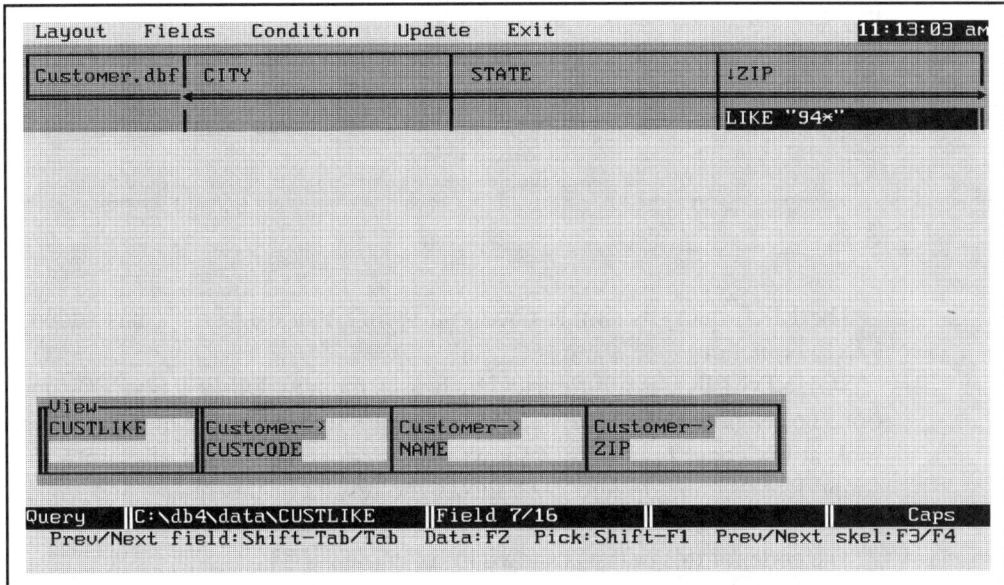

Figure 2-22   LIKE Query

data you need, you won't have to create a special calculated field to generate it; just pick "Include indexes," and the compound index will be automatically added to the example form.

LIKE and SOUNDS LIKE Queries

QBE includes two approximate match operators: LIKE and SOUNDS LIKE. LIKE lets you use DOS wildcard characters in examples. Figure 2-22 shows an example in which all zip codes starting with 94 are selected. The example LIKE "94*" will select those records. Example 2-9 shows the code generated by this query.

Example 2-9   QBE Code for the LIKE Query

```
* dBASE IV .QBE file
SET FIELDS TO
SELECT 1
```

(continued)

```
USE CUSTOMER.DBF AGAIN
SET EXACT ON
SET FILTER TO ((LIKE("94*",A->ZIP)))
GO TOP
SET FIELDS TO A->CUSTCODE,A->NAME,A->ZIP
```

The LIKE query is simple once you realize that dBASE IV has added a LIKE() function!

SOUNDS LIKE is a little trickier. It uses the new DIFFERENCE() function. To see how DIFFERENCE() works, let's first set up the query and then look at the code. Figure 2-23 shows the query setup to find all names that sound like "Lima." Figure 2-24 shows the results of this query, and Figure 2-25 shows the entire database.

The code for this query is shown in Example 2-10.

Example 2-10   Code for the SOUNDS LIKE Query

```
* dBASE IV .QBE file
SET FIELDS TO
SELECT 1
USE NAMELIST.DBF AGAIN
SET EXACT ON
SET FILTER TO ((DIFFERENCE("Lima",A->LASTNAME)>=4))
GO TOP
```

Here's how the DIFFERENCE(<string1,string2>) function works. Both strings are converted to SOUNDEX() phonetic equivalents (see the next section). DIFFERENCE() compares the results of the two SOUNDEX() calculations and returns a value from 0 to 4. A value of 4 indicates a nearly perfect soundalike; a value of 0 indicates, theoretically, little sound resemblance. Note that in the query in Example 2-10, DIFFERENCE() is set to 4. This is the default value unless you specifically enter the DIFFERENCE() function in the example. In that case, you can specify a different value. However, the key phrase SOUNDS LIKE always tells dBASE IV to use a value of 4 for the DIFFERENCE() comparison.

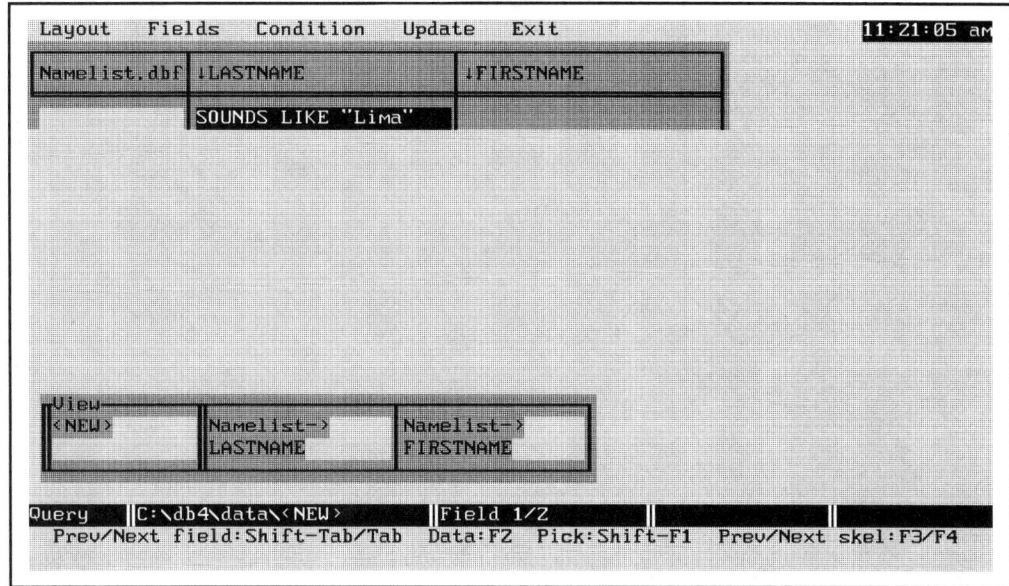

Figure 2-23   SOUNDS LIKE Query

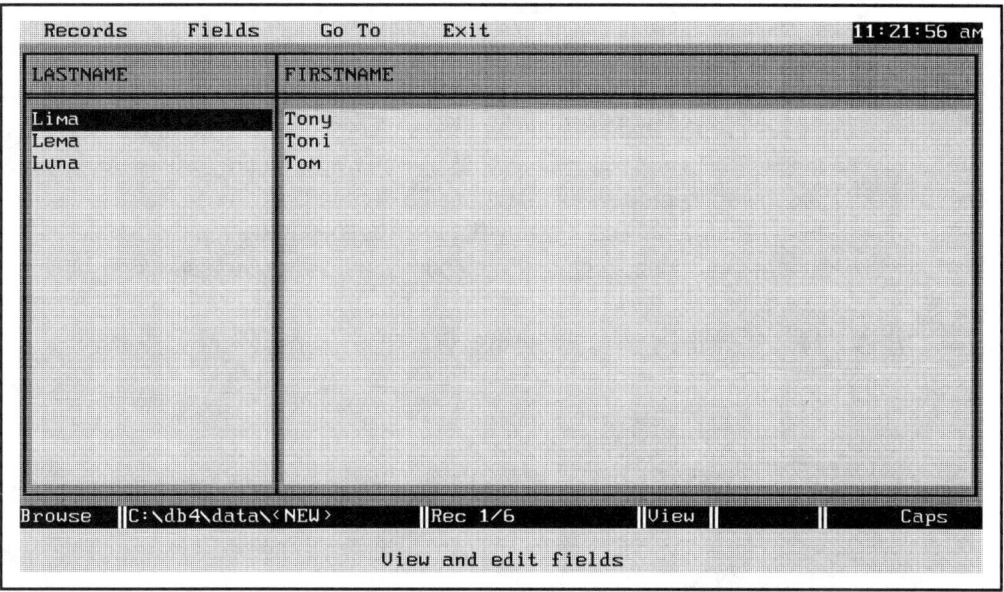

Figure 2-24   SOUNDS LIKE Query Results

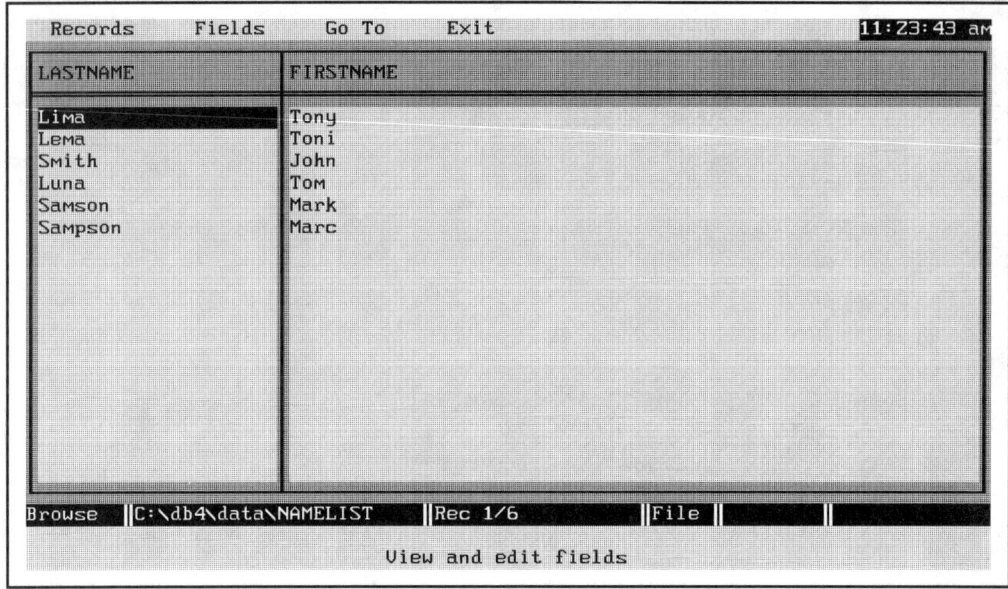

Figure 2-25   Database for SOUNDS LIKE Query

The SOUNDEX() Function

Here's how SOUNDEX(<expC>) works. First, it retains the first letter of the character expression <expC>, skipping over any leading blanks. DIFFER-ENCE() never produces a match if the first characters of the strings are different; thus, *xenix* and *zenith* will never be matched even though their first characters are both *z* sounds. It also parses the expression and stops when it reaches a nonalphabetic character. If the first character is nonalphabetic, SOUNDEX() stops and returns the character string 0000 as a value.

Second, SOUNDEX() drops the following letters from the expression: a, e, h, i, o, u, w, and y. Of course, if one of these characters is the first in the expression, it is not dropped.

Third, a number is assigned to the remaining letters according to this scheme:

b, f, p, v   : 1
c, g, j, k, q, s, x, z   : 2
d, t   : 3

l	: 4
m, n	: 5
r	: 6

Fourth, if two or more adjacent letters have the same code number, all but the first occurrence are dropped.

Finally, SOUNDEX() returns a value of the form A999 (as it would be expressed in a PICTURE clause). That is, the first character is the first character of <expC>, followed by a three-digit number. Any digits beyond the third are dropped. If there are fewer than three digits, the result is padded with trailing zeroes. The four-character code returned can then be matched with codes for other words. In fact, that's what DIFFERENCE() does.

Update Queries

There are four kinds of Update queries: Append, Replace, Mark (for deletion), and Unmark (remove marks for deletion). All of them use examples, much like those we've seen already. The code produced by Mark and Unmark is exactly what you'd expect, simply using the DELETE and RECALL commands with a FILTER set. There's no point in looking at code that simple. Instead, let's concentrate on Append and Replace queries.

Append Query

An Append query has a unique characteristic — only fields for which actual examples are included will be added. Thus, Append queries are a good way to move selected fields from one database to another when you don't want to move the entire record or deal with arrays. Figure 2-26 shows an Append query that will move only the CUSTCODE and NAME fields from a temporary customer database to the permanent file. Example 2-11 shows the code produced by this query.

Note that you cannot execute this query by pressing F2. Instead you must select "Perform the update operation" from the Update menu. Or, if you're in the Control Center, you can execute an Update query by highlighting the query and pressing Enter. Update queries are marked with asterisks in the Control Center query column to help prevent you from executing them accidentally. Remember — these queries change data!

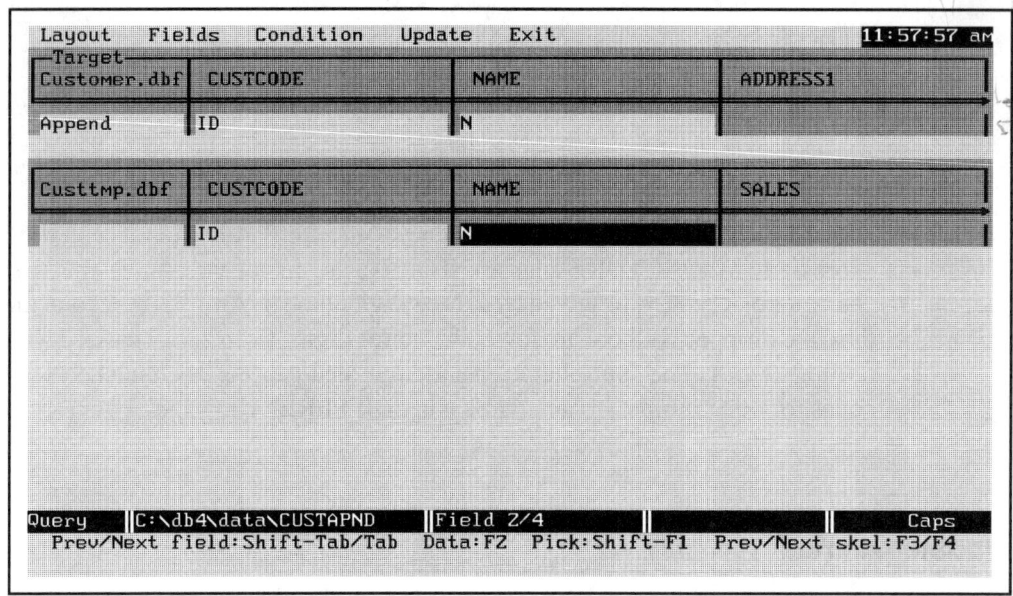

Figure 2-26   Append Query

Example 2-11   Code for Append Query

```
* dBASE IV .UPD file
SET TALK ON
SELECT 1
USE CUSTOMER.DBF AGAIN
SET FIELDS TO
SELECT 2
USE CUSTTMP.DBF AGAIN
SET EXACT ON
SET FILTER TO
GO TOP
DO WHILE .NOT. EOF()
SELECT 1
APPEND BLANK
REPLACE CUSTCODE WITH B->CUSTCODE,NAME WITH B->NAME
SELECT 2
SKIP
ENDDO
```

(continued)

```
SELECT 2
SET FILTER TO                        .
SET FIELDS TO
SET SKIP TO
SET RELATION TO
SELECT 2                                                      .
USE
```

There's nothing surprising about the code for the Append query. Instead of using APPEND FROM, the program uses APPEND BLANK, followed by REPLACE, to perform field-specific operations. Again, SCAN ... END-SCAN would be more efficient than the DO WHILE construct used.

Replace Queries

Replace queries are probably the most useful of all the Updates. Replace lets you easily and quickly perform operations such as posting invoices to customer balances. Figure 2-27 shows a Replace query that does just that. The linking examples (LINK1 in the CUSTCODE field of the CUSTOMER example form and EVERY LINK1 in the CUSTCODE field of the INVOICE example form) are not shown.

Example 2-12 shows the code generated by this query. This program is very straightforward — and also very inefficient. Example 2-13 shows a better way to do the same thing.

Example 2-12   Code for Replace Query

```
* dBASE IV .UPD file
SET TALK ON
SET FIELDS TO
SELECT 2
USE INVOICE.DBF AGAIN NOUPDATE
USE CUSTOMER.DBF AGAIN IN 1 ORDER CUSTCODE
SET EXACT ON
SET FILTER TO
SET RELATION TO B->CUSTCODE INTO A
SET SKIP TO A
```

(continued)

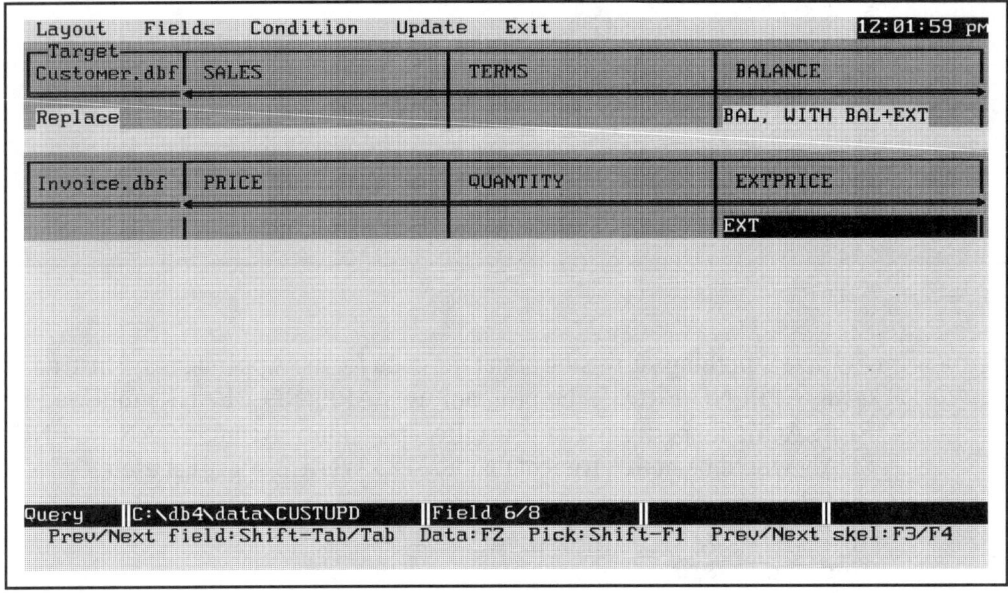

Figure 2-27   A Replace Query

```
GO TOP
DO WHILE .NOT. EOF()
SELECT 1
REPLACE BALANCE WITH A->BALANCE+B->EXTPRICE
SELECT 2
SKIP
ENDDO
SELECT 2
SET FILTER TO
SET FIELDS TO
SET SKIP TO
SET RELATION TO
SELECT 2
USE
```

Example 2-13   Better Code for Replace Query

```
* CUSTPOST.PRG
SET TALK ON
SET FIELDS TO
SELECT 1
USE CUSTOMER.DBF AGAIN ORDER CUSTCODE
USE INVOICE.DBF AGAIN IN 2 NOUPDATE
SET EXACT ON
SET FILTER TO
SET RELATION TO CUSTCODE INTO INVOICE
SET SKIP TO INVOICE, CUSTOMER
GO TOP
SCAN
  REPLACE BALANCE WITH A->BALANCE+B->EXTPRICE
ENDSCAN
SELECT 2
SET FILTER TO
SET FIELDS TO
SET SKIP TO
SET RELATION TO
SELECT 2
USE
```

By setting the SKIP this way, the pointer is automatically moved through the INVOICE database for every invoice for each customer. Thus, all we have to do is the SCAN ... ENDSCAN with a simple REPLACE in between! Based on tests with small databases (posting 1,000 invoices to three customers), this program runs about 30 percent faster than the Replace query.

Conclusion

Query By Example is a powerful, easy-to-use feature of dBASE IV that has the added advantage of producing program code. The relational select and project operators are easily accomplished, along with inner and outer joins.

Approximate match queries are also supported. Finally, Update queries let you change data easily. However, we saw that the code generated by QBE is not always the most efficient, largely due to its use of the archaic DO WHILE .NOT. EOF() ... SKIP ... ENDDO construct instead of the more efficient SCAN ... ENDSCAN.

Chapter 3

An Overview of Templates

Before plunging into the intricacies of the dBASE IV templates, let's first take a look at the major parts of a template program. We'll be looking at many of the details in the following chapters, so don't worry about them for the moment.

Elements of a Template Program

There are six basic sections in a template program:

- File header
- Inclusion section, where external program files are read into the main program
- Variable initialization section
- Processing section
- File closing and housekeeping section
- User-defined functions

Let's look at each of these.

The Template Header

Every template program begins with a header that looks something like Example 3-1. The header gives the file name, purpose of the file, version number and date, and initials of the developer. Unfortunately, as is so often the case with software, the version number and date of last modification are not kept up to date. In fact, since the October 1988 release there have been at least two updates to REPORT.COD and LABEL.COD. If you want to be sure you have the latest version of all templates, call Ashton-Tate to find out how to get access to their computer bulletin board. Updated versions of all dBASE IV templates are contained in the DB4 conference and available for downloading from there. These files are also available in the Ashton-Tate conference on CompuServe and The Source.

Example 3-1   Template File Header (FORM.COD)

```
 1 // $Header: /a/CCS/apgentc/cod/form.cod,v 1.47 88/08/24 19:21:43
      joeg Dev$
 2 // Module Name: FORM.COD
 3 // Description: This module is for producing dBASE IV .FMT files
 4 //
 5
 6 Format (.fmt) File Template
 7 --------------------------
 8 Version 1.47
 9 Ashton-Tate (c) 1987, 1988
10
```

The point is to check the DOS date stamp on the file to see if it is different from that in your directory. I always keep new template files in a directory separate from the old versions and always, always archive the old templates before replacing them with the new ones. Table 3-1 shows the dates on the template source code files used in this book.

These updates cause slight problems for readers of this book. If a source code file has been updated with a later version, its code might not exactly match the code shown here. However, the changes we'll be making are generic enough that they can easily be incorporated in the correct places. Far more important is to be sure you have the latest versions of the templates and to keep archive copies of the previous versions.

Table 3-1

Template	*Date*
FORM.COD	11/20/88
REPORT.COD	2/01/89
LABEL.COD	2/22/89
QUICKAPP.COD	8/29/88
DS_*.COD, DD_*.COD	8/29/88
(DOCUMENT.GEN files)	
AS_*.COD, AD_*.COD	8/29/88
(Applications Generator file)	

Include Section

All template commands must be enclosed in curly braces ({ }). Within command lines, comments can be included if they are preceded by a double slash (//). The first commands in virtually every template program file are the include commands. There are usually two of them. The file BUILTIN.DEF, which contains constants and functions used in all template modules, is always included. Usually there will be a second file included that contains constants and functions specific to the type of object being processed. This file will have the same name as the template file, with the extension DEF instead of COD. Example 3-2 shows the include section of FORM.COD. (Don't worry about what's in these files, for now; these files will be discussed in detail in subsequent chapters.)

Example 3-2   Include Section (FORM.COD)

```
11 {
12 include "form.def";    // Form selectors
13 include "builtin.def"; // Builtin functions
14
```

The template language relies on a large number of "selectors." These are data names defined as numeric constants. There are four classes of selectors:

- Elements that make up the design object file, such as Box_element
- Attributes of an element, such as Row_Positn
- Functions such as DATE() and SUBSTR()
- Miscellaneous names such as TREE and DOSFILE

Selectors are declared with the SELECTOR statement. They are generally initialized in the DEF files. Using the selector in a template returns information about the item referenced. Most return strings or constants. If you want to find out the identification number for a selector, use the IIDC() function or attach an @ sign to the beginning of the selector name.

There are six selector (DEF) files included with dBASE IV. BUILTIN.DEF is used in all template files. FORM.DEF, REPORT.DEF, and LABEL.DEF are each used with the appropriate template. QUICKAPP.DEF is used with the quick applications generator, while APPLCTN.DEF is used with the full applications generator. I strongly recommend printing all of these files and using them for reference while you read this book. Selectors are referenced frequently in the text.

Variable Initialization Section

Every template program has to define a number of variables and initialize them. The template language has "strong data typing," meaning that variables must be defined before they can be used (rather than defined when they are first used, as with dBASE IV). Example 3-3 shows part of the variable initialization section of FORM.COD.

Example 3-3   Variable Initialization Section (FORM.COD)

```
15 //
16 // Enum string constants for international translation
17 //
18 enum wrong_class = "Can't use FORM.GEN on non-form objects ",
19       form_empty = "Form design was empty ";
20 //
```

(continued)

```
21
22 if Frame_class != form then // We are not processing a form object
23   pause(wrong_class + any_key);
24   goto NoGen;
25 endif
26
27 var  fmt_name,    // Format file name
28      crlf,        // line feed
29      carry_flg,   // Flag to test carry loop
30      carry_cnt,   // Count of the number of fields to carry
31      carry_len,   // Cumulative length of carry line until 75
                        characters
32      carry_lent,  // Total cumulative length of carry line
33      carry_first, // Flag to test "," output for carry fields
34      color_flg,   // Flag to if color should stay on am line
35      line_cnt,    // Count for total lines processed (Mulitple page
                        forms)
36      page_cnt,    // Count for total pages processed (Mulitple page
                        forms)
37      temp,        // tempory work variable
38      cnt,         // Foreach loop variable
39      wnd_cnt,     // Window counter
40      wnd_names,   // Window names so I can clear them at the bottom
                        of the file
41      default_drv, // dBASE default drive
42      dB_status,   // dBASE status before entering designer
43      scrn_size,   // Screen size when generation starts
44      display,     // Type of display screen we are on
45      color;       // Color returned from getcolor function
46
47 //----------------------------------------------
48 // Assign default values to some of the variables
49 //----------------------------------------------
50 crlf = chr(10);
51 temp = "";
52 carry_flg = carry_first = carry_cnt = carry_len = carry_lent =
53 wnd_cnt = line_cnt =  color_flg = cnt = 0;
54 page_cnt = 1;
55
```

Example 3-3 also contains the first of several error traps, shown on lines
22–25. Here the type of object is tested. If it is not a form, the template returns
an error message and aborts.

Processing Section

Naturally, most of the template program is devoted to processing. Example
3-4 shows ninety-one lines of FORM.COD. Let's see what these do.

Example 3-4   Processing Section (FORM.COD)

```
56  // Test screen size if display > 2 screen is 43 lines
57  display = numset(_flgcolor);
58  if display > ega25 then scrn_size = 39 else scrn_size = 21 endif;
59
60  // Test to see if status was off before going into form designer
61  dB_status = numset(_flgstatus);
62  if scrn_size == 21 and !db_status then
63     scrn_size = 24;
64  endif
65  if scrn_size == 39 and !db_status then // status is off
66     scrn_size = 42;
67  endif
68  //-----------------------------
69  // Create Format file
70  //-----------------------------
71  default_drv = strset(_defdrive);  // grab default drive from
       dBASE
72  if filedrive(Name) or !default_drv then
73     fmt_name = alltrim(Name);
74  else
75     fmt_name = default_drv + ":" +alltrim(Name);
76  endif
77  fmt_name = upper(fmt_name);
78  create(fmt_name+".FMT");
79  }
80  //
```

(continued)

```
 81 {print(replicate("*",80)+crlf);}
 82 *-- Name....: {filename(fmt_name)}FMT
 83 *-- Date....: {ltrim(SUBSTR(date(),1,8))}
 84 *-- Version.: dBASE IV, Format {Frame_ver}.44
 85 *-- Notes...: Format files use "" as delimiters!
 86 {print(replicate("*",80)+crlf);}
 87 //
 88
 89 *-- Format file initialization code -----------------------------
 90
 91 IF SET("TALK")="ON"
 92    SET TALK OFF
 93    lc_talk="ON"
 94 ELSE
 95    lc_talk="OFF"
 96 ENDIF
 97 {   case display of
 98       mono:   temp="MONO";
 99       cga:    temp="COLOR";
100       ega25:  temp="EGA25";
101       mono43: temp="MONO43";
102       ega43:  temp="EGA43";
103    endcase
104 }
105
106 *-- This form was created in {temp} mode
107 SET DISPLAY TO {temp}
108 {  temp="";}
109
110 lc_status=SET("STATUS")
111 *-- SET STATUS was \
112 {if dB_status then}
113 ON when you went into the Forms Designer.
114 IF lc_status = "OFF"
115    SET STATUS ON
116 {else}
117 OFF when you went into the Forms Designer.
118 IF lc_status = "ON"
119    SET STATUS OFF
```

(continued)

```
120 {endif}
121 ENDIF
122 //-------------------------------------------------------------
123 // Process fields to build "SET CARRY" and WINDOW commands.
124 //-------------------------------------------------------------
125 {
126  foreach Fld_element flds
127    if Row_positn-line_cnt > scrn_size then
128       line_cnt = line_cnt+scrn_size+1;
129    endif
130    if Fld_carry then carry_flg = 1; ++carry_cnt; endif
131    if chr(Fld_value_type) == "M" and Fld_mem_typ and wnd_cnt < 16
then
132       ++wnd_cnt; wnd_names = wnd_names + "Wndow" + wnd_cnt + ",";
133 }
134
135 *-- Window for memo field {lower(Fld_fieldname)}.
136 DEFINE WINDOW Wndow{wnd_cnt} FROM {nul2zero(Box_top) - line_cnt},\
137 {   nul2zero(Box_left)} TO \
138 {   temp = nul2zero(Box_top) + Box_height - line_cnt - 1;
139    if temp > scrn_size then scrn_size else temp endif},\
140 {   nul2zero(Box_left) + Box_width - 1} \
141 {   outbox(Box_type, Box_special_char);
142    color = getcolor(Fld_display, Fld_editable);
143    outcolor();
144   endif
145  next flds;
146  print(crlf);
```

Lines 56–58 test the display type:

```
56  // Test screen size if display > 2 screen is 43 lines
57  display = numset(_flgcolor);
58  if display > ega25 then scrn_size = 39 else scrn_size = 21
     endif;
```

To see how this works, it helps to know that the constant _flgcolor is defined in BUILTIN.DEF:

```
_flgcolor ,          //  8 Color set flag 0=b/w 1=cga 2=ega24
4=mono43
                     //                      6=ega43   3 & 5=N/A

   .

   .

   .

// Enum for Monitor types
// Values returned by numset(_flgcolor)
 enum mono = 0,
      cga,
      ega25,
      mono43 = 4,
      ega43  = 6

 ;
```

Writing the FMT file actually starts at line 78 with the CREATE() function. Note that the format file name is stored and converted to uppercase before this point. After that, the file header is written. In the next chapter, we'll see how to easily modify this file header to produce your own personalized header. That way, your copyright notices, and so on, will be automatically inserted in the program whenever a new version is generated. Lines 81–86 of Example 3-4 show this code.

Finally, the last part of the code we'll look at here sets the display to match the mode your computer was in when you generated the code. We'll see how to modify this to make your program code relatively independent of monitor or graphics board type.

```
 97 {   case display of
 98       mono:   temp="MONO";
 99       cga:    temp="COLOR";
100       ega25:  temp="EGA25";
101       mono43: temp="MONO43";
102       ega43:  temp="EGA43";
103     endcase
104 }
105
106 *-- This form was created in {temp} mode
107 SET DISPLAY TO {temp}
108 {   temp="";}
109
```

File Closing Section

Finally, the housekeeping commands and FMT file exit code must be generated. Example 3-5 shows the section of FORM.COD that generates this
program code.

Example 3-5   File Closing (FORM.COD)

```
319 *-- Format file exit code ----------------------------------------
320
321 *-- SET STATUS was \
322 {if dB_status then}
323 ON when you went into the Forms Designer.
324 IF lc_status = "OFF"  && Entered form with status off
325    SET STATUS OFF      && Turn STATUS "OFF" on the way out
326 {else}
327 OFF when you went into the Forms Designer.
328 IF lc_status = "ON"  && Entered form with status on
329    SET STATUS ON     && Turn STATUS "ON" on the way out
330 {endif}
331 ENDIF
332 {if carry_flg then}
333
334 IF lc_carry = "OFF"
335    SET CARRY OFF
336 ENDIF
337 {endif}
338 {if wnd_names then}
339
340 RELEASE WINDOWS {substr(wnd_names, 1, (len(wnd_names) - 1))}
341 {endif}
342
343 IF lc_talk="ON"
344    SET TALK ON
345 ENDIF
346
347 RELEASE {if carry_flg
        then}lc_carry,{endif}lc_talk,lc_fields,lc_status
348 *-- EOP: {filename(fmt_name)}FMT
349 {if cnt == 0 then
```

(continued)

```
350      pause(form_empty + any_key);
351  endif;
352  fileerase(fmt_name+".FMO");
353  nogen:
354  return 0;}
```

The dBASE IV code generated is pretty standard. There's an error trap in lines 349–351 to handle the case when the screen form is empty. The nogen: label on line 353 is where the program jumps if the error trap near the beginning of the COD file that checks to be sure the file is processing a form object returns a false. The "return 0;" statement returns to the calling program with a value of 0, indicating no generation errors.

User-defined Functions

These functions are defined for use in the template file. Example 3-6 shows the beginning of a UDF that handles processing colors. All template UDFs begin with the keyword DEFINE and end with ENDDEF.

Example 3-6   User-defined Functions (FORM.COD)

```
355 //----------------------------
356 // User defined functions follow
357 //----------------------------
358 {
359  define getcolor(f_display, f_editable);
360
361  enum  Foreground   =    7,
362        Intensity    =    8,  // Color
363        Background    =  112,
364
365        MIntensity   =  256,
366        Reverse      =  512,  // Mono
367        Underline    = 1024,
368        Blink        = 2048,
369        default      =32768; // Screen set to default
370
```

(continued)

```
371  var forgrnd, enhanced, backgrnd, blnk, underln, revrse,
        use_colors, incolor;
372  incolor="";
373
```

BUILTIN.DEF

The one file that is used by all other templates is BUILTIN.DEF. This contains the global selectors required by virtually all dBASE programs. As mentioned earlier, I strongly recommend that you print this and all other DEF files for reference while reading this book.

Conclusion

This chapter has been an introduction to the structure of template files. Along the way, you have probably picked up some of the syntax of template commands and functions. However, the basic structure of template programs does not change. The same six elements are always present, as is the definition file BUILTIN.DEF. With this as an introduction, let's look at FORM.COD.

Chapter 4

Screen Forms and Templates

This chapter discusses how the template language processes screen form objects; it also suggests several possible changes to the basic template file. You will also learn the rudiments of working with the template compiler, DTC.EXE, and the fine art (and believe me, it's an art) of substituting your own template for FORM.GEN.

FORM.GEN is discussed first because it's the simplest of all the templates. The complexities of other templates will be discussed in following chapters.

In this chapter you will actually look at a template language program, FORM.COD. This is the source code version of the compiled file FORM.GEN. FORM.GEN takes about 8.4K of disk space. FORM.COD is a 478-line template program that uses the "selectors" defined in FORM.DEF, which is actually a second program of about 150 lines. The file BUILTIN.DEF is called by all main template files and is about three hundred lines of code. A complete listing of the latest version of FORM.COD with line numbers is included in Appendix B to this chapter. If you haven't already done it, print FORM.DEF so you can look up the selectors as they're referenced throughout this chapter.

A word of warning: this chapter is very long because you are going to go through FORM.COD in great detail as a way of learning many of the elements of the template language. Stick with it and read the whole thing. You'll find the chapters after this are much easier going.

What Must a Template Do?

The idea is for the template program to recognize different screen objects and produce program code to handle them appropriately. Thus, FORM.GEN must be able to recognize a field. More important, once it has spotted a field it must be able to figure out what specifically to do with it. For example if the field has been marked "read only" in the Edit options menu, the template has to be intelligent enough to generate an @...SAY rather than an @...GET. Naturally, all the other Edit options, picture functions, colors, and so on must be fully supported.

dBASE IV can operate in a variety of video modes, including forty three-line EGA mode. The template must be able to recognize the current video mode and produce appropriate code. One thing we'll be concerned with is producing more generic code that can check for the current video mode and adjust the display appropriately.

If there are boxes or lines drawn on the screen, the template must recognize and process them using the correct color combinations. Similarly, memory variables must be correctly handled. Even a simple template like FORM.COD has quite a bit to keep track of!

A Simple Data Entry Screen

Figures 4-1 and 4-2 show a simple two-page data entry screen for CUSTO-MER.DBF, the structure of which is shown in Example 4-1. Without going into too many details, Example 4-2 shows the code generated by this screen.

Example 4-1   Structure of CUSTOMER.DBF

```
Structure for database: C:\DB4\DATA\CUSTOMER.DBF
Number of data records:        3
Date of last update   : 04/01/89
Field   Field Name  Type      Width    Dec    Index
    1   CUSTCODE    Character    11             Y
    2   NAME        Character    28             Y
    3   ADDRESS1    Character    28             N
    4   ADDRESS2    Character    28             N
    5   CITY        Character    17             N
    6   STATE       Character     2             Y
    7   ZIP         Character    10             Y
```

(continued)

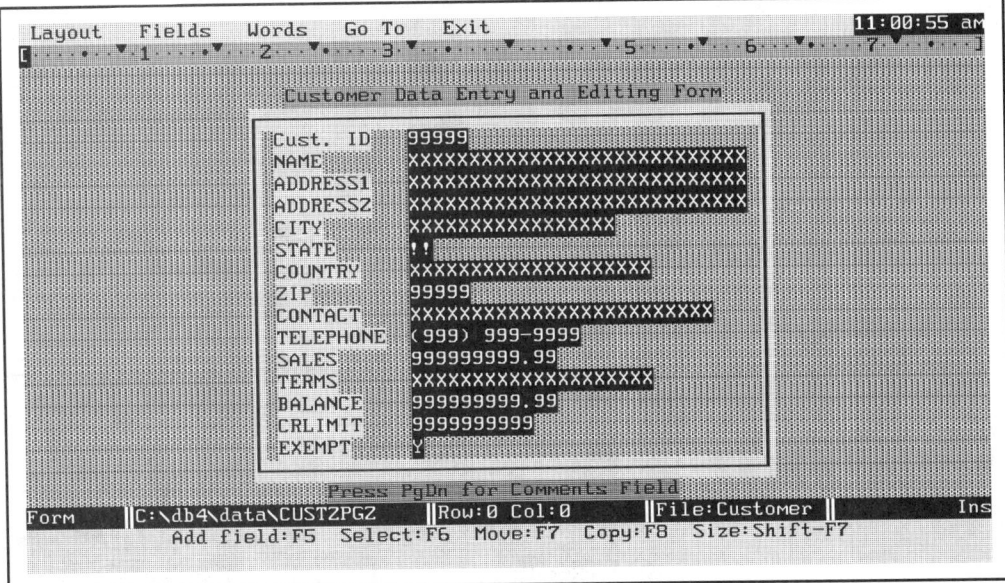

Figure 4-1   Data Entry Screen for CUSTOMER.DBF (Page 1)

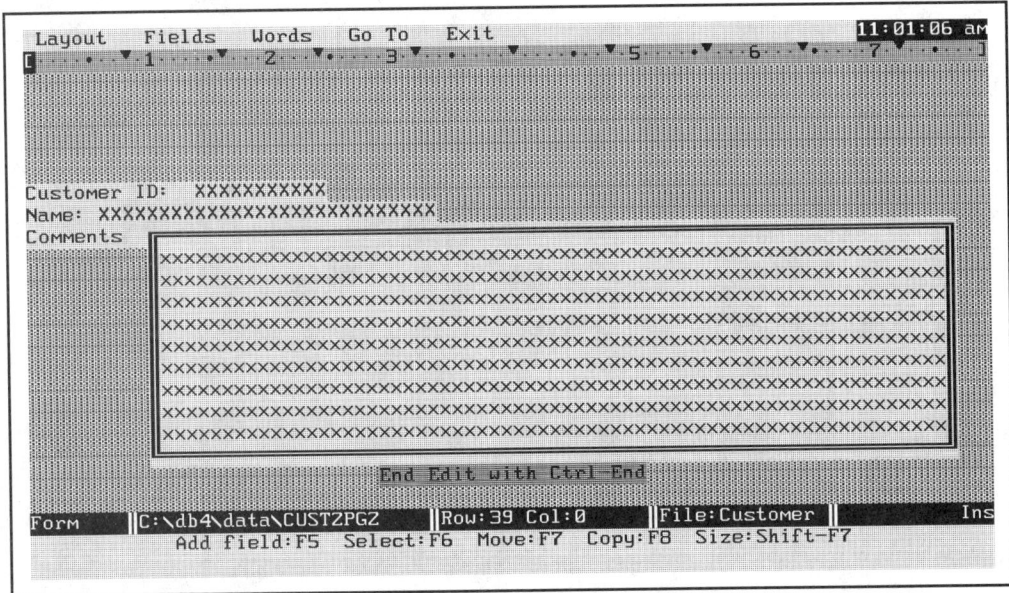

Figure 4-2   Data Entry Screen for CUSTOMER.DBF (Page 2)

8	CONTACT	Character	25		N
9	TELEPHONE	Character	20		N
10	SALES	Numeric	12	2	N
11	TERMS	Character	20		N
12	BALANCE	Numeric	12	2	Y
13	CRLIMIT	Numeric	10		N
14	COUNTRY	Character	20		N
15	EXEMPT	Logical	1		N
16	COMMENTS	Memo	10		N
** Total **			255		

Example 4-2 Generated Code for CUST2PG2.SCR

```
 1 ********************************************************************
 2 *-- Name....: CUST2PG2.FMT
 3 *-- Date....: 4-08-89
 4 *-- Version.: dBASE IV, Format 1.0
 5 *-- Notes...: Format files use "" as delimiters!
 6 ********************************************************************
 7
 8 *-- Format file initialization code ------------------------------
 9
10 IF SET("TALK")="ON"
11    SET TALK OFF
12    lc_talk="ON"
13 ELSE
14    lc_talk="OFF"
15 ENDIF
16
17 *-- This form was created in EGA25 mode
18 SET DISPLAY TO EGA25
19
20 lc_status=SET("STATUS")
21 *-- SET STATUS was ON when you went into the Forms Designer.
22 IF lc_status = "OFF"
23    SET STATUS ON
24 ENDIF
25
```

(continued)

```
26 *-- Window for memo field comments.
27 DEFINE WINDOW Wndow1 FROM 5,10 TO 15,76 DOUBLE
28
29 lc_carry = SET("CARRY")
30 *-- Fields to carry forward during APPEND.
31 SET CARRY TO custcode ADDITIVE
32
33 *-- @ SAY GETS Processing. ---------------------------------------
34
35 *--  Format Page: 1
36
37 @ 1,22 SAY "Customer Data Entry and Editing Form" COLOR b/bg
38 @ 2,19 TO 18,61
39 @ 3,21 SAY "C" COLOR w/b
40 @ 3,22 SAY "ust. ID"
41 @ 3,32 GET custcode PICTURE "99999" ;
42    VALID VAL(CUSTCODE) > 10000 ;
43    ERROR "Customer ID number must be greater than 10000" ;
44    MESSAGE "Enter the 5 digit customer ID number"
45 @ 4,21 SAY "NAME"
46 @ 4,32 GET name PICTURE "XXXXXXXXXXXXXXXXXXXXXXXXXXX"
47 @ 5,21 SAY "ADDRESS1"
48 @ 5,32 GET address1 PICTURE "XXXXXXXXXXXXXXXXXXXXXXXXXXXX"
49 @ 6,21 SAY "ADDRESS2"
50 @ 6,32 GET address2 PICTURE "XXXXXXXXXXXXXXXXXXXXXXXXXXXX"
51 @ 7,21 SAY "CITY"
52 @ 7,32 GET city PICTURE "XXXXXXXXXXXXXXXX"
53 @ 8,21 SAY "STATE"
54 @ 8,32 GET state PICTURE "@!M CA,AZ,AK,OH"
55 @ 9,21 SAY "COUNTRY"
56 @ 9,32 GET country PICTURE "XXXXXXXXXXXXXXXXXXX" ;
57    DEFAULT "U.S."
58 @ 10,21 SAY "ZIP"
59 @ 10,32 GET zip PICTURE "99999" ;
60    WHEN COUNTRY = "U.S." .OR. TRIM(COUNTRY) = ""
61 @ 11,21 SAY "CONTACT"
62 @ 11,32 GET contact PICTURE "XXXXXXXXXXXXXXXXXXXXXXXXX"
63 @ 12,21 SAY "TELEPHONE"
64 @ 12,32 GET telephone PICTURE "(999) 999-9999"
65 @ 13,21 SAY "SALES"
```

(continued)

```
66 @ 13,32 GET sales PICTURE "999999999.99"
67 @ 14,21 SAY "TERMS"
68 @ 14,32 GET terms PICTURE "XXXXXXXXXXXXXXXXXXXX"
69 @ 15,21 SAY "BALANCE"
70 @ 15,32 GET balance PICTURE "999999999.99"
71 @ 16,21 SAY "CRLIMIT"
72 @ 16,32 GET crlimit PICTURE "9999999999" ;
73    RANGE 0,100000
74 @ 17,21 SAY "EXEMPT"
75 @ 17,32 GET exempt PICTURE "Y"
76 @ 19,25 SAY "Press PgDn for Comments Field" COLOR b/r
77 READ
78
79 *-- Format Page: 2
80
81 @ 3,0 SAY "Customer ID:  "
82 @ 3,14 SAY custcode PICTURE "XXXXXXXXXXX"
83 @ 4,0 SAY "Name: "
84 @ 4,6 SAY name PICTURE "XXXXXXXXXXXXXXXXXXXXXXXXXXXX"
85 @ 5,0 SAY "Comments   "
86 @ 5,10 GET comments OPEN WINDOW Wndow1 ;
87    MESSAGE "Press Ctrl-Home to edit"
88 @ 16,29 SAY "End Edit with Ctrl-End" COLOR b/r
89
90 *-- Format file exit code ----------------------------------------
91
92 *-- SET STATUS was ON when you went into the Forms Designer.
93 IF lc_status = "OFF"  && Entered form with status off
94    SET STATUS OFF     && Turn STATUS "OFF" on the way out
95 ENDIF
96
97 IF lc_carry = "OFF"
98    SET CARRY OFF
99 ENDIF
100
101 RELEASE WINDOWS Wndow1
102
103 IF lc_talk="ON"
104    SET TALK ON
105 ENDIF
```

(continued)

```
106
107 RELEASE lc_carry,lc_talk,lc_fields,lc_status
108 *-- EOP: CUST2PG2.FMT
109
```

Note that a number of Edit options that haven't been discussed were used to create CUST2PG2. These include displaying and editing the memo data in a window; using the MESSAGE, RANGE, DISPLAY ONLY, WHEN, and DEFAULT clauses; and using the multiple-choice picture function @M. In addition, this screen form was created in EGA25 (EGA with a twenty-five line screen) mode, so the SET DISPLAY TO command reflects this. Finally, CARRY is SET ON for the CUSTCODE field only. If you are interested in writing programs that must run on a number of different systems (with different monitors and display types), the best thing you can do is simply delete all references to SET DISPLAY from the COD files and let dBASE decide which to select.

Setting Display Modes: A Brief Digression

For the more ambitious, a short routine (AUTODISP.PRG) is shown in Example 4-3 that detects the current display type. First the program uses the ISCOLOR() function to determine whether the display is monochrome. If it is, DISPLAY is set to MONO and the program terminates. If not, by SETting consecutive display types and trapping for error 216 ("Display mode not available"), we can set the mode to the first available. Ideally, of course, the SET("DISPLAY") function would return the current display type set for dBASE, making AUTODISP redundant. Unfortunately this does not work in dBASE IV 1.0. Because of an apparent bug in 1.0, AUTODISP may not work either, depending on the color graphics adapter your machine uses. So test carefully.

Example 4-3   Routine to Automatically Detect Display Mode

```
**********************************************************************
* Program AUTODISP.PRG - Tests automatic setting of display mode
* Tony Lima, April 6, 1989
* Copyright, 1989, Pacific System Design Workshop, Inc.
```

(continued)

```
* All Rights Reserved.
* Pacific System Design Workshop, Inc. 415-593-6431
* Permission is granted to make unlimited copies of these
*  routines providing this header is left intact.
*****************************************************************
gc_lmode = "COLOR"
gl_break = .F.
ON ERROR DO Errproc WITH gc_lmode
PUBLIC gl_break
DO Pstart
DO Wndowdef
***************************************
* Start application
ACTIVATE WINDOW full
@ 10,10 SAY "Test display mode..."
WAIT "Hit the space bar to continue..."
gl_break = .T.
IF .NOT. ISCOLOR()
  SET DISPLAY TO MONO
 ELSE
  gc_lmode="COLOR"
  SET DISPLAY TO COLOR
  DO WHILE ERROR()=216
    SET DISPLAY TO &gc_lmode
  ENDDO
ENDIF && .NOT. ISCOLOR()
RELEASE WINDOW full
***************************************
DO Pstop
RETURN
* EOP: AUTODISP.PRG
*********************************************************************
* Following are procedures in alpha order
*********************************************************************
*--------------------------------------
* Procedure Errproc - Resets display mode
* Call:  ON ERROR DO Errproc WITH gc_lmode
PROCEDURE Errproc
PARAMETERS gc_lmode
```

(continued)

```
*-- Parameters : gc_lmode = last attempted display mode value
ln_err=ERROR()
IF ln_err=216
  DO CASE
    CASE gc_lmode="COLOR"
      gc_lmode="EGA25"
    CASE gc_lmode="EGA25"
      gc_lmode="COLOR"
  ENDCASE
ENDIF && ln_err=216
RETURN
*------------------------------------
* Procedure Pstart - Initializes
PROCEDURE Pstart
SET COLOR TO
@ 0 , 0 CLEAR
SET CONSOLE ON
IF ISCOLOR()
  SET COLOR TO RB+/R,G+/N
  SET COLOR OF BOX TO G+/N
  SET COLOR OF FIELDS TO RB+/R
ENDIF
SET BELL OFF
SET CARRY OFF
SET CLOCK TO 0,66
SET CLOCK ON
SET CENTURY OFF
SET CONFIRM OFF
SET DELIMITERS OFF
SET DELIMITERS TO ""
SET ESCAPE ON
SET INSTRUCT OFF
SET SAFETY ON
SET STATUS OFF
SET SCOREBOARD OFF
SET TALK OFF
RETURN
* --------------------
* Procedure Pstop
```

(continued)

```
PROCEDURE Pstop
SET FORMAT TO
SET COLOR TO
CLEAR WINDOW
CLEAR POPUP
CLEAR ALL
CLOSE ALL
ON ERROR
SET BELL ON
SET CARRY ON
SET CLOCK TO 0,66
SET CLOCK ON
SET CENTURY OFF
SET CONFIRM OFF
SET DELIMITERS ON
SET ESCAPE ON
SET INSTRUCT OFF
SET SAFETY ON
SET STATUS ON
SET SCOREBOARD ON
SET TALK ON
CLEAR
RETURN
* ---------------------
* Procedure WNDOWDEF
PROCEDURE Wndowdef
* NONE parameter refers to window border. Other legal arguments
*  are DOUBLE and PANEL. The default is a single line window.
*  full and full2 are the names of the windows.
*-- Window to cover work surface during edit, append, etc.
DEFINE WINDOW full  FROM 0,0 TO 19,79 NONE
DEFINE WINDOW full2  FROM 0,0 TO 19,79 NONE
*-- Window to cover work surface during edit, append, etc.
DEFINE WINDOW dot FROM 1,0 TO 19,79
*-- Window for area below menu heading & for running reports/labels in
DEFINE WINDOW desktop FROM 4,0 TO 19,79
*-- Window for area for browsing
DEFINE WINDOW Browse FROM 10,05 TO 19,79
RETURN
* End program AUTODISP.PRG
```

Back to Format Files

The format file CUST2PG2.FMT will be more than adequate to reflect changes made to FORM.COD. Ideally, of course, we would incorporate code in FORM.COD to produce the kind of routines suggested in the previous section. I can make suggestions about where such code should be placed and what it should look like, but our objective is to produce a modified version of FORM.COD that will produce *working* dBASE IV programs. Because there's a chance that AUTODISP.PRG may not work on your machine, I'll omit further references to automatic display detection. (However, feel free to experiment on your own.)

Before Making Changes . . .

Because of the way dBASE IV handles templates, it's easier to make a backup of the original FORM.COD than it is to work with a form template with a different file name. (Appendix A shows how to substitute different template file names for the defaults for screen forms, reports, and labels.)

Therefore, make a directory called ORIGCOD (for ORIGinal COD), and copy FORM.COD, REPORT.COD, LABEL.COD, and QUICKAPP.COD into it. (Actually, you might want to copy all the COD files, since we'll get around to most of them sooner or later.) Copy all the DEF files, too.

Then copy the contents of that directory to floppy disks. Remember, except for your original dBASE IV disks this is your only backup, so be careful with it.

Hints: *(1) Can't find the COD files? The dBASE IV installation program will copy them only if you selected the option to install the "Template Language Toolkit" when you installed dBASE IV. This procedure puts all the COD files, the template compiler and interpreter, and the DEF files into a subdirectory called DTL. If there's no such directory on your disk, you probably skipped that step in the installation process. You can either run DBSETUP from the directory where you installed dBASE IV and select the "Install other files" option or (easier) just make the subdirectory DTL and copy the two template language disks into it. They're the last two disks in the dBASE IV disk manual.*

(2) The COD files are shipped only with the Developer's Edition of dBASE IV. If you have the User's Edition, call Ashton-Tate about upgrading.

Personalizing Your Program

The easiest thing you can do with template files is to make them produce code with your personalized header attached. Let's make this change to FORM.COD and see what it does to our code.

Here's what we want the new header to look like:

```
*******************************************************************
* Name.........: CUST2PG2.FMT
* Author.......: Tony Lima
* Date.........: 4-06-89
* dBASE Ver....: dBASE IV, Format 1.0
* Notice.......: Copyright, 1989, Tony Lima
* Description..:
* Notes........: Format files use "" as delimiters!
*******************************************************************
```

You have to add the description manually — you can't expect the templates to do everything for you! And be sure to use your own name.

The program header is generated on lines 88–95 of FORM.COD:

```
88 //
89 {print(replicate("*",80)+crlf);}
90 *-- Name....: {filename(fmt_name)}FMT
91 *-- Date....: {ltrim(SUBSTR(date(),1,8))}
92 *-- Version.: dBASE IV, Format {Frame_ver}.0
93 *-- Notes...: Format files use "" as delimiters!
94 {print(replicate("*",80)+crlf);}
95 //
```

Change this to read:

```
88 //
89 {print(replicate("*",65)+crlf);}
90 * Name.........: {filename(fmt_name)}FMT
   * Author.......: Tony Lima
91 * Date.........: {ltrim(SUBSTR(date(),1,8))}
92 * dBASE Ver....: dBASE IV, Format {Frame_ver}.0
   * Notice.......: Copyright, 1989, Tony Lima
   * Description..:
```

```
93 * Notes........: Format files use "" as delimiters!
94 {print(replicate("*",65)+crlf);}
95 //
```

If you don't like the style of my program headers, change them to suit your purpose. For the moment, though, stick to adding text. Don't try any functions or commands. And don't type in line numbers or use the curly brace characters ({ }). The template language uses those as delimiters for commands, and adding them here will produce a spate of error messages when you try to compile FORM.COD. (Note: If you use the MODIFY COMMAND editor in dBASE IV, you can use the GO TO menu to move the cursor directly to line 88.)

Note that I have changed the {PRINT(REPLICATE ... commands to output only sixty-five asterisks instead of eighty. That leaves room for line numbers and generally fits my printer a little better. In general this is a change I'd recommend, although it isn't always possible to stick to lines of that length.

Compiling and Using the New Form Template

This is your first change to a template, so let's compile it and see how to use it. First, be sure DTC.EXE, FORM.DEF, and BUILTIN.DEF are in the directory with the modified FORM.COD. Since you'll usually want to compile the entire program, create a DOS batch file to do this. Call it "DT.BAT." It has exactly one command line:

```
dtc -i form.cod -o form.gen -l form.out
```

The -i option is the name of the input file (with path, if any), -o is the output file, and -l is a listing file that includes all included files in their entirety, error messages, and line numbers. Generally it's a good idea to generate this file as a record of compiler errors. That way, you can browse through them at your leisure.

If you don't want to bother with a batch file, just type the above command line from the DOS prompt. After a few seconds, you should see a message to the effect that the compilation is complete with no errors. If errors occurred, FORM.GEN will not be produced.

If you want assembly language output, include the option -a as the last argument on the DTC command line. You must include the -l option if you use -a.

If you want, you can have the compiler write FORM.GEN to the dBASE directory by changing the DTC command to:

```
dtc -i form.cod -o \dbase\form.gen -l form.out
```

Procedures like this always make me nervous because they automatically overwrite the old FORM.GEN, but you might be more adventurous than I am.

Once you have FORM.GEN compiled, copy it to the dBASE IV directory, change to your data directory, and run dBASE. Pick an existing screen form and modify it. The easiest way to modify a form is to press Ctrl-Y to delete the (presently blank) top line of the form, then press Ctrl-N to add the blank line back again. You must make a change to the SCR file; otherwise, the FMT file will not be generated. Like the dBASE IV compiler, the template generators check for changes in the SCR files. If no changes have been made, new code is not generated. Check to be sure the new header looks the way you want it to look; if it doesn't, go back and fix the template. Never make manual changes to a program file header — fix the template and make the change permanently.

Defining Constants

There are three data types in the template language: numbers (long integers, positive or negative), character strings (237-character limit per string; may include ASCII graphic characters), and cursors. The first two are self-explanatory. We'll cover cursors as the topic arises in this and the next few chapters. However, if you're accustomed to SQL cursors, you should know that template cursors are completely different animals.

The template language supports strong data typing. That is, variables and constants must be defined and/or initialized before they are used. However, this can be done in one step. For example, consider lines 18 and 19 of FORM.COD:

```
18 enum wrong_class = "Can't use FORM.GEN on non-form objects. ",
19       form_empty = "Form design was empty. "
```

The ENUM command is used to substitute a numeric or string constant for a symbol when the code is compiled. In this case, the two variables wrong_class and form_empty are defined as string constants that are error messages. ENUM can also be used to initialize numeric variables. For example, consider the following code from FORM.DEF:

```
139 //
140 // Values returned by Fld_Fieldtype
141 //
142 enum dbf = 0,    // Field from a database
143      calc,       // Calculated expression
144      sum,        // Summary ie. Average, Count, etc.
145      predef,     // Predefined ie. Date, Page, etc.
146      memvar;     // Memvar reference
```

This ENUM statement assigns the value 0 to the variable DBF. More importantly, it assigns consecutive integers to the subsequent variables, 2 to CALC, 3 to SUM, and so on. The terminator for the command is a semicolon; the separator between variables is a comma. All IBM ASCII characters (decimal 0–255) are available to ENUM.

Since the values are assigned at compile time, these are really just constants.

Error Trapping

Lines 23–26 check to be sure FORM.GEN is processing a form object:

```
23 if Frame_class != form then // We are not processing a form
     object
24   pause(wrong_class + any_key);
25   goto NoGen;
26 endif
```

The symbol != means "not equal to." In other words, if the selector Frame_class isn't a form, then use the PAUSE function to put an error message on the screen followed by the message "Press any key to continue." PAUSE(<expC>) is a built-in function that automatically displays a message on either line 24 or line 42 of the monitor, depending on display size. The value of any_key is defined in BUILTIN.DEF:

```
311 enum any_key = "Press any key ...",
312     read_only = " can't be opened - possible read-only file. ";
```

Finally, the line label NoGen will be found on the next to last line of
FORM.COD. Its purpose is obvious.

Variables and User-defined Functions

The VAR command is used to declare variable names for later use. Lines 28
through 46 of FORM.COD define the variables with comments to tell what
they are for. However, these variables are not assigned data types until they
are initialized. Variable names must begin with a letter or underscore. After
that, letters, numbers, and underscores are allowed. A variable name can be
up to two hundred characters long. Local variables are defined within a
DEFINE command. Variables defined outside a DEFINE are global and
available to all template modules.

DEFINE is used to set up a user-defined function (UDF). Without going
into too many details, its syntax is:

```
DEFINE <function name> ([<varname][, <varname> ...]) ... RETURN
      ENDDEF
```


We saw UDFs earlier in this chapter and we'll see UDFs again when we get
to the end of FORM.COD.

Initializing Variables

Variables are initialized on lines 51–55 of FORM.COD. The syntax on lines
53–54 is interesting:

```
53  carry_flg = carry_first = carry_cnt = carry_len = carry_lent =
54  wnd_cnt = line_cnt =  color_flg = cnt = 0;
```

Variables can be initialized in one fell swoop if they all have the same
value.

Testing Display Values

The next step is to see what kind of display is being used. The variable _flgcolor is defined in BUILTIN.DEF:

```
210     _flgcolor ,   //  8 Color set flag 0=b/w 1=cga 2=ega24
                                           4=mono43
211                   //                   6=ega43  3 & 5=N/A
```

Since _flgcolor is defined as part of an ENUM statement, it is initialized with a value of 8.

The NUMSET(<expN>) function is a built-in function that lets your program see the internal numeric settings of dBASE selectors. As we've seen before, these selectors are defined and documented in the various DEF files. For example, NUMSET(_flgcolor) returns a 0 for a monochrome monitor, 1 for CGA, and so on. Similarly, the value of the constant EGA25 is set to 3 in BUILTIN.DEF. This allows the easy test of the screen size shown in lines 57–59 of FORM.COD:

```
57  // Test screen size if display > 2 screen is 43 lines
58  display = numset(_flgcolor);
59  if display > ega25 then scrn_size = 39 else scrn_size = 21
      endif;
```

However, if the status bar is to be turned off while the FMT file is in use, the screen size will be three lines larger. Lines 61–68 handle this. NUMSET(_flgstatus) returns a value of 0 if STATUS is OFF and 1 if it is ON. The == operator on line 63 is merely the comparison equals operator. In this case, it tests whether scrn_size is equal to 21. The ! sign in front of the db_status variable is the logical not operator, as you might expect.

```
61  // Test to see if status was off before going into form
      designer
62  dB_status = numset(_flgstatus);
63  if scrn_size == 21 and !db_status then
64     scrn_size = 24;
65  endif
66  if scrn_size == 39 and !db_status then // status is off
67     scrn_size = 42;
68  endif
```

Creating the Format File

At last, we can start to generate the format file. Line 72 gets the current default drive:

```
72  default_drv = strset(_defdrive);  // grab default drive from
                                          dBASE
```

The STRSET(<expN>) function is similar to NUMSET() except that it is used to determine character settings. Again, _defdrive is initialized in BUILTIN.DEF.

The name for the FMT file, the value of fmt_name, is built on line 74. There are two parts, both selectors defined in FORM.DEF. The selector frame_path returns the current path, while name returns the file name. These two are concatenated to produce the file name with a path. Then, on line 75, the FILEOK(<filename>) function is used to check for a valid DOS file name. If the value of fmt_name is not a valid DOS file name, FILEOK() will return false. In that case, the program checks to see if anything was entered in the default_drv variable initialized in line 72. If not, fmt_name is reset to simply the file name. On the other hand, if a default_drv was entered, the program tries to construct a valid file name by adding a colon between the drive and the name. Finally, the UPPER() function converts the name to uppercase.

Next, the template creates and opens the named file. Lines 83–87 are particularly interesting:

```
83  if not create(fmt_name+".FMT") then
84      pause(fileroot(fmt_name) +".FMT" + read_only + any_key);
85      goto nogen;
86  endif
87  }
```

Normally the CREATE(<filename>) function creates a file and opens it. Here, the program takes advantage of the fact that it also returns an error if it is unable to create the named file — for example, if <filename> is an illegal name. In that case, an error message is displayed and generation is aborted. For example, suppose you named your file "M:DATA." Neither dBASE nor DOS will be able to tell whether M: is part of the name or a drive designator. In that case, CREATE() will return an error and generation will abort. Note the FILEROOT(<filename>) function, which returns the file name stripped of any drive designator or extension.

The FMT File Header and Initialization Code

We've already changed the format file header, so we can ignore this section of the program. The only point of lines 99–104 is to store the current value of SET TALK to the memory variable lc_talk so that when the program exits the FMT file, TALK will be restored to its proper value.

```
 99 IF SET("TALK")="ON"
100    SET TALK OFF
101    lc_talk="ON"
102 ELSE
103    lc_talk="OFF"
104 ENDIF
```

The code immediately following puts the current value of the display type into a memory variable:

```
105 {   case display of
106        mono:   temp="MONO";
107        cga:    temp="COLOR";
108        ega25:  temp="EGA25";
109        mono43: temp="MONO43";
110        ega43:  temp="EGA43";
111     endcase
112 }
113
114 *-- This form was created in {temp} mode
115 SET DISPLAY TO {temp}
116 {   temp=""; }
```

Of course, this is perfectly understandable as the template equivalent of a dBASE DO CASE command. Lines 114–115 use the variable temp to add two lines to the program file. The first is a comment telling what display mode was in effect when the FMT file was created. The second line generates the SET DISPLAY TO command.

Here's a suggestion: Why not let the CONFIG.DB file handle which display mode to use with a DISPLAY = <mode> command? This will make your FMT files somewhat system-independent. Modify lines 114–115 as follows to comment them out:

```
114 // *-- This form was created in {temp} mode
115 // SET DISPLAY TO {temp}
```

> ### *Warning! Danger!*
> **DOS users may be inclined to type \\ instead of // to comment out**
> **lines. Be sure you use //. Typing \\ will add those characters to the**
> **beginning of the line in the generated program file, causing the**
> **dBASE IV compiler no end of confusion.**

Actually, you can comment out all of lines 105–115. Leave line 116 ({ temp="";}) alone, however, as it resets the value of the variable temp, which might be used later in the program.

The last block of initialization code (lines 118–129) grabs the current value of STATUS from db_status, stores it to the variable lc_status, and produces the appropriate code.

Processing Fields

Most of the main body of the program is devoted to processing fields. Since SET CARRY and DEFINE WINDOW commands must be executed before any @ . . . SAY . . . GETs, the fields are first scanned for any references to those commands. This begins on line 134:

```
133 {
134  foreach Fld_element flds
135    if Row_positn-line_cnt > scrn_size then
136       line_cnt = line_cnt+scrn_size+1;
137    endif
138    if Fld_carry then carry_flg = 1; ++carry_cnt; endif
139    if chr(Fld_value_type) == "M" and
          Fld_mem_typ and wnd_cnt < 20 then
140       ++wnd_cnt; wnd_names = wnd_names
             + "Wndow" + wnd_cnt + ",";
141 }
```

The selector Fld_element is defined in FORM.DEF. The FOREACH-NEXT construct allows the program to move sequentially through repeated occurrences of DOS files, design object files, elements, and attributes. Elements available for screen forms are Element, Box_element, Fld_element, and Text_element. The cursor variable flds is defined on the fly by the FOREACH command and is used to simply keep track of which field is currently being processed. A cursor variable simply holds the current processing position for the interpreter. (You can explicitly create a cursor variable using the MAKEC() function.)

Line 135 checks to see if the row position (Row_positn) minus the total number of lines processed is greater than the number of lines on the screen (scrn_size). The variable line_cnt is reset later in the program at the beginning of each new screen. Therefore, to get the correct value of line_cnt on multi-screen forms, you must add scrn_size + 1 to the current line_cnt.

Line 138 tests whether this field has CARRY set ON or not. The selector Fld_carry contains this information. If CARRY is set ON for this field, the variable carry_flg will be set to 1. The expression "++carry_cnt" simply increments the value of the variable carry_cnt by 1. Those of you who know the C language will be familiar with this construct. (The - - sign works in the opposite direction. Alternative syntax is "carry_cnt += 1.")

Doing the Windows Lines 139–140 tests the field type (selector Fld_value_type) to see if it is a memo field ("M"). The selector Fld_mem_type is tested to see if the memo field is a window or not. Finally, the number of windows already defined must be less than twenty, the de facto limit in dBASE IV.

If each of those conditions is true, the variable wnd_cnt is incremented and the string wnd_names has the new window name added to it followed by a comma. After that, code to define the window is written to the FMT file:

```
143 *-- Window for memo field {lower(Fld_fieldname)}.
144 DEFINE WINDOW Wndow{wnd_cnt} FROM
      {nul2zero(Box_top) - line_cnt},\
145 {   nul2zero(Box_left)} TO \
146 {     temp = nul2zero(Box_top) + Box_height - line_cnt - 1;
147       if temp > scrn_size then scrn_size else temp endif},\
148 {     nul2zero(Box_left) + Box_width - 1} \
149 {     outbox(Box_type, Box_special_char);
150       color = getcolor(Fld_display, Fld_editable);
151       outcolor();
152     endif
```

Lines 143–144 are simply output to the file. The expression "Wndow{wnd_cnt}" merely appends the value of wnd_cnt to the string

Wndow. In line 143, the selector Fld_fieldname is used to generate the field name. The LOWER() function is identical to the dBASE IV of the same name.

Next, the program must figure out the dimensions of the box for the window. The NUL2ZERO() function is a UDF defined in lines 471–476. It merely converts null values to zeroes. If the screen line number of the top row of the window has a null value, it is converted to zero. If the value is already a number, it remains unchanged. Therefore, the row value for the window is output, followed by the column value separated by a comma. This defines the upper left corner of the window. Note that when a text expression is continued onto a new line, the continuation character is a backslash (\ ).

Lines 146–147 show some of the true power of the template language. The variable temp is defined as what should be the bottom row of the window. However, there's a possible problem here: what if the bottom row is beyond the bottom of the screen? The IF statement on line 147 handles this. If the calculated bottom row is beyond the bottom of the screen, the selector scrn_size is output; otherwise, the value of temp is used.

Note the space preceding the \ at the end of line 148. This blank will be output and will precede the output from the OUTBOX(<box type>,<box special character>) function. OUTBOX() is a user-defined function defined in lines 447–455. The selector Box_type, defined in FORM.COD, returns a value of 0 for single line, 1 for double line, and 2 for special characters. If the value returned is 0, nothing is added to the window definition clause, since single is the default. For a value of 2, the word "DOUBLE" is returned by OUTBOX() and is added to the DEFINE WINDOW command. For special characters, the character itself is returned.

The GETCOLOR(<display type>,<field edit?>) user-defined function, used on line 150, determines the color to be used for the window. The second parameter determines whether the field can be edited; that is, whether it is a SAY or GET. Basically, this UDF processes combinations of foreground and background colors, returning the correct string in the variable incolor. The UDF OUTCOLOR() adds a semicolon, a carriage return–line feed, and indents three spaces. It then outputs the word "color" followed by the string returned from GETCOLOR().

Finally, on line 153, the next flds statement tells the template to look for the next field and process it. This statement closes the FOREACH loop on line 134.

Line 154 outputs a carriage return–line feed to put a blank line at the end of the section that defines the windows.

Handling SET CARRY   The SET CARRY command is the next command to be output:

```
158 lc_carry = SET("CARRY")
159 *-- Fields to carry forward during APPEND.
160 SET CARRY TO \
161 {  carry_len = 13; carry_first = 0;
162    foreach Fld_element flds
163       if Fld_carry then
164           carry_len = carry_len + len(Fld_fieldname + ",");
165           carry_lent = carry_lent + carry_len;
166           if carry_lent > 1000 then
167               print(crlf + "SET CARRY TO ");
168               carry_len = 13; carry_lent = 0;
169           endif
170           if carry_len > 75 then print(";" + crlf + "  ");
                  carry_len = 2; endif
171           temp = lower(Fld_fieldname);
172           if !carry_first then
173               print(temp);
174               carry_first = 1;
175           else
176               print("," + temp);
177           endif
178       endif
179    next flds;
180    print(" ADDITIVE" + crlf);
181  endif
182 }
```

Line 158 outputs the line that stores the current value of CARRY to the variable lc_carry, followed by a comment and the SET CARRY TO command on subsequent lines. The variable carry_len is used to keep track of the length of the current line of the command. It is initialized with a value of 13 on line 161 because that is the number of characters in "SET CARRY TO ". Another FOREACH Fld_element loop begins on line 162. Line 163 tests for whether this field has the selector Fld_carry set or not. If so, the new length of the SET CARRY command is calculated by adding LEN(Fld_fieldname+",") to its current value. A second variable, carry_lent, is defined incorrectly. Its purpose is to store the total length of the current SET CARRY command. However, it adds the running total of the current line (carry_len) rather than the length of the current clause.

Here's the problem this causes: the variable carry_lent will be larger than the actual length of the current SET CARRY command. This means the length of SET CARRY will not be anywhere near one thousand characters. If you use this feature from the Edit options menu quite a bit, you will generate multiple SET CARRY commands when fewer would have been required.

There will probably be a new version of FORM.COD that corrects this error. But if you have an old version, change line 165 to read like this (leave out the line number):

```
165         carry_lent = carry_lent + len(Fld_fieldname + ",");
```

Basically, carry_lent checks to make sure the total length of the command is less than the dBASE IV limit of 1,000 (actually, 1,024) characters. You might want to change 1,000 to 1,024 in line 166, too. If the command is longer than that, the template simply begins a new SET CARRY TO command, terminating the previous one with a carriage return–line feed, reinitializes carry_len and carry_lent, and proceeds. If carry_len is greater than 75, the template adds a semicolon, carriage return–line feed, and two blank spaces on the next line, resets carry_len (this time to 2), and proceeds. The selector Fld_fieldname is used to grab the field name. If it's the first field in the CARRY (i.e., if !carry_first is true — remember, ! is the not operator), then the field name is simply output. If it's not the first field, the template prefaces the field name with a comma. If you like blank spaces between your variable names, change line 176 to read:

```
176         print(", " + temp);
```

Finally, on line 180, the word ADDITIVE is tacked on (so the command doesn't wipe out any existing SET CARRYs), followed by a carriage return–line feed.

And the Result Is ... All this translates into some pretty straightforward code from CUST2PG2.FMT (Example 4-2):

```
26 *-- Window for memo field comments.
27 DEFINE WINDOW Wndow1 FROM 5,10 TO 15,76 DOUBLE
28
```

```
29 lc_carry = SET("CARRY")
30 *-- Fields to carry forward during APPEND.
31 SET CARRY TO custcode ADDITIVE
```

Adding Multiuser Code

This is the place to add any multiuser code you might want. Let's consider how to rewrite the template to write the following code to your FMT file:

```
IF NETWORK()
  SET REPROCESS TO 10
  IF .NOT. RLOCK()
    SET STATUS ON
    SET MESSAGE TO "Record is locked by " + ;
      TRIM(LKSYS(2)) + ". Hit the space bar."
    WAIT " "
    SET STATUS &lc_status
  ENDIF && .NOT. RLOCK()
ENDIF && NETWORK()
```

Looks straightforward, doesn't it? But you don't want to lock anything if all the fields are read-only. In other words, there must be at least one GET before you add this code. But you already know how to do that. Here's the template code to add after line 182. (Note: LKSYS(2) will return the network name of the user who has locked the record only if the database has been processed by the dBASE IV CONVERT command.)

However, we also don't always want to include multiuser code. To keep the volume of code generated to a minimum, we'll use the ASKUSER() function to let the user decide whether or not multiuser functionality is to be included in the generated program.

```
{VAR tlresp;
ASKUSER("Do you want to include multiuser commands",
        "Y",1)};
if tlresp == "Y" then}

{ll_getcnt = 0;
  foreach Fld_element flds
    if Fld_editable then ++ll_getcnt endif;
  next flds;
```

```
      if ll_getcnt > 0 then; // We have at least one GET}

 * Code to process network operations

IF NETWORK()
  SET REPROCESS TO 10
  IF .NOT. RLOCK()
    SET STATUS ON
    SET MESSAGE TO "Record is locked by " + ;
    TRIM(LKSYS(2)) + ". Hit the space bar."
    WAIT " "
    IF lc_status = "OFF"
      SET STATUS OFF
    ELSE
      SET STATUS ON
    ENDIF
  ENDIF && .NOT. RLOCK()
ENDIF && NETWORK()
{ endif;
endif}
```

Next, be sure you add the variable ll_getcnt to the variables list on line 46:

```
color,     // Color returned from getcolor function
ll_getcnt; // Counter for gets
```

Compile the new FORM.COD, run an SCR file through it, and you'll see the network code added automatically.

You may want to incorporate this procedure into a more general procedure file for handling multiuser locking. However, this illustrates the power of the template language (not to mention of dBASE IV itself).

@ . . . SAY . . . GETs Processing

Processing the actual @ . . . SAY . . . GETs begins by outputting the comments on lines 184–186. The variable page_cnt, initialized to 1 on line 55, performs the obvious function.

Lines 201–202 check the type of object being examined. The selector Element_type can have three values: Box_element, Fld_element, or Text_element. The == sign is a logical comparison operator, while the @ sign in front of a selector is an operator that converts the selector into its integer value. Line 201 checks to see whether the Element_type is text or a field; line 202 checks to see whether the field type is calculated.

```
201     if Element_type == @Text_element or
            Element_type == @Fld_element then
202        if Fld_fieldtype == calc}
```

Calculated Fields and Memory Variables

If the field is calculated, a comment is output on line 203 that includes the selectors Fld_fieldname and Fld_descript. If you assigned a name or description to the calculated field when you set it up in the form designer, those will be output here. Line 204 closes the IF for calculated fields.

```
203 *-- Calculated field: {lower(Fld_fieldname)} - {Fld_descript}
204 {    endif
```

Next, the template checks to see if the field is a memory variable. If so, the appropriate comment is output.

```
205        if Fld_fieldtype == memvar then}
206 *-- Memory variable: {lower(Fld_fieldname)}
207 {    endif}
```

Handling Boxes   Lines 208–215 handle boxes. This is the first place where row-column coordinates are output. Note the use of NUL2ZERO(). Thus, line 208 will produce output like "@ 10,15." (The ENDIF on line 209 closes the IF from line 201.)

```
208 @ {nul2zero(Row_positn) - line_cnt},{nul2zero(Col_positn)} \
209 {   endif
```

Boxes are handled by checking the Element_type selector on line 210. The same algorithm used to define windows and make sure they don't run off the bottom of the screen (lines 144–149) is used here to calculate where to place the box frame.

```
210    if ELEMENT_TYPE == @Box_element then}
211 @ {nul2zero(Box_top) - line_cnt},{nul2zero(Box_left)} TO \
212 {    temp = nul2zero(Box_top) + Box_height - line_cnt - 1;
213      if temp > scrn_size then scrn_size else temp endif},\
214 {    nul2zero(Box_left) + Box_width - 1} \
215 {  endif}
216 //
```

Handling SAYs   The first step in handling a SAY command is to get the correct element type. The case statement in line 217 does this. This case statement lasts for most of the rest of the program, closing on line 315.

```
217 {  case ELEMENT_TYPE of
```

If the element type is text, things can get more complicated than you might expect. The comments on lines 219–222 indicate the kind of problems that might be encountered, notably problems with the lower part of the ASCII table. For example, ASCII character 13 (decimal) is a carriage return. The template handles this potential problem cleverly by outputting the dBASE IV CHR() function for any text_item that has an ASCII value less than 32 (line 225). In all this confusion, note that line 224 outputs a "SAY ".

```
218    @Text_element:
219    // Certain control characters can cause dBASE problems ie,
          ASCII(13,26,0)
220    // so the form designer will either send them to us as a
          string if they are
221    // all the same character or as individual characters if
          they differ. We
222    // handle this by using the chr() function to "SAY" them in
          dBASE.
223 }
224 SAY \
225 {    if asc(text_item) < 32 then
226        if len(text_item) == 1 then}
227 CHR({asc(text_item)}) \
228 {      else}
229 REPLICATE(CHR({asc(text_item)}), {len(text_item)}) \
230 {      endif
```

On the other hand, if it's not a special ASCII character, simply output the Text_item selector in double quotes:

```
231        else}
232 "{Text_Item}" \
233 {      endif
```

Naturally, the template has to worry about the color using the UDF OUT-COLOR():

```
234        outcolor();
```

The next part of the case structure checks for the Box_element selector. If the element is a box, the UDF OUTBOX(<box type>,<box special character>) is called. OUTBOX() is defined on lines 447–455. We saw in the window definition section that it outputs either nothing for a single-line border, the word "DOUBLE" for a double-line border, or the appropriate character for a user-defined border. Again, OUTCOLOR() is used to generate the correct color.

```
235    @Box_element:
236        outbox(Box_type, Box_special_char);
237        outcolor();
```

Finally (at last!), an actual database field is processed. The first thing to check for is whether editing is allowed (selected from the Edit options menu). The expression "if !Fld_editable" means "if the field is not editable" in which case it's a SAY.

```
238    @Fld_element:
239        if !Fld_editable then; // its a SAY}
240 SAY \
```

Next, the program checks for a calculated field. The first thing to do is test whether the calculated field expression is longer than 237 characters, the maximum allowed by dBASE IV. The FOREACH loop that begins on line 243 actually is two loops in one. The clause "in k" means only ELEMENTs will be examined. (The variable k was defined in the master FOREACH ELEMENT k loop command on line 189.) The variable fcursor stores the result. As it's counting, it outputs the Fld_expression to the FMT file.

```
241 {        if Fld_fieldtype == calc then
242              // Loop thru expression in case it is longer
                    than 237
243              foreach Fld_expression fcursor in k
244                  Fld_expression}
245 {            next}
```

Finally, the template outputs a space after the Fld_expression

```
246 // Output a space after the Fld_expression and get ready for
        picture clause
247  \
```

If it's not editable and not calculated, it must be a plain old SAY, either a
field or memory variable. If it's a memory variable, the code just has to
include an m-> in front of the variable name to indicate that.

```
248 {        else // not a editable field
249              if Fld_fieldtype == dbf then temp = ""
                    else temp = "m->" endif;
250                  lower(temp + Fld_fieldname)} \
251 {        endif
```

PICTUREs   The selector Fld_template is the picture template holder. After
storing its value in the (now well-known) temp variable, a complicated little
bit of logic occurs on lines 253–254. Let's go through this in some detail.
First, the && operator is a logical *and* operator. The | operator is a bitwise
numeric inclusive *or*. This IF statement means if the Fld_template indicates a
picture clause is present and none of the following are present, DO next
statements. The first four AT() functions check for the presence of the strings
DD, HH, MM, and SS in the Fld_template selector. If any of those are present,
the IF is false. These four tests correspond to picture functions for dates (DD),
hours (HH), minutes (MM), and seconds (SS). (Clearly, Ashton-Tate has a
few new things in mind for the near future!) Using the string DD to check for
date-type data is sensible because the two-digit day number is always present
regardless of the date format currently in effect. Finally, the expression
'chr(Fld_value_type) == "M"' checks to see if it is a memo-type field, in
which case also the IF is false.

```
252          temp = Fld_template;
253          if Fld_template && !(AT("DD",temp) | AT("HH",temp) |
             AT("MM",temp)
254             | AT("SS",temp) | chr(Fld_value_type) == "M") then}
```

If none of these is true, the PICTURE is output, along with any picture function. If it's a horizontal-scrolled picture function (@S), output the selector Fld_pic_scroll. If it's not a horizontal-scrolled or multiple-choice function, output the field template. Line 261 adds a closing double quote, and line 263 carries the program to the GETs section.

```
255 PICTURE "{  if Fld_picfun then}@{Fld_picfun}\
256 {              if AT("S", Fld_picfun)
                      then}{Fld_pic_scroll}{endif}\
257 {//leave this space}\
258 {          endif
259            if !AT("S", Fld_picfun) and !AT("M", Fld_picfun)
                  then
260                Fld_template}\
261 {          endif}" \
262 {       endif
263      else // it's a get}
```

GETs   GETs processing is pretty straightforward and very similar to what we've seen already. If Fld_fieldtype is a DBF field, the variable temp is a null string; otherwise it's a memory variable, and temp is "m->". Either way, output temp in front of the field name. If it's a memo field (line 267) and the number of windows so far is less than twenty, then increment the window counter on line 268 and output the OPEN WINDOW command on line 269. Lines 271–273 duplicate the exclusion we saw earlier for the PICTURE for SAYs.

```
264 GET \
265 {          if Fld_fieldtype == dbf then temp = "" else temp =
               "m->" endif;
266            lower(temp + Fld_fieldname)} \
267 {          if chr(Fld_value_type) == "M" && Fld_mem_typ then
268              if wnd_cnt < 20  then ++wnd_cnt endif;
269              if Fld_mem_typ == 1}OPEN {endif}WINDOW
                   Wndow{wnd_cnt} \
270 {          endif
```

```
271          temp = Fld_template;
272          if Fld_template && !(AT("DD",temp) | AT("HH",temp) |
             AT("MM",temp)
273             | AT("SS",temp) | chr(Fld_value_type) == "M") then}
```

Lines 274–282 duplicate the previous process for SAYs. You may want to convert this block of code to a UDF to save space. Call it "PICOUT()"; it doesn't need any parameters. Just move the block of code to a UDF.

```
274 PICTURE "{if Fld_picfun then}@{Fld_picfun}\
275 {          if AT("S", Fld_picfun)
                  then}{Fld_pic_scroll}{endif}\
276  {//leave this space}\
277 {          endif
278            if AT("M", Fld_picfun)}{Fld_pic_choice}{endif}\
279 {          if !AT("S", Fld_picfun) and !AT("M", Fld_picfun)
then
280               Fld_template}\
281 {          endif}" \
282 {          endif
```

RANGE Processing   Line 283 checks the selectors Fld_l_bound and Fld_u_bound, the lower and upper bounds on field values, corresponding to the presence of a RANGE clause. If either of these is set, the variable color_flg is set to 1 and the template proceeds to the RANGE clause.

```
283            if Fld_l_bound or Fld_u_bound then color_flg = 1;}
284 ;
```

The IF on line 283 continues in that the RANGE clause will be output only if it is true. The RANGE clause is pretty straightforward. The only point to the "if Fld_u_bound then" statement is to put a comma between the two range values or leave it out if there's no upper bound.

```
285    RANGE {Fld_l_bound}{if Fld_u_bound
          then},{Fld_u_bound}{endif} \
286 {       endif
```

VALIDs   The VALID clause is processed next. First, the Fld_ok_cond selector is output as the condition for the VALID. Next, if there is a Fld_rej_msg (message for violating VALIDs), the ERROR clause is output.

Lines 293–294 check for the presence of an IIF() function in the Fld_hlp_msg. If there isn't one, Fld_rej_msg is simply output after a double quote. The purpose of line 294 is to output the closing double quote. The !AT() is used so that if an IIF() function is present, it will not be placed in quotation marks.

```
287              if Fld_ok_cond then color_flg = 1;}
288 ;
289    VALID {Fld_ok_cond} \
290 {           if Fld_rej_msg then}
291 ;
292    ERROR \
293 {              if !AT("IIF", upper(Fld_hlp_msg))}"
                    {endif}{Fld_rej_msg}\
294 {              if !AT("IIF", upper(Fld_hlp_msg))}"{endif} \
295 {           endif
296           endif // Fld_ok_cond
```

WHENs and DEFAULTs   The IF on line 297 determines whether the selector Fld_ed_cond contains anything. If so, a WHEN is output followed by the Edit condition.

```
297              if Fld_ed_cond then color_flg = 1;}
298 ;
299    WHEN {Fld_ed_cond} \
300 {      endif
```

Similarly, the DEFAULT clause is processed. Neither of these clauses requires error checking, because that is handled within the form generator.

```
301              if Fld_def_val then color_flg = 1;}
302 ;
303    DEFAULT {Fld_def_val} \
304 {      endif
```

MESSAGEs   You may have been bothered by the semicolons on lines such as 306 below. In the template language, a semicolon indicates the end of a command when the command is not terminated with a }. Messages are processed just like the previous cases, with the exception of checking for an IIF() function. Note the implicit suggestion to use an IIF() to output different messages conditional on (perhaps) the contents of previous fields.

```
305              if Fld_hlp_msg then color_flg = 1;}
306 ;
307    MESSAGE \
308 {          if !AT("IIF", upper(Fld_hlp_msg))}"{endif}
                  {Fld_hlp_msg}\
309 {          if !AT("IIF", upper(Fld_hlp_msg))}"{endif} \
310 {       endif
311       endif // Fld_editable
```

Finally, the OUTCOLOR() UDF is used to generate a semicolon to continue the @ . . . SAY . . . GET within the main processing loop.

```
312        outcolor();
313        color_flg=0;
314    otherwise: goto getnext;
315    endcase
316 }
317
318 //Leave the above blank line, it forces a line feed!
319 //-----------------
320 // End of @ SAY GET
321 //-----------------
322 {   ++cnt;
323    getnext:
324  next k;
325 }
326
```

The format file exit code is straightforward and duplicates what's at the beginning of the template file. The only complicating factor is the check to see whether the variable cnt is zero, in which case the form is empty and no code is generated (line 357). Line 360 erases the existing FMO file, causing dBASE IV to automatically recompile the new FMT file after it is generated.

```
327 *-- Format file exit code ------------------------------------
328
329 *-- SET STATUS was \
330 {if dB_status then}
331 ON when you went into the Forms Designer.
```

```
332 IF lc_status = "OFF"  && Entered form with status off
333    SET STATUS OFF      && Turn STATUS "OFF" on the way out
334 {else}
335 OFF when you went into the Forms Designer.
336 IF lc_status = "ON"  && Entered form with status on
337    SET STATUS ON      && Turn STATUS "ON" on the way out
338 {endif}
339 ENDIF
340 {if carry_flg then}
341
342 IF lc_carry = "OFF"
343    SET CARRY OFF
344 ENDIF
345 {endif}
346 {if wnd_names then}
347
348 RELEASE WINDOWS {substr(wnd_names, 1, (len(wnd_names) - 1))}
349 {endif}
350
351 IF lc_talk="ON"
352    SET TALK ON
353 ENDIF
354
355 RELEASE {if carry_flg
then}lc_carry,{endif}lc_talk,lc_fields,lc_status
356 *-- EOP: {filename(fmt_name)}FMT
357 {if cnt == 0 then
358    pause(form_empty + any_key);
359  endif;
360  fileerase(fmt_name+".FMO");
361  nogen:
362  return 0;
```

The New Format File

Example 4-4 shows the new version of CUST2PG2.FMT. This is what all your format files will look like in the future.

Example 4-4   CUST2PG2.FMT (Revised Version)

```
 1 ********************************************************************
 2 * Name.........: CUST2PG2.FMT
 3 * Author.......: Tony Lima
 4 * Date.........: 4-09-89
 5 * dBASE Ver....: dBASE IV, Format 1.0
 6 * Notice.......: Copyright, 1989, Tony Lima
 7 * Description..:
 8 * Notes........: Format files use "" as delimiters!
 9 ********************************************************************
10
11 *-- Format file initialization code ----------------------------
12
13 IF SET("TALK")="ON"
14    SET TALK OFF
15    lc_talk="ON"
16 ELSE
17    lc_talk="OFF"
18 ENDIF
19
20
21 lc_status=SET("STATUS")
22 *-- SET STATUS was ON when you went into the Forms Designer.
23 IF lc_status = "OFF"
24    SET STATUS ON
25 ENDIF
26
27 *-- Window for memo field comments.
28 DEFINE WINDOW Wndow1 FROM 5,10 TO 15,76 DOUBLE
29
30 lc_carry = SET("CARRY")
31 *-- Fields to carry forward during APPEND.
32 SET CARRY TO custcode ADDITIVE
33
34
35 * Code to process network operations
36
37 IF NETWORK()
38    SET REPROCESS TO 10
```

(continued)

```
39  IF .NOT. RLOCK()
40    SET STATUS ON
41    SET MESSAGE TO "Record is locked by " + ;
42    TRIM(LKSYS(2)) + ". Hit the space bar."
43    WAIT " "
44    IF lc_status = "OFF"
45      SET STATUS OFF
46    ELSE
47      SET STATUS ON
48    ENDIF
49  ENDIF && .NOT. RLOCK()
50 ENDIF && NETWORK()
51
52 *-- @ SAY GETS Processing. ----------------------------------------
53
54 *--  Format Page: 1
55
56 @ 1,22 SAY "Customer Data Entry and Editing Form" COLOR b/bg
57 @ 2,19 TO 18,61
58 @ 3,21 SAY "C" COLOR w/b
59 @ 3,22 SAY "ust. ID"
60 @ 3,32 GET custcode PICTURE "99999" ;
61    VALID VAL(CUSTCODE) > 10000 ;
62    ERROR "Customer ID number must be greater than 10000" ;
63    MESSAGE "Enter the 5 digit customer ID number"
64 @ 4,21 SAY "NAME"
65 @ 4,32 GET name PICTURE "XXXXXXXXXXXXXXXXXXXXXXXXXXX"
66 @ 5,21 SAY "ADDRESS1"
67 @ 5,32 GET address1 PICTURE "XXXXXXXXXXXXXXXXXXXXXXXXXXXX"
68 @ 6,21 SAY "ADDRESS2"
69 @ 6,32 GET address2 PICTURE "XXXXXXXXXXXXXXXXXXXXXXXXXXXX"
70 @ 7,21 SAY "CITY"
71 @ 7,32 GET city PICTURE "XXXXXXXXXXXXXXXX"
72 @ 8,21 SAY "STATE"
73 @ 8,32 GET state PICTURE "@!M CA,AZ,AK,OH"
74 @ 9,21 SAY "COUNTRY"
75 @ 9,32 GET country PICTURE "XXXXXXXXXXXXXXXXXXX" ;
76    DEFAULT "U.S."
77 @ 10,21 SAY "ZIP"
78 @ 10,32 GET zip PICTURE "99999" ;
```

(continued)

```
 79     WHEN COUNTRY = "U.S." .OR. TRIM(COUNTRY) = " "
 80 @ 11,21 SAY "CONTACT"
 81 @ 11,32 GET contact PICTURE "XXXXXXXXXXXXXXXXXXXXXXXXXX"
 82 @ 12,21 SAY "TELEPHONE"
 83 @ 12,32 GET telephone PICTURE "(999) 999-9999"
 84 @ 13,21 SAY "SALES"
 85 @ 13,32 GET sales PICTURE "999999999.99"
 86 @ 14,21 SAY "TERMS"
 87 @ 14,32 GET terms PICTURE "XXXXXXXXXXXXXXXXXXXX"
 88 @ 15,21 SAY "BALANCE"
 89 @ 15,32 GET balance PICTURE "999999999.99"
 90 @ 16,21 SAY "CRLIMIT"
 91 @ 16,32 GET crlimit PICTURE "9999999999" ;
 92     RANGE 0,100000
 93 @ 17,21 SAY "EXEMPT"
 94 @ 17,32 GET exempt PICTURE "Y"
 95 @ 19,25 SAY "Press PgDn for Comments Field" COLOR b/r
 96 READ
 97
 98 *-- Format Page: 2
 99
100 @ 3,0 SAY "Customer ID:   "
101 @ 3,14 SAY custcode PICTURE "XXXXXXXXXXX"
102 @ 4,0 SAY "Name: "
103 @ 4,6 SAY name PICTURE "XXXXXXXXXXXXXXXXXXXXXXXXXXXXX"
104 @ 5,0 SAY "Comments   "
105 @ 5,10 GET comments OPEN WINDOW Wndow1 ;
106     MESSAGE "Press Ctrl-Home to edit"
107 @ 16,29 SAY "End Edit with Ctrl-End" COLOR b/r
108
109 *-- Format file exit code -------------------------------------
110
111 *-- SET STATUS was ON when you went into the Forms Designer.
112 IF lc_status = "OFF"  && Entered form with status off
113    SET STATUS OFF      && Turn STATUS "OFF" on the way out
114 ENDIF
115
116 IF lc_carry = "OFF"
117    SET CARRY OFF
118 ENDIF
```

(continued)

```
119
120 RELEASE WINDOWS Wndow1
121
122 IF lc_talk="ON"
123    SET TALK ON
124 ENDIF
125
126 RELEASE lc_carry,lc_talk,lc_fields,lc_status
127 *-- EOP: CUST2PG2.FMT
128
```

Conclusion

This chapter has been a lengthy, detailed explanation of FORM.COD. But it's been more than that. You have looked at the concept of selectors and seen how they are used, along with various operators, commands, and functions. Later chapters cover additional selectors, operators, commands, and functions, but you now understand the fundamentals of template programs and how they work. In the next chapter, you will look at a slightly more complex file, LABEL.COD, and see how to work with it.

Appendix A

Substituting for Default GEN Files

One alternative to making copies of your COD, GEN, and DEF files is to use a different file at the generation step. Unfortunately, this is not particularly easy. Suppose, for instance, you wanted to generate FMT files using MYFORM.GEN instead of FORM.GEN. To do this, you must type:

```
SET DTL_FORM=C:\DB4\MYFORM.GEN
```

from the DOS prompt or in your AUTOEXEC.BAT file — not from the dot prompt. The DOS environmental variable DTL_FORM controls the name of the file used to process screen forms. For reports and labels, the commands are:

```
SET DTL_REPORT=<path\file name>
SET DTL_LABEL=<path\file name>
```

Yes, you have to include the complete path with the file name. Once you have set the default GEN files in DOS, you must exit to DOS to change the defaults again. (You can try using the RUN command from dBASE IV, but I would advise closing all files first.)

To change applications generator templates, select that option from the Generate menu.

Appendix B

FORM.COD

```
1 //
2 // Module Name: FORM.COD
3 // Description: This module is for producing dBASE IV .FMT files
4 //
5
6 Format (.fmt) File Template
7 ----------------------------
8 Version 1.0
9 Ashton-Tate (c) 1987, 1988
10
11 {
12 include "form.def";   // Form selectors
13 include "builtin.def"; // Builtin functions
14
15 //
16 // Enum string constants for international translation
17 //
18 enum wrong_class = "Can't use FORM.GEN on non-form objects. ",
19       form_empty = "Form design was empty. "
20 ;
21 //
22
23 if Frame_class != form then // We are not processing a form object
24   pause(wrong_class + any_key);
25   goto NoGen;
26 endif
27
28 var  fmt_name,    // Format file name
29      crlf,        // line feed
30      carry_flg,   // Flag to test carry loop
31      carry_cnt,   // Count of the number of fields to carry
32      carry_len,   // Cumulative length of carry line until 75 characters
33      carry_lent,  // Total cumulative length of carry line
34      carry_first,// Flag to test "," output for carry fields
35      color_flg,   // Flag to if color should stay on am line
36      line_cnt,    // Count for total lines processed (Mulitple page forms)
37      page_cnt,    // Count for total pages processed (Mulitple page forms)
38      temp,        // tempory work variable
39      cnt,         // Foreach loop variable
40      wnd_cnt,     // Window counter
41      wnd_names,   // Window names so I can clear them
42      default_drv,// dBASE default drive
43      dB_status,   // dBASE status before entering designer
44      scrn_size,   // Screen size when generation starts
45      display,     // Type of display screen we are on
```

(continued)

```
46      color;        // Color returned from getcolor function
47
48  //-----------------------------------------------
49  // Assign default values to some of the variables
50  //-----------------------------------------------
51  crlf = chr(10);
52  temp = "";
53  carry_flg = carry_first = carry_cnt = carry_len = carry_lent =
54  wnd_cnt = line_cnt =  color_flg = cnt = 0;
55  page_cnt = 1;
56
57  // Test screen size if display > 2 screen is 43 lines
58  display = numset(_flgcolor);
59  if display > ega25 then scrn_size = 39 else scrn_size = 21 endif;
60
61  // Test to see if status was off before going into form designer
62  dB_status = numset(_flgstatus);
63  if scrn_size == 21 and !db_status then
64     scrn_size = 24;
65  endif
66  if scrn_size == 39 and !db_status then // status is off
67     scrn_size = 42;
68  endif
69  //------------------------------
70  // Create Format file
71  //------------------------------
72
74  fmt_name = frame_path + name;
75  if not FILEOK(fmt_name) then
76     if !default_drv then
77        fmt_name = name;
78     else
79        fmt_name = default_drv + ":" + NAME;
80     endif
81  endif
82  fmt_name = upper(fmt_name);
83  if not create(fmt_name+".FMT") then
84     pause(fileroot(fmt_name) +".FMT" + read_only + any_key);
85     goto nogen;
86  endif
87  }
88  //
89  {print(replicate("*",80)+crlf);}
90  *-- Name....: {filename(fmt_name)}FMT
91  *-- Date....: {ltrim(SUBSTR(date(),1,8))}
92  *-- Version.: dBASE IV, Format {Frame_ver}.0
93  *-- Notes...: Format files use "" as delimiters!
94  {print(replicate("*",80)+crlf);}
95  //
96
97  *-- Format file initialization code -----------------------------
98
```

(continued)

```
 99 IF SET("TALK")="ON"
100    SET TALK OFF
101    lc_talk="ON"
102 ELSE
103    lc_talk="OFF"
104 ENDIF
105 {   case display of
106       mono:    temp="MONO";
107       cga:     temp="COLOR";
108       ega25:   temp="EGA25";
109       mono43:  temp="MONO43";
110       ega43:   temp="EGA43";
111     endcase
112 }
113
114 *-- This form was created in {temp} mode
115 SET DISPLAY TO {temp}
116 {   temp="";}
117
118 lc_status=SET("STATUS")
119 *-- SET STATUS was \
120 {if dB_status then}
121 ON when you went into the Forms Designer.
122 IF lc_status = "OFF"
123    SET STATUS ON
124 {else}
125 OFF when you went into the Forms Designer.
126 IF lc_status = "ON"
127    SET STATUS OFF
128 {endif}
129 ENDIF
130 //----------------------------------------------------------------
131 // Process fields to build "SET CARRY" and WINDOW commands.
132 //----------------------------------------------------------------
133 {
134  foreach Fld_element flds
135    if Row_positn-line_cnt > scrn_size then
136        line_cnt = line_cnt+scrn_size+1;
137    endif
138    if Fld_carry then carry_flg = 1; ++carry_cnt; endif
139    if chr(Fld_value_type) == "M" and Fld_mem_typ and wnd_cnt < 20 then
140        ++wnd_cnt; wnd_names = wnd_names + "Wndow" + wnd_cnt + ",";
141 }
142
143 *-- Window for memo field {lower(Fld_fieldname)}.
144 DEFINE WINDOW Wndow{wnd_cnt} FROM {nul2zero(Box_top) - line_cnt},\
145 {   nul2zero(Box_left)} TO \
146 {    temp = nul2zero(Box_top) + Box_height - line_cnt - 1;
147    if temp > scrn_size then scrn_size else temp endif},\
148 {    nul2zero(Box_left) + Box_width - 1} \
149 {    outbox(Box_type, Box_special_char);
150        color = getcolor(Fld_display, Fld_editable);
```

(continued)

```
151        outcolor();
152     endif
153  next flds;
154  print(crlf);
155  if carry_flg then
156 }
157
158 lc_carry = SET("CARRY")
159 *-- Fields to carry forward during APPEND.
160 SET CARRY TO \
161 {  carry_len = 13; carry_first = 0;
162    foreach Fld_element flds
163       if Fld_carry then
164          carry_len = carry_len + len(Fld_fieldname + ",");
165          carry_lent = carry_lent + carry_len;
166          if carry_lent > 1000 then
167             print(crlf + "SET CARRY TO ");
168             carry_len = 13; carry_lent = 0;
169          endif
170          if carry_len > 75
                then print(";" + crlf + "   "); carry_len = 2; endif
171          temp = lower(Fld_fieldname);
172          if !carry_first then
173             print(temp);
174             carry_first = 1;
175          else
176             print("," + temp);
177          endif
178       endif
179    next flds;
180    print(" ADDITIVE" + crlf);
181  endif
182 }
183
184 *-- @ SAY GETS Processing. ---------------------------------------
185
186 *--  Format Page: {page_cnt}
187
188 {line_cnt = wnd_cnt = 0;
189  foreach ELEMENT k
190    color = getcolor(Fld_display, Fld_editable); // get color of element
191    if nul2zero(Row_positn) - line_cnt > scrn_size then
192       line_cnt = line_cnt + scrn_size + 1;
193       ++page_cnt;
194 }
195 READ
196
197 *--  Format Page: {page_cnt}
198
199 {  endif
200 //
201    if Element_type == @Text_element or Element_type == @Fld_element then
```

(continued)

```
202       if Fld_fieldtype == calc}
203 *-- Calculated field: {lower(Fld_fieldname)} - {Fld_descript}
204 {     endif
205       if Fld_fieldtype == memvar then}
206 *-- Memory variable: {lower(Fld_fieldname)}
207 {     endif}
208 @ {nul2zero(Row_positn) - line_cnt},{nul2zero(Col_positn)} \
209 {  endif
210    if ELEMENT_TYPE == @Box_element then}
211 @ {nul2zero(Box_top) - line_cnt},{nul2zero(Box_left)} TO \
212 {    temp = nul2zero(Box_top) + Box_height - line_cnt - 1;
213      if temp > scrn_size then scrn_size else temp endif},\
214 {    nul2zero(Box_left) + Box_width - 1} \
215 {  endif}
216 //
217 {  case ELEMENT_TYPE of
218    @Text_element:
219    // Certain control characters can cause dBASE problems ie, ASCII(13,26,0)
220    // so the form designer will either send them to us as a string if they
          are
221    // all the same character or as individual characters if they differ. We
222    // handle this by using the chr() function to "SAY" them in dBASE.
223 }
224 SAY \
225 {     if asc(text_item) < 32 then
226          if len(text_item) == 1 then}
227 CHR({asc(text_item)}) \
228 {        else}
229 REPLICATE(CHR({asc(text_item)}), {len(text_item)}) \
230 {        endif
231        else}
232 "{Text_Item}" \
233 {      endif
234      outcolor();
235    @Box_element:
236      outbox(Box_type, Box_special_char);
237      outcolor();
238    @Fld_element:
239      if !Fld_editable then; // its a SAY}
240 SAY \
241 {      if Fld_fieldtype == calc then
242          // Loop thru expression in case it is longer than 237
243          foreach Fld_expression fcursor in k
244            Fld_expression}
245 {        next}
246 // Output a space after the Fld_expression and get ready for picture clause
247 \
248 {      else // not a editable field
249          if Fld_fieldtype == dbf then temp = "" else temp = "m->" endif;
250            lower(temp + Fld_fieldname)} \
251 {        endif
252        temp = Fld_template;
```

(continued)

```
253            if Fld_template && !(AT("DD",temp) | AT("HH",temp) | AT("MM",temp)
254            | AT("SS",temp) | chr(Fld_value_type) == "M") then}
255 PICTURE "{  if Fld_picfun then}@{Fld_picfun}\
256 {             if AT("S", Fld_picfun) then}{Fld_pic_scroll}{endif}\
257  {//leave this space}\
258 {          endif
259            if !AT("S", Fld_picfun) and !AT("M", Fld_picfun) then
260            Fld_template}\
261 {          endif}" \
262 {        endif
263      else // it's a get}
264 GET \
265 {        if Fld_fieldtype == dbf then temp = "" else temp = "m->" endif;
266          lower(temp + Fld_fieldname)} \
267 {        if chr(Fld_value_type) == "M" && Fld_mem_typ then
268            if wnd_cnt < 20  then ++wnd_cnt endif;
269            if Fld_mem_typ == 1}OPEN {endif}WINDOW Wndow{wnd_cnt} \
270 {        endif
271          temp = Fld_template;
272          if Fld_template && !(AT("DD",temp) | AT("HH",temp) | AT("MM",temp)
273            | AT("SS",temp) | chr(Fld_value_type) == "M") then}
274 PICTURE "{if Fld_picfun then}@{Fld_picfun}\
275 {          if AT("S", Fld_picfun) then}{Fld_pic_scroll}{endif}\
276  {//leave this space}\
277 {          endif
278            if AT("M", Fld_picfun)}{Fld_pic_choice}{endif}\
279 {          if !AT("S", Fld_picfun) and !AT("M", Fld_picfun) then
280            Fld_template}\
281 {          endif}" \
282 {        endif
283          if Fld_l_bound or Fld_u_bound then color_flg = 1;}
284 ;
285    RANGE {Fld_l_bound}{if Fld_u_bound then},{Fld_u_bound}{endif} \
286 {        endif
287          if Fld_ok_cond then color_flg = 1;}
288 ;
289    VALID {Fld_ok_cond} \
290 {          if Fld_rej_msg then}
291 ;
292    ERROR \
293 {            if !AT("IIF", upper(Fld_hlp_msg))}"{endif}{Fld_rej_msg}\
294 {            if !AT("IIF", upper(Fld_hlp_msg))}"{endif} \
295 {          endif
296          endif // Fld_ok_cond
297          if Fld_ed_cond then color_flg = 1;}
298 ;
299    WHEN {Fld_ed_cond} \
300 {        endif
301          if Fld_def_val then color_flg = 1;}
302 ;
303    DEFAULT {Fld_def_val} \
304 {        endif
```

(continued)

```
305           if Fld_hlp_msg then color_flg = 1;}
306 ;
307    MESSAGE \
308 {            if !AT("IIF", upper(Fld_hlp_msg))}"{endif}{Fld_hlp_msg}\
309 {            if !AT("IIF", upper(Fld_hlp_msg))}"{endif} \
310 {        endif
311      endif // Fld_editable
312      outcolor();
313      color_flg=0;
314    otherwise: goto getnext;
315    endcase
316 }
317
318 //Leave the above blank line, it forces a line feed!
319 //-----------------
320 // End of @ SAY GET
321 //-----------------
322 {  ++cnt;
323    getnext:
324  next k;
325 }
326
327 *-- Format file exit code ----------------------------------------
328
329 *-- SET STATUS was \
330 {if dB_status then}
331 ON when you went into the Forms Designer.
332 IF lc_status = "OFF"  && Entered form with status off
333    SET STATUS OFF     && Turn STATUS "OFF" on the way out
334 {else}
335 OFF when you went into the Forms Designer.
336 IF lc_status = "ON"  && Entered form with status on
337    SET STATUS ON      && Turn STATUS "ON" on the way out
338 {endif}
339 ENDIF
340 {if carry_flg then}
341
342 IF lc_carry = "OFF"
343    SET CARRY OFF
344 ENDIF
345 {endif}
346 {if wnd_names then}
347
348 RELEASE WINDOWS {substr(wnd_names, 1, (len(wnd_names) - 1))}
349 {endif}
350
351 IF lc_talk="ON"
352    SET TALK ON
353 ENDIF
354
355 RELEASE {if carry_flg then}lc_carry,{endif}lc_talk,lc_fields,lc_status
356 *-- EOP: {filename(fmt_name)}FMT
```

(continued)

```
357 {if cnt == 0 then
358     pause(form_empty + any_key);
359 endif;
360 fileerase(fmt_name+".FMO");
361 nogen:
362 return 0;
363 //---------------------------------------
364 // Template user defined functions follow
365 //---------------------------------------
366
367 define getcolor(f_display, f_editable);
368 // Determines the color from f_display and f_editable (GET or SAY)
369 enum  Foreground =    7,
370       Intensity   =    8,  // Color
371       Background   = 112,
372       MIntensity   = 256,
373       Reverse      = 512,  // Mono
374       Underline    =1024,
375       Blink        =2048,
376       default      =32768; // Screen set to default
377
378 var forgrnd, enhanced, backgrnd, blnk, underln,
       revrse, use_colors, incolor;
379 incolor="";
380
381 use_colors = default & f_display;
382 forgrnd  = Foreground & f_display;
383 enhanced = (Intensity & f_display) || (MIntensity & f_display);
384 backgrnd = Background & f_display;
385 blnk     = Blink  & f_display;
386 underln  = Underline & f_display;
387 revrse   = Reverse & f_display;
388
389 if not use_colors then // Use system colors, no colors set in designer
390
391     if backgrnd then backgrnd = backgrnd/16 endif;
392
393     if (display != mono and display != mono43) then
394        case forgrnd of
395          0: incolor = "n";
396          1: incolor = "b";
397          2: incolor = "g";
398          3: incolor = "bg";
399          4: incolor = "r";
400          5: incolor = "rb";
401          6: incolor = "gr";
402          7: incolor = "w";
403        endcase
404     else
405        incolor = "w";
406     endif
407
```

(continued)

```
408     if revrse then
409        incolor = incolor + "i";
410     endif
411     if underln then
412        incolor = incolor + "u";
413     endif
414     if enhanced then
415        incolor = incolor + "+";
416     endif
417     if blnk then
418        incolor = incolor + "*";
419     endif
420
421     incolor = incolor + "/";
422
423     if (display != mono and display != mono43) then
424        case backgrnd of
425          0: incolor = incolor + "n";
426          1: incolor = incolor + "b";
427          2: incolor = incolor + "g";
428          3: incolor = incolor + "bg";
429          4: incolor = incolor + "r";
430          5: incolor = incolor + "rb";
431          6: incolor = incolor + "gr";
432          7: incolor = incolor + "w";
433        endcase
434     else
435        incolor = incolor + "n";
436     endif
437
438     if f_editable and incolor then
439        incolor = incolor + "," + incolor;
440     endif
441
442  endif // use no colors
443  return alltrim(incolor);
444 enddef;
445
446 //----------------------------------------------------------------
447 define outbox(mbox, mchar);
448    // Output the of Box border and charater if any
449    case mbox of
450       0: // single}\
451 {    1:}DOUBLE \
452 {       2:}CHR({mchar}) \
453 {    endcase
454      return;
455    enddef
456
457  //----------------------------------------------------------------
458    define outcolor();
459    // Output the of color of the @ SAY GET
```

(continued)

```
460     if LEN(color) > 0 then
461        if color_flg then
462           // If flag is set output a dBASE continuation ";"
463           print(";"+crlf+space(3));
464        endif}
465 COLOR {color} \
466 {  endif
467    return;
468  enddef
469
470 //------------------------------------------------------------
471   define nul2zero(numbr);
472     // if number is nul and we are expecting a zero - convert the nul to 0
473     if !numbr then numbr=0 endif;
474     return numbr;
475   enddef
476 }
477  // EOP FORM.COD
478
```

Appendix C

Constants File FORM.DEF

```
 1 //-----------------------------------------------------------------------
 2 // FORM.DEF              NPI form object data selectors
 3 // Ashton-Tate (c) 1987, 1988
 4 //
 5 // Updated 9-21-88 KJN
 6 //
 7 // This include file contains all the selectors required for forms.
 8 // *** DO NOT CHANGE ANY OF THE NUMBERS BELOW ***
 9 //
10 //-----------------------------------------------------------------------
11 // NOTE:
12 // Selectors listed in the following table which are shown to have
13 // "Value: Number" will sometimes return the null string instead
14 // of the numeric zero. For logical compares, null is the same
15 // as zero, however when emitting the value to the output file
16 // the null string must be converted to a numeric zero explicitly.
17 // A user defined function is used in the FORM.COD template program
18 // called NUL2ZERO() for converting null strings to explicit numeric
19 // zeros.
20 //-----------------------------------------------------------------------
21 {
22 selectors
23 #lstoff
24 //
25 // ELEMENT selectors (FOREACH loop elements)
26 //
27 ELEMENT            1000, // All elements types by row & column
28 BOX_ELEMENT        1086, // Box element
29 FLD_ELEMENT        1130, // Field element
30 TEXT_ELEMENT       1085, // Text element
31 //
32 // Selectors common to all elements
33 //
34 ELEMENT_TYPE       001, // Element types found in forms are:
35                         //     BOX_ELEMENT
36                         //     FLD_ELEMENT
37                         //     TEXT_ELEMENT
38                         // Menu Path: None
39 ROW_POSITN         225, // Row number of Element
40                         // Menu Path: None - Value: Number
41 COL_POSITN         093, // Column number of Element
42                         // Menu Path: None - Value: Number
43 SYS_FLEN           053, // Element length in layout
44 SYS_INAME          068, // reserved
45 SYS_FMT            071, // reserved
```

(continued)

```
46 SYS_PAGE              090, // reserved
47 SYS_ROW               092, // reserved
48 SYS_ATRB              094, // reserved
49 //
50 // Frame level selectors - can be accessed at any time
51 //
52 NAME                  040, // Name of NPI form object
53                            // Menu Path: None - Value: String
54 FRAME_CLASS           181, // Object type (called MENU_TYPE in
                                    application.def)
55                            // Menu Path: None - Value:11=form, 12=label,
                                            13=report
56 FRAME_VER             150, // Version #
57                            // Menu Path: None - Value: Number
58 FRAME_FILE_TYPE       151, // File type of object
59                            // Menu Path: None - Value: Number
60 FRAME_PATH            042, // Path of object
61                            // Menu Path: None - Value: String
62 FRAME_NUM_OF_FIELDS 153, // Number of fields
63                            // Menu Path: None - Value: Number
64 //
65 // Text attribute selectors (FOREACH Text_element x .... NEXT)
66 //
67 TEXT_ITEM             095, // Static text data
68                            // Menu Path: None - Value: String
69 //
70 // Field attribute selectors (FOREACH Fld_element x .... NEXT)
71 //
72 FLD_FILENAME          060, // File name (Alias) of current field
73                            // Menu Path: None - Value: String
74 FLD_FIELDNAME         061, // Field name of Element
75                            // Menu Path: None - Value: String
76 FLD_FIELDTYPE         063, // Where the data coming from
77                            // Menu Path: None - Value: 0:dBF field 1:calc'ed
78                            //                  2:sum 3:predefined
                                            4:memory var
79 FLD_VALUE_TYPE        064, // Field data type in dBF
80                            // Menu Path: None - Value: 67:char 68:date
                                        70:float
81                            //           76:logical 77:memo
                                        78:numeric
82                            //  Try chr(fld_value_type) return C:char
                                        D:date etc.
83 FLD_LENGTH            065, // Length of field in dBF
84                            // Menu Path: None - Value: Number
85 FLD_DECIMALS          066, // Number of decimal positions for numeric data
86                            // Menu Path: None - Value: Number
87 FLD_TEMPLATE          074, // Picture template
88                            // Menu Path: FMT - Value: String
89 FLD_PICFUN            075, // Picture functions
90                            // Menu Path: FMP - Value: String
91 FLD_PIC_CHOICE        180, // Picture function sting for (M) picture
```

(continued)

```
 92                          // Menu Path: FMP - Value: String
 93 FLD_PIC_SCROLL      183, // Picture function scroll with for (S) picture
 94                          // Menu Path: FMP - Value: String
 95 FLD_DESCRIPT        076, // Calc & sum description
 96                          // Menu Path: FMD - Value: String
 97 FLD_EXPRESSION      077, // Calculated field expression
 98                          // Menu Path: FME - Value: String
 99 FLD_L_BOUND         079, // Lower field range bound
100                          // Menu Path: FMES - Value: String
101 FLD_U_BOUND         080, // Upper field range bound
102                          // Menu Path: FMEL - Value: String
103 FLD_DEF_VAL         081, // Default field value
104                          // Menu Path: FMED - Value: String
105 FLD_ED_COND         082, // Edit if condition
106                          // Menu Path: FMEE - Value: String
107 FLD_OK_COND         083, // Satisfy condition
108                          // Menu Path: FMEA - Value: String
109 FLD_REJ_MSG         084, // Reject message
110                          // Menu Path: FMEU - Value: String
111 FLD_HLP_MSG         099, // Help message
112                          // Menu Path: FMEM - Value: String
113 FLD_MEM_TYP         170, // Memo window type
114                          // Menu Path: FMED - Value: 1:Open 2:Marker
115 FLD_EDITABLE        087, // Say or Get data
116                          // Menu Path: FMED - Value: 0:say 1:get
117 FLD_CARRY           088, // Carry value forward
118                          // Menu Path: FMEC - Value: 0:no 1:yes
119 FLD_DISPLAY         171, // Field display
120                          // Menu Path: WD - Value: number See udf() at
121                          //     bottom of form.cod for values
122 //
123 // Box Attribute Selectors (FOREACH Box_element x .... NEXT)
124 //
125 BOX_TYPE            160, // 0:single 1:double 2:special
126                          // Menu Path: LB - Value: 0:single 1:double 2:spe-
cial
127 BOX_SPECIAL_CHAR    161, // Box character
128                          // Menu Path: LBU - Value: Number
129 BOX_LEFT            162, // Left column for box
130                          // Menu Path: None - Value: Number
131 BOX_TOP             163, // Top row of box
132                          // Menu Path: None - Value: Number
133 BOX_WIDTH           164, // Box width in columns
134                          // Menu Path: None - Value: Number
135 BOX_HEIGHT          165, // Box height in rows
136                          // Menu Path: None - Value: Number
137 #lston
138 ;
139 //
140 // Values returned by Fld_Fieldtype
141 //
142 enum dbf = 0,     // Field from a database
```

(continued)

```
143     calc,       // Calculated expression
144     sum,        // Summary ie. Average, Count, etc.
145     predef,     // Predefined ie. Date, Page, etc.
146     memvar;     // Memvar reference
147 }
148
```

Chapter 5

Labels and Templates

This chapter discusses how the template language processes label objects and suggests several possible changes to the basic template file. As you might expect, the template file LABEL.COD is the source code for LABEL.GEN. The selectors are defined in the file LABEL.DEF along with the usual BUILTIN.DEF. These files process labels saved in the special-format LBL file. LABEL.GEN takes about 14K of disk space. LABEL.COD is a 966-line template program that uses the selectors defined in LABEL.DEF, 164 lines long. A partial listing (that omits the selectors) of the latest version of LABEL.COD with line numbers is included in the appendix to this chapter. (If you want to substitute a different name for LABEL.GEN, see Appendix A of Chapter 4.)

The particular version of LABEL.COD we'll be using here has the date February 22, 1989, on the source code file. If your LABEL.COD has an earlier date, you should contact Ashton-Tate to obtain the latest version. Probably the easiest way to do this is to download it from the dBASE IV conference on the Ashton-Tate bulletin board. Contact Ashton-Tate for access.

What Does a Label Template Do?

LABEL.COD is basically a straightforward program. The complexities arise from having to deal with the different printer drivers, user-defined fonts, functions, and so on. Also, remember that the code has to provide the option to produce sample labels. These complexities increase the size of

LABEL.COD, but they don't make the structure that much more difficult to understand.

The label template must first determine which fields, calculated fields, functions, text, and so on are contained in the LBL file. A good deal of code is spent worrying about not printing blank fields as blank lines. The basic strategy is to create a separate user-defined function for each line of each label in a row, then to call those functions to output the particular line (or not output the line if it is blank). Thus, the function _ _ _21() will output the second line of the first column of labels. The function _ _ _32() will output the third line of the second column. All variables are reset when the next row of labels is printed. The procedure Chk4null calls the line-printing functions.

You saw in Chapter 4 how many of the template commands work. This chapter focuses on new commands and functions used in the label template.

A Simple Label Setup

Figure 5-1 shows a simple label setup. The fields are from CUSTO-MER.DBF. Each uses a simple "XXX" picture clause and the T picture function to trim trailing blanks. The field names are:

```
NAME
ADDRESS1
ADDRESS2
CITY, STATE   ZIP
```

In other words, it's a typical label layout.

A Digression on Blank Lines

Some versions of LABEL.GEN and REPORT.GEN don't omit blank lines in address fields. For example, if the ADDRESS2 field is blank, perhaps because there is no suite number, a blank line may still be printed. This produces an unprofessional-looking label. If printed addresses show up with blank lines in your reports, try using the IIF() function instead. Figure 5-2 shows how to include the IIF() in a label. The question is what the expression should look like.

The trick to omitting blank lines is to fool dBASE IV into thinking they're all one line. Use the IIF() to determine whether there's anything in the field. If there is, print a carriage return–line feed and the contents of the field. If the

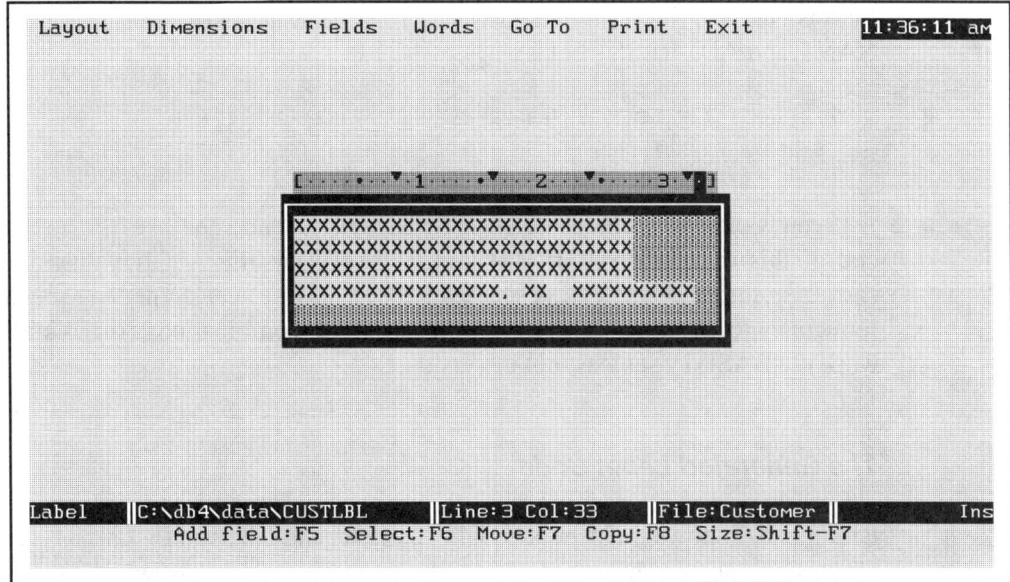

Figure 5-1   The Label Generation Screen

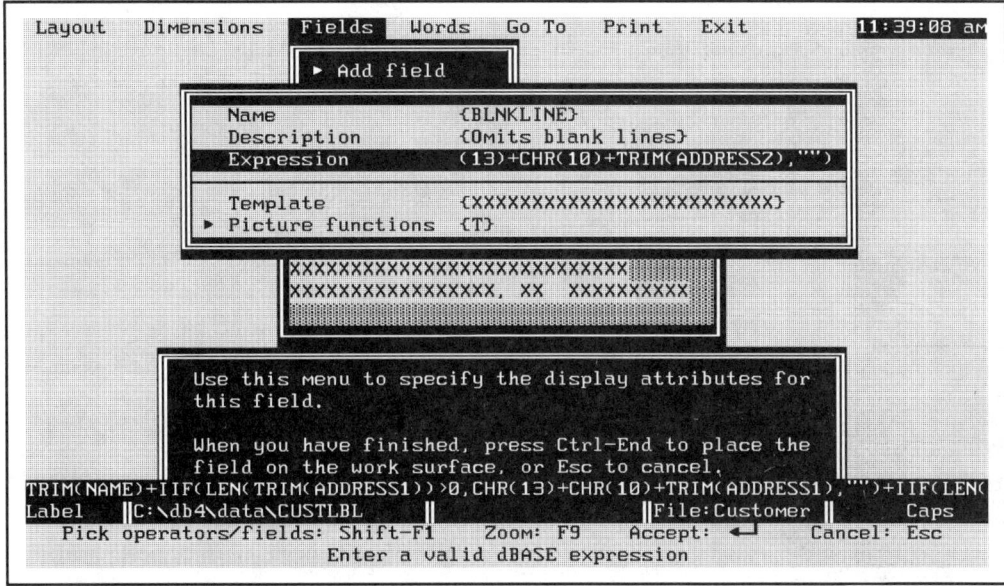

Figure 5-2   An Expression to Omit Blank Lines

field is empty, print a null character. Here's the exact expression using the NAME and ADDRESS1 fields:

```
TRIM(NAME)+IIF(LEN(TRIM(ADDRESS1))>0,CHR(13)+CHR(10)
  +TRIM(ADDRESS1),"")
```

If you wanted to include ADDRESS2 as well, just add another IIF() to the end of this expression. CHR(13) and CHR(10) are the ASCII values for carriage return and line feed, respectively. You may be accustomed to using a semicolon to generate carriage return–line feed combinations; that won't work in dBASE IV, at least not in version 1.0.

The Generated Label Code

Example 5-1 shows the generated label code for the labels in Figure 5-1. As usual, line numbers have been added to make discussion easier. We won't discuss this code right now, but will refer back to it later in this chapter. Put a paper clip at this page so you can easily find the generated code to see where it comes from in LABEL.COD.

Example 5-1   The Generated Label Program CUSTLBL.LBG

```
 1 * Program............: C:\DB4\DATA\CUSTLBL.LBG
 2 * Date...............: 4-16-89
 3 * Version............: dBASE IV, Label 1
 4 *
 5 * Label Specifics:
 6 *    Wide - 35
 7 *    Tall - 5
 8 *    Indentation - 0
 9 *    Number across - 1
10 *    Space between - 0
11 *    Lines between - 1
12 *    Blankable lines - 4
13 *    Print formatted - 4
14 *
15 PARAMETER ll_sample
16 *-- Set printer variables for this procedure only
17 PRIVATE _peject, _ploffset, _wrap
```

(continued)

```
18
19 *-- Test for End of file
20 IF EOF()
21    RETURN
22 ENDIF
23
24 IF SET("TALK")="ON"
25    SET TALK OFF
26    gc_talk="ON"
27 ELSE
28     gc_talk="OFF"
29 ENDIF
30 gc_space = SET("SPACE")
31 SET SPACE OFF
32 gc_time=TIME()      && system time for predefined field
33 gd_date=DATE()      && system date   "     "    "     "
34 gl_fandl=.F.        && first and last record flag
35 gl_prntflg=.T.      && Continue printing flag
36 gn_column=1
37 gn_element=0
38 gn_line=1
39 gn_memowid=SET("MEMOWIDTH")
40 SET MEMOWIDTH TO 254
41 gn_page=_pageno     && capture page number for multiple copies
42 _plineno=0
43 _wrap = .F.
44
45 IF ll_sample
46    DO Sample
47    IF LASTKEY() = 27
48       RETURN
49    ENDIF
50 ENDIF
51
52 *-- Setup Environment
53 ON ESCAPE DO prnabort
54
55 DECLARE gn_line2[1]
56
57 PRINTJOB
```

(continued)

```
58
59
60 *-- set page number for multiple copies
61 _pageno=gn_page
62
63 DO WHILE FOUND() .AND. .NOT. EOF() .AND. gl_prntflg
64
65    gn_line=0
66    *-- Check for blank lines
67    DO chk4null WITH 0, 4, 4
68
69    DO WHILE gn_line < 6
70       ?
71       gn_line=gn_line+1
72    ENDDO
73    CONTINUE
74 ENDDO
75
76 IF .NOT. gl_prntflg
77    SET MEMOWIDTH TO gn_memowid
78    SET SPACE &gc_space.
79    SET TALK &gc_talk.
80    ON ESCAPE
81    RETURN
82 ENDIF
83
84 ENDPRINTJOB
85
86 SET MEMOWIDTH TO gn_memowid
87 SET SPACE &gc_space.
88 SET TALK &gc_talk.
89 ON ESCAPE
90 RETURN
91 * EOP: C:\DB4\DATA\CUSTLBL.LBG
92
93 PROCEDURE prnabort
94 gl_prntflg=.F.
95 RETURN
96 * EOP: prnabort
97
```

(continued)

```
 98 FUNCTION ___01
 99 lc_ret=.F.
100 *-- Test for blank line
101 IF LEN(TRIM( NAME )) > 0
102    ll_output=.T.
103    _pcolno = 0
104    ?? NAME PICTURE "@T" AT 0
105 ELSE
106    lc_ret=.T.
107 ENDIF
108 RETURN lc_ret
109
110 FUNCTION ___11
111 lc_ret=.F.
112 *-- Test for blank line
113 IF LEN(TRIM( ADDRESS1 )) > 0
114    ll_output=.T.
115    _pcolno = 0
116    ?? ADDRESS1 PICTURE "@T" AT 0
117 ELSE
118    lc_ret=.T.
119 ENDIF
120 RETURN lc_ret
121
122 FUNCTION ___21
123 lc_ret=.F.
124 *-- Test for blank line
125 IF LEN(TRIM( ADDRESS2 )) > 0
126    ll_output=.T.
127    _pcolno = 0
128    ?? ADDRESS2 PICTURE "@T" AT 0
129 ELSE
130    lc_ret=.T.
131 ENDIF
132 RETURN lc_ret
133
134 FUNCTION ___31
135 lc_ret=.F.
136 *-- Test for blank line
137 IF LEN(TRIM( CITY + STATE + ZIP )) > 0
```

(continued)

```
138     ll_output=.T.
139     _pcolno = 0
140     ?? CITY PICTURE "@T" AT 0 ;
141     ,IIF(LEN(TRIM(CITY )) > 0,", " ,"" ) ,
142     ?? STATE PICTURE "@T" ;
143     ,IIF(LEN(TRIM(STATE )) > 0," " ,"" ) ,
144     ?? ZIP PICTURE "@T"
145 ENDIF
146 RETURN lc_ret
147
148
149 PROCEDURE chk4null
150 *-- Parameters:
151 *
152 *-- 1) line number on the design surface
153 *-- 2) maximum number of printable lines
154 *-- 3) parameter 2 times number of labels across
155 *
156 PARAMETERS ln_line, ln_nolines, ln_element
157 gn_element=0
158 gn_line2[1]=ln_line
159 lc_temp=SPACE(7)
160 ll_output=.F.
161 DO WHILE gn_element < ln_element
162    gn_column=1
163    ll_output=.F.
164    DO WHILE gn_column <= 1
165       IF gn_line2[gn_column] < ln_line+ln_nolines
166          lc_temp=LTRIM(STR(gn_line2[gn_column]))+;
                   LTRIM(STR(gn_column))
167          DO WHILE ___&lc_temp.()
168             gn_element=gn_element+1
169             gn_line2[gn_column]=gn_line2[gn_column]+1
170             lc_temp=LTRIM(STR(gn_line2[gn_column]))+;
                      LTRIM(STR(gn_column))
171          ENDDO
172          gn_element=gn_element+1
173          gn_line2[gn_column]=gn_line2[gn_column]+1
174       ENDIF
```

(continued)

```
175      gn_column=gn_column+1
176    ENDDO
177    IF ll_output
178      ?
179      gn_line=gn_line+1
180    ENDIF
181 ENDDO
182 RETURN
183 * EOP: chk4null
184
185 PROCEDURE SAMPLE
186 PRIVATE x,y,choice
187 DEFINE WINDOW w4sample FROM 15,20 TO 17,60 DOUBLE
188 choice="Y"
189 x=0
190 DO WHILE choice = "Y"
191    y=0
192    ?
193    DO WHILE y < 5
194       x=0
195       DO WHILE x < 1
196          ?? REPLICATE("X",35)
197          x=x+1
198       ENDDO
199       ?
200       y=y+1
201    ENDDO
202    x=0
203    DO WHILE x < 1
204       ?
205       x=x+1
206    ENDDO
207    ACTIVATE WINDOW w4sample
208    @ 0,3 SAY "Do you want more samples? (Y/N)";
209    GET choice PICTURE "!" VALID choice $ "NY"
210    READ
211    DEACTIVATE WINDOW w4sample
212    IF LASTKEY() = 27
213       EXIT
```

(continued)

```
214    ENDIF
215 ENDDO
216 RELEASE WINDOW w4sample
217 RETURN
218 * EOP: SAMPLE
219
```

The Label Template Code

With that as background, let's look at the code for LABEL.COD.

Initialization

The label template file begins with the usual comments that make up the program header. Next, LABEL.DEF and BUILTIN.DEF selectors are read in.

```
11 {include "label.def";
12  include "builtin.def";
```

String constants are defined for different basic error messages. Any of these errors will cause program generation to abort.

```
14  // Enum string constants for international translation
15  //
16  enum wrong_class = "Can't use LABEL.GEN on non-label objects. ",
17      label_empty = "Label design was empty. ",
18    more_samples = "Do you want more samples? (Y/N)",
19    gen_request  = "Generation request cancelled. ";
20  //
21  if frame_class != label then
22    pause(wrong_class + any_key);
23    return 0;
24  endif
```

A set of variables is defined on lines 26–60, and some of them are initialized. We'll refer back to these variables as we discuss the program further, so take a look at them now.

Figure Out the Number of Lines in the Label

The FOREACH loop that starts on line 80 determines how many lines are to be in the label. It examines each element in the label, tracking it with the cursor variable ecursor. This FOREACH loop terminates on line 119. Note the use of the EOC() function, which tests whether the cursor variable has reached the end of the set. If there are more elements to process, ecursor returns a 0, otherwise a 1. Thus, this loop processes each element in the label and stores the number of elements in the ecursor variable.

The COUNTC() function on line 81 returns the number of elements in a cursor variable. In this case, it is used to determine whether the four variables referenced in line 82 need to be reset. The first time through the loop they will be set to 0. After that, they will be set to the current value of the selector Row_positn, the row number of the element.

```
80  foreach ELEMENT ecursor
81    if COUNTC(ecursor) > 1 && !eoc(ecursor) then
82      temp_row = previous_row = current_row =
            nul2zero(Row_Positn);
```

The DO WHILE loop in line 83 processes each cursor element. If the element is on a new line (line 84), then the program increments the number of lines that might be blank, resets some variables, and increments the printed_lines variable by 1 (line 89).

```
83        do while !eoc(ecursor)
84          if Row_Positn > previous_row then
85            number_of_blankable_lines=
                number_of_blankable_lines+blank_line;
86            blank_line=1;
87            previous_element=0;
88            previous_row=Row_Positn;
89            ++printed_lines;
90          endif
```

Next, check to see whether this is a blank line or not. If it is, the selector Fld_value_type is checked. Fld_value_type is defined on line 125 of LABEL.DEF:

```
122 FLD_FIELDTYPE        063, // Where the data is coming from
123                           // Menu Path: None - Value: 0:dBF
                                             field 1:calc'ed
124                           //            2:sum 3:predefined
                                             4:memory var
125 FLD_VALUE_TYPE       064, // Field data type in dBF
126                           // Menu Path: None - Value: 67:char
                                             68:date 70:float
127                           //            76:logical 77:memo
                                             78:numeric
128                           //  Try chr(fld_value_type) return
                                  C:char D:date etc.
```

In other words, a Fld_value_type of 78 means we are working with a numeric field. In that case, check to see whether the picture function Z has been used. If so, set the blank line indicator variable to 0. (The Z picture function displays zero numeric values as a blank string.) In other words, if the line is blank, the field is numeric, and it's not to be printed as a blank string, then keep the line blank.

```
91      if blank_line then
92        if FLD_VALUE_TYPE == 78 then
93          if not AT("Z",FLD_PICFUN) then
94            blank_line=0;
95          endif
```

If the field is not numeric, check to see whether it is text. The variable previous_element checks to see whether the previous element inspected was a field with a type of either character or numeric with a Z picture function. If it was, the value of blank_line is not changed. However, if the previous element was either of those, the value of blank_line is set to 0. Similarly, on line 100, if the element is a field that is not a character field, the value of blank_line is set to 0.

```
96      else
97        if Text_Item && !previous_element then
98          blank_line=0;
99        endif
```

```
100            if ELEMENT_TYPE == @Fld_Element &&
                FLD_VALUE_TYPE != 67 then
101               blank_line=0;
102            endif
103          endif
104        endif
```

The next block of code sets the value of previous_element for the next iteration of the DO WHILE !EOC(cursor) loop. The value of the cursor variable ecursor is incremented just before the ENDDO statement that closes the DO WHILE loop.

```
105        if ELEMENT_TYPE == @Fld_Element &&
            FLD_VALUE_TYPE == 67 ||
106        (FLD_VALUE_TYPE == 78 && AT("Z",FLD_PICFUN)) then
107          previous_element=1;
108        else
109          previous_element=0;
110        endif
111        ++ecursor;
112      enddo
```

Next, the number of lines that could be blank, stored in the aptly named variable number_of_blankable_lines, is incremented by the value of blank_line. If the line is not blank or is simply the continuation of a character variable, blank_line will be 0. Otherwise, it will be 1. The variable printed_lines (again, self-explanatory) is incremented, the cursor variable ecursor is decremented by 1 (the -- operator), the variables previous_row and last_row are modified, the FOREACH loop is closed with the next command on line 119, and blank_line is reinitialized to 0.

```
113        number_of_blankable_lines=
              number_of_blankable_lines+blank_line;
114        ++printed_lines;
115        --ecursor;
116        previous_row=Row_Positn+1;
117        last_row=Row_Positn;
118      endif
119  next
120  blank_line=0;
```

Create and Check File Names

The block of code from lines 122–143 sets default drive names and the name and path of the label file. The file name and path are checked, and correction attempts are made in the same way as they were handled by FORM.COD.

```
121
122   default_drive = STRSET(_defdrive);
123   lblname = FRAME_PATH + NAME;
124   lblpath = FRAME_PATH;
125   if not FILEOK(lblname) then
126     if FILEDRIVE(NAME) || !default_drive then
127       lblname=NAME;
128       if FILEDRIVE(NAME) then
129         lblpath=FILEDRIVE(NAME)+":"+FILEPATH(NAME);
130       else
131         lblpath=FILEPATH(NAME);
132       endif
133     else
134       lblname=default_drive + ":" + NAME;
135       lblpath=default_drive + ":";
136     endif
137   endif
138
139   if not CREATE(lblname+".LBG") then;
140     PAUSE(fileroot(lblname)+".LBG"+read_only+any_key);
141     return 0;
142   endif
143 }
```

Output Initial Label Code

As with most report code, label programs include many variables and a lot of standardized code. The usual header information, including label dimensions, is included in lines 144–157. Note the special selectors for labels, such as Lbl_wide, Label_tall, Label_marg, and so on. The comments explain what these selectors do. Read this code carefully and make sure you understand what each selector is measuring before going on through LABEL.COD.

```
144 * Program............: {lblname}.LBG
145 * Date...............: {LTRIM(SUBSTR(DATE(),1,8))}
146 * Version............: dBASE IV, Label {FRAME_VER}
147 *
148 * Label Specifics:
149 *    Wide - {lbl_wide}
150 *    Tall - {label_tall}
151 *    Indentation - {nul2zero(label_lmarg)}
152 *    Number across - {label_nup}
153 *    Space between - {lbl_hspace}
154 *    Lines between - {lbl_vspace}
155 *    Blankable lines - {number_of_blankable_lines}
156 *    Print formatted - {printed_lines}
157 *
```

Lines 144–146 are totally inadequate as a file header. I strongly recommend you replace them with something similar to what we did with FORM.COD.

```
//
{print(replicate("*",65)+crlf);}
* Name.........: {lblname}.LBG
* Author.......: Tony Lima
* Date.........: {LTRIM(SUBSTR(DATE(),1,8))}
* dBASE Ver....: dBASE IV, Label {FRAME_VER}
* Notice.......: Copyright, 1989, Tony Lima
* Description..:
* Notes........:
{print(replicate("*",65)+crlf);}
//
```

The next block is output directly to the file as well. It sets up some memory variables, declares three print-system memory variables PRIVATE, checks to see whether there are any records in the database (IF EOF()), and does the usual trick with SET TALK.

```
158 PARAMETER ll_sample
159 *-- Set printer variables for this procedure only
160 PRIVATE _peject, _ploffset, _wrap
```

```
161
162 *-- Test for End of file
163 IF EOF()
164     RETURN
165 ENDIF
166
167 IF SET("TALK")="ON"
168     SET TALK OFF
169     gc_talk="ON"
170 ELSE
171     gc_talk="OFF"
172 ENDIF
```

The next block of code uses the SET() function with the SET SPACE ON/OFF command. SET SPACE OFF means that fields and memory variables printed with the ?? command will not be automatically separated by a blank space. Thus, ?? TRIM(FNAME),LNAME would result in "Tony Lima" with SPACE set ON (the default) and TonyLima with SPACE OFF. Lines 182–183 capture the current memo width and reset it to 254, the maximum width allowed in a report.

```
173 gc_space = SET("SPACE")
174 SET SPACE OFF
175 gc_time=TIME()        && system time for predefined field
176 gd_date=DATE()        && system date  "     "      "       "
177 gl_fandl=.F.          && first and last record flag
178 gl_prntflg=.T.        && Continue printing flag
179 gn_column=1
180 gn_element=0
181 gn_line=1
182 gn_memowid=SET("MEMOWIDTH")
183 SET MEMOWIDTH TO 254
184 gn_page=_pageno       && capture page number for multiple copies
185 _plineno=0
```

Some template processing is done on lines 186–188. The selector Label_lmarg stores the value of any left margin set in the LBL file. If the value of this selector is 0, the IF takes the value false, and the value of the print-system variable _ploffset is left unchanged. Otherwise, it is incremented by the left margin entered in the LBL file.

```
186 {if LABEL_LMARG then}
187 _ploffset = _ploffset + {LABEL_LMARG}
188 {endif}
189 _wrap = .F.
190
```

Next, check to see if the user has requested sample labels, stored in the variable ll_sample. This memory variable can be passed from a calling program (note the PARAMETERS statement output by line 158) so programmers can write their own sample labels routines. Therefore, it's important to check for this before actually starting the label printing.

Line 199 sets the switch to trap for the Esc key and runs the procedure Prnabort if that key is pressed. The LASTKEY() function is used for the same purpose on line 193, except it returns to the calling program instead of trapping. (Try DO CUSTLBL WITH .T. from the dot prompt to see how this works.)

```
191 IF ll_sample
192    DO Sample
193    IF LASTKEY() = 27
194       RETURN
195    ENDIF
196 ENDIF
197
198 *-- Setup Environment
199 ON ESCAPE DO prnabort
200
```

Line 201 stores the value of the selector Frame_num_of_fields (the number of fields in the label) in the variable numflds. The next line checks to see whether more than one column of labels are to be printed (selector Label_nup, named for the expression "three up labels" to refer to printing three across). Note that the number of fields has to be greater than zero; if the labels are pure text, the next block of code will not be included. That code DECLAREs three arrays to handle labels that are more than one column.

Line 209 begins printing labels with the PRINTJOB command.

```
201 {numflds=FRAME_NUM_OF_FIELDS;}
202 {if LABEL_NUP > 1 && numflds then}
203 *-- Initialize array(s) for {LABEL_NUP} across labels
```

```
204 DECLARE isfound[{LABEL_NUP-1}]
205 DECLARE tmp4lbl[{LABEL_NUP-1},{numflds}]
206 {endif}
207 DECLARE gn_line2[{label_nup}]
208
209 PRINTJOB
210
```

Adding Multiuser Code

The appropriate place to add multiuser code is after line 208. I recommend something like this:

```
{VAR tlresp;
ASKUSER("Do you want to include multiuser commands",
        "Y",1);
{if tlresp == "Y" then}

* Code to process network operations

IF NETWORK()
  DEFINE WINDOW Lockwin FROM 12,10 TO 21,70 DOUBLE
  lc_lock=SET("LOCK")
  IF lc_lock="ON"
  SET REPROCESS TO 10
  ll_lock=FLOCK()
  IF .NOT. ll_lock
    lc_time=LKSYS(0)
    ld_date=LKSYS(1)
    lc_name=LKSYS(2)
    ACTIVATE WINDOW Lockwin
    @ 01,02 SAY "Unable to lock file. Already in use by"
    @ 02,02 SAY lc_name
    @ 03,02 SAY "Locked on "+DTOC(ld_date)+" at "+lc_time
    WAIT "  Hit the space bar to continue..."
    DEACTIVATE WINDOW Lockwin
    RETURN
  ENDIF && .NOT. ll_lock
ELSE
```

```
        ACTIVATE WINDOW Lockwin
        @ 01,02 SAY "WARNING!"
        @ 02,02 SAY "Database not locked, data may change"
        @ 03,02 SAY "while printing is in process."
        @ 04,02 SAY "SET LOCK ON to correct this problem."
        WAIT "  Hit the space bar to continue or press Esc to exit..."
        DEACTIVATE WINDOW Lockwin
     ENDIF && lc_lock="ON"
     RELEASE WINDOW Lockwin
     ENDIF && NETWORK()
     {endif}
```

Note that LKSYS(0) and LKSYS(1) will not return the date or time in dBASE IV version 1.0.

Label Printing Code

The label printing code is the next major block of LABEL.COD. It generates the code to print labels. The first step is to check all calculated fields.

Calculated Fields

Each field element is scanned with the cursor variable k. If the field is calculated and a name has been assigned (and x is not 0, meaning it's not the first time through the loop), then output the code to initialize the calculated variable. The comment is output on line 218, followed by the name of the field on the next line. (The \ at the end of line 220 is the continuation character for output to the program file. It prevents a carriage return–line feed from being generated.)

```
211 {x=0;}
212 {foreach FLD_ELEMENT k}
213 //
214 // only if there is a fieldname assigned to the calculated
        field
215 //
216 {if FLD_FIELDTYPE == Calc_data && FLD_FIELDNAME then}
217 {  if !x then}
218 *-- Initialize calculated variables.
```

```
219 {  endif}
220 {FLD_FIELDNAME}=\
```

The case statement on line 221 checks the field type and outputs the appropriate initialization code. If the field type is not one of these four, the variable is initialized with a null string. The variable *x* is incremented by 1, and the FOREACH loop is closed on line 230.

```
221 {case FLD_VALUE_TYPE of}
222 {68: // Date    }CTOD(SPACE(8))
223 {70: // Float   }FLOAT(0)
224 {76: // Logical}.F.
225 {78: // Numeric}INT(0)
226 {otherwise:}""
227 {endcase}
228 {   ++x;}
229 {endif}
230 {next k;}
231
```

Initializing date-type calculated fields is done on line 222 using the archaic CTOD() function. It's easier and more efficient to use the date delimiters '{ / / }' instead. However, there's a dilemma here: curley braces ({,}) are used as command delimiters in the template language, so how can you output them to a file? Although it's not documented, the following trick will work:

```
222 {68: // Date    }{"{ / / }"}
```

In other words, putting quotation marks around the string inside the command curly braces will output that exact string. I recommend making this minor change in any template file where you find the expression CTOD(SPACE(8)).

Multiple Copies and Columns

dBASE IV allows printing of multiple copies from within the label and report generators. Multiple copies are also collated automatically, meaning that the report program has to keep track of which page it's on. This is set on line 233. Line 235 is the main DO WHILE loop for printing labels. The LMARG(4) function on line 236 sets the left margin for program file output. In this case, subsequent lines will be indented four spaces.

```
232 *-- set page number for multiple copies
233 _pageno=gn_page
234
235 DO WHILE FOUND() .AND. .NOT. EOF() .AND. gl_prntflg
236 {LMARG(4);}
```

Next, the template checks to see if there is more than one column of labels (and at least one field). If so, the variables isfirst and *x* are initialized to 1, and the array ISFOUND[] has all its elements initialized to false. The expression "{init_array:}" on line 241 defines a line label. It is referenced on line 249 where the value of *x* is compared to the number of label columns and, if there are more array elements to be initialized, transfers control back to init_array:.

The IF statement on line 237 is closed on line 315. Most of the code in between is designed to process multicolumn labels, as we'll see later.

```
237 {if LABEL_NUP > 1 and numflds then}
238 {isfirst=1;}
239 {x=1;}
240 STORE .F. TO \
241 {init_array:}
242 {if isfirst then}
243 {  isfirst=0;}
244 {else}
245 ,\
246 {endif}
247 isfound[{x}]\
248 {++x;}
249 {if x < LABEL_NUP then goto init_array endif}
250
```

Output from this expression will be (assuming three up labels):

```
STORE .F. TO isfound[1],isfound[2],isfound[3]
```

The ISFOUND[] array keeps track of whether there is data for each label in any given row of labels. If an element is false at print time, printing for that label is skipped.

Next, the label arcopy: defines a loop that will place values in arrays. Since *x* is 0 the first time through the loop, lines 254–257 will be skipped.

```
251 {x=0;}
252 {i=1;}
253 {arcopy:}
254 {  if x then}
255 IF FOUND() .AND. .NOT. EOF()
256 {    LMARG(7);}
257 {  endif}
258 {  calcflds();}
259 //
```

The user-defined function CALCFLDS() is defined in lines 935–946. It scans the field elements using the cursor variable *k* as a counter. If the field has a name and it is calculated, then output the name. Scan the expressions in the current cursor element and output the field expression after the = sign. CALCFLDS() is used throughout LABEL.COD.

```
935 {define calcflds();}
936 {foreach FLD_ELEMENT k}
937 {  if FLD_FIELDNAME && FLD_FIELDTYPE == Calc_data then}
938 {FLD_FIELDNAME}=\
939 {foreach FLD_EXPRESSION j in k}
940 {FLD_EXPRESSION}
941 {next}
942
943 {  endif}
944 {next k;}
945 {return;}
946 {enddef}
```

Setting Up the Data Array

The next step is to set up the data array TMP4LBL[] for output. The variable *x* is used as the column counter, while *i* is the fields counter.

```
260 {foreach FLD_ELEMENT i}
261 tmp4lbl[{x+1},{i}]=\
```

Next, determine the field type and output the appropriate expression. The first type is database fields (Tabl_data). A field value type of 77 means the field is memo type, in which case the dBASE IV MLINE() function is used to print the first line of the memo field only. (If you want more than one line of memo data printed, change the 1 on line 265 to the number of lines you want.) If the data is not memo type, the name of the field is output.

```
262 {case FLD_FIELDTYPE of}
263 {Tabl_data:}
264 {  if FLD_VALUE_TYPE == 77 then}
265 MLINE({FLD_FIELDNAME},1)
266 {  else}
267 {    FLD_FIELDNAME}
268
269 {  endif}
```

If the field is calculated and you've given it a name, output the field name. If not, just output the field expression one element at a time. Similarly, if the field is predefined, output the appropriate variable.

```
270 {Calc_data:}
271 {  if FLD_FIELDNAME then}
272 {    FLD_FIELDNAME}
273
274 {  else}
275 {    foreach FLD_EXPRESSION exp in i}
276 {      FLD_EXPRESSION}\
277 {    next}
278
279 {  endif}
280 {Pred_data:}
281 {  case FLD_PREDEFINE of}
282 {  0: // Date}
283 gd_date
284 {  1: // Time}
285 gc_time
286 {  2: // Recno}
287 RECNO()
288 {  3: // Pageno}
289 _pageno
290 {  endcase}
```

```
291 {endcase}
292 {next i;}
293 //
```

Next, the value of *x* is checked. If it's 1, the isfound[] array element is changed to true. The CONTINUE command is output, and the output left margin is changed to 4. (The CONTINUE means you must perform a LO-CATE before running the labels.) Finally, *x* is incremented by 1 and compared to Label_nup. If there are still labels across the page, the program transfers to arcopy:.

```
294 {  if x then}
295 isfound[{x}]=.T.
296 {  endif}
297 CONTINUE
298 {  if x then}
299 {    LMARG(4);}
300 ENDIF
301 {  endif}
302 {  ++x;}
303 {  if x < LABEL_NUP-1 then
304     goto arcopy;
305     endif
306 }
```

Next, the command IF FOUND .AND. .NOT. EOF() is output, and the output left margin is changed to 7. CALCFLDS() is called to output the field name and expression for calculated fields. The element of ISFOUND[] corresponding to this data element is set to true.

On the other hand, if this is not a multicolumn label program, CALCFLDS() is called only on line 314, bypassing all processing between lines 237 and 313.

```
307 IF FOUND() .AND. .NOT. EOF()
308 {LMARG(7);}
309 {calcflds();}
310 isfound[{x}]=.T.
311 {LMARG(4);}
312 ENDIF
313 {else}
314 {calcflds();}
```

```
315 {endif}
316
```

The variable *x* is used to output a blank line (? command) if there are unused lines in a label. Next, the procedure Chk4null is called to check for blank fields. Chk4null in turn calls the procedures that output each row and column of a label.

```
317 {x=0;
318   do while x < temp_row}
319 ?
320 {   ++x;
321   enddo
322 }
323 gn_line={temp_row}
324 *-- Check for blank lines
325 DO chk4null WITH {temp_row}, {last_row+1},
        {(last_row-temp_row+1)*label_nup}
326
```

Next, enough ? commands are output to move the printer to the top of the next label. The memory variable gn_line stores the last line number printed. The remainder of the main program is output, resetting SET commands to their original values and other housekeeping.

```
327 DO WHILE gn_line < {label_tall+lbl_vspace}
328    ?
329    gn_line=gn_line+1
330 ENDDO
331 CONTINUE
332 {LMARG(1);}
333 ENDDO
334
335 IF .NOT. gl_prntflg
336    SET MEMOWIDTH TO gn_memowid
337    SET SPACE &gc_space.
338    SET TALK &gc_talk.
339    ON ESCAPE
340    RETURN
341 ENDIF
342
```

```
343 ENDPRINTJOB
344
345 SET MEMOWIDTH TO gn_memowid
346 SET SPACE &gc_space.
347 SET TALK &gc_talk.
348 ON ESCAPE
349 RETURN
350 * EOP: {lblname}.LBG
351
```

The standardized code continues with the procedure Prnabort, defined on lines 352–355.

Output User-defined Functions

The UDFs and the procedure Chk4null created by LABEL.COD are the heart of the label output. In fact, on line 358 this is referred to as the start of the main loop. The FOREACH loop scans all the elements in the label definition file. First, check to see if the element is a band element. If so, increment the cursor k, the variable item_number, and reset the temp_row variable to the Row_positn selector. If k is at the last value of the cursor, the EOC(k) function will exit the FOREACH loop.

```
357 //
358 // Main loop (inner loop to handles fields on each line by #
        of columns)
359 //
360 {foreach ELEMENT k}
361 {   if ELEMENT_TYPE == @Band_Element then}
362 {     ++k; ++item_number;}
363 {     if eoc(k) then}
364 {       exit;}
365 {     endif}
366 {     temp_row=Row_Positn;}
367 {   endif}
368 {   ++count;}
369 {   LMARG(1);}
370 {   blank_line=0;}
371 //
```

If the number of blankable lines is greater than zero, several variables are initialized.

```
372 {
373   if number_of_blankable_lines then
374
375     long_line=0;
376     blank_line=1;
377     current_element=COUNTC(k);
378     previous_element=0;
379     previous_row=Row_Positn;
380
```

Next the elements are scanned to the current value of the cursor *k*. If it's a new row, the program exits from this loop. The usual check on blank lines and field types is done to reset the variable blank_line. This block of code is identical to that seen earlier.

```
381     do while !eoc(k);
382       if Row_Positn > previous_row then
383         exit
384       endif
385       if blank_line then
386         if FLD_VALUE_TYPE == 78 then
387           if not AT("Z",FLD_PICFUN) then
388             blank_line=0;
389           endif
390         else
391           if Text_Item && !previous_element then
392             blank_line=0;
393           endif
394           if ELEMENT_TYPE == @Fld_Element &&
              FLD_VALUE_TYPE != 67 then
395             blank_line=0;
396           endif
397         endif
398       endif
399       if !blank_line then
400         exit
401       endif
```

```
402        if ELEMENT_TYPE == @Fld_Element &&
             FLD_VALUE_TYPE == 67 ||
403        (FLD_VALUE_TYPE == 78 && AT("Z",FLD_PICFUN)) then
404          previous_element=1;
405        else
406          previous_element=0;
407        endif
408        ++k;
409      enddo
```

If the cursor *k* is at its last element, decrement its value by 1, then decrement it by enough to match the value for the current element.

The ENDIF on line 418 closes the IF on line 373 that checked for the number of blankable lines.

```
410      if eoc(k) then
411        --k;
412      endif
413
414      do while COUNTC(k) > current_element;
415        --k;
416      enddo
417
418    endif}
```

Process Blank Lines

Again, we must process blank lines. The variables line and *x* are set to define the name of the function to be output. The FUNCTION command on line 427 defines the function name. Since this is a blank line, the function simply sets ll_output to true and returns a false. Finally, the value of the variables *x* and line are incremented by 1.

```
419 //
420 //--------------------
421 // Process blank lines
422 //--------------------
423 {  line=temp_row+1; }
424 {  do while line < Row_Positn}
```

```
425 {     x=1;}
426 {     do while x <= LABEL_NUP}
427 FUNCTION ___{line}{x}
428 ll_output=.T.
429 RETURN .F.
430
431 {        ++x;}
432 {     enddo}
433 {     ++line;}
434 {  enddo}
435 //-------------------
436 // End of blank lines
437 //-------------------
```

The UDF for Nonblank Lines

Next, nonblank lines are handled. The function name is defined as before. The variable mrows defines the number of labels across.

```
439 {  mrows = 0;}
440 {  first_item = item_number;}
441 {  line = temp_row;}
442 //
443 {  repeat:}
444 //
445 {  if new_line then}
446 FUNCTION ___{nul2zero(Row_Positn)}{mrows+1}
447 lc_ret=.F.
448 {     if mrows then}
449 *-- Column {mrows+1}
```

The array element ISFOUND[{mrows}] is output to be checked to see if it is true or false. If true, the values of blank_line and mrows are tested. The UDF conditional_if_for_blank_line(<cursor>,<page offset>) is called. This UDF is defined on lines 868–925 of LABEL.COD. The <page offset> is simply the column in the output file where you want commands to appear. In this case, the function is called with the cursor *k* that is associated with the main FOREACH loop. This function, while apparently complex, merely outputs a statement like the following from our sample label LBG file:

```
100 *-- Test for blank line
101 IF LEN(TRIM( NAME )) > 0
102    ll_output=.T.
```

The complexity of the UDF is due to the fact that it must deal with picture functions and templates, as well as the TRANSFORM() function. However, there is one interesting bit of syntax used regularly:

```
884 {cursor2.FLD_FIELDNAME},"\
```

Note how the cursor is used to define the element to be used for the particular selector.

On the other hand, if mrows is 0, then the statement "ll_output=.T." is simply output to the file.

```
450 IF isfound[{mrows}]
451 {LMARG(4);}
452 {    endif}
453 {    if blank_line then}
454 {      if mrows then}
455 {        conditional_if_for_blank_line(k,7);}
456 {      else}
457 {        conditional_if_for_blank_line(k,4);}
458 {      endif}
459 {    else}
460 ll_output=.T.
461 {    endif}
```

The variable first_combine tests whether a text or field element is the first in a series of chained data. If so, initialize the column-position print-system variable _pcolno. Output a ?? and check the variable long_line, which is set if a calculated field might exceed the width of the label. If it's not the first element and not a long line, output a comma (line 471).

```
462 {    if first_combine then}
463 _pcolno = {Col_Positn+(mrows*(lbl_wide+lbl_hspace))}
464 {    endif}
465 ?? \
466 {  else}
467 {    if long_line then}
468 ?? \
```

```
469 {      long_line=0;}
470 {    else}
471 ,\
472 {    endif}
473 { endif}
474 //
```

Determine Print Width

The CASE statement that starts on line 476 determines the width of the printed data. If it's text, the LEN() function determines how long it is. The maximum value of LEN() is 237, the block size used by the templates. If LEN() returns that value, the entire element *k* must be scanned. The FOREACH statement from lines 483–489 handles this. Field elements are handled similarly.

```
475 {ni=0;}
476 {   case ELEMENT_TYPE of}
477 //
478 {   @Text_Element:}
479 //
480 {x=Col_Positn;}
481 {i=LEN(Text_Item);}
482 {if i == 237 then}
483 {   foreach Text_Item fcursor in k}
484 {     if ni then}
485 {        i=i+LEN(Text_Item);}
486 {        temp=Text_Item;}
487 {     endif}
488 {     ++ni;}
489 {   next}
490 {endif}
491 {current_column=x+i;}
492 //
493 {   @Fld_Element:}
494 //
495 {x=Col_Positn;}
496 {i=FLD_REPWIDTH;}
497 {if i > 237 then}
498 {   foreach FLD_TEMPLATE fcursor in k}
```

```
499 {    if ni then}
500 {       temp=FLD_TEMPLATE;}
501 {    endif}
502 {    ++ni;}
503 {  next}
504 {endif}
505 {current_column=x+i;}
506 //
507 {  endcase}
```

Next, the template checks to see whether the next element is on the same line and whether it is flush with the previous element. The variables new_line and combine are used to track this. Since the cursor *k* is incremented on line 512, it is decremented to compensate on line 526.

```
509 // is the next element on the same line
510 //
511 {  line=Row_Positn;}
512 {  ++k;}
513 {  if (not EOC(k)) && line == Row_Positn then}
514 {    new_line=0;}
515 //
516 // is the next element flush with previous element
517 //
518 {    if current_column == Col_Positn then}
519 {       combine=1;}
520 {    else}
521 {       combine=0;}
522 {    endif}
523 {  else}
524 {    new_line=1;}
525 {  endif}
526 {  --k;}
```

Lines 527–576 are pretty routine. The case statement looks at text and field elements. Two new user-defined functions are introduced. PUTFLD() places fields in the output file. SEPERATE() (*sic*) separates long output lines.

```
527 //----------------------------------------------
528 // Determine what type of data we are processing
529 //----------------------------------------------
```

```
530 {  case ELEMENT_TYPE of}
531 //
532 {  @Text_Element:}
533 //
534 {if blank_line then}
535 IIF(LEN(TRIM(\
536 {  --k;}
537 {  if FLD_VALUE_TYPE == 78 then}
538 TRANSFORM(\
539 {  endif}
540 {  if mrows+1 < LABEL_NUP then}
541 tmp4lbl[{mrows+1},{mcolumns-1}] \
542 {  else}
543 {     putfld(k);}
544 {  endif}
545 {  if FLD_VALUE_TYPE == 78 then}
546 ,"@{FLD_PICFUN}")\
547 {  endif}
548 {  ++k;}
549 )) > 0,\
550 {  long_line=1;
551  endif}
552 //
553 {if i > 70 then}
554 ;
555 {  seperate(Text_Item);}
556 {  if ni then}
557 + "{temp}";
558 {  endif}
559 {else}
560 "{Text_Item}" \
561 {endif}
562 //
563 {if blank_line then}
564 ,"" ) \
565 {endif}
566 //
567 {  @Fld_Element:}
568 //
569 {    if mrows+1 < LABEL_NUP then}
570 tmp4lbl[{mrows+1},{mcolumns}] \
```

```
571 {    else}
572 {       putfld(k);}
573 {    endif}
574 {    ++mcolumns;}
575 {  endcase}
576 //
```

The next block of code adds picture functions and templates. Line 577
checks to see whether the element is a field element. If so, it looks at three
conditions. If any one of these three is true, control will pass to the then
clause. First, the selector Fld_fieldtype will have a value of 0 if this is a
database field. Hence, the expression !Fld_fieldtype means we are not working with a database field. The second condition is that the field type be
calculated. The third is that it be predefined.

If any one of those conditions is true, line 582 checks to see whether the
data type is character (Fld_value_type == 67). If so, the variable *j* is set to any
field template. (The variable temp contains any previously defined field
templates from line 500. On line 584, if the length of the field is equal to the
width of its template in the label (Fld_repwidth) and the picture template is
equal to a string of *X*s equal to the length of the field, no template is necessary,
so set *j* to a null string. Note the ability of the template program to figure out
whether a picture template is necessary. If those conditions don't hold, *j* is set
to the character 1.

```
577 {   if ELEMENT_TYPE == @Fld_Element then}
578 //
579 {     if !FLD_FIELDTYPE || FLD_FIELDTYPE == Calc_data ||
580          (FLD_FIELDTYPE == Pred_data && FLD_PREDEFINE > 1) then}
581 //
582 {       if FLD_VALUE_TYPE == 67 then
583            j=FLD_TEMPLATE+temp;
584            if FLD_LENGTH == FLD_REPWIDTH &&
                  j == REPLICATE("X",FLD_LENGTH) then
585              j="";
586            endif
587          else
588            j="1";
589          endif}
```

Next, check the picture functions (selector Fld_picfun) and the variable *j*. If
either is non-null, output the word PICTURE and wait for the next clause. If

there is a picture function (line 595), output the "@ string followed by the value of the picture function. If *j* is not null (line 597), continue; otherwise output a closing quotation mark (").

```
590 //
591 {       if FLD_PICFUN || j then}
592 PICTURE \
593 {       endif}
594 //
595 {       if FLD_PICFUN then}
596 "@{FLD_PICFUN}\
597 {        if j then}
598  \
599 {        else}
600 " \
601 {        endif}
602 {       endif}
```

If there's a picture clause, we have to output it as well. Check *j*, then look at the variable *i* (line length counter) to see if it's greater than 70. If so and there's a picture function, output the string "+;. Otherwise, merely output the continuation character (;).

```
603 //
604 {       if j then}
605 {        if i > 70 then}
606 {          if FLD_PICFUN then}
607 "+;
608 {          else}
609 ;
610 {          endif}
```

Next, the SEPERATE() UDF is used to split the picture template if necessary. The ni flag variable tracks whether the variable temp contains a picture template. If so, the template is output followed by a semicolon. Finally, on line 619, the field template itself is output.

```
611 {          seperate(FLD_TEMPLATE);}
612 {          if ni then}
```

```
613 + "{temp}";
614 {         endif}
615 {         else}
616 {             if !FLD_PICFUN then}
617 "\
618 {             endif}
619 {FLD_TEMPLATE}" \
620 {         endif}
621 {       endif}
622 {     endif}
623 //
624 { endif}
625 //
```

The STYLE Clause

The ability to access printer drivers and their fonts is a major feature of dBASE IV. The STYLE clause is used for this. GETSTYLE(<style var>) is a user-defined function that handles output for this clause. It's defined on lines 808–824 of LABEL.COD. Basically, all it does is look at each possibility and add the appropriate character to the string "outstyle" returned by the UDF. The variable (style) contains this string, which is simply output to the file after the word "STYLE". Line 630 checks to see whether this is the first element of a combination. If it is, the template program outputs the word "AT" followed by the row and column positions (referred to, unfortunately, by the variables col_positn and mrows respectively).

```
626 {  if FLD_STYLE then}
627 {      style=getstyle(FLD_STYLE);}
628 STYLE "{style}" \
629 { endif}
630 {  if first_combine then}
631 AT {Col_Positn+(mrows*(lbl_wide+lbl_hspace))} \
632 {     if combine then}
633 {        first_combine=0;}
634 {     endif}
635 {  else}
636 {     if not combine then first_combine=1; endif}
637 { endif}
```

Iterating

Next, position the pointer to the next element and increment the cursor k and the item_number variable. Check to see whether it's a new line, or the end of the cursor k and the same row. If it is neither, then check to see whether it's a long line. If it is, output a comma. Otherwise, output a semicolon. The remainder of the code through line 654 is straightforward and merely there to determine whether the correct character for output is a comma or semicolon.

```
638 //
639 // position to next element
640 //
641 {   temp_row=Row_Positn;}
642 {   ++k; ++item_number;}
643 //
644 {   if !new_line || (!EOC(k) && temp_row == Row_Positn) then
645       if !new_line then}
646 {       if long_line then}
647 ,
648 {       else}
649 ;
650 {       endif}
651 {     else}
652 ,
653 {       long_line=0;}
654 {     endif
```

Looping

The program checks to see whether this is the end of the cursor k. If it isn't, control transfers to the repeat label (line 443). The remainder of this code is the closing code for the user-defined function. Line 718 closes the main FOREACH loop that defines each output UDF.

```
655       if !EOC(k) then
656         goto repeat;
657       endif}
658 {   else}
659 {     long_line=0;}
660 {   endif}
```

```
661 //
662 {   combine=0;}
663 {   first_combine=1;}
664 //
665 {   if LABEL_NUP-1 > mrows then}
666 ,
667 {     if blank_line && mrows then}
668 {        LMARG(4);}
669 {     else}
670 {        LMARG(1);}
671 {     endif}
672 {     if blank_line then}
673 {        if temp_row != last_row then}
674 ELSE
675    lc_ret=.T.
676 {        endif}
677 ENDIF
678 {     endif}
679 {     if mrows then}
680 {        LMARG(1);}
681 ENDIF
682 {     endif}
683 RETURN lc_ret
684
685 {     ++mrows;}
686 {     do while item_number > first_item}
687 {        --k; --item_number;}
688 {        if ELEMENT_TYPE == @Fld_Element then}
689 {           --mcolumns;}
690 {        endif}
691 {     enddo}
692 {     new_line=1;}
693 {     goto repeat;}
694 {   else}
695
696 {     if mrows then}
697 {        LMARG(4);}
698 {     else}
699 {        LMARG(1);}
700 {     endif}
701 {     if blank_line then}
```

```
702 {        if temp_row != last_row then}
703 ELSE
704    lc_ret=.T.
705 {        endif}
706 ENDIF
707 {    endif}
708 {    if mrows then}
709 {        LMARG(1);}
710 ENDIF
711 {    endif}
712 RETURN lc_ret
713
714 {    mrows=0;}
715 {    --k; --item_number;}
716 {  endif}
717 //
718 {next k;}
719
```

Procedure CHK4NULL

The procedures Chk4null (lines 720–758) and SAMPLE (760–800) are almost pure dBASE IV code, and they are not particularly complex or instructive in the template language. One bit of syntax reveals the power of dBASE IV user-defined functions, however:

```
742        DO WHILE ___&lc_temp.()
743            gn_element=gn_element+1
744            gn_line2[gn_column]=gn_line2[gn_column]+1
745            lc_temp=LTRIM(STR(gn_line2[gn_column]))+;
                    LTRIM(STR(gn_column))
746        ENDDO
```

The memory variable lc_temp contains the row and column number of the UDF that outputs that label row and column. Each of these UDFs returns a logical true or false. Note how the UDFs are called in order using macro substitution: ___&lc_temp.(). They will be called in sequence until a false is returned. This will be done by the UDF that outputs the last line on the last label in that row of labels.

Conclusion

LABEL.COD is interesting because it illustrates several important points about the template language. First, it shows how dBASE IV user-defined functions can be defined in an iterative process. Second, it shows some interesting elements of error trapping and processing, especially the use of cursors. This chapter serves as an introduction to the more general report generator in Chapter 6.

Appendix

LABEL.COD

```
1 //
2 // Module Name: LABEL.COD
3 // Description: Define Application menus and program structure.
4 //
5
6 Label (.lbg) Program Template
7 ----------------------------
8 Version 1.0
9 Ashton-Tate (c) 1987
10
11 {include "label.def";
12  include "builtin.def";
13  //
14  // Enum string constants for international translation
15  //
16  enum wrong_class = "Can't use LABEL.GEN on non-label objects. ",
17       label_empty = "Label design was empty. ",
18      more_samples = "Do you want more samples? (Y/N)",
19       gen_request = "Generation request cancelled. ";
20  //
21  if frame_class != label then
22    pause(wrong_class + any_key);
23    return 0;
24  endif
25
26  //--------------------------
27  // Declare working variables
28  //--------------------------
29  var lblname,        // Name of label file program
30      lblpath,        // Path to write label file
31      default_drive,  // dBASE default drive
32      crlf,           // line feed
33      line,           // Line counter for outputing number of "?'s"
34      isfirst,        // Logical work variable
35      mrows,          // Number of rows that the label uses
36      mcolumns,       // Number of columns in label
37      lbl_vspace,     // Number of characters between labels
38      lbl_wide,       // Label width
39      lbl_hspace,     // How tall the label is
40      numflds,        // Number of fields used in label
41      style,          // Style attribute assigned to the field/text
42      current_column, // Current column number
43      first_combine,  // text or field is first in the chain of combined data
44      combine,        // combine fields flag
45      new_line,       // is the next field on a new line
```

(continued)

```
46  i, j, x, temp, ni, // temporary usage variables
47     first_item,    // relative element number when repeating columns
48     item_number,   // current item number
49     count,         // number of text and field items
50    last_row,
51    temp_row,
52   current_row,
53  previous_row,
54   blank_line,
55   printed_lines,
56  previous_element,
57 number_of_blankable_lines,
58  current_element,
59    response,
60   long_line        // calculated expression possibly exceeds line
61 ;
62  //-------------------------------------------------
63  // Assign starting values to some of the variables
64  //-------------------------------------------------
65  crlf = chr(10);
66  current_element=2;
67  item_number = isfirst = mcolumns = first_combine = new_line = 1;
68  count = line = mrows = numflds = current_column = combine = long_line = 0;
69  lbl_vspace = nul2zero(LABEL_VSPACE);
70  lbl_wide = LABEL_WIDE;
71  lbl_hspace = nul2zero(LABEL_HSPACE);
72
73  blank_line = 1;
74  current_row = 0;
75  previous_row = -1;
76  printed_lines = 0;
77  previous_element = 0;
78  number_of_blankable_lines=0;
79
80  foreach ELEMENT ecursor
81    if COUNTC(ecursor) > 1 && !eoc(ecursor) then
82      temp_row = previous_row = current_row = nul2zero(Row_Positn);
83      do while !eoc(ecursor)
84        if Row_Positn > previous_row then
85          number_of_blankable_lines=number_of_blankable_lines+blank_line;
86          blank_line=1;
87          previous_element=0;
88          previous_row=Row_Positn;
89          ++printed_lines;
90        endif
91        if blank_line then
92          if FLD_VALUE_TYPE == 78 then
93            if not AT("Z",FLD_PICFUN) then
94              blank_line=0;
95            endif
96          else
97            if Text_Item && !previous_element then
```

(continued)

```
 98              blank_line=0;
 99            endif
100            if ELEMENT_TYPE == @Fld_Element && FLD_VALUE_TYPE != 67 then
101              blank_line=0;
102            endif
103          endif
104        endif
105        if ELEMENT_TYPE == @Fld_Element && FLD_VALUE_TYPE == 67 ||
106        (FLD_VALUE_TYPE == 78 && AT("Z",FLD_PICFUN)) then
107          previous_element=1;
108        else
109          previous_element=0;
110        endif
111        ++ecursor;
112      enddo
113      number_of_blankable_lines=number_of_blankable_lines+blank_line;
114      ++printed_lines;
115      --ecursor;
116      previous_row=Row_Positn+1;
117      last_row=Row_Positn;
118    endif
119 next
120 blank_line=0;
121
122 default_drive = STRSET(_defdrive);
123 lblname = FRAME_PATH + NAME;
124 lblpath = FRAME_PATH;
125 if not FILEOK(lblname) then
126   if FILEDRIVE(NAME) || !default_drive then
127     lblname=NAME;
128     if FILEDRIVE(NAME) then
129       lblpath=FILEDRIVE(NAME)+":"+FILEPATH(NAME);
130     else
131       lblpath=FILEPATH(NAME);
132     endif
133   else
134     lblname=default_drive + ":" + NAME;
135     lblpath=default_drive + ":";
136   endif
137 endif
138
139 if not CREATE(lblname+".LBG") then;
140   PAUSE(fileroot(lblname)+".LBG"+read_only+any_key);
141   return 0;
142 endif
143 }
144 * Program............: {lblname}.LBG
145 * Date...............: {LTRIM(SUBSTR(DATE(),1,8))}
146 * Version............: dBASE IV, Label {FRAME_VER}
147 *
148 * Label Specifics:
149 *    Wide - {lbl_wide}
```

(continued)

```
150 *    Tall - {label_tall}
151 *    Indentation - {nul2zero(label_lmarg)}
152 *    Number across - {label_nup}
153 *    Space between - {lbl_hspace}
154 *    Lines between - {lbl_vspace}
155 *    Blankable lines - {number_of_blankable_lines}
156 *    Print formatted - {printed_lines}
157 *
158 PARAMETER ll_sample
159 *-- Set printer variables for this procedure only
160 PRIVATE _peject, _ploffset, _wrap
161
162 *-- Test for End of file
163 IF EOF()
164    RETURN
165 ENDIF
166
167 IF SET("TALK")="ON"
168    SET TALK OFF
169    gc_talk="ON"
170 ELSE
171    gc_talk="OFF"
172 ENDIF
173 gc_space = SET("SPACE")
174 SET SPACE OFF
175 gc_time=TIME()      && system time for predefined field
176 gd_date=DATE()      && system date  "    "    "    "
177 gl_fandl=.F.      && first and last record flag
178 gl_prntflg=.T.    && Continue printing flag
179 gn_column=1
180 gn_element=0
181 gn_line=1
182 gn_memowid=SET("MEMOWIDTH")
183 SET MEMOWIDTH TO 254
184 gn_page=_pageno      && capture page number for multiple copies
185 _plineno=0
186 {if LABEL_LMARG then}
187 _ploffset = _ploffset + {LABEL_LMARG}
188 {endif}
189 _wrap = .F.
190
191 IF ll_sample
192    DO Sample
193    IF LASTKEY() = 27
194       RETURN
195    ENDIF
196 ENDIF
197
198 *-- Setup Environment
199 ON ESCAPE DO prnabort
200
201 {numflds=FRAME_NUM_OF_FIELDS;}
```

(continued)

```
202 {if LABEL_NUP > 1 && numflds then}
203 *-- Initialize array(s) for {LABEL_NUP} across labels
204 DECLARE isfound[{LABEL_NUP-1}]
205 DECLARE tmp4lbl[{LABEL_NUP-1},{numflds}]
206 {endif}
207 DECLARE gn_line2[{label_nup}]
208
209 PRINTJOB
210
211 {x=0;}
212 {foreach FLD_ELEMENT k}
213 //
214 // only if there is a fieldname assigned to the calculated field
215 //
216 {if FLD_FIELDTYPE == Calc_data && FLD_FIELDNAME then}
217 {  if !x then}
218 *-- Initialize calculated variables.
219 {  endif}
220 {FLD_FIELDNAME}=\
221 {case FLD_VALUE_TYPE of}
222 {68: // Date   }CTOD(SPACE(8))
223 {70: // Float  }FLOAT(0)
224 {76: // Logical}.F.
225 {78: // Numeric}INT(0)
226 {otherwise:}""
227 {endcase}
228 {  ++x;}
229 {endif}
230 {next k;}
231
232 *-- set page number for multiple copies
233 _pageno=gn_page
234
235 DO WHILE FOUND() .AND. .NOT. EOF() .AND. gl_prntflg
236 {LMARG(4);}
237 {if LABEL_NUP > 1 and numflds then}
238 {isfirst=1;}
239 {x=1;}
240 STORE .F. TO \
241 {init_array:}
242 {if isfirst then}
243 {  isfirst=0;}
244 {else}
245 ,\
246 {endif}
247 isfound[{x}]\
248 {++x;}
249 {if x < LABEL_NUP then goto init_array endif}
250
251 {x=0;}
252 {i=1;}
253 {arcopy:}
```

(continued)

```
254 {  if x then}
255 IF FOUND() .AND. .NOT. EOF()
256 {     LMARG(7);}
257 {  endif}
258 {  calcflds();}
259 //
260 {foreach FLD_ELEMENT i}
261 tmp4lbl[{x+1},{i}]=\
262 {case FLD_FIELDTYPE of}
263 {Tabl_data:}
264 {  if FLD_VALUE_TYPE == 77 then}
265 MLINE({FLD_FIELDNAME},1)
266 {  else}
267 {     FLD_FIELDNAME}
268
269 {  endif}
270 {Calc_data:}
271 {  if FLD_FIELDNAME then}
272 {     FLD_FIELDNAME}
273
274 {  else}
275 {     foreach FLD_EXPRESSION exp in i}
276 {        FLD_EXPRESSION}\
277 {     next}
278
279 {  endif}
280 {Pred_data:}
281 {  case FLD_PREDEFINE of}
282 {  0: // Date}
283 gd_date
284 {  1: // Time}
285 gc_time
286 {  2: // Recno}
287 RECNO()
288 {  3: // Pageno}
289 _pageno
290 {  endcase}
291 {endcase}
292 {next i;}
293 //
294 {  if x then}
295 isfound[{x}]=.T.
296 {  endif}
297 CONTINUE
298 {  if x then}
299 {     LMARG(4);}
300 ENDIF
301 {  endif}
302 {  ++x;}
303 {  if x < LABEL_NUP-1 then
304      goto arcopy;
305    endif
```

(continued)

```
306 }
307 IF FOUND() .AND. .NOT. EOF()
308 {LMARG(7);}
309 {calcflds();}
310 isfound[{x}]=.T.
311 {LMARG(4);}
312 ENDIF
313 {else}
314 {calcflds();}
315 {endif}
316
317 {x=0;
318   do while x < temp_row}
319 ?
320 {   ++x;
321   enddo
322 }
323 gn_line={temp_row}
324 *-- Check for blank lines
325 DO chk4null WITH {temp_row}, {last_row+1}, {(last_row-temp_row+1)*label_nup}
326
327 DO WHILE gn_line < {label_tall+lbl_vspace}
328     ?
329     gn_line=gn_line+1
330 ENDDO
331 CONTINUE
332 {LMARG(1);}
333 ENDDO
334
335 IF .NOT. gl_prntflg
336     SET MEMOWIDTH TO gn_memowid
337     SET SPACE &gc_space.
338     SET TALK &gc_talk.
339     ON ESCAPE
340     RETURN
341 ENDIF
342
343 ENDPRINTJOB
344
345 SET MEMOWIDTH TO gn_memowid
346 SET SPACE &gc_space.
347 SET TALK &gc_talk.
348 ON ESCAPE
349 RETURN
350 * EOP: {lblname}.LBG
351
352 PROCEDURE prnabort
353 gl_prntflg=.F.
354 RETURN
355 * EOP: prnabort
356
357 //
```

(continued)

```
358  // Main loop (inner loop to handles fields on each line by # of columns)
359  //
360  {foreach ELEMENT k}
361  {  if ELEMENT_TYPE == @Band_Element then}
362  {     ++k; ++item_number;}
363  {    if eoc(k) then}
364  {      exit;}
365  {    endif}
366  {    temp_row=Row_Positn;}
367  {  endif}
368  {  ++count;}
369  {  LMARG(1);}
370  {  blank_line=0;}
371  //
372  {
373     if number_of_blankable_lines then
374
375        long_line=0;
376        blank_line=1;
377        current_element=COUNTC(k);
378        previous_element=0;
379        previous_row=Row_Positn;
380
381        do while !eoc(k);
382          if Row_Positn > previous_row then
383            exit
384          endif
385          if blank_line then
386            if FLD_VALUE_TYPE == 78 then
387              if not AT("Z",FLD_PICFUN) then
388                blank_line=0;
389              endif
390            else
391              if Text_Item && !previous_element then
392                blank_line=0;
393              endif
394              if ELEMENT_TYPE == @Fld_Element && FLD_VALUE_TYPE != 67 then
395                blank_line=0;
396              endif
397            endif
398          endif
399          if !blank_line then
400            exit
401          endif
402          if ELEMENT_TYPE == @Fld_Element && FLD_VALUE_TYPE == 67 ||
403          (FLD_VALUE_TYPE == 78 && AT("Z",FLD_PICFUN)) then
404            previous_element=1;
405          else
406            previous_element=0;
407          endif
408          ++k;
409        enddo
```

(continued)

```
410     if eoc(k) then
411        --k;
412     endif
413
414     do while COUNTC(k) > current_element;
415        --k;
416     enddo
417
418   endif}
419 //
420 //--------------------
421 // Process blank lines
422 //--------------------
423 {   line=temp_row+1;}
424 {   do while line < Row_Positn}
425 {     x=1;}
426 {     do while x <= LABEL_NUP}
427 FUNCTION ___{line}{x}
428 ll_output=.T.
429 RETURN .F.
430
431 {        ++x;}
432 {      enddo}
433 {      ++line;}
434 {   enddo}
435 //--------------------
436 // End of blank lines
437 //--------------------
438 //
439 {   mrows = 0;}
440 {   first_item = item_number;}
441 {   line = temp_row;}
442 //
443 {   repeat:}
444 //
445 {   if new_line then}
446 FUNCTION ___{nul2zero(Row_Positn)}{mrows+1}
447 lc_ret=.F.
448 {     if mrows then}
449 *-- Column {mrows+1}
450 IF isfound[{mrows}]
451 {LMARG(4);}
452 {     endif}
453 {     if blank_line then}
454 {       if mrows then}
455 {         conditional_if_for_blank_line(k,7);}
456 {       else}
457 {         conditional_if_for_blank_line(k,4);}
458 {       endif}
459 {     else}
460 ll_output=.T.
461 {     endif}
```

(continued)

```
462 {    if first_combine then}
463 _pcolno = {Col_Positn+(mrows*(lbl_wide+lbl_hspace))}
464 {    endif}
465 ?? \
466 {  else}
467 {    if long_line then}
468 ?? \
469 {      long_line=0;}
470 {    else}
471 ,\
472 {    endif}
473 {  endif}
474 //
475 {ni=0;}
476 {  case ELEMENT_TYPE of}
477 //
478 {  @Text_Element:}
479 //
480 {x=Col_Positn;}
481 {i=LEN(Text_Item);}
482 {if i == 237 then}
483 {  foreach Text_Item fcursor in k}
484 {    if ni then}
485 {      i=i+LEN(Text_Item);}
486 {      temp=Text_Item;}
487 {    endif}
488 {    ++ni;}
489 {  next}
490 {endif}
491 {current_column=x+i;}
492 //
493 {  @Fld_Element:}
494 //
495 {x=Col_Positn;}
496 {i=FLD_REPWIDTH;}
497 {if i > 237 then}
498 {  foreach FLD_TEMPLATE fcursor in k}
499 {    if ni then}
500 {      temp=FLD_TEMPLATE;}
501 {    endif}
502 {    ++ni;}
503 {  next}
504 {endif}
505 {current_column=x+i;}
506 //
507 {  endcase}
508 //
509 // is the next element on the same line
510 //
511 {  line=Row_Positn;}
512 {  ++k;}
513 {  if (not EOC(k)) && line == Row_Positn then}
```

(continued)

```
514 {     new_line=0;}
515 //
516 // is the next element flush with previous element
517 //
518 {     if current_column == Col_Positn then}
519 {        combine=1;}
520 {     else}
521 {        combine=0;}
522 {     endif}
523 {  else}
524 {     new_line=1;}
525 {  endif}
526 {  --k;}
527 //-----------------------------------------------
528 // Determine what type of data we are processing
529 //-----------------------------------------------
530 {  case ELEMENT_TYPE of}
531 //
532 {  @Text_Element:}
533 //
534 {if blank_line then}
535 IIF(LEN(TRIM(\
536 {  --k;}
537 {  if FLD_VALUE_TYPE == 78 then}
538 TRANSFORM(\
539 {  endif}
540 {  if mrows+1 < LABEL_NUP then}
541 tmp4lbl[{mrows+1},{mcolumns-1}] \
542 {  else}
543 {     putfld(k);}
544 {  endif}
545 {  if FLD_VALUE_TYPE == 78 then}
546 ,"@{FLD_PICFUN}")\
547 {  endif}
548 {  ++k;}
549 )) > 0,\
550 {  long_line=1;
551  endif}
552 //
553 {if i > 70 then}
554 ;
555 {  seperate(Text_Item);}
556 {  if ni then}
557 + "{temp}";
558 {  endif}
559 {else}
560 "{Text_Item}" \
561 {endif}
562 //
563 {if blank_line then}
564 ,"" ) \
565 {endif}
```

(continued)

```
566 //
567 {  @Fld_Element:}
568 //
569 {    if mrows+1 < LABEL_NUP then}
570 tmp4lbl[{mrows+1},{mcolumns}] \
571 {    else}
572 {       putfld(k);}
573 {    endif}
574 {    ++mcolumns;}
575 {  endcase}
576 //
577 {  if ELEMENT_TYPE == @Fld_Element then}
578 //
579 {    if !FLD_FIELDTYPE || FLD_FIELDTYPE == Calc_data ||
580         (FLD_FIELDTYPE == Pred_data && FLD_PREDEFINE > 1) then}
581 //
582 {       if FLD_VALUE_TYPE == 67 then
583          j=FLD_TEMPLATE+temp;
584          if FLD_LENGTH == FLD_REPWIDTH && j == REPLICATE("X",FLD_LENGTH)
then
585             j="";
586          endif
587       else
588          j="1";
589       endif}
590 //
591 {       if FLD_PICFUN || j then}
592 PICTURE \
593 {       endif}
594 //
595 {       if FLD_PICFUN then}
596 "@{FLD_PICFUN}\
597 {          if j then}
598   \
599 {          else}
600 " \
601 {          endif}
602 {       endif}
603 //
604 {       if j then}
605 {          if i > 70 then}
606 {             if FLD_PICFUN then}
607 "+;
608 {             else}
609 ;
610 {             endif}
611 {             seperate(FLD_TEMPLATE);}
612 {             if ni then}
613 + "{temp}";
614 {             endif}
615 {          else}
616 {             if !FLD_PICFUN then}
```

(continued)

```
617 "\
618 {           endif}
619 {FLD_TEMPLATE}" \
620 {         endif}
621 {       endif}
622 {     endif}
623 //
624 {  endif}
625 //
626 {  if FLD_STYLE then}
627 {     style=getstyle(FLD_STYLE);}
628 STYLE "{style}" \
629 {  endif}
630 {  if first_combine then}
631 AT {Col_Positn+(mrows*(lbl_wide+lbl_hspace))} \
632 {     if combine then}
633 {        first_combine=0;}
634 {     endif}
635 {  else}
636 {     if not combine then first_combine=1; endif}
637 {  endif}
638 //
639 // position to next element
640 //
641 {  temp_row=Row_Positn;}
642 {  ++k; ++item_number;}
643 //
644 {  if !new_line || (!EOC(k) && temp_row == Row_Positn) then
645      if !new_line then}
646 {       if long_line then}
647 ,
648 {       else}
649 ;
650 {       endif}
651 {     else}
652 ,
653 {       long_line=0;}
654 {     endif
655      if !EOC(k) then
656        goto repeat;
657      endif}
658 {  else}
659 {     long_line=0;}
660 {  endif}
661 //
662 {  combine=0;}
663 {  first_combine=1;}
664 //
665 {  if LABEL_NUP-1 > mrows then}
666 ,
667 {     if blank_line && mrows then}
668 {        LMARG(4);}
```

(continued)

```
669 {     else}
670 {        LMARG(1);}
671 {     endif}
672 {     if blank_line then}
673 {        if temp_row != last_row then}
674 ELSE
675    lc_ret=.T.
676 {        endif}
677 ENDIF
678 {     endif}
679 {     if mrows then}
680 {        LMARG(1);}
681 ENDIF
682 {     endif}
683 RETURN lc_ret
684
685 {     ++mrows;}
686 {     do while item_number > first_item}
687 {        --k; --item_number;}
688 {        if ELEMENT_TYPE == @Fld_Element then}
689 {           --mcolumns;}
690 {        endif}
691 {     enddo}
692 {     new_line=1;}
693 {     goto repeat;}
694 {  else}
695
696 {     if mrows then}
697 {        LMARG(4);}
698 {     else}
699 {        LMARG(1);}
700 {     endif}
701 {     if blank_line then}
702 {        if temp_row != last_row then}
703 ELSE
704    lc_ret=.T.
705 {        endif}
706 ENDIF
707 {     endif}
708 {     if mrows then}
709 {        LMARG(1);}
710 ENDIF
711 {     endif}
712 RETURN lc_ret
713
714 {     mrows=0;}
715 {     --k; --item_number;}
716 {  endif}
717 //
718 {next k;}
719
720 PROCEDURE chk4null
```

(continued)

```
721 *-- Parameters:
722 *
723 *-- 1) line number on the design surface
724 *-- 2) maximum number of printable lines
725 *-- 3) parameter 2 times number of labels across
726 *
727 PARAMETERS ln_line, ln_nolines, ln_element
728 gn_element=0
729 {    x=1;
730      do while x <= label_nup}
731 gn_line2[{x}]=ln_line
732 {      ++x;
733      enddo}
734 lc_temp=SPACE(7)
735 ll_output=.F.
736 DO WHILE gn_element < ln_element
737    gn_column=1
738    ll_output=.F.
739    DO WHILE gn_column <= {label_nup}
740      IF gn_line2[gn_column] < ln_line+ln_nolines
741        lc_temp=LTRIM(STR(gn_line2[gn_column]))+LTRIM(STR(gn_column))
742        DO WHILE ___&lc_temp.()
743          gn_element=gn_element+1
744          gn_line2[gn_column]=gn_line2[gn_column]+1
745          lc_temp=LTRIM(STR(gn_line2[gn_column]))+LTRIM(STR(gn_column))
746        ENDDO
747        gn_element=gn_element+1
748        gn_line2[gn_column]=gn_line2[gn_column]+1
749      ENDIF
750      gn_column=gn_column+1
751    ENDDO
752    IF ll_output
753      ?
754      gn_line=gn_line+1
755    ENDIF
756 ENDDO
757 RETURN
758 * EOP: chk4null
759
760 PROCEDURE SAMPLE
761 PRIVATE x,y,choice
762 DEFINE WINDOW w4sample FROM 15,20 TO 17,60 DOUBLE
763 choice="Y"
764 x=0
765 DO WHILE choice = "Y"
766    y=0
767    ?
768    DO WHILE y < {LABEL_TALL}
769      x=0
770      DO WHILE x < {LABEL_NUP}
771          ?? REPLICATE("X",{LABEL_WIDE})\
772 {if LABEL_HSPACE then}
```

(continued)

```
773 +SPACE({LABEL_HSPACE})
774 {else}
775
776 {endif}
777         x=x+1
778      ENDDO
779      ?
780      y=y+1
781    ENDDO
782 {if LABEL_VSPACE then}
783    x=0
784    DO WHILE x < {LABEL_VSPACE}
785      ?
786      x=x+1
787    ENDDO
788 {endif}
789    ACTIVATE WINDOW w4sample
790    @ 0,3 SAY "{more_samples}";
791    GET choice PICTURE "!" VALID choice $ "NY"
792    READ
793    DEACTIVATE WINDOW w4sample
794    IF LASTKEY() = 27
795      EXIT
796    ENDIF
797 ENDDO
798 RELEASE WINDOW w4sample
799 RETURN
800 * EOP: SAMPLE
801 {if !count then pause(label_empty + any_key); endif}
802 {return 0;}
803 //-------------------------------
804 // End of main template procedure
805 // User defined function follows
806 //-------------------------------
807 {
808  define getstyle(mstyle);
809   var outstyle;
810   outstyle="";
811   if Bold        & mstyle then outstyle=outstyle+"B"; endif
812   if Italic      & mstyle then outstyle=outstyle+"I"; endif
813   if Underline   & mstyle then outstyle=outstyle+"U"; endif
814   if Superscript & mstyle then outstyle=outstyle+"R"; endif
815   if Subscript   & mstyle then outstyle=outstyle+"L"; endif
816   if User_Font   & mstyle then
817     if  1 & mstyle then outstyle=outstyle+"1"; endif
818     if  2 & mstyle then outstyle=outstyle+"2"; endif
819     if  4 & mstyle then outstyle=outstyle+"3"; endif
820     if  8 & mstyle then outstyle=outstyle+"4"; endif
821     if 16 & mstyle then outstyle=outstyle+"5"; endif
822   endif
823 return outstyle;
824 enddef;
```

(continued)

```
825 }
826 {define putfld(cursor);
827  var value,value2;
828  value=cursor.FLD_FIELDTYPE;}
829 {        if mrows+1 < LABEL_NUP then}
830 tmp4lbl[{mrows+1},{mcolumns}] \
831 {        else}
832 {case value of}
833 {Tabl_data:}
834 {  if cursor.FLD_VALUE_TYPE == 77 then}
835 MLINE({cursor.FLD_FIELDNAME},1)\
836 {  else}
837 {    cursor.FLD_FIELDNAME}\
838 {  endif}
839 {Calc_data:}
840 {  if cursor.FLD_FIELDNAME then}
841 {    cursor.FLD_FIELDNAME }\
842 {  else}
843 {    foreach FLD_EXPRESSION exp in cursor}
844 {       FLD_EXPRESSION}\
845 {    next}
846  ;
847 {    long_line=1;}
848 {  endif}
849 {Pred_data:}
850 {  value2=cursor.FLD_PREDEFINE;}
851 {  case value2 of}
852 {  0: // Date}
853 gd_date\
854 {  1: // Time}
855 gc_time\
856 {  2: // Recno}
857 RECNO()\
858 {  3: // Pageno}
859 _pageno\
860 {  endcase}
861 {endcase}
862  \
863 {        endif}
864 {return;
865 enddef;
866 }
867 {
868  define conditional_if_for_blank_line(cursor2, page_offset);
869  var current_column, current_row;
870 }
871 *-- Test for blank line
872 IF LEN(TRIM( \
873 {       current_column=cursor2.Col_Positn;
874         current_element=COUNTC(cursor2);
875         current_row=cursor2.Row_Positn;
876         do while !eoc(cursor2) && cursor2.Row_Positn == current_row}
```

(continued)

```
877  {          if cursor2.Col_Positn > current_column then}+ {endif}\
878  {          if cursor2.FLD_VALUE_TYPE == 78 then}
879  TRANSFORM(\
880  {             if mrows+1 < LABEL_NUP then}
881  tmp4lbl[{mrows+1},{mcolumns}],"\
882  {          else}
883  {             if cursor2.FLD_FIELDNAME then}
884  {cursor2.FLD_FIELDNAME},"\
885  {          else}
886  {             foreach FLD_EXPRESSION exp in cursor2}
887  {                FLD_EXPRESSION}\
888  {             next}
889  ;
890  {          endif}
891  {          endif}
892  {          if cursor2.FLD_PICFUN then}
893  {             if not cursor2.FLD_FIELDNAME then}
894  ,"\
895  {          endif}
896  @{cursor2.FLD_PICFUN} \
897  {          endif}
898  {cursor2.FLD_TEMPLATE}") \
899  {//
900          else
901            if cursor2.ELEMENT_TYPE == @Fld_element then
902              putfld(cursor2);
903            else
904              ++cursor2;
905              if !eoc(cursor2) then current_column=cursor2.Col_Positn; endif
906              --cursor2;
907            endif
908          endif
909          if cursor2.ELEMENT_TYPE == @Fld_element then
910            ++mcolumns;
911          endif
912          ++cursor2;
913        enddo
914        do while eoc(cursor2) || COUNTC(cursor2) > current_element;
915          --cursor2;
916          if cursor2.ELEMENT_TYPE == @Fld_element then
917            --mcolumns;
918          endif
919        enddo}
920  )) > 0
921  {LMARG(page_offset);}
922  ll_output=.T.
923  {  return;
924   enddef
925  }
926  {
927  define nul2zero(numbr);
928  //
```

(continued)

```
929 // if number is null convert to 0
930 //
931 if !numbr then numbr=0 endif;
932  return numbr;
933  enddef
934 }
935 {define calcflds();}
936 {foreach FLD_ELEMENT k}
937 {  if FLD_FIELDNAME && FLD_FIELDTYPE == Calc_data then}
938 {FLD_FIELDNAME}=\
939 {foreach FLD_EXPRESSION j in k}
940 {FLD_EXPRESSION}
941 {next}
942
943 {  endif}
944 {next k;}
945 {return;}
946 {enddef}
947 {
948  define seperate(string);
949  var x,y,length;
950  x=1;
951  length=LEN(string);
952  moreleft:
953  if x < length then
954    if x != 1 then}
955 + \
956 {  endif
957    if x+70 <= length then y=70; else y=length-x+1; endif}
958 "{SUBSTR(string,x,y)}";
959 {  x=x+70;
960    goto moreleft;
961  endif
962  return;
963  enddef
964 }
965 // EOP: LABEL.COD
966
```

Chapter 6

The Report Generator

The report template, REPORT.COD, is quite a bit more complex than LABEL.COD. This chapter discusses the major features of the report generator and shows how they relate to a generated report program. As usual, changes to the basic template file for a new program header and multiuser commands are included. REPORT.GEN takes about 34K of disk space. REPORT.COD is a 2,170-line template program that uses the selectors defined in REPORT.DEF, 240 lines long. These files process reports saved in the special-format FRM file. A complete listing of the latest version of REPORT.COD with line numbers is included in the appendix to this chapter. (If you want to substitute a different name for REPORT.GEN, see Appendix A of Chapter 4.)

The particular version of REPORT.COD we'll be using here has the date February 1, 1989, on the source code file. As was the case with LABEL.COD, if your REPORT.COD has an earlier date, you should contact Ashton-Tate to obtain the latest version or download it from the dBASE IV conference on the Ashton-Tate bulletin board.

What Does a Report Template Do?

REPORT.COD is a very complicated program. But consider what it has to work with. Items such a page headers and footers, report headers and footers, and the detail band are relatively easy to work with. The complexities arise from having to deal with groupings, group headers and footers, summary operations, the different printer drivers, user-defined fonts, functions, and so

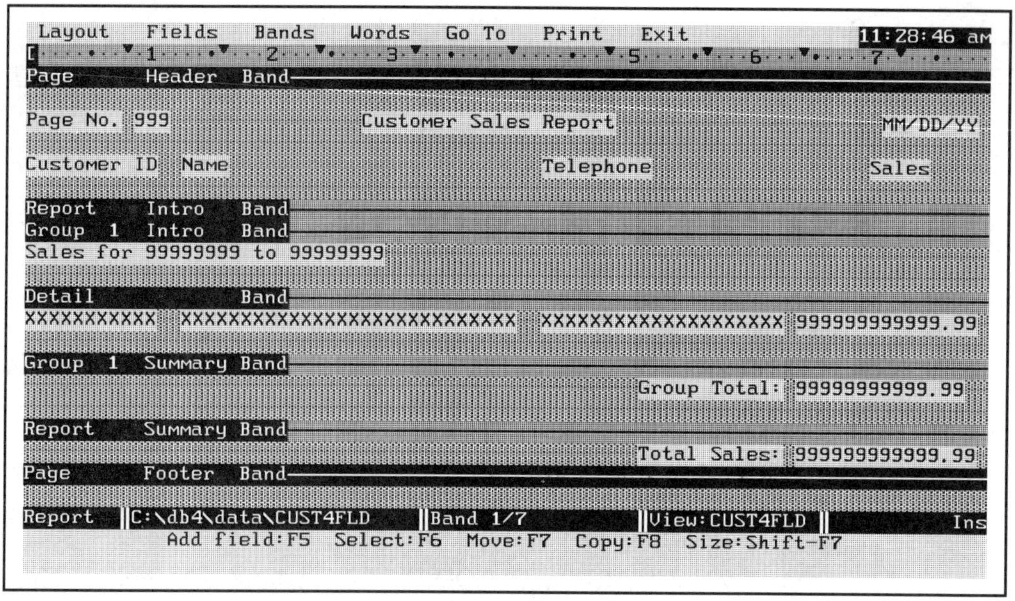

```
   Layout    Fields    Bands    Words    Go To    Print    Exit        11:28:46 am
[          1         2         3                  5          6          7
Page       Header    Band

Page No. 999                      Customer Sales Report                  MM/DD/YY

Customer ID  Name                             Telephone                  Sales

Report      Intro     Band
Group  1    Intro     Band
Sales for 99999999 to 99999999

Detail              Band
XXXXXXXXXX  XXXXXXXXXXXXXXXXXXXXXXXXX    XXXXXXXXXXXXXXXXXXXX  999999999999.99

Group  1    Summary Band
                                            Group Total:  99999999999.99

Report      Summary Band
                                            Total Sales:  999999999999.99
Page        Footer    Band

Report    C:\db4\data\CUST4FLD      Band 1/7          View:CUST4FLD          Ins
          Add field:F5  Select:F6  Move:F7  Copy:F8  Size:Shift-F7
```

Figure 6-1   The Report Generation Screen

on. These complexities increase the size of REPORT.COD, making its structure extremely difficult to understand.

Figure 6-1 shows a typical report layout with four fields and one group
band. The group header shows the range of values included in the group, and
the group footer shows subtotals.

A Second Digression on Blank Lines

As mentioned in the previous chapter, your version of REPORT.GEN may
have a problem processing blank lines, particularly in mailmerge format
which may output addresses containing blank lines. If printed addresses show
up with blank lines in your reports, try using the IIF() function instead. Figure
5-2 showed you how to include the IIF() in a label. The same expression will
work for a report.

The trick to omitting blank lines is to fool dBASE IV into thinking they're
all one line. Use the IIF() function to determine whether there's anything in
the field. If there is, print a carriage return–line feed and the contents of the
field. If the field is empty, print a null character. Here's the exact expression
using the NAME and ADDRESS1 fields:

```
TRIM(NAME)+IIF(LEN(TRIM(ADDRESS1))>0,CHR(13)+CHR(10)+
  TRIM(ADDRESS1),"")
```

To include ADDRESS2 as well, just add another IIF() to the end of this expression. CHR(13) and CHR(10) are the ASCII values for carriage return and line feed, respectively. You may be accustomed to using a semicolon to generate CR–LF combinations; that won't work in dBASE IV, at least not in version 1.0.

The Generated Report Code

Example 6-1 shows the generated label code for the labels in Figure 6-1. As usual, line numbers have been added to make discussion easier. We won't discuss this code right now, but will refer back to it later in this chapter. Put a paper clip at this page so you can easily find the generated code to see where it comes from in REPORT.COD.

Example 6-1   The Generated Report Program CUST4FLD.FRG

```
 1 * Program...........: C:\DB4\DATA\CUST4FLD.FRG
 2 * Date..............: 4-16-89
 3 * Versions..........: dBASE IV, Report 1
 4 *
 5 * Notes:
 6 * ------
 7 * Prior to running this procedure with the DO command
 8 * it is necessary use LOCATE because the CONTINUE
 9 * statement is in the main loop.
10 *
11 *-- Parameters
12 PARAMETERS gl_noeject, gl_plain, gl_summary, gc_heading, gc_extra
13 ** The first three parameters are of type Logical.
14 ** The fourth parameter is a string.  The fifth is extra.
15 PRIVATE _peject, _wrap
16
17 *-- Test for no records found
18 IF EOF() .OR. .NOT. FOUND()
19    RETURN
```

(continued)

```
20 ENDIF
21
22 *-- turn word wrap mode off
23 _wrap=.F.
24
25 IF _plength < 8
26    SET DEVICE TO SCREEN
27    DEFINE WINDOW gw_report FROM 7,17 TO 11,62 DOUBLE
28    ACTIVATE WINDOW gw_report
29    @ 0,1 SAY "Increase the page length for this report."
30    @ 2,1 SAY "Press any key ..."
31    x=INKEY(0)
32    DEACTIVATE WINDOW gw_report
33    RELEASE WINDOW gw_report
34    RETURN
35 ENDIF
36
37 _plineno=0          && set lines to zero
38 *-- NOEJECT parameter
39 IF gl_noeject
40    IF _peject="BEFORE"
41       _peject="NONE"
42    ENDIF
43    IF _peject="BOTH"
44       _peject="AFTER"
45    ENDIF
46 ENDIF
47
48 *-- Set-up environment
49 ON ESCAPE DO prnabort
50 IF SET("TALK")="ON"
51    SET TALK OFF
52    gc_talk="ON"
53 ELSE
54    gc_talk="OFF"
55 ENDIF
56 gc_space=SET("SPACE")
57 SET SPACE OFF
58 gc_time=TIME()      && system time for predefined field
59 gd_date=DATE()      && system date  "    "    "    "
```

(continued)

```
60 gl_fandl=.F.          && first and last page flag
61 gl_prntflg=.T.        && Continue printing flag
62 gl_widow=.T.          && flag for checking widow bands
63 gn_length=LEN(gc_heading)  && store length of the HEADING
64 gn_level=2            && current band being processed
65 gn_page=_pageno       && grab current page number
66 gn_pspace=_pspacing   && get current print spacing
67
68
69 *-- Initialize calculated variables.
70 LOWSALES=0
71 HIGHSALES=0
72
73 *-- Set up procedure for page break
74 gn_atline=_plength - (_pspacing + 1)
75 ON PAGE AT LINE gn_atline EJECT PAGE
76
77 *-- Print Report
78
79 PRINTJOB
80
81 *-- Initialize group break vars.
82 r_mvar4=INT(SALES/10000)
83
84 *-- Initialize summary variables.
85 r_msum1=0
86 r_msum2=0
87
88 *-- Assign initial values to calculated variables.
89 LOWSALES=IIF(SALES>0,10000*(INT(SALES/10000)),10*(INT(SALES/10)))
90 HIGHSALES=10000*(INT(SALES/10000)+1)
91
92 IF gl_plain
93    ON PAGE AT LINE gn_atline DO Pgplain
94 ELSE
95    ON PAGE AT LINE gn_atline DO Pgfoot
96 ENDIF
97
98 DO Pghead
99
```

(continued)

```
100 gl_fandl=.T.          && first physical page started
101
102 DO Grphead
103
104 *-- File Loop
105 DO WHILE FOUND() .AND. .NOT. EOF() .AND. gl_prntflg
106    DO CASE
107    CASE .NOT. (INT(SALES/10000) = r_mvar4)
108       gn_level=4
109    OTHERWISE
110       gn_level=0
111    ENDCASE
112    *-- test whether an expression didn't match
113    IF gn_level <> 0
114       DO Grpfoot WITH 100-gn_level
115       DO Grpinit
116    ENDIF
117    *-- Repeat group intros
118    IF gn_level <> 0
119       DO Grphead
120    ENDIF
121    DO Upd_Vars
122    *-- Detail lines
123    IF .NOT. gl_summary
124       DO __Detail
125    ENDIF
126    CONTINUE
127 ENDDO
128
129 IF gl_prntflg
130    gn_level=3
131    DO Grpfoot WITH 97
132    DO Rsumm
133    IF _plineno <= gn_atline
134       EJECT PAGE
135    ENDIF
136 ELSE
137    gn_level=3
138    DO Rsumm
139    DO Reset
```

(continued)

```
140    RETURN
141 ENDIF
142
143 ON PAGE
144
145 ENDPRINTJOB
146
147 DO Reset
148 RETURN
149 * EOP: C:\DB4\DATA\CUST4FLD.FRG
150
151 *-- Determine height of group bands and detail band for widow
        checking
152 FUNCTION Gheight
153 PARAMETER Group_Band
154 retval=0              && return value
155 IF Group_Band <= 4
156    retval = retval + 2 * gn_pspace
157 ENDIF
158 *-- add height of detail band
159 retval = retval + 2 * gn_pspace
160 RETURN retval
161 * EOP: Gheight
162
163 *-- Update summary fields and/or calculated fields in the detail
        band.
164 PROCEDURE Upd_Vars
165 *-- Sum
166 r_msum1=r_msum1+SALES
167 *-- Sum
168 r_msum2=r_msum2+SALES
169 RETURN
170 * EOP: Upd_Vars
171
172 *-- Set flag to get out of DO WHILE loop when escape is pressed.
173 PROCEDURE prnabort
174 gl_prntflg=.F.
175 RETURN
176 * EOP: prnabort
177
```

(continued)

```
178 *-- Reset group break variables.  Reinit summary
179 *-- fields with reset set to a particular group band.
180 PROCEDURE Grpinit
181 IF gn_level <= 4
182    r_msum1=0
183 ENDIF
184 IF gn_level <= 4
185    r_mvar4=INT(SALES/10000)
186 ENDIF
187 RETURN
188 * EOP: Grpinit
189
190 *-- Process Group Intro bands during group breaks
191 PROCEDURE Grphead
192 IF EOF()
193    RETURN
194 ENDIF
195 PRIVATE _pspacing
196 _pspacing=gn_pspace
197 gl_widow=.T.        && enable widow checking
198 IF gn_level <= 4
199    DO Head4
200 ENDIF
201 gn_level=0
202 RETURN
203 * EOP: Grphead.PRG
204
205 *-- Process Group Summary bands during group breaks
206 PROCEDURE Grpfoot
207 PARAMETER ln_level
208 IF ln_level >= 96
209    DO Foot96
210 ENDIF
211 RETURN
212 * EOP: Grpfoot.PRG
213
214 PROCEDURE Pghead
215 ?
216 ?? IIF(gl_plain,'' , "Page No." ) AT 0,
```

(continued)

```
217 ?? IIF(gl_plain,'',_pageno) PICTURE "999" AT 9,
218 ?? "Customer Sales Report" AT 28,
219 ?? IIF(gl_plain,'',gd_date) AT 71
220 ?
221 ?
222 *-- Print HEADING parameter ie. REPORT FORM <name> HEADING <expC>
223 IF .NOT. gl_plain .AND. gn_length > 0
224    ?? gc_heading FUNCTION "I;V"+LTRIM(STR(_rmargin-_lmargin))
225    ?
226 ENDIF
227 ?? "Customer ID" AT 0,
228 ?? "Name" AT 13,
229 ?? "Telephone" AT 43,
230 ?? "Sales" AT 70
231 ?
232 ?
233 RETURN
234 * EOP: Pghead
235
236
237 PROCEDURE Head4
238 IF gn_level=1
239    RETURN
240 ENDIF
241 LOWSALES=IIF(SALES>0,10000*(INT(SALES/10000)),10*(INT(SALES/10)))
242 HIGHSALES=10000*(INT(SALES/10000)+1)
243 IF 2 * gn_pspace < _plength
244    IF (gl_widow .AND. _plineno+Gheight(4) > gn_atline + 1) ;
245    .OR. (gl_widow .AND. _plineno+2 * gn_pspace > gn_atline)
246       EJECT PAGE
247    ENDIF
248 ENDIF
249 ?? "Sales for " AT 0,
250 ?? LOWSALES FUNCTION "$T" PICTURE "99999999" ,
251 ?? " to " ,
252 ?? HIGHSALES FUNCTION "$T" PICTURE "99999999"
253 ?
254 ?
255 RETURN
```

(continued)

```
256
257 PROCEDURE __Detail
258 IF 2 * gn_pspace < _plength
259    IF gl_widow .AND. _plineno+2 * gn_pspace > gn_atline + 1
260       EJECT PAGE
261    ENDIF
262 ENDIF
263 ?? CUSTCODE FUNCTION "T" AT 0,
264 ?? NAME FUNCTION "T" AT 13,
265 ?? TELEPHONE FUNCTION "T" AT 43,
266 ?? SALES FUNCTION "$T" PICTURE "999999999999.99" AT 64
267 ?
268 ?
269 RETURN
270 * EOP: __Detail
271
272 PROCEDURE Foot96
273 ?? "Group Total:" AT 51,
274 ?? r_msum1 FUNCTION "$T" PICTURE "99999999999.99" AT 64
275 ?
276 ?
277 RETURN
278
279 PROCEDURE Rsumm
280 ?? "Total Sales:" AT 51,
281 ?? r_msum2 FUNCTION "$T" PICTURE "999999999999.99" AT 64
282 gl_fandl=.F.        && last page finished
283 ?
284 RETURN
285 * EOP: Rsumm
286
287 PROCEDURE Pgfoot
288 PRIVATE _box, _pspacing
289 gl_widow=.F.        && disable widow checking
290 _pspacing=1
291 ?
292 IF .NOT. gl_plain
293 ENDIF
294 EJECT PAGE
```

(continued)

```
295 *-- is the page number greater than the ending page
296 IF _pageno > _pepage
297    GOTO BOTTOM
298    SKIP
299    gn_level=0
300 ENDIF
301 IF .NOT. gl_plain .AND. gl_fandl
302    _pspacing=gn_pspace
303    DO Pghead
304 ENDIF
305 IF gn_level = 0 .AND. gl_fandl
306    gn_level=1
307    DO Grphead
308 ENDIF
309 gl_widow=.T.           && enable widow checking
310 RETURN
311 * EOP: Pgfoot
312
313 *-- Process page break when PLAIN option is used.
314 PROCEDURE Pgplain
315 PRIVATE _box
316 EJECT PAGE
317 IF gn_level = 0 .AND. gl_fandl
318    gn_level=1
319    DO Grphead
320 ENDIF
321 RETURN
322 * EOP: Pgplain
323
324 *-- Reset dBASE environment prior to calling report
325 PROCEDURE Reset
326 SET SPACE &gc_space.
327 SET TALK &gc_talk.
328 ON ESCAPE
329 ON PAGE
330 RETURN
331 * EOP: Reset
332
333
```

Example 6-2 shows the finished report output.

Example 6-2   Report CUST4FLD

```
Page No.   1                Customer Sales Report              04/16/89
Customer ID   Name                           Telephone              Sales
Sales for $0000 to $10000
10003         Accounting Technology Ltd.     513-555-6666        $1234.56
                                             Group Total: $1234.56
Sales for $10000 to $20000
10001         Pacific Sys. Des. Workshop     415/593-6431       $11231.78
                                             Group Total: $11231.78
Sales for $980000 to $990000
10002         SBT                            415/331-9900       $987654.32
                                             Group Total:   $987654.32
                                             Total Sales: $1000120.66
```

The Report Template Code

With that as background, let's look at the code for REPORT.COD. Because the program is so long, we'll stick to the salient features and bypass discussion of many details.

Initialization

The report template file begins with the usual comments that make up the program header. Next, REPORT.DEF and BUILTIN.DEF selectors are read in.

```
12   include "report.def";
13   include "builtin.def";
```

String constants are defined for different basic error messages. Three of these errors will cause program generation to abort. The fourth, whose message is demo_string, is intended to be used with evaluation copies of the report generator and dBASE IV.

```
15 // Enum string constants for international translation
16 //
17  enum wrong_class =
       "Can't use REPORT.GEN on non-report objects.  ",
18     report_empty = "Report design was empty.  ",
19     demo_string  =
           "dBASE IV SAMPLE REPORT - FOR EVALUATION PURPOSES ONLY",
20     increase_page = "Increase the page length for this report.",
21     demo_version = 0;
```

A set of variables is defined, and some of them are initialized (lines 30–81). We will refer to these variables in the discussion, but there are too many of them to list them all here. Similarly, lines 82–96 check the file name to be sure it is valid, aborting generation if it is not. Lines 97–111 initialize a number of variables, most of them to 0. (If you want to shorten REPORT.COD slightly and make generation a little more efficient, you might initialize all of these variables with a single assignment statement, viz., {bandrow=bsrv=combine=...=0;}. However, note that a single variable, first_combine, is initialized to 1, not to 0. Do not include it in any multiple-assignment statement you may create.

The Report File Header

Once again, the template generates a file header that is pretty inadequate:

```
113 * Program............: {rptname}.FRG
114 * Date...............: {LTRIM(SUBSTR(DATE(),1,8))}
115 * Versions...........: dBASE IV, Report {FRAME_VER}
116 *
117 * Notes:
118 * ------
119 * Prior to running this procedure with the DO command
120 * it is necessary use LOCATE because the CONTINUE
121 * statement is in the main loop.
122 *
123 *-- Parameters
124 PARAMETERS gl_noeject, gl_plain, gl_summary, gc_heading,;
        gc_extra
125 ** The first three parameters are of type Logical.
```

```
126 ** The fourth parameter is a string.  The fifth is extra.
127 PRIVATE _peject\
```

I recommend changing lines 113–115 to this:

```
//
{print(replicate("*",65)+crlf);}
* Name.........: {rptname}.FRG
* Author.......: Tony Lima
* Date.........: {LTRIM(SUBSTR(DATE(),1,8))}
* dBASE Ver....: dBASE IV, Report {FRAME_VER}
* Notice.......: Copyright, 1989, Tony Lima
* Description..:
* Notes........:
{print(replicate("*",65)+crlf);}
//
```

However, if you're going to do this, note that the variable crlf is not defined. Therefore, you have two choices: (1) replace the variable crlf in the above block of code with CHR(10);, or (2) add crlf to the variables list (lines 30–81) and initialize it somewhere in lines 97–111 with the expression crlf=CHR(10); . In the version of REPORT.COD we're using, CHR(10) is not called anywhere else, so you can save one variable by using the CHR() function instead. For clarity, I prefer using the variable.

Check for dBASE III Plus FRM File

Next, the template checks to see whether this is a dBASE III Plus FRM file. If it is, it adds the variables _plength and _ploffset to the PRIVATE command being output to the file.

```
128 {if dBASE_III_PLUS == 2 then}
129 , _plength, _ploffset\
130 {endif}
131 , _wrap
132
```

More Initialization Code

Lines 132–140 output the code that checks to be sure the database or query is not empty and turns word wrap off. Similarly, lines 141–156 initialize a number of additional variables to 0. Again, note that these assignment statements can be combined into a single statement to reduce program length and slightly improve generation performance.

Adding Multiuser Code

This is the appropriate place to add the same sort of multiuser code we used in the label template. After line 156, add this code to REPORT.COD:

```
{VAR tlresp;
ASKUSER("Do you want to include multiuser commands",
        "Y",1);
if tlresp == "Y" then}

* Code to process network operations

IF NETWORK()
DEFINE WINDOW Lockwin FROM 12,10 TO 21,70 DOUBLE
lc_lock=SET("LOCK")
IF lc_lock="ON"
  SET REPROCESS TO 10
  ll_lock=FLOCK()
  IF .NOT. ll_lock
    lc_time=LKSYS(0)
    ld_date=LKSYS(1)
    lc_name=LKSYS(2)
    ACTIVATE WINDOW Lockwin
    @ 01,02 SAY "Unable to lock file.  Already in use by"
    @ 02,02 SAY lc_name
    @ 03,02 SAY "Locked on "+DTOC(ld_date)+" at "+lc_time
    WAIT "  Hit the space bar to continue..."
    DEACTIVATE WINDOW Lockwin
    RETURN
  ENDIF && .NOT. ll_lock
```

```
    ELSE
        ACTIVATE WINDOW Lockwin
        @ 01,02 SAY "WARNING!"
        @ 02,02 SAY "Database not locked, data may change"
        @ 03,02 SAY "while printing is in process."
        @ 04,02 SAY "SET LOCK ON to correct this problem."
        WAIT "  Hit the space bar to continue or press Esc to exit..."
        DEACTIVATE WINDOW Lockwin
    ENDIF && lc_lock="ON"
    RELEASE WINDOW Lockwin
    ENDIF && NETWORK()
    {endif}
```

Note that LKSYS(0) and LKSYS(1) will not return the date or time in dBASE IV version 1.0.

Scan FRM File to Determine Band Types

The command "FOREACH BAND_ELEMENT k" on line 157 scans all report bands. It checks each for word wrap, checks whether it is a page-break band, and tracks the different band types by setting different variables to 1 if the band type is present. Read this code to see which variables are being set. However, there are only a couple of blocks worth discussing in depth.

First, the Group_Intro band type has to consider the possibility that this might be a dBASE III Plus FRM file:

```
174    Group_Intro:
175       if dBASE_III_PLUS == 2 then
176          if GROUP == 4 then intro_band_one_height = BAND_HEIGHT;
                endif
177          if GROUP == 5 then intro_band_two_height = BAND_HEIGHT;
                endif
178       endif
179 //
```

Since dBASE III Plus was limited to two levels of grouping, the selector GROUP stores this information (4 for one level, 5 for two). The Band_height selector stores the number of lines in the band. Note that for conversion purposes the default band-height is used. You can modify this if you want your dBASE III Plus reports converted with a different number of lines in the group introduction band.

Next, the detail band is analyzed. The selector Band_openflg is set to 1 if the band contains any actual data lines, and 0 otherwise. The variable bandlen50 is the height of the detail band. Similarly, the Band_spacing selector is 1, 2, 3, or 0 to select the printer default.

```
180    Detail:
181      if BAND_OPENFLG then bandlen50=BAND_HEIGHT; endif
182      if BAND_SPACING then
183        bandspacing=BAND_SPACING;
184      endif
185 //
```

If the demo version of the report generator is being run, the variable bandlen98 is incremented by 1, changing it to a logical true. Next, the program checks to see if there are any group summaries (number_of_open_group_summarys), any report summaries (is_rsumm_open), or the demo version is running. If so, field elements are scanned with the cursor variable k. The selector GROUP is tested. Then the selector Fld_fieldtype is examined. If it's Tabl_data (a database field), the variable d is set to 1. If it's a calculated field, the GROUP selector is checked, the field cannot be hidden, it must have a name, and it must be a character type field (Fld_value_type == 67). In that case, d is set to 1. If it's a predefined field, GROUP must be less than 97 and it must be the record number (Fld_predefine == 2). Again, d is set to 1. The purpose of the variable d is to increment the number_of_group_footer_fields variable in case any of these conditions are met (lines 210–212).

```
199 if demo_version then ++bandlen98; endif
200
201 if number_of_open_group_summarys || is_rsumm_open ||
        bandlen98 then
202   foreach FLD_ELEMENT k
203     if GROUP > 50 then
204       d=0;
205       case FLD_FIELDTYPE of
206       Tabl_data: d=1;
207       Calc_data: if GROUP < 97 && !FLD_HIDDEN &&
              FLD_FIELDNAME && FLD_VALUE_TYPE == 67
              then d=1; endif
```

```
208        Pred_data: if GROUP < 97 && FLD_PREDEFINE == 2 then
              d=1; endif
209        endcase
210        if d then
211           ++number_of_group_footer_fields;
212        endif
213     endif
214   next k;
215  endif
216 }
```

Check Page Length and Page Eject

Lines 217–227 output the code to check the page length (_plength) against the sum of the variables bandlen2 and bandlen98 with two lines added for margins. (If you don't want one-line top and bottom margins, get rid of the number 2 on line 217; but I don't recommend this, because reports are difficult enough to work with even with an extra line at the top and bottom.)

Lines 229–240 output certain values for the print-system memory variables to the file, depending on the value of the selectors. It's worth including the code here without comment because it uses a number of report-specific selectors. Note that lines 231–241 are output only if this is a dBASE III Plus FRM file. In that case, the numeric value of the Print_new_page selector must be checked. A similar scheme is used in lines 243–251 for the "plain" option in the dBASE III Plus report generator.

```
229 _plineno=0            && set lines to zero
230 {if dBASE_III_PLUS == 2 then}
231 *-- dBASE III PLUS report setup
232 _peject=\
233 {case PRINT_NEW_PAGE of}
234 {0:}"AFTER"
235 {1:}"BEFORE"
236 {2:}"BOTH"
237 {3:}"NONE"
238 {endcase}
239 _plength={PRINT_PAGE_LENGTH}
240 _ploffset={nul2zero(PRINT_LEFT_OFFSET)}
241
242 {endif}
```

However, for dBASE IV, the gl_noeject variable is set coming into the FRG file using the SET() function. Lines 252–260 output the code to handle this. Lines 262–280 set up the environment and initialize variables.

Group Footers

Line 283 checks the variable number_of_group_footer_fields. If it's greater than 0, the variables current_group_footer_field and x are set to 1. The comment on line 286 is output, and the code to initialize the memory variables r_foot<x> is created.

```
282 {x=0;
283  if number_of_group_footer_fields then
284    current_group_footer_field=1;
285    x=1;}
286 *-- Initialize group footer field variables
287 {  do while x <= number_of_group_footer_fields}
288 r_foot{x}=.F.
289 {    ++x;
290    enddo
291  endif
292 }
```

When to Reset Summary Variables

Lines 294–320 scan the field elements with a cursor k. If the field type is summary and the summary is to be reset every page (FLD_RESET == 1), then increment the appropriately named variable. If the field is to have repeated values suppressed, increment that variable.

```
294 {x=0;}
295 {foreach FLD_ELEMENT k}
296 //
297 // Reset Summary (on page) and Suppress repeated values
298 //
299 {if FLD_FIELDTYPE == Summ_data && FLD_RESET == 1 then
300    ++number_of_reset_on_page
301  endif}
302 {if FLD_SUPPRESS then ++number_of_fld_suppress endif}
```

The next block of code cries out for the same change you may have made to LABEL.COD. Change line 312 to read

```
312 {68: // Date   }{"{  /  /  }"}
303 //
304 // only if there is a fieldname assigned to the calculated
        field
305 //
306 {if FLD_FIELDTYPE == Calc_data && FLD_FIELDNAME then}
307 {  if !x then}
308 *-- Initialize calculated variables.
309 {  endif}
310 {FLD_FIELDNAME}=\
311 {case FLD_VALUE_TYPE of}
312 {68: // Date   }CTOD("  /  /  ")
313 {70: // Float  }FLOAT(0)
314 {76: // Logical}.F.
315 {78: // Numeric}0
316 {otherwise:}""
317 {endcase}
318 {   ++x;}
319 {endif}
320 {next k;}
```

Calculating Page Length

The next block of code calculates the page length, taking into account the length of various page and group footers. Note that the variable being computed is the one that is used to control the ON PAGE AT <line number> switch command, output on line 354. There isn't anything particularly complicated about this code, so we'll go on to look at the report output.

Report Body

The report is actually printed beginning with the PRINTJOB command on line 358. The first thing to be done is to determine the number of group bands. This is done on lines 365–397. Band element selectors are scanned with the cursor variable *k*. If the band type is a group introduction, the program must initialize the group break variables as noted by the comment output on line 372.

```
365  x=1;  // to obtain number of group bands
366  number_of_open_group_intros=0;
367
368  foreach BAND_ELEMENT k
369 //
370    if BAND_BANDTYPE == Group_Intro then
371      if x == 1 then}
372 *-- Initialize group break vars.
373 {    endif
374      if BAND_OPENFLG then ++number_of_open_group_intros; endif}
```

Next the band group type is checked. A value of 1 indicates the grouping is done on a field, in which case the memory variable that tracks the groups by field is output. Line 380 checks for the > character in the group field expression (selector Band_gfield). If it's there, the alias is removed in line 381 and output. If not, the field name is simply output (line 384).

```
375 //
376 {case BAND_GROUPTYPE of}
377 {1: // by field}
378 {// initialize Group by field variable}
379 r_mvar{GROUP}=\
380 {      if AT(">",BAND_GFIELD) then  // Check for ALIAS}
381 {SUBSTR(BAND_GFIELD,AT(">",BAND_GFIELD)+1)}
382
383 {    else}
384 {BAND_GFIELD}
385
386 {    endif}
```

If the band group type is 3, the group is on record count and the appropriate code to initialize the correct memory variable is output. If it's not 1 or 3, the group is on an expression. The selector Band_expression is scanned for the current value of the cursor *k*, and the expression is output as entered with no further error checking.

```
387 //
388 {3: // by record count}
389 {// initialize Group by record variable}
390 r_mvar{GROUP}=1
391 //
392 {otherwise: // by expression}
393 {// initialize Group by expression variable}
394 r_mvar{GROUP}=\
395 {foreach BAND_EXPRESSION fcursor in k}
396 {BAND_EXPRESSION}
397 {next}
```

The FOREACH clause on line 368 is closed on line 404. Note the line immediately before that:

```
403     if BAND_BANDTYPE == Detail then exit endif
404  next k;}
```

If the template has reached the detail band, exit from the FOREACH loop. Group footers and so on will be handled later.

Lines 406–408 simply output a blank line if there are any group bands in the report.

Initialize Summary Variables

Next, the code to initialize the summary variables is output starting on line 409. Lines 411–412 check to see whether the field is a summary field. If it is, and if *x* is 0, it's the first summary field found and the comment on line 413 is output.

```
409 {x=0;}
410 {foreach FLD_ELEMENT k}
411 {  if FLD_FIELDTYPE == Summ_data then}
412 {    if !x then}
413 *-- Initialize summary variables.
414 {    endif}
415 {     ++x;}
416 //
```

Next, a repetitive block of code is used to assign names to summary variables if the user hasn't already assigned them. The summary variable names are stored in the template variable priv_vars. The selector Fld_operation (line 425) will be greater than 4 only for standard deviation or variance operations. (Other values are shown on line 145 of REPORT.DEF.) If one of the statistical measures is selected, a series of summary variables is initialized to 0. Note how the counter variable xxsum can be incremented with the ++ operator at the same time as it is defining a variable name.

For those who are curious, the code generated by this block is shown on lines 85–86 of CUST4FLD.FRG, where there are two subtotal variables. The actual code was produced by lines 440–447 of REPORT.COD.

```
417 // standard deviation or variance?
418 //
419 {    if !FLD_FIELDNAME then}
420 {      ++xsum;}
421 {      priv_vars="r_msum"+STR(xsum);}
422 {    else}
423 {      priv_vars=FLD_FIELDNAME;}
424 {    endif}
425 {    if FLD_OPERATION > 4 then}
426 STORE 0 TO r_sum{++xxsum},r_sum{++xxsum},\
427 r_sum{++xxsum},r_sum{++xxsum},{priv_vars}
428 // DECLARE {priv_vars}[5]
429 // STORE 0 TO {priv_vars}[3]
430 // STORE 0 TO {priv_vars}[1],{priv_vars}[2],
        {priv_vars}[4],{priv_vars}[5]
431 {    else}
432 {      case FLD_OPERATION of}
433 {        0: // Average}
434 STORE 0 TO r_sum{++xxsum},r_sum{++xxsum},{priv_vars}
435 // DECLARE {priv_vars}[3]
436 // STORE 0 TO {priv_vars}[1]
437 // STORE 0 TO {priv_vars}[2],{priv_vars}[3]
438 {        1: // Count}
439 {priv_vars}=0
440 {      otherwise: // Max, Min or Sum}
441 {priv_vars}=\
442 {        if FLD_OPERATION == 3 then // Minimum}
443 {FLD_SUMFIELD}
```

```
444
445 {       else}
446 0
447 {         endif}
448 {        endcase}
449 {    endif}
450 {  endif}
451 {next k;}
```

Similar code is used to initialize the variables that suppress repeated values (lines 458–485), calculated variables (491–506), and maximum and minimum summary variables (511–530).

Report Introduction

The variable isrepo determines whether there is a report introduction or group introduction. If there is and it is open (is_rintro_open > 0), the selector Frame_pageheadings is checked. It will have the value 1 if the page heading is to be included in the report introduction, and 0 otherwise. If these three conditions are true, the command DO Rintro is output. The remainder of the code output by this block is pretty straightforward. However, note the role of the memory variable gn_atline in the ON PAGE command. This was defined starting on line 323. You may wish to use more complicated code than on line 547 if you have complex page footers. If you are going to have to regenerate this report a number of times, change the template and let it do the hard work.

```
535 {if isrepo && is_rintro_open then}
536 {  if not FRAME_PAGEHEADINGS then}
537 DO Rintro
538
539 *-- reset page number in case report intro spanned two pages
540 _pageno=gn_page
541
542 {  endif}
543 {endif}
544 IF gl_plain
545    ON PAGE AT LINE gn_atline DO Pgplain
546 ELSE
547    ON PAGE AT LINE gn_atline DO Pgfoot
```

```
548 ENDIF
549
```

Next, the template checks to see whether the page header is open; or the report introduction is open and the page heading is included in it; or the number of open group introductions is greater than 0. If any of these are true, the DO Pghead command is output.

```
550 {if is_page_header_open || (is_rintro_open &&
        FRAME_PAGEHEADINGS)
551 || number_of_open_group_intros then}
552 DO Pghead
553
554 {endif}
```

The same sort of procedure is used for report introduction (Rintro) and group headers (Grphead) (lines 555–569).

Next, the loop for the database is output on line 571.

Handling Group Bands

If there are multiple group bands, a DO CASE is output to handle them. The variable maxgrp contains the maximum number of groups for this report. It must be more than 3, and there must be an open group introduction or an open group summary before the DO CASE will be output. The structure of this dBASE DO CASE statement will be familiar, as it is similar to the template structure used earlier for the same purpose.

```
573 // If there are group bands
574 // set up the CASE structure to test
575 // the group band values
576 //
577 {if maxgrp > 3 &&
578   (number_of_open_group_intros ||
        number_of_open_group_summarys) then}
579     DO CASE
580 {   foreach BAND_ELEMENT k}
581 {     if BAND_BANDTYPE == Group_Intro then}
582 //
583 // Group by field
```

```
584 //
585 {       if BAND_GFIELD then}
586   CASE .NOT. (\
587 {         if AT(">",BAND_GFIELD) then  // Check for ALIAS}
588 {SUBSTR(BAND_GFIELD,AT(">",BAND_GFIELD)+1)}
589 {         else}
590 {BAND_GFIELD}
591 {         endif}
592  = r_mvar{GROUP})
593 {       endif}
594 //
595 // Group by expression
596 //
597 {       if BAND_EXPRESSION then}
598   CASE .NOT. (\
599 {foreach BAND_EXPRESSION fcursor in k}
600 {BAND_EXPRESSION}
601 {next}
602  = r_mvar{GROUP})
603 {       endif}
604 //
605 // Group by record count
606 //
607 {       if BAND_GROUP_REC then}
608   CASE r_mvar{GROUP} > {BAND_GROUP_REC}
609 {       endif}
610      gn_level={GROUP}
611 {    endif}
612 {  next k;}
613    OTHERWISE
614      gn_level=0
615    ENDCASE
616    *-- test whether an expression didn't match
617    IF gn_level <> 0
618 {  if number_of_open_group_summarys then}
619      DO Grpfoot WITH 100-gn_level
620 {  endif}
621      DO Grpinit
622    ENDIF
623 {  if number_of_open_group_intros then}
624    *-- Repeat group intros
```

```
625    IF gn_level <> 0
626        DO Grphead
627    ENDIF
628 {  endif}
629 {endif}
630 {LMARG(4);}
631 DO Upd_Vars
```

Detail Lines

The detail lines are the easiest of all. Lines 632–637 manage them entirely by checking to be sure the detail band has at least one line (bandlen50 > 0), then outputting code to check for a summary report. If the report is not a summary, the procedure __DETAIL is called to print a detail line.

Group, Page, and Report Footers

Lines 638–713 handle these three items. Since the code is so similar to that used for the headers, we won't discuss it here, leaving it to the interested reader to pursue. Lines 718–724 close the PRINTJOB, reset the environment, and end the main program.

```
718 ON PAGE
719
720 ENDPRINTJOB
721
722 DO Reset
723 RETURN
724 * EOP: {rptname}.FRG
```

Procedures and Functions

The remainder of REPORT.COD generates procedures and functions called by the main program. Note how the section of the template that generates the main program must interact with the functions and procedures. When designing a new template, it's important to see how the functional parts of the generated program interact.

We won't explore all the functions and procedures, but will instead sample them to see the general philosophy used.

Group Band Height

Lines 725–779 generate the code to calculate the group band height. The band element selectors are scanned with the cursor *k*. If it's "greater than" a group introduction band, exit from the loop without adding any code. Line 161 of REPORT.DEF tells us that this means it is a detail element, a group summary, a report summary, or a page footer. If it's not any of those and is a group introduction and is the first introduction (!x), output a comment followed by the FUNCTION and PARAMETER commands, followed by initializing the memory variable retval to 0.

```
725 {x=0;
726  foreach BAND_ELEMENT k
727    if BAND_BANDTYPE > Group_Intro then exit endif
728    if BAND_BANDTYPE == Group_Intro then
729      if !x then}
730
731 *-- Determine height of group bands and detail band for widow
        checking
732 FUNCTION Gheight
733 PARAMETER Group_Band
734 retval=0              && return value
735 {    endif}
```

The next block of code worries about both the number of lines in the group band and the line spacing. If you read this carefully, you'll see something similar to lines 155–161 of CUST4FLD.FRG will be generated.

```
736 IF Group_Band <= {GROUP}
737    retval = retval +\
738 {    if BAND_HEIGHT > 1 then}
739  {BAND_HEIGHT}\
740 {    endif}
741 {    if !BAND_SPACING && !bandspacing then}
742 {if BAND_HEIGHT > 1 then} *{endif} gn_pspace
743 {    else
744        if !BAND_SPACING && bandspacing > 1 then}
```

```
745 {if BAND_HEIGHT > 1 then} *{endif} {bandspacing}
746 {      else
747              if BAND_SPACING > 1 then}
748 {if BAND_HEIGHT > 1 then} *{endif} {BAND_SPACING}
749 {      else}
750 {             if BAND_HEIGHT < 2 then}
751  {BAND_HEIGHT}\
752 {            endif}
753
754 {        endif
755        endif
756     endif}
757 ENDIF
758 {     ++x;
759    endif
760  next k;
761  if x then
762    if bandlen50 then}
763 *-- add height of detail band
764 retval = retval + \
765 {    if !bandspacing then}
766 {if bandlen50 > 1 then}{bandlen50} * {endif}gn_pspace
767 {    else}
768 {       if bandspacing > 1 then}
769 {bandspacing*bandlen50}
770
771 {       else}
772 {bandlen50}
773
774 {       endif
775        endif
776    endif}
777 RETURN retval
778 * EOP: Gheight
779 {endif}
```

Let's take a look at the generated code for reference.

```
151 *-- Determine height of group bands and detail band for widow
        checking
152 FUNCTION Gheight
```

```
153 PARAMETER Group_Band
154 retval=0                 && return value
155 IF Group_Band <= 4
156     retval = retval + 2 * gn_pspace
157 ENDIF
158 *-- add height of detail band
159 retval = retval + 2 * gn_pspace
160 RETURN retval
161 * EOP: Gheight
```

Update Variables

The procedure Upd_Vars is generated next. This updates summary variables. There is nothing particularly new here with one exception: lines 837–865 calculate the variance and standard deviation. You may be tempted to change these to use the STD() and VAR() function built in to dBASE IV. Don't do it. The program has to calculate the variable one record at a time. This is an incremental calculation that adds the value of summary field from the next record in the appropriate way.

Abort Printing

The Prnabort procedure is the same in all generated programs. It simply sets the print flag memory variable gl_prntflg to false and returns. Exiting the main DO WHILE loop in the FRG file will execute the ENDPRINTJOB, reset all SET commands, and handle any exit housekeeping.

Reset Group Break Variables

Lines 879–976 handle this procedure. First, the template checks for open group introduction bands or open group summary bands (line 879). If there are none of these, the entire procedure is omitted from the output file. If there are some open bands, the PROCEDURE command is output with appropriate comments. Field elements are scanned with the cursor *k*. The code to generate the procedure is very familiar. The only thing new is the selector Fld_reset, which is 0 for never, 1 for each page, and 2 for each group.

Reset On Page

The procedure Pageinit (lines 979–1042) resets summary variables at the beginning of each page and suppresses repeated values. As usual, line 979 uses the CTOD() function rather than {"{ / / }"}. Make this change.

Once again, there is nothing especially new about the template code for this procedure.

Group Headers, Footers, and Other Things

The procedure Grphead (lines 1043–1078) prints group headers. The only two things worth noting about this are on line 1057, where the memory variable gl_widow is set to true to enable widow checking, and on line 1059, where the FRM file is checked to see whether it is a dBASE III Plus file. If it is a dBASE III Plus file, the program must generate blank lines to compensate for those automatically produced by dBASE IV.

Grpfoot (lines 1079–1098) generates the code to print the group footer. Again, there is nothing particularly new about this template code.

However, note the FOREACH statement on line 1064. It is closed on line 1097. This loop processes the last part of the Grphead procedure and all of Grpfoot. This illustrates how the template need not be logically connected to the output code.

```
1064 {foreach BAND_ELEMENT k}
1065 {  case BAND_BANDTYPE of}
1066 {  Group_Intro:}
1067 {    if BAND_OPENFLG then}
1068 IF gn_level <= {GROUP}
1069    DO Head{GROUP}
1070 ENDIF
1071 {    endif}
1072 {  Detail:}
1073 {    if number_of_open_group_intros then}
1074 gn_level=0
1075 RETURN
1076 * EOP: Grphead.PRG
1077
1078 {    endif}
```

Serial Procedure Generation

Beginning on line 1220, procedures are generated serially. This process ends 1,015 lines later on line 2035. Lines 1223 and 1227 output the word PROCE-DURE. After that, the template determines the name of the procedure and what code it is to include. Serial procedure generation is used for the procedures Pghead, Rintro, Head{GROUP} (one header for each group), __Detail, Foot{GROUP}, Rsumm, and Pgfoot. The reason for using this is that all these procedures do basically the same thing: print data on a page. They must access print-system memory variables, different text pitches and styles, word wrap, and so on. Rather than write massively duplicated code (which would result if there were one template procedure for each of the FRG procedures), the authors cleverly chose to generate them in this serial fashion. Fortunately, there is nothing particularly new in this process except its length. Those who are curious about the exact implementation easily know enough to study the code.

Plain Reports and Resetting

The procedures to process plain reports and reset the system before exiting are in lines 2037–2062. These basically output straight dBASE IV code and are not particularly complex. The only change I'd suggest would be to add some commands to the Reset procedure if you normally SET a number of environmental variables before running your report.

The remainder of REPORT.COD is user-defined functions that we have examined already.

Conclusion

This chapter has examined the most important elements of the report generator template. What makes the template so large is the number of details it must handle, not any inherent complexity. If you understand this template, you have a good idea of nearly all the tricks available in the language.

Appendix

REPORT.COD

```
1  //
2  // Module Name: REPORT.COD
3  // Description: Define Application menus and program structure.
4  //
5
6  Report (.frg) Program Template
7  -----------------------------
8  Version 1.0
9  Ashton-Tate (c) 1987, 1988
10
11 {
12  include "report.def";
13  include "builtin.def";
14 //
15 // Enum string constants for international translation
16 //
17  enum wrong_class = "Can't use REPORT.GEN on non-report objects.  ",
18      report_empty = "Report design was empty.  ",
19      demo_string  =
            "dBASE IV SAMPLE REPORT - FOR EVALUATION  PURPOSES ONLY",
20      increase_page = "Increase the page length for this report.",
21      demo_version = 0;
22 //
23  if frame_class != report then
24    pause(wrong_class + any_key);
25    return 0;
26  endif
27 //
28 // temporary storage variables
29 //
30  var count,x,a,d,i,ni,j,k,temp,temp2,
31 //
32      rptname,    // Report name
33  default_drive, // dBASE default drive
34      isfirst,    // first system memvar? (handles commas)
35      isnew,      // is this a new band?
36      isopen,     // is the band open?
37      priv_vars,  // system memvars list
38     priv_vars2, // if FLD_EXPRESSION is broken into 2 strings
39      bandedit,   // word wrap off or on
40      bandgrp,    // GROUP id for bands
41      bandhgt,    // band row position plus height plus one
42      bandlen2,   // length of page header (0 if band is closed)
43      bandlen50,  // length of detail band          "
44    bandspacing, // spacing on detail band
```

(continued)

```
45       bandlen98, // length of page footer         "
46   bandspacing98, // spacing on footer band
47       bandtype,  // type of band ie. page footer, report intro, etc.
48   band_previous, // previous bandtype
49       length,    // length of field or text
50       maxgrp,    // maximum number of bands
51       isrepo,    // is there report intro/summary bands
52       maxrow,    // maximum row
53       nextrow,   // next row when looking ahead ie. ++<cursor>
54 current_column, // current text or field plus length
55       bsrv,      // beginning of band suppress repeated value
56       xsrv,      // current suppress repeated value var
57       xsum,      // current "noname" summary field
58       xxsum,     // subset of either an average, std. deviation or variancey
59       samerow,   // flag set for items occuring on the same row
60       bandrow,   // band row plus one
61   first_combine, // text or field is the first in the chain of combined data
62       combine,   // combine fields flag
63   suppress_line, // if the text "Page no." appears first on the line
64   previous_row,  // previous elements' row
65     pre_type,    // previous element type was field or text
66    inner_loop,   // elements inside the band encountered
67   optl_heading,  // flag to test whether optional heading has been output
68 is_rintro_open, // is the Report Intro band open
69  is_rsumm_open, // is the Report Summary band open
70 number_of_open_group_intros,   // none open,
     Grphead procedure is suppressed
71 number_of_open_group_summarys, // none open,
     Grpfoot procedure is suppressed
72 is_page_header_open, // if Page Header band is open
73 number_of_reset_on_page, // summary fields reset on page
74 number_of_fld_suppress,  // suppressed fields
75 intro_band_one_height,   // footer widow checking for
76 intro_band_two_height,   // dBASE III PLUS reports
77 number_of_word_wrap_bands,
78 number_of_group_footer_fields,
79 current_group_footer_field,
80 number_of_begin_new_pages
81 ;
82  default_drive = STRSET(_defdrive);
83  rptname = FRAME_PATH + NAME;
84  if not FILEOK(rptname) then
85    if FILEDRIVE(NAME) || !default_drive then
86      rptname=NAME;
87    else
88      rptname=default_drive + ":" + NAME;
89    endif
90  endif
91
92  if not CREATE(rptname+".FRG") then;
93    PAUSE(fileroot(rptname)+".FRG"+read_only+any_key);
94    return 0;
```

(continued)

```
 95  endif
 96  }
 97  {bandrow=0;
 98   bsrv=0;
 99   combine=0;
100   current_column=0;
101   first_combine=1;
102   isopen=0;
103   maxrow=0;
104   nextrow=0;
105   optl_heading=0;
106   previous_row=0;
107   pre_type=0;
108   samerow=0;
109   xsrv=0;
110   xsum=0;
111   xxsum=0;
112  }
113  * Program............: {rptname}.FRG
114  * Date...............: {LTRIM(SUBSTR(DATE(),1,8))}
115  * Versions...........: dBASE IV, Report {FRAME_VER}
116  *
117  * Notes:
118  * ------
119  * Prior to running this procedure with the DO command
120  * it is necessary use LOCATE because the CONTINUE
121  * statement is in the main loop.
122  *
123  *-- Parameters
124  PARAMETERS gl_noeject, gl_plain, gl_summary, gc_heading, gc_extra
125  ** The first three parameters are of type Logical.
126  ** The fourth parameter is a string.  The fifth is extra.
127  PRIVATE _peject\
128  {if dBASE_III_PLUS == 2 then}
129  , _plength, _ploffset\
130  {endif}
131  , _wrap
132
133  *-- Test for no records found
134  IF EOF() .OR. .NOT. FOUND()
135     RETURN
136  ENDIF
137
138  *-- turn word wrap mode off
139  _wrap=.F.
140
141  {
142   isrepo=0;
143   is_rintro_open=0;
144   bandlen2=0;
145   is_page_header_open=0;
146   bandlen50=0;
```

(continued)

```
147   number_of_begin_new_pages=0;
148   number_of_group_footer_fields=0;
149   number_of_open_group_summarys=0;
150   number_of_word_wrap_bands=0;
151   bandlen98=0;
152   bandspacing=0;
153   bandspacing98=0;
154   is_rsumm_open=0;
155   intro_band_one_height=0;
156   intro_band_two_height=0;
157   foreach BAND_ELEMENT k
158
159      if BAND_BANDEDIT then ++number_of_word_wrap_bands; endif
160
161      if BAND_NEWPAGE then ++number_of_begin_new_pages; endif
162
163      case BAND_BANDTYPE of
164      Report_Intro:
165         isrepo=1;
166         if BAND_OPENFLG then is_rintro_open = 1; endif
167 //
168      Page_Header:
169        if BAND_OPENFLG then
170          is_page_header_open = 1;
171          bandlen2=BAND_HEIGHT;
172        endif
173 //
174      Group_Intro:
175        if dBASE_III_PLUS == 2 then
176          if GROUP == 4 then intro_band_one_height = BAND_HEIGHT; endif
177          if GROUP == 5 then intro_band_two_height = BAND_HEIGHT; endif
178        endif
179 //
180      Detail:
181        if BAND_OPENFLG then bandlen50=BAND_HEIGHT; endif
182        if BAND_SPACING then
183          bandspacing=BAND_SPACING;
184        endif
185 //
186      Group_Summary:
187        if BAND_OPENFLG then ++number_of_open_group_summarys; endif
188 //
189      Page_Footer:
190        if BAND_OPENFLG then bandlen98=BAND_HEIGHT; endif
191        if BAND_SPACING then
192          bandspacing98=BAND_SPACING;
193        endif
194 //
195      Report_Summary:
196        if BAND_OPENFLG then is_rsumm_open = 1; endif
197      endcase
198   next k;
```

(continued)

```
199  if demo_version then ++bandlen98; endif
200
201  if number_of_open_group_summarys || is_rsumm_open || bandlen98 then
202    foreach FLD_ELEMENT k
203      if GROUP > 50 then
204        d=0;
205        case FLD_FIELDTYPE of
206        Tabl_data: d=1;
207        Calc_data: if GROUP < 97 && !FLD_HIDDEN && FLD_FIELDNAME &&
               FLD_VALUE_TYPE == 67 then d=1; endif
208        Pred_data: if GROUP < 97 && FLD_PREDEFINE == 2 then d=1; endif
209        endcase
210        if d then
211          ++number_of_group_footer_fields;
212        endif
213      endif
214    next k;
215  endif
216 }
217 IF _plength < {bandlen2+bandlen98+2}
218    SET DEVICE TO SCREEN
219    DEFINE WINDOW gw_report FROM 7,17 TO 11,62 DOUBLE
220    ACTIVATE WINDOW gw_report
221    @ 0,1 SAY "{increase_page}"
222    @ 2,1 SAY "{any_key}"
223    x=INKEY(0)
224    DEACTIVATE WINDOW gw_report
225    RELEASE WINDOW gw_report
226    RETURN
227 ENDIF
228
229 _plineno=0          && set lines to zero
230 {if dBASE_III_PLUS == 2 then}
231 *-- dBASE III PLUS report setup
232 _peject=\
233 {case PRINT_NEW_PAGE of}
234 {0:}"AFTER"
235 {1:}"BEFORE"
236 {2:}"BOTH"
237 {3:}"NONE"
238 {endcase}
239 _plength={PRINT_PAGE_LENGTH}
240 _ploffset={nul2zero(PRINT_LEFT_OFFSET)}
241
242 {endif}
243 {if dBASE_III_PLUS == 2 then}
244 *-- PLAIN option to screen only
245 IF gl_plain
246    IF SET("PRINT") = "OFF" .AND. SET("ALTERNATE") = "OFF"
247        gl_noeject=.T.
248    ENDIF
249 ENDIF
```

(continued)

```
250
251 {endif}
252 *-- NOEJECT parameter
253 IF gl_noeject
254    IF _peject="BEFORE"
255       _peject="NONE"
256    ENDIF
257    IF _peject="BOTH"
258       _peject="AFTER"
259    ENDIF
260 ENDIF
261
262 *-- Set-up environment
263 ON ESCAPE DO prnabort
264 IF SET("TALK")="ON"
265    SET TALK OFF
266    gc_talk="ON"
267 ELSE
268    gc_talk="OFF"
269 ENDIF
270 gc_space=SET("SPACE")
271 SET SPACE OFF
272 gc_time=TIME()        && system time for predefined field
273 gd_date=DATE()        && system date  "    "    "    "
274 gl_fandl=.F.          && first and last page flag
275 gl_prntflg=.T.        && Continue printing flag
276 gl_widow=.T.          && flag for checking widow bands
277 gn_length=LEN(gc_heading)  && store length of the HEADING
278 gn_level=2            && current band being processed
279 gn_page=_pageno       && grab current page number
280 gn_pspace=_pspacing && get current print spacing
281
282 {x=0;
283  if number_of_group_footer_fields then
284    current_group_footer_field=1;
285    x=1;}
286 *-- Initialize group footer field variables
287 {  do while x <= number_of_group_footer_fields}
288 r_foot{x}=.F.
289 {     ++x;
290    enddo
291  endif
292 }
293
294 {x=0;}
295 {foreach FLD_ELEMENT k}
296 //
297 // Reset Summary (on page) and Suppress repeated values
298 //
299 {if FLD_FIELDTYPE == Summ_data && FLD_RESET == 1 then
300    ++number_of_reset_on_page
301  endif}
```

(continued)

```
302 {if FLD_SUPPRESS then ++number_of_fld_suppress endif}
303 //
304 // only if there is a fieldname assigned to the calculated field
305 //
306 {if FLD_FIELDTYPE == Calc_data && FLD_FIELDNAME then}
307 {  if !x then}
308 *-- Initialize calculated variables.
309 {  endif}
310 {FLD_FIELDNAME}=\
311 {case FLD_VALUE_TYPE of}
312 {68: // Date   }CTOD("  /  /  ")
313 {70: // Float  }FLOAT(0)
314 {76: // Logical}.F.
315 {78: // Numeric}0
316 {otherwise:}""
317 {endcase}
318 {  ++x;}
319 {endif}
320 {next k;}
321
322 *-- Set up procedure for page break
323 gn_atline=_plength - \
324 {
325 // Page footer set to default spacing?
326  if !bandspacing98 then
327
328 // Detail band set to default?
329    if !bandspacing then
330
331 // Page footer height greater than 1?
332      if bandlen98 > 1 then
333 }
334 (_pspacing * {bandlen98} + 1)
335 {    else}
336 {      if bandlen98 then}
337 (_pspacing + 1)
338 {      else}
339 1
340 {      endif
341      endif
342
343 // Detail band is not default
344    else
345      bandspacing * bandlen98 +1}
346
347 {  endif
348
349 // Page footer is not default
350  else
351    bandspacing98 * bandlen98 +1}
352
353 {endif}
```

(continued)

```
354 ON PAGE AT LINE gn_atline EJECT PAGE
355
356 *-- Print Report
357
358 PRINTJOB
359
360 {if number_of_begin_new_pages then}
361 gl_newpage=.T.       && ok to begin band on new page
362
363 {endif}
364 {
365  x=1;  // to obtain number of group bands
366  number_of_open_group_intros=0;
367
368  foreach BAND_ELEMENT k
369 //
370    if BAND_BANDTYPE == Group_Intro then
371      if x == 1 then}
372 *-- Initialize group break vars.
373 {     endif
374      if BAND_OPENFLG then ++number_of_open_group_intros; endif}
375 //
376 {case BAND_GROUPTYPE of}
377 {1: // by field}
378 {// initialize Group by field variable}
379 r_mvar{GROUP}=\
380 {     if AT(">",BAND_GFIELD) then  // Check for ALIAS}
381 {SUBSTR(BAND_GFIELD,AT(">",BAND_GFIELD)+1)}
382
383 {     else}
384 {BAND_GFIELD}
385
386 {     endif}
387 //
388 {3: // by record count}
389 {// initialize Group by record variable}
390 r_mvar{GROUP}=1
391 //
392 {otherwise: // by expression}
393 {// initialize Group by expression variable}
394 r_mvar{GROUP}=\
395 {foreach BAND_EXPRESSION fcursor in k}
396 {BAND_EXPRESSION}
397 {next}
398
399 //
400 {endcase}
401 {     ++x;
402    endif
403    if BAND_BANDTYPE == Detail then exit endif
404  next k;}
405 {maxgrp=x+2;}
```

(continued)

```
406 {if x > 1 then}
407
408 {endif}
409 {x=0;}
410 {foreach FLD_ELEMENT k}
411 {   if FLD_FIELDTYPE == Summ_data then}
412 {     if !x then}
413 *-- Initialize summary variables.
414 {     endif}
415 {     ++x;}
416 //
417 // standard deviation or variance?
418 //
419 {     if !FLD_FIELDNAME then}
420 {       ++xsum;}
421 {       priv_vars="r_msum"+STR(xsum);}
422 {     else}
423 {       priv_vars=FLD_FIELDNAME;}
424 {     endif}
425 {     if FLD_OPERATION > 4 then}
426 STORE 0 TO r_sum{++xxsum},r_sum{++xxsum},\
427 r_sum{++xxsum},r_sum{++xxsum},{priv_vars}
428 // DECLARE {priv_vars}[5]
429 // STORE 0 TO {priv_vars}[3]
430 // STORE 0 TO {priv_vars}[1],{priv_vars}[2],{priv_vars}[4],{priv_vars}[5]
431 {     else}
432 {       case FLD_OPERATION of}
433 {       0: // Average}
434 STORE 0 TO r_sum{++xxsum},r_sum{++xxsum},{priv_vars}
435 // DECLARE {priv_vars}[3]
436 // STORE 0 TO {priv_vars}[1]
437 // STORE 0 TO {priv_vars}[2],{priv_vars}[3]
438 {       1: // Count}
439 {priv_vars}=0
440 {       otherwise: // Max, Min or Sum}
441 {priv_vars}=\
442 {         if FLD_OPERATION == 3 then // Minimum}
443 {FLD_SUMFIELD}
444
445 {         else}
446 0
447 {         endif}
448 {       endcase}
449 {     endif}
450 {   endif}
451 {next k;}
452 {xsum=0; xxsum=0;}
453 {if x then}
454
455 {endif}
456 {x=0;   // to offset each suppress repeated value variable}
457 //
```

(continued)

```
458 {foreach FLD_ELEMENT k}
459 //
460 // suppress repeated values?
461 //
462 {if FLD_SUPPRESS then}
463 {  if !x then}
464 *-- Initialize suppress repeated value variables.
465 {  endif}
466 {++x;}
467 r_msrv{x}=\
468 {case FLD_VALUE_TYPE of}
469 {68: // Date   }CTOD(" / / ")
470 {70: // Float  }FLOAT(0)
471 {76: // Logical}.NOT. \
472 {  if FLD_FIELDNAME then}
473 {FLD_FIELDNAME}
474
475 {  else}
476 {     foreach FLD_EXPRESSION fcursor in k}
477 {FLD_EXPRESSION}
478 {     next}
479
480 {  endif}
481 {78: // Numeric}0
482 {otherwise:}""
483 {endcase}
484 {endif}
485 {next k;}
486 {if x then}
487
488 {endif}
489 //
490 {x=0;}
491 {foreach FLD_ELEMENT k}
492 //
493 // only if there is a fieldname assigned to the calculated field
494 //
495 {if FLD_FIELDTYPE == Calc_data && FLD_FIELDNAME then}
496 {  if !x then}
497 *-- Assign initial values to calculated variables.
498 {  endif}
499 {FLD_FIELDNAME}=\
500 {foreach FLD_EXPRESSION fcursor in k}
501 {FLD_EXPRESSION}
502 {next}
503
504 {   ++x;}
505 {endif}
506 {next k;}
507 {if x then}
508
509 {endif}
```

(continued)

```
510 {x=0;}
511 {foreach FLD_ELEMENT k}
512 {  if FLD_FIELDTYPE == Summ_data then}
513 {     if !FLD_FIELDNAME then}
514 {        ++xsum;}
515 {     endif}
516 {     if FLD_OPERATION == 2 || FLD_OPERATION == 3 then}
517 {        if !x then}
518 *-- Initialize min/max summary variables again,
519 *-- in case it's based on a calculated field.
520 {        endif}
521 {        ++x;}
522 {        if !FLD_FIELDNAME then}
523 {          priv_vars="r_msum"+STR(xsum);}
524 {        else}
525 {          priv_vars=FLD_FIELDNAME;}
526 {        endif}
527 {        priv_vars}={FLD_SUMFIELD}
528 {     endif}
529 {  endif}
530 {next k;}
531 {xsum=0;}
532 {if x then}
533
534 {endif}
535 {if isrepo && is_rintro_open then}
536 {  if not FRAME_PAGEHEADINGS then}
537 DO Rintro
538
539 *-- reset page number in case report intro spanned two pages
540 _pageno=gn_page
541
542 {  endif}
543 {endif}
544 IF gl_plain
545    ON PAGE AT LINE gn_atline DO Pgplain
546 ELSE
547    ON PAGE AT LINE gn_atline DO Pgfoot
548 ENDIF
549
550 {if is_page_header_open || (is_rintro_open && FRAME_PAGEHEADINGS)
551 || number_of_open_group_intros then}
552 DO Pghead
553
554 {endif}
555 gl_fandl=.T.          && first physical page started
556
557 {if isrepo && is_rintro_open then}
558 {  if FRAME_PAGEHEADINGS then}
559 DO Rintro
560 {     if number_of_begin_new_pages then}
561 gl_newpage=.F.
```

(continued)

```
562 {    endif}
563
564 {  endif}
565 {endif}
566 {if maxgrp > 3 && number_of_open_group_intros then}
567 DO Grphead
568
569 {endif}
570 *-- File Loop
571 DO WHILE FOUND() .AND. .NOT. EOF() .AND. gl_prntflg
572 //
573 // If there are group bands
574 // set up the CASE structure to test
575 // the group band values
576 //
577 {if maxgrp > 3 &&
578  (number_of_open_group_intros || number_of_open_group_summarys) then}
579    DO CASE
580 {  foreach BAND_ELEMENT k}
581 {    if BAND_BANDTYPE == Group_Intro then}
582 //
583 // Group by field
584 //
585 {      if BAND_GFIELD then}
586    CASE .NOT. (\
587 {      if AT(">",BAND_GFIELD) then  // Check for ALIAS}
588 {SUBSTR(BAND_GFIELD,AT(">",BAND_GFIELD)+1)}
589 {      else}
590 {BAND_GFIELD}
591 {      endif}
592  = r_mvar{GROUP})
593 {      endif}
594 //
595 // Group by expression
596 //
597 {      if BAND_EXPRESSION then}
598    CASE .NOT. (\
599 {foreach BAND_EXPRESSION fcursor in k}
600 {BAND_EXPRESSION}
601 {next}
602  = r_mvar{GROUP})
603 {      endif}
604 //
605 // Group by record count
606 //
607 {      if BAND_GROUP_REC then}
608    CASE r_mvar{GROUP} > {BAND_GROUP_REC}
609 {      endif}
610      gn_level={GROUP}
611 {    endif}
612 {  next k;}
613    OTHERWISE
```

(continued)

```
614        gn_level=0
615     ENDCASE
616     *-- test whether an expression didn't match
617     IF gn_level <> 0
618  {  if number_of_open_group_summarys then}
619        DO Grpfoot WITH 100-gn_level
620  {  endif}
621        DO Grpinit
622     ENDIF
623  {  if number_of_open_group_intros then}
624     *-- Repeat group intros
625     IF gn_level <> 0
626        DO Grphead
627     ENDIF
628  {  endif}
629  {endif}
630  {LMARG(4);}
631  DO Upd_Vars
632  {if bandlen50 then}
633  *-- Detail lines
634  IF .NOT. gl_summary
635      DO __Detail
636  ENDIF
637  {endif}
638  {if number_of_group_footer_fields || is_rsumm_open || bandlen98 then
639      x=1;
640      foreach FLD_ELEMENT k
641        if GROUP > 50 then
642           d=0;
643           case FLD_FIELDTYPE of
644           Tabl_data: d=1;
645           Calc_data: if GROUP < 97 && !FLD_HIDDEN && FLD_FIELDNAME &&
                 FLD_VALUE_TYPE == 67 then d=1; endif
646           Pred_data: if GROUP < 97 && FLD_PREDEFINE == 2 then d=1; endif
647           endcase
648           if d then}
649  r_foot{x}=\
650  {         case FLD_FIELDTYPE of}
651  {         Tabl_data:}
652  {            FLD_FIELDNAME}
653
654  {         Calc_data:}
655  {            FLD_FIELDNAME}
656
657  {         Pred_data:}
658  RECNO()
659  {         endcase}
660  {         ++x;}
661  {      endif
662        endif
663     next k;
664   endif}
```

(continued)

```
665 CONTINUE
666 {if number_of_open_group_intros || number_of_open_group_summarys then}
667 {foreach BAND_ELEMENT k}
668 {   if BAND_BANDTYPE == Group_Intro then}
669 //
670 // increment any group by record count vars.
671 //
672 {     if BAND_GROUP_REC then}
673 r_mvar{GROUP}=r_mvar{GROUP}+1
674 {     endif}
675 {   else}
676 {     if BAND_BANDTYPE > Group_Intro then exit endif}
677 {   endif}
678 {next k;}
679 {endif}
680 {LMARG(1);}
681 ENDDO
682
683 IF gl_prntflg
684 //
685 // If there are group bands
686 //
687 {if maxgrp > 3 then}
688    gn_level=3
689 {   if number_of_open_group_summarys then}
690    DO Grpfoot WITH 97
691 {   endif}
692 {endif}
693 //
694 // Report summary?
695 //
696 {if isrepo && is_rsumm_open then}
697    DO Rsumm
698 {endif}
699 {   if bandlen98 then}
700 {     if !is_rsumm_open then}
701    gl_fandl=.F.      && last page finished
702 {     endif}
703    IF _plineno <= gn_atline
704       EJECT PAGE
705    ENDIF
706 {   endif}
707 ELSE
708 {if isrepo && is_rsumm_open then}
709 {   if maxgrp > 3 then}
710    gn_level=3
711 {   endif}
712    DO Rsumm
713 {endif}
714    DO Reset
715    RETURN
716 ENDIF
```

(continued)

```
717
718 ON PAGE
719
720 ENDPRINTJOB
721
722 DO Reset
723 RETURN
724 * EOP: {rptname}.FRG
725 {x=0;
726  foreach BAND_ELEMENT k
727    if BAND_BANDTYPE > Group_Intro then exit endif
728    if BAND_BANDTYPE == Group_Intro then
729      if !x then}
730
731 *-- Determine height of group bands and detail band for widow checking
732 FUNCTION Gheight
733 PARAMETER Group_Band
734 retval=0                 && return value
735 {    endif}
736 IF Group_Band <= {GROUP}
737    retval = retval +\
738 {    if BAND_HEIGHT > 1 then}
739 {BAND_HEIGHT}\
740 {    endif}
741 {    if !BAND_SPACING && !bandspacing then}
742 {if BAND_HEIGHT > 1 then} *{endif} gn_pspace
743 {    else
744        if !BAND_SPACING && bandspacing > 1 then}
745 {if BAND_HEIGHT > 1 then} *{endif} {bandspacing}
746 {    else
747          if BAND_SPACING > 1 then}
748 {if BAND_HEIGHT > 1 then} *{endif} {BAND_SPACING}
749 {      else}
750 {        if BAND_HEIGHT < 2 then}
751  {BAND_HEIGHT}\
752 {        endif}
753
754 {      endif
755        endif
756      endif}
757 ENDIF
758 {    ++x;
759    endif
760  next k;
761  if x then
762    if bandlen50 then}
763 *-- add height of detail band
764 retval = retval + \
765 {    if !bandspacing then}
766 {if bandlen50 > 1 then}{bandlen50} * {endif}gn_pspace
767 {    else}
768 {      if bandspacing > 1 then}
```

(continued)

```
769 {bandspacing*bandlen50}
770
771 {      else}
772 {bandlen50}
773
774 {      endif
775     endif
776   endif}
777 RETURN retval
778 * EOP: Gheight
779 {endif}
780
781 *-- Update summary fields and/or calculated fields in the detail band.
782 PROCEDURE Upd_Vars
783 {x=0;}
784 {foreach FLD_ELEMENT k}
785 //
786 // Initialize calculated fields for Detail band
787 //
788 {  if GROUP == 50 && FLD_FIELDTYPE == Calc_data && FLD_FIELDNAME then}
789 {FLD_FIELDNAME}=\
790 {     foreach FLD_EXPRESSION fcursor in k}
791 {FLD_EXPRESSION}
792 {     next}
793
794 {  endif}
795 //
796 // Summary field?
797 //
798 {if FLD_FIELDTYPE == Summ_data then}
799 {  if !FLD_FIELDNAME then}
800 {     ++x;}
801 {     priv_vars="r_msum"+STR(x);}
802 {  else}
803 {     priv_vars=FLD_FIELDNAME;}
804 {  endif}
805 *-- \
806 {case FLD_OPERATION of}
807 {0: // AVG}
808 Average
809 r_sum{++xxsum}=r_sum{xxsum}+1{tabto(40)}&& count
810 // {priv_vars}[1]={priv_vars}[1]+1{tabto(40)}&& count
811 r_sum{++xxsum}=r_sum{xxsum}+{FLD_SUMFIELD}{tabto(40)}&& sum
812 // {priv_vars}[2]={priv_vars}[2]+{FLD_SUMFIELD}{tabto(40)}&& sum
813 {priv_vars}=r_sum{xxsum}/r_sum{xxsum-1}{tabto(40)}&& average
814 // {priv_vars}[3]={priv_vars}[2]/{priv_vars}[1]{tabto(40)}&& average
815 {1: // COUNT}
816 Count
817 {priv_vars}={priv_vars}+1
818 {2: // MAX}
819 Max
820 IF {FLD_SUMFIELD} > {priv_vars}
```

(continued)

```
821     {priv_vars}={FLD_SUMFIELD}
822 ENDIF
823 {3: // MIN}
824 Min
825 IF {FLD_SUMFIELD} < {priv_vars}
826     {priv_vars}={FLD_SUMFIELD}
827 ENDIF
828 {4: // SUM}
829 Sum
830 {priv_vars}={priv_vars}+{FLD_SUMFIELD}
831 {otherwise: // STD or VAR}
832 {if FLD_OPERATION == 5 then}
833 Std deviation
834 {else}
835 Variance
836 {endif}
837 r_sum{++xxsum}=r_sum{xxsum}+{FLD_SUMFIELD}^2\
838 {tabto(40)}&& sum of squares
839 // {priv_vars}[1]={priv_vars}[1]+{FLD_SUMFIELD}^2\
840 // {tabto(40)}&& sum of squares
841 r_sum{++xxsum}=r_sum{xxsum}+{FLD_SUMFIELD}\
842 {tabto(40)}&& sum
843 // {priv_vars}[2]={priv_vars}[2]+{FLD_SUMFIELD}\
844 // {tabto(40)}&& sum
845 r_sum{++xxsum}=r_sum{xxsum}+1\
846 {tabto(40)}&& count
847 // {priv_vars}[3]={priv_vars}[3]+1\
848 // {tabto(40)}&& count
849 r_sum{++xxsum}=r_sum{xxsum-2}/r_sum{xxsum-1}\
850 {tabto(40)}&& average
851 // {priv_vars}[4]={priv_vars}[2]/{priv_vars}[3]\
852 // {tabto(40)}&& average
853 *-- variance
854 {priv_vars}=\
855 (r_sum{xxsum-3}+r_sum{xxsum-1}*(r_sum{xxsum}^2);
856     -(2*r_sum{xxsum}*r_sum{xxsum-2}))/r_sum{xxsum-1}
857 // {priv_vars}[5]=\
858 // ({priv_vars}[1]+{priv_vars}[3]*({priv_vars}[4]^2);
859 //    -(2*{priv_vars}[4]*{priv_vars}[2]))/{priv_vars}[3]
860 {if FLD_OPERATION == 5 then}
861 {priv_vars}=SQRT({priv_vars})\
862 {tabto(40)}&& std deviation
863 // {priv_vars}[5]=SQRT({priv_vars}[5])\
864 // {tabto(40)}&& std deviation
865 {endif}
866 {endcase}
867 {endif}
868 {next k;}
869 {xxsum=0;}
870 RETURN
871 * EOP: Upd_Vars
872
```

(continued)

```
873 *-- Set flag to get out of DO WHILE loop when escape is pressed.
874 PROCEDURE prnabort
875 gl_prntflg=.F.
876 RETURN
877 * EOP: prnabort
878
879 {if number_of_open_group_intros || number_of_open_group_summarys then}
880 *-- Reset group break variables.  Reinit summary
881 *-- fields with reset set to a particular group band.
882 PROCEDURE Grpinit
883 {i=0;
884  x=0;}
885 {foreach FLD_ELEMENT k}
886 //
887 // Summary field and reset on group?
888 //
889 {  if FLD_FIELDTYPE == Summ_data && FLD_RESET >= Each_Group then}
890 {    if i && FLD_RESET > Each_Group && i != FLD_RESET then}
891 {       i=0;
892         lmarg(1);}
893 ENDIF
894 {     endif}
895 {    if FLD_RESET > Each_Group && i != FLD_RESET then}
896 IF gn_level <= {FLD_RESET}
897 {       i=FLD_RESET;
898         lmarg(4);}
899 {    endif}
900 {    if !FLD_FIELDNAME then}
901 {      ++x;}
902 {      priv_vars="r_msum"+STR(x);}
903 {    else}
904 {      priv_vars=FLD_FIELDNAME;}
905 {    endif}
906 //
907 // standard deviation or variance?
908 //
909 {    if FLD_OPERATION > 4 then}
910 STORE 0 TO r_sum{++xxsum},r_sum{++xxsum},\
911 r_sum{++xxsum},r_sum{++xxsum},{priv_vars}
912 // STORE 0 TO {priv_vars}[3]
913 // STORE 0 TO {priv_vars}[1],{priv_vars}[2],\
914 // {priv_vars}[4],{priv_vars}[5]
915 {    else}
916 {      case FLD_OPERATION of}
917 {      0: // Average}
918 STORE 0 TO r_sum{++xxsum},r_sum{++xxsum},{priv_vars}
919 // STORE 0 TO {priv_vars}[1]
920 // STORE 0 TO {priv_vars}[2],{priv_vars}[3]
921 {      1: // Count}
922 {priv_vars}=0
923 {      otherwise: // Min, Max or Sum}
924 {priv_vars}=\
```

(continued)

```
925 {         if FLD_OPERATION == 3 then  // Minimum}
926 {FLD_SUMFIELD}
927
928 {         else}
929 0
930 {         endif}
931 {       endcase}
932 {     endif}
933 {  endif}
934 {next k;}
935 {xxsum=0;}
936 {if i then
937    i=0;
938    lmarg(1);}
939 ENDIF
940 {endif}
941 {foreach BAND_ELEMENT k}
942 {  if BAND_BANDTYPE == Group_Intro then}
943 //
944 // Reset Group break vars on group intro bands
945 //
946 IF gn_level <= {GROUP}
947 //
948 {     lmarg(4);}
949 {     if BAND_GFIELD then}
950 r_mvar{GROUP}=\
951 {       if AT(">",BAND_GFIELD) then  // Check for ALIAS}
952 {SUBSTR(BAND_GFIELD,AT(">",BAND_GFIELD)+1)}
953
954 {       else}
955 {BAND_GFIELD}
956
957 {       endif}
958 {     endif}
959 {     if BAND_GROUP_REC then}
960 r_mvar{GROUP}=1
961 {     endif}
962 {     if BAND_EXPRESSION then}
963 r_mvar{GROUP}=\
964 {foreach BAND_EXPRESSION fcursor in k}
965 {BAND_EXPRESSION}
966 {next}
967
968 {     endif}
969 {     lmarg(1);}
970 ENDIF
971 {  else}
972 {     if BAND_BANDTYPE > Group_Intro then exit endif}
973 {  endif}
974 {next k;}
975 RETURN
976 * EOP: Grpinit
```

(continued)

```
 977
 978 {endif}
 979 {if number_of_reset_on_page || number_of_fld_suppress then}
 980 *-- Reset summary fields (on page) and suppress repeated values.
 981 PROCEDURE Pageinit
 982 {i=0;}
 983 {x=0;}
 984 {foreach FLD_ELEMENT k}
 985 {   if FLD_SUPPRESS then}
 986 {      ++x;}
 987 r_msrv{x}=\
 988 {    case FLD_VALUE_TYPE of}
 989 {      68: // Date}CTOD("  /  /  ")
 990 {      70: // Float}FLOAT(0)
 991 {      76: // Logical}.NOT. \
 992 {         if FLD_FIELDNAME then}
 993 {FLD_FIELDNAME}
 994
 995 {         else}
 996 {            foreach FLD_EXPRESSION fcursor in k}
 997 {FLD_EXPRESSION}
 998 {            next}
 999
1000 {         endif}
1001 {      78: // Numeric}0
1002 {      otherwise:}""
1003 {      endcase}
1004 {   endif}
1005 {   if FLD_FIELDTYPE == Summ_data && FLD_RESET == Each_Page then}
1006 {      if !FLD_FIELDNAME then}
1007 {         ++i;}
1008 {         priv_vars="r_msum"+STR(i);}
1009 {      else}
1010 {         priv_vars=FLD_FIELDNAME;}
1011 {      endif}
1012 {      if FLD_OPERATION > 4 then}
1013 STORE 0 TO r_sum{++xxsum},r_sum{++xxsum},\
1014 r_sum{++xxsum},r_sum{++xxsum},{priv_vars}
1015 // STORE 0 TO {priv_vars}[3]
1016 // STORE 0 TO {priv_vars}[1],{priv_vars}[2],\
1017 // {priv_vars}[4],{priv_vars}[5]
1018 {      else}
1019 {         case FLD_OPERATION of}
1020 {         0: // Average}
1021 STORE 0 TO r_sum{++xxsum},r_sum{++xxsum},{priv_vars}
1022 // STORE 0 TO {priv_vars}[1]
1023 // STORE 0 TO {priv_vars}[2],{priv_vars}[3]
1024 {         1: // Count}
1025 {priv_vars}=0
1026 {         otherwise: // Min,Max or Sum}
1027 {priv_vars}=\
1028 {            if FLD_OPERATION == 3 then // Minimum}
```

(continued)

```
1029 {FLD_SUMFIELD}
1030
1031 {        else}
1032 0
1033 {        endif}
1034 {      endcase}
1035 {    endif}
1036 {  endif}
1037 {next k;}
1038 {xxsum=0;}
1039 RETURN
1040 * EOP: Pageinit
1041
1042 {endif}
1043 {if maxgrp > 3 &&
1044  (number_of_open_group_intros || number_of_open_group_summarys) then}
1045 {  if number_of_open_group_intros then}
1046 *-- Process Group Intro bands during group breaks
1047 PROCEDURE Grphead
1048 IF EOF()
1049    RETURN
1050 ENDIF
1051 PRIVATE _pspacing
1052 {if bandspacing then}
1053 _pspacing={bandspacing}
1054 {else}
1055 _pspacing=gn_pspace
1056 {endif}
1057 gl_widow=.T.          && enable widow checking
1058 {  endif}
1059 {  if dBASE_III_PLUS == 2 && !number_of_open_group_summarys then}
1060 IF gn_level > 3
1061    ?
1062 ENDIF
1063 {  endif}
1064 {foreach BAND_ELEMENT k}
1065 {  case BAND_BANDTYPE of}
1066 {  Group_Intro:}
1067 {    if BAND_OPENFLG then}
1068 IF gn_level <= {GROUP}
1069    DO Head{GROUP}
1070 ENDIF
1071 {    endif}
1072 {  Detail:}
1073 {    if number_of_open_group_intros then}
1074 gn_level=0
1075 RETURN
1076 * EOP: Grphead.PRG
1077
1078 {    endif}
1079 {    if number_of_open_group_summarys then}
1080 *-- Process Group Summary bands during group breaks
```

(continued)

```
1081 PROCEDURE Grpfoot
1082 PARAMETER ln_level
1083 {     endif}
1084 {   Group_Summary:}
1085 {     if BAND_OPENFLG then}
1086 IF ln_level >= {GROUP}
1087    DO Foot{GROUP}
1088 ENDIF
1089 {     endif}
1090 {   Page_Footer:}
1091 {     if number_of_open_group_summarys then}
1092 RETURN
1093 * EOP: Grpfoot.PRG
1094
1095 {     endif}
1096 {   endcase}
1097 {next k;}
1098 {endif}
1099 {bandtype=99;}
1100 //
1101 {foreach ELEMENT ecursor}
1102 {   inner_loop=0;}
1103 {   pre_type=0;}
1104 //
1105 // List type is a BAND?
1106 //
1107 {if ELEMENT_TYPE == @Band_Element then}
1108 {   band_previous=bandtype;
1109      bandtype=BAND_BANDTYPE;}
1110 //
1111 // reset samerow to zero if set and output a carriage return
1112 //
1113 {   if samerow then}
1114 {     samerow=0;}
1115 //
1116 {   endif}
1117 {   combine=0;}
1118 {   first_combine=1;}
1119 //
1120 // Output carriage returns for dBASE report to handle blank lines
1121 //
1122 {   nextline2:}
1123 {   if maxrow < bandhgt then}
1124 {     if isopen then}
1125 ?
1126 {     endif}
1127 {     ++maxrow;}
1128 {     goto nextline2;}
1129 {   endif}
1130 //
1131 // beyond the first band?
1132 //
```

(continued)

```
1133 {   if band_previous != 99 then}
1134 //
1135 {     if number_of_begin_new_pages then
1136         if band_previous == Group_Intro
1137         || band_previous == Detail
1138         || band_previous == Group_Summary then}
1139 gl_newpage=.F.
1140 {       endif}
1141 {     endif}
1142 {    if band_previous == Page_Header || band_previous == Page_Footer
1143  || isopen then}
1144 {     case band_previous of}
1145 {     Page_Header:}
1146 //
1147 {       if suppress_line then
1148       suppress_line=0;}
1149 //
1150 {          lmarg(1);}
1151 ENDIF
1152 {       endif}
1153 //
1154 {       if isopen || (is_rintro_open && FRAME_PAGEHEADINGS)
1155           || number_of_open_group_intros then}
1156 //
1157 // Insert heading code for no page number
1158 //
1159 {          if !optl_heading then}
1160 *-- Print HEADING parameter ie. REPORT FORM <name> HEADING <expC>
1161 IF .NOT. gl_plain .AND. gn_length > 0
1162     ?? gc_heading FUNCTION "I;V"+LTRIM(STR(_rmargin-_lmargin))
1163     ?
1164 ENDIF
1165 {            optl_heading=1;}
1166 {          endif}
1167 //
1168 RETURN
1169 * EOP: Pghead
1170 {       endif}
1171 {     Report_Intro:}
1172 RETURN
1173 * EOP: Rintro                          \
1174 {     Group_Intro:}
1175 RETURN
1176 {     Detail:}
1177 RETURN
1178 * EOP: __Detail
1179 {     Group_Summary:}
1180 {if dBASE_III_PLUS == 2 then}
1181 IF ln_level < 9{if GROUP == 96 then}6{else}7{endif}
1182    ?
1183 ENDIF
1184 {endif}
```

(continued)

```
1185 RETURN
1186 {       Report_Summary:}
1187 gl_fandl=.F.          && last page finished
1188 ?
1189 RETURN
1190 * EOP: Rsumm
1191 {       Page_Footer:}
1192 {          finish_page_footer();}
1193 {       endcase}
1194 {    endif}
1195
1196 {  endif}
1197 //
1198 // capture band attributes
1199 // ----------------------
1200 // bandrow and maxrow for row position
1201 // bandedit for word wrap band
1202 // isopen for band open or closed
1203 //
1204 {  if Row_Positn then
1205       bandhgt=Row_Positn+BAND_HEIGHT+1;
1206       bandrow=Row_Positn+1;
1207       maxrow=Row_Positn+1;
1208    else
1209       bandhgt=BAND_HEIGHT+1;
1210       bandrow=1;
1211       maxrow=1;
1212    endif
1213 }
1214 {  bandedit=BAND_BANDEDIT;}
1215 {  bandgrp=GROUP;}
1216 {  bsrv=xsrv;}
1217 {  isnew=1;}
1218 {  isopen=BAND_OPENFLG;}
1219 //
1220 {  if BAND_BANDTYPE == Page_header || BAND_BANDTYPE == Page_Footer
1221    || BAND_OPENFLG then}
1222 {    if BAND_BANDTYPE then}
1223 PROCEDURE \
1224 {    else}
1225 {       if BAND_OPENFLG || (is_rintro_open && FRAME_PAGEHEADINGS)
1226          || number_of_open_group_intros then}
1227 PROCEDURE \
1228 {       endif}
1229 {    endif}
1230 {    case bandtype of}
1231 {    Page_Header:}
1232 {       if BAND_OPENFLG || (is_rintro_open && FRAME_PAGEHEADINGS)
1233          || number_of_open_group_intros then}
1234 Pghead
1235 {       endif}
1236 {    Report_Intro:}
```

(continued)

```
1237 Rintro
1238 {    Group_Intro:}
1239 Head{GROUP}
1240 {      if not BAND_INTROEACH then}
1241 IF gn_level=1
1242   RETURN
1243 ENDIF
1244 {      endif}
1245 {      if dBASE_III_PLUS == 2 && GROUP == 4 &&
1246       intro_band_one_height && intro_band_two_height then
1247        ++bandhgt;
1248      endif}
1249 {    Detail:}
1250 __Detail
1251 {    Group_Summary:}
1252 Foot{GROUP}
1253 {      if dBASE_III_PLUS == 2 then}
1254 ln_lines=IIF(ln_level < 97, \
1255 {      case GROUP of
1256        96:}
1257 {intro_band_one_height+intro_band_two_height+2}, \
1258 {intro_band_one_height+intro_band_two_height+1})
1259 {      95:}
1260 {intro_band_two_height+2}, \
1261 {intro_band_two_height+1})
1262 {      endcase}
1263 IF _plineno+ln_lines > gn_atline
1264   _plineno=gn_atline
1265   ?
1266 ENDIF
1267 {      endif}
1268 {    Report_Summary:}
1269 Rsumm
1270 {      --bandhgt;}
1271 {    Page_Footer:}
1272 Pgfoot
1273 PRIVATE _box{if isopen}, _pspacing{endif}
1274 gl_widow=.F.          && disable widow checking
1275 {      if isopen then}
1276 _pspacing=1
1277 ?
1278 {      endif}
1279 {      --bandhgt;}
1280 {      if BAND_OPENFLG && BAND_HEIGHT then}
1281 IF .NOT. gl_plain
1282 {      endif}
1283 {    endcase}
1284 {  endif}
1285 //
1286 // is the band open?
1287 // make system memvars PRIVATE
1288 // only if the values change
```

(continued)

```
1289 //
1290 {  if isopen then}
1291 //
1292 // BAND_NEWPAGE  - Begin band on new page:  No, Yes|
1293 //
1294 {    if BAND_NEWPAGE then}
1295 IF .NOT. gl_newpage
1296    gl_newpage=.T.
1297    EJECT PAGE
1298 ENDIF
1299 {    endif}
1300 //
1301 // BAND_TEXTPITCH - Text pitch for band:  Pica, Elite, Condensed, Default|
1302 //
1303 {    if BAND_TEXTPITCH != 3 then}
1304 IF SET("PRINT") = "ON" .AND. _ppitch <> \
1305 {        case BAND_TEXTPITCH of}
1306 {        0:}
1307 "PICA"
1308 {        1:}
1309 "ELITE"
1310 {        2:}
1311 "CONDENSED"
1312 {        3:}
1313 "DEFAULT"
1314 {        endcase}
1315    PRIVATE _ppitch
1316    _ppitch = \
1317 {        case BAND_TEXTPITCH of}
1318 {        0:}
1319 "PICA"
1320 {        1:}
1321 "ELITE"
1322 {        2:}
1323 "CONDENSED"
1324 {        3:}
1325 "DEFAULT"
1326 {        endcase}
1327 ENDIF
1328 {    endif}
1329 //
1330 // BAND_QUALITY - Quality pitch for band:  Yes, No|
1331 //
1332 {    if BAND_QUALITY < 2 then}
1333 IF SET("PRINT") = "ON" .AND. {if !BAND_QUALITY then}.NOT. {endif}_pquality
1334    PRIVATE _pquality
1335    _pquality = \
1336 {        if BAND_QUALITY then}
1337 .F.
1338 {        else}
1339 .T.
1340 {        endif}
```

(continued)

```
1341 ENDIF
1342 {    endif}
1343 //
1344 // BAND_SPACING - Default, single, double or triple
1345 //
1346 {    if BAND_SPACING then}
1347 IF _pspacing <> {BAND_SPACING}
1348    PRIVATE _pspacing
1349    _pspacing={BAND_SPACING}
1350 ENDIF
1351 {    endif}
1352 //
1353 // BAND_BANDEDIT - Wordwrap band:  Yes, No|
1354 //
1355 {    if number_of_word_wrap_bands then}
1356 {       if BAND_BANDEDIT then}
1357 PRIVATE _indent, _lmargin, _rmargin, _tabs
1358 {       endif}
1359 IF {    if BAND_BANDEDIT then}.NOT. {endif}_wrap
1360    PRIVATE _wrap
1361    _wrap = \
1362 {       if BAND_BANDEDIT then}
1363 .T.
1364 {       else}
1365 .F.
1366 {       endif}
1367 ENDIF
1368 {    endif}
1369 //
1370 {    i=GROUP;}
1371 //
1372 // Initialize calculated fields
1373 // in case they are used in the group break procedure
1374 //
1375 {    if BAND_BANDTYPE != Detail then}
1376 {       foreach FLD_ELEMENT k}
1377 {          if GROUP == i && FLD_FIELDTYPE == Calc_data && FLD_FIELDNAME then}
1378 {FLD_FIELDNAME}=\
1379 {          foreach FLD_EXPRESSION fcursor in k}
1380 {FLD_EXPRESSION}
1381 {          next}
1382
1383 {       endif}
1384 {       next k;}
1385 {    endif}
1386 //
1387 // Check for possible widow band
1388 //
1389 {    if BAND_BANDTYPE == Group_Intro then}
1390 //
1391 {       x=0;
1392       i=GROUP;
```

(continued)

```
1393         foreach BAND_ELEMENT k
1394 //
1395 // GROUP >= i means current Group intro
1396 //
1397         if k.BAND_OPENFLG && k.GROUP >= i then
1398           if k.BAND_BANDTYPE <= Detail then
1399             x=x+k.BAND_HEIGHT;
1400           else
1401             exit
1402           endif
1403         endif
1404       next k;
1405 }
1406 //
1407 {     ni="";
1408       if x then
1409         if !BAND_SPACING && !bandspacing then
1410           ni=" * gn_pspace";
1411         else
1412           if !BAND_SPACING && bandspacing > 1 then
1413             ni=" * "+STR(bandspacing);
1414           else
1415             if BAND_SPACING > 1 then
1416               ni=" * "+STR(BAND_SPACING);
1417             endif
1418           endif
1419         endif
1420         if BAND_HEIGHT > 1 then
1421           a=STR(BAND_HEIGHT)+ni+" ";
1422         else
1423           if ni then
1424             a=SUBSTR(ni,4)+" ";
1425           else
1426             a="";
1427           endif
1428         endif
1429         if a then}
1430 IF {a} < _plength
1431 {         lmarg(4);}
1432 IF (gl_widow .AND. _plineno+Gheight({GROUP}) > gn_atline + 1)\
1433 {         if BAND_HEIGHT then}
1434   ;
1435 .OR. (gl_widow .AND. _plineno+\
1436 {         if BAND_HEIGHT > 1 then}
1437 {BAND_HEIGHT}{ni}\
1438 {         else}
1439 {           if !BAND_SPACING then}
1440 {             if ni then}
1441 {SUBSTR(ni,4)}\
1442 {           else}
1443 1\
1444 {           endif}
```

(continued)

```
1445 {            else}
1446 {BAND_SPACING}\
1447 {            endif
1448            endif}
1449  > gn_atline)
1450 {        else}
1451
1452 {        endif
1453            endif}
1454    EJECT PAGE
1455 ENDIF
1456 {        lmarg(1);}
1457 ENDIF
1458 {       endif}
1459 {     endif}
1460 //
1461 {    ni="";
1462      if BAND_BANDTYPE == Detail then
1463        if BAND_HEIGHT then
1464          if !bandspacing then
1465            if BAND_HEIGHT > 1 then
1466              ni=STR(BAND_HEIGHT)+" * gn_pspace";
1467            else
1468              ni="gn_pspace";
1469            endif
1470          else
1471            if bandspacing > 1 then
1472              ni=STR(BAND_HEIGHT * BAND_SPACING);
1473            else
1474              if BAND_HEIGHT > 1 then
1475                ni=STR(BAND_HEIGHT);
1476              endif
1477            endif
1478          endif
1479          if ni then}
1480 IF {ni} < _plength
1481    IF gl_widow .AND. _plineno+{ni} > gn_atline + 1
1482        EJECT PAGE
1483    ENDIF
1484 ENDIF
1485 {        endif
1486          endif
1487        endif}
1488 {    if Row_Positn then previous_row=Row_Positn endif;}
1489 {   endif}
1490 {   loop}
1491 {else}
1492 {   ++count;}
1493 {endif}
1494 {do while ELEMENT_TYPE != @Band_Element && !eoc(ecursor)}
1495 {   inner_loop=1;}
1496 //
```

(continued)

```
1497 {   if FLD_SUPPRESS then}
1498 {      ++xsrv;}
1499 {   endif}
1500 //
1501 {   if FLD_HIDDEN || not isopen goto noprint endif}
1502 //
1503 // List type is TEXT or FIELD?
1504 //
1505 {   if ELEMENT_TYPE == @Text_Element || ELEMENT_TYPE == @Fld_Element then}
1506 {      if pre_type && maxrow == Row_Positn then}
1507 {         samerow=1;}
1508 {      else}
1509 {         samerow=0;}
1510 {         combine=0;}
1511 {         first_combine=1;}
1512 {      endif}
1513 {   endif}
1514 //
1515 // Output carriage returns for dBASE report
1516 //
1517 {   if !bandedit then}
1518 {      nextline1:}
1519 {      if maxrow < Row_Positn then}
1520 ?
1521 {         ++maxrow;}
1522 {         goto nextline1;}
1523 {      endif}
1524 {   else}
1525 {      maxrow=Row_Positn;}
1526 {   endif}
1527 //
1528 // Insert heading code for no page number
1529 //
1530 {      if !optl_heading && bandtype == Page_Header &&
1531       Row_Positn > bandrow+1 && !suppress_line then}
1532 *-- Print HEADING parameter ie. REPORT FORM <name> HEADING <expC>
1533 IF .NOT. gl_plain .AND. gn_length > 0
1534    ?? gc_heading FUNCTION "I;V"+LTRIM(STR(_rmargin-_lmargin))
1535    ?
1536 ENDIF
1537 {         optl_heading=1;}
1538 {      endif}
1539 //
1540 {   pre_type=0;}
1541 //
1542 {   case ELEMENT_TYPE of}
1543 {   @Text_Element:}
1544 //
1545 {      x=Col_Positn;}
1546 {      i=LEN(Text_Item);}
1547 {      ni=0;}
1548 {      pre_type=1;}
```

(continued)

```
1549 {    if i == 237 then}
1550 {      foreach Text_Item fcursor in ecursor}
1551 {        if ni then}
1552 {          i=i+LEN(Text_Item);}
1553 {          temp=Text_Item;}
1554 {        endif}
1555 {        ++ni;}
1556 {      next}
1557 {    endif}
1558 {    current_column=x+i;}
1559 {  ++ecursor;}
1560 {  nextrow=Row_Positn;}
1561 {  if ELEMENT_TYPE == @Text_Element || ELEMENT_TYPE == @Fld_Element then}
1562 {    if current_column == Col_Positn && maxrow == Row_Positn then}
1563 {      combine=1;}
1564 {    else}
1565 {      combine=0;}
1566 {    endif}
1567 {    if (bandtype == Page_Header || bandtype == Page_Footer) &&
1568        ELEMENT_TYPE == @Fld_Element && nextrow == maxrow then}
1569 {      if FLD_FIELDTYPE == Pred_data && FLD_PREDEFINE == 3 then}
1570 {        --ecursor;}
1571 {        if SUBSTR(UPPER(Text_Item),1,4) == "PAGE" then
1572            suppress_line=1;
1573          endif}
1574 {        ++ecursor;}
1575 {        if suppress_line then}
1576 {          ++ecursor;}
1577 {          if !eoc(ecursor) && Row_Positn == nextrow then}
1578 {            suppress_line=2;}
1579 {          endif}
1580 {          --ecursor;}
1581 {        endif}
1582 {      endif}
1583 {    endif}
1584 {  endif}
1585 {  --ecursor;}
1586 //
1587 {.   if suppress_line == 1 &&
1588      (bandtype == Page_Header || bandtype == Page_Footer) then
1589        plainopt(ecursor);
1590      endif}
1591 {  if isnew then}
1592 {    isnew=0;}
1593 ?? \
1594 {  else}
1595 {    if samerow then}
1596 ?? \
1597 {    else}
1598 ?? \
1599 {    endif}
1600 {  endif}
```

(continued)

```
1601 {    if suppress_line == 2 then}
1602 IIF(gl_plain,'' , \
1603 {    endif}
1604 {    if i > 70 then}
1605 ;
1606 {       seperate(Text_Item);}
1607 {       if ni then}
1608 + "{temp}";
1609 {          endif}
1610 {    else}
1611 "{Text_Item}" \
1612 {    endif}
1613 {    if suppress_line == 2 then}
1614 ) \
1615 {       suppress_line=0;}
1616 {    endif}
1617 {  @Box_Element:}
1618 DEFINE BOX FROM {nul2zero(BOX_LEFT)} TO {nul2zero(BOX_LEFT)+BOX_WIDTH-1} \
1619 HEIGHT {BOX_HEIGHT} \
1620 {    case BOX_TYPE of}
1621 {    0: // Single}
1622 SINGLE
1623 {    1: // Double}
1624 DOUBLE
1625 {    2: // Defined}
1626 CHR({BOX_SPECIAL_CHAR})
1627 {    endcase}
1628 {    nextrow=Row_Positn;}
1629 {  @Page_Element:}
1630 EJECT PAGE
1631 {  @Para_Element:}
1632 ?
1633 {  @Ruler_Element:}
1634 _indent={nul2zero(RULER_INDENT)}
1635 _lmargin={nul2zero(RULER_LEFTM)}
1636 _pcolno={nul2zero(RULER_LEFTM)}
1637 _rmargin={RULER_RIGHTM}
1638 _tabs=\
1639 {    if LEN(RULER_TABS) > 70 then}
1640 ;
1641 {       seperate(RULER_TABS);}
1642
1643 {    else}
1644 "{RULER_TABS}"
1645 {    endif}
1646 {  @Fld_Element:}
1647 //
1648 {    x=Col_Positn;}
1649 {    i=FLD_REPWIDTH;}
1650 {    ni=0;}
1651 {    pre_type=1;}
1652 {    if i > 237 then}
```

(continued)

```
1653 {       foreach FLD_TEMPLATE fcursor in ecursor}
1654 {          if ni then}
1655 {             temp2=FLD_TEMPLATE; }
1656 {          endif}
1657 {          ++ni; }
1658 {       next}
1659 {     endif}
1660 {     current_column=x+i; }
1661 //
1662 {     ++ecursor; }
1663 {     nextrow=Row_Positn; }
1664 {     if ELEMENT_TYPE == @Text_Element || ELEMENT_TYPE == @Fld_Element then}
1665 {       if current_column == Col_Positn && maxrow == Row_Positn then}
1666 {          combine=1; }
1667 {       else}
1668 {          combine=0; }
1669 {       endif}
1670 {     endif}
1671 {     --ecursor; }
1672 //
1673 {     k=0; }
1674 {     x=0; }
1675 {     priv_vars2=""; }
1676 {     if dBASE_III_PLUS == 2 && CHR(FLD_VALUE_TYPE) == "C" &&
1677        (FLD_FIELDTYPE == Tabl_data || FLD_FIELDTYPE == Calc_data) then}
1678 {       priv_vars="TRIM("; }
1679 {       x=1; }
1680 {     else}
1681 {       priv_vars=""; }
1682 {     endif}
1683 {     d=0;
1684       if GROUP > 50 then
1685         case FLD_FIELDTYPE of
1686         Tabl_data: d=1;
1687         Calc_data: if GROUP < 97 && !FLD_HIDDEN && FLD_FIELDNAME &&
1688             FLD_VALUE_TYPE == 67 then d=1; endif
1688         Pred_data: if GROUP < 97 && FLD_PREDEFINE == 2 then d=1; endif
1689         endcase
1690       endif
1691       if d then}
1692 {       priv_vars="r_foot"+STR(current_group_footer_field); }
1693 {       ++current_group_footer_field; }
1694 {     else}
1695 {     case FLD_FIELDTYPE of}
1696 {     Tabl_data:}
1697 // With ALIAS
1698 //{      priv_vars=priv_vars+FLD_FILENAME+"->"+FLD_FIELDNAME; }
1699 // Without ALIAS
1700 {       priv_vars=priv_vars+FLD_FIELDNAME; }
1701 {     Calc_data:}
1702 {       if FLD_FIELDNAME then}
1703 {          priv_vars=priv_vars+FLD_FIELDNAME; }
```

(continued)

```
1704 {       else}
1705 {         foreach FLD_EXPRESSION fcursor in ecursor}
1706 {           if k then}
1707 {             priv_vars2=FLD_EXPRESSION;}
1708 {           endif}
1709 {           ++k;}
1710 {         next}
1711 {         if (UPPER(SUBSTR(LTRIM(FLD_EXPRESSION),1,5))) != "TRIM(" then}
1712 {           priv_vars=priv_vars+FLD_EXPRESSION;}
1713 {         else}
1714 {           priv_vars=FLD_EXPRESSION;}
1715 {           x=0;}
1716 {         endif}
1717 {       endif}
1718 {    Pred_data:}
1719 {       case FLD_PREDEFINE of}
1720 {       0: // Date}
1721 {         priv_vars="gd_date";}
1722 {       1: // Time}
1723 {         priv_vars="gc_time";}
1724 {       2: // Recno}
1725 {         priv_vars="RECNO()";}
1726 {       3: // Pageno}
1727 {         priv_vars="_pageno";}
1728 {       endcase}
1729 {    Summ_data:}
1730 {       if !FLD_FIELDNAME then}
1731 {         ++xsum;}
1732 {         priv_vars="r_msum"+STR(xsum);}
1733 //{       case FLD_OPERATION of}
1734 //{       0: // Average}
1735 //{         priv_vars=priv_vars+"[3]";}
1736 //{       5: // standard deviation}
1737 //{         priv_vars=priv_vars+"[5]";}
1738 //{       6: // variance}
1739 //{         priv_vars=priv_vars+"[5]";}
1740 //{       endcase}
1741 {       else}
1742 {         priv_vars=FLD_FIELDNAME;}
1743 //{       case FLD_OPERATION of}
1744 //{       0: // Average}
1745 //{         priv_vars=FLD_FIELDNAME+"[3]";}
1746 //{       5: // standard deviation}
1747 //{         priv_vars=FLD_FIELDNAME+"[5]";}
1748 //{       6: // variance}
1749 //{         priv_vars=FLD_FIELDNAME+"[5]";}
1750 //{       otherwise: // count, min, max or sum}
1751 //{         priv_vars=FLD_FIELDNAME;}
1752 //{       endcase}
1753 {       endif}
1754 {    endcase}
```

(continued)

```
1755 {    endif}
1756 {    if x then}
1757 {      priv_vars2=priv_vars2+")";}
1758 {    endif}
1759 {    if !suppress_line &&
1760      (bandtype == Page_Header || bandtype == Page_Footer) then}
1761 {      plainopt(ecursor);}
1762 {    endif}
1763 //
1764 // For output of suppress repeated value memo fields
1765 //
1766 {    if FLD_SUPPRESS && CHR(FLD_VALUE_TYPE) == "M" then}
1767 lf_temp=\
1768 {      goto memo_patch1}
1769 {    endif}
1770 {    memo_patch2:}
1771 {    if isnew then}
1772 {      isnew=0;}
1773 ?? \
1774 {    else}
1775 {      if samerow then}
1776 , \
1777 {      else}
1778 ?? \
1779 {      endif}
1780 {    endif}
1781 {    if FLD_SUPPRESS && CHR(FLD_VALUE_TYPE) == "M" then}
1782 &lf_temp. \
1783 {      goto memo_patch3}
1784 {    endif}
1785 {    memo_patch1:}
1786 //
1787 // Suppress repeated values?
1788 //
1789 {    if FLD_SUPPRESS then}
1790 IIF(\
1791 //
1792 // Date field?
1793 //
1794 {      if CHR(FLD_VALUE_TYPE) == "D" then}
1795 DTOS(r_msrv{xsrv}) \
1796 {      else}
1797 r_msrv{xsrv} \
1798 {      endif}
1799 <> \
1800 //
1801 // Date field?
1802 //
1803 {      if CHR(FLD_VALUE_TYPE) == "D" then}
1804 DTOS({priv_vars}{priv_vars2})\
1805 {      else}
```

(continued)

```
1806 //
1807 // Memo field?   ·
1808 //
1809 {       if CHR(FLD_VALUE_TYPE) == "M" then}
1810 LEFT({priv_vars},254)\
1811 {       else}
1812 {priv_vars}{priv_vars2}
1813 {       endif}
1814 {     endif}
1815 //
1816 // Memo field?
1817 //
1818 {       if CHR(FLD_VALUE_TYPE) == "M" then}
1819 ,[{priv_vars}],[""])
1820 {       else}
1821 ,{priv_vars}{priv_vars2},"") \
1822 {       endif}
1823 {     else}
1824 {       priv_vars}{priv_vars2} \
1825 {     endif}
1826 {     if FLD_SUPPRESS && CHR(FLD_VALUE_TYPE) == "M" then}
1827 {       goto memo_patch2}
1828 {     endif}
1829 {     memo_patch3:}
1830 {     j=0;}
1831 {     if FLD_PICFUN then}
1832 {       temp=FLD_PICFUN;}
1833 {       j=AT("V",temp) | AT("H",temp);}
1834 {       if not j then}
1835 FUNCTION "{FLD_PICFUN}" \
1836 {       else}
1837 {         if not AT("H",temp) then
1838             if j < LEN(FLD_PICFUN) then
1839               temp=SUBSTR(temp,1,j)+STR(i)+SUBSTR(temp,j+1);
1840             else
1841               temp=temp+STR(i);
1842             endif
1843           endif}
1844 FUNCTION "{temp}" \
1845 {       endif}
1846 {     endif}
1847 {     temp=FLD_TEMPLATE+temp2;}
1848 {     if FLD_VALUE_TYPE == 67 then
1849         if FLD_LENGTH == FLD_REPWIDTH && temp == REPLICATE("X",FLD_LENGTH)
              then
1850           j=FLD_LENGTH;
1851         endif
1852       endif}
1853 {     if not j then}
1854 //
1855 // test for invalid picture templates
```

(continued)

```
1856 //
1857 {       if temp && (FLD_FIELDTYPE != Pred_data || FLD_PREDEFINE != 1) &&
1858         CHR(FLD_VALUE_TYPE) != "D" then}
1859 {        if i > 70 then}
1860 PICTURE ;
1861 {            seperate(temp);}
1862 {         else}
1863 PICTURE "{FLD_TEMPLATE}" \
1864 {         endif}
1865 {       endif}
1866 {     endif}
1867 {  endcase}
1868 //
1869 // Style of output ie. BOLD, UNDERLINE and ITALICS.
1870 //
1871 {  if FLD_STYLE then}
1872 STYLE "\
1873 {    if Bold & FLD_STYLE then}
1874 B\
1875 {    endif}
1876 {    if Italic & FLD_STYLE then}
1877 I\
1878 {    endif}
1879 {    if Underline & FLD_STYLE then}
1880 U\
1881 {    endif}
1882 {    if Superscript & FLD_STYLE then}
1883 R\
1884 {    endif}
1885 {    if Subscript & FLD_STYLE then}
1886 L\
1887 {    endif}
1888 {    if User_Font & FLD_STYLE then}
1889 {      if  1 & FLD_STYLE then}1{endif}\
1890 {      if  2 & FLD_STYLE then}2{endif}\
1891 {      if  4 & FLD_STYLE then}3{endif}\
1892 {      if  8 & FLD_STYLE then}4{endif}\
1893 {      if 16 & FLD_STYLE then}5{endif}\
1894 {    endif}
1895 " \
1896 {  endif}
1897 //
1898 // List type is TEXT or FIELD?
1899 //
1900 {  if (ELEMENT_TYPE == @Text_Element || ELEMENT_TYPE == @Fld_Element) then}
1901 //
1902 // not a word wrap band?
1903 //
1904 {     if !bandedit && first_combine then}
1905 AT {Col_Positn}\
1906 {        if maxrow == nextrow then}
```

(continued)

```
1907 ,
1908 {       else}
1909
1910 {       endif}
1911 {       isnew=1;}
1912 {     else}
1913 {       if maxrow == nextrow then}
1914 ,
1915 {         isnew=1;}
1916 {       else}
1917
1918 {       endif}
1919 {     endif}
1920 //
1921 // ***********************
1922 //
1923 {     if FLD_SUPPRESS && bsrv != xsrv then}
1924 //
1925 IF .NOT. (r_msrv{xsrv} = \
1926 //
1927 {       if !FLD_FIELDNAME then}
1928 {         if FLD_FIELDTYPE == Calc_data then}
1929 {           foreach FLD_EXPRESSION fcursor in k}
1930 {FLD_EXPRESSION}
1931 {           next}
1932 {         endif}
1933 {         if FLD_FIELDTYPE == Summ_data then}
1934 r_msum{xsum}\
1935 {         endif}
1936 {       else}
1937 {         if CHR(FLD_VALUE_TYPE) == "M" then}
1938 LEFT({FLD_FIELDNAME},254)\
1939 {         else}
1940 {FLD_FIELDNAME}
1941 {         endif}
1942 {       endif}
1943 )
1944 {       if !FLD_FIELDNAME then}
1945    r_msrv{xsrv}=\
1946 {         if FLD_FIELDTYPE == Calc_data then}
1947 {           foreach FLD_EXPRESSION fcursor in k}
1948 {FLD_EXPRESSION}
1949 {           next}
1950
1951 {         endif}
1952 {         if FLD_FIELDTYPE == Summ_data then}
1953 r_msum{xsum}
1954 {         endif}
1955 {       else}
1956    r_msrv{xsrv}={FLD_FIELDNAME}
1957 {       endif}
```

(continued)

```
1958 ENDIF
1959 {    endif}
1960 //
1961 {    samerow=1;}
1962 {    if first_combine && combine then}
1963 {       first_combine=0;}
1964 {    endif}
1965 //
1966 {    if !combine && !first_combine then}
1967 {       first_combine=1;}
1968 {    endif}
1969 {  endif}
1970 {  if bandtype == Page_Header || bandtype == Page_Footer then}
1971 {    x=0;}
1972 {    if previous_row < maxrow && nextrow > maxrow &&
1973        FLD_FIELDTYPE == Pred_data &&
1974        (!FLD_PREDEFINE || FLD_PREDEFINE == 3) then
1975        x=1;
1976      endif}
1977 {    if x || (suppress_line && nextrow > maxrow) then}
1978 {       if suppress_line && nextrow > maxrow then suppress_line=0; endif}
1979 //
1980 {       if optl_heading && nextrow > maxrow then}
1981 ?
1982 {          ++maxrow;}
1983 {       endif}
1984 {       lmarg(1);}
1985 ENDIF
1986 //
1987 // Insert heading code if pageno exists
1988 //
1989 {       if !optl_heading && bandtype == Page_Header && bandrow+1 ==
              Row_Positn
1990         && FLD_FIELDTYPE == Pred_data && FLD_PREDEFINE == 3 then}
1991 *-- Print HEADING parameter ie. REPORT FORM <name> HEADING <expC>
1992 IF .NOT. gl_plain .AND. gn_length > 0
1993    ?? " "
1994    ?? gc_heading FUNCTION "I;V"+;
1995    LTRIM(STR(_rmargin-_lmargin-(_pcolno*2+2)))
1996 ENDIF
1997 {       if nextrow > maxrow then}
1998 IF .NOT. gl_plain
1999    ?
2000 ENDIF
2001 {          ++maxrow;}
2002 {          isnew=1;}
2003 {       endif}
2004 {       optl_heading=1;}
2005 {     endif}
2006 //
2007 {    endif}
```

(continued)

```
2008 {  endif}
2009 {  noprint:}
2010 {  x=0;}
2011 {  previous_row=Row_Positn;}
2012 {  ++ecursor;}
2013 {enddo}
2014 {if inner_loop then --ecursor; endif}
2015 {next ecursor;}
2016 //
2017 // Output carriage returns for dBASE report to handle blank lines
2018 //
2019 {nextline3:}
2020 {if maxrow < bandhgt then}
2021 {  if isopen then}
2022 ?
2023 {  endif}
2024 {  ++maxrow;}
2025 {  goto nextline3;}
2026 {endif}
2027 {if bandtype == Report_Summary && is_rsumm_open then}
2028 gl_fandl=.F.
2029 ?
2030 RETURN
2031 * EOP: Rsumm
2032 {endif}
2033 {if bandtype == Page_Footer then}
2034 {  finish_page_footer();}
2035 {endif}
2036
2037 *-- Process page break when PLAIN option is used.
2038 PROCEDURE Pgplain
2039 PRIVATE _box
2040 EJECT PAGE
2041 {if number_of_reset_on_page || number_of_fld_suppress then}
2042 IF gl_fandl
2043    DO Pageinit
2044 ENDIF
2045 {endif}
2046 {if maxgrp > 3 && number_of_open_group_intros then}
2047 IF gn_level = 0 .AND. gl_fandl
2048    gn_level=1
2049    DO Grphead
2050 ENDIF
2051 {endif}
2052 RETURN
2053 * EOP: Pgplain
2054
2055 *-- Reset dBASE environment prior to calling report
2056 PROCEDURE Reset
2057 SET SPACE &gc_space.
2058 SET TALK &gc_talk.
```

(continued)

```
2059 ON ESCAPE
2060 ON PAGE
2061 RETURN
2062 * EOP: Reset
2063
2064 {if !count then pause(report_empty + any_key); endif}
2065 {Nogen:}
2066 {return 0;}
2067 //------------------------------
2068 // End of main template procedure
2069 // User defined functions follow
2070 //------------------------------
2071 {define nul2zero(number);
2072  if !number then
2073    number=0;
2074  endif
2075  return number;
2076  enddef
2077 }
2078 //
2079 {
2080  define seperate(string);
2081  var x,y,length;
2082  x=1;
2083  length=LEN(string);
2084  moreleft:
2085  if x <= length then
2086    if x != 1 then}
2087 + \
2088 {  endif
2089    if x+70 <= length then y=70; else y=length-x+1; endif}
2090 "{SUBSTR(string,x,y)}";
2091 {  x=x+70;
2092    goto moreleft;
2093  endif
2094  return;
2095  enddef
2096 }
2097 {define plainopt(cursor);
2098  var temp; temp=0;
2099    if previous_row < maxrow && nextrow > maxrow &&
2100    cursor.FLD_FIELDTYPE == Pred_data &&
2101    (!cursor.FLD_PREDEFINE || cursor.FLD_PREDEFINE == 3) then
2102      temp=1;
2103    endif}
2104 {  if temp || suppress_line then}
2105 IF .NOT. gl_plain
2106 {    LMARG(4);
2107    else
2108      if cursor.FLD_FIELDTYPE == Pred_data &&
2109      (!cursor.FLD_PREDEFINE || cursor.FLD_PREDEFINE == 3) then
```

(continued)

```
2110         if !cursor.FLD_PREDEFINE then
2111           priv_vars="IIF(gl_plain,'',gd_date)";
2112         else
2113           priv_vars="IIF(gl_plain,'',_pageno)";
2114         endif
2115       endif
2116     endif
2117  return;
2118  enddef}
2119 {define finish_page_footer();}
2120 {   if suppress_line then
2121       suppress_line=0;}
2122 //
2123 {     LMARG(1);}
2124 ENDIF
2125 {   endif}
2126 {   if isopen && bandhgt+1 then}
2127 ENDIF
2128 {   endif}
2129 {   if demo_version then}
2130 ? "{demo_string}" FUNCTION "IV"+LTRIM(STR(_rmargin-_lmargin))
2131 {   endif}
2132 EJECT PAGE
2133 {   if number_of_begin_new_pages then}
2134 gl_newpage=.T.
2135 {   endif}
2136 *-- is the page number greater than the ending page
2137 IF _pageno > _pepage
2138     GOTO BOTTOM
2139     SKIP
2140     gn_level=0
2141 ENDIF
2142 {   if number_of_reset_on_page || number_of_fld_suppress then}
2143 IF gl_fandl
2144     DO Pageinit
2145 ENDIF
2146 {   endif}
2147 {   if is_page_header_open || (is_rintro_open && FRAME_PAGEHEADINGS)
2148     || number_of_open_group_intros then}
2149 IF .NOT. gl_plain .AND. gl_fandl
2150 {if bandspacing then}
2151     _pspacing={bandspacing}
2152 {else}
2153     _pspacing=gn_pspace
2154 {endif}
2155     DO Pghead
2156 ENDIF
2157 {   endif}
2158 {   if maxgrp > 3 && number_of_open_group_intros then}
2159 IF gn_level = 0 .AND. gl_fandl
2160     gn_level=1
```

(continued)

```
2161    DO Grphead
2162 ENDIF
2163 {  endif}
2164 gl_widow=.T.          && enable widow checking
2165 RETURN
2166 * EOP: Pgfoot
2167 {return;
2168  enddef}
2169 // EOP: REPORT.COD
2170
```

Part II

Building and Documenting Applications

In this section, we're going to shift gears and focus on using the three major elements of the applications generator: quick applications, the full applications generator, and the applications documentation template. Although each of these three chapters will include full listings of the three COD files, the listings will be there for reference rather than for the kind of detailed analysis we went through in Part I.

One note on the source code listings (contained in the Appendix to each chapter). These listings were created by specifying the -o <file name> option with the template compiler. The output file will include complete listings of all modules referenced with the include template command and with the line numbers from each file printed. The output file was loaded into the dBASE IV MODIFY COMMAND editor and listed to a file with line numbers. This produces a file with unique line numbers to the left of the line numbers in each of the included files. While this may sound confusing, take a look at this bit of code to see how it works:

```
 6      6:   Quick Application Template
 7      7:   -------------------------
 8      8:   Version 1.58
 9      9:   Ashton-Tate (c) 1987, 1988
10     10:
11     11:   {
12     12:    include "applctn.def";  // Applicaton selectors
13      1:   //-------------------------------------------------
```

```
14     2:  // APPLCTN.DEF                Application object(s) data
               selectors
15     3:  // Ashton-Tate (c) 1987, 1988
16     4:  //
17     5:  // Updated 9-21-88 KJN
18     6:  //
19     7:  // This include file contains all the selectors required
               for applications.
20     8:  // *** DO NOT CHANGE ANY OF THE NUMBERS BELOW ***
21     9:  //
```

Note that line 12 (12:) in the file QUICKAPP.COD is an include statement. The following line in the output file is numbered 1:, the line number in APPLCTN.DEF. Our line numbers for the two lines are 12 and 13, thus making for easy reference.

To shorten the listings, I have removed from each the listing of selectors. If you use this technique, some selectors will be listed depending on the placement of the #lstoff and #lston commands.

Chapter 7

Quick Applications

One of the greatest things about the dBASE IV applications generator (Apps-Gen) is the quick application template, QUICKAPP.COD. Think about a basic database application and what you want it to do. First, it will manage a single database file. It allows data display, appending, browsing, and editing using a custom screen format when appropriate. It lets you search records using an index or a non-indexed search (LOCATE). It lets you print reports and mailing labels. And it does all this from a menu system that's easy to use.

That's basically what the quick application module does for you. All you have to do is fill in the names of the database, the primary index (if any), the screen form file, the report format file, the label format file, and pick "Generate quick application." (There are a couple of other things to fill in, but they're simple items like your name.)

This chapter discusses the major features of the quick applications generator and shows how they relate to a generated application program. A few changes to the basic template file are included. However, in general the AppsGen templates handle special procedures much better than the object-specific ones.

There are several deficiencies in the quick application generator. Later, we'll correct a number of them.

QUICKAPP.GEN takes about 21K of disk space. In that sense, it is shorter than either LABEL.GEN or REPORT.GEN. However, the quick application presumes you have already built any screen forms, reports, and labels you want to use. Its main function is to put together a menu system and searching capabilities. QUICKAPP.COD is a short template program that uses the selectors defined in a number of DEF and COD files. After including all these

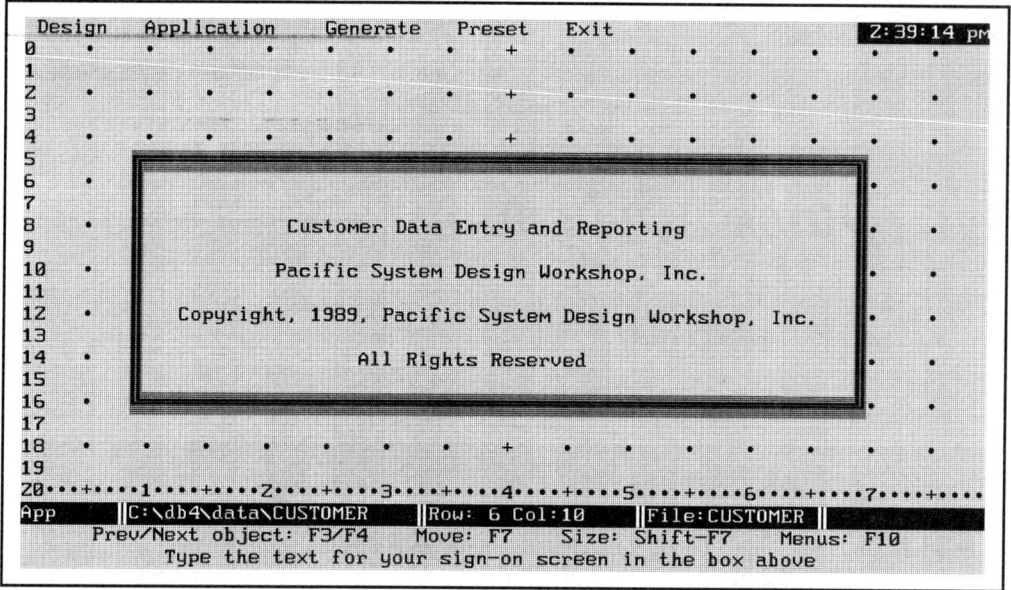

Figure 7-1   A Splash Screen

files, the total length is 1,032 lines. A complete listing of the August 29, 1988, version with line numbers is included in Appendix A.

The applications generator is the only activity in the Control Center that lets you pick the template you want to use for generation. However, for the quick application, the file QUICKAPP.GEN must still be used. The next chapter discusses switching templates in the context of a general-purpose application program. Note that there is no DOS SET command that will let you easily switch to a QUICKAPP.GEN under a different name.

A Quick Application

Using CUSTOMER.DBF, a typical quick application is easy to build. Figures 7-1 through 7-5 show the basic setup. Note that several of the application objects (screen form, report, labels) were developed in previous chapters. Also note that the option to display the "splash screen" (the sign-on banner) is switched on or off using the Application/Display sign-on banner menu.

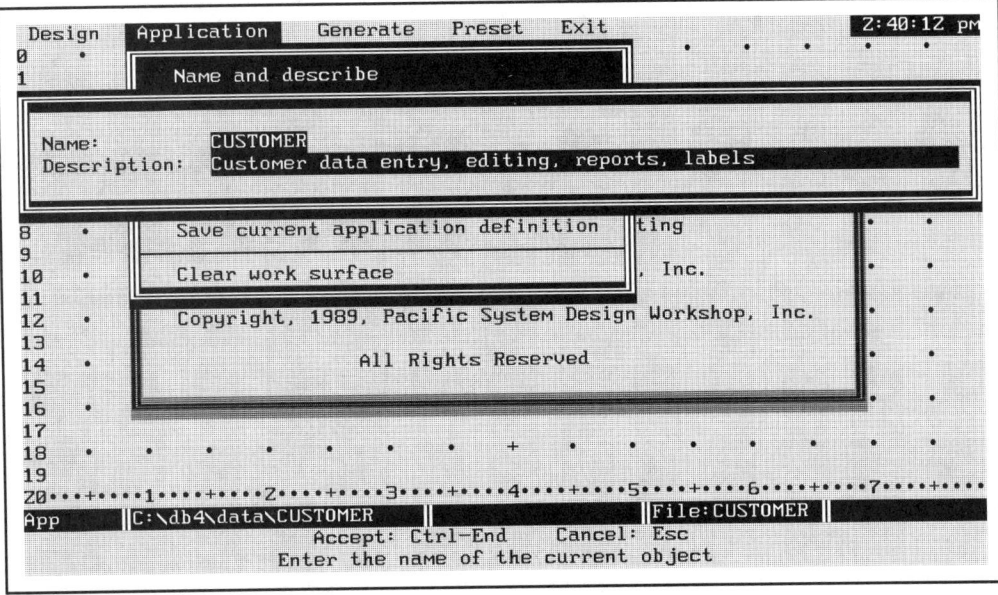

Figure 7-2 The Application/Name and Describe Menu

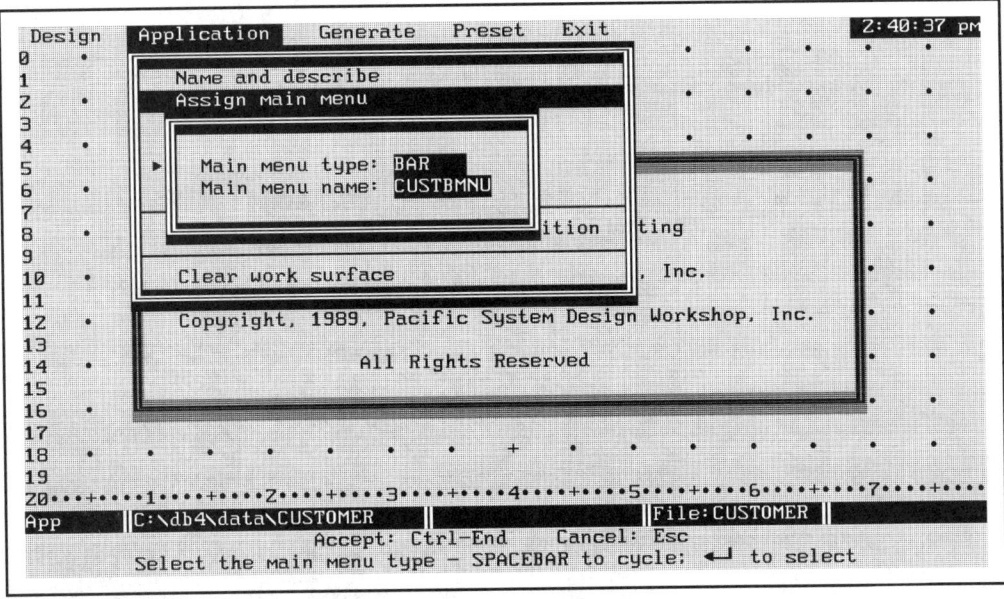

Figure 7-3 The Application/Assign Main Menu Menu

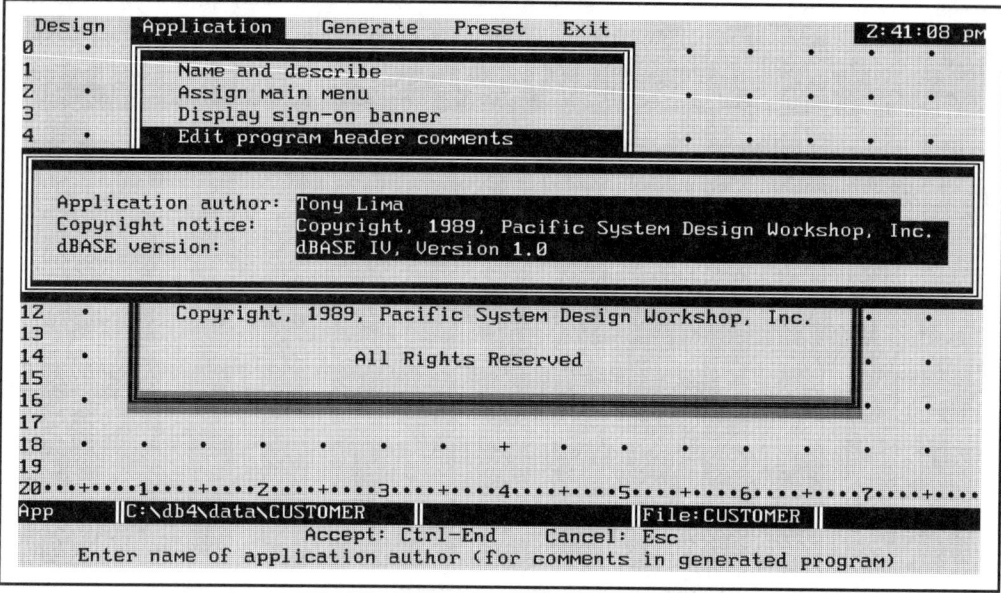

Figure 7-4 The Application/Edit Program Header Comments Menu

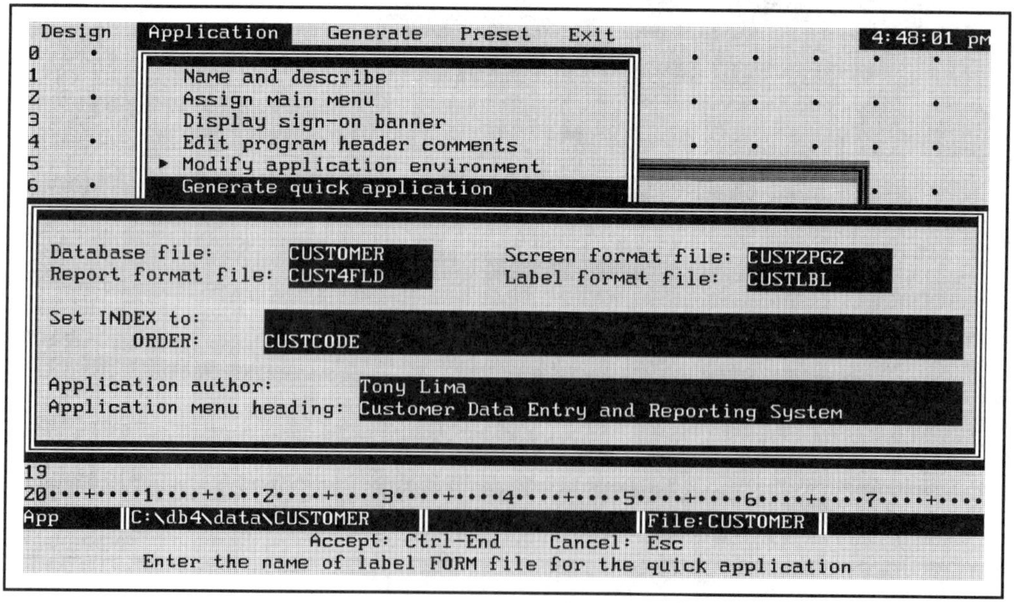

Figure 7-5 The Application/Generate Quick Application Menu

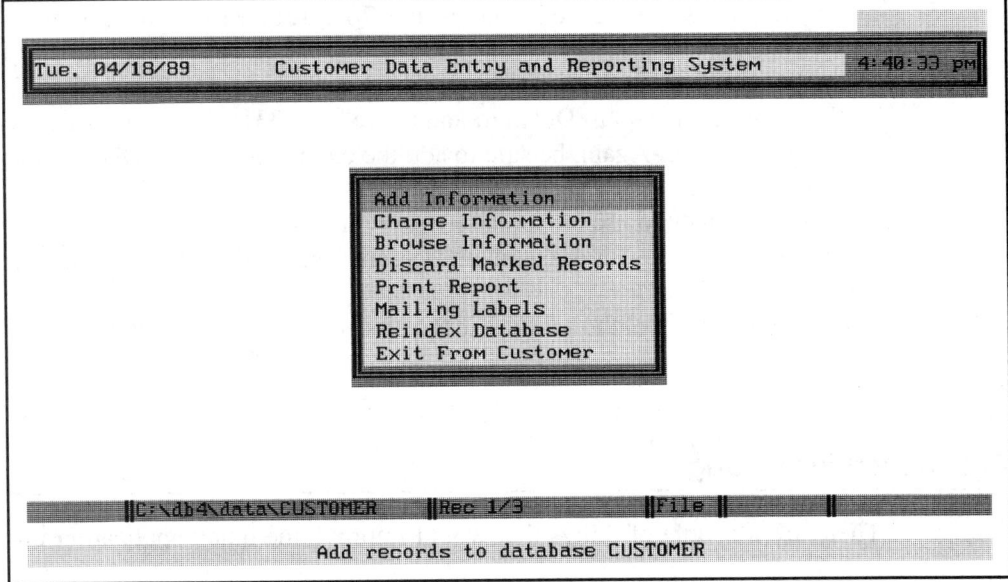

Figure 7-6   The Quick Application Main Menu

Once the quick-application definition screen (Figure 7-5) is set up, press Ctrl-End to generate the application. Appendix B shows a listing of the finished program. Figure 7-6 shows the opening menu for this application.

Comments and Fixes

There are several changes that you should make to the different source code files that make up QUICKAPP.COD. First, note lines 30–42 and 44–64. The first block stores the current values of different SET commands to memory variables. The second block is basic housekeeping. Both are best placed in procedures rather than the main program. This means moving lines 317–329 and 331–363 of QUICKAPP.COD (combined file line numbers) to the procedure generating section of the program. I recommend changing line 318 to read:

```
DO Setstore WITH gc_bell,gc_carry,gc_clock,gc_century,gc_confirm,;
   gc_deli,gc_escape,gc_instruc,gc_safety,gc_status,;
   gc_score,gc_talk
```

and moving lines 317–329 to just below line 764. Be sure to add the command PROCEDURE Setstore before the code and a RETURN at the end. Also add the WITH clause unless you're going to declare all these variables PUBLIC.

Next, change line 44 to DO Start and move lines 331–363 to just after the Setstore procedure. Again, be sure to add the command PROCEDURE Start and a RETURN.

You might want to use the same process with lines 480–494 and 496–507. There's no reason to clutter the main program with all these SET commands and functions.

Fortunately, most of the action is in the procedures. Let's look at them next.

Recommended Changes

There are a couple of things that would improve the quick application immensely:

- Fix a number of errors and clean up the generated code.
- Currently, only one index is used throughout the program. However, for printing reports with groups, a different index may be required. The quick application should let you swap indexes with an easy menu selection.
- Omit the sample labels bar from the report menu popup.

Rather than going through QUICKAPP.COD in minute detail, let's see how to implement the above four changes. The program header produced by the applications generator is already pretty good, so we don't have to fool around with that. (If you like, you can add the multiuser code developed in Chapters 4, 5, and 6 to QUICKAPP. However, we won't go through the details here.)

Fixes

The most obvious problem is with lines 101–102 in CUSTOMER.PRG:

```
101 USE CUSTOMER
102 SET ORDER TO CUSTCODE
```

More efficient code is simply:

```
USE CUSTOMER ORDER CUSTCODE
```

This is an easy change to QUICKAPP.COD. The user-defined template function DBFOPEN() sets up the USE command. Change lines 970–976 (Appendix A line numbers) to read:

```
// USE {mdbf} {if mndx then}INDEX {mndx}{endif}
USE {mdbf} {if mndx then}\
INDEX {mndx}
{             else}\
{    if mord then}
// Following code modified by Tony Lima, April 20, 1989
// SET ORDER TO {mord}
ORDER {mord}
{    endif
        endif
   endif
  return;
 enddef;
```

Feel free to leave out the lines I've commented out with //. They're included above so you can see what the original code was and what I've changed it to. I'll leave it to you to sort out the variables and selectors — their meaning is pretty obvious.

The next problem is with reports and labels. When you send them to the screen instead of the printer, they scroll right off the screen. This is easily fixed by using the print-system memory variables _plength (numeric type, page length) and _pwait (pause after each page). First, let's add code to figure out the screen size. We'll also add a couple of new variables. This code block should be inserted after line 232 in QUICKAPP.COD. Add the comma after the display variable, then add the three new variables mdxchoice, dB_status and scrn_size.

```
        display, // Type of display
        mdxchoice, // Added by Tony Lima to handle order menu
        dB_status, // Added by Tony Lima to handle status
        scrn_size  // Added by Tony Lima to handle screen size
    ;
```

The next block of code is borrowed from FORM.COD. Place it after line 252 in QUICKAPP. It determines the screen size, and stores it to the variable.

```
// Following line commented out and replaced with
//  block after that, Tony Lima, April 21, 1989
// display = numset(_flgcolor);

// Test screen size if display > 2 screen is 43 lines
display = numset(_flgcolor);
if display > ega25 then scrn_size = 39 else scrn_size = 21 endif;

// Test to see if status was off before going into form designer
dB_status = numset(_flgstatus);
if scrn_size == 21 and !db_status then
   scrn_size = 24;
endif
if scrn_size == 39 and !db_status then // status is off
   scrn_size = 42;
endif
// End of Tony Lima block
```

Next, we have to store the scrn_size template variable to a dBASE memory variable. Place the following code after line 316 in QUICKAPP. By subtracting 3 from the screen size, we allow enough room for the screen header block.

```
*-- Initialize screen size variable
ln_scrsize = {scrn_size} - 3
```

In setting up pop-up menus, the template variable barcnt is used to keep track of the current bar number. In much of the code, this variable is incremented with the syntax barcnt=barcnt+1. I recommend changing this to ++barcnt, using the operator rather than a command. This will slightly increase the efficiency of generating code.

Better Reports and Labels

Let's see how to improve reports and labels next. Virtually all the changes are included in the following DO CASE structure. Use this code to replace lines 448–459 of QUICKAPP. The variables ln_plength and ln_pwait are used to store the current values of the print system variables _plength and _pwait. Those are then set to the screen length and .T. if the report is to be sent to the screen, then reset after the report or label is run.

This block of code also corrects a minor error in the report and label generation code. The correction is:

```
{
        // Following fix by Tony Lima, April 21, 1989
        // lc_toprnt = 'TO PRINT'
}
        lc_toprnt = lc_toprnt+'TO PRINT'
        ON ERROR DO prntrtry
```

In the original version, any scope stored in the variable lc_toprnt was overwritten if the 'TO PRINT' clause was included. The correction appends TO PRINT to any scope already there.

```
        {  if Quick_FRM}
    CASE gn_barv = {rptchoice}
        *-- Run report form {lower(Quick_FRM)}
        SET MESSAGE TO 'Pick an option to locate a record or <ESC>
          for default'
        ACTIVATE WINDOW work
        gn_recno = RECNO()
        DO position
        DEACTIVATE WINDOW work
        ln_plength = _plength
        ll_pwait = _pwait
        lc_toprnt = IIF(gn_recno <> recno(),'REST ','')
        STORE 0 TO gn_send, gn_pkey
        ACTIVATE POPUP prntchk
{
        // Following IF added by Tony Lima to correct
        // for screen size when report sent to screen
}
        IF gn_send = 3
          _plength = ln_scrsize
          _pwait = .T.
        ENDIF && gn_send = 3
        IF gn_send = 4
{
        // Following fix by Tony Lima, April 21, 1989
        // lc_toprnt = 'TO PRINT'
}
```

```
                    lc_toprnt = lc_toprnt+'TO PRINT'
                    ON ERROR DO prntrtry
              ENDIF && gn_send = 4
              IF .NOT. gn_send = 6
                  ACTIVATE WINDOW desktop
                  IF gc_escape="OFF"
                     SET ESCAPE ON
                  ENDIF
                  REPORT FORM {Quick_FRM} &lc_toprnt.
                  IF gn_pkey <> 27
                     WAIT
                  ENDIF
                  SET ESCAPE &gc_escape.
                  _plength = ln_plength
                  _pwait = ll_pwait
                  DEACTIVATE WINDOW desktop
              ENDIF && .NOT. gn_send = 6
              GOTO gn_recno
              ON ERROR DO PAUSE WITH "Error occurred on line
      "+LTRIM(STR(LINE())) +" of procedure "+Program()
      { endif
        if Quick_LBL}
        CASE gn_barv = {lblchoice}
           *-- Run label form {lower(Quick_LBL)}
           SET MESSAGE TO 'Pick an option to locate a record or <ESC>
             for default'
           ACTIVATE WINDOW work
           gn_recno = RECNO()
           DO position
           DEACTIVATE WINDOW work
           STORE 0 TO gn_send, gn_pkey
           ln_plength = _plength
           ll_pwait = _pwait
           lc_toprnt = IIF(gn_recno <> recno(),'REST ','')
           ACTIVATE POPUP lbltchk
           DO CASE
      {
      // Following IF added by Tony Lima to correct
      // for screen size when labels sent to screen
      }
              CASE gn_send = 3
```

```
            _plength = ln_scrsize
             _pwait = .T.
         CASE gn_send = 4
{
// Following couple of lines changed to
// preserve existing value of lc_toprnt
// Tony Lima, April 21, 1989
}
             lc_toprnt = lc_toprnt+'TO PRINT'
          CASE gn_send = 5
             lc_toprnt = lc_torpnt+'TO PRINT SAMPLE'
        ENDCASE
        IF .NOT. gn_send = 6
           ACTIVATE WINDOW desktop
           IF gc_escape="OFF"
              SET ESCAPE ON
           ENDIF
           ON ERROR DO prntrtry
           LABEL FORM {Quick_LBL} &lc_toprnt.
           IF gn_pkey <> 27
              WAIT
           ENDIF
           _plength = ln_plength
           _pwait = ll_pwait
           SET ESCAPE &gc_escape.
           DEACTIVATE WINDOW desktop
        ENDIF
        GOTO gn_recno
        ON ERROR DO PAUSE WITH "Error occurred on line";
           +LTRIM(STR(LINE())) +" of procedure "+Program()
{  endif
```

Naturally, we have to change the menu as well. Replace the code from lines 440–459 with the following. Note the use of ++barcnt. Again, the code is lengthy but not especially complex. Feel free to leave out my comments. And note the use of the variable mdxchoice to keep track of whether there is an MDX file in use. (Note that the reports pop-up now omits the option to print sample labels.)

```
        DEFINE BAR {barcnt} OF quick PROMPT " Reindex Database";
          MESSAGE "Reindex database {Quick_DBF}"
```

```
{ endif
   ++barcnt;
// barcnt=barcnt+1;
// Following menu bar added by Tony Lima, April 20, 1989
   if Quick_Ordr then
      mdxchoice=barcnt;}
DEFINE BAR {barcnt} OF quick PROMPT " Select new key";
   MESSAGE "Select new primary key for {Quick_DBF}"
{ endif
      ++barcnt;
// barcnt=barcnt+1;
 strng=fileroot(quickapp);
 strng=upper(substr(strng,1,1))+lower(substr(strng,2,7));}
DEFINE BAR {barcnt} OF quick PROMPT " Exit From {strng}";
   MESSAGE "Exit program to dBASE"
ON SELECTION POPUP quick DO Action WITH BAR()
// Following code changed by Tony Lima, April 20, 1989
// Allow different menus for reports and labels
{if Quick_LBL then}
*-- Define the popup menu for label redirection
DEFINE POPUP lbltchk FROM 10,55
DEFINE BAR 1 OF lbltchk PROMPT " Send to..." SKIP
DEFINE BAR 2 OF lbltchk PROMPT REPLICATE(CHR(196),14) SKIP
DEFINE BAR 3 OF lbltchk PROMPT " Screen " MESSAGE "Screen only"
DEFINE BAR 4 OF lbltchk PROMPT " Printer" MESSAGE "Printer LPT1:"
DEFINE BAR 5 OF lbltchk PROMPT " Label Sample ";
   MESSAGE "Printer LPT1: with \
Sample label" SKIP{if Quick_LBL} FOR gn_barv <> {lblchoice}{endif}
DEFINE BAR 6 OF lbltchk PROMPT " Return";
   MESSAGE "Return to Main Menu"
ON SELECTION POPUP lbltchk DO get_sele
{endif}

{if Quick_FRM then}
*-- Define the popup menu for print redirection
DEFINE POPUP prntchk FROM 10,55
DEFINE BAR 1 OF prntchk PROMPT " Send to..." SKIP
DEFINE BAR 2 OF prntchk PROMPT REPLICATE(CHR(196),14) SKIP
DEFINE BAR 3 OF prntchk PROMPT " Screen " MESSAGE "Screen only"
DEFINE BAR 4 OF prntchk PROMPT " Printer" MESSAGE "Printer LPT1:"
DEFINE BAR 5 OF prntchk PROMPT REPLICATE(CHR(196),14) SKIP
```

```
DEFINE BAR 6 OF prntchk PROMPT " Return";
  MESSAGE "Return to Main Menu"
ON SELECTION POPUP prntchk DO get_sele
{endif}
```

Allow Index Swaps

Currently, only one index key is used throughout the application. The problem is that reports, especially those that use groups, may need a different index. You may want labels indexed on zip code rather than customer ID number. Let's add a module to allow swapping index tags. (We'll ignore the more complicated problem of swapping index files. It's easier to simply check to see if the user has selected an index file and use COPY INDEXES to add it to an existing MDX file.)

Here's how the module will work. We've already added the "Select new key" bar to the main menu. We want to automatically read every index tag and its associated key expression into two arrays, display the tags and keys in a menu, and allow the user to make the selection from the menu. The only complicating factor in all this is how to fit forty-seven of them on one screen. That's not hard — we just display the menu in three columns.

Replace line 706 with the following. Note the use of the TYPE() function to ensure that we only initialize TAGLIST[] and KEYLIST[] once. Also note the use of the dBASE ORDER() function to determine the current index key and store it to the variable lc_order. This variable is used to set the default value in the GET statement and to put an asterisk next to the current key value.

```
{  endif
if Quick_Ordr}
CASE gn_barv = {mdxchoice}
   *-- Select new primary key for {lower(Quick_DBF)}
   ACTIVATE WINDOW work
   IF TYPE("TAGLIST[1]") = "U"
     DECLARE TAGLIST[47],KEYLIST[47]
     ln_keyno = 1
     lc_order = TRIM(ORDER())
     DO WHILE LEN(TRIM(TAG(ln_keyno))) <> 0
       TAGLIST[ln_keyno] = TAG(ln_keyno)
       KEYLIST[ln_keyno] = KEY(ln_keyno)
```

```
      IF TRIM(TAGLIST[ln_keyno]) = TRIM(ORDER())
        ln_ordno = ln_keyno
      ENDIF && TRIM(TAGLIST[ln_keyno]) = TRIM(ORDER())
      ln_keyno = ln_keyno + 1
    ENDDO  &&  TAG(ln_keyno) <> ""
    ln_maxkey = ln_keyno - 1
ENDIF && TYPE("TAGLIST[1]") = "U"
@ 01,20 SAY "Select an index key to use for this report."
ln_keyno = 1
ll_break = .T.
DO WHILE ln_keyno <= ln_maxkey
  DO CASE
    CASE ln_keyno <= 16
      @ 02,04 SAY "Index Tag"
      @ 02,16 SAY "Key"
      IF TRIM(TAGLIST[ln_keyno]) = lc_order
        @ ln_keyno+2,00 SAY STR(ln_keyno,2)+".*"+;
            TAGLIST[ln_keyno]+;
          SPACE(10-LEN(TAGLIST[ln_keyno]))+"  "+;
          SUBSTR(KEYLIST[ln_keyno],1,11)
      ELSE
        @ ln_keyno+2,00 SAY STR(ln_keyno,2)+". "+;
            TAGLIST[ln_keyno]+;
          SPACE(10-LEN(TAGLIST[ln_keyno]))+"  "+;
          SUBSTR(KEYLIST[ln_keyno],1,11)
      ENDIF && TAG(ln_keyno) = lc_order
    CASE ln_keyno <= 32
      @ 02,30 SAY "Index Tag"
      @ 02,42 SAY "Key"
      IF TRIM(TAGLIST[ln_keyno]) = lc_order
        @ ln_keyno-14,26 SAY STR(ln_keyno,2)+".*"+;
            TAGLIST[ln_keyno]+;
          SPACE(10-LEN(TAGLIST[ln_keyno]))+"  "+;
          SUBSTR(KEYLIST[ln_keyno],1,11)
      ELSE
        @ ln_keyno-14,26 SAY STR(ln_keyno,2)+". "+;
            TAGLIST[ln_keyno]+;
          SPACE(10-LEN(TAGLIST[ln_keyno]))+"  "+;
          SUBSTR(KEYLIST[ln_keyno],1,11)
      ENDIF && TAG(ln_keyno) = lc_order
    CASE ln_keyno <= 47
```

```
          @ 02,56 SAY "Index Tag"
          @ 02,68 SAY "Key"
          IF TRIM(TAGLIST[ln_keyno]) = lc_order
            @ ln_keyno-30,52 SAY STR(ln_keyno,2)+".*"+;
                TAGLIST[ln_keyno]+;
              SPACE(10-LEN(TAGLIST[ln_keyno]))+"  "+;
              SUBSTR(KEYLIST[ln_keyno],1,11)
           ELSE
            @ ln_keyno-30,52 SAY STR(ln_keyno,2)+".  "+;
                TAGLIST[ln_keyno]+;
              SPACE(10-LEN(TAGLIST[ln_keyno]))+"  "+;
              SUBSTR(KEYLIST[ln_keyno],1,11)
          ENDIF && ORDER(ln_keyno) = lc_order
        ENDCASE
      ln_keyno = ln_keyno + 1
      ENDDO && WHILE ln_keyno <= ln_maxkey
      lc_choice =
IIF(LEN(STR(ln_ordno))=1,"0"+STR(ln_ordno,1),STR(ln_ordno,2))
      DO WHILE ln_keyno > ln_maxkey
        @ 19,23 SAY "Which index? " GET lc_choice PICTURE '#9' ;
          DEFAULT lc_order ;
          MESSAGE "Current tag is "+TRIM(TAGLIST[ln_ordno])+;
          " with key "+TRIM(KEYLIST[ln_ordno])+;
          ". Be sure to enter leading blank."
        READ
        ln_keyno = VAL(lc_choice)
      ENDDO
      SET ORDER TO &TAGLIST[ln_keyno]
      DEACTIVATE WINDOW work
  {  endif}
```

Now if you want to do a seek using a different key, all you have to do is switch keys first, then select the option to locate a record.

Automatically Set Data Type for SEEK

The last thing we want to do is automatically set the data type for the SEEK option for reports and labels. (Currently, the user must supply the data type guided by the fields list at the top of the screen.) Replace the code from lines

837–850 with the following. Note that these correspond to lines 73–84 in
AS_POSIT.COD.

```
              DO CASE
        CASE lc_option='3'
            *-- Seek
            IF LEN(NDX(1))=0 .AND. LEN(MDX(1))=0
                DO Pause WITH
                  "Can't use this option - No index files are open."
                LOOP
            ENDIF
  {
  // Following block added by Tony Lima, April 21, 1989
  }
            IF TYPE(ORDER()) <> "U"
              lc_type=TYPE(ORDER())
              DO CASE
                CASE lc_type = "C"
                  ln_type = 1
                CASE lc_type = "N" .OR. lc_type = "F"
                  ln_type = 2
                CASE lc_type = "D"
                  ln_type = 3
                OTHERWISE
                  ln_type = 1
              ENDCASE
            ENDIF && TYPE(ORDER()) <> "U"
            ln_type=1
            lc_ln1=SPACE(40)
            DEFINE WINDOW Posit2 FROM {ln_frow},{ln_fcol-11} TO;
              {ln_frow+7},{ln_fcol+32} DOUBLE
            ACTIVATE WINDOW Posit2
            @ 1,1 SAY "Enter the type of expression:" GET ln_type PICT;
              "#" RANGE 1,3
            @ 2,1 SAY "(1=character, 2=numeric (N/F) and 3=date.)"
            READ
```

It would be fairly easy to simply omit the READ. I leave it to you to handle
that.

Note that AS_POSIT.COD is also INCLUDEd in the larger applications
generator system, so the code to automatically detect the data type of the key

will be used there as well. Recompile AS_MENU.COD to produce MENU.GEN if you want this.

Conclusion

There are a number of other changes that could be made to the quick application. For example, adding the ability to do a SEEK or LOCATE before an edit would be useful. This could be easily accomplished by adding a "Position record pointer" option to the main menu. Since this is not particularly difficult, I leave it to the reader to complete this exercise.

This chapter has made some fairly extensive changes to the quick application. These could be easily transferred to the general applications generator as well. However, rather than do that, the next chapter will focus on using the applications generator and suggesting modifications that could be made along the way. For those who are interested, Appendix C to this chapter contains the version of CUSTOMER.PRG produced by the revised QUICKAPP template.

Appendix A

QUICKAPP.COD
(Including all submodules)

```
 1    1:  // $Header: /a/CCS/apgentc/cod/quickapp.cod,v 1.58 88/08/08
                08:11:16 kirkn Dev $
 2    2:  // Module name: Quickapp.cod
 3    3:  // Description: Quick application template for dBASE IV 1.0
 4    4:  //
 5    5:
 6    6:  Quick Application Template
 7    7:  -------------------------
 8    8:  Version 1.58
 9    9:  Ashton-Tate (c) 1987, 1988
10   10:
11   11:  {
12   12:   include "applctn.def";   // Applicaton selectors
223  15:   // Check menu type
224  16:   if Menu_Type != app then
225  17:     pause("Please position to the application object and restart
                  generation.");
226  18:       goto NoGen;
227  19:   endif
228  20:
229  21:   // Declare variables
230  22:   var quickapp, barcnt, rptchoice, lblchoice, ndxchoice, file,
                crlf, x, color,
231  23:       ask_user, strng, author, copyright, dbVersion, default_drv,
232  24:       display // Type of display
233  25:   ;
234  26:
235  27:   // Grab default drive from dBASE
236  28:   // See bottom of Builtin.def for numset & strset enum's
237  29:   default_drv = strset(_defdrive);
238  30:
239  31:   if filedrive(menu_name) or !default_drv then
240  32:     quickapp = alltrim(menu_name);
241  33:   else
242  34:     quickapp = default_drv + ":" + alltrim(menu_name);
243  35:   endif
244  36:   quickapp = upper(quickapp);
245  37:
246  38:   // Assign default values to some of the variables
247  39:   barcnt = 4;
248  40:   crlf = chr(10);
249  41:   author = Appl_Authr;
250  42:   copyright = Appl_cpyrt;
251  43:   dbVersion = Appl_Versn;
```

(continued)

```
252   44:    display = numset(_flgcolor);
253   45:
254   46:    // Check to see if file exists and safety is on
255   47:    if fileexist(quickapp+".PRG") and numset(_safety) then
256   48:       do while not at(upper(ask_user),"YN")
257   49:          ask_user = askuser("Application "+quickapp+".prg already
                      exists...Overwrite (Y/N)","N",1);
258   50:       enddo
259   51:       if upper(ask_user) == "N" then
260   52:          pause("Generation request cancelled -- press any key to
                      continue");
261   53:          goto NoGen;
262   54:       endif
263   55:    endif
264   56:    }
265   57:    //
266   58:    //---------------------------------
267   59:    //Create Quickapp main program
268   60:    //---------------------------------
269   61:    //
270   62:    {create(quickapp+".PRG");
271   63:     print(replicate("*",80)+crlf);
272   64:    }
273   65:    * Program......: {quickapp}
274   66:    {include "as_headr.cod";}
275    1:    // $Header: /a/CCS/apgentc/cod/as_headr.cod,v 1.8 88/03/28
                      10:07:35 kirkn Dev $
276    2:    // Module Name: AS_HEADR.COD
277    3:    // Current incident (atomname):
278    4:    // Atoms used : Appl_Authr, Appl_Cpyrt, Appl_versn
279    5:    // Date       : March 23, 1987
280    6:    // Description: Used as a include to produce Program Header
                      Information
281    7:    // Notes      : AS_HEADR IS AN INCLUDE FILE  DO NOT RUN ALONE!!!
282    8:    // Syntax     :
283    9:    //
284   10:    // Module Change Log
285   11:    //   Date          Initials        Short Change Description
286   12:    //   03/23/87      KJN             Created Module
287   13:    //   04/07/87      KJN             Changed to new atoms
288   14:    //
289   15:    //
290   16:    {strng=STR(VERSION());}
291   17:    * Author.......: {if author then}{author}{endif}
292   18:    * Date.........: {ltrim(SUBSTR(DATE(),1,8))}
293   19:    * Notice.......: {if Copyright then}{Copyright}{endif}
294   20:    * dBASE Ver....: {if dBVersion then}{dBVersion}{endif}
295   21:    * Generated by.: APGEN version {strng}
296   22:    * Description..: {if Menu_Desc then}{Menu_Desc}{endif}
297   23:    // EOP AS_HEADR.COD
298   67:    * Notes........:
299   68:    {print(replicate("*",80)+crlf);}
```

(continued)

```
300   69:
301   70:   SET CONSOLE OFF
302   71:   IF TYPE("gn_apgen") = "U"   && We were not called from another
                 APGEN program
303   72:      CLEAR ALL
304   73:      CLEAR WINDOW
305   74:      CLOSE ALL
306   75:      gn_apgen = 1
307   76:   ELSE
308   77:      gn_apgen = gn_apgen + 1
309   78:      PRIVATE gc_bell, gc_carry, gc_clock, gc_century, gc_confirm,
                 gc_deli,;
310   79:            gc_escape, gc_instruc, gc_safety, gc_status, gc_score,
                     gc_talk
311   80:   ENDIF
312   81:
313   82:   *-- Window for pause message box (ON ERROR)
314   83:   DEFINE WINDOW Pause FROM 15,00 TO 19,79 DOUBLE
315   84:   ON ERROR DO PAUSE WITH "Error occurred on line
                 "+LTRIM(STR(LINE())) +" of procedure "+Program()
316   85:
317   86:   *-- Store initial SETs to variables
318   87:   gc_bell   =SET("BELL")
319   88:   gc_carry  =SET("CARRY")
320   89:   gc_clock  =SET("CLOCK")
321   90:   gc_century=SET("CENTURY")
322   91:   gc_confirm=SET("CONFIRM")
323   92:   gc_deli   =SET("DELIMITERS")
324   93:   gc_escape =SET("ESCAPE")
325   94:   gc_instruc=SET("INSTRUCT")
326   95:   gc_safety =SET("SAFETY")
327   96:   gc_status =SET("STATUS")
328   97:   gc_score  =SET("SCOREBOARD")
329   98:   gc_talk   =SET("TALK")
330   99:
331  100:   SET CLOCK OFF
332  101:   SET COLOR TO
333  102:   CLEAR
334  103:   SET CONSOLE ON
335  104:
336  105:   *-- Sets for application
337  106:   SET BELL {if Set_Bell then}OFF{else}ON{endif}
338  107:   {if Set_BellFr and Set_BellDr then}
339  108:   SET BELL TO {Set_BellFr},{Set_BellDr}
340  109:   {endif}
341  110:   SET CARRY {if Set_Carry then}ON{else}OFF{endif}
342  111:   SET CENTURY {if Set_Centry then}ON{else}OFF{endif}
343  112:   SET CONFIRM {if Set_Confrm then}ON{else}OFF{endif}
344  113:   SET DELIMITERS TO \
345  114:   {if not AT(CHR(34),Set_DelChr) then}"{Set_DelChr}"
346  115:   {  goto deliok;
347  116:    endif
```

(continued)

```
348  117:    if not AT("'",Set_DelChr) then}'{Set_DelChr}'
349  118:    {  goto deliok;
350  119:    endif
351  120:    if not AT("[",Set_DelChr) or not AT("]",Set_DelChr) then}
            [{Set_DelChr}]
352  121:    {  goto deliok;
353  122:    endif
354  123:    }
355  124:    ""
356  125:    {deliok:}
357  126:    SET DELIMITER {if Set_Delim then}ON{else}OFF{endif}
358  127:    SET ESCAPE {if Set_Escape then}OFF{else}ON{endif}
359  128:    SET INSTRUCT OFF
360  129:    SET SAFETY {if Set_Safety then}OFF{else}ON{endif}
361  130:    SET SCOREBOARD OFF
362  131:    SET STATUS OFF
363  132:    SET TALK OFF
364  133:    //
365  134:    {if Run_Drive then}
366  135:    SET DEFAULT TO {UPPER(Run_Drive)}:
367  136:    {endif}
368  137:    {if Run_Path then}
369  138:    SET PATH TO {Run_Path}
370  139:    {endif}
371  140:
372  141:    *-- Set global variables
373  142:    gn_barv  = 0{tabto(30)}&& Initialize bar value variable
374  143:    gn_error = 0{tabto(30)}&& Variable to store error() number
375  144:    gn_send  = 0{tabto(30)}&& Return variable from popup
376  145:    gc_brdr  = "2"{tabto(30)}&& Border style for menu box
                - See Procedure
377  146:    lc_heading = "{if quick_hdng then
378  147:      alltrim(Quick_Hdng)
379  148:    else
380  149:      fileroot(Upper(quickapp))
381  150:    endif}" && Menu heading string
382  151:    lc_color = ISCOLOR()
383  152:    //
384  153:
385  154:    {if Disp_Sign then}
386  155:    // Display Signon Banner
387  156:    SET ESCAPE OFF
388  157:
389  158:    *-- Signon Banner
390  159:    tmpcolor = IIF(lc_color,"{color(Clr_box)}", "W+/N")
391  160:    @ {row1()},{col1()} TO {row2()},{col2()} \
392  161:    {   case Mnu_Border of}
393  162:    {   0: // Panel}
394  163:    PANEL \
395  164:    {   1: // Single}
396  165:    \
397  166:    {   2: // Double}
```

(continued)

```
398  167:  DOUBLE \
399  168:  {   endcase}
400  169:  COLOR &tmpcolor.
401  170:  {   foreach text_element}
402  171:  @ {row1()+Row_Positn},{col1()+Col_Positn} SAY "{Text_Item}"
403  172:  {   next;}
404  173:  IF lc_color
405  174:     @ {row1()+1},{col1()+1} FILL TO {row2()-1},{col2()-1} COLOR
                  {color(Clr_Text)}
406  175:  ENDIF
407  176:  ln_inkey = inkey(5)
408  177:  {endif}
409  178:  CLEAR
410  179:  SET ESCAPE {if Set_Escape then}OFF{else}ON{endif}
411  180:  SET STATUS ON
412  181:  *-- Set colors
413  182:  IF lc_color
414  183:     SET COLOR OF NORMAL TO {color(Clr_Text)}
415  184:     SET COLOR OF MESSAGES TO {color(Clr_Messages)}
416  185:     SET COLOR OF TITLES TO {color(Clr_Heading)}
417  186:     SET COLOR OF HIGHLIGHT TO {color(Clr_Hghlight)}
418  187:     SET COLOR OF BOX TO {color(Clr_Box)}
419  188:     SET COLOR OF INFORMATION TO {color(Clr_Info)}
420  189:     SET COLOR OF FIELDS TO {color(Clr_Fields)}
421  190:  ENDIF
422  191:  //
423  192:
424  193:  {dBFOpen(Quick_DBF, Quick_NDX, Quick_Ordr);}
425  194:
426  195:  *-- Define the main popup menu for Quickapp
427  196:  SET BORDER TO DOUBLE
428  197:  DEFINE POPUP quick FROM 7,27
429  198:  DEFINE BAR 1 OF quick PROMPT " Add Information"
                  MESSAGE "Add records to database {Quick_DBF}"
430  199:  DEFINE BAR 2 OF quick PROMPT " Change Information"
                  MESSAGE "Edit records in database {Quick_DBF}"
431  200:  DEFINE BAR 3 OF quick PROMPT " Browse Information"
                  MESSAGE "Browse database {Quick_DBF}"
432  201:  DEFINE BAR 4 OF quick PROMPT " Discard Marked Records "
                  MESSAGE "Purge deleted records in database {Quick_DBF}"
433  202:  { if Quick_FRM then barcnt=barcnt+1; rptchoice=barcnt;}
434  203:  DEFINE BAR {barcnt} OF quick PROMPT " Print Report"
                  MESSAGE "Run report form {Quick_FRM}"
435  204:  { endif
436  205:     if Quick_LBL then barcnt=barcnt+1; lblchoice=barcnt;}
437  206:  DEFINE BAR {barcnt} OF quick PROMPT " Mailing Labels"
                  MESSAGE "Run label form {Quick_LBL}"
438  207:  { endif
439  208:     if Quick_NDX or Quick_Ordr then barcnt=barcnt+1;
                  ndxchoice=barcnt;}
440  209:  DEFINE BAR {barcnt} OF quick PROMPT " Reindex Database"
                  MESSAGE "Reindex database {Quick_DBF}"
```

(continued)

```
441   210:  { endif
442   211:    barcnt=barcnt+1;
443   212:   strng=fileroot(quickapp);
444   213:   strng=upper(substr(strng,1,1))+lower(substr(strng,2,7));}
445   214:  DEFINE BAR {barcnt} OF quick PROMPT " Exit From {strng}"
             MESSAGE "Exit program to dBASE"
446   215:  ON SELECTION POPUP quick DO Action WITH BAR()
447   216:
448   217:  {if Quick_LBL or Quick_FRM then}
449   218:  *-- Define the popup menu for print redirection
450   219:  DEFINE POPUP prntchk FROM 10,55
451   220:  DEFINE BAR 1 OF prntchk PROMPT " Send to..." SKIP
452   221:  DEFINE BAR 2 OF prntchk PROMPT REPLICATE(CHR(196),14) SKIP
453   222:  DEFINE BAR 3 OF prntchk PROMPT " Screen " MESSAGE "Screen only"
454   223:  DEFINE BAR 4 OF prntchk PROMPT " Printer" MESSAGE "Printer LPT1:"
455   224:  DEFINE BAR 5 OF prntchk PROMPT " Label Sample "
             MESSAGE "Printer LPT1: with \
456   225:  Sample label" SKIP{if Quick_LBL} FOR gn_barv <> {lblchoice}{endif}
457   226:  DEFINE BAR 6 OF prntchk PROMPT " Return"
             MESSAGE "Return to Main Menu"
458   227:  ON SELECTION POPUP prntchk DO get_sele
459   228:  {endif}
460   229:
461   230:  *-- Window to cover work surface during edit, append, etc.
462   231:  DEFINE WINDOW work FROM 0,0 TO 21,79 NONE
463   232:
464   233:  *-- Window for area below menu heading & for running
             reports/labels in
465   234:  DEFINE WINDOW desktop FROM 4,0 TO 21,79 NONE
466   235:
467   236:  DEFINE WINDOW printemp FROM 10,25 TO 15,56
468   237:
469   238:  *-- Display heading centered on the screen.
470   239:  DO menubox WITH lc_heading
471   240:
472   241:  *-- Show the menu so we don't get a flash if the user hits arrow
             keys or ESC
473   242:  SHOW POPUP quick
474   243:  SAVE SCREEN TO quick
475   244:  *-- Display Quickapp menu centered on the screen.
476   245:  DO WHILE gn_barv <> {barcnt} && Prevent user from exiting with
             arrow keys or ESC
477   246:    ACTIVATE POPUP quick
478   247:  ENDDO
479   248:
480   249:  * Restore SET environment the best we can
481   250:  SET BELL &gc_bell.
482   251:  SET CARRY &gc_carry.
483   252:  SET CLOCK TO
484   253:  SET CLOCK &gc_clock.
485   254:  SET CENTURY &gc_century.
486   255:  SET CONFIRM &gc_confirm.
```

(continued)

```
487   256:   SET DELIMITERS &gc_deli.
488   257:   SET ESCAPE &gc_escape.
489   258:   SET INSTRUCT &gc_instruc.
490   259:   SET STATUS &gc_status.
491   260:   SET SAFETY &gc_safety.
492   261:   SET SCORE  &gc_score.
493   262:   SET TALK   &gc_talk.
494   263:   SET FORMAT TO
495   264:
496   265:   IF gn_apgen = 1 && We were not called from another APGEN program
497   266:      CLEAR WINDOW
498   267:      CLEAR POPUP
499   268:      CLEAR ALL
500   269:      CLOSE ALL
501   270:   ELSE
502   271:      RELEASE WINDOWS work, desktop
503   272:      RELEASE SCREEN quick
504   273:      RELEASE POPUP quick
505   274:      gn_apgen = gn_apgen - 1
506   275:   ENDIF
507   276:   ON ERROR
508   277:   RETURN
509   278:   * EOP: {Quickapp}.PRG
510   279:
511   280:   //
512   281:   //------------------------------------------------------------------
513   282:   //  Create Quickapp procedure file
514   283:   //  Since the dBASE compiler does not care that their are
             procedures in the
515   284:   //  same file as the program we tack the procedures onto the
             bottom.
516   285:   //------------------------------------------------------------------
517   286:   //
518   287:   {print(replicate("*",80)+crlf);}
519   288:   * Procedures...: {quickapp}.Prc
520   289:   {include "as_headr.cod";}
521     1:   // $Header: /a/CCS/apgentc/cod/as_headr.cod,v 1.8 88/03/28
             10:07:35 kirkn Dev $
522     2:   // Module Name: AS_HEADR.COD
523     3:   // Current incident (atomname):
524     4:   // Atoms used : Appl_Authr, Appl_Cpyrt, Appl_versn
525     5:   // Date       : March 23, 1987
526     6:   // Description: Used as a include to produce Program Header
             Information
527     7:   // Notes      : AS_HEADR IS AN INCLUDE FILE  DO NOT RUN ALONE!!!
528     8:   // Syntax     :
529     9:   //
530    10:   // Module Change Log
531    11:   //  Date         Initials        Short Change Description
532    12:   //  03/23/87     KJN             Created Module
533    13:   //  04/07/87     KJN             Changed to new atoms
534    14:   //
```

(continued)

```
535    15:  //
536    16:  {strng=STR(VERSION());}
537    17:  * Author.......: {if author then}{author}{endif}
538    18:  * Date.........: {ltrim(SUBSTR(DATE(),1,8))}
539    19:  * Notice.......: {if Copyright then}{Copyright}{endif}
540    20:  * dBASE Ver....: {if dBVersion then}{dBVersion}{endif}
541    21:  * Generated by.: APGEN version {strng}
542    22:  * Description..: {if Menu_Desc then}{Menu_Desc}{endif}
543    23:  // EOP AS_HEADR.COD
544   290:  * Notes........:
545   291:  {print(replicate("*",80)+crlf);}
546   292:
547   293:  *-- Here is a sample procedure file to show the beginning user what
548   294:  *   the power of procdures will do for him.
549   295:  *-- This example - Menubox displays a menu heading box with
                  a centered heading.
550   296:  {include "as_menub.cod";}
551    1:  // $Header: /a/CCS/apgentc/cod/as_menub.cod,v 1.17 88/04/26
                  07:57:51 kirkn Dev $
552    2:  // Module Name: AS_MENUB.COD
553    3:  // Current incident (atomname):
554    4:  // Atoms used :
555    5:  // Date       : December 10, 1986
556    6:  // Description: Used to build a menu heading box with date,
                  name, time
557    7:  // Notes      : as_menub IS AN INCLUDE FILE
558    8:  // Syntax     :
559    9:  //
560   10:  // Module Change Log
561   11:  //  Date         Initials        Short Change Description
562   12:  //  12/10/86      KJN             Created Module
563   13:  //
564   14:  PROCEDURE MenuBox
565   15:  PARAMETER lc_m_name
566   16:  *-- Parameter lc_m_name - is the title variable for the menu
567   17:  SET CLOCK OFF
568   18:  @ 1,0 FILL TO 2,79 COLOR n/n
569   19:  DO CASE
570   20:  CASE gc_brdr = "0"
571   21:     @ 1,0 CLEAR TO 3,79
572   22:  CASE gc_brdr = "1"
573   23:     @ 1,0 TO 3,79
574   24:  CASE gc_brdr = "2"
575   25:     lc_color = IIF(ISCOLOR(),"{color(Clr_box)}", "W+/N")
576   26:     @ 1,0 TO 3,79 DOUBLE COLOR &lc_color.
577   27:  ENDCASE
578   28:  SET CLOCK TO 2,68
579   29:  @ 2,1 SAY SUBSTR(CDOW(DATE()),1,3)+'. '+DTOC(DATE())+' '
580   30:  // Because of the length of the heading in the generator I am
                  using 41 so that
581   31:  // the date display does not touch the heading.
582   32:  @ 2,41 - (LEN(lc_m_name)/2) SAY lc_m_name
```

(continued)

```
583   33:   lc_color = IIF(ISCOLOR(),"{color(Clr_Text)}", "W+/N")
584   34:   @ 2,1 FILL TO 2,78 COLOR &lc_color.
585   35:   RETURN
586   36:   // EOP AS_MENUB.COD
587  297:
588  298:   PROCEDURE get_sele
589  299:   *-- Get the user selection & store BAR into variable
590  300:   gn_send = BAR()   && Variable for print testing
591  301:   DEACTIVATE POPUP
592  302:   RETURN
593  303:
594  304:   PROCEDURE Action
595  305:   PARAMETERS bar
596  306:   *-- Get the user selection & store BAR into variable
597  307:   gn_barv = bar
598  308:   SET MESSAGE TO ' '
599  309:   {if Quick_FMT then}
600  310:   IF LTRIM( STR( gn_barv)) $ "123"
601  311:      *-- Set format file {Quick_FMT} for edit/append/browse
602  312:      SET FORMAT TO {Quick_FMT}
603  313:   ENDIF
604  314:   {endif}
605  315:   DO CASE
606  316:      CASE gn_barv = 1
607  317:         *-- Add information
608  318:         SET MESSAGE TO 'Appending records to file {Quick_DBF}'
609  319:         APPEND
610  320:      CASE gn_barv = 2
611  321:         *-- Change information
612  322:         SET MESSAGE TO 'Editing file {Quick_DBF}'
613  323:         EDIT
614  324:      CASE gn_barv = 3
615  325:         *-- Browse information
616  326:         SET MESSAGE TO 'Browsing file {Quick_DBF}'
617  327:         BROWSE {if Quick_FMT then}FORMAT {endif}
618  328:      CASE gn_barv = 4
619  329:         *-- Remove information (Pack file {lower(Quick_DBF)})
620  330:         ACTIVATE WINDOW desktop
621  331:         @ 2,0 SAY 'Packing database {Quick_DBF} to REMOVE records
                     marked for deletion...'
622  332:         @ 3,0
623  333:         SET TALK ON
624  334:         PACK
625  335:         GO TOP
626  336:         ?
627  337:         WAIT
628  338:         SET TALK OFF
629  339:         DEACTIVATE WINDOW desktop
630  340:   {  if Quick_FRM}
631  341:      CASE gn_barv = {rptchoice}
632  342:         *-- Run report form {lower(Quick_FRM)}
```

(continued)

```
633  343:       SET MESSAGE TO 'Pick an option to locate a record or <ESC>
                   for default'
634  344:       ACTIVATE WINDOW work
635  345:       gn_recno = RECNO()
636  346:       DO position
637  347:       DEACTIVATE WINDOW work
638  348:       lc_toprnt = IIF(gn_recno <> recno(),'REST ','')
639  349:       STORE 0 TO gn_send, gn_pkey
640  350:       ACTIVATE POPUP prntchk
641  351:       IF gn_send = 4
642  352:          lc_toprnt = 'TO PRINT'
643  353:          ON ERROR DO prntrtry
644  354:       ENDIF
645  355:       IF .NOT. gn_send = 6
646  356:          ACTIVATE WINDOW desktop
647  357:          IF gc_escape="OFF"
648  358:             SET ESCAPE ON
649  359:          ENDIF
650  360:          REPORT FORM {Quick_FRM} &lc_toprnt.
651  361:          IF gn_pkey <> 27
652  362:             WAIT
653  363:          ENDIF
654  364:          SET ESCAPE &gc_escape.
655  365:          DEACTIVATE WINDOW desktop
656  366:       ENDIF
657  367:       GOTO gn_recno
658  368:       ON ERROR DO PAUSE WITH "Error occurred on line
                   "+LTRIM(STR(LINE())) +" of procedure "+Program()
659  369:  {  endif
660  370:     if Quick_LBL}
661  371:    CASE gn_barv = {lblchoice}
662  372:       *-- Run label form {lower(Quick_LBL)}
663  373:       SET MESSAGE TO 'Pick an option to locate a record or <ESC>
                   for default'
664  374:       ACTIVATE WINDOW work
665  375:       gn_recno = RECNO()
666  376:       DO position
667  377:       DEACTIVATE WINDOW work
668  378:       STORE 0 TO gn_send, gn_pkey
669  379:       lc_toprnt = IIF(gn_recno <> recno(),'REST ','')
670  380:       ACTIVATE POPUP prntchk
671  381:       DO CASE
672  382:        CASE gn_send = 4
673  383:           lc_toprnt = 'TO PRINT'
674  384:        CASE gn_send = 5
675  385:           lc_toprnt = 'TO PRINT SAMPLE'
676  386:       ENDCASE
677  387:       IF .NOT. gn_send = 6
678  388:          ACTIVATE WINDOW desktop
679  389:          IF gc_escape="OFF"
680  390:             SET ESCAPE ON
```

(continued)

```
681  391:          ENDIF
682  392:          ON ERROR DO prntrtry
683  393:          LABEL FORM {Quick_LBL} &lc_toprnt.
684  394:          IF gn_pkey <> 27
685  395:             WAIT
686  396:          ENDIF
687  397:          SET ESCAPE &gc_escape.
688  398:          DEACTIVATE WINDOW desktop
689  399:       ENDIF
690  400:       GOTO gn_recno
691  401:       ON ERROR DO PAUSE WITH "Error occurred on line"
                    +LTRIM(STR(LINE())) +" of procedure "+Program()
692  402: {  endif
693  403:    if Quick_NDX or Quick_Ordr}
694  404:    CASE gn_barv = {ndxchoice}
695  405:       *-- Reindex {lower(Quick_DBF)}
696  406:       ACTIVATE WINDOW desktop
697  407:       @ 3,0 SAY 'Reindexing database {Quick_DBF}...'
698  408:       @ 4,0
699  409:       SET TALK ON
700  410:       REINDEX
701  411:       GO TOP
702  412:       ?
703  413:       WAIT
704  414:       SET TALK OFF
705  415:       DEACTIVATE WINDOW desktop
706  416: {  endif}
707  417:    CASE gn_barv = {barcnt}
708  418:       DEACTIVATE POPUP
709  419: ENDCASE
710  420: SET MESSAGE TO ' '
711  421: {if Quick_FMT then}
712  422: IF gc_status = "OFF"
713  423:    SET STATUS ON
714  424: ENDIF
715  425: SET FORMAT TO
716  426: {endif}
717  427: IF LTRIM( STR( gn_barv)) $ "123"
718  428:    RESTORE SCREEN FROM quick
719  429: ENDIF
720  430: RETURN
721  431:
722  432: {include "as_pause.cod"}
723    1: // $Header: /a/CCS/apgentc/cod/as_pause.cod,v 1.14 88/06/22
                22:03:27 dough Dev $
724    2: // Module Name: AS_PAUSE.COD
725    3: // Current incident (atomname):
726    4: // Atoms used :
727    5: // Date       : November 24, 1986
728    6: // Description: Display message on line 19
729    7: // Notes      :
730    8: // Syntax     :
```

(continued)

```
731     9:  //
732    10:  // Module Change Log
733    11:  //    Date       Initials    Short Change Description
734    12:  //  12/01/86     KJN           Created Module
735    13:  //  01/27/87     DCH           Moved message to line 18 thru 20
736    14:  //                             instead of 22 thru 24
737    15:  //  04/06/87     DCH         variable lc_option for AS_POSIT.COD
738    16:  //  07/06/87     DCH         changed to run in Nova
739    17:  //  09/30/87     KJN         Changed - MOVE REGION to WINDOWS
740    18:  //  06/10/88     KJN         Move window to main procedure
                                         because define
741    19:  //                          window can't be in a ON ERROR routine
742    20:  //
743    21:  PROCEDURE Pause
744    22:  PARAMETER lc_msg
745    23:  *-- Parameters : lc_msg = message line
746    24:  IF TYPE("lc_message")="U"
747    25:     gn_error=ERROR()
748    26:  ENDIF
749    27:  lc_msg = lc_msg
750    28:  lc_option='0'
751    29:  ACTIVATE WINDOW Pause
752    30:  IF gn_error > 0
753    31:     IF TYPE("lc_message")="U"
754    32:        @ 0,1 SAY "An error has occurred !! - Error message: "+
                         MESSAGE()
755    33:     ELSE
756    34:        @ 0,1 SAY "Error # "+lc_message
757    35:     ENDIF
758    36:  ENDIF
759    37:  @ 1,1 SAY lc_msg
760    38:  WAIT " Press any key to continue..."
761    39:  DEACTIVATE WINDOW Pause
762    40:  RETURN
763    41:  // EOP AS_PAUSE.COD
764   433:
765   434:  {if Quick_LBL or Quick_FRM then
766   435:     include "as_posit.cod";}
767     1:  // $Header: /a/CCS/apgentc/cod/as_posit.cod,v 1.19 88/06/21
                 12:07:20 dough Dev $
768     2:  // Module Name: AS_POSIT.COD
769     3:  // Current incident (atomname):
770     4:  // Atoms used :
771     5:  // Date        : April 7, 1987
772     6:  // Description: Record positioning (Ask at runtime)
773     7:  // Notes     :
774     8:  // Syntax    :
775     9:  //
776    10:  // Module Change Log
777    11:  //    Date       Initials    Short Change Description
778    12:  //  04/07/87     DCH           Created Module
779    13:  //  09/30/87     KJN         Changed  MOVE REGION to WINDOWS
```

(continued)

```
780   14:  //
781   15:  //
782   16:  {var ln_frow, ln_fcol;}
783   17:  PROCEDURE Position
784   18:  IF LEN(DBF()) = 0
785   19:     DO Pause WITH "Database not in use. "
786   20:     RETURN
787   21:  ENDIF
788   22:  SET SPACE ON
789   23:  SET DELIMITERS OFF
790   24:  // Frame row position
791   25:  {ln_frow=8;}
792   26:  // Frame col position
793   27:  {ln_fcol=30;//28}
794   28:  ln_type=0            && sublevel selection
795   29:  ln_rkey=READKEY()    && test for ESC or Return
796   30:  ln_rec=RECNO()       && DBF record number
797   31:  ln_num=0             && for input of a number
798   32:  ld_date=DATE()       && for input of a date
799   33:  lc_option='0'        && main option ie. Seek, Goto and Locate
800   34:  *-- Scope ie. ALL, REST, NEXT <n>
801   35:  STORE SPACE(10) TO lc_scp
802   36:  *-- 1 = Character SEEK, 2 = For clause, 3 = While clause
803   37:  STORE SPACE(40) TO lc_ln1, lc_ln2, lc_ln3
804   38:  lc_temp=""
805   39:  @ 0,00 SAY "Index order: "+IIF(""=ORDER(),"Database is in natural
           order",ORDER())
806   40:  @ 1,00 SAY "Listed below are the first 16 fields."
807   41:  lc_temp=REPLICATE(CHR(196),19)
808   42:  @ 2,0 SAY CHR(218)+lc_temp+CHR(194)+lc_temp+
           CHR(194)+lc_temp+CHR(194)+lc_temp
809   43:  ln_num=240
810   44:  DO WHILE ln_num < 560
811   45:     lc_temp=FIELD( (ln_num-240)/20 +1)
812   46:     @ (ln_num/80),MOD(ln_num,80) SAY CHR(179)+;
813   47:  lc_temp+SPACE(11-LEN(lc_temp))+;
814   48:  SUBSTR("= Char  = Date  = Logic = Num   = Float = Memo        ",;
815   49:  AT(TYPE(lc_temp),"CDLNFMU")*8-7,8)
816   50:     ln_num=ln_num+20
817   51:  ENDDO
818   52:  ln_num=1
819   53:
820   54:  DEFINE POPUP Posit1 FROM {ln_frow},{ln_fcol}
821   55:  DEFINE BAR 1 OF Posit1 PROMPT " Position by " SKIP
822   56:  DEFINE BAR 2 OF Posit1 PROMPT REPLICATE(CHR(196),15) SKIP
823   57:  DEFINE BAR 3 OF Posit1 PROMPT " SEEK Record"
           MESSAGE "Search on index key" SKIP FOR ""=ORDER()
824   58:  DEFINE BAR 4 OF Posit1 PROMPT " GOTO Record"
           MESSAGE "Position to specific record"
825   59:  DEFINE BAR 5 OF Posit1 PROMPT " LOCATE Record "
           MESSAGE "Locate record for condition"
```

(continued)

```
826    60:  DEFINE BAR 6 OF Posit1 PROMPT " Return"
                 MESSAGE "Return without positioning"
827    61:  ON SELECTION POPUP Posit1 DO get_sele
828    62:
829    63:  SET CONFIRM ON
830    64:  DO WHILE lc_option='0'
831    65:     ACTIVATE POPUP Posit1
832    66:     lc_option = ltrim(str(gn_send))   && for popup
833    67:      IF LASTKEY() = 27 .OR. lc_option="6"
834    68:         GOTO ln_rec
835    69:         EXIT
836    70:      ENDIF
837    71:      DO CASE
838    72:      CASE lc_option='3'
839    73:         *-- Seek
840    74:         IF LEN(NDX(1))=0 .AND. LEN(MDX(1))=0
841    75:            DO Pause WITH "Can't use this option - No index files are
                         open."
842    76:            LOOP
843    77:         ENDIF
844    78:         ln_type=1
845    79:         lc_ln1=SPACE(40)
846    80:         DEFINE WINDOW Posit2 FROM {ln_frow},{ln_fcol-11} TO
                      {ln_frow+7},{ln_fcol+32} DOUBLE
847    81:         ACTIVATE WINDOW Posit2
848    82:         @ 1,1 SAY "Enter the type of expression:" GET ln_type PICT
                      "#" RANGE 1,3
849    83:         @ 2,1 SAY "(1=character, 2=numeric and 3=date.)"
850    84:         READ
851    85:         IF .NOT. (READKEY() = 12 .OR. READKEY() = 268)
852    86:            SET CONFIRM ON
853    87:            @ 3,1 SAY "Enter the key expression to search for:"
854    88:            IF ln_type=3
855    89:               @ 4,1 GET ld_date PICT "@D"
856    90:            ELSE
857    91:               IF ln_type=2
858    92:                  @ 4,1 GET ln_num PICT "##########"
859    93:               ELSE
860    94:                  @ 4,1 GET lc_ln1
861    95:               ENDIF
862    96:            ENDIF
863    97:            READ
864    98:            SET CONFIRM OFF
865    99:            IF .NOT. (READKEY() = 12 .OR. READKEY() = 268)
866   100:               lc_temp=IIF(ln_type=1,"TRIM(lc_ln1)",
                            IIF(ln_type=2,"ln_num","ld_date"))
867   101:               SEEK &lc_temp.
868   102:            ENDIF
869   103:         ENDIF
870   104:         RELEASE WINDOWS Posit2
871   105:      CASE lc_option='4'
```

(continued)

```
872   106:        *-- Goto
873   107:        ln_type=1
874   108:        DEFINE POPUP Posit2 FROM {ln_frow},{ln_fcol}
875   109:        DEFINE BAR 1 OF Posit2 PROMPT " GOTO:" SKIP
876   110:        DEFINE BAR 2 OF Posit2 PROMPT REPLICATE(CHR(196),10) SKIP
877   111:        DEFINE BAR 3 OF Posit2 PROMPT " TOP"
                      MESSAGE "GOTO Top of File"
878   112:        DEFINE BAR 4 OF Posit2 PROMPT " BOTTOM"
                      MESSAGE "GOTO Bottom of File"
879   113:        DEFINE BAR 5 OF Posit2 PROMPT " Record # "
                      MESSAGE "GOTO A Specific Record"
880   114:        ON SELECTION POPUP Posit2 DO get_sele
881   115:        ACTIVATE POPUP posit2
882   116:        ln_type = gn_send
883   117:        IF LASTKEY() <> 27
884   118:           IF ln_type=5
885   119:              DEFINE WINDOW Posit2 FROM {ln_frow},{ln_fcol-4} TO
                            {ln_frow+5},{ln_fcol+20} DOUBLE
886   120:              ACTIVATE WINDOW Posit2
887   121:              ln_num=0
888   122:              @ 3,1 SAY "Max. Record # = "+LTRIM(STR(RECCOUNT()))
889   123:              @ 1,1 SAY "Record to GOTO" GET ln_num PICT "######"
                            RANGE 1,RECCOUNT()
890   124:              READ
891   125:              IF .NOT. (READKEY() = 12 .OR. READKEY() = 268)
892   126:                 GOTO ln_num
893   127:              ENDIF
894   128:              RELEASE WINDOWS Posit2
895   129:           ELSE
896   130:              lc_temp=IIF(ln_type=3,"TOP","BOTTOM")
897   131:              GOTO &lc_temp.
898   132:           ENDIF
899   133:        ENDIF
900   134:     CASE lc_option='5'
901   135:        *-- Locate
902   136:        DEFINE WINDOW Posit2 FROM {ln_frow},{ln_fcol-14} TO
                      {ln_frow+6},{ln_fcol+36} DOUBLE
903   137:        ACTIVATE WINDOW Posit2
904   138:        @ 1,19 SAY "ie. ALL, NEXT <n>, and REST"
905   139:        @ 1,1 SAY "Scope:" GET lc_scp
906   140:        @ 2,1 SAY "For:  " GET lc_ln2
907   141:        @ 3,1 SAY "While:" GET lc_ln3
908   142:        READ
909   143:        IF .NOT. (READKEY() = 12 .OR. READKEY() = 268)
910   144:           lc_temp=TRIM(lc_scp)
911   145:           lc_temp=lc_temp + IIF(LEN(TRIM(lc_ln2)) > 0," FOR "
                         +TRIM(lc_ln2),"")
912   146:           lc_temp=lc_temp + IIF(LEN(TRIM(lc_ln3)) > 0," WHILE "
                         +TRIM(lc_ln3),"")
913   147:           IF LEN(lc_temp) > 0
914   148:              LOCATE &lc_temp.
915   149:           ELSE
```

(continued)

```
916   150:                  DO Pause WITH "All fields were blank."
917   151:              ENDIF
918   152:            ENDIF
919   153:            RELEASE WINDOW Posit2
920   154:         ENDCASE
921   155:      IF EOF()
922   156:         DO Pause WITH "Record not found."
923   157:         GOTO ln_rec
924   158:      ENDIF
925   159:      IF READKEY()=12 .OR. READKEY()= 268 .OR. LASTKEY()=27  && Esc
                 was hit
926   160:         lc_option='0'
927   161:      ENDIF
928   162: ENDDO
929   163: SET DELIMITERS &gc_deli.
930   164: SET CONFIRM {if Set_Confrm then}ON{else}OFF{endif}
931   165: RETURN
932   166: // EOP AS_POSIT.COD
933   436:
934   437: PROC prntrtry
935   438: IF .NOT. PRINTSTATUS()
936   439:    ACTIVATE WINDOW printemp
937   440:    @ 1,0 SAY " Please ready your printer or"
938   441:    @ 2,0 SAY "    press ESC to cancel"
939   442:    DO WHILE ( .NOT. PRINTSTATUS()) .AND. gn_pkey <> 27
940   443:       gn_pkey = INKEY()
941   444:    ENDDO
942   445:    DEACTIVATE WINDOW printemp
943   446:    RETRY
944   447: ENDIF
945   448: RETURN
946   449: { endif}
947   450: * EOF: {quickapp}.PRG
948   451: {pause("Generation is complete -- press any key to continue");
949   452:  fileerase(quickapp+".DBO");
950   453:  NoGen:
951   454:  return 0;
952   455: }
953   456: //
954   457: //------------------------------
955   458: // End of quickapp
956   459: // User defined functions include
957   460: //------------------------------
958   461: //
959   462: {
960   463:  define dbfOpen(mdbf,mndx,mord)}
961   464: { if at(upper(filetype(mdbf)), ".QBE,.QBO,.VUE") then}
962   465: SET VIEW TO {mdbf}
963   466: {    if mndx then}
964   467: SET INDEX TO {mndx}
965   468: {    endif
966   469:      if mord then}
```

(continued)

```
 967   470:  SET ORDER TO {mord}
 968   471:  {    endif
 969   472:    else}
 970   473:  USE {mdbf} {if mndx then}INDEX {mndx}{endif}
 971   474:  {    if mord then}
 972   475:  SET ORDER TO {mord}
 973   476:  {    endif
 974   477:    endif
 975   478:   return;
 976   479:  enddef;
 977   480:
 978   481:  define color(getcolor);
 979   482:  //
 980   483:  // This udf is used for processing colors from the apgen.
 981   484:  //  The foreground and background colors are stored in one byte.
 982   485:  //  The formulas below show how to get the foreground and
                    background color
 983   486:  //  out of the variable passed in.
 984   487:  //
 985   488:  var blink, forground, background, enhanced, incolor;
 986   489:  //
 987   490:  forground = background = enhanced = 0;
 988   491:  //
 989   492:  if getcolor != 255 then          // N/N in apgen (black on black)
 990   493:    blink = getcolor >> 7;          // high order bit set?
 991   494:    if blink then
 992   495:       getcolor = getcolor - 128;   // Shift high order bit back
 993   496:    endif
 994   497:    background = getcolor >> 4;
 995   498:    forground  = getcolor - (background << 4);
 996   499:    //
 997   500:    if forground > 7 then
 998   501:       enhanced = 1;
 999   502:       forground = forground - 8;
1000   503:    endif
1001   504:  endif
1002   505:  // Set your dBASE manual for an explanation of the colors below
1003   506:  case forground of
1004   507:   0: incolor = "n";
1005   508:   1: incolor = "b";
1006   509:   2: incolor = "g";
1007   510:   3: incolor = "bg";
1008   511:   4: incolor = "r";
1009   512:   5: incolor = "rb";
1010   513:   6: incolor = "gr";
1011   514:   7: incolor = "w";
1012   515:  endcase
1013   516:  if blink then incolor = incolor + "*"; endif
1014   517:  if enhanced then
1015   518:    incolor = incolor + "+/";
1016   519:  else
1017   520:    incolor = incolor + "/";
```

(continued)

```
1018   521:    endif
1019   522:    case background of
1020   523:     0: incolor = incolor + "n";
1021   524:     1: incolor = incolor + "b";
1022   525:     2: incolor = incolor + "g";
1023   526:     3: incolor = incolor + "bg";
1024   527:     4: incolor = incolor + "r";
1025   528:     5: incolor = incolor + "rb";
1026   529:     6: incolor = incolor + "gr";
1027   530:     7: incolor = incolor + "w";
1028   531:    endcase
1029   532:    return incolor;
1030   533:   enddef;
1031   534:   }
1032   535:   // EOP QUICKAPP.COD
1033 Compilation complete (no errors).
1034
```

Appendix B

CUSTOMER.PRG

```
 1 ******************************************************************************
 2 * Program......: C:CUSTOMER
 3 * Author.......: Tony Lima
 4 * Date.........: 4-18-89
 5 * Notice.......: Copyright, 1989, Pacific System Design Workshop, Inc.
 6 * dBASE Ver....: dBASE IV, Version 1.0
 7 * Generated by.: APGEN version 1.0
 8 * Description..: Customer data entry, editing, reports, labels
 9
10 * Notes........:
11 ******************************************************************************
12
13 SET CONSOLE OFF
14 IF TYPE("gn_apgen") = "U"   && We were not called from another APGEN program
15    CLEAR ALL
16    CLEAR WINDOW
17    CLOSE ALL
18    gn_apgen = 1
19 ELSE
20    gn_apgen = gn_apgen + 1
21    PRIVATE gc_bell, gc_carry, gc_clock, gc_century, gc_confirm, gc_deli,;
22            gc_escape, gc_instruc, gc_safety, gc_status, gc_score, gc_talk
23 ENDIF
24
25 *-- Window for pause message box (ON ERROR)
26 DEFINE WINDOW Pause FROM 15,00 TO 19,79 DOUBLE
27 ON ERROR DO PAUSE WITH [Error occurred on line ]+LTRIM(STR(LINE())) +[ of
    procedure ]+Program()
28 ON KEY LABEL F1 DO quickhlp
29
30 *-- Store initial SETs to variables
31 gc_bell   =SET("BELL")
32 gc_carry  =SET("CARRY")
33 gc_clock  =SET("CLOCK")
34 gc_century=SET("CENTURY")
35 gc_confirm=SET("CONFIRM")
36 gc_deli   =SET("DELIMITERS")
37 gc_escape =SET("ESCAPE")
38 gc_instruc=SET("INSTRUCT")
39 gc_safety =SET("SAFETY")
40 gc_status =SET("STATUS")
41 gc_score  =SET("SCOREBOARD")
42 gc_talk   =SET("TALK")
43
44 SET CLOCK OFF
```

(continued)

```
45 SET COLOR TO
46 CLEAR
47 SET CONSOLE ON
48
49 *-- Sets for application
50 SET BELL ON
51 SET BELL TO 220,2
52 SET CARRY OFF
53 SET CENTURY OFF
54 SET CONFIRM OFF
55 SET DELIMITERS TO "  "
56 SET DELIMITER OFF
57 SET ESCAPE ON
58 SET INSTRUCT OFF
59 SET SAFETY OFF
60 SET SCOREBOARD OFF
61 SET STATUS OFF
62 SET TALK OFF
63 SET DEFAULT TO C:
64 SET PATH TO c:\db4\data
65
66 *-- Set global variables
67 gn_barv  = 0              && Initialize bar value variable
68 gn_error = 0              && Variable to store error() number
69 gn_send  = 0              && Return variable from popup
70 gc_brdr  = "2"            && Border style for menu box - See Procedure
71 lc_heading = "Customer Data Entry and Reporting System" && Menu heading
     string
72 ll_color = ISCOLOR()
73
74 SET ESCAPE OFF
75
76 *-- Signon Banner
77 tmpcolor = IIF(ll_color,"b/r", "W+/N")
78 @ 5,9 TO 16,69 DOUBLE COLOR &tmpcolor.
79 @ 8,10 SAY "            Customer Data Entry and Reporting"
80 @ 10,10 SAY "         Pacific System Design Workshop, Inc."
81 @ 12,10 SAY "   Copyright, 1989, Pacific System Design Workshop, Inc."
82 @ 14,10 SAY "              All Rights Reserved"
83 IF ll_color
84    @ 6,10 FILL TO 15,68 COLOR w+/b
85 ENDIF
86 ln_inkey = INKEY(5)
87 CLEAR
88 SET ESCAPE ON
89 SET STATUS ON
90 *-- Set colors
91 IF ll_color
92    SET COLOR OF NORMAL TO w+/b
93    SET COLOR OF MESSAGES TO bg+/b
94    SET COLOR OF TITLES TO gr/w
95    SET COLOR OF HIGHLIGHT TO gr+/bg
```

(continued)

```
 96     SET COLOR OF BOX TO b/r
 97     SET COLOR OF INFORMATION TO g/r
 98     SET COLOR OF FIELDS TO b/rb
 99 ENDIF
100
101 USE CUSTOMER
102 SET ORDER TO CUSTCODE
103
104 *-- Define the main popup menu for Quickapp
105 SET BORDER TO DOUBLE
106 DEFINE POPUP quick FROM 7,27
107 DEFINE BAR 1 OF quick PROMPT " Add Information"
        MESSAGE "Add records to database CUSTOMER"
108 DEFINE BAR 2 OF quick PROMPT " Change Information"
        MESSAGE "Edit records in database CUSTOMER"
109 DEFINE BAR 3 OF quick PROMPT " Browse Information"
        MESSAGE "Browse database CUSTOMER"
110 DEFINE BAR 4 OF quick PROMPT " Discard Marked Records "
        MESSAGE "Purge deleted records in database CUSTOMER"
111 DEFINE BAR 5 OF quick PROMPT " Print Report"
        MESSAGE "Run report form CUST4FLD"
112 DEFINE BAR 6 OF quick PROMPT " Mailing Labels"
        MESSAGE "Run label form CUSTLBL"
113 DEFINE BAR 7 OF quick PROMPT " Reindex Database"
        MESSAGE "Reindex database CUSTOMER"
114 DEFINE BAR 8 OF quick PROMPT " Exit From Customer"
        MESSAGE "Exit program to dBASE"
115 ON SELECTION POPUP quick DO Action WITH BAR()
116
117 *-- Define the popup menu for print redirection
118 DEFINE POPUP prntchk FROM 10,55
119 DEFINE BAR 1 OF prntchk PROMPT " Send to..." SKIP
120 DEFINE BAR 2 OF prntchk PROMPT REPLICATE(CHR(196),14) SKIP
121 DEFINE BAR 3 OF prntchk PROMPT " Screen " MESSAGE "Screen only"
122 DEFINE BAR 4 OF prntchk PROMPT " Printer " MESSAGE "Printer LPT1:"
123 DEFINE BAR 5 OF prntchk PROMPT " Label Sample "
      MESSAGE "Printer LPT1: with Sample label"  SKIP FOR gn_barv <> 6
124 DEFINE BAR 6 OF prntchk PROMPT " Return" MESSAGE "Return to Main Menu"
125 ON SELECTION POPUP prntchk DO get_sele
126
127 *-- Window to cover work surface during edit, append, etc.
128 DEFINE WINDOW work FROM 0,0 TO 21,79 NONE
129
130 *-- Window for area below menu heading & for running reports/labels in
131 DEFINE WINDOW desktop FROM 4,0 TO 21,79 NONE
132
133 DEFINE WINDOW printemp FROM 10,25 TO 15,56
134
135 *-- Display heading centered on the screen.
136 DO menubox WITH lc_heading
137
138 *-- Show the menu so we don't get a flash if the user hits arrow keys or ESC
```

(continued)

```
139 SHOW POPUP quick
140 SAVE SCREEN TO quick
141 *-- Display Quickapp menu centered on the screen.
142 DO WHILE gn_barv <> 8 && Prevent user from exiting with arrow keys or ESC
143   ACTIVATE POPUP quick
144 ENDDO
145
146 * Restore SET environment the best we can
147 SET BELL &gc_bell.
148 SET CARRY &gc_carry.
149 SET CLOCK TO
150 SET CLOCK &gc_clock.
151 SET CENTURY &gc_century.
152 SET CONFIRM &gc_confirm.
153 SET DELIMITERS &gc_deli.
154 SET ESCAPE &gc_escape.
155 SET INSTRUCT &gc_instruc.
156 SET STATUS &gc_status.
157 SET SAFETY &gc_safety.
158 SET SCORE  &gc_score.
159 SET TALK   &gc_talk.
160 SET FORMAT TO
161
162 IF gn_apgen = 1 && We were not called from another APGEN program
163    CLEAR WINDOW
164    CLEAR POPUP
165    CLEAR ALL
166    CLOSE ALL
167 ELSE
168    RELEASE WINDOWS work, desktop
169    RELEASE SCREEN quick
170    RELEASE POPUP quick
171    gn_apgen = gn_apgen - 1
172 ENDIF
173 ON ERROR
174 ON KEY LABEL F1
175 RETURN
176 * EOP: C:CUSTOMER.PRG
177
178 **********************************************************************
179 * Procedures...: C:CUSTOMER.Prc
180 * Author.......: Tony Lima
181 * Date.........: 4-18-89
182 * Notice.......: Copyright, 1989, Pacific System Design Workshop, Inc.
183 * dBASE Ver....: dBASE IV, Version 1.0
184 * Generated by.: APGEN version 1.0
185 * Description..: Customer data entry, editing, reports, labels
186
187 * Notes........:
188 **********************************************************************
189
190 *-- Here is a sample procedure file to show the power of procdures.
```

(continued)

```
191 *-- This example - Menubox displays a menu heading box with a centered
           heading.
192 PROCEDURE MenuBox
193 PARAMETER lc_m_name
194 *-- Parameter lc_m_name - is the title variable for the menu
195 SET CLOCK OFF
196 @ 1,0 FILL TO 2,79 COLOR n/n
197 DO CASE
198 CASE gc_brdr = "0"
199    @ 1,0 CLEAR TO 3,79
200 CASE gc_brdr = "1"
201    @ 1,0 TO 3,79
202 CASE gc_brdr = "2"
203    lc_color = IIF(ISCOLOR(),"b/r", "W+/N")
204    @ 1,0 TO 3,79 DOUBLE COLOR &lc_color.
205 ENDCASE
206 SET CLOCK TO 2,68
207 @ 2,1 SAY SUBSTR(CDOW(DATE()),1,3)+'. '+DTOC(DATE())+' '
208 @ 2,41 - (LEN(lc_m_name)/2) SAY lc_m_name
209 lc_color = IIF(ISCOLOR(),"w+/b", "W+/N")
210 @ 2,1 FILL TO 2,78 COLOR &lc_color.
211 RETURN
212
213
214 PROCEDURE get_sele
215 *-- Get the user selection & store BAR into variable
216 gn_send = BAR()   && Variable for print testing
217 DEACTIVATE POPUP
218 RETURN
219
220 PROCEDURE Action
221 PARAMETERS bar
222 *-- Get the user selection & store BAR into variable
223 gn_barv = bar
224 SET MESSAGE TO
225 IF LTRIM( STR( gn_barv)) $ "123"
226    *-- Set format file CUST2PG2 for edit/append/browse
227    SET FORMAT TO CUST2PG2
228 ENDIF
229 DO CASE
230    CASE gn_barv = 1
231       *-- Add information
232       SET MESSAGE TO 'Appending records to file CUSTOMER'
233       APPEND
234    CASE gn_barv = 2
235       *-- Change information
236       SET MESSAGE TO 'Editing file CUSTOMER'
237       EDIT
238    CASE gn_barv = 3
239       *-- Browse information
240       SET MESSAGE TO 'Browsing file CUSTOMER'
241       BROWSE FORMAT
242    CASE gn_barv = 4
```

```
243        *-- Remove information (Pack file customer)
244        ACTIVATE WINDOW desktop
245        @ 2,0 SAY "Packing database CUSTOMER to REMOVE records marked for
              deletion..."
246        @ 3,0
247        SET TALK ON
248        PACK
249        GO TOP
250        ?
251        WAIT
252        SET TALK OFF
253        DEACTIVATE WINDOW desktop
254     CASE gn_barv = 5
255        *-- Run report form cust4fld
256        SET MESSAGE TO 'Pick an option to locate a record or <ESC> for
              default'
257        ACTIVATE WINDOW work
258        gn_recno = RECNO()
259        DO position
260        DEACTIVATE WINDOW work
261        lc_toprnt = IIF(gn_recno <> recno(),'REST ','')
262        STORE 0 TO gn_send, gn_pkey
263        ACTIVATE POPUP prntchk
264        IF gn_send = 4
265           lc_toprnt = 'TO PRINT'
266           ON ERROR DO prntrtry
267        ENDIF
268        IF .NOT. gn_send = 6
269           SET MESSAGE TO 'Printing report CUST4FLD'
270           ACTIVATE WINDOW desktop
271           SET ESCAPE ON
272           REPORT FORM CUST4FLD &lc_toprnt.
273           IF gn_pkey <> 27
274              WAIT
275           ENDIF
276           SET ESCAPE ON
277           DEACTIVATE WINDOW desktop
278        ENDIF
279        GOTO gn_recno
280        ON ERROR DO PAUSE WITH [Error occurred on line ]+LTRIM(STR(LINE()))
              +[ of procedure ]+Program()
281     CASE gn_barv = 6
282        *-- Run label form custlbl
283        SET MESSAGE TO 'Pick an option to locate a record or <ESC> for
              default'
284        ACTIVATE WINDOW work
285        gn_recno = RECNO()
286        DO position
287        DEACTIVATE WINDOW work
288        STORE 0 TO gn_send, gn_pkey
289        lc_toprnt = IIF(gn_recno <> recno(),'REST ','')
290        ACTIVATE POPUP prntchk
```

(continued)

```
291        DO CASE
292         CASE gn_send = 4
293           lc_toprnt = 'TO PRINT'
294         CASE gn_send = 5
295           lc_toprnt = 'TO PRINT SAMPLE'
296        ENDCASE
297        IF .NOT. gn_send = 6
298           SET MESSAGE TO 'Printing labels'
299           ACTIVATE WINDOW desktop
300           SET ESCAPE ON
301           ON ERROR DO prntrtry
302           LABEL FORM CUSTLBL &lc_toprnt.
303           IF gn_pkey <> 27
304              WAIT
305           ENDIF
306           SET ESCAPE ON
307           DEACTIVATE WINDOW desktop
308        ENDIF
309        GOTO gn_recno
310        ON ERROR DO PAUSE WITH [Error occurred on line ]+LTRIM(STR(LINE()))
              +[ of procedure ]+Program()
311     CASE gn_barv = 7
312        *-- Reindex customer
313        ACTIVATE WINDOW desktop
314        @ 3,0 SAY "Reindexing database CUSTOMER..."
315        @ 4,0
316        SET TALK ON
317        REINDEX
318        GO TOP
319        ?
320        WAIT
321        SET TALK OFF
322        DEACTIVATE WINDOW desktop
323     CASE gn_barv = 8
324        DEACTIVATE POPUP
325 ENDCASE
326 SET MESSAGE TO
327 IF gc_status = "OFF"
328    SET STATUS ON
329 ENDIF
330 SET FORMAT TO
331 RESTORE SCREEN FROM quick
332 RETURN
333
334 PROCEDURE Pause
335 PARAMETER lc_msg
336 *-- Parameters : lc_msg = message line
337 IF TYPE("lc_message")="U"
338    gn_error=ERROR()
339 ENDIF
340 lc_msg = lc_msg
```

(continued)

```
341 lc_option='0'
342 ACTIVATE WINDOW Pause
343 IF gn_error > 0
344    IF TYPE("lc_message")="U"
345       @ 0,1 SAY [An error has occurred !! - Error message: ]+MESSAGE()
346    ELSE
347       @ 0,1 SAY [Error # ]+lc_message
348    ENDIF
349 ENDIF
350 @ 1,1 SAY lc_msg
351 WAIT " Press any key to continue..."
352 DEACTIVATE WINDOW Pause
353 RETURN
354
355
356 PROCEDURE quickhlp
357 *-- If you want to include help for a quickapp uncomment the lines below and
358 *-- put your help @ say's into the case statements
359 *ACTIVATE WINDOW desktop
360 *CLEAR
361 DO CASE
362    CASE BAR() = 1
363    CASE BAR() = 2
364    CASE BAR() = 3
365    CASE BAR() = 4
366    CASE BAR() = 5
367    CASE BAR() = 6
368    CASE BAR() = 7
369    CASE BAR() = 8
370 ENDCASE
371 *WAIT
372 *DEACTIVATE WINDOW desktop
373 RETURN
374
375 PROCEDURE Position
376 IF LEN(DBF()) = 0
377    DO Pause WITH "Database not in use. "
378    RETURN
379 ENDIF
380 SET SPACE ON
381 SET DELIMITERS OFF
382 ln_type=0          && sublevel selection
383 ln_rkey=READKEY()  && test for ESC or Return
384 ln_rec=RECNO()     && DBF record number
385 ln_num=0           && for input of a number
386 ld_date=DATE()     && for input of a date
387 lc_option='0'      && main option ie. Seek, Goto and Locate
388 *-- Scope ie. ALL, REST, NEXT <n>
389 STORE SPACE(10) TO lc_scp
390 *-- 1 = Character SEEK, 2 = For clause, 3 = While clause
391 STORE SPACE(40) TO lc_ln1, lc_ln2, lc_ln3
```

(continued)

```
392 lc_temp=""
393 @ 0,00 SAY "Index order: "+IIF(""=ORDER(),"Database is in natural
       order",ORDER())
394 @ 1,00 SAY "Listed below are the first 16 fields."
395 lc_temp=REPLICATE(CHR(196),19)
396 @ 2,0 SAY
       CHR(218)+lc_temp+CHR(194)+lc_temp+CHR(194)+lc_temp+CHR(194)+lc_temp
397 ln_num=240
398 DO WHILE ln_num < 560
399    lc_temp=FIELD( (ln_num-240)/20 +1)
400    @ (ln_num/80),MOD(ln_num,80) SAY CHR(179)+;
401 lc_temp+SPACE(11-LEN(lc_temp))+;
402 SUBSTR("= Char  = Date  = Logic = Num   = Float = Memo          ",;
403 AT(TYPE(lc_temp),"CDLNFMU")*8-7,8)
404    ln_num=ln_num+20
405 ENDDO
406 ln_num=1
407
408 DEFINE POPUP Posit1 FROM 8,30
409 DEFINE BAR 1 OF Posit1 PROMPT " Position by " SKIP
410 DEFINE BAR 2 OF Posit1 PROMPT REPLICATE(CHR(196),15) SKIP
411 DEFINE BAR 3 OF Posit1 PROMPT " SEEK Record"
       MESSAGE "Search on index key" SKIP FOR ""=ORDER()
412 DEFINE BAR 4 OF Posit1 PROMPT " GOTO Record"
       MESSAGE "Position to specific record"
413 DEFINE BAR 5 OF Posit1 PROMPT " LOCATE Record "
       MESSAGE "Locate record for condition"
414 DEFINE BAR 6 OF Posit1 PROMPT " Return" MESSAGE "Return without positioning"
415 ON SELECTION POPUP Posit1 DO get_sele
416
417 SET CONFIRM ON
418 DO WHILE lc_option='0'
419   ACTIVATE POPUP Posit1
420   lc_option = ltrim(str(gn_send))  && for popup
421     IF LASTKEY() = 27 .OR. lc_option="6"
422        GOTO ln_rec
423        EXIT
424     ENDIF
425     DO CASE
426     CASE lc_option='3'
427        *-- Seek
428        IF LEN(NDX(1))=0 .AND. LEN(MDX(1))=0
429           DO Pause WITH "Can't use this option - No index files are open."
430           LOOP
431        ENDIF
432        ln_type=1
433        lc_ln1=SPACE(40)
434        DEFINE WINDOW Posit2 FROM 8,19 TO 15,62 DOUBLE
435        ACTIVATE WINDOW Posit2
436        @ 1,1 SAY "Enter the type of expression:" GET ln_type PICT
              "#" RANGE 1,3
437        @ 2,1 SAY "(1=character, 2=numeric and 3=date.)"
```

(continued)

```
438        READ
439        IF .NOT. (READKEY() = 12 .OR. READKEY() = 268)
440           SET CONFIRM ON
441           @ 3,1 SAY "Enter the key expression to search for:"
442           IF ln_type=3
443              @ 4,1 GET ld_date PICT "@D"
444           ELSE
445              IF ln_type=2
446                 @ 4,1 GET ln_num PICT "##########"
447              ELSE
448                 @ 4,1 GET lc_ln1
449              ENDIF
450           ENDIF
451           READ
452           SET CONFIRM OFF
453           IF .NOT. (READKEY() = 12 .OR. READKEY() = 268)
454              lc_temp=IIF(ln_type=1,"TRIM(lc_ln1)",;
                    IIF(ln_type=2,"ln_num","ld_date"))
455              SEEK &lc_temp.
456           ENDIF
457        ENDIF
458        RELEASE WINDOWS Posit2
459     CASE lc_option='4'
460        *-- Goto
461        ln_type=1
462        DEFINE POPUP Posit2 FROM 8,30
463        DEFINE BAR 1 OF Posit2 PROMPT " GOTO:" SKIP
464        DEFINE BAR 2 OF Posit2 PROMPT REPLICATE(CHR(196),10) SKIP
465        DEFINE BAR 3 OF Posit2 PROMPT " TOP" MESSAGE "GOTO Top of File"
466        DEFINE BAR 4 OF Posit2 PROMPT " BOTTOM" MESSAGE "GOTO Bottom of File"
467        DEFINE BAR 5 OF Posit2 PROMPT " Record # ";
              MESSAGE "GOTO A Specific Record"
468        ON SELECTION POPUP Posit2 DO get_sele
469        ACTIVATE POPUP posit2
470        ln_type = gn_send
471        IF LASTKEY() <> 27
472           IF ln_type=5
473              DEFINE WINDOW Posit2 FROM 8,26 TO 13,50 DOUBLE
474              ACTIVATE WINDOW Posit2
475              ln_num=0
476              @ 3,1 SAY "Max. Record # = "+LTRIM(STR(RECCOUNT()))
477              @ 1,1 SAY "Record to GOTO" GET ln_num PICT "######";
                    RANGE 1,RECCOUNT()
478              READ
479              IF .NOT. (READKEY() = 12 .OR. READKEY() = 268)
480                 GOTO ln_num
481              ENDIF
482              RELEASE WINDOWS Posit2
483           ELSE
484              lc_temp=IIF(ln_type=3,"TOP","BOTTOM")
485              GOTO &lc_temp.
486           ENDIF
```

(continued)

```
487         ENDIF
488     CASE lc_option='5'
489         *-- Locate
490         DEFINE WINDOW Posit2 FROM 8,16 TO 14,66 DOUBLE
491         ACTIVATE WINDOW Posit2
492         @ 1,19 SAY "ie. ALL, NEXT <n>, and REST"
493         @ 1,01 SAY "Scope:" GET lc_scp
494         @ 2,01 SAY "For:  " GET lc_ln2
495         @ 3,01 SAY "While:" GET lc_ln3
496         READ
497         IF .NOT. (READKEY() = 12 .OR. READKEY() = 268)
498            lc_temp=TRIM(lc_scp)
499            lc_temp=lc_temp + IIF(LEN(TRIM(lc_ln2)) > 0," FOR "
                 +TRIM(lc_ln2),"")
500            lc_temp=lc_temp + IIF(LEN(TRIM(lc_ln3)) > 0," WHILE "
                 +TRIM(lc_ln3),"")
501            IF LEN(lc_temp) > 0
502                LOCATE &lc_temp.
503            ELSE
504                DO Pause WITH "All fields were blank."
505            ENDIF
506         ENDIF
507         RELEASE WINDOW Posit2
508     ENDCASE
509     IF EOF()
510         DO Pause WITH "Record not found."
511         GOTO ln_rec
512     ENDIF
513     IF READKEY()=12 .OR. READKEY()= 268 .OR. LASTKEY()=27  && Esc was hit
514         lc_option='0'
515     ENDIF
516 ENDDO
517 SET DELIMITERS &gc_deli.
518 SET CONFIRM OFF
519 RETURN
520
521
522 PROC prntrtry
523 PRIVATE lc_escape
524 lc_escape = SET("ESCAPE")
525 IF .NOT. PRINTSTATUS()
526    IF lc_escape = "ON"
527            SET ESCAPE OFF
528        ENDIF
529    gn_pkey = 0
530    ACTIVATE WINDOW printemp
531    @ 1,0 SAY "Please ready your printer or"
532    @ 2,0 SAY "     press ESC to cancel"
533    DO WHILE ( .NOT. PRINTSTATUS()) .AND. gn_pkey <> 27
534       gn_pkey = INKEY()
535    ENDDO
536    DEACTIVATE WINDOW printemp
```

(continued)

```
537     SET ESCAPE &lc_escape
538     IF gn_pkey <> 27
539        RETRY
540     ENDIF
541 ENDIF
542 RETURN
543 * EOF: C:CUSTOMER.PRG
544
```

Appendix C

New CUSTOMER.PRG

```
 1  ******************************************************************************
 2  * Program......: C:CUSTOMER
 3  * Author.......: Tony Lima
 4  * Date.........: 4-23-89
 5  * Notice.......: Copyright, 1989, Pacific System Design Workshop, Inc.
 6  * dBASE Ver....: dBASE IV, Version 1.0
 7  * Generated by.: APGEN version 0.96
 8  * Description..: Customer data entry, editing, reports, labels
 9
10  * Notes........:
11  ******************************************************************************
12
13  SET CONSOLE OFF
14  IF TYPE("gn_apgen") = "U"  && We were not called from another APGEN program
15     CLEAR ALL
16     CLEAR WINDOW
17     CLOSE ALL
18     gn_apgen = 1
19  ELSE
20     gn_apgen = gn_apgen + 1
21     PRIVATE gc_bell, gc_carry, gc_clock, gc_century, gc_confirm, gc_deli,;
22             gc_escape, gc_instruc, gc_safety, gc_status, gc_score, gc_talk
23  ENDIF
24
25  *-- Window for pause message box (ON ERROR)
26  DEFINE WINDOW Pause FROM 15,00 TO 19,79 DOUBLE
27  ON ERROR DO PAUSE WITH "Error occurred on line "+LTRIM(STR(LINE())) +
28     " of procedure "+Program()
29  *-- Initialize screen size variable
30  ln_scrsize = 17
31
32  *-- Store initial SETs to variables
33  STORE "" TO gc_bell,gc_carry,gc_clock,gc_century,gc_confirm,;
34             gc_deli,gc_escape,gc_instruc,gc_safety,gc_status,;
35             gc_score,gc_talk
36
37  DO Setstore WITH gc_bell,gc_carry,gc_clock,gc_century,gc_confirm,;
38             gc_deli,gc_escape,gc_instruc,gc_safety,gc_status,;
39             gc_score,gc_talk
40
41  *-- SET environment
42  DO Start WITH gc_bell,gc_carry,gc_clock,gc_century,gc_confirm,;
43             gc_deli,gc_escape,gc_instruc,gc_safety,gc_status,;
44             gc_score,gc_talk
```

(continued)

```
45
46 *-- Set global variables
47 gn_barv  = 0              && Initialize bar value variable
48 gn_error = 0              && Variable to store error() number
49 gn_send  = 0              && Return variable from popup
50 gc_brdr = "2"             && Border style for menu box - See Procedure
51 lc_heading = "Customer Data Entry and Reporting System" && Menu heading
   string
52 lc_color = ISCOLOR()
53
54 SET ESCAPE OFF
55
56 *-- Signon Banner
57 tmpcolor = IIF(lc_color,"b/r", "W+/N")
58 @ 5,9 TO 16,69 DOUBLE COLOR &tmpcolor.
59 @ 8,10 SAY "           Customer Data Entry and Reporting"
60 @ 10,10 SAY "          Pacific System Design Workshop, Inc."
61 @ 12,10 SAY "   Copyright, 1989, Pacific System Design Workshop, Inc."
62 @ 14,10 SAY "              All Rights Reserved"
63 IF lc_color
64    @ 6,10 FILL TO 15,68 COLOR w+/b
65 ENDIF
66 ln_inkey = inkey(5)
67 CLEAR
68 SET ESCAPE ON
69 SET STATUS ON
70 *-- Set colors
71 IF lc_color
72    SET COLOR OF NORMAL TO w+/b
73    SET COLOR OF MESSAGES TO bg+/b
74    SET COLOR OF TITLES TO gr/w
75    SET COLOR OF HIGHLIGHT TO gr+/bg
76    SET COLOR OF BOX TO b/r
77    SET COLOR OF INFORMATION TO g/r
78    SET COLOR OF FIELDS TO b/rb
79 ENDIF
80
81 USE CUSTOMER ORDER CUSTCODE
82
83 *-- Define the main popup menu for Quickapp
84 SET BORDER TO DOUBLE
85 DEFINE POPUP quick FROM 7,27
86 DEFINE BAR 1 OF quick PROMPT " Add Information"
      MESSAGE "Add records to database CUSTOMER"
87 DEFINE BAR 2 OF quick PROMPT " Change Information"
      MESSAGE "Edit records in database CUSTOMER"
88 DEFINE BAR 3 OF quick PROMPT " Browse Information"
      MESSAGE "Browse database CUSTOMER"
89 DEFINE BAR 4 OF quick PROMPT " Discard Marked Records "
      MESSAGE "Purge deleted records in database CUSTOMER"
90 DEFINE BAR 5 OF quick PROMPT " Print Report"
      MESSAGE "Run report form CUST4FLD"
```

(continued)

```
 91 DEFINE BAR 6 OF quick PROMPT " Mailing Labels"
       MESSAGE "Run label form CUSTLBL"
 92 DEFINE BAR 7 OF quick PROMPT " Reindex Database"
       MESSAGE "Reindex database CUSTOMER"
 93 DEFINE BAR 8 OF quick PROMPT " Select new key"
       MESSAGE "Select new primary key for CUSTOMER"
 94 DEFINE BAR 9 OF quick PROMPT " Exit From Customer"
       MESSAGE "Exit program to dBASE"
 95 ON SELECTION POPUP quick DO Action WITH BAR()
 96
 97 *-- Define the popup menu for label redirection
 98 DEFINE POPUP lbltchk FROM 10,55
 99 DEFINE BAR 1 OF lbltchk PROMPT " Send to..." SKIP
100 DEFINE BAR 2 OF lbltchk PROMPT REPLICATE(CHR(196),14) SKIP
101 DEFINE BAR 3 OF lbltchk PROMPT " Screen " MESSAGE "Screen only"
102 DEFINE BAR 4 OF lbltchk PROMPT " Printer" MESSAGE "Printer LPT1:"
103 DEFINE BAR 5 OF lbltchk PROMPT " Label Sample "
       MESSAGE "Printer LPT1: with Sample label" SKIP FOR gn_barv <> 6
104 DEFINE BAR 6 OF lbltchk PROMPT " Return" MESSAGE "Return to Main Menu"
105 ON SELECTION POPUP lbltchk DO get_sele
106
107 *-- Define the popup menu for print redirection
108 DEFINE POPUP prntchk FROM 10,55
109 DEFINE BAR 1 OF prntchk PROMPT " Send to..." SKIP
110 DEFINE BAR 2 OF prntchk PROMPT REPLICATE(CHR(196),14) SKIP
111 DEFINE BAR 3 OF prntchk PROMPT " Screen " MESSAGE "Screen only"
112 DEFINE BAR 4 OF prntchk PROMPT " Printer" MESSAGE "Printer LPT1:"
113 DEFINE BAR 5 OF prntchk PROMPT REPLICATE(CHR(196),14) SKIP
114 DEFINE BAR 6 OF prntchk PROMPT " Return" MESSAGE "Return to Main Menu"
115 ON SELECTION POPUP prntchk DO get_sele
116
117 *-- Window to cover work surface during edit, append, etc.
118 DEFINE WINDOW work FROM 0,0 TO 21,79 NONE
119
120 *-- Window for area below menu heading & for running reports/labels in
121 DEFINE WINDOW desktop FROM 4,0 TO 21,79 NONE
122
123 DEFINE WINDOW printemp FROM 10,25 TO 15,56
124
125 *-- Display heading centered on the screen.
126 DO menubox WITH lc_heading
127
128 *-- Show the menu so we don't get a flash if the user hits arrow keys or ESC
129 SHOW POPUP quick
130 SAVE SCREEN TO quick
131 *-- Display Quickapp menu centered on the screen.
132 DO WHILE gn_barv <> 9 && Prevent user from exiting with arrow keys or ESC
133    ACTIVATE POPUP quick
134 ENDDO
135
136 DO Stop WITH gc_bell,gc_carry,gc_clock,gc_century,gc_confirm,;
137          gc_deli,gc_escape,gc_instruc,gc_safety,gc_status,;
```

(continued)

```
138              gc_score,gc_talk
139
140 RETURN
141 * EOP: C:CUSTOMER.PRG
142
143 *****************************************************************************
144 * Procedures...: C:CUSTOMER.Prc
145 * Author.......: Tony Lima
146 * Date.........: 4-23-89
147 * Notice.......: Copyright, 1989, Pacific System Design Workshop, Inc.
148 * dBASE Ver....: dBASE IV, Version 1.0
149 * Generated by.: APGEN version 0.96
150 * Description..: Customer data entry, editing, reports, labels
151
152 * Notes........:
153 *****************************************************************************
154
155 *-- Here is a sample procedure file to show the beginning user what
156 *    the power of procdures will do for him.
157 *-- This example - Menubox displays a menu heading box with a centered
        heading.
158 PROCEDURE MenuBox
159 PARAMETER lc_m_name
160 *-- Parameter lc_m_name - is the title variable for the menu
161 SET CLOCK OFF
162 @ 1,0 FILL TO 2,79 COLOR n/n
163 DO CASE
164 CASE gc_brdr = "0"
165    @ 1,0 CLEAR TO 3,79
166 CASE gc_brdr = "1"
167    @ 1,0 TO 3,79
168 CASE gc_brdr = "2"
169    lc_color = IIF(ISCOLOR(),"b/r", "W+/N")
170    @ 1,0 TO 3,79 DOUBLE COLOR &lc_color.
171 ENDCASE
172 SET CLOCK TO 2,68
173 @ 2,1 SAY SUBSTR(CDOW(DATE()),1,3)+'. '+DTOC(DATE())+' '
174 @ 2,41 - (LEN(lc_m_name)/2) SAY lc_m_name
175 lc_color = IIF(ISCOLOR(),"w+/b", "W+/N")
176 @ 2,1 FILL TO 2,78 COLOR &lc_color.
177 RETURN
178
179
180 PROCEDURE get_sele
181 *-- Get the user selection & store BAR into variable
182 gn_send = BAR()   && Variable for print testing
183 DEACTIVATE POPUP
184 RETURN
185
186 PROCEDURE Action
187 PARAMETERS bar
188 *-- Get the user selection & store BAR into variable
```

(continued)

```
189 gn_barv = bar
190 SET MESSAGE TO ' '
191 IF LTRIM( STR( gn_barv)) $ "123"
192    *-- Set format file CUST2PG2 for edit/append/browse
193    SET FORMAT TO CUST2PG2
194 ENDIF
195 DO CASE
196    CASE gn_barv = 1
197       *-- Add information
198       SET MESSAGE TO 'Appending records to file CUSTOMER'
199       APPEND
200    CASE gn_barv = 2
201       *-- Change information
202       SET MESSAGE TO 'Editing file CUSTOMER'
203       EDIT
204    CASE gn_barv = 3
205       *-- Browse information
206       SET MESSAGE TO 'Browsing file CUSTOMER'
207       BROWSE FORMAT
208    CASE gn_barv = 4
209       *-- Remove information (Pack file customer)
210       ACTIVATE WINDOW desktop
211       @ 2,0 SAY 'Packing database CUSTOMER to REMOVE records marked for
            deletion...'
212       @ 3,0
213       SET TALK ON
214       PACK
215       GO TOP
216       ?
217       WAIT
218       SET TALK OFF
219       DEACTIVATE WINDOW desktop
220    CASE gn_barv = 5
221       *-- Run report form cust4fld
222       SET MESSAGE TO 'Pick an option to locate a record or <ESC> for
            default'
223       ACTIVATE WINDOW work
224       gn_recno = RECNO()
225       DO position
226       DEACTIVATE WINDOW work
227       ln_plength = _plength
228       ll_pwait = _pwait
229       lc_toprnt = IIF(gn_recno <> recno(),'REST ','')
230       STORE 0 TO gn_send, gn_pkey
231       ACTIVATE POPUP prntchk
232       IF gn_send = 3
233          _plength = ln_scrsize
234          _pwait = .T.
235       ENDIF && gn_send = 3
236       IF gn_send = 4
237          lc_toprnt = lc_toprnt+'TO PRINT'
238          ON ERROR DO prntrtry
```

(continued)

```
239        ENDIF && gn_send = 4
240        IF .NOT. gn_send = 6
241           ACTIVATE WINDOW desktop
242           IF gc_escape="OFF"
243              SET ESCAPE ON
244           ENDIF
245           REPORT FORM CUST4FLD &lc_toprnt.
246           IF gn_pkey <> 27
247              WAIT
248           ENDIF
249           SET ESCAPE &gc_escape.
250           _plength = ln_plength
251           _pwait = ll_pwait
252           DEACTIVATE WINDOW desktop
253        ENDIF && .NOT. gn_send = 6
254        GOTO gn_recno
255        ON ERROR DO PAUSE WITH "Error occurred on line "+LTRIM(STR(LINE()))
             +" of procedure "+Program()
256     CASE gn_barv = 6
257        *-- Run label form custlbl
258        SET MESSAGE TO 'Pick an option to locate a record or <ESC> for
             default'
259        ACTIVATE WINDOW work
260        gn_recno = RECNO()
261        DO position
262        DEACTIVATE WINDOW work
263        STORE 0 TO gn_send, gn_pkey
264        ln_plength = _plength
265        ll_pwait = _pwait
266        lc_toprnt = IIF(gn_recno <> recno(),'REST ','')
267        ACTIVATE POPUP lbltchk
268        DO CASE
269         CASEgn_send = 3
270           _plength = ln_scrsize
271           _pwait = .T.
272         CASE gn_send = 4
273           lc_toprnt = lc_toprnt+'TO PRINT'
274         CASE gn_send = 5
275           lc_toprnt = lc_torpnt+'TO PRINT SAMPLE'
276        ENDCASE
277        IF .NOT. gn_send = 6
278           ACTIVATE WINDOW desktop
279           IF gc_escape="OFF"
280              SET ESCAPE ON
281           ENDIF
282           ON ERROR DO prntrtry
283           LABEL FORM CUSTLBL &lc_toprnt.
284           IF gn_pkey <> 27
285              WAIT
286           ENDIF
287           _plength = ln_plength
288           _pwait = ll_pwait
```

(continued)

```
289            SET ESCAPE &gc_escape.
290            DEACTIVATE WINDOW desktop
291        ENDIF
292        GOTO gn_recno
293        ON ERROR DO PAUSE WITH "Error occurred on line "+LTRIM(STR(LINE()))
           +" of procedure "+Program()
294    CASE gn_barv = 7
295        *-- Reindex customer
296        ACTIVATE WINDOW desktop
297        @ 3,0 SAY 'Reindexing database CUSTOMER...'
298        @ 4,0
299        SET TALK ON
300        REINDEX
301        GO TOP
302        ?
303        WAIT
304        SET TALK OFF
305        DEACTIVATE WINDOW desktop
306    CASE gn_barv = 8
307        *-- Select new primary key for customer
308        ACTIVATE WINDOW work
309        IF TYPE("TAGLIST[1]") = "U"
310          DECLARE TAGLIST[47],KEYLIST[47]
311          ln_keyno = 1
312          lc_order = TRIM(ORDER())
313          DO WHILE LEN(TRIM(TAG(ln_keyno))) <> 0
314            TAGLIST[ln_keyno] = TAG(ln_keyno)
315            KEYLIST[ln_keyno] = KEY(ln_keyno)
316            IF TRIM(TAGLIST[ln_keyno]) = TRIM(ORDER())
317              ln_ordno = ln_keyno
318            ENDIF && TRIM(TAGLIST[ln_keyno]) = TRIM(ORDER())
319            ln_keyno = ln_keyno + 1
320          ENDDO && TAG(ln_keyno) <> ""
321          ln_maxkey = ln_keyno - 1
322        ENDIF && TYPE("TAGLIST[1]") = "U"
323        @ 01,20 SAY "Select an index key to use for this report."
324        ln_keyno = 1
325        ll_break = .T.
326        DO WHILE ln_keyno <= ln_maxkey
327          DO CASE
328          CASE ln_keyno <= 16
329            @ 02,04 SAY "Index Tag"
330            @ 02,16 SAY "Key"
331            IF TRIM(TAGLIST[ln_keyno]) = lc_order
332              @ ln_keyno+2,00 SAY STR(ln_keyno,2)+".*"+TAGLIST[ln_keyno]+;
333                SPACE(10-LEN(TAGLIST[ln_keyno]))+"  "+;
334                SUBSTR(KEYLIST[ln_keyno],1,11)
335            ELSE
336              @ ln_keyno+2,00 SAY STR(ln_keyno,2)+". "+TAGLIST[ln_keyno]+;
337                SPACE(10-LEN(TAGLIST[ln_keyno]))+"  "+;
338                SUBSTR(KEYLIST[ln_keyno],1,11)
339            ENDIF && TAG(ln_keyno) = lc_order
```

(continued)

```
340              CASE ln_keyno <= 32
341                 @ 02,30 SAY "Index Tag"
342                 @ 02,42 SAY "Key"
343                 IF TRIM(TAGLIST[ln_keyno]) = lc_order
344                    @ ln_keyno-14,26 SAY STR(ln_keyno,2)+".*"+TAGLIST[ln_keyno]+;
345                       SPACE(10-LEN(TAGLIST[ln_keyno]))+"  "+;
346                       SUBSTR(KEYLIST[ln_keyno],1,11)
347                  ELSE
348                    @ ln_keyno-14,26 SAY STR(ln_keyno,2)+". "+TAGLIST[ln_keyno]+;
349                       SPACE(10-LEN(TAGLIST[ln_keyno]))+"  "+;
350                       SUBSTR(KEYLIST[ln_keyno],1,11)
351                 ENDIF && TAG(ln_keyno) = lc_order
352              CASE ln_keyno <= 47
353                 @ 02,56 SAY "Index Tag"
354                 @ 02,68 SAY "Key"
355                 IF TRIM(TAGLIST[ln_keyno]) = lc_order
356                    @ ln_keyno-30,52 SAY STR(ln_keyno,2)+".*"+TAGLIST[ln_keyno]+;
357                       SPACE(10-LEN(TAGLIST[ln_keyno]))+"  "+;
358                       SUBSTR(KEYLIST[ln_keyno],1,11)
359                  ELSE
360                    @ ln_keyno-30,52 SAY STR(ln_keyno,2)+". "+TAGLIST[ln_keyno]+;
361                       SPACE(10-LEN(TAGLIST[ln_keyno]))+"  "+;
362                       SUBSTR(KEYLIST[ln_keyno],1,11)
363                 ENDIF && ORDER(ln_keyno) = lc_order
364              ENDCASE
365           ln_keyno = ln_keyno + 1
366           ENDDO && WHILE ln_keyno <= ln_maxkey
367           lc_choice = IIF(LEN(STR(ln_ordno))=1,"0"+STR(ln_ordno,1),;
              STR(ln_ordno,2))
368           DO WHILE ln_keyno > ln_maxkey
369              @ 19,23 SAY "Which index? " GET lc_choice PICTURE '#9' ;
370                 DEFAULT lc_order ;
371                 MESSAGE "Current tag is "+TRIM(TAGLIST[ln_ordno])+;
372                 " with key "+TRIM(KEYLIST[ln_ordno])+;
373                 ". Be sure to enter leading blank."
374              READ
375              ln_keyno = VAL(lc_choice)
376           ENDDO
377           SET ORDER TO &TAGLIST[ln_keyno]
378           ****************************************
379           DEACTIVATE WINDOW work
380        CASE gn_barv = 9
381           DEACTIVATE POPUP
382 ENDCASE
383 SET MESSAGE TO ' '
384 IF gc_status = "OFF"
385    SET STATUS ON
386 ENDIF
387 SET FORMAT TO
388 IF LTRIM( STR( gn_barv)) $ "123"
389    RESTORE SCREEN FROM quick
390 ENDIF
```

(continued)

```
391 RETURN
392
393 PROCEDURE Pause
394 PARAMETER lc_msg
395 *-- Parameters : lc_msg = message line
396 IF TYPE("lc_message")="U"
397    gn_error=ERROR()
398 ENDIF
399 lc_msg = lc_msg
400 lc_option='0'
401 ACTIVATE WINDOW Pause
402 IF gn_error > 0
403    IF TYPE("lc_message")="U"
404       @ 0,1 SAY "An error has occurred !! - Error message: "+MESSAGE()
405    ELSE
406       @ 0,1 SAY "Error # "+lc_message
407    ENDIF
408 ENDIF
409 @ 1,1 SAY lc_msg
410 WAIT " Press any key to continue..."
411 DEACTIVATE WINDOW Pause
412 RETURN
413
414
415 PROCEDURE Setstore
416 PARAMETERS gc_bell,gc_carry,gc_clock,gc_century,gc_confirm,;
417            gc_deli,gc_escape,gc_instruc,gc_safety,gc_status,;
418            gc_score,gc_talk
419
420 gc_bell   =SET("BELL")
421 gc_carry  =SET("CARRY")
422 gc_clock  =SET("CLOCK")
423 gc_century=SET("CENTURY")
424 gc_confirm=SET("CONFIRM")
425 gc_deli   =SET("DELIMITERS")
426 gc_escape =SET("ESCAPE")
427 gc_instruc=SET("INSTRUCT")
428 gc_safety =SET("SAFETY")
429 gc_status =SET("STATUS")
430 gc_score  =SET("SCOREBOARD")
431 gc_talk   =SET("TALK")
432 RETURN
433
434 PROCEDURE Start
435 PARAMETERS gc_bell,gc_carry,gc_clock,gc_century,gc_confirm,;
436            gc_deli,gc_escape,gc_instruc,gc_safety,gc_status,;
437            gc_score,gc_talk
438
439 SET CLOCK OFF
440 SET COLOR TO
441 CLEAR
442 SET CONSOLE ON
```

(continued)

```
443
444 *-- Sets for application
445 SET BELL ON
446 SET BELL TO 220,2
447 SET CARRY OFF
448 SET CENTURY OFF
449 SET CONFIRM OFF
450 SET DELIMITERS TO "  "
451 SET DELIMITER OFF
452 SET ESCAPE ON
453 SET INSTRUCT OFF
454 SET SAFETY OFF
455 SET SCOREBOARD OFF
456 SET STATUS OFF
457 SET TALK OFF
458 SET DEFAULT TO C:
459 SET PATH TO c:\db4\data
460 RETURN
461
462 PROCEDURE Stop
463 PARAMETERS gc_bell,gc_carry,gc_clock,gc_century,gc_confirm,;
464            gc_deli,gc_escape,gc_instruc,gc_safety,gc_status,;
465            gc_score,gc_talk
466
467 * Restore SET environment the best we can
468 SET BELL &gc_bell.
469 SET CARRY &gc_carry.
470 SET CLOCK TO
471 SET CLOCK &gc_clock.
472 SET CENTURY &gc_century.
473 SET CONFIRM &gc_confirm.
474 SET DELIMITERS &gc_deli.
475 SET ESCAPE &gc_escape.
476 SET INSTRUCT &gc_instruc.
477 SET STATUS &gc_status.
478 SET SAFETY &gc_safety.
479 SET SCORE  &gc_score.
480 SET TALK   &gc_talk.
481 SET FORMAT TO
482
483 IF gn_apgen = 1 && We were not called from another APGEN program
484    CLEAR WINDOW
485    CLEAR POPUP
486    CLEAR ALL
487    CLOSE ALL
488 ELSE
489    RELEASE WINDOWS work, desktop
490    RELEASE SCREEN quick
491    RELEASE POPUP quick
492    gn_apgen = gn_apgen - 1
493 ENDIF
494 ON ERROR
```

(continued)

```
495 RETURN
496
497 PROCEDURE Position
498 IF LEN(DBF()) = 0
499    DO Pause WITH "Database not in use. "
500    RETURN
501 ENDIF
502 SET SPACE ON
503 SET DELIMITERS OFF
504 ln_type=0          && sublevel selection
505 ln_rkey=READKEY()  && test for ESC or Return
506 ln_rec=RECNO()     && DBF record number
507 ln_num=0           && for input of a number
508 ld_date=DATE()     && for input of a date
509 lc_option='0'      && main option ie. Seek, Goto and Locate
510 *-- Scope ie. ALL, REST, NEXT <n>
511 STORE SPACE(10) TO lc_scp
512 *-- 1 = Character SEEK, 2 = For clause, 3 = While clause
513 STORE SPACE(40) TO lc_ln1, lc_ln2, lc_ln3
514 lc_temp=""
515 @ 0,00 SAY "Index order: "+IIF(""=ORDER(),"Database is in natural
       order",ORDER())
516 @ 1,00 SAY "Listed below are the first 16 fields."
517 lc_temp=REPLICATE(CHR(196),19)
518 @ 2,0 SAY CHR(218)+lc_temp+CHR(194)+lc_temp+CHR(194)+
       lc_temp+CHR(194)+lc_temp
519 ln_num=240
520 DO WHILE ln_num < 560
521    lc_temp=FIELD( (ln_num-240)/20 +1)
522    @ (ln_num/80),MOD(ln_num,80) SAY CHR(179)+;
523 lc_temp+SPACE(11-LEN(lc_temp))+;
524 SUBSTR("= Char  = Date  = Logic = Num   = Float = Memo          ",;
525 AT(TYPE(lc_temp),"CDLNFMU")*8-7,8)
526    ln_num=ln_num+20
527 ENDDO
528 ln_num=1
529
530 DEFINE POPUP Posit1 FROM 8,30
531 DEFINE BAR 1 OF Posit1 PROMPT " Position by " SKIP
532 DEFINE BAR 2 OF Posit1 PROMPT REPLICATE(CHR(196),15) SKIP
533 DEFINE BAR 3 OF Posit1 PROMPT " SEEK Record"
       MESSAGE "Search on index key" SKIP FOR ""=ORDER()
534 DEFINE BAR 4 OF Posit1 PROMPT " GOTO Record"
       MESSAGE "Position to specific record"
535 DEFINE BAR 5 OF Posit1 PROMPT " LOCATE Record "
       MESSAGE "Locate record for condition"
536 DEFINE BAR 6 OF Posit1 PROMPT " Return"
       MESSAGE "Return without positioning"
537 ON SELECTION POPUP Posit1 DO get_sele
538
539 SET CONFIRM ON
540 DO WHILE lc_option='0'
```

(continued)

```
541    ACTIVATE POPUP Posit1
542    lc_option = ltrim(str(gn_send))   && for popup
543    IF LASTKEY() = 27 .OR. lc_option="6"
544       GOTO ln_rec
545       EXIT
546    ENDIF
547    DO CASE
548    CASE lc_option='3'
549       *-- Seek
550       IF LEN(NDX(1))=0 .AND. LEN(MDX(1))=0
551          DO Pause WITH "Can't use this option - No index files are open."
552          LOOP
553       ENDIF
554       IF TYPE(ORDER()) <> "U"
555         lc_type=TYPE(ORDER())
556         DO CASE
557          CASE lc_type = "C"
558            ln_type = 1
559          CASE lc_type = "N" .OR. lc_type = "F"
560            ln_type = 2
561          CASE lc_type = "D"
562            ln_type = 3
563          OTHERWISE
564            ln_type = 1
565         ENDCASE
566       ENDIF && TYPE(ORDER()) <> "U"
567       ln_type=1
568       lc_ln1=SPACE(40)
569       DEFINE WINDOW Posit2 FROM 8,19 TO 15,62 DOUBLE
570       ACTIVATE WINDOW Posit2
571       @ 1,1 SAY "Enter the type of expression:" GET ln_type PICT "#"
              RANGE 1,3
572       @ 2,1 SAY "(1=character, 2=numeric (N/F) and 3=date.)"
573       READ
574       IF .NOT. (READKEY() = 12 .OR. READKEY() = 268)
575          SET CONFIRM ON
576          @ 3,1 SAY "Enter the key expression to search for:"
577          IF ln_type=3
578             @ 4,1 GET ld_date PICT "@D"
579          ELSE
580             IF ln_type=2
581                @ 4,1 GET ln_num PICT "##########"
582             ELSE
583                @ 4,1 GET lc_ln1
584             ENDIF
585          ENDIF
586          READ
587          SET CONFIRM OFF
588          IF .NOT. (READKEY() = 12 .OR. READKEY() = 268)
589             lc_temp=IIF(ln_type=1,"TRIM(lc_ln1)",
                   IIF(ln_type=2,"ln_num","ld_date"))
590             SEEK &lc_temp.
```

(continued)

```
591            ENDIF
592         ENDIF
593         RELEASE WINDOWS Posit2
594      CASE lc_option='4'
595         *-- Goto
596         ln_type=1
597         DEFINE POPUP Posit2 FROM 8,30
598         DEFINE BAR 1 OF Posit2 PROMPT " GOTO:" SKIP
599         DEFINE BAR 2 OF Posit2 PROMPT REPLICATE(CHR(196),10) SKIP
600         DEFINE BAR 3 OF Posit2 PROMPT " TOP" MESSAGE "GOTO Top of File"
601         DEFINE BAR 4 OF Posit2 PROMPT " BOTTOM" MESSAGE "GOTO Bottom of File"
602         DEFINE BAR 5 OF Posit2 PROMPT " Record # "
              MESSAGE "GOTO A Specific Record"
603         ON SELECTION POPUP Posit2 DO get_sele
604         ACTIVATE POPUP posit2
605         ln_type = gn_send
606         IF LASTKEY() <> 27
607            IF ln_type=5
608               DEFINE WINDOW Posit2 FROM 8,26 TO 13,50 DOUBLE
609               ACTIVATE WINDOW Posit2
610               ln_num=0
611               @ 3,1 SAY "Max. Record # = "+LTRIM(STR(RECCOUNT()))
612               @ 1,1 SAY "Record to GOTO" GET ln_num PICT "######"
                    RANGE 1,RECCOUNT()
613               READ
614               IF .NOT. (READKEY() = 12 .OR. READKEY() = 268)
615                  GOTO ln_num
616               ENDIF
617               RELEASE WINDOWS Posit2
618            ELSE
619               lc_temp=IIF(ln_type=3,"TOP","BOTTOM")
620               GOTO &lc_temp.
621            ENDIF
622         ENDIF
623      CASE lc_option='5'
624         *-- Locate
625         DEFINE WINDOW Posit2 FROM 8,16 TO 14,66 DOUBLE
626         ACTIVATE WINDOW Posit2
627         @ 1,19 SAY "ie. ALL, NEXT <n>, and REST"
628         @ 1,1 SAY "Scope:" GET lc_scp
629         @ 2,1 SAY "For:  " GET lc_ln2
630         @ 3,1 SAY "While:" GET lc_ln3
631         READ
632         IF .NOT. (READKEY() = 12 .OR. READKEY() = 268)
633            lc_temp=TRIM(lc_scp)
634            lc_temp=lc_temp + IIF(LEN(TRIM(lc_ln2)) > 0," FOR "
                 +TRIM(lc_ln2),"")
635            lc_temp=lc_temp + IIF(LEN(TRIM(lc_ln3)) > 0," WHILE "
                 +TRIM(lc_ln3),"")
636            IF LEN(lc_temp) > 0
637               LOCATE &lc_temp.
638            ELSE
```

(continued)

```
639              DO Pause WITH "All fields were blank."
640           ENDIF
641       ENDIF
642       RELEASE WINDOW Posit2
643    ENDCASE
644    IF EOF()
645       DO Pause WITH "Record not found."
646       GOTO ln_rec
647    ENDIF
648    IF READKEY()=12 .OR. READKEY()= 268 .OR. LASTKEY()=27  && Esc was hit
649       lc_option='0'
650    ENDIF
651 ENDDO
652 SET DELIMITERS &gc_deli.
653 SET CONFIRM OFF
654 RETURN
655
656 PROC prntrtry
657 IF .NOT. PRINTSTATUS()
658    ACTIVATE WINDOW printemp
659    @ 1,0 SAY " Please ready your printer or"
660    @ 2,0 SAY "     press ESC to cancel"
661    DO WHILE ( .NOT. PRINTSTATUS()) .AND. gn_pkey <> 27
662       gn_pkey = INKEY()
663    ENDDO
664    DEACTIVATE WINDOW printemp
665    RETRY
666 ENDIF
667 RETURN
668 * EOF: C:CUSTOMER.PRG
669
```

Chapter 8

The Applications Generator

This chapter focuses on using the dBASE IV applications generator to pull the elements of a system together into a menu-driven whole. We'll see that the applications generator is amazingly powerful to the point of allowing the programmer to include blocks of code before or after any menu item. We won't, however, abandon the tweaking process entirely. There are some problems with the way applications are handled that must be corrected.

Appendix D, as usual, contains a complete listing of the applications generator template system. In the previous chapter, we modified the routine AS_POSIT.COD to automatically detect the data type of the primary key expression. However, it is the original version that is included here. If you made the change suggested in Chapter 7, the line numbers in Appendix D will not correspond to those in your output file from compiling the applications generator system.

The applications generator uses the COD files that begin with AS_ and AD_. Files that begin with AS_ generate code for menus and other applications objects. The AD_ files generate code for application actions. For example, AD_BROW.COD generates the code for the Browse database action.

The AD_ files are generally pretty useful and easy to understand. When you decide to write your own templates, you'll find the AD_ files invaluable because they generate the code to handle many fundamental database actions automatically.

The Applications Generator Templates

The main program for the applications generator is AS_MENU.COD. This is the first occasion where the main program has a name different from the name of the output file. I use a batch file called DM.BAT to compile. It looks like this:

```
dtc -i as_menu.cod -o menu.gen -l menu.out
```

If you're going to work with a number of templates, I recommend creating a set of these batch files, one per major template, named appropriately. The following names are short, to the point, and remind you of what each file does:

df.bat   Forms
dl.bat   Labels
dr.bat   Reports
dq.bat   Quick application
dm.bat   Applications generator

Fixing Two Major Problems

Although the focus of this chapter will be on using the applications generator, there are numerous examples of code that could be improved. Many of these are similar or identical to those proposed in the previous chapter, so I won't repeat them here. Instead, I encourage you to read the template file in Appendix D, play with the applications generator, and look at the code that's produced. When you find things that are wrong or code that is inefficient, change the template. I always try to make good change notes in the file. But (as may be true for you, too), sometimes time pressure means I don't document changes adequately. That's why it's important to keep backups of the originals of the template files.

Positioning the Pointer

The first significant and interesting problem arises if you pick the option to switch indexes before a report or set of labels is printed (the Item/Reassign index-order menu bar). The generated code does not add a GOTO TOP command after setting the new index order. In fact, it doesn't even add the

SET ORDER TO <tag name> or SET INDEX TO <index file name> command at all. Therefore, the pointer is likely to be left in the middle of the file and not all the data will be printed. Or worse yet the data may be printed in the incorrect order.

There are two solutions to this problem. First, you can select the option to switch the database, using the same database with a new order. The problem is that this closes and opens the files, slowing performance.

The second, better, solution is to add the GOTO TOP and SET commands to the appropriate places in the template file. The block of code that defines reports is in the file AD_REPT.COD:

```
1999    1:  // $Header: /a/CCS/apgentc/cod/ad_rept.cod,v 1.19
                88/08/16 20:39:15 dough Dev $
2000    2:  // Module Name: AD_REPT.COD - Menu_Act = 4
2001    3:  // Selectors  : FRM_Dest, FRM_File, FRM_Headng,
                               FRM_Plain, FRM_Eject,
2002    4:  //             : FRM_Summry, Flter_Cond, Scope,
                               For_Expr, While_Exp
2003    5:  // Description: Call to REPORT
2004    6:  // Syntax     : REPORT FORM <report form file>/?
2005    7:  //                   [PLAIN] [SUMMARY] [NOEJECT]
                                 [HEADING <expC>]
2006    8:  //                   [<scope>] [FOR <expL>]
                                 [WHILE <expL>]
2007    9:  //                   [TO [PRINT]/[FILE <expFN>]]
2008   10:  //
2009   11:  *-- Desc: Report
2010   12:  //
2011   13:  {if Flter_Cond then}
2012   14:  SET FILTER TO {Flter_Cond}
2013   15:  GOTO TOP
2014   16:  {endif}
2015   17:  //
2016   18:  {case FRM_Dest of}
2017   19:  {0: // Printer}
2018   20:  SET PRINT ON
2019   21:  {1: // File}
2020   22:  SET ALTERNATE TO {FRM_File}.prt
2021   23:  SET ALTERNATE ON
2022   24:  {3: // Ask at runtime}
2023   25:  gn_pkey = 0
```

```
2024    26:    DO PrintSet
2025    27:    IF gn_pkey <> 27  && esc
2026    28:       \
2027    29:    {endcase}
2028    30:    REPORT FORM {FRM_File}\
2029    31:    {if not FRM_Plain} PLAIN {endif}\
2030    32:    {if FRM_Headng} HEADING "{FRM_Headng}"{endif}\
2031    33:    {if FRM_Eject} NOEJECT {endif}\
2032    34:    {if FRM_Summry} SUMMARY {endif}\
2033    35:    {if Scope} {upper(Scope)} {endif}\
2034    36:    {if For_Expr} FOR {For_Expr}{endif}\
2035    37:    {if While_Exp} WHILE {While_Exp}{endif}\
2036    38:
2037    39:    {case FRM_Dest of}
2038    40:    {0:}
2039    41:    SET PRINT OFF
2040    42:    {1:}
2041    43:    CLOSE ALTERNATE
2042    44:    {2:}
2043    45:    WAIT
2044    46:    {3:}
2045    47:       DO Cleanup
2046    48:    ENDIF
2047    49:    {endcase}
2048    50:    //
2049    51:    {if Flter_Cond then}
2050    52:    SET FILTER TO
2051    53:    {endif}
2052    54:    //
2053    55:    // EOP AD_REPT.COD
```

There's one other problem with this code. It uses SET PRINT ON/OFF instead of the superior REPORT FORM...TO PRINT. Here's a replacement version of AD_REPT.COD that handles both problems.

```
// $Header: /a/CCS/apgentc/cod/ad_rept.cod,v 1.19 88/08/16
   20:39:15 dough Dev $
// Module Name: AD_REPT.COD - Menu_Act = 4
// Selectors  : FRM_Dest, FRM_File, FRM_Headng, FRM_Plain,
                FRM_Eject,
//             : FRM_Summry, Flter_Cond, Scope, For_Expr, While_Exp
```

```
// Description: Call to REPORT
// Syntax     : REPORT FORM <report form file>/?
//                  [PLAIN] [SUMMARY] [NOEJECT] [HEADING <expC>]
//                  [<scope>] [FOR <expL>] [WHILE <expL>]
//                  [TO [PRINT]/[FILE <expFN>]]
//
*-- Desc: Report
//
{if Flter_Cond then}
SET FILTER TO {Flter_Cond}
GOTO TOP
{endif}
{
// Following block added by Tony Lima, April 25, 1989
}
{if ndx_file or ndx_order then;
  if ndx_file then
}
SET INDEX TO {ndx_file}
GOTO TOP
{   else
}
SET ORDER TO {ndx_order}
GOTO TOP
{  endif;
 endif
}
{
// Following block commented out and replaced
// Tony Lima, April 25, 1989
}
{case FRM_Dest of}
{// 0: // Printer}
{
// SET PRINT ON
}
{// 1: // File}
{
// SET ALTERNATE TO {FRM_File}.prt
// SET ALTERNATE ON
}
```

```
{3: // Ask at runtime}
gn_pkey = 0
DO PrintSet
IF gn_pkey <> 27   && esc
   \
{endcase}
REPORT FORM {FRM_File}\
{if not FRM_Plain} PLAIN {endif}\
{if FRM_Headng} HEADING "{FRM_Headng}"{endif}\
{if FRM_Eject} NOEJECT {endif}\
{if FRM_Summry} SUMMARY {endif}\
{if Scope} {upper(Scope)} {endif}\
{if For_Expr} FOR {For_Expr}{endif}\
{if While_Exp} WHILE {While_Exp}{endif}\
{
// Following block added by Tony Lima, April 25, 1989
}
{case FRM_Dest of}
{0:}
 TO PRINT
{1:}
 TO FILE {FRM_File}.prt
{// 2:}
{
// WAIT
}
{// 3:}
{
//    DO Cleanup
// ENDIF
}
{endcase}
{case FRM_Dest of}
{// 0:}
{
// SET PRINT OFF
}
{// 1:}
{
// CLOSE ALTERNATE
}
```

```
{2:}
WAIT
{3:}
   DO Cleanup
ENDIF
{endcase}
//
{if Flter_Cond then}
SET FILTER TO
{endif}
{
// Following block added by Tony Lima, April 25, 1989
}
{if ndx_file or ndx_order then;
   if ndx_file then
}
SET INDEX TO {global_NDX}
GOTO TOP
{   else
}
SET ORDER TO {global_Ord}
GOTO TOP
{  endif;
 endif
}
//
// EOP AD_REPT.COD
```

The variables global_NDX and global_ORD store the values of the primary key index file or tag set with the initial application definition. The selectors ndx_file and ndx_order contain the currently active index file or order. You change these variables from the Item/Reassign index-order menu in the applications generator. Feel free to remove the lines that are commented out. I left them in so you could see the changes clearly.

And Here's Another One

For some reason, the Ashton-Tate template programmers are enamoured of SET INDEX TO and SET ORDER TO. The following code will look familiar to those who read the previous chapter.

```
2796    38:    USE {mdbf}
2797    39:    {  endif}
2798    40:    {endif}
2799    41:    {if mndx then}
2800    42:    IF "" <> DBF()
2801    43:       SET INDEX TO {mndx}
2802    44:    ENDIF
2803    45:    {endif}
2804    46:    {if mord then}
2805    47:    SET ORDER TO {mord}
2806    48:    {endif}
```

I strongly recommend changing this so it produces clean code like USE <dbf file> ORDER <mdx tag name>. Here's how to do it.

```
USE {mdbf} /
{  endif}
{endif}
{if mndx then}
INDEX {mndx}
{endif}
{if mord then}
ORDER {mord}
{endif}
```

That's a lot easier and more efficient.

Even though I really recommend making those two changes, the code in Appendixes A, B, and C uses the original template. Note that the index order is not reset before or after reports are printed. This block of code is from Appendix C:

```
261 CASE BAR() = 1
262    ACTIVATE WINDOW Savescr
263    SET MESSAGE TO "Report on Customer Balances"
264    *-- Desc: Report
265    SET PRINT ON
266    REPORT FORM CUST4FLD NOEJECT
267    SET PRINT OFF
268    DEACTIVATE WINDOW Savescr
```

```
269 CASE BAR() = 2
270    ACTIVATE WINDOW Savescr
271    SET MESSAGE TO "Customer Name, Address, Phone"
272    *-- Desc: Report
273    SET PRINT ON
274    REPORT FORM CUSTOMER
275    SET PRINT OFF
276    DEACTIVATE WINDOW Savescr
```

After implementing the changes suggested, the same block of code looks like this:

```
CASE BAR() = 1
   ACTIVATE WINDOW Savescr
   SET MESSAGE TO "Report on Customer Balances"
   *-- Desc: Report
   SET ORDER TO BALANCE
   GOTO TOP
   REPORT FORM CUST4FLD NOEJECT  TO PRINT
   SET ORDER TO CUSTCODE
   GOTO TOP
   DEACTIVATE WINDOW Savescr
CASE BAR() = 2
   ACTIVATE WINDOW Savescr
   SET MESSAGE TO "Customer Name, Address, Phone"
   *-- Desc: Report
   SET ORDER TO CUSTCODE
   GOTO TOP
   REPORT FORM CUSTOMER TO PRINT
   SET ORDER TO CUSTCODE
   GOTO TOP
   DEACTIVATE WINDOW Savescr
```

One additional thing you might add is a check to see whether the current index order is the same as the global order. If it is, leave out the SET ORDER TO commands. In any case, this code is certainly better than the original.

Finally, make the same changes to AD_LABL.COD, the label generation module.

Leave Out Code You Don't Need

A major problem with the applications generator is that all modules are
included whether you need them or not. A prime example are various procedures and templates that deal with multiuser operations. For example, consider the procedure file AS_PROC.COD. The first procedure defined is
multiuser file and record locking:

```
504    273:   {include "as_proc.cod";}
505      1:   // $Header: /a/CCS/apgentc/cod/as_proc.cod,v 1.27
                    88/07/13 17:00:42 dough Dev $
506      2:   // Module name: as_proc.cod
507      3:   // Date        : August 10, 1987 2:28 PM
508      4:   // Description: Procedure file for the generated
                    application
509      5:   //
510      6:   //
511      7:   // Module Change Log
512      8:   //   Date     Initials   Short Change description
513      9:   //
514     10:   // 08/10/87    KJN         Created module
515     11:   // 10/02/87    DCH         Removed askuser and CREATE
                    functions
516     12:   //
517     13:   {  replicate("*",79)}
518     14:
519     15:   * Description..: Procedure files for generated menu
                    system.
520     16:   * The programs that follow are common to main routines
521     17:   * The last procedure is the Menu Process DEFinition
522     18:   {  replicate("*",79)}
523     19:
524     20:   PROCEDURE Lockit
525     21:   PARAMETER ltype
526     22:   IF NETWORK()
527     23:      gn_error=0
528     24:      ON ERROR DO Multerr
529     25:      IF ltype = "1"
530     26:         ll_lock=FLOCK()
531     27:      ENDIF
532     28:      IF ltype = "2"
```

```
533    29:        ll_lock=RLOCK()
534    30:     ENDIF
535    31:     ON ERROR
536    32:  ENDIF
537    33:  RETURN
538    34:
```

We should not include this code if we're not going to use it, so let's use the same trick we saw in earlier chapters. Between lines 523 and 524, insert the following code:

```
{VAR tlmult;
 tlmult=ASKUSER("Do you need multiuser code (Y/N) ? ",
 "Y",1);
 if tlmult == "Y" then}
```

And don't forget the {endif} after line 538. Also, don't forget the variable tlmult. We'll use it again.

Consider the template file AS_MUSER.COD:

```
642    84:  {  include "as_muser.cod";}
643     1:  // $Header: /a/CCS/apgentc/cod/as_muser.cod,v 1.5
                88/06/27 21:09:16 dough Dev $
644     2:  // Module name: as_muser.cod
645     3:  // Date        : August 21, 1987
646     4:  // Description: Multi-User error handler
647     5:  //
648     6:  //
649     7:  // Module Change Log
650     8:  //    Date     Initials    Short Change description
651     9:  //
652    10:  // 08/21/87    DCH          Created module
653    11:  //
654    12:  // ERROR() MESSAGE()                          File,
                record error, critical
655    13:  // ==================================================
656    14:  //    148 Network server busy            critical
657    15:  //    217 Lock table full               critical
658    16:  //    131 Database is encrypted          file
659    17:  //    110 Exclusive open of file is required file
660    18:  //    108 File is in use by another       file
```

```
661   19:   //      129 Unable to lock
                                                    file/record
662   20:   //      133 Unauthorized access level
                                                    file/record
663   21:   //      124 Invalid printer redirection    N/A
664   22:   //      132 Unauthorized login             N/A
665   23:   //      111 Cannot write to a read-only file  record
666   24:   //      109 Record is in use by another   record
667   25:   //      130 Record is not locked          record
668   26:   //      128 Unable to skip                record
669   27:   //
670   28:   // Errors will be handled in one of two ways:
671   29:   //
672   30:   // 1) Display message and return to menu
673   31:   // 2) Dialog box for options Try again and Return to
                    menu
674   32:   //
675   33:   PROCEDURE Multerr
676   34:   *-- set the global error variable
677   35:   gn_error=ERROR()
678   36:   *-- contains error number to test
679   37:   lc_erno=STR(ERROR(),3)+','
680   38:   *-- option var.
681   39:   lc_opt='T'
682   40:   *-- Dialog box for options Try again and Return to
                 menu.
683   41:   IF lc_erno $ "108,109,128,129,"
684   42:      ACTIVATE WINDOW Pause
685   43:      @ 0,2 SAY lc_erno+" "+MESSAGE()
686   44:      @ 2,22 SAY "T = Try again, R = Return to menu."
                 GET lc_opt ;
687   45:   PICTURE "!" VALID lc_opt $ "TR"
688   46:      READ
689   47:      DEACTIVATE WINDOW Pause
690   48:      IF lc_opt = "R"
691   49:         RETURN
692   50:      ENDIF
693   51:   ENDIF
694   52:   *-- Display message and return to menu.
695   53:   IF .NOT. lc_erno $ "108,109,128,129,"
696   54:      DO PAUSE WITH ERROR()
```

```
697   55:    RETURN
698   56:  ENDIF
699   57:  *-- reset global variable
700   58:  gn_error=0
701   59:  *-- Try the command again
702   60:  RETRY
703   61:  RETURN
704   85:  * EOP: Multerr
705   86:
```

While this is a wonderful list of multi-user error messages and numbers, you don't need this code if you're not going to run the program on a network. However, this time you don't have to ask the user whether or not to include the code, since you already have that information in the variable tlmult. Note that if you never run your applications on a network, the most efficient way to handle this is to comment out the statement on line 642 so AS_MUSER.COD is never even included in MENU.GEN. Or, you may want to have single and multiuser versions of MENU.GEN. Since you can switch templates in the applications generator, you can generate single-user and multi-user for the same application without even leaving the applications generator.

Warning (and a hint)!
If you're going to generate single- and multi-user code in the same run of the applications generator, change the default output file name as well. Here's a strategy to do that efficiently. First, ask the user if a multi-user application is wanted at the beginning of AS_MENU.COD. Change the applications generator so that the first character of any generated file is either S (for single user) or M (for multi-user). Pick the correct letter at generation time depending on the answer to the question. Then include or leave out code as shown here.

Commenting out code is easy. What we want to do is selectively include or leave out code. Before line 675, add the usual code:

```
{if tlmult == "Y"}
```

and insert an {endif} after line 705.

There are a few other places where multi-user code is added. The block of code between lines 1663 and 1778 is devoted exclusively to multi-user operations. Omit it from single user applications.

Leave the Application?

There's a confusing omission in AS_MENU.COD. Find the following code (lines 463–464) and add the ERROR clause as shown below. Otherwise, you will get a cryptic dBASE IV error message "Editing condition not satisfied" if you type anything other than a Y or N.

```
@ 1,2 SAY "Do you want to leave this application?" ;
      GET gc_key PICT "!" VALID gc_key $ "NY" ;
      ERROR "Press Y or N..."
```

Procedure TRACE

There is a procedure called TRACE that is included for programmers. It allows the programmer to simply insert the command DO TRACE in a generated program at a point where problems are cropping up. However, you may want to leave it out when generating finished code. The procedure is contained in the file AS_TRCE.COD and is included in the template at line 706. If you don't want this procedure, just comment out the include statement. Note that you could also ask the user at generation time if the procedure TRACE was to be included.

Printer Ready?

Although it's not a bug, there is a procedure called PRNTRTRY that checks the status of the printer. It's on lines 833–846 and is part of AD_PRIN.COD. A procedure like this should be included in every application that uses a printer (which is just about every application ever written).

Finished?

Once you've made the changes to the template, recompile it.

A Sample Application

The rest of this chapter will be devoted to putting together the application that produced the code in Appendixes A and C. (Appendix B, KEYSET.PRG, was written by hand. Nobody ever promised that you'd never have to write *any* code.)

The application allows the user to do the following things:

- Add records using a format file (CUST2PG2 developed in Chapter 3).
- Browse the database with certain options set.
- Reposition the record pointer and edit the record. Either a SEEK or a LOCATE is performed.
- Select a new index key from a menu.
- Print two different reports.
- Back up the first one hundred records of the database.
- Exit to dBASE IV.

You can create a new application by selecting "create" from the Applications column of the Control Center or with the CREATE APPLICATION <application name> command from the dot prompt. Similarly, you can modify an existing application by highlighting its name in the Control Center and pressing F2. Those addicted to the dot prompt will prefer the MODIFY APPLICATION <application name> command. Finally, to run an application, highlight its name and press Enter. You're probably intimately familiar with the DO command from the dot prompt.

The Application Definition Screen

Once in the AppsGen, you'll see the Applications Definition screen shown in Figure 8-1. Most of it is pretty self-explanatory. The application name will be the name assigned to the main PRG file generated. The description will be included in the file header. You can cycle through the different menu types (BAR, POPUP, and BATCH) by pressing the space bar. Don't forget to press Enter when you get to the one you want.

Note that you can use either a database or QBE view. This means your applications can access fields from multiple databases. However, you don't have to use a view even if some objects were created with it. For example, the report we'll use with this application, CUST4FLD, was actually built as a Quick Layout from the view CUST4FLD. This was an easy way to select four fields from customer and build a report. However, since all fields are from the same database, you can run the report directly from that database without switching to a view.

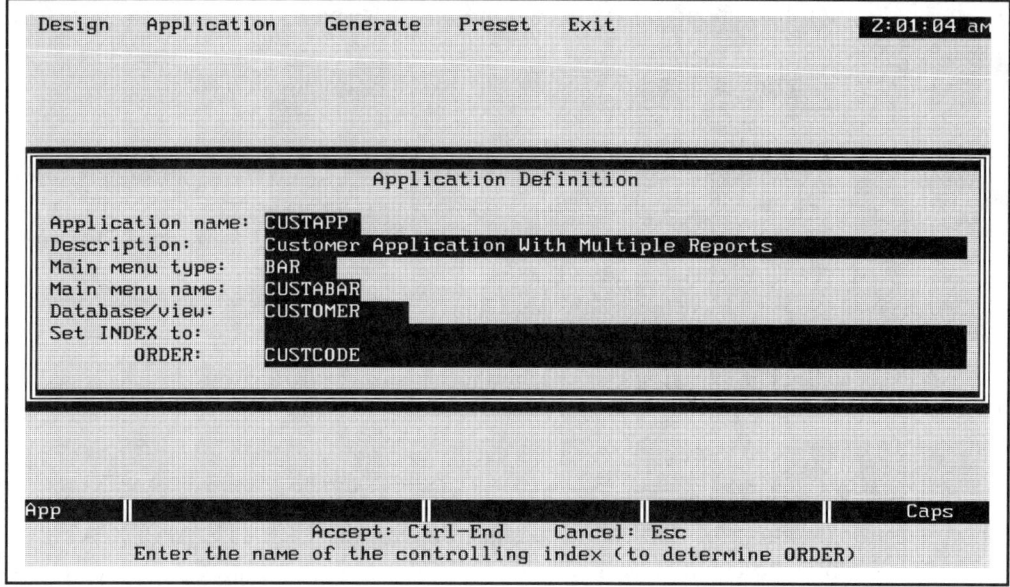

Figure 8-1   Applications Definition Screen

Finally, always select a primary key for the application. You can swap index keys on the fly — at least, you can in theory! If you find your index key switches not "taking," track down the problem in the template files and fix it.

"Splash"

When you're done with this screen, press Ctrl-End. You'll be asked to put together a "splash screen" similar to the one constructed in the previous chapter. Figure 8-2 shows a minimal opening screen. As always, feel free to use your own text. The Application/Display sign-on banner will let you choose to display this message or not when the program begins.

The Application Menu

It's a good idea to check each item in the Application pop-up menu to be sure it's OK. Some information is pulled from the Applications Definition screen. However, some is not. A case in point is the program header contents, which must be filled in by hand. Figure 8-3 shows a typical screen. This information

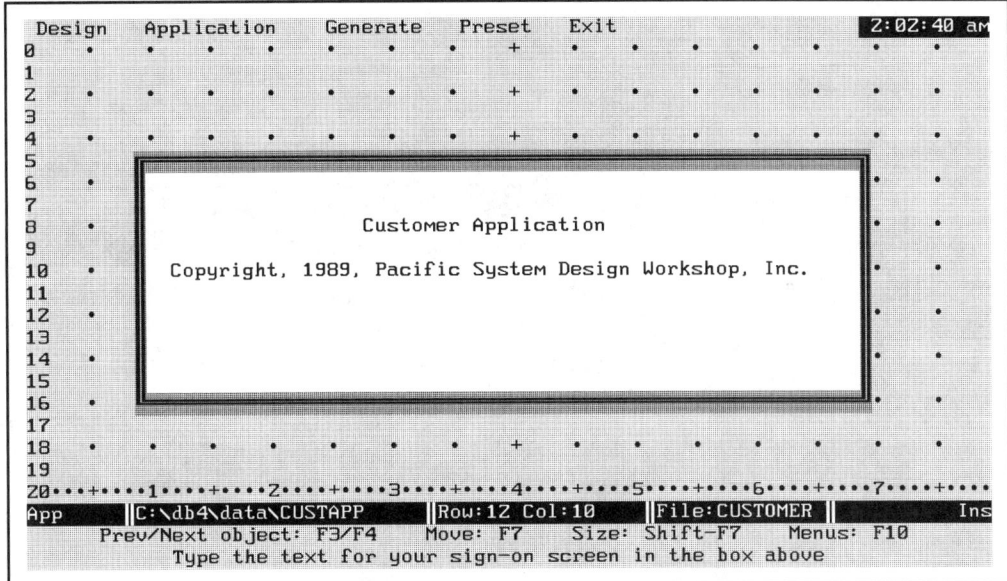

Figure 8-2   Splash Screen

will be placed at the beginning of each program file and major procedure block.

I also recommend checking the application environment variables. I usually SET the BELL ON with a frequency of 220 and a duration of 2. Most people find that tone much more pleasant than the IBM standard beep. Figure 8-4 shows the environment setup for our sample application.

The Main Menu

The next step is to design the main menu for the application. Pick the Design/Horizontal bar menu option (Figure 8-5). The name you assign will be the name of the program file and/or procedure, so be sure it is unique. The description will be inserted in the program file. The message line prompt will be centered on the bottom line of the screen. However, you will probably want to assign different messages to each bar of the menu, so it's OK to leave this blank.

Next, design the menu itself. To start a new menu item, move the cursor to the position you want and press F5. Type in the menu bar prompt and press F5

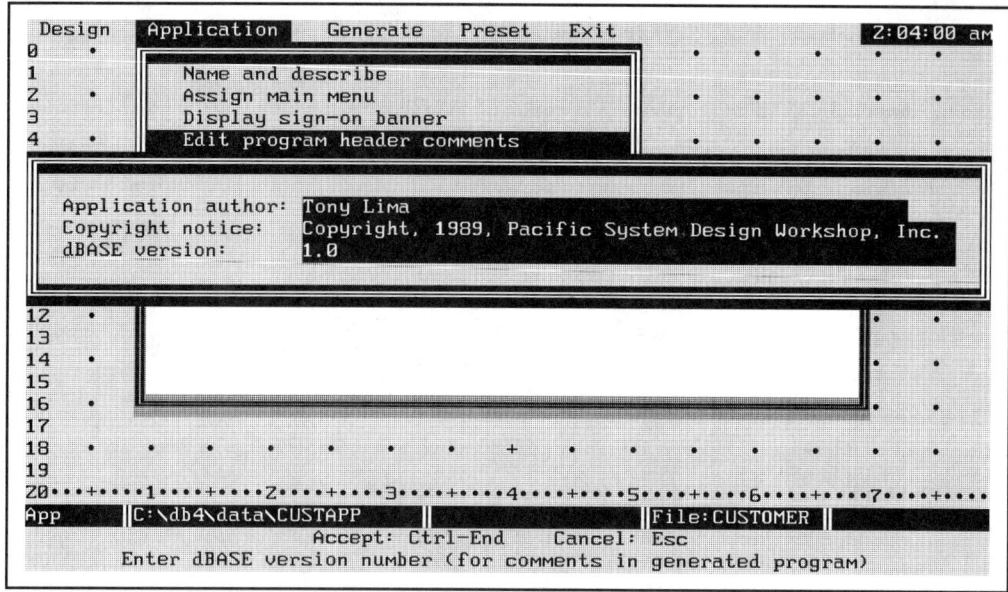

Figure 8-3   Edit Program Header Comments Screen

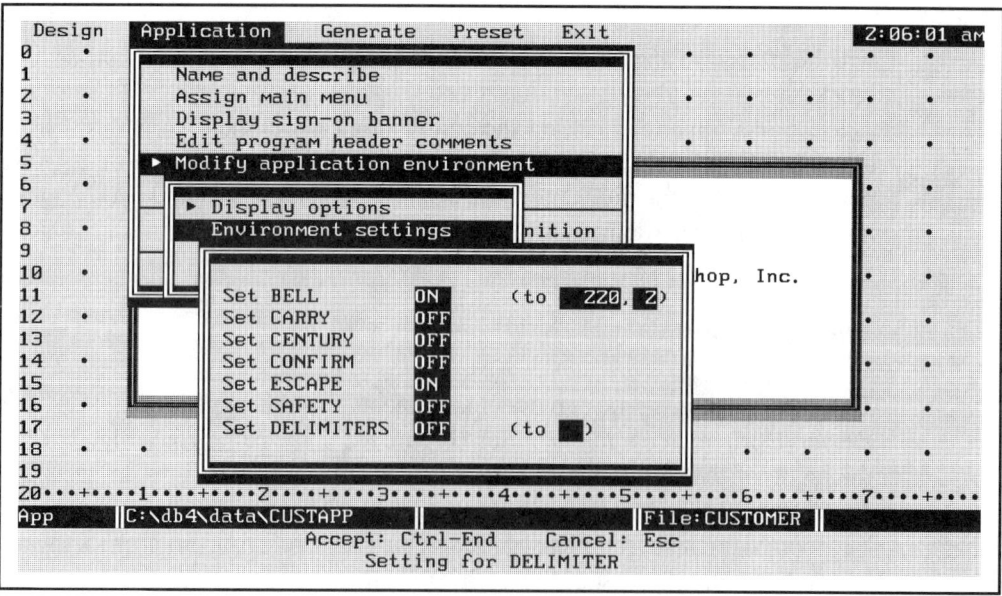

Figure 8-4   Modify Application Environment Screen

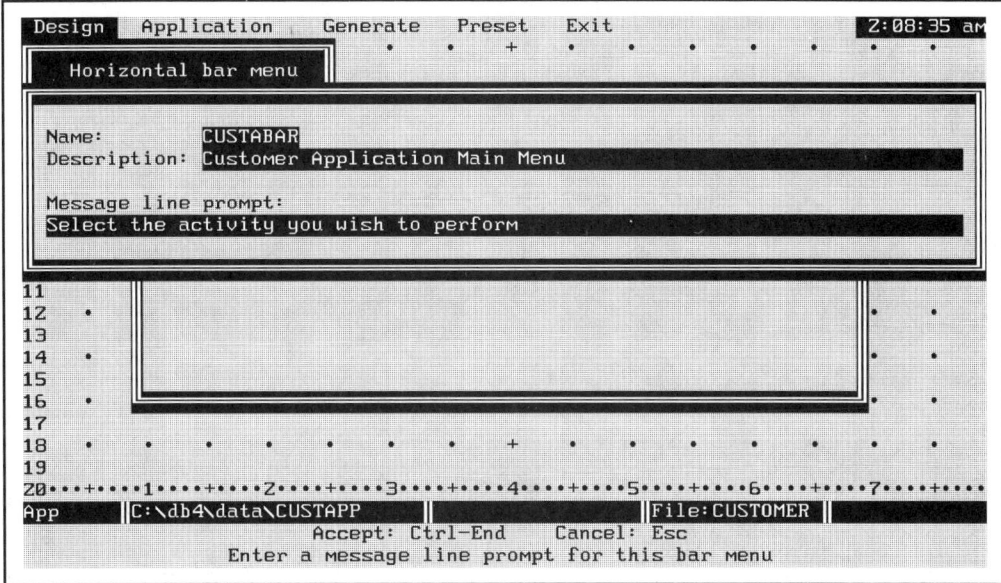

Figure 8-5　Menu Definition Screen

again to conclude that menu item. Note that as you move the cursor back over items already created, each is highlighted as the cursor hits it.

Two Hints: *First, you can use Ctrl-RightArrow and Ctrl-LeftArrow to move right and left one pad at a time.*

Second, when deciding the names of menu bars, try to use a different first letter for each. That way, the user can move directly to any menu item by pressing Alt-<letter>. In other words, don't have items like Browse and Backup (as will eventually be the case on our sample menu!)

Note that there is a bug in dBASE IV version 1.0 that prevents you from using Alt-<letter> to access a light-bar menu pad when a pop-up menu is active. (When no pop-ups are active, Alt-<letter> works just fine.)

Figure 8-6 shows a sample menu setup. To move a pad, just move the cursor into its area and press F7. Or you can use F6 to mark several items and move them with F7. It's easy to make changes, so don't be afraid to wing it. Select "Item only" from the dialog box. (If you select "Entire frame," dBASE IV will want you to move the whole menu box. We'll see how that works later in this chapter.)

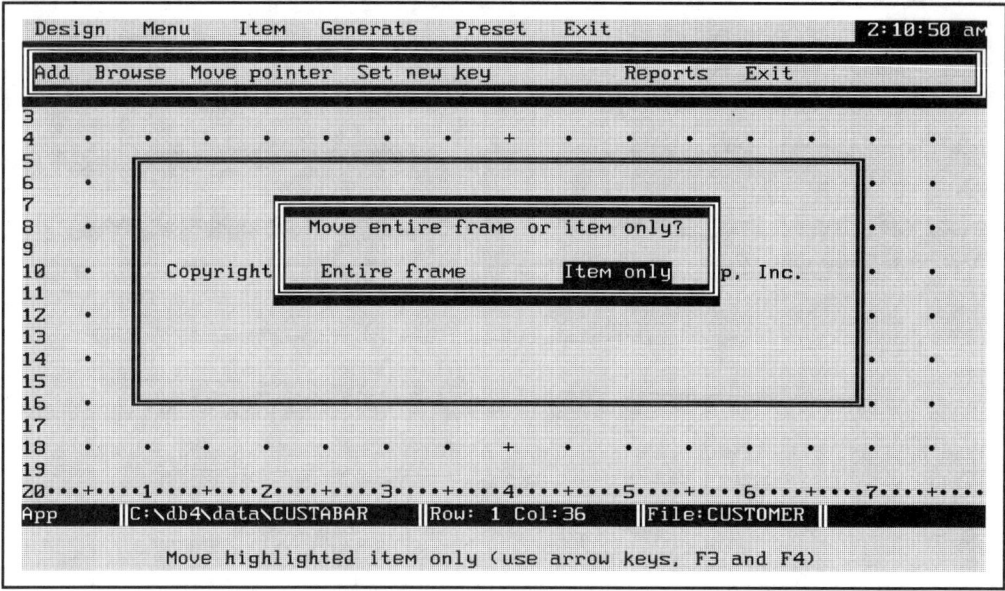

Figure 8-6   Light Bar Menu Design Screen

Setting Actions for Bars

The next thing to do is assign an action to each menu bar. Figure 8-7 shows an Item/Change action menu. There are a number of submenus, so don't worry about how limited this list looks. Also, the Item menu itself lets you alter the environment in a number of ways without actually making those alterations an action. For example, earlier in this chapter we saw that the index order could be changed in the context of the actions of a single light-bar pad.

The Add Bar

To add data to the database (APPEND), select "Edit form" from the menu in Figure 8-7. You'll see the Append/Edit Via Form File setup screen shown in Figure 8-8. You can specify a format file. The Mode options are APPEND and EDIT. You can give a FIELDS list, a FILTER, a SCOPE, or FOR and WHILE clauses. Since this is the Add bar on the menu, I recommend you leave the "Allow record ADD?" option at YES. I also recommend setting "FOLLOW record after update?" to NO. This will keep the pointer from following the record to its new position in the primary index key. The other

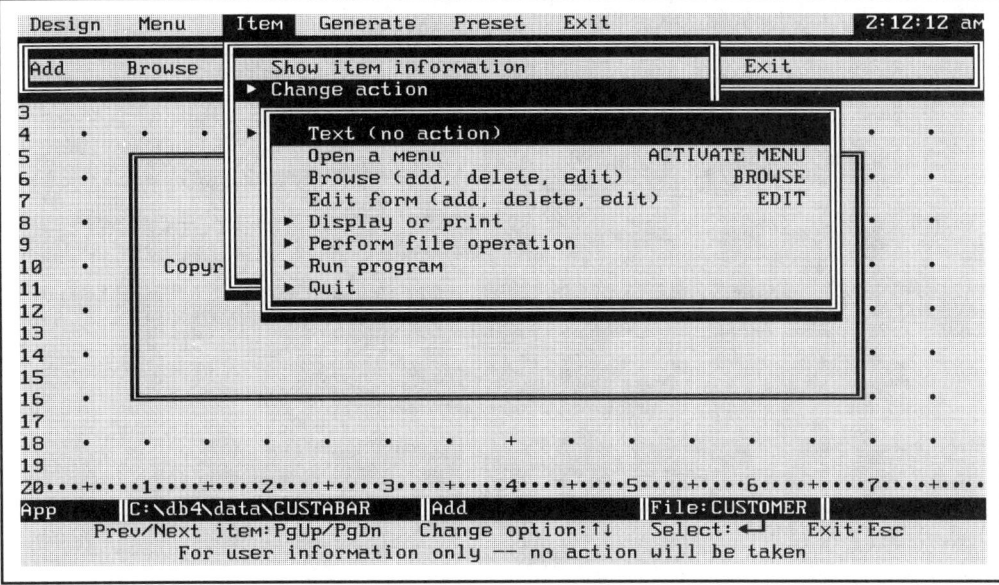

Figure 8-7   Item/Change Action Screen

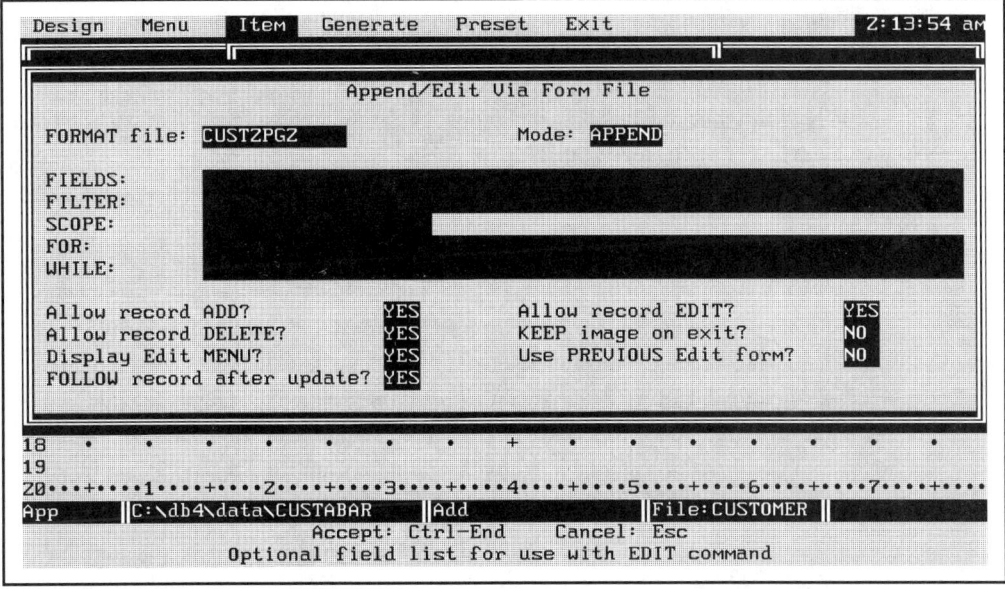

Figure 8-8   Append/Edit Via Form Screen

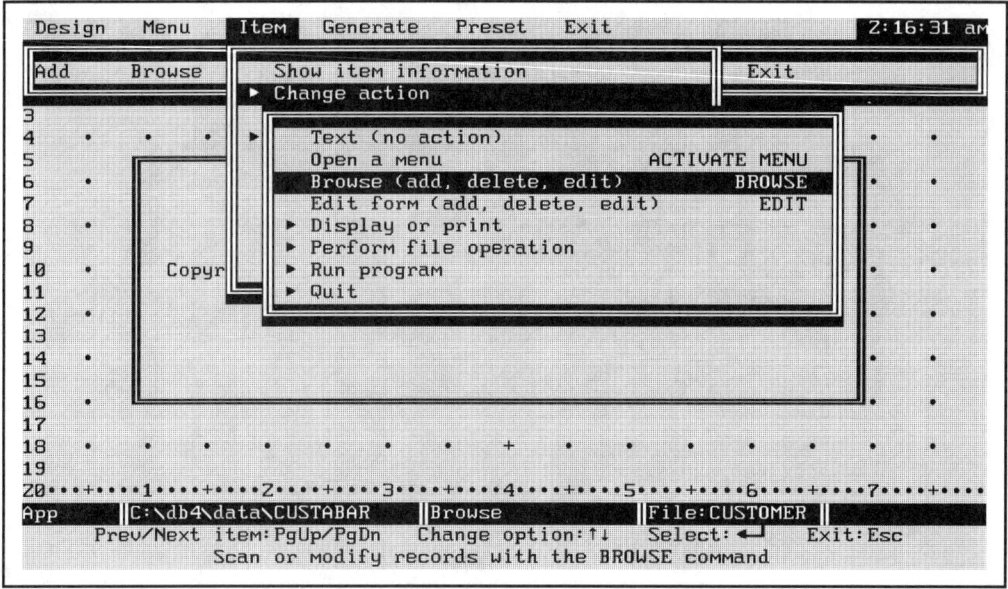

Figure 8-9   Item/Change action/Browse Screen

options are pretty much self-explanatory. Note that if you just want to display a record but want the field values to appear in their designated colors, just set all items to NO except "KEEP image on exit?" Set this to YES and the record's data will appear but will be completely display-only.

When finished with this screen, press Ctrl-End to save. If you want to quit and start over with the defaults, just press Esc.

The Browse Pad

Next let's set the action for the Browse pad. Move the cursor to Browse, then press Alt-I to bring up the Item menu (Figure 8-9). Select "Browse" from this menu and press Enter.

Figure 8-10 shows the Browse setup screen. It's similar in many ways to the Add/Edit screen. Since I want this screen mainly for display, I have set every option except "Display Browse MENU?" to NO.

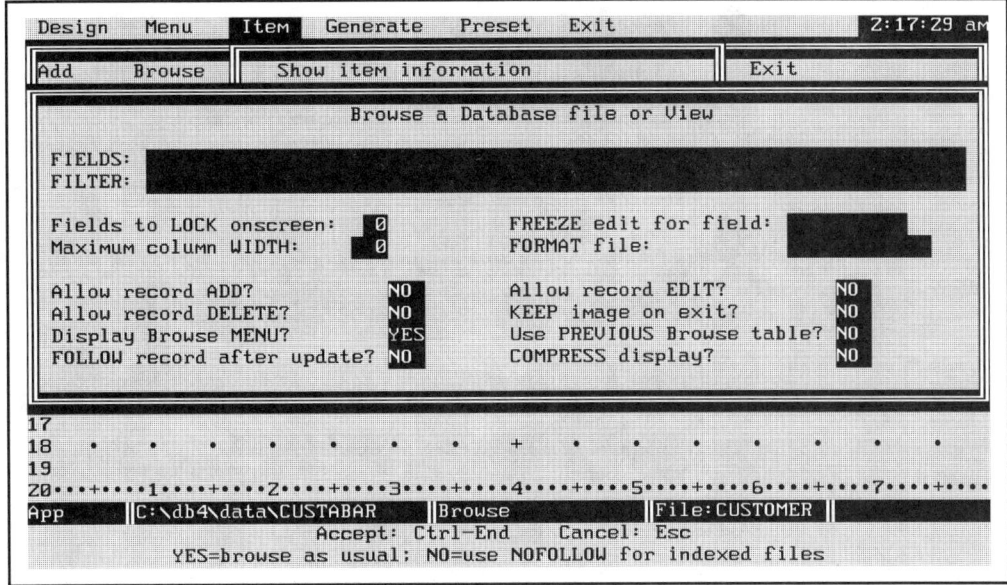

Figure 8-10   The Browse Setup Screen

The Set New Key Pad

This pad is designed to let the user select a new key from a list of available TAGs. To use it, we want to run the program KEYSET.PRG (Appendix B). Therefore, select the Item/Change action/Run program/Do dBASE program option (Figure 8-11).

Note the other available options, including running a batch file; simply inserting dBASE code into the file at the current location (there isn't an option to read in an ASCII file); run a DOS program; load/call a binary file; or play back a previously recorded keyboard macro.

Figure 8-12 shows the setup screen for running a dBASE program. The setup is simple, requiring only a program file name (with extension if it's not PRG) and any parameters to be passed to the program using a WITH clause. If you wish, you can use the DBO file from a previously compiled program, thus preventing automatic change detection and recompilation.

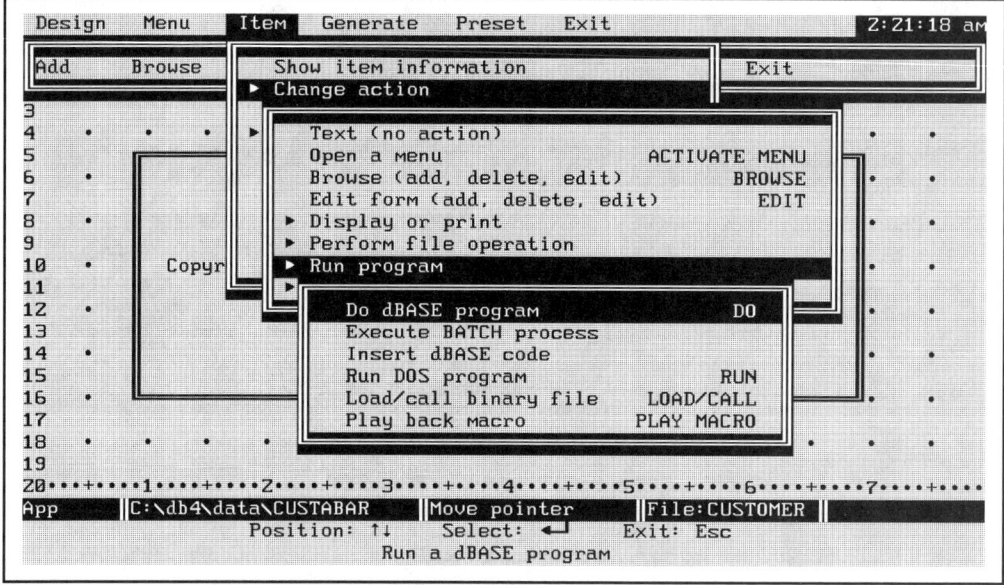

Figure 8-11   Run Program Screen

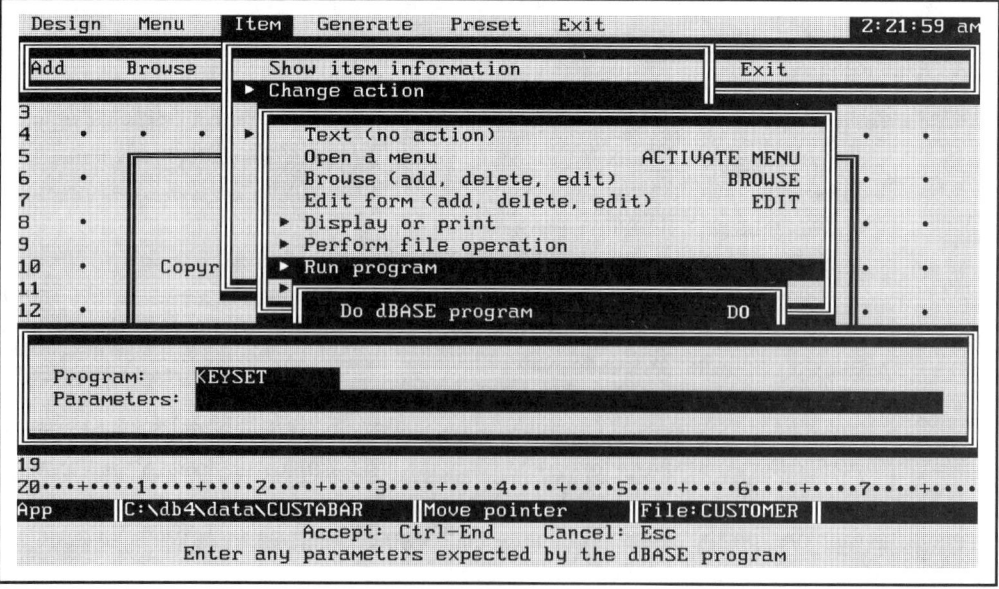

Figure 8-12   Run dBASE Program Setup Screen

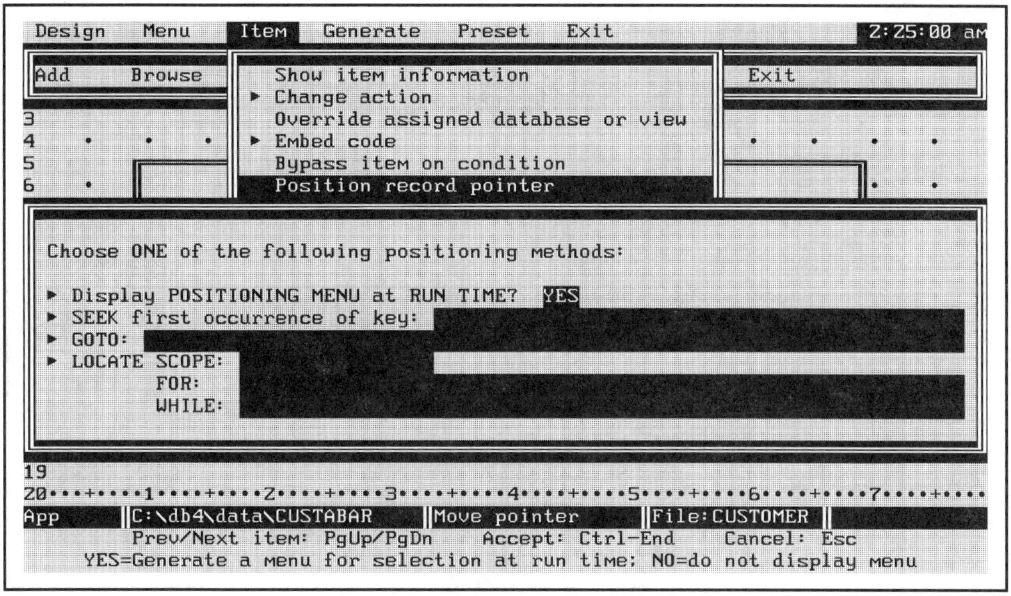

```
 Design    Menu   Item   Generate   Preset   Exit              2:25:00 am
┌─────────────────────────────────────────────────────────────────────────┐
│Add      Browse      Show item information              Exit              │
│3                  ► Change action                                        │
│4    •    •    •     Override assigned database or view    •    •    •    •│
│5                  ► Embed code                                           │
│6    •               Bypass item on condition                    •    •  │
│                     Position record pointer                              │
├─────────────────────────────────────────────────────────────────────────┤
│ Choose ONE of the following positioning methods:                         │
│                                                                          │
│ ► Display POSITIONING MENU at RUN TIME?  YES                             │
│ ► SEEK first occurrence of key:                                          │
│ ► GOTO:                                                                  │
│ ► LOCATE SCOPE:                                                          │
│         FOR:                                                             │
│         WHILE:                                                           │
│                                                                          │
├─────────────────────────────────────────────────────────────────────────┤
│19                                                                        │
│20•••+••••1••••+••••2••••+••••3••••+••••4••••+••••5••••+••••6••••+••••7••••+••••│
│App    ║C:\db4\data\CUSTABAR    ║Move pointer    ║File:CUSTOMER ║         │
│       Prev/Next item: PgUp/PgDn    Accept: Ctrl-End    Cancel: Esc       │
│   YES=Generate a menu for selection at run time; NO=do not display menu  │
└─────────────────────────────────────────────────────────────────────────┘
```

Figure 8-13   Position Record Pointer Screen

Moving the Pointer

The option to move the record pointer is simple. Figure 8-13 shows the setup screen.

The Exit Pad

Even easier is the Exit pad. Move the cursor to "Exit" and press Alt-I to bring up the Item menu. Select "Change action and Quit" as shown in Figure 8-14.

Figure 8-15 shows the two options available: RETURN and QUIT. While this might seem straightforward, remember that dBASE IV always tries to reset the environment to what it was before you ran the application, so there is more code than you might think. A good deal of this code is SET commands, which I recommend you place in procedures as we did with QUICKAPP.COD (Chapter 7).

For this application, I selected RETURN.

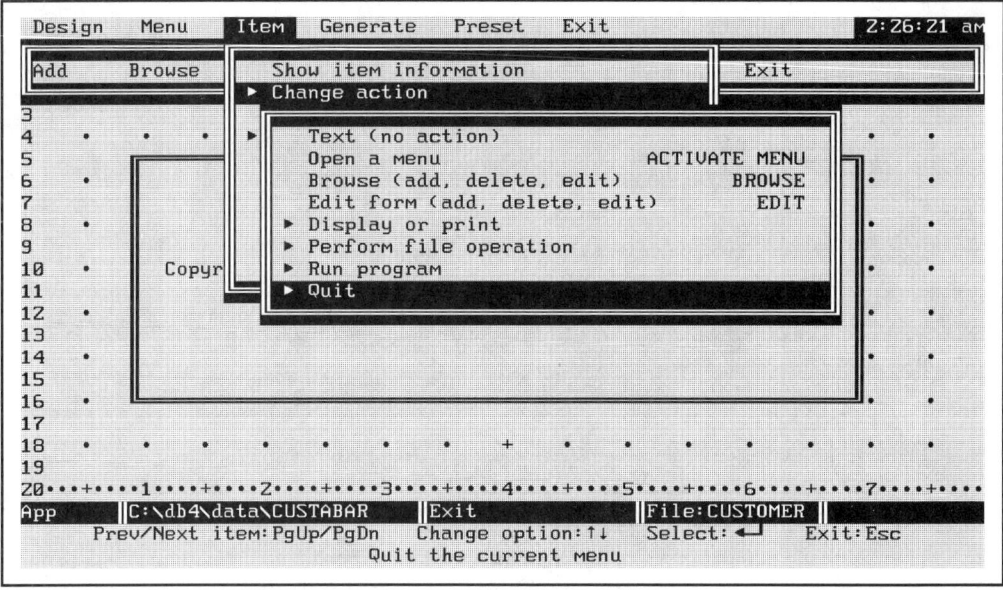

Figure 8-14   Quit Screen

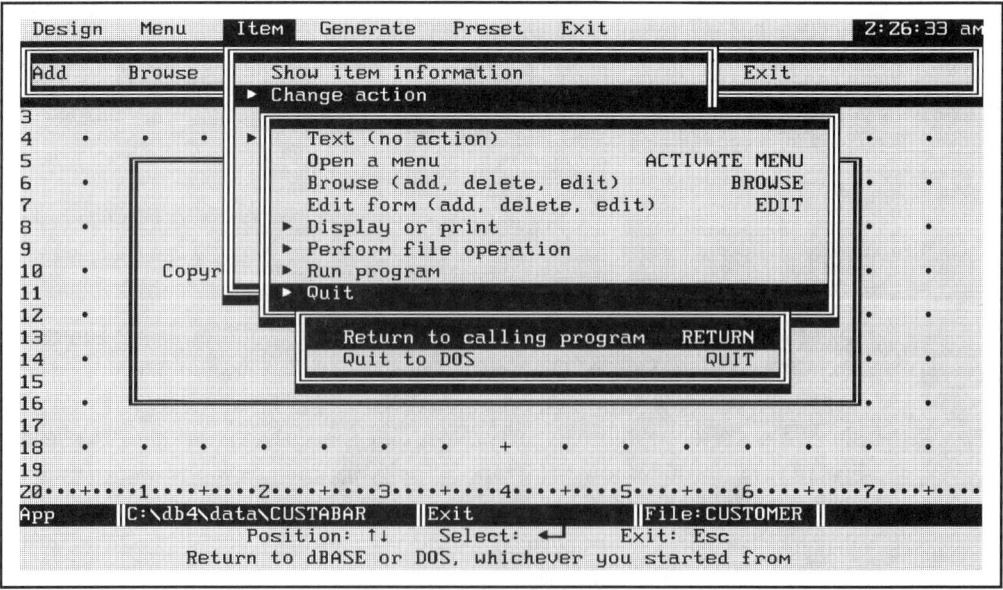

Figure 8-15   Quit Setup Screen

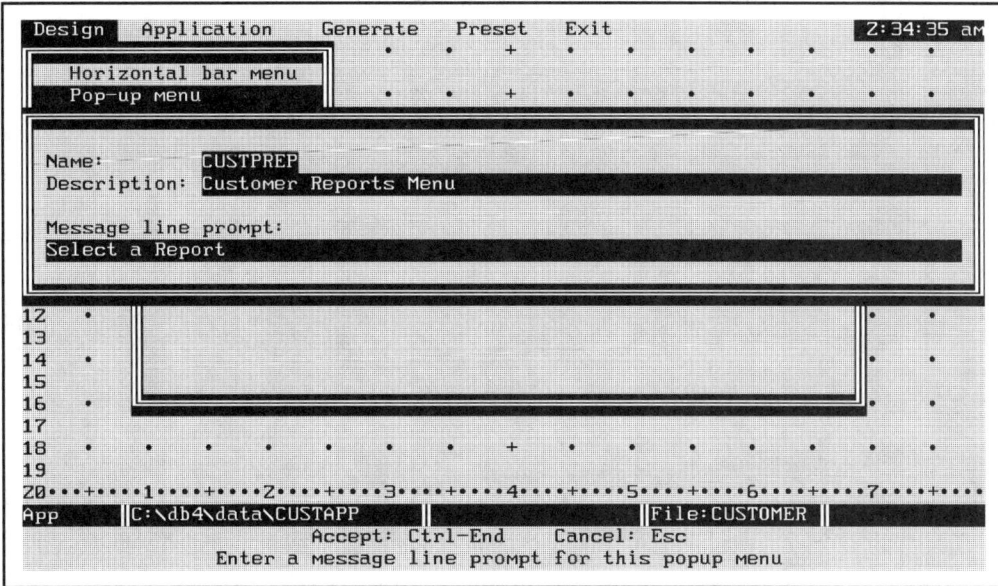

Figure 8-16   Pop-up Menu Setup Screen

Adding a Pop-up

Next, let's add a pop-up menu for the Reports pad. Since we want to let the user select one of two reports, it's easier to use a pop-up than add layer upon layer of menus. First, put away the light bar menu by selecting "Menu/Put away menu." This clears the screen leaving only the splash screen signon box. Select "Design/Pop-up menu," and you'll see the setup screen shown in Figure 8-16. As usual, the name you assign the pop-up will be the name given the program or procedure, so be sure the name is unique. The description is added to the program file. You'll probably assign messages to each pop-up element, so you can leave the message-line prompt blank.

Figure 8-17 shows the pop-up menu definition screen. Since each new line defines a pop-up bar, just type the entries as you want them to appear. It's a good idea to use different first characters for each bar (although I haven't followed my own advice here); that way, the user can access a bar by pressing its first letter.

This pop-up will be attached to a light bar pad, so it's a good idea to have the light bar on the screen at the same time. This is easy. Just select "Design/Horizontal bar menu" and pick the menu you just saved. Then select "Design/Popup menu." This will place both menus on the screen at once.

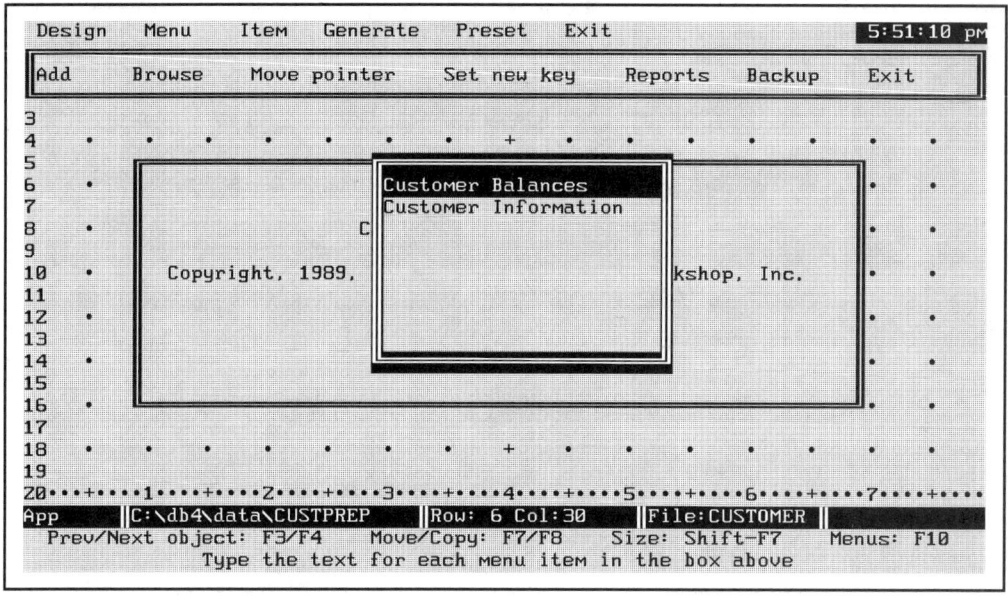

Figure 8-17   Pop-up Setup Screen

However, only the pop-up will be active. (Press F3 and F4 to change the currently active screen object. You can only modify the active object.)

Once all the bars are in place, the menu size should be changed. Press Shift-F7, then use the cursor keys to set the new box size. Press Enter when you're done. Figure 8-18 shows the menu box just before Enter was pressed.

Next, let's move the pop-up. Press F7 and you'll see the dialog box shown in Figure 8-19. Select "Entire frame" and use the cursor keys to move the pop-up to an appropriate location such as the one shown in Figure 8-20.

Press Enter and the pop-up will be moved as shown in Figure 8-21. This is the finished menu system.

The next step is to attach the pop-up to the pad. There are two parts to this. First, we must tell dBASE IV we want to open the menu when the Reports pad is highlighted. Figure 8-22 shows the "Open a menu" option. You will have to give the name of the pop-up you want opened.

Next, we have to say that we want the pop-up activated. To do this, select "Menu/Attach pull-down menus" as shown in Figure 8-23. And that's all there is to it.

Menu design is one of the great strengths of the applications generator. Moving boxes and pad elements around is much easier than worrying about the syntax of DEFINE MENU and DEFINE BAR.

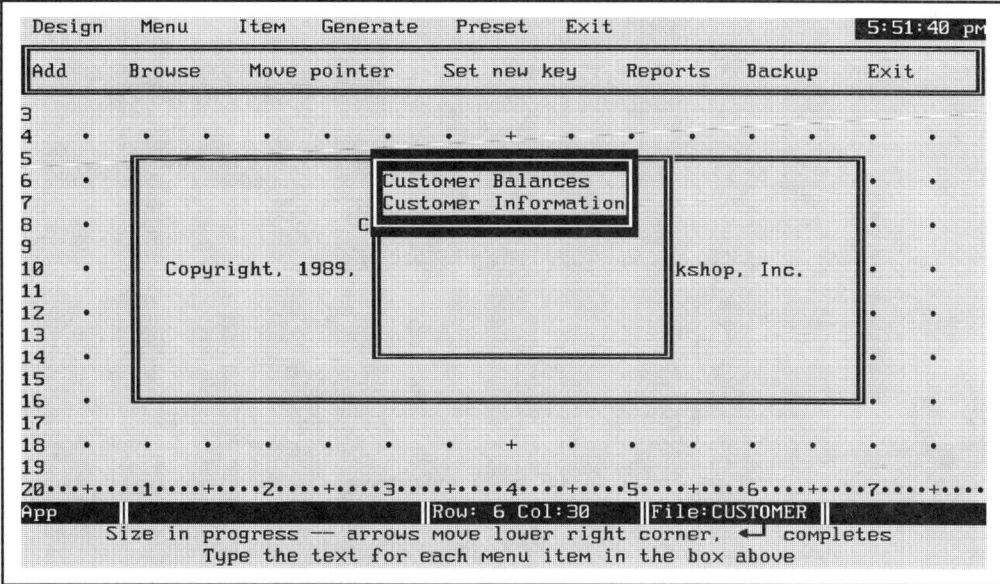

Figure 8-18   Resizing the Pop-up

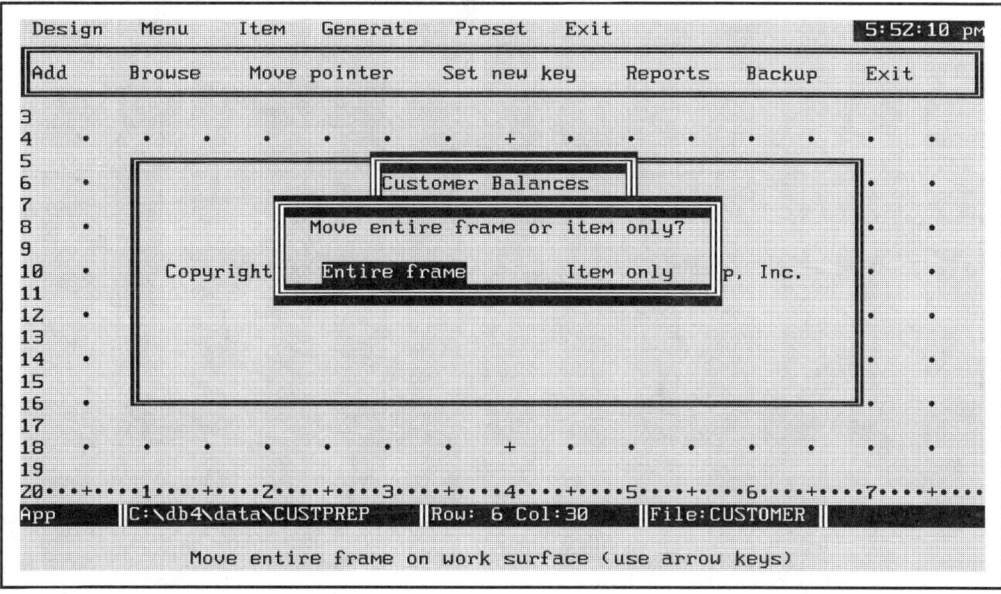

Figure 8-19   Moving the Pop-up

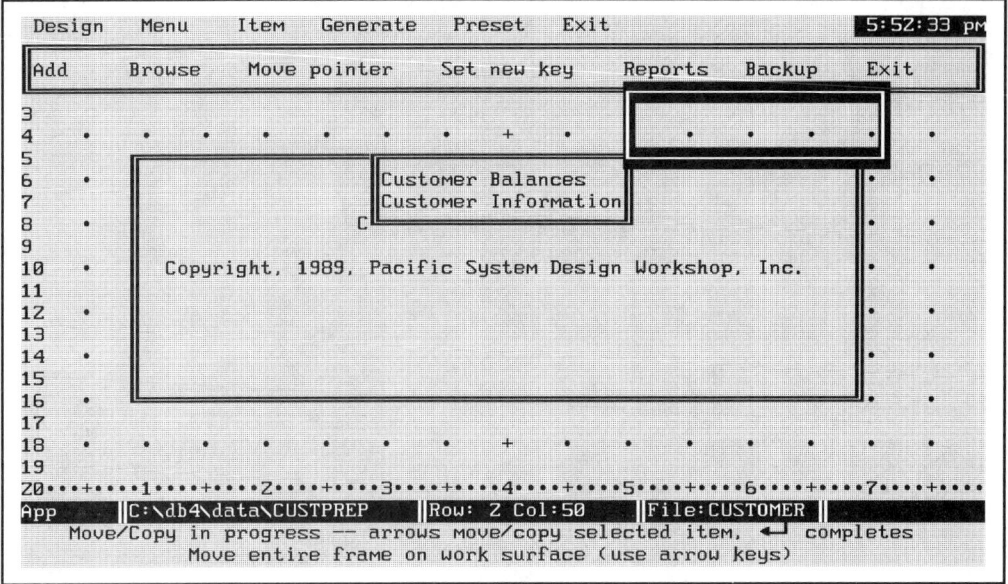

Figure 8-20   Moving the Pop-up

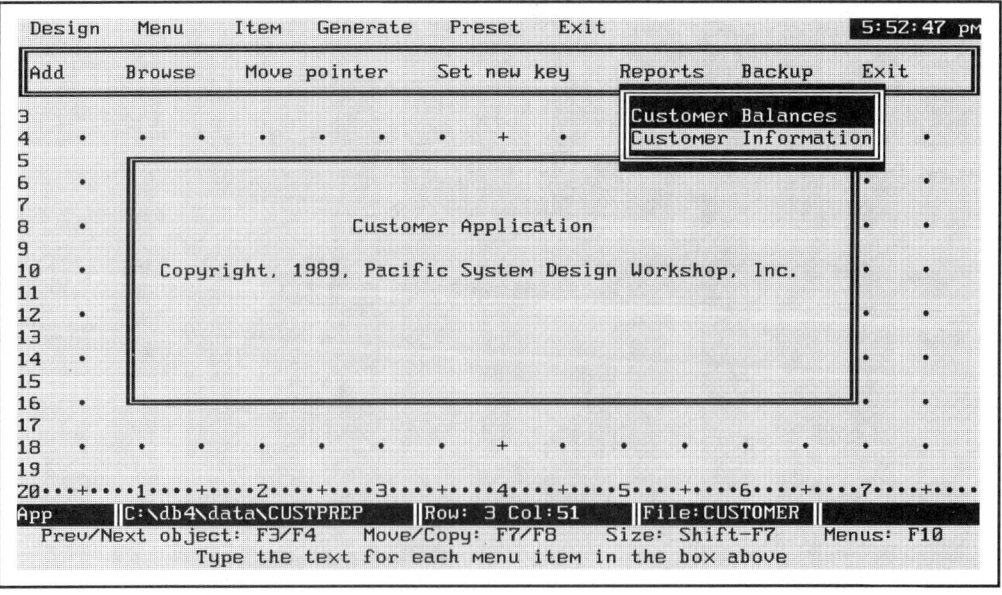

Figure 8-21   The Light-Bar Pop-up Menu System

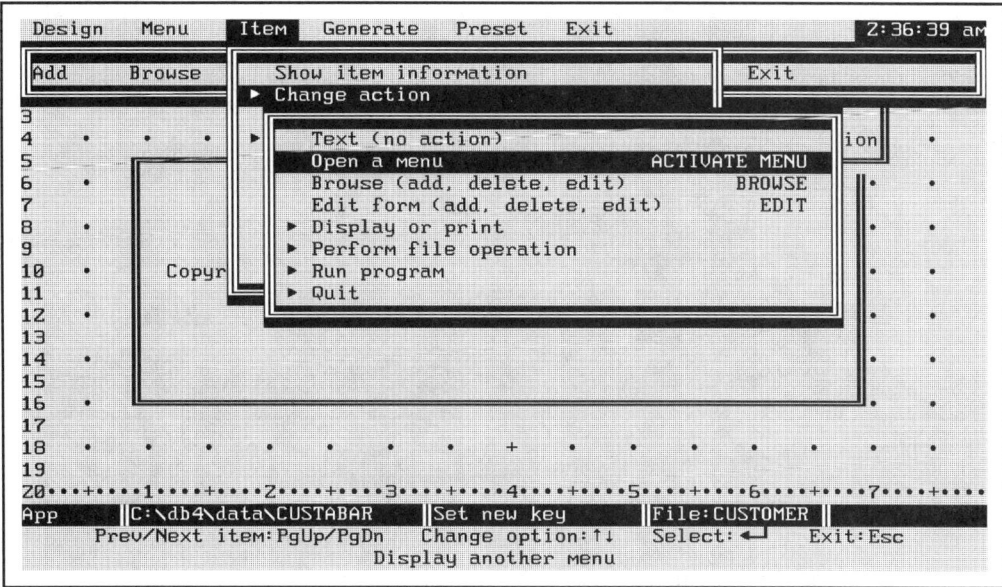

Figure 8-22   Attaching the Pop-up to the Pad

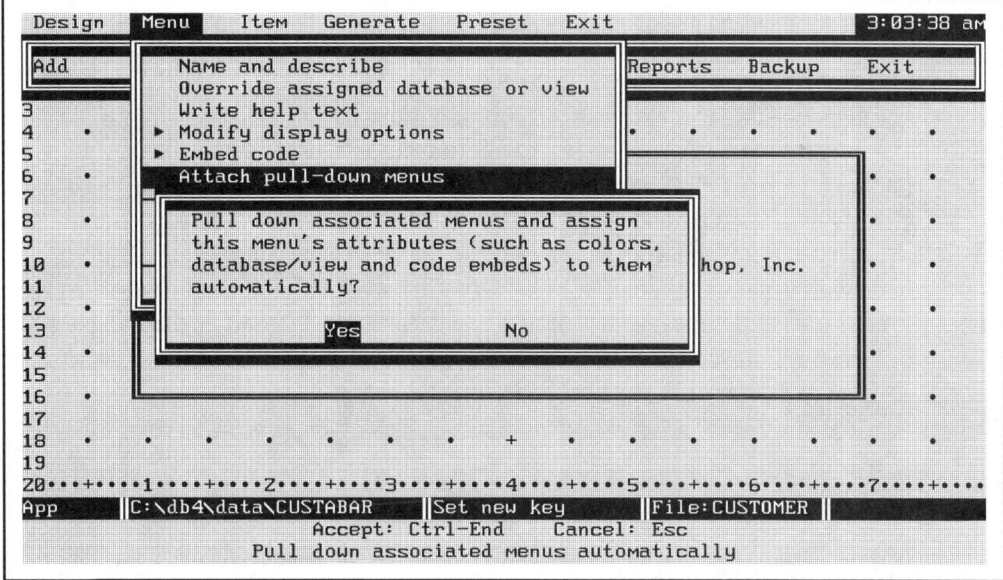

Figure 8-23   Attaching the Pop-up to the Pad

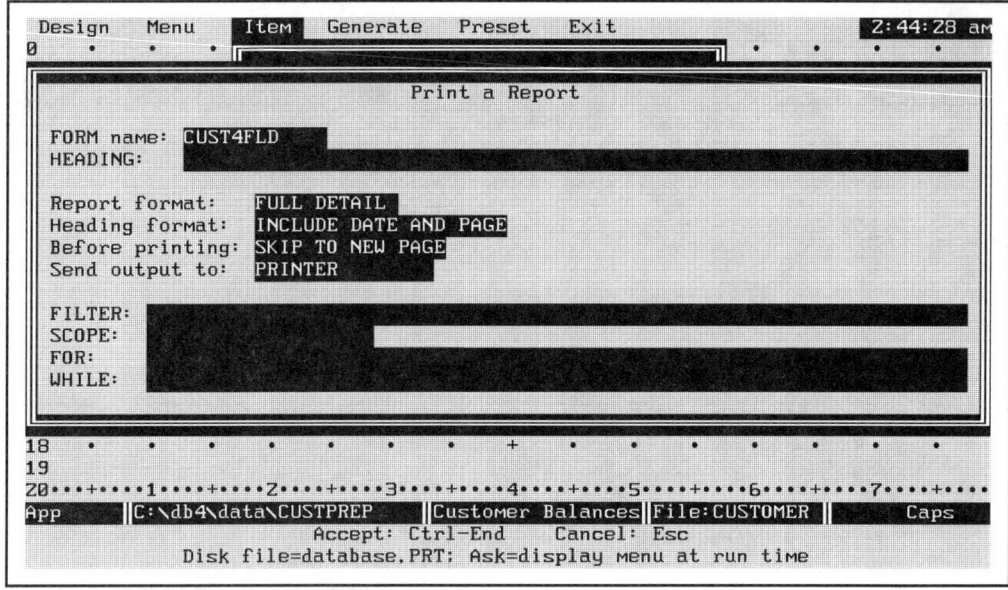

Figure 8-24   Actions for the Report Bar

Finally, we have to specify what to do when a report is selected. To do this, select "Item/Change action/Display or print" with the pop-up as the active screen object and the light bar on the first report (CUSTOMER BALANCE). Figure 8-24 shows the various report options.

Since the CUST4FLD report is grouped on CUSTOMER BALANCE, we have to reset the index order to that field. If you've made the changes to AD_REPT.COD and AD_LABL.COD suggested earlier in this chapter, you can use Item/Reassign index order to do this as shown in Figure 8-25. If you haven't made this change, use "Override assigned database or view to reset the index." However, this option is not particularly good as the database and view are closed, then reopened. If you use this option, the screen shown in Figure 8-26 will be the one you use.

Backup

The last pad to worry about is Backup. Figure 8-27 shows the complete light bar with this pad highlighted.

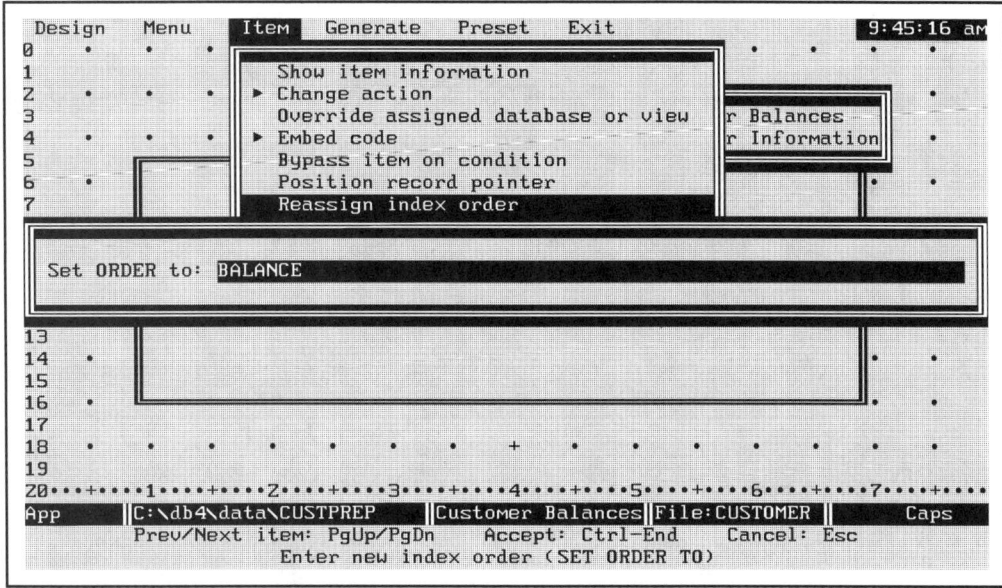

Figure 8-25   Resetting the Primary Key

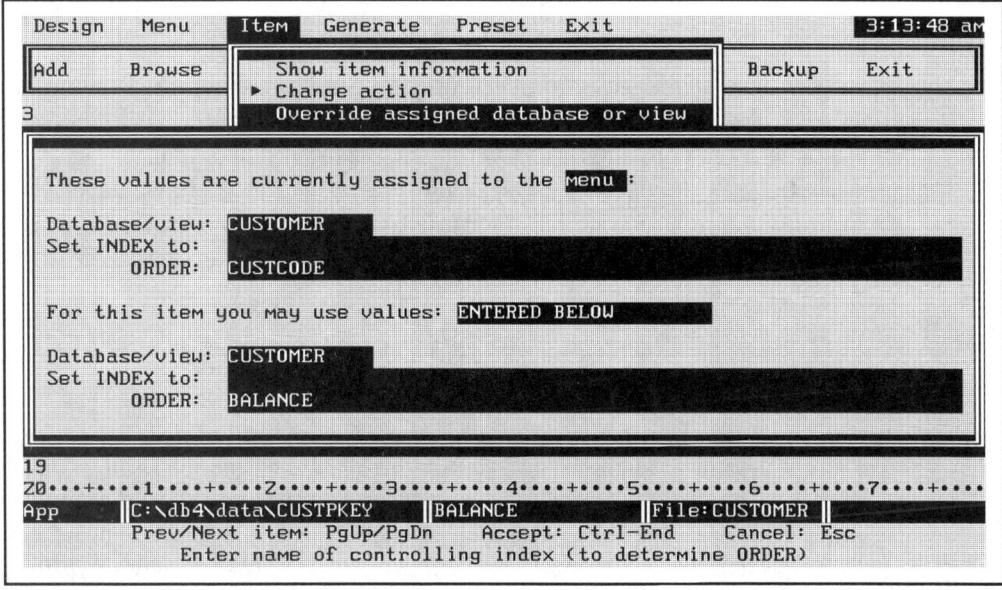

Figure 8-26   Overriding the Database and Index

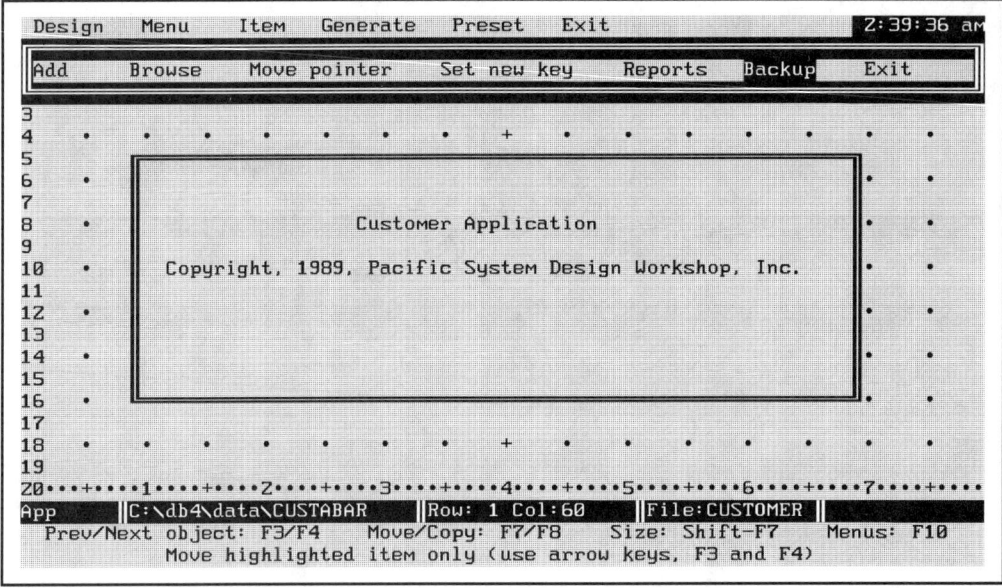

Figure 8-27   The Complete Menu

Select "Item/Change action/Perform file operation." Figure 8-28 shows the menu of file operations. As you can see, they are quite extensive. In this case, we just want to copy the file, so we'll pick the highlighted item.

Figure 8-29 shows the file operation screen filled in. Here we have specified only the next one hundred records to be copied. The user will have to select the Backup option until all records in the database are exhausted.

Defining a Window

There's a somewhat misleading option on the Items menu: Define logical window. The screen to do this is straightforward, but you should know that you are not only defining a window but opening it at the same time. At least that's the way the applications generator handles it. If you want to define a window without opening it, you'll have to write a little template code. By now that should be nothing to you.

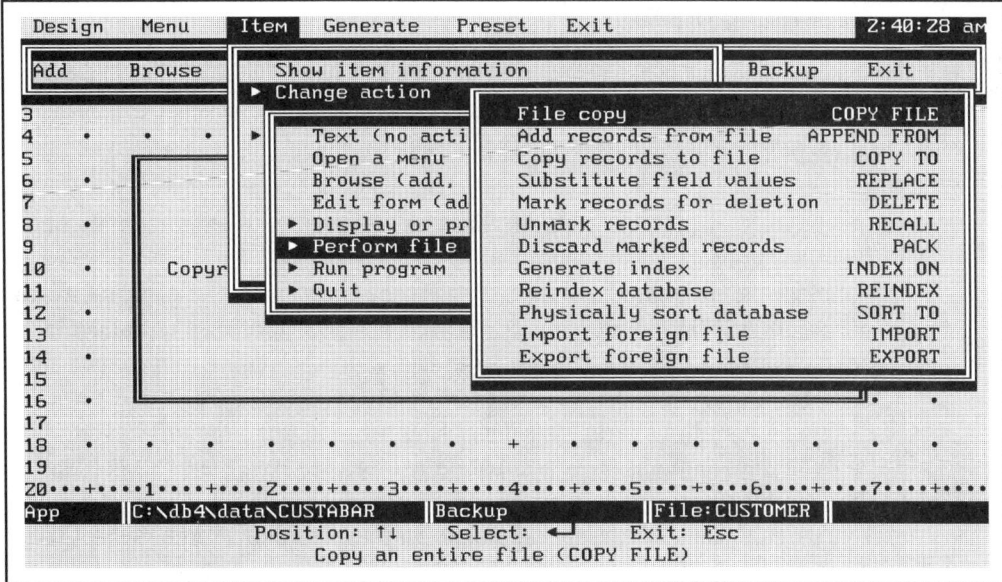

Figure 8-28   Backing Up Data

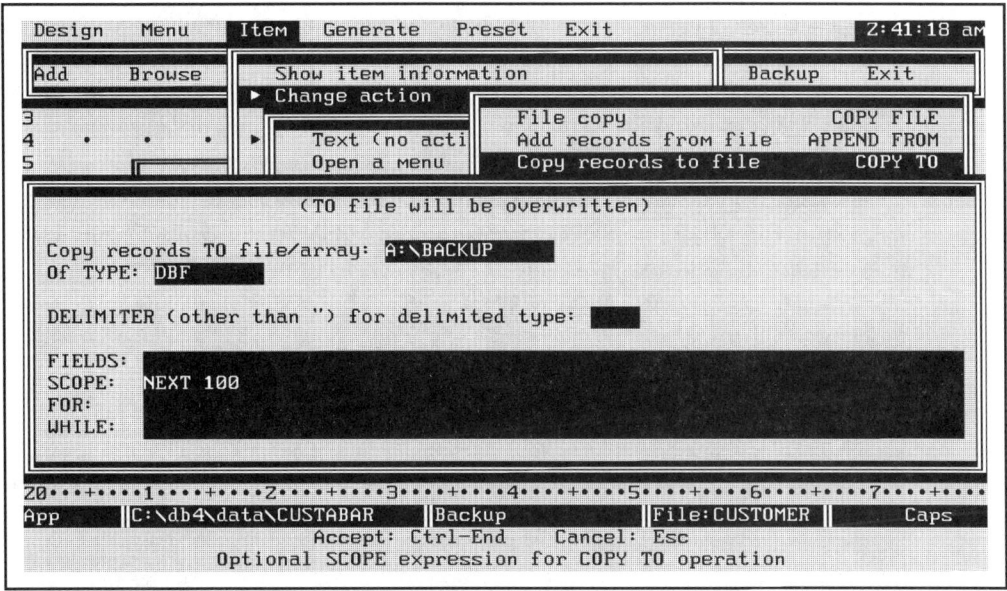

Figure 8-29   The File Operation Setup Screen

Generating Code

At long last we get to generate the program. Select "Application/Put away menu" to get both menus off the screen. Then select "Generate/Display program" and set this to NO so the code won't be displayed on the screen while it's being generated. (Actually, showing the code just slows the process down, so go ahead and watch if you want. Be warned — there are about one thousand lines in the application.)

Select the template MENU.GEN. The applications generator is the only part of dBASE IV where you are allowed to select your own template. In the next chapter, we'll see how to use DOCUMENT.GEN to produce quite different output from dBASE program code.

When everything is ready, select "Begin generating." You'll have to hit a key when the generation is completed and select "Exit/Save" to get back to the Control Center or dot prompt. Once there, run the application. I'll bet you'll agree that this is a lot easeir than sitting in front of a screen writing code one line at a time.

Conclusion

This chapter has suggested some minor changes to the Applications Generator templates to correct some obvious deficiencies. In addition, you could incorporate the changes made in the last chapter to QUICKAPP.COD. However, keep in mind the central point: if you're ever going to use a particular command again, it's probably easier to track it down and change it in the templates than fix the code every time in a program.

Going through the process of putting an application together should give you some idea of the power of the applications generator. I strongly recommend using it whenever possible. If you think the code it produces is inefficient, fix the template.

Appendix A

CUSTAPP.PRG

```
1  ********************************************************************
2  * Program......: CUSTAPP.PRG
3  * Author.......: Tony Lima
4  * Date.........: 4-24-89
5  * Notice.......: Copyright, 1989, Pacific System Design Workshop, Inc.
6  * dBASE Ver....: 1.0
7  * Generated by.: APGEN version 1.0
8  * Description..: Customer Application With Multiple Reports
9
10 * Description..: Main routine for menu system
11 ********************************************************************
12
13 *-- Setup environment
14 SET CONSOLE OFF
15 IF TYPE("gn_ApGen")="U"
16    CLEAR ALL
17    CLEAR WINDOWS
18    CLOSE ALL
19    CLOSE PROCEDURE
20    gn_ApGen=1
21 ELSE
22    gn_ApGen=gn_ApGen+1
23    IF gn_ApGen > 4
24       Do Pause WITH "Maximum level of Application nesting exceeded."
25       RETURN
26    ENDIF
27    PRIVATE gc_bell, gc_carry, gc_clock, gc_century, gc_confirm, gc_deli,;
28            gc_instruc, gc_safety, gc_status, gc_score, gc_talk, gc_key
29 ENDIF
30 *-- Store some sets to variables
31 gc_bell   =SET("BELL")
32 gc_carry  =SET("CARRY")
33 gc_clock  =SET("CLOCK")
34 gc_century=SET("CENTURY")
35 gc_confirm=SET("CONFIRM")
36 gc_deli   =SET("DELIMITERS")
37 gc_instruc=SET("INSTRUCT")
38 gc_safety =SET("SAFETY")
39 gc_status =SET("STATUS")
40 gc_score  =SET("SCOREBOARD")
41 gc_talk   =SET("TALK")
42 SET CONSOLE ON
43
44 SET BELL TO 220,2
45 SET BELL ON
```

(continued)

```
46 SET CARRY OFF
47 SET CENTURY OFF
48 SET CLOCK OFF
49 SET CONFIRM OFF
50 SET DELIMITERS TO "  "
51 SET DELIMITERS OFF
52 SET DEVICE TO SCREEN
53 SET ESCAPE ON
54 SET EXCLUSIVE OFF
55 SET ECHO OFF
56 SET LOCK ON
57 SET MESSAGE TO ""
58 SET PRINT OFF
59 SET REPROCESS TO 4
60 SET SAFETY OFF
61 SET TALK OFF
62
63 *-- Initialize global variables
64 gn_error=0          && 0 if no error, otherwise an error occurred
65 gn_ikey=0           && keypress returned from the INKEY() function
66 gn_send=0           && return value from popup of position menus
67 gn_trace=1          && sets trace level, however you need to change template
68 gc_brdr='1'         && border to use when drawing boxes
69 gc_dev='CON'        && Device to use for printing - See Proc. PrintSet
70 gc_key='N'          && leave the application
71 gc_prognum='  '     && internal program counter to handle nested menus
72 gc_quit=' '         && memvar for return to caller
73 listval='NO_FIELD'  && Pick List value
74
75 *-- remove asterisk to turn clock on
76 * SET CLOCK TO
77 SET INSTRUCT OFF
78
79 *-- Blank the screen
80 SET COLOR TO
81 CLEAR
82 SET SCOREBOARD OFF
83 SET STATUS OFF
84
85 *-- Define menus
86 DO MPDEF            && execute Menu Process DEFinition
87
88 *-- Execute main menu
89 DO WHILE gc_key = 'N'
90    DO CUSTABAR WITH "B00"
91    IF gc_quit = 'Q'
92       EXIT
93    ENDIF
94    ACTIVATE WINDOW Exit_App
95    lc_conf=SET("CONFIRM")
96    lc_deli=SET("DELIMITER")
97    SET CONFIRM OFF
```

(continued)

```
 98     SET DELIMITER OFF
 99     @ 1,2 SAY "Do you want to leave this application?" ;
100         GET gc_key PICT "!" VALID gc_key $ "NY"
101     READ
102     SET CONFIRM &lc_conf.
103     SET DELIMITER &lc_deli.
104     RELEASE lc_conf, lc_deli
105     DEACTIVATE WINDOW Exit_App
106 ENDDO
107
108 *-- Reset environment
109 gn_ApGen=gn_ApGen-1
110 SET BELL   &gc_bell.
111 SET CARRY  &gc_carry.
112 SET CLOCK  &gc_clock.
113 SET CENTURY &gc_century.
114 SET CONFIRM &gc_confirm.
115 SET DELIMITERS &gc_deli.
116 SET INSTRUCT &gc_instruc.
117 SET STATUS &gc_status.
118 SET SAFETY &gc_safety.
119 SET SCORE  &gc_score.
120 SET TALK   &gc_talk.
121
122 IF gn_Apgen < 1
123     ON KEY LABEL F1
124     CLEAR ALL
125     CLEAR WINDOWS
126     CLOSE ALL
127     CLOSE PROCEDURE
128     SET CLOCK OFF
129     SET ESCAPE ON
130     SET MESSAGE TO ""
131     CLEAR
132 ENDIF
133 RETURN
134
135 ************************************************************************
136 * Description..: Procedure files for generated menu system.
137 * The programs that follow are common to main routines
138 * The last procedure is the Menu Process DEFinition
139 ************************************************************************
140 PROCEDURE Lockit
141 PARAMETER ltype
142 IF NETWORK()
143     gn_error=0
144     ON ERROR DO Multerr
145     IF ltype = "1"
146         ll_lock=FLOCK()
147     ENDIF
148     IF ltype = "2"
149         ll_lock=RLOCK()
```

(continued)

```
150    ENDIF
151    ON ERROR
152 ENDIF
153 RETURN
154
155 PROCEDURE Info_Box
156 PARAMETERS lc_say
157 ? lc_say
158 ? REPLICATE("-",LEN(lc_say))
159 ?
160 RETURN
161 * EOP: Info_Box
162
163 PROCEDURE get_sele
164 *-- Get the user selection & store BAR into variable
165 gn_send = BAR()  && Variable for print testing
166 DEACTIVATE POPUP
167 RETURN
168
169 PROCEDURE ShowPick
170 listval=PROMPT()
171 IF LEFT(entryflg,1)="B"
172    lc_file=POPUP()
173    DO &lc_file. WITH "A"
174    RETURN
175 ENDIF
176 IF TYPE("lc_window")="U"
177    ACTIVATE WINDOW ShowPick
178 ELSE
179    ACTIVATE WINDOW &lc_window.
180 ENDIF
181 STORE 0 TO ln_ikey,x1,x2
182 ln_ikey=LASTKEY()
183 IF ln_ikey=13
184    x1=AT(TRIM(listval)+',',lc_fldlst)
185    IF x1 = 0
186       lc_fldlst=lc_fldlst+TRIM(listval)+','
187    ELSE
188       x2=AT(',',SUBSTR(lc_fldlst,x1))
189       lc_fldlst=STUFF(lc_fldlst,x1,x2,'')
190    ENDIF
191    CLEAR
192    ? lc_fldlst
193 ENDIF
194 ACTIVATE SCREEN
195 RETURN
196 * EOP: ShowPick
197
198 PROCEDURE Cleanup
199 *-- test whether report option was selected
200 DO CASE
201 CASE gc_dev='CON'
```

(continued)

```
202    WAIT
203 CASE gc_dev='PRN'
204    SET PRINT OFF
205    SET PRINTER TO
206 CASE gc_dev='TXT'
207    CLOSE ALTERNATE
208 ENDCASE
209 RETURN
210
211 * EOP: Cleanup
212
213 PROCEDURE Pause
214 PARAMETER lc_msg
215 *-- Parameters : lc_msg = message line
216 IF TYPE("lc_message")="U"
217    gn_error=ERROR()
218 ENDIF
219 lc_msg = lc_msg
220 lc_option='0'
221 ACTIVATE WINDOW Pause
222 IF gn_error > 0
223    IF TYPE("lc_message")="U"
224       @ 0,1 SAY [An error has occurred !! - Error message: ]+MESSAGE()
225    ELSE
226       @ 0,1 SAY [Error # ]+lc_message
227    ENDIF
228 ENDIF
229 @ 1,1 SAY lc_msg
230 WAIT " Press any key to continue..."
231 DEACTIVATE WINDOW Pause
232 RETURN
233
234 * EOP: Pause
235
236 PROCEDURE Multerr
237 *-- set the global error variable
238 gn_error=ERROR()
239 *-- contains error number to test
240 lc_erno=STR(ERROR(),3)+','
241 *-- option var.
242 lc_opt='T'
243 *-- Dialog box for options Try again and Return to menu.
244 IF lc_erno $ "108,109,128,129,"
245    ACTIVATE WINDOW Pause
246    @ 0,2 SAY lc_erno+" "+MESSAGE()
247    @ 2,22 SAY "T = Try again, R = Return to menu." GET lc_opt ;
248 PICTURE "!" VALID lc_opt $ "TR"
249    READ
250    DEACTIVATE WINDOW Pause
251    IF lc_opt = "R"
252       RETURN
253    ENDIF
```

(continued)

```
254 ENDIF
255 *-- Display message and return to menu.
256 IF .NOT. lc_erno $ "108,109,128,129,"
257    DO PAUSE WITH ERROR()
258    RETURN
259 ENDIF
260 *-- reset global variable
261 gn_error=0
262 *-- Try the command again
263 RETRY
264 RETURN
265
266 * EOP: Multerr
267
268 PROCEDURE Trace
269 *  Desc: Trace procedure - to let programmer know what module
270 *             is about to execute and what module has executed.
271 PARAMETERS p_msg, p_lvl
272 *-- Parameters : p_msg = message line, p_lvl = trace level
273 lc_msg = p_msg
274 ln_lvl = p_lvl
275 lc_trp = ' '
276 IF gn_trace < ln_lvl
277    RETURN
278 ENDIF
279 DEFINE WINDOW trace FROM 11,00 TO 16,79 DOUBLE
280 DO WHILE lc_trp <> 'Q'
281    @ 2,40-LEN(lc_msg)/2 SAY lc_msg
282    @ 4,05 SAY 'S - Set trace level, D - Display status, M - display Memory'
283    @ 5,05 SAY 'P - Turn printer on, Q - to Quit'
284    lc_trp = 'Q'
285    @ 5,38 GET lc_trp PICTURE "!"
286    READ
287    DO CASE
288    CASE lc_trp = 'S'
289       @ 2,01 CLEAR
290       @ 2,33 SAY 'Set trace level'
291       @ 4,05 SAY 'Enter trace level to change to:' GET gn_trace PICTURE '#'
292       @ 5,05 SAY '                    '
293       READ
294       IF gn_trace=0
295          @ 2,01 CLEAR
296          @ 3,05 SAY 'Trace is now turned off..To reactivate Trace
                - Press [F3]'
297          @ 4,05 say 'Press any key to continue...'
298          WAIT ''
299       ENDIF
300    CASE lc_trp = 'D'
301       DISPLAY STATUS
302       WAIT
303    CASE lc_trp = 'M'
304       DISPLAY MEMORY
```

(continued)

```
305     WAIT
306   CASE lc_trp = 'P'
307       SET PRINT ON
308   ENDCASE
309 ENDDO
310 SET PRINT OFF
311 @ 24,79 SAY " "
312 RELEASE WINDOW trace
313 RETURN
314
315 * EOP: Trace
316
317 PROCEDURE PrintSet
318 *-- Initialize variables
319 gc_dev='CON'
320 lc_choice=' '
321 gn_pkey=0
322 gn_send=0
323
324 DEFINE WINDOW printemp FROM 08,25 TO 17,56
325
326 DEFINE POPUP SavePrin FROM 10,40
327 DEFINE BAR 1 OF SavePrin PROMPT " Send output to ..." SKIP
328 DEFINE BAR 2 OF SavePrin PROMPT REPLICATE(CHR(196),24) SKIP
329 DEFINE BAR 3 OF SavePrin PROMPT " CON:   Console"
      MESSAGE "Send output to Screen"
330 DEFINE BAR 4 OF SavePrin PROMPT " LPT1:  Parallel port 1 "
      MESSAGE "Send output to LPT1:"
331 DEFINE BAR 5 OF SavePrin PROMPT " LPT2:  Parallel port 2"
      MESSAGE "Send output to LPT2:"
332 DEFINE BAR 6 OF SavePrin PROMPT " COM1:  Serial port 1"
      MESSAGE "Send output to COM1:"
333 DEFINE BAR 7 OF SavePrin PROMPT " FILE = REPORT.TXT"
      MESSAGE "Send output to File Report.txt"
334 ON SELECTION POPUP SavePrin DO get_sele
335
336 ACTIVATE POPUP SavePrin
337 RELEASE POPUP SavePrin
338
339 IF gn_send = 7
340    gc_dev = 'TXT'
341    SET ALTERNATE TO REPORT.TXT
342    SET ALTERNATE ON
343 ELSE
344    IF .NOT. (gn_send = 3 .OR. LASTKEY() = 27)
345       gc_dev = 'PRN'
346       temp = SUBSTR("    LPT1LPT2COM1 ",((gn_send-2)-1)*4,4)
347       ON ERROR DO prntrtry
348       SET PRINTER TO &temp.
349       IF gn_pkey <> 27
350          SET PRINT ON
351       ENDIF
```

(continued)

```
352        ON ERROR
353     ENDIF
354 ENDIF
355 RELEASE WINDOW printemp
356 RETURN
357
358 PROCEDURE prntrtry
359 PRIVATE lc_escape
360 lc_escape = SET("ESCAPE")
361 IF .NOT. PRINTSTATUS()
362    IF lc_escape = "ON"
363       SET ESCAPE OFF
364    ENDIF
365    gn_pkey = 0
366    ACTIVATE WINDOW printemp
367    @ 1,0 SAY "Please ready your printer or"
368    @ 2,0 SAY "    press ESC to cancel"
369    DO WHILE ( .NOT. PRINTSTATUS()) .AND. gn_pkey <> 27
370       gn_pkey = INKEY()
371    ENDDO
372    DEACTIVATE WINDOW printemp
373    SET ESCAPE &lc_escape.
374    IF gn_pkey <> 27
375       RETRY
376    ENDIF
377 ENDIF
378 RETURN
379
380 * EOP: PrintSet
381
382 PROCEDURE Position
383 IF LEN(DBF()) = 0
384    DO Pause WITH "Database not in use. "
385    RETURN
386 ENDIF
387 SET SPACE ON
388 SET DELIMITERS OFF
389 ln_type=0          && sublevel selection
390 ln_rkey=READKEY()  && test for ESC or Return
391 ln_rec=RECNO()     && DBF record number
392 ln_num=0           && for input of a number
393 ld_date=DATE()     && for input of a date
394 lc_option='0'      && main option ie. Seek, Goto and Locate
395 *-- Scope ie. ALL, REST, NEXT <n>
396 STORE SPACE(10) TO lc_scp
397 *-- 1 = Character SEEK, 2 = For clause, 3 = While clause
398 STORE SPACE(40) TO lc_ln1, lc_ln2, lc_ln3
399 lc_temp=""
400 @ 0,00 SAY "Index order: "+IIF(""=ORDER(),"Database is in natural
       order",ORDER())
401 @ 1,00 SAY "Listed below are the first 16 fields."
402 lc_temp=REPLICATE(CHR(196),19)
```

(continued)

```
403 @ 2,0 SAY CHR(218)+lc_temp+CHR(194)+lc_temp+CHR(194)+
    lc_temp+CHR(194)+lc_temp
404 ln_num=240
405 DO WHILE ln_num < 560
406    lc_temp=FIELD( (ln_num-240)/20 +1)
407    @ (ln_num/80),MOD(ln_num,80) SAY CHR(179)+;
408 lc_temp+SPACE(11-LEN(lc_temp))+;
409 SUBSTR("= Char  = Date  = Logic = Num   = Float = Memo      ",;
410 AT(TYPE(lc_temp),"CDLNFMU")*8-7,8)
411    ln_num=ln_num+20
412 ENDDO
413 ln_num=1
414
415 DEFINE POPUP Posit1 FROM 8,30
416 DEFINE BAR 1 OF Posit1 PROMPT " Position by " SKIP
417 DEFINE BAR 2 OF Posit1 PROMPT REPLICATE(CHR(196),15) SKIP
418 DEFINE BAR 3 OF Posit1 PROMPT " SEEK Record"
       MESSAGE "Search on index key" SKIP FOR ""=ORDER()
419 DEFINE BAR 4 OF Posit1 PROMPT " GOTO Record"
       MESSAGE "Position to specific record"
420 DEFINE BAR 5 OF Posit1 PROMPT " LOCATE Record "
       MESSAGE "Locate record for condition"
421 DEFINE BAR 6 OF Posit1 PROMPT " Return" MESSAGE "Return without positioning"
422 ON SELECTION POPUP Posit1 DO get_sele
423
424 SET CONFIRM ON
425 DO WHILE lc_option='0'
426    ACTIVATE POPUP Posit1
427    lc_option = ltrim(str(gn_send))  && for popup
428     IF LASTKEY() = 27 .OR. lc_option="6"
429        GOTO ln_rec
430        EXIT
431     ENDIF
432     DO CASE
433     CASE lc_option='3'
434        *-- Seek
435        IF LEN(NDX(1))=0 .AND. LEN(MDX(1))=0
436           DO Pause WITH "Can't use this option - No index files are open."
437           LOOP
438        ENDIF
439        ln_type=1
440        lc_ln1=SPACE(40)
441        DEFINE WINDOW Posit2 FROM 8,19 TO 15,62 DOUBLE
442        ACTIVATE WINDOW Posit2
443        @ 1,1 SAY "Enter the type of expression:" GET ln_type PICT
             "#" RANGE 1,3
444        @ 2,1 SAY "(1=character, 2=numeric and 3=date.)"
445        READ
446        IF .NOT. (READKEY() = 12 .OR. READKEY() = 268)
447           SET CONFIRM ON
448           @ 3,1 SAY "Enter the key expression to search for:"
449           IF ln_type=3
```

(continued)

```
450              @ 4,1 GET ld_date PICT "@D"
451           ELSE
452              IF ln_type=2
453                 @ 4,1 GET ln_num PICT "##########"
454              ELSE
455                 @ 4,1 GET lc_ln1
456              ENDIF
457           ENDIF
458           READ
459           SET CONFIRM OFF
460           IF .NOT. (READKEY() = 12 .OR. READKEY() = 268)
461              lc_temp=IIF(ln_type=1,"TRIM(lc_ln1)",
                    IIF(ln_type=2,"ln_num","ld_date"))
462              SEEK &lc_temp.
463           ENDIF
464        ENDIF
465        RELEASE WINDOWS Posit2
466     CASE lc_option='4'
467        *-- Goto
468        ln_type=1
469        DEFINE POPUP Posit2 FROM 8,30
470        DEFINE BAR 1 OF Posit2 PROMPT " GOTO:" SKIP
471        DEFINE BAR 2 OF Posit2 PROMPT REPLICATE(CHR(196),10) SKIP
472        DEFINE BAR 3 OF Posit2 PROMPT " TOP" MESSAGE "GOTO Top of File"
473        DEFINE BAR 4 OF Posit2 PROMPT " BOTTOM" MESSAGE "GOTO Bottom of File"
474        DEFINE BAR 5 OF Posit2 PROMPT " Record # "
              MESSAGE "GOTO A Specific Record"
475        ON SELECTION POPUP Posit2 DO get_sele
476        ACTIVATE POPUP posit2
477        ln_type = gn_send
478        IF LASTKEY() <> 27
479           IF ln_type=5
480              DEFINE WINDOW Posit2 FROM 8,26 TO 13,50 DOUBLE
481              ACTIVATE WINDOW Posit2
482              ln_num=0
483              @ 3,1 SAY "Max. Record # = "+LTRIM(STR(RECCOUNT()))
484              @ 1,1 SAY "Record to GOTO" GET ln_num PICT "######"
                    RANGE 1,RECCOUNT()
485              READ
486              IF .NOT. (READKEY() = 12 .OR. READKEY() = 268)
487                 GOTO ln_num
488              ENDIF
489              RELEASE WINDOWS Posit2
490           ELSE
491              lc_temp=IIF(ln_type=3,"TOP","BOTTOM")
492              GOTO &lc_temp.
493           ENDIF
494        ENDIF
495     CASE lc_option='5'
496        *-- Locate
497        DEFINE WINDOW Posit2 FROM 8,16 TO 14,66 DOUBLE
498        ACTIVATE WINDOW Posit2
```

(continued)

```
499         @ 1,19 SAY "ie. ALL, NEXT <n>, and REST"
500         @ 1,01 SAY "Scope:" GET lc_scp 501        @ 2,01 SAY "For:  "
              GET lc_ln2
502         @ 3,01 SAY "While:" GET lc_ln3
503         READ
504         IF .NOT. (READKEY() = 12 .OR. READKEY() = 268)
505            lc_temp=TRIM(lc_scp)
506            lc_temp=lc_temp + IIF(LEN(TRIM(lc_ln2)) > 0," FOR "
                 +TRIM(lc_ln2),"")
507            lc_temp=lc_temp + IIF(LEN(TRIM(lc_ln3)) > 0," WHILE "
                 +TRIM(lc_ln3),"")
508            IF LEN(lc_temp) > 0
509               LOCATE &lc_temp.
510            ELSE
511               DO Pause WITH "All fields were blank."
512            ENDIF
513         ENDIF
514         RELEASE WINDOW Posit2
515      ENDCASE
516      IF EOF()
517         DO Pause WITH "Record not found."
518         GOTO ln_rec
519      ENDIF
520      IF READKEY()=12 .OR. READKEY()= 268 .OR. LASTKEY()=27  && Esc was hit
521         lc_option='0'
522      ENDIF
523 ENDDO
524 SET DELIMITERS &gc_deli.
525 SET CONFIRM OFF
526 RETURN
527
528 * EOP: Position
529
530 PROCEDURE Postnhlp
531 ln_getkey=INKEY()
532 DO CASE
533 CASE "SEEK" $ PROMPT()
534    HELP SEEK
535 CASE "GOTO" $ PROMPT()
536    HELP GOTO
537 CASE "LOCATE" $ PROMPT()
538    HELP LOCATE
539 ENDCASE
540 RETURN
541 * EOP: Postnhlp
542
543
544 **********************************************************************
545 * Program......: MPDEF
546 * Author.......: Tony Lima
547 * Date.........: 4-24-89
548 * Notice.......: Copyright, 1989, Pacific System Design Workshop, Inc.
```

(continued)

```
549 * dBASE Ver....: 1.0
550 * Generated by.: APGEN version 1.0
551 * Description..: Customer Application With Multiple Reports
552
553 * Description..: Defines all menus in the system
554 ***********************************************************************
555 PROCEDURE MPDEF
556 IF ISCOLOR()
557    SET COLOR OF NORMAL TO W+/B
558    SET COLOR OF MESSAGES TO R/B
559    SET COLOR OF TITLES TO GR+/B
560    SET COLOR OF HIGHLIGHT TO B+/W
561    SET COLOR OF BOX TO R/W
562    SET COLOR OF INFORMATION TO RB/W
563    SET COLOR OF FIELDS TO N/W
564 ENDIF
565 CLEAR
566
567 *-- Sign-on banner
568
569 SET BORDER TO
570 @ 5,9 TO 16,69 DOUBLE COLOR R/W
571 @ 6,10 CLEAR TO 15,68
572 @ 8,10 SAY "                 Customer Application"
573 @ 10,10 SAY " Copyright, 1989, Pacific System Design Workshop, Inc."
574 @ 24,30 SAY " Press "+CHR(17)+CHR(196)+CHR(217)+" to continue. "
575 gn_ikey=INKEY(4)
576
577 CLEAR
578
579 DEFINE WINDOW FullScr FROM 0,0 TO 24,79 NONE
580 DEFINE WINDOW Savescr FROM 0,0 TO 21,79 NONE
581 DEFINE WINDOW Helpscr FROM 0,0 TO 21,79 NONE
582 DEFINE WINDOW Browscr FROM 1,0 TO 21,79 NONE
583 IF gn_ApGen=1
584    DEFINE WINDOW Exit_App FROM 11,17 TO 15,62 DOUBLE
585 ENDIF
586 *-- Window for pause message box
587 DEFINE WINDOW Pause FROM 15,00 TO 19,79 DOUBLE
588
589 ACTIVATE WINDOW FullScr
590 @ 24,00
591 @ 23,00 SAY "Loading..."
592 SET BORDER TO DOUBLE
593 *-- Bar
594 DEFINE MENU CUSTABAR MESSAGE "Select the activity you wish to perform"
595 DEFINE PAD PAD_1 OF CUSTABAR PROMPT "Add" AT 1,1
       MESSAGE "Add records to the Customer file."
596 ON SELECTION PAD PAD_1 OF CUSTABAR DO ACT01
597 DEFINE PAD PAD_2 OF CUSTABAR PROMPT "Browse" AT 1,9
       MESSAGE "Browse Customer Records"
```

(continued)

```
598 ON SELECTION PAD PAD_2 OF CUSTABAR DO ACT01
599 DEFINE PAD PAD_3 OF CUSTABAR PROMPT "Move pointer" AT 1,19
      MESSAGE "Locate and display a record.  (You may want to Select new
      key first.)"
600 ON SELECTION PAD PAD_3 OF CUSTABAR DO ACT01
601 DEFINE PAD PAD_4 OF CUSTABAR PROMPT "Set new key" AT 1,35
      MESSAGE "Select a new index key.  A menu of available indexes will be
      displayed."
602 ON SELECTION PAD PAD_4 OF CUSTABAR DO ACT01
603 DEFINE PAD PAD_5 OF CUSTABAR PROMPT "Reports" AT 1,50
604 ON PAD PAD_5 OF CUSTABAR ACTIVATE POPUP CUSTPREP
605 DEFINE PAD PAD_6 OF CUSTABAR PROMPT "Backup" AT 1,60
      MESSAGE "Copy Customer database to BACKUP.DBF."
606 ON SELECTION PAD PAD_6 OF CUSTABAR DO ACT01
607 DEFINE PAD PAD_7 OF CUSTABAR PROMPT "Exit" AT 1,70
      MESSAGE "Return to dBASE IV"
608 ON SELECTION PAD PAD_7 OF CUSTABAR DO ACT01
609 ?? "."
610 SET BORDER TO DOUBLE
611 *-- Popup
612 DEFINE POPUP CUSTPREP FROM 2,50 TO 5,71 ;
613 MESSAGE "Select a Report"
614 DEFINE BAR 1 OF CUSTPREP PROMPT "Customer Balances"
      MESSAGE "Report on Customer Balances"
615 DEFINE BAR 2 OF CUSTPREP PROMPT "Customer Information"
      MESSAGE "Customer Name, Address, Phone"
616 ON SELECTION POPUP CUSTPREP DO ACT02
617 ?? "."
618 @ 23,00 CLEAR
619 RETURN
620 *-- EOP: MPDEF.PRG
621
622 PROCEDURE 1HELP1
623 ACTIVATE WINDOW Helpscr
624 SET ESCAPE OFF
625 ACTIVATE SCREEN
626 @ 0,0 CLEAR TO 21,79
627 @ 1,0 TO 21,79 COLOR R/W
628 @ 24,00
629 @ 24,26 SAY "Press any key to continue..."
630 @ 0,0 SAY ""
631 ln_row=INKEY()
632 DO CASE
633 *-- help for menu CUSTABAR
634 CASE "01"=gc_prognum
635    @ 2,2 SAY "No Help defined."
636    ln_row=INKEY(0)
637 *-- help for menu CUSTPREP
638 CASE "02"=gc_prognum
639    @ 2,2 SAY "No Help defined."
640    ln_row=INKEY(0)
```

(continued)

```
641 ENDCASE
642 SET ESCAPE ON
643 @ 24,00
644 DEACTIVATE WINDOW Helpscr
645 RETURN
646 *-- EOP: 1HELP1
647
```

Appendix B

KEYSET.PRG

```
1  ******************************************************************
2  * Program KEYSET.PRG
3  * Stores tags and keys in arrays, then allows user to pick one
4  * Tony Lima, April 24, 1989
5  ******************************************************************
6  *-- Select new primary key
7  ACTIVATE WINDOW Savescr
8  IF TYPE("TAGLIST[1]") = "U"
9    DECLARE TAGLIST[47],KEYLIST[47]
10   ln_keyno = 1
11   lc_order = TRIM(ORDER())
12   DO WHILE LEN(TRIM(TAG(ln_keyno))) <> 0
13     TAGLIST[ln_keyno] = TAG(ln_keyno)
14     KEYLIST[ln_keyno] = KEY(ln_keyno)
15     IF TRIM(TAGLIST[ln_keyno]) = TRIM(ORDER())
16       ln_ordno = ln_keyno
17     ENDIF && TRIM(TAGLIST[ln_keyno]) = TRIM(ORDER())
18     ln_keyno = ln_keyno + 1
19   ENDDO  && TAG(ln_keyno) <> ""
20   ln_maxkey = ln_keyno - 1
21 ENDIF && TYPE("TAGLIST[1]") = "U"
22 @ 01,20 SAY "Select an index key to use for this report."
23 ln_keyno = 1
24 ll_break = .T.
25 DO WHILE ln_keyno <= ln_maxkey
26   DO CASE
27   CASE ln_keyno <= 16
28     @ 02,04 SAY "Index Tag"
29     @ 02,16 SAY "Key"
30     IF TRIM(TAGLIST[ln_keyno]) = lc_order
31       @ ln_keyno+2,00 SAY STR(ln_keyno,2)+".*"+TAGLIST[ln_keyno]+;
32         SPACE(10-LEN(TAGLIST[ln_keyno]))+"  "+;
33         SUBSTR(KEYLIST[ln_keyno],1,11)
34      ELSE
35       @ ln_keyno+2,00 SAY STR(ln_keyno,2)+". "+TAGLIST[ln_keyno]+;
36         SPACE(10-LEN(TAGLIST[ln_keyno]))+"  "+;
37         SUBSTR(KEYLIST[ln_keyno],1,11)
38     ENDIF && TAG(ln_keyno) = lc_order
39   CASE ln_keyno <= 32
40     @ 02,30 SAY "Index Tag"
41     @ 02,42 SAY "Key"
42     IF TRIM(TAGLIST[ln_keyno]) = lc_order
43       @ ln_keyno-14,26 SAY STR(ln_keyno,2)+".*"+TAGLIST[ln_keyno]+;
44         SPACE(10-LEN(TAGLIST[ln_keyno]))+"  "+;
45         SUBSTR(KEYLIST[ln_keyno],1,11)
```

(continued)

```
46     ELSE
47       @ ln_keyno-14,26 SAY STR(ln_keyno,2)+". "+TAGLIST[ln_keyno]+;
48         SPACE(10-LEN(TAGLIST[ln_keyno]))+"   "+;
49         SUBSTR(KEYLIST[ln_keyno],1,11)
50     ENDIF && TAG(ln_keyno) = lc_order
51     CASE ln_keyno <= 47
52     @ 02,56 SAY "Index Tag"
53     @ 02,68 SAY "Key"
54     IF TRIM(TAGLIST[ln_keyno]) = lc_order
55       @ ln_keyno-30,52 SAY STR(ln_keyno,2)+".*"+TAGLIST[ln_keyno]+;
56         SPACE(10-LEN(TAGLIST[ln_keyno]))+"   "+;
57         SUBSTR(KEYLIST[ln_keyno],1,11)
58     ELSE
59       @ ln_keyno-30,52 SAY STR(ln_keyno,2)+". "+TAGLIST[ln_keyno]+;
60         SPACE(10-LEN(TAGLIST[ln_keyno]))+"   "+;
61         SUBSTR(KEYLIST[ln_keyno],1,11)
62     ENDIF && ORDER(ln_keyno) = lc_order
63   ENDCASE
64   ln_keyno = ln_keyno + 1
65 ENDDO && WHILE ln_keyno <= ln_maxkey
66 lc_choice = IIF(LEN(STR(ln_ordno))=1,"0"+STR(ln_ordno,1),STR(ln_ordno,2))
67 DO WHILE ln_keyno > ln_maxkey
68   @ 19,23 SAY "Which index? " GET lc_choice PICTURE '#9' ;
69     DEFAULT lc_order ;
70     MESSAGE "Current tag is "+TRIM(TAGLIST[ln_ordno])+;
71     " with key "+TRIM(KEYLIST[ln_ordno])+;
72     ". Be sure to enter leading blank."
73   READ
74   ln_keyno = VAL(lc_choice)
75 ENDDO && WHILE ln_keyno > ln_maxkey
76 SET ORDER TO &TAGLIST[ln_keyno]
77 DEACTIVATE WINDOW Savescr
78 RETURN
79 * EOP:  KEYSET.PRG
80
```

Appendix C

CUSTABAR.PRG

```
 1 ************************************************************************
 2 * Program......: CUSTABAR.PRG
 3 * Author.......: Tony Lima
 4 * Date.........: 4-24-89
 5 * Notice.......: Copyright, 1989, Pacific System Design Workshop, Inc.
 6 * dBASE Ver....: 1.0
 7 * Generated by.: APGEN version 1.0
 8 * Description..: Customer Application Main Menu
 9
10 * Description..: Menu actions
11 ************************************************************************
12 PROCEDURE CUSTABAR
13 PARAMETER entryflg
14 PRIVATE gc_prognum
15 gc_prognum="01"
16
17 DO SET01
18 IF gn_error > 0
19    gn_error=0
20    RETURN
21 ENDIF
22
23 *-- Before menu code
24
25
26 ACTIVATE MENU CUSTABAR
27
28 @ 0,0 CLEAR TO 2,79
29
30 *-- After menu
31
32 RETURN
33 *-- EOP CUSTABAR
34
35 PROCEDURE SET01
36 ON KEY LABEL F1 DO 1HELP1
37
38 DO DBF01 && open menu level database
39
40 IF gn_error = 0
41    IF ISCOLOR()
42       SET COLOR OF NORMAL TO W+/B
43       SET COLOR OF MESSAGES TO R/B
44       SET COLOR OF TITLES TO GR+/B
45       SET COLOR OF HIGHLIGHT TO B+/W
46       SET COLOR OF BOX TO R/W
```

```
47      SET COLOR OF INFORMATION TO RB/W
48       SET COLOR OF FIELDS TO N/W
49    ENDIF
50
51    SET BORDER TO
52    @ 0,0 TO 2,79 DOUBLE COLOR R/W
53    @ 1,1 CLEAR TO 1,78
54    @ 1,1 FILL TO 1,78 COLOR R/B
55    @ 1,2 SAY "Add" COLOR R/B
56    @ 1,10 SAY "Browse" COLOR R/B
57    @ 1,20 SAY "Move pointer" COLOR R/B
58    @ 1,36 SAY "Set new key" COLOR R/B
59    @ 1,51 SAY "Reports" COLOR R/B
60    @ 1,61 SAY "Backup" COLOR R/B
61    @ 1,71 SAY "Exit" COLOR R/B
62    @ 22,00
63 ENDIF
64 RETURN
65
66 PROCEDURE DBF01
67 CLOSE DATABASES
68 *-- Open menu level view/database
69 lc_message="0"
70 ON ERROR lc_message=LTRIM(STR(ERROR()))+" "+MESSAGE()
71 USE CUSTOMER
72 SET ORDER TO CUSTCODE
73 ON ERROR
74 gn_error=VAL(lc_message)
75 IF gn_error > 0
76    DO Pause WITH ;
77    "Error opening CUSTOMER.DBF"
78    lc_new='Y'
79    RETURN
80 ENDIF
81 lc_new='Y'
82 RELEASE lc_message
83 RETURN
84
85 PROCEDURE ACT01
86 *-- Begin CUSTABAR: BAR Menu Actions.
87 *-- (before item, action, and after item)
88 *
89 PRIVATE lc_new, lc_dbf
90 lc_new=' '
91 lc_dbf=' '
92 DO CASE
93 CASE "PAD_1" = PAD()
94    ACTIVATE WINDOW Browscr
95    SET SCOREBOARD ON
96    SET MESSAGE TO "Add records to the Customer file."
97    *-- Desc: attach format file CUST2PG2
98    SET FORMAT TO CUST2PG2
```

(continued)

```
 99    APPEND
100
101    *-- close format file so as not to affect READ's
102    SET FORMAT TO
103    SET SCOREBOARD OFF
104    DEACTIVATE WINDOW Browscr
105 CASE "PAD_2" = PAD()
106    ACTIVATE WINDOW Browscr
107    SET SCOREBOARD ON
108    SET MESSAGE TO "Browse Customer Records"
109    *-- Desc: Browse file -
110    BROWSE NOFOLLOW NOAPPEND NODELETE NOEDIT
111    SET SCOREBOARD OFF
112    DEACTIVATE WINDOW Browscr
113 CASE "PAD_3" = PAD()
114    ON KEY LABEL F1 DO Postnhlp
115    ACTIVATE WINDOW Savescr
116    Do Position
117    DEACTIVATE WINDOW Savescr
118    ON KEY LABEL F1 DO 1HELP1
119    ACTIVATE WINDOW Browscr
120    SET SCOREBOARD ON
121    SET MESSAGE TO "Locate and display a record.  (You may want to Select
          new key first.)"
122    *-- Desc: attach format file CUST2PG2
123    SET FORMAT TO CUST2PG2
124    EDIT NOFOLLOW NOAPPEND NODELETE
125    *-- close format file so as not to affect READ's
126    SET FORMAT TO
127    SET SCOREBOARD OFF
128    DEACTIVATE WINDOW Browscr
129 CASE "PAD_4" = PAD()
130    ACTIVATE WINDOW Savescr
131    SET SCOREBOARD ON
132    SET MESSAGE TO "Select a new index key.  A menu of available indexes
          will be displayed."
133    DO KEYSET.PRG
134
135    SET SCOREBOARD OFF
136    DEACTIVATE WINDOW Savescr
137 CASE "PAD_5" = PAD()
138    lc_new='Y'
139    DO CUSTPREP WITH " 01"
140 CASE "PAD_6" = PAD()
141    *-- Multi user file lock
142    DO Lockit WITH "1"
143    IF gn_error <> 0
144       gn_error=0
145       RETURN
146    ENDIF
147    ACTIVATE WINDOW Savescr
148    SET MESSAGE TO "Copy Customer database to BACKUP.DBF."
```

(continued)

```
149    lc_say='Copying records to BACKUP'
150    DO info_box WITH lc_say
151    SET TALK ON
152    *--  Desc: Copy records to BACKUP
153    COPY TO BACKUP NEXT 100
154    SET TALK OFF
155
156    DEACTIVATE WINDOW Savescr
157    IF NETWORK()
158       UNLOCK
159    ENDIF
160 CASE "PAD_7" = PAD()
161    *-- Return to caller
162    gc_quit='Q'
163    DEACTIVATE MENU && CUSTABAR
164    RETURN
165 OTHERWISE
166    @ 24,00
167    @ 24,21 SAY "This item has no action. Press a key."
168    x=INKEY(0)
169    @ 24,00
170 ENDCASE
171 SET MESSAGE TO
172 IF SET("STATUS")="ON"
173    SET STATUS OFF
174 ENDIF
175 IF gc_quit='Q'
176    DEACTIVATE MENU && CUSTABAR
177 ENDIF
178 IF lc_new='Y'
179    lc_file="SET"+gc_prognum
180    DO &lc_file.
181 ENDIF
182 RETURN
183 ***********************************************************************
184 * Program......: CUSTPREP.PRG
185 * Author.......: Tony Lima
186 * Date.........: 4-24-89
187 * Notice.......: Copyright, 1989, Pacific System Design Workshop, Inc.
188 * dBASE Ver....: 1.0
189 * Generated by.: APGEN version 1.0
190 * Description..: Customer Reports Menu
191
192 * Description..: Menu actions
193 ***********************************************************************
194 PROCEDURE CUSTPREP
195 PARAMETER entryflg
196 PRIVATE gc_prognum
197 gc_prognum="02"
198
199 DO SET02
200 IF gn_error > 0
```

(continued)

```
201    gn_error=0
202    RETURN
203 ENDIF
204
205 *-- Before menu code
206
207
208 ACTIVATE POPUP CUSTPREP
209
210 *-- After menu
211
212 RETURN
213 *-- EOP CUSTPREP
214
215 PROCEDURE SET02
216 ON KEY LABEL F1 DO 1HELP1
217
218 DO DBF02 && open menu level database
219
220 IF gn_error = 0
221    IF ISCOLOR()
222       SET COLOR OF NORMAL TO W+/B
223       SET COLOR OF MESSAGES TO R/B
224       SET COLOR OF TITLES TO GR+/B
225       SET COLOR OF HIGHLIGHT TO B+/W
226       SET COLOR OF BOX TO R/W
227       SET COLOR OF INFORMATION TO RB/W
228       SET COLOR OF FIELDS TO N/W
229    ENDIF
230    @ 22,00
231 ENDIF
232 RETURN
233
234 PROCEDURE DBF02
235 CLOSE DATABASES
236 *-- Open menu level view/database
237 lc_message="0"
238 ON ERROR lc_message=LTRIM(STR(ERROR()))+" "+MESSAGE()
239 USE CUSTOMER
240 SET ORDER TO CUSTCODE
241 ON ERROR
242 gn_error=VAL(lc_message)
243 IF gn_error > 0
244    DO Pause WITH ;
245    "Error opening CUSTOMER.DBF"
246    lc_new='Y'
247    RETURN
248 ENDIF
249 lc_new='Y'
250 RELEASE lc_message
251 RETURN
252
```

(continued)

```
253 PROCEDURE ACT02
254 *-- Begin CUSTPREP: POPUP Menu Actions.
255 *-- (before item, action, and after item)
256 *
257 PRIVATE lc_new, lc_dbf
258 lc_new=' '
259 lc_dbf=' '
260 DO CASE
261 CASE BAR() = 1
262    ACTIVATE WINDOW Savescr
263    SET MESSAGE TO "Report on Customer Balances"
264    *-- Desc: Report
265    SET PRINT ON
266    REPORT FORM CUST4FLD NOEJECT
267    SET PRINT OFF
268    DEACTIVATE WINDOW Savescr
269 CASE BAR() = 2
270    ACTIVATE WINDOW Savescr
271    SET MESSAGE TO "Customer Name, Address, Phone"
272    *-- Desc: Report
273    SET PRINT ON
274    REPORT FORM CUSTOMER
275    SET PRINT OFF
276    DEACTIVATE WINDOW Savescr
277 ENDCASE
278 SET MESSAGE TO
279 IF SET("STATUS")="ON"
280    SET STATUS OFF
281 ENDIF
282 IF gc_quit='Q'
283    DEACTIVATE POPUP && CUSTPREP
284 ENDIF
285 IF lc_new='Y'
286    lc_file="SET"+gc_prognum
287    DO &lc_file.
288 ENDIF
289 RETURN
290
```

Appendix D

Applications Generator Template

```
 1      1:  // $Header: /a/CCS/apgentc/cod/as_menu.cod,v 1.96 88/08/19
               00:00:06 dough Dev $
 2      2:  // Module Name: AS_MENU.COD
 3      3:  // Description: Define Application menus and program structure.
 4      4:  //
 5      5:
 6      6:  Application Template
 7      7:  --------------------
 8      8:  Version 1.96
 9      9:  Ashton-Tate (c) 1987, 1988
10     10:
11     11:  {include "applctn.def";
75     12:   include "builtin.def";
222    14:   var strng,       // temporary string storage
223    15:       strng1,      // menus to call
224    16:       mainmenu,    // name of main menu
225    17:       mnuname,     // current menu name
226    18:       padmenu,     // padmenu name to deactivate
227    19:       pulldown,    // flag indicating pad is a pulldown
228    20:       mnu_messag,  // dBASE message string variable
229    21:       color,       // Used to grab menu colors
230    22:       cnt,         // incremental counter for items in menus
231    23:       count,       // temporary counter
232    24:       prgcnt,      // counter for actions and help
233    25:       muser,       // multi user switch
234    26:       mactions,    // menu actions
235    27:       x,           // temporary numeric variable
236    28:       ask_user,    // string for askuser function
237    29:       appl_name,   // application name
238    30:     default_drive, // dBASE default drive
239    31:       mpath,       // DOS path
240    32:       file,        // DOS file
241    33:       itemdbf,     // flag to indicate whether database changed
                                 during a batch
242    34:       exclflg,     // flag for exclusive use of database needed
243    35:       mtype,       // Menu TYPE - converted to a character
244    36:       display,     // monitor display type
245    37:       scrn_size,   // number of rows of monitor display type
246    38:       midentify,   // Identify string for structure pick list
247    39:       windowvar    // whether to declare lc_window private or not
248    40:   ;
249    41:  // Used in as_help.cod
250    42:   var rowpoint,menucnt;
251    43:  // vars below used to compare Menu & Item view/ndx's to open
252    44:   var global_view, global_ndx, global_ord, gc_view, gc_ndx, gc_ord;
```

(continued)

```
253   45:   var itemview, itemndx, itemord, lc_view, lc_ndx, lc_ord;
254   46:   // vars for global use of author, copyright & db Version
255   47:   var author,copyright,dbVersion;
256   48:   // foreach variables
257   49:   var flds,j,k,m,mtree;
258   50:   }
259   51:   //
260   52:   // Some initial environment testing follows
261   53:   //
262   54:   {display = numset(_flgcolor);
263   55:    if display > ega25 then scrn_size = 40 else scrn_size = 21 endif;
264   56:    default_drive = STRSET(_defdrive);
265   57:    if FILEDRIVE(Menu_Name) || !default_drive then
266   58:      appl_name=Menu_Name;
267   59:    else
268   60:      appl_name=default_drive + ":" + Menu_Name;
269   61:    endif
270   62:   }
271   63:   {if Menu_Type != app then
272   64:      PAUSE("Please position to the application object and restart
                   generation.");
273   65:      GOTO NoGen;
274   66:    endif
275   67:   }
276   68:   { if not FILEEXIST(Menu_Main) then
277   69:      pause("Could not find main menu under appl. definition...Please
                   try again");
278   70:      return 8; // resource file not found
279   71:    endif
280   72:   }
281   73:   { if fileexist(appl_name+".prg") && NUMSET(_safety) then}
282   74:   { retry:}
283   75:   {  ask_user = ASKUSER("Program "+appl_name+".PRG already
                   exists...Overwrite (Y/N)?","N",1);
284   76:      if not at(upper(ask_user),"YN") then GOTO retry endif
285   77:      if upper(ask_user) == "N" then
286   78:        pause("Generation request cancelled -- press any key to
                     continue");
287   79:        GOTO NoGen;
288   80:      endif
289   81:    endif
290   82:   }
291   83:   //
292   84:   // Initialize some variables
293   85:   //
294   86:   {count=1;
295   87:    prgcnt=1;
296   88:    itemdbf=0;
297   89:    muser=0;
298   90:    pulldown=0;
299   91:    mnu_messag="'Position: '+CHR(27)+CHR(26)+CHR(25)+CHR(24)+'
                   Select: '"+
```

(continued)

```
300    92:        "+CHR(17)+CHR(196)+CHR(217)+'  Help: F1'";
301    93:     author=appl_Authr;
302    94:     copyright=appl_cpyrt;
303    95:     dbVersion=Appl_Versn;
304    96:     global_View=Appl_View;   // Set global application dbf/view
305    97:     global_NDX=Appl_NDX;     // Set global application ndx
306    98:     global_Ord=Appl_Order;   // Set global application Order
307    99:     mtype="";
308   100:     padmenu="";
309   101:   }
310   102:   //-----------------------------------
311   103:   // Create application startup program
312   104:   //-----------------------------------
313   105:   {fileerase(appl_name+".DBO");}
314   106:   {CREATE(appl_name+".PRG");}
315   107:   {replicate("*",70)}
316   108:
317   109:   * Program......: {fileroot(appl_name)}.PRG
318   110:   {INCLUDE "AS_HEADR.COD";}
319     1:   // $Header: /a/CCS/apgentc/cod/as_headr.cod,v 1.8 88/03/28
                  10:07:35 kirkn Dev $
320     2:   // Module Name: AS_HEADR.COD
321     3:   // Current incident (atomname):
322     4:   // Atoms used : Appl_Authr, Appl_Cpyrt, Appl_versn
323     5:   // Date        : March 23, 1987
324     6:   // Description: Used as a include to produce Program Header
                  Information
325     7:   // Notes       : AS_HEADR IS AN INCLUDE FILE  DO NOT RUN ALONE!!!
326     8:   // Syntax      :
327     9:   //
328    10:   // Module Change Log
329    11:   //  Date          Initials          Short Change Description
330    12:   //  03/23/87      KJN               Created Module
331    13:   //  04/07/87      KJN               Changed to new atoms
332    14:   //
333    15:   //
334    16:   {strng=STR(VERSION());}
335    17:   * Author.......: {if author then}{author}{endif}
336    18:   * Date.........: {ltrim(SUBSTR(DATE(),1,8))}
337    19:   * Notice.......: {if Copyright then}{Copyright}{endif}
338    20:   * dBASE Ver....: {if dBVersion then}{dBVersion}{endif}
339    21:   * Generated by.: APGEN version {strng}
340    22:   * Description..: {if Menu_Desc then}{Menu_Desc}{endif}
341    23:   // EOP AS_HEADR.COD
342   111:   * Description..: Main routine for menu system
343   112:   {replicate("*",70)}
344   113:
345   114:
346   115:   *-- Setup environment
347   116:   SET CONSOLE OFF
348   117:   IF TYPE("gn_ApGen")="U"
349   118:      CLEAR ALL
```

(continued)

```
350   119:     CLEAR WINDOWS
351   120:     CLOSE ALL
352   121:     CLOSE PROCEDURE
353   122:     gn_ApGen=1
354   123:  ELSE
355   124:     gn_ApGen=gn_ApGen+1
356   125:     IF gn_ApGen > 4
357   126:        Do Pause WITH "Maximum level of Application nesting
                       exceeded."
358   127:        RETURN
359   128:     ENDIF
360   129:     PRIVATE gc_bell, gc_carry, gc_clock, gc_century, gc_confirm,
                   gc_deli,;
361   130:               gc_instruc, gc_safety, gc_status, gc_score, gc_talk,
                           gc_key
362   131:  ENDIF
363   132:  *-- Store some sets to variables
364   133:  gc_bell   =SET("BELL")
365   134:  gc_carry  =SET("CARRY")
366   135:  gc_clock  =SET("CLOCK")
367   136:  gc_century=SET("CENTURY")
368   137:  gc_confirm=SET("CONFIRM")
369   138:  gc_deli   =SET("DELIMITERS")
370   139:  gc_instruc=SET("INSTRUCT")
371   140:  gc_safety =SET("SAFETY")
372   141:  gc_status =SET("STATUS")
373   142:  gc_score  =SET("SCOREBOARD")
374   143:  gc_talk   =SET("TALK")
375   144:  SET CONSOLE ON
376   145:
377   146:  {if !Set_Bell then}
378   147:  {  if Set_BellFR and Set_BellDr then}
379   148:  SET BELL TO {Set_BellFR},{Set_BellDr}
380   149:  {  endif}
381   150:  {endif}
382   151:  SET BELL {if Set_Bell}OFF{else}ON{endif}
383   152:  SET CARRY {if Set_Carry}ON{else}OFF{endif}
384   153:  SET CENTURY {if Set_Centry}ON{else}OFF{endif}
385   154:  SET CLOCK OFF
386   155:  SET CONFIRM {if Set_Confrm}ON{else}OFF{endif}
387   156:  {if Run_Drive then}
388   157:  SET DEFAULT TO {UPPER(Run_Drive)}
389   158:  {endif}
390   159:  SET DELIMITERS TO \
391   160:  {if not AT(CHR(34),Set_DelChr) then}"{Set_DelChr}"
392   161:  {  goto deliok;
393   162:   endif
394   163:   if not AT("'",Set_DelChr) then}'{Set_DelChr}'
395   164:  {  goto deliok;
396   165:   endif
397   166:   if !AT("[",Set_DelChr) or !AT("]",Set_DelChr) then}[{Set_DelChr}]
398   167:  {  goto deliok;
```

(continued)

```
399   168:   endif
400   169:   }
401   170:   ""
402   171:   {deliok:}
403   172:   SET DELIMITERS {if Set_Delim}ON{else}OFF{endif}
404   173:   SET DEVICE TO SCREEN
405   174:   SET ESCAPE {if Set_Escape}OFF{else}ON{endif}
406   175:   SET EXCLUSIVE OFF
407   176:   SET ECHO OFF
408   177:   SET LOCK ON
409   178:   SET MESSAGE TO ""
410   179:   {if Run_Path then}
411   180:   SET PATH TO {Run_Path}
412   181:   {endif}
413   182:   SET PRINT OFF
414   183:   SET REPROCESS TO 4
415   184:   SET SAFETY {if Set_Safety}OFF{else}ON{endif}
416   185:   SET TALK OFF
417   186:
418   187:   *-- Initialize global variables
419   188:   gn_error=0         && 0 if no error, otherwise an error occurred
420   189:   gn_ikey=0          && keypress returned from the INKEY() function
421   190:   gn_send=0          && return value from popup of position menus
422   191:   gn_trace=1         && sets trace level, however you need to
                                  change template
423   192:   gc_brdr='1'        && border to use when drawing boxes
424   193:   gc_dev='CON'       && Device to use for printing - See Proc.
                                  PrintSet
425   194:   gc_key='N'         && leave the application
426   195:   gc_prognum=' '     && internal program counter to handle nested
                                  menus
427   196:   gc_quit=' '        && memvar for return to caller
428   197:   listval='NO_FIELD' && Pick List value
429   198:
430   199:   *-- remove asterisk to turn clock on
431   200:   * SET CLOCK TO
432   201:   SET INSTRUCT OFF
433   202:
434   203:   *-- Blank the screen
435   204:   SET COLOR TO
436   205:   {if display > ega25 then}
437   206:   SET DISPLAY TO \
438   207:   {  if display == mono43 then}
439   208:   MONO43
440   209:   {  endif}
441   210:   {  if display == ega43 then}
442   211:   EGA43
443   212:   {  endif}
444   213:   {endif}
445   214:   CLEAR
446   215:   SET SCOREBOARD OFF
447   216:   SET STATUS OFF
```

(continued)

```
448  217:
449  218:  *-- Define menus
450  219:  DO MPDEF            && execute Menu Process DEFinition
451  220:
452  221:  *-- Execute main menu
453  222:  DO WHILE gc_key = 'N'
454  223:      DO {Appl_Menu} WITH "{if !Appl_Type then}B{else} {endif}00"
455  224:      IF gc_quit = 'Q'
456  225:         EXIT
457  226:      ENDIF
458  227:      ACTIVATE WINDOW Exit_App
459  228:      lc_conf=SET("CONFIRM")
460  229:      lc_deli=SET("DELIMITER")
461  230:      SET CONFIRM OFF
462  231:      SET DELIMITER OFF
463  232:      @ 1,2 SAY "Do you want to leave this application?" ;
464  233:          GET gc_key PICT "!" VALID gc_key $ "NY"
465  234:      READ
466  235:      SET CONFIRM &lc_conf.
467  236:      SET DELIMITER &lc_deli.
468  237:      RELEASE lc_conf, lc_deli
469  238:      DEACTIVATE WINDOW Exit_App
470  239:  ENDDO
471  240:
472  241:  *-- Reset environment
473  242:  gn_ApGen=gn_ApGen-1
474  243:  SET BELL   &gc_bell.
475  244:  SET CARRY &gc_carry.
476  245:  SET CLOCK &gc_clock.
477  246:  SET CENTURY &gc_century.
478  247:  SET CONFIRM &gc_confirm.
479  248:  SET DELIMITERS &gc_deli.
480  249:  SET INSTRUCT &gc_instruc.
481  250:  SET STATUS &gc_status.
482  251:  SET SAFETY &gc_safety.
483  252:  SET SCORE  &gc_score.
484  253:  SET TALK   &gc_talk.
485  254:
486  255:  IF gn_Apgen < 1
487  256:     ON KEY LABEL F1
488  257:     CLEAR ALL
489  258:     CLEAR WINDOWS
490  259:     CLOSE ALL
491  260:     CLOSE PROCEDURE
492  261:     SET CLOCK OFF
493  262:     SET ESCAPE ON
494  263:     SET MESSAGE TO ""
495  264:     CLEAR
496  265:  ENDIF
497  266:  RETURN
498  267:
499  268:  //-------------------------------
```

(continued)

```
500   269:  // Add Application Procedure file
501   270:  // contains common programs
502   271:  //-------------------------------
503   272:  //
504   273:  {include "as_proc.cod";}
505     1:  // $Header: /a/CCS/apgentc/cod/as_proc.cod,v 1.27 88/07/13
                17:00:42 dough Dev $
506     2:  // Module name: as_proc.cod
507     3:  // Date        : August 10, 1987 2:28 PM
508     4:  // Description: Procedure file for the generated application
509     5:  //
510     6:  //
511     7:  // Module Change Log
512     8:  //   Date     Initials    Short Change description
513     9:  //
514    10:  // 08/10/87    KJN           Created module
515    11:  // 10/02/87    DCH           Removed askuser and CREATE functions
516    12:  //
517    13:  {  replicate("*",79)}
518    14:
519    15:  * Description..: Procedure files for generated menu system.
520    16:  * The programs that follow are common to main routines
521    17:  * The last procedure is the Menu Process DEFinition
522    18:  {  replicate("*",79)}
523    19:
524    20:  PROCEDURE Lockit
525    21:  PARAMETER ltype
526    22:  IF NETWORK()
527    23:     gn_error=0
528    24:     ON ERROR DO Multerr
529    25:     IF ltype = "1"
530    26:       ll_lock=FLOCK()
531    27:     ENDIF
532    28:     IF ltype = "2"
533    29:       ll_lock=RLOCK()
534    30:     ENDIF
535    31:     ON ERROR
536    32:  ENDIF
537    33:  RETURN
538    34:
539    35:  PROCEDURE Info_Box
540    36:  PARAMETERS lc_say
541    37:  ? lc_say
542    38:  ? REPLICATE("-",LEN(lc_say))
543    39:  ?
544    40:  RETURN
545    41:  * EOP: Info_Box
546    42:
547    43:  PROCEDURE get_sele
548    44:  *-- Get the user selection & store BAR into variable
549    45:  gn_send = BAR()   && Variable for print testing
550    46:  DEACTIVATE POPUP
```

(continued)

```
551    47:  RETURN
552    48:
553    49:  PROCEDURE ShowPick
554    50:  listval=PROMPT()
555    51:  IF LEFT(entryflg,1)="B"
556    52:     lc_file=POPUP()
557    53:     DO &lc_file. WITH "A"
558    54:     RETURN
559    55:  ENDIF
560    56:  IF TYPE("lc_window")="U"
561    57:     ACTIVATE WINDOW ShowPick
562    58:  ELSE
563    59:     ACTIVATE WINDOW &lc_window.
564    60:  ENDIF
565    61:  STORE 0 TO ln_ikey,x1,x2
566    62:  ln_ikey=LASTKEY()
567    63:  IF ln_ikey=13
568    64:     x1=AT(TRIM(listval)+',',lc_fldlst)
569    65:     IF x1 = 0
570    66:        lc_fldlst=lc_fldlst+TRIM(listval)+','
571    67:     ELSE
572    68:        x2=AT(',',SUBSTR(lc_fldlst,x1))
573    69:        lc_fldlst=STUFF(lc_fldlst,x1,x2,'')
574    70:     ENDIF
575    71:     CLEAR
576    72:     ? lc_fldlst
577    73:  ENDIF
578    74:  ACTIVATE SCREEN
579    75:  RETURN
580    76:  * EOP: ShowPick
581    77:
582    78:  {  include "as_clnup.cod";}
583     1:  // $Header: /a/CCS/apgentc/cod/as_clnup.cod,v 1.4 88/06/10
                21:31:02 dough Dev $
584     2:  PROCEDURE Cleanup
585     3:  *-- test whether report option was selected
586     4:  DO CASE
587     5:  CASE gc_dev='CON'
588     6:     WAIT
589     7:  CASE gc_dev='PRN'
590     8:     SET PRINT OFF
591     9:     SET PRINTER TO
592    10:  CASE gc_dev='TXT'
593    11:     CLOSE ALTERNATE
594    12:  ENDCASE
595    13:  RETURN
596    79:  * EOP: Cleanup
597    80:
598    81:  {  include "as_pause.cod";}
599     1:  // $Header: /a/CCS/apgentc/cod/as_pause.cod,v 1.14 88/06/22
                22:03:27 dough Dev $
600     2:  // Module Name: AS_PAUSE.COD
```

(continued)

```
601    3:   // Current incident (atomname):
602    4:   // Atoms used :
603    5:   // Date        : November 24, 1986
604    6:   // Description: Display message on line 19
605    7:   // Notes     :
606    8:   // Syntax    :
607    9:   //
608   10:   // Module Change Log
609   11:   //   Date       Initials     Short Change Description
610   12:   //   12/01/86    KJN           Created Module
611   13:   //   01/27/87    DCH           Moved message to line 18 thru 20
612   14:   //                             instead of 22 thru 24
613   15:   //   04/06/87    DCH           variable lc_option for AS_POSIT.COD
614   16:   //   07/06/87    DCH           changed to run in Nova
615   17:   //   09/30/87    KJN           Changed - MOVE REGION to WINDOWS
616   18:   //   06/10/88    KJN           Move window to main procedure
                                           because define
617   19:   //                             window can't be in a ON ERROR routine
618   20:   //
619   21:   PROCEDURE Pause
620   22:   PARAMETER lc_msg
621   23:   *-- Parameters : lc_msg = message line
622   24:   IF TYPE("lc_message")="U"
623   25:      gn_error=ERROR()
624   26:   ENDIF
625   27:   lc_msg = lc_msg
626   28:   lc_option='0'
627   29:   ACTIVATE WINDOW Pause
628   30:   IF gn_error > 0
629   31:      IF TYPE("lc_message")="U"
630   32:         @ 0,1 SAY "An error has occurred !! - Error message: "+
                       MESSAGE()
631   33:      ELSE
632   34:         @ 0,1 SAY "Error # "+lc_message
633   35:      ENDIF
634   36:   ENDIF
635   37:   @ 1,1 SAY lc_msg
636   38:   WAIT " Press any key to continue..."
637   39:   DEACTIVATE WINDOW Pause
638   40:   RETURN
639   41:   // EOP AS_PAUSE.COD
640   82:   * EOP: Pause
641   83:
642   84:   {  include "as_muser.cod";}
643    1:   // $Header: /a/CCS/apgentc/cod/as_muser.cod,v 1.5 88/06/27
                21:09:16 dough Dev $
644    2:   // Module name: as_muser.cod
645    3:   // Date        : August 21, 1987
646    4:   // Description: Multi-User error handler
647    5:   //
648    6:   //
649    7:   // Module Change Log
```

(continued)

```
650     8:  //    Date      Initials    Short Change description
651     9:  //
652    10:  // 08/21/87    DCH             Created module
653    11:  //
654    12:  // ERROR() MESSAGE()                                   File, record error,
                                                                       critical
655    13:  // ================================================================
656    14:  //      148 Network server busy            critical
657    15:  //      217 Lock table full                critical
658    16:  //      131 Database is encrypted          file
659    17:  //      110 Exclusive open of file is required file
660    18:  //      108 File is in use by another      file
661    19:  //      129 Unable to lock                 file/record
662    20:  //      133 Unauthorized access level      file/record
663    21:  //      124 Invalid printer redirection    N/A
664    22:  //      132 Unauthorized login             N/A
665    23:  //      111 Cannot write to a read-only file  record
666    24:  //      109 Record is in use by another    record
667    25:  //      130 Record is not locked           record
668    26:  //      128 Unable to skip                 record
669    27:  //
670    28:  // Errors will be handled in one of two ways:
671    29:  //
672    30:  // 1) Display message and return to menu
673    31:  // 2) Dialog box for options Try again and Return to menu
674    32:  //
675    33:  PROCEDURE Multerr
676    34:  *-- set the global error variable
677    35:  gn_error=ERROR()
678    36:  *-- contains error number to test
679    37:  lc_erno=STR(ERROR(),3)+','
680    38:  *-- option var.
681    39:  lc_opt='T'
682    40:  *-- Dialog box for options Try again and Return to menu.
683    41:  IF lc_erno $ "108,109,128,129,"
684    42:     ACTIVATE WINDOW Pause
685    43:     @ 0,2 SAY lc_erno+" "+MESSAGE()
686    44:     @ 2,22 SAY "T = Try again, R = Return to menu." GET lc_opt ;
687    45:  PICTURE "!" VALID lc_opt $ "TR"
688    46:     READ
689    47:     DEACTIVATE WINDOW Pause
690    48:     IF lc_opt = "R"
691    49:        RETURN
692    50:     ENDIF
693    51:  ENDIF
694    52:  *-- Display message and return to menu.
695    53:  IF .NOT. lc_erno $ "108,109,128,129,"
696    54:     DO PAUSE WITH ERROR()
697    55:     RETURN
698    56:  ENDIF
699    57:  *-- reset global variable
700    58:  gn_error=0
```

(continued)

```
701   59:  *-- Try the command again
702   60:  RETRY
703   61:  RETURN
704   85:  * EOP: Multerr
705   86:
706   87:  {  include "as_trce.cod";}
707    1:  // $Header: /a/CCS/apgentc/cod/as_trce.cod,v 1.7 87/12/28 14:22:52
                 dough Dev $
708    2:  // Module Name: AS_TRCE.COD - currently (atomname):
709    3:  // Atoms used : None - data independent
710    4:  // Date        : December 1, 1986
711    5:  // Description: Used for stubs and status level
712    6:  // Notes      :
713    7:  //
714    8:  //
715    9:  // Module Change Log
716   10:  //   Date         Initials           Short Change Description
717   11:  //   12/01/86      DCH                Created Module
718   12:  //   12/16/86      KJN                Put set print on into trace
719   13:  //   12/16/86      KJN                Added message about turning
                                                 trace off also
720   14:  //                                   [F3] turns trace back on
721   15:  //   01/05/86      DCH                Removed additional screen save
                                                 because,
722   16:  //                                   each screen save takes up 3850
                                                 bytes.
723   17:  //   07/06/87      DCH                changed for Nova - MOVE REGION
724   18:  //   09/30/87      KJN                changed for Nova - MOVE REGION
                                                 to WINDOWS
725   19:  //
726   20:  PROCEDURE Trace
727   21:  *  Desc: Trace procedure - to let programmer know what module
728   22:  *           is about to execute and what module has executed.
729   23:  PARAMETERS p_msg, p_lvl
730   24:  *-- Parameters : p_msg = message line, p_lvl = trace level
731   25:  lc_msg = p_msg
732   26:  ln_lvl = p_lvl
733   27:  lc_trp = ' '
734   28:  IF gn_trace < ln_lvl
735   29:     RETURN
736   30:  ENDIF
737   31:  DEFINE WINDOW trace FROM 11,00 TO 16,79 DOUBLE
738   32:  DO WHILE lc_trp <> 'Q'
739   33:     @ 2,40-LEN(lc_msg)/2 SAY lc_msg
740   34:     @ 4,05 SAY 'S - Set trace level, D - Display status,
                   M - display Memory'
741   35:     @ 5,05 SAY 'P - Turn printer on, Q - to Quit'
742   36:     lc_trp = 'Q'
743   37:     @ 5,38 GET lc_trp PICTURE "!"
744   38:     READ
745   39:     DO CASE
746   40:        CASE lc_trp = 'S'
```

(continued)

```
747   41:        @ 2,01 CLEAR
748   42:        @ 2,33 SAY 'Set trace level'
749   43:        @ 4,05 SAY 'Enter trace level to change to:' GET gn_trace
                    PICTURE '#'
750   44:        @ 5,05 SAY '           "0" turns trace off'
751   45:        READ
752   46:        IF gn_trace=0
753   47:           @ 2,01 CLEAR
754   48:           @ 3,05 SAY 'Trace is now turned off..To reactivate Trace
                      - Press [F3]'
755   49:           @ 4,05 say 'Press any key to continue...'
756   50:           WAIT ''
757   51:        ENDIF
758   52:      CASE lc_trp = 'D'
759   53:        DISPLAY STATUS
760   54:        WAIT
761   55:      CASE lc_trp = 'M'
762   56:        DISPLAY MEMORY
763   57:        WAIT
764   58:      CASE lc_trp = 'P'
765   59:        SET PRINT ON
766   60:      ENDCASE
767   61:    ENDDO
768   62:    SET PRINT OFF
769   63:    @ 24,79 SAY " "
770   64:    RELEASE WINDOW trace
771   65:    RETURN
772   66:    // EOP AS_TRCE.COD
773   88:    * EOP: Trace
774   89:
775   90:    {  include "as_prin.cod";}
776    1:    // $Header: /a/CCS/apgentc/cod/as_prin.cod,v 1.11 88/06/16
                 15:33:34 dough Dev $
777    2:    // Module Name: AS_PRIN.COD
778    3:    // Current incident (atomname):
779    4:    // Atoms used :
780    5:    // Date       : March 20, 1987
781    6:    // Description: Procedure for toggling printer output
782    7:    // Notes      : Written for dBASE III PLUS
783    8:    // Syntax     :
784    9:    //
785   10:    // Module Change Log
786   11:    //   Date       Initials        Short Change Description
787   12:    //   03/20/87    DCH             Created Module
788   13:    //   07/06/87    DCH             Changed for Nova - MOVE REGION
789   14:    //   05/05/88    KJN             Changed to a popup menu
790   15:    //   06/15/88    KJN             Moved window from ON ERROR to
                                             Printset
791   16:    //
792   17:    PROCEDURE PrintSet
793   18:    *-- Initialize variables
794   19:    gc_dev='CON'
```

(continued)

```
795    20:   lc_choice=' '
796    21:   gn_pkey=0
797    22:   gn_send=0
798    23:
799    24:   DEFINE WINDOW printemp FROM 08,25 TO 17,56
800    25:
801    26:   DEFINE POPUP SavePrin FROM 10,40
802    27:   DEFINE BAR 1 OF SavePrin PROMPT " Send output to ..." SKIP
803    28:   DEFINE BAR 2 OF SavePrin PROMPT REPLICATE(CHR(196),24) SKIP
804    29:   DEFINE BAR 3 OF SavePrin PROMPT " CON:   Console"
                 MESSAGE "Send output to Screen"
805    30:   DEFINE BAR 4 OF SavePrin PROMPT " LPT1:  Parallel port 1 "
                 MESSAGE "Send output to LPT1:"
806    31:   DEFINE BAR 5 OF SavePrin PROMPT " LPT2:  Parallel port 2"
                 MESSAGE "Send output to LPT2:"
807    32:   DEFINE BAR 6 OF SavePrin PROMPT " COM1:  Serial port 1"
                 MESSAGE "Send output to COM1:"
808    33:   DEFINE BAR 7 OF SavePrin PROMPT " FILE = REPORT.TXT"
                 MESSAGE "Send output to File Report.txt"
809    34:   ON SELECTION POPUP SavePrin DO get_sele
810    35:
811    36:   ACTIVATE POPUP SavePrin
812    37:   RELEASE POPUP SavePrin
813    38:
814    39:   IF gn_send = 7
815    40:      gc_dev = 'TXT'
816    41:      SET ALTERNATE TO REPORT.TXT
817    42:      SET ALTERNATE ON
818    43:   ELSE
819    44:      IF .NOT. (gn_send = 3 .OR. LASTKEY() = 27)
820    45:         gc_dev = 'PRN'
821    46:         temp = SUBSTR("    LPT1LPT2COM1 ",((gn_send-2)-1)*4,4)
822    47:         ON ERROR DO prntrtry
823    48:         SET PRINTER TO &temp.
824    49:         IF gn_pkey <> 27
825    50:            SET PRINT ON
826    51:         ENDIF
827    52:         ON ERROR
828    53:      ENDIF
829    54:   ENDIF
830    55:   RELEASE WINDOW printemp
831    56:   RETURN
832    57:
833    58:   PROC prntrtry
834    59:   IF .NOT. PRINTSTATUS()
835    60:      ACTIVATE WINDOW printemp
836    61:      @ 1,0 SAY " Please ready your printer or"
837    62:      @ 3,0 SAY "     press ESC to cancel"
838    63:      @ 6,0 SAY "     Printing to "+temp
839    64:      DO WHILE (.NOT. PRINTSTATUS()) .AND. gn_pkey <> 27
840    65:         gn_pkey = INKEY()
841    66:      ENDDO
```

(continued)

```
842   67:       IF gn_pkey <> 27
843   68:          RETRY
844   69:       ENDIF
845   70:    ENDIF
846   71:    RETURN
847   72:    // EOP AD_PRIN.COD
848   91:    * EOP: PrintSet
849   92:
850   93:    {  include "as_posit.cod";}
851    1:    // $Header: /a/CCS/apgentc/cod/as_posit.cod,v 1.19 88/06/21
                  12:07:20 dough Dev $
852    2:    // Module Name: AS_POSIT.COD
853    3:    // Current incident (atomname):
854    4:    // Atoms used :
855    5:    // Date       : April 7, 1987
856    6:    // Description: Record positioning (Ask at runtime)
857    7:    // Notes      :
858    8:    // Syntax     :
859    9:    //
860   10:    // Module Change Log
861   11:    //    Date        Initials     Short Change Description
862   12:    //  04/07/87      DCH          Created Module
863   13:    //  09/30/87      KJN          Changed  MOVE REGION to WINDOWS
864   14:    //
865   15:    //
866   16:    {var ln_frow, ln_fcol;}
867   17:    PROCEDURE Position
868   18:    IF LEN(DBF()) = 0
869   19:       DO Pause WITH "Database not in use. "
870   20:       RETURN
871   21:    ENDIF
872   22:    SET SPACE ON
873   23:    SET DELIMITERS OFF
874   24:    // Frame row position
875   25:    {ln_frow=8;}
876   26:    // Frame col position
877   27:    {ln_fcol=30;//28}
878   28:    ln_type=0           && sublevel selection
879   29:    ln_rkey=READKEY()   && test for ESC or Return
880   30:    ln_rec=RECNO()      && DBF record number
881   31:    ln_num=0            && for input of a number
882   32:    ld_date=DATE()      && for input of a date
883   33:    lc_option='0'       && main option ie. Seek, Goto and Locate
884   34:    *-- Scope ie. ALL, REST, NEXT <n>
885   35:    STORE SPACE(10) TO lc_scp
886   36:    *-- 1 = Character SEEK, 2 = For clause, 3 = While clause
887   37:    STORE SPACE(40) TO lc_ln1, lc_ln2, lc_ln3
888   38:    lc_temp=""
889   39:    @ 0,00 SAY "Index order: "+IIF(""=ORDER(),"Database is in natural
                  order",ORDER())
890   40:    @ 1,00 SAY "Listed below are the first 16 fields."
891   41:    lc_temp=REPLICATE(CHR(196),19)
```

(continued)

```
892   42:   @ 2,0 SAY CHR(218)+lc_temp+CHR(194)+lc_temp+CHR(194)+
                lc_temp+CHR(194)+lc_temp
893   43:   ln_num=240
894   44:   DO WHILE ln_num < 560
895   45:      lc_temp=FIELD( (ln_num-240)/20 +1)
896   46:      @ (ln_num/80),MOD(ln_num,80) SAY CHR(179)+;
897   47:   lc_temp+SPACE(11-LEN(lc_temp))+;
898   48:   SUBSTR("= Char  = Date  = Logic = Num   = Float = Memo      ",;
899   49:   AT(TYPE(lc_temp),"CDLNFMU")*8-7,8)
900   50:      ln_num=ln_num+20
901   51:   ENDDO
902   52:   ln_num=1
903   53:
904   54:   DEFINE POPUP Posit1 FROM {ln_frow},{ln_fcol}
905   55:   DEFINE BAR 1 OF Posit1 PROMPT " Position by " SKIP
906   56:   DEFINE BAR 2 OF Posit1 PROMPT REPLICATE(CHR(196),15) SKIP
907   57:   DEFINE BAR 3 OF Posit1 PROMPT " SEEK Record"
                MESSAGE "Search on index key" SKIP FOR ""=ORDER()
908   58:   DEFINE BAR 4 OF Posit1 PROMPT " GOTO Record"
                MESSAGE "Position to specific record"
909   59:   DEFINE BAR 5 OF Posit1 PROMPT " LOCATE Record "
                MESSAGE "Locate record for condition"
910   60:   DEFINE BAR 6 OF Posit1 PROMPT " Return"
                MESSAGE "Return without positioning"
911   61:   ON SELECTION POPUP Posit1 DO get_sele
912   62:
913   63:   SET CONFIRM ON
914   64:   DO WHILE lc_option='0'
915   65:      ACTIVATE POPUP Posit1
916   66:      lc_option = ltrim(str(gn_send))   && for popup
917   67:      IF LASTKEY() = 27 .OR. lc_option="6"
918   68:         GOTO ln_rec
919   69:         EXIT
920   70:      ENDIF
921   71:      DO CASE
922   72:      CASE lc_option='3'
923   73:         *-- Seek
924   74:         IF LEN(NDX(1))=0 .AND. LEN(MDX(1))=0
925   75:            DO Pause WITH "Can't use this option - No index files are
                        open."
926   76:            LOOP
927   77:         ENDIF
928   78:         ln_type=1
929   79:         lc_ln1=SPACE(40)
930   80:         DEFINE WINDOW Posit2 FROM {ln_frow},{ln_fcol-11} TO
                     {ln_frow+7},{ln_fcol+32} DOUBLE
931   81:         ACTIVATE WINDOW Posit2
932   82:         @ 1,1 SAY "Enter the type of expression:" GET ln_type PICT
                     "#" RANGE 1,3
933   83:         @ 2,1 SAY "(1=character, 2=numeric and 3=date.)"
934   84:         READ
935   85:         IF .NOT. (READKEY() = 12 .OR. READKEY() = 268)
```

(continued)

```
936   86:        SET CONFIRM ON
937   87:        @ 3,1 SAY "Enter the key expression to search for:"
938   88:        IF ln_type=3
939   89:           @ 4,1 GET ld_date PICT "@D"
940   90:        ELSE
941   91:           IF ln_type=2
942   92:              @ 4,1 GET ln_num PICT "##########"
943   93:           ELSE
944   94:              @ 4,1 GET lc_ln1
945   95:           ENDIF
946   96:        ENDIF
947   97:        READ
948   98:        SET CONFIRM OFF
949   99:        IF .NOT. (READKEY() = 12 .OR. READKEY() = 268)
950  100:           lc_temp=IIF(ln_type=1,"TRIM(lc_ln1)",
                        IIF(ln_type=2,"ln_num","ld_date"))
951  101:           SEEK &lc_temp.
952  102:        ENDIF
953  103:     ENDIF
954  104:     RELEASE WINDOWS Posit2
955  105:  CASE lc_option='4'
956  106:     *-- Goto
957  107:     ln_type=1
958  108:     DEFINE POPUP Posit2 FROM {ln_frow},{ln_fcol}
959  109:     DEFINE BAR 1 OF Posit2 PROMPT " GOTO:" SKIP
960  110:     DEFINE BAR 2 OF Posit2 PROMPT REPLICATE(CHR(196),10) SKIP
961  111:     DEFINE BAR 3 OF Posit2 PROMPT " TOP"
                 MESSAGE "GOTO Top of File"
962  112:     DEFINE BAR 4 OF Posit2 PROMPT " BOTTOM"
                 MESSAGE "GOTO Bottom of File"
963  113:     DEFINE BAR 5 OF Posit2 PROMPT " Record # "
                 MESSAGE "GOTO A Specific Record"
964  114:     ON SELECTION POPUP Posit2 DO get_sele
965  115:     ACTIVATE POPUP posit2
966  116:     ln_type = gn_send
967  117:     IF LASTKEY() <> 27
968  118:        IF ln_type=5
969  119:           DEFINE WINDOW Posit2 FROM {ln_frow},{ln_fcol-4} TO
                        {ln_frow+5},{ln_fcol+20} DOUBLE
970  120:           ACTIVATE WINDOW Posit2
971  121:           ln_num=0
972  122:           @ 3,1 SAY "Max. Record # = "+LTRIM(STR(RECCOUNT()))
973  123:           @ 1,1 SAY "Record to GOTO" GET ln_num PICT "######"
                        RANGE 1,RECCOUNT()
974  124:           READ
975  125:           IF .NOT. (READKEY() = 12 .OR. READKEY() = 268)
976  126:              GOTO ln_num
977  127:           ENDIF
978  128:           RELEASE WINDOWS Posit2
979  129:        ELSE
980  130:           lc_temp=IIF(ln_type=3,"TOP","BOTTOM")
981  131:           GOTO &lc_temp.
```

(continued)

```
982   132:           ENDIF
983   133:         ENDIF
984   134:     CASE lc_option='5'
985   135:       *-- Locate
986   136:       DEFINE WINDOW Posit2 FROM {ln_frow},{ln_fcol-14} TO
                  {ln_frow+6},{ln_fcol+36} DOUBLE
987   137:       ACTIVATE WINDOW Posit2
988   138:       @ 1,19 SAY "ie. ALL, NEXT <n>, and REST"
989   139:       @ 1,1 SAY "Scope:" GET lc_scp
990   140:       @ 2,1 SAY "For:  " GET lc_ln2
991   141:       @ 3,1 SAY "While:" GET lc_ln3
992   142:       READ
993   143:       IF .NOT. (READKEY() = 12 .OR. READKEY() = 268)
994   144:           lc_temp=TRIM(lc_scp)
995   145:           lc_temp=lc_temp + IIF(LEN(TRIM(lc_ln2)) > 0," FOR "
                      +TRIM(lc_ln2),"")
996   146:           lc_temp=lc_temp + IIF(LEN(TRIM(lc_ln3)) > 0," WHILE "
                      +TRIM(lc_ln3),"")
997   147:           IF LEN(lc_temp) > 0
998   148:               LOCATE &lc_temp.
999   149:           ELSE
1000  150:               DO Pause WITH "All fields were blank."
1001  151:           ENDIF
1002  152:       ENDIF
1003  153:       RELEASE WINDOW Posit2
1004  154:     ENDCASE
1005  155:     IF EOF()
1006  156:       DO Pause WITH "Record not found."
1007  157:       GOTO ln_rec
1008  158:     ENDIF
1009  159:     IF READKEY()=12 .OR. READKEY()= 268 .OR. LASTKEY()=27  && Esc
                was hit
1010  160:       lc_option='0'
1011  161:     ENDIF
1012  162:   ENDDO
1013  163:   SET DELIMITERS &gc_deli.
1014  164:   SET CONFIRM {if Set_Confrm then}ON{else}OFF{endif}
1015  165:   RETURN
1016  166:   // EOP AS_POSIT.COD
1017   94:   * EOP: Position
1018   95:
1019   96:   PROCEDURE Postnhlp
1020   97:   ln_getkey=INKEY()
1021   98:   DO CASE
1022   99:   CASE "SEEK" $ PROMPT()
1023  100:      HELP SEEK
1024  101:   CASE "GOTO" $ PROMPT()
1025  102:      HELP GOTO
1026  103:   CASE "LOCATE" $ PROMPT()
1027  104:      HELP LOCATE
1028  105:   ENDCASE
1029  106:   RETURN
```

(continued)

```
1030   107:   * EOP: Postnhlp
1031   108:   // EOP AS_PROC.COD
1032   274:
1033   275:   {replicate("*",70)}
1034   276:
1035   277:   * Program......: MPDEF
1036   278:   {include "AS_HEADR.COD";}
1037     1:   // $Header: /a/CCS/apgentc/cod/as_headr.cod,v 1.8 88/03/28
                   10:07:35 kirkn Dev $
1038     2:   // Module Name: AS_HEADR.COD
1039     3:   // Current incident (atomname):
1040     4:   // Atoms used : Appl_Authr, Appl_Cpyrt, Appl_versn
1041     5:   // Date       : March 23, 1987
1042     6:   // Description: Used as a include to produce Program Header
                   Information
1043     7:   // Notes      : AS_HEADR IS AN INCLUDE FILE  DO NOT RUN ALONE!!!
1044     8:   // Syntax     :
1045     9:   //
1046    10:   // Module Change Log
1047    11:   //   Date        Initials        Short Change Description
1048    12:   //   03/23/87    KJN             Created Module
1049    13:   //   04/07/87    KJN             Changed to new atoms
1050    14:   //
1051    15:   //
1052    16:   {strng=STR(VERSION());}
1053    17:   * Author.......: {if author then}{author}{endif}
1054    18:   * Date.........: {ltrim(SUBSTR(DATE(),1,8))}
1055    19:   * Notice.......: {if Copyright then}{Copyright}{endif}
1056    20:   * dBASE Ver....: {if dBVersion then}{dBVersion}{endif}
1057    21:   * Generated by.: APGEN version {strng}
1058    22:   * Description..: {if Menu_Desc then}{Menu_Desc}{endif}
1059    23:   // EOP AS_HEADR.COD
1060   279:   * Description..: Defines all menus in the system
1061   280:   {replicate("*",70)}
1062   281:
1063   282:   PROCEDURE MPDEF
1064   283:   IF ISCOLOR()
1065   284:   {LMARG(4);}
1066   285:   SET COLOR OF NORMAL TO {color(Clr_Text)}
1067   286:   SET COLOR OF MESSAGES TO {color(Clr_Messages)}
1068   287:   SET COLOR OF TITLES TO {color(Clr_Heading)}
1069   288:   SET COLOR OF HIGHLIGHT TO {color(Clr_Hghlight)}
1070   289:   SET COLOR OF BOX TO {color(Clr_Box)}
1071   290:   SET COLOR OF INFORMATION TO {color(Clr_Info)}
1072   291:   SET COLOR OF FIELDS TO {color(Clr_Fields)}
1073   292:   {LMARG(1);}
1074   293:   ENDIF
1075   294:   CLEAR
1076   295:
1077   296:   {if Disp_Sign then}
1078   297:   *-- Sign-on banner
1079   298:
```

(continued)

```
1080   299:   //
1081   300:   // Draw border
1082   301:   //
1083   302:   SET BORDER TO
1084   303:   {if Mnu_Border != 3 then}
1085   304:   @ {row1()},{col1()} TO {row2()},{col2()}\
1086   305:   {case Mnu_Border of}
1087   306:   {0: // Panel}
1088   307:    PANEL\
1089   308:   {2: // Double}
1090   309:    DOUBLE\
1091   310:   {endcase}
1092   311:    COLOR {color(Clr_Box)}
1093   312:   {endif}
1094   313:   @ {row1()+1},{col1()+1} CLEAR TO {row2()-1},{col2()-1}
1095   314:   //
1096   315:   // Display text
1097   316:   //
1098   317:   {foreach TEXT_ELEMENT flds}
1099   318:   @ {row1()+Row_Positn},{col1()+Col_Positn} SAY "{Text_Item}"
1100   319:   {next flds;}
1101   320:   //
1102   321:   // Wait for a return key
1103   322:   //
1104   323:   @ {scrn_size+3},30 SAY " Press "+CHR(17)+CHR(196)+CHR(217)+" to
                  continue. "
1105   324:   gn_ikey=INKEY(4)
1106   325:
1107   326:   CLEAR
1108   327:   {endif // if Disp_Sign}
1109   328:
1110   329:   //
1111   330:   // default window if none defined for action
1112   331:   //
1113   332:   DEFINE WINDOW FullScr FROM 0,0 TO {scrn_size+3},79 NONE
1114   333:   DEFINE WINDOW Savescr FROM 0,0 TO {scrn_size},79 NONE
1115   334:   DEFINE WINDOW Helpscr FROM 0,0 TO {scrn_size},79 NONE
1116   335:   DEFINE WINDOW Browscr FROM 1,0 TO {scrn_size},79 NONE
1117   336:   IF gn_ApGen=1
1118   337:      DEFINE WINDOW Exit_App FROM 11,17 TO 15,62 DOUBLE
1119   338:   ENDIF
1120   339:   *-- Window for pause message box
1121   340:   DEFINE WINDOW Pause FROM 15,00 TO 19,79 DOUBLE
1122   341:
1123   342:   ACTIVATE WINDOW FullScr
1124   343:   @ {scrn_size+3},00
1125   344:   @ {scrn_size+2},00 SAY "Loading..."
1126   345:   //
1127   346:   {x=LEN(Menu_Main) - 4;
1128   347:    if FILEDRIVE(Menu_Main) || !default_drive then
1129   348:      mainmenu=SUBSTR(Menu_Main,1,x);
1130   349:    else
```

(continued)

```
1131   350:      mainmenu=default_drive + ":" + SUBSTR(Menu_Main,1,x);
1132   351:   endif
1133   352:   }
1134   353:   //
1135   354:   // Put first menu on black board before fortree loop
1136   355:   //
1137   356:   {x=newframe(Menu_Main);}
1138   357:   //
1139   358:   // If the main menu is not on disk
1140   359:   //
1141   360:   {if !x then
1142   361:      PAUSE("Couldn't find "+menu_main+", generation halted.")
1143   362:      goto NoGen;
1144   363:   endif
1145   364:   fileerase(mainmenu+".DBO");
1146   365:   CREATE(mainmenu+".PRG");
1147   366:   CREATE("0HLP$$$");
1148   367:   }
1149   368:   //
1150   369:   // Top half of help
1151   370:   //
1152   371:   PROCEDURE 1HELP1
1153   372:   ACTIVATE WINDOW Helpscr
1154   373:   SET ESCAPE OFF
1155   374:   ACTIVATE SCREEN
1156   375:   @ 0,0 CLEAR TO 21,79
1157   376:   @ 1,0 TO 21,79 COLOR {color(Clr_Box)}
1158   377:   @ {scrn_size+3},00
1159   378:   @ {scrn_size+3},26 SAY "Press any key to continue..."
1160   379:   @ 0,0 SAY ""
1161   380:   ln_row=INKEY()
1162   381:   DO CASE
1163   382:   //
1164   383:   // end of top half
1165   384:   //
1166   385:   // FORTREE statement
1167   386:   {foreach TREE mtree}
1168   387:   {x=1;
1169   388:     strng1="";
1170   389:     mactions="";
1171   390:     itemview=0;
1172   391:     itemndx=0;
1173   392:     itemord=0;
1174   393:     mnuname=Menu_Name;
1175   394:     mtype=STR(Menu_Type);
1176   395:     prgcnt=COUNTC(mtree);
1177   396:     midentify="";
1178   397:   }
1179   398:   {LMARG(1);}
1180   399:   //
1181   400:   // Write Menu definition program
1182   401:   //
```

(continued)

```
1183   402:   {APPEND(appl_name+".PRG");}
1184   403:   SET BORDER TO \
1185   404:   {case Mnu_Border of}
1186   405:   {0: // Panel}
1187   406:   PANEL
1188   407:   {1: // Single}
1189   408:   SINGLE
1190   409:   {2: // Double}
1191   410:   DOUBLE
1192   411:   {3: // None}
1193   412:   NONE
1194   413:   {endcase}
1195   414:   {case Menu_Type of
1196   415:    2: // Popup define
1197   416:   }
1198   417:   *-- Popup
1199   418:   DEFINE POPUP {mnuname} FROM {row1()},{col1()} TO {row2()},{col2()} ;
1200   419:   MESSAGE {if Menu_Prmpt then}"{Menu_Prmpt}"{else}{mnu_messag}{endif}
1201   420:   //
1202   421:   {  foreach FLD_ELEMENT flds}
1203   422:   //
1204   423:   DEFINE BAR {Row_Positn} OF {mnuname} PROMPT "{Fld_Pictur}" \
1205   424:   {if Item_Prmpt then}MESSAGE "{Item_Prmpt}"{endif} \
1206   425:   {if ItemSkipIf then}SKIP FOR\
1207   426:    {ItemSkipIf}{else}{if !Menu_Act then} SKIP{endif}{endif}
1208   427:   {if Item_Ovride == 1 then itemover(flds); endif}
1209   428:   {  next flds;}
1210   429:   //
1211   430:   // set call to action procedure.
1212   431:   //
1213   432:   ON SELECTION POPUP {mnuname} DO ACT0{prgcnt}
1214   433:   //
1215   434:   // File, Structure and Value pick lists all make use of a variable
1216          listval.
1216   435:   // -----------------------------------------------------------------
1217   436:   {  3: // Files}
1218   437:   DEFINE POPUP {mnuname} FROM {row1()},{col1()} TO {row2()},{col2()} \
1219   438:   PROMPT FILES LIKE {if Pick_File then}{Pick_File} {else}*.* {endif};
1220   439:   MESSAGE \
1221   440:   {  foreach FLD_ELEMENT flds}
1222   441:   {     strng=Item_Prmpt;}
1223   442:   {  next flds;}
1224   443:   {if strng then}
1225   444:   "{strng}"
1226   445:   {else}
1227   446:   {  if Menu_Prmpt then}
1228   447:   "{Menu_Prmpt}"
1229   448:   {  else}
1230   449:   {mnu_messag}
1231   450:
1232   451:   {  endif}
1233   452:   {endif}
```

(continued)

```
1234   453:   ON SELECTION POPUP {mnuname} DO ACT0{prgcnt}
1235   454:   {  foreach FLD_ELEMENT flds}
1236   455:   {if Item_Ovride == 1 then itemover(flds); endif}
1237   456:   {  next flds;}
1238   457:   //
1239   458:   { 4: // Structure}
1240   459:   DEFINE POPUP {mnuname} FROM {row1()},{col1()} TO {row2()},{col2()}\
1241   460:   PROMPT STRUCTURE ;
1242   461:   MESSAGE \
1243   462:   {  foreach FLD_ELEMENT flds}
1244   463:   {    strng=Item_Prmpt;}
1245   464:   {  next flds;}
1246   465:   {if strng then}
1247   466:   "{strng}"
1248   467:   {else}
1249   468:   {  if Menu_Prmpt then}
1250   469:   "{Menu_Prmpt}"
1251   470:   {  else}
1252   471:   {mnu_messag}
1253   472:
1254   473:   {  endif}
1255   474:   {endif}
1256   475:   ON SELECTION POPUP {mnuname} DO ShowPick
1257   476:   {  foreach FLD_ELEMENT flds}
1258   477:   {if Item_Ovride == 1 then itemover(flds); endif}
1259   478:   {midentify=PICK_FIELD;}
1260   479:   {  next flds;}
1261   480:   //
1262   481:   { 5: // Values}
1263   482:   {  if !Pick_Value || UPPER(Pick_Value) == "&LISTVAL" then}
1264   483:   DEFINE POPUP {mnuname} FROM {row1()},{col1()}
1265   484:   DEFINE BAR 1 OF {mnuname} PROMPT "  No Field defined " SKIP
1266   485:   {  else}
1267   486:   DEFINE POPUP {mnuname} FROM {row1()},{col1()} TO {row2()},{col2()}\
1268   487:   PROMPT FIELD {Pick_Value} ;
1269   488:   MESSAGE \
1270   489:   {    foreach FLD_ELEMENT flds}
1271   490:   {      strng=Item_Prmpt;}
1272   491:   {    next flds;}
1273   492:   {    if strng then}
1274   493:   "{strng}"
1275   494:   {    else}
1276   495:   {      if Menu_Prmpt then}
1277   496:   "{Menu_Prmpt}"
1278   497:   {      else}
1279   498:   {mnu_messag}
1280   499:
1281   500:   {      endif}
1282   501:   {    endif}
1283   502:   {  endif}
1284   503:   ON SELECTION POPUP {mnuname} DO ACT0{prgcnt}
1285   504:   {  foreach FLD_ELEMENT flds}
```

(continued)

```
1286   505:   {if Item_Ovride == 1 then itemover(flds); endif}
1287   506:   {  next flds;}
1288   507:   // --------------------------------------------------------------
1289   508:   //
1290   509:   { 7: // Bar define}
1291   510:   *-- Bar
1292   511:   DEFINE MENU {mnuname} MESSAGE \
1293   512:   {  if Menu_Prmpt then}
1294   513:   "{Menu_Prmpt}"
1295   514:   {  else}
1296   515:   'Position with: '+CHR(27)+CHR(26)+' - <Enter> to select choice
               - <F1> Help'
1297   516:   {  endif}
1298   517:   {   x=0;
1299   518:       pulldown=0;
1300   519:   }
1301   520:   {   foreach FLD_ELEMENT flds}
1302   521:   {      ++x;}
1303   522:   //
1304   523:   // if for some reason there is an entry in the list
1305   524:   // without text ie. corrupted data, skip it.
1306   525:   //
1307   526:   {      if !Fld_Pictur goto loophpad;}
1308   527:   //
1309   528:   // use the menu name and the letter option on each pad
1310   529:   //
1311   530:   DEFINE PAD PAD_{x} OF {mnuname} PROMPT "{Fld_Pictur}" \
1312   531:   AT {Row_Positn+Row1()},{Col_Positn+Col1()} \
1313   532:   {      if Item_Prmpt then}MESSAGE "{Item_Prmpt}"{endif}
1314   533:   //
1315   534:   // if the action is to open a menu then find out whether it's a
               popup
1316   535:   //
1317   536:   {      if Menu_Act == 1 && Open_Type then}
1318   537:   //
1319   538:   // if it is a popup is it a pulldown or not.
1320   539:   //
1321   540:   ON {if Pldwn_Menu then}SELECTION {endif}\
1322   541:   PAD PAD_{x} OF {mnuname} \
1323   542:   {if Pldwn_Menu then}
1324   543:   DO ACT0{prgcnt}
1325   544:   {else}
1326   545:   ACTIVATE POPUP {Open_Menu}
1327   546:   {endif}
1328   547:   {      else}
1329   548:   {if Item_Ovride == 1 then itemover(flds); endif}
1330   549:   //
1331   550:   // set call to action procedure.
1332   551:   //
1333   552:   ON SELECTION PAD PAD_{x} OF {mnuname} DO ACT0{prgcnt}
1334   553:   {      endif}
1335   554:   {      loophpad:}
```

(continued)

```
1336    555:  {    next flds;}
1337    556:  { otherwise:}
1338    557:  *-- {mnuname} - not a defined object yet.
1339    558:  {endcase // endcase Menu_Type}
1340    559:  ?? "."
1341    560:  //-------------------------------------------
1342    561:  // Create program control loop for each menu.
1343    562:  //-------------------------------------------
1344    563:  {
1345    564:    APPEND(mainmenu+".PRG");
1346    565:  }
1347    566:  {replicate("*",70)}
1348    567:
1349    568:  * Program......: {mnuname}.PRG
1350    569:  {include "AS_HEADR.COD";}
1351      1:  // $Header: /a/CCS/apgentc/cod/as_headr.cod,v 1.8 88/03/28
                    10:07:35 kirkn Dev $
1352      2:  // Module Name: AS_HEADR.COD
1353      3:  // Current incident (atomname):
1354      4:  // Atoms used : Appl_Authr, Appl_Cpyrt, Appl_versn
1355      5:  // Date        : March 23, 1987
1356      6:  // Description: Used as a include to produce Program Header
                    Information
1357      7:  // Notes       : AS_HEADR IS AN INCLUDE FILE  DO NOT RUN ALONE!!!
1358      8:  // Syntax      :
1359      9:  //
1360     10:  // Module Change Log
1361     11:  //   Date          Initials        Short Change Description
1362     12:  //   03/23/87       KJN            Created Module
1363     13:  //   04/07/87       KJN            Changed to new atoms
1364     14:  //
1365     15:  //
1366     16:  {strng=STR(VERSION());}
1367     17:  * Author.......: {if author then}{author}{endif}
1368     18:  * Date.........: {ltrim(SUBSTR(DATE(),1,8))}
1369     19:  * Notice.......: {if Copyright then}{Copyright}{endif}
1370     20:  * dBASE Ver....: {if dBVersion then}{dBVersion}{endif}
1371     21:  * Generated by.: APGEN version {strng}
1372     22:  * Description..: {if Menu_Desc then}{Menu_Desc}{endif}
1373     23:  // EOP AS_HEADR.COD
1374    570:  * Description..: Menu actions
1375    571:  {replicate("*",70)}
1376    572:
1377    573:  PROCEDURE {mnuname}
1378    574:  PARAMETER entryflg
1379    575:  PRIVATE gc_prognum
1380    576:  gc_prognum="0{prgcnt}"
1381    577:  {if Menu_Type == s_pick then}
1382    578:
1383    579:  IF LEFT(entryflg,1)="A"
1384    580:     DO ACT0{prgcnt}
1385    581:     RETURN
```

(continued)

```
1386   582:   ENDIF
1387   583:   {endif}
1388   584:
1389   585:   DO SET0{prgcnt // global counter tracks number of procedures}
1390   586:   IF gn_error > 0
1391   587:      gn_error=0
1392   588:      RETURN
1393   589:   ENDIF
1394   590:
1395   591:   *-- Before menu code
1396   592:   {foreach Menu_Before
1397   593:      print(Menu_Before+CHR(10));
1398   594:    next
1399   595:   }
1400   596:
1401   597:   {if Menu_Type == s_pick then}
1402   598:   lc_fldlst=''
1403   599:   {  if midentify then}
1404   600:   SET FIELDS TO {midentify}
1405   601:
1406   602:   {  endif}
1407   603:   IF TYPE("lc_window")="U"
1408   604:      DEFINE WINDOW ShowPick FROM 1,0 TO 5,79 DOUBLE
1409   605:      ACTIVATE WINDOW ShowPick
1410   606:   ENDIF
1411   607:   ACTIVATE SCREEN
1412   608:   {endif}
1413   609:   {if Menu_Type == btch then // batch process}
1414   610:   //
1415   611:   // Perform batch actions
1416   612:   //
1417   613:   ACTIVATE WINDOW Savescr
1418   614:   DO ACT0{prgcnt}
1419   615:   DEACTIVATE WINDOW Savescr
1420   616:   {else}
1421   617:   //
1422   618:   // Pick_Value has the field the pick list is based on
1423   619:   //
1424   620:   {  if Menu_Type == v_pick then}
1425   621:   DEFINE POPUP {mnuname} FROM {row1()},{col1()} TO {row2()},{col2()} \
1426   622:   PROMPT FIELD {if Pick_Value then}{Pick_Value} {else}&listval.
                 {endif}\
1427   623:   MESSAGE \
1428   624:   {  foreach FLD_ELEMENT flds}
1429   625:   {     strng=Item_Prmpt;}
1430   626:   {  next flds;}
1431   627:   {if strng then}
1432   628:   "{strng}"
1433   629:   {else}
1434   630:   {  if Menu_Prmpt then}
1435   631:   "{Menu_Prmpt}"
1436   632:   {  else}
```

(continued)

```
1437   633:   {mnu_messag}
1438   634:
1439   635:   {  endif}
1440   636:   {endif}
1441   637:   ON SELECTION POPUP {mnuname} DO ACT0{prgcnt}
1442   638:   {  endif}
1443   639:   //
1444   640:   // Activate the pad menu or popup.
1445   641:   //
1446   642:
1447   643:   ACTIVATE {if Menu_Type == bar then}MENU {else}POPUP
                   {endif}{mnuname}
1448   644:   {endif}
1449   645:
1450   646:   {if Menu_Type == bar then}
1451   647:   {  if Mnu_Border == 3 then}
1452   648:   @ {row1()+1},{col1()+1} CLEAR TO {row2()-1},{col2()-1}
1453   649:   @ {row1()+1},{col1()+1} FILL TO {row2()-1},{col2()-1} COLOR N/N
1454   650:   {  else}
1455   651:   @ {row1()},{col1()} CLEAR TO {row2()},{col2()}
1456   652:   @ {row1()},{col1()} FILL TO {row2()},{col2()} COLOR N/N
1457   653:   {  endif}
1458   654:
1459   655:   {endif}
1460   656:   {if Menu_Type == s_pick then}
1461   657:   IF TYPE("lc_window")="U"
1462   658:      DEACTIVATE WINDOW ShowPick
1463   659:      RELEASE WINDOW ShowPick
1464   660:   ENDIF
1465   661:   IF RIGHT(lc_fldlst,1)=","
1466   662:      listval=LEFT(lc_fldlst,LEN(lc_fldlst)-1)
1467   663:      DO ACT0{prgcnt}
1468   664:   ENDIF
1469   665:
1470   666:   {endif}
1471   667:   *-- After menu
1472   668:   {foreach Menu_After
1473   669:      print(Menu_After+CHR(10));
1474   670:    next
1475   671:   }
1476   672:
1477   673:   //
1478   674:   // if the menu is a file, structure, value or batch,
1479   675:   // set the key to escape so that the menu is exited.
1480   676:   //
1481   677:   {if AT(mtype,"3459") then}
1482   678:   gn_ikey=27
1483   679:   {endif}
1484   680:   RETURN
1485   681:   *-- EOP {mnuname}
1486   682:
1487   683:   // Setup procedure
```

(continued)

```
1488   684:   // 1) Set help file to call
1489   685:   // 2) set colors
1490   686:   // 3) ? menu level database
1491   687:   // 4 conditional before code (flag var to handle calls to other
                   menus)
1492   688:   //
1493   689:   {include "AS_SETUP.COD"}
1494     1:   // $Header: /a/CCS/apgentc/cod/as_setup.cod,v 1.21 88/08/17
                   19:57:41 dough Dev $
1495     2:   // Module Name: AS_SETUP.COD
1496     3:   // Description: Setup for current menu
1497     4:   //
1498     5:   PROCEDURE SET0{prgcnt}
1499     6:   ON KEY LABEL F1 DO 1HELP1
1500     7:   //
1501     8:   // capture the menu level database/view
1502     9:   //
1503    10:   {if (not Menu_Ovride) or (not Menu_View) or (global_view ==
                   Menu_View) then
1504    11:     gc_view = global_view;
1505    12:   //
1506    13:   // capture the menu level index(es)
1507    14:   //
1508    15:     if (not Menu_Ovride) or (not Menu_NDX) or (global_ndx ==
                   Menu_NDX) then
1509    16:       gc_ndx = global_ndx;
1510    17:     else
1511    18:       gc_ndx = Menu_NDX;
1512    19:     endif
1513    20:   //
1514    21:   // capture the menu level index order(s)
1515    22:   //
1516    23:     if (not Menu_Ovride) or (not Menu_Order) or (global_ord ==
                   Menu_Order) then
1517    24:       gc_ord = global_ord;
1518    25:     else
1519    26:       gc_ord = Menu_Order;
1520    27:     endif
1521    28:   else
1522    29:     gc_view = Menu_View;
1523    30:     gc_ndx  = Menu_NDX;
1524    31:     gc_ord  = Menu_Order;
1525    32:   endif
1526    33:   }
1527    34:   {if Menu_Ovride != 2 then}
1528    35:
1529    36:   DO DBF0{prgcnt} && open menu level database
1530    37:   {endif}
1531    38:   {if Menu_Type != btch then}
1532    39:
1533    40:   IF gn_error = 0
1534    41:   {LMARG(4);}
```

(continued)

```
1535    42:   IF ISCOLOR()
1536    43:   {LMARG(7);}
1537    44:   SET COLOR OF NORMAL TO {color(Clr_Text)}
1538    45:   SET COLOR OF MESSAGES TO {color(Clr_Messages)}
1539    46:   SET COLOR OF TITLES TO {color(Clr_Heading)}
1540    47:   SET COLOR OF HIGHLIGHT TO {color(Clr_Hghlight)}
1541    48:   SET COLOR OF BOX TO {color(Clr_Box)}
1542    49:   SET COLOR OF INFORMATION TO {color(Clr_Info)}
1543    50:   SET COLOR OF FIELDS TO {color(Clr_Fields)}
1544    51:   {LMARG(4);}
1545    52:   ENDIF
1546    53:   {endif}
1547    54:   //
1548    55:   // if the pad menu has a box around it, draw it.
1549    56:   //
1550    57:   {if Menu_Type == bar then}
1551    58:
1552    59:   SET BORDER TO
1553    60:   {  if Mnu_Border != 3 then}
1554    61:   @ {row1()},{col1()} TO {row2()},{col2()}\
1555    62:   {    case Mnu_Border of}
1556    63:   {      0:}
1557    64:    PANEL\
1558    65:   {      2:}
1559    66:    DOUBLE\
1560    67:   {      endcase}
1561    68:    COLOR {color(Clr_Box)}
1562    69:   {  endif}
1563    70:   @ {row1()+1},{col1()+1} CLEAR TO {row2()-1},{col2()-1}
1564    71:   @ {row1()+1},{col1()+1} FILL TO {row2()-1},{col2()-1} \
1565    72:   COLOR {color(Clr_Messages)}
1566    73:   {endif}
1567    74:   {if Menu_Type != btch then}
1568    75:   {LMARG(1);}
1569    76:   ENDIF
1570    77:   {endif}
1571    78:   RETURN
1572    79:
1573    80:   {if Menu_Ovride != 2 then}
1574    81:   PROCEDURE DBF0{prgcnt}
1575    82:   CLOSE DATABASES
1576    83:   *-- Open menu level view/database
1577    84:   {  dbfOpen(gc_view,gc_ndx,gc_ord,1);}
1578    85:   RETURN
1579    86:
1580    87:   {endif}
1581    690:  {nosub:}
1582    691:  //
1583    692:  // Actions procedure
1584    693:  //
```

(continued)

```
1585    694:  {include "AS_ACTN.COD"}
1586      1:  // $Header: /a/CCS/apgentc/cod/as_actn.cod,v 1.49 88/08/18
                   23:59:03 dough Dev $
1587      2:  // Module Name: AS_ACTN.COD
1588      3:  // Description: Menu item actions (taken out of AS_MENU.COD)
1589      4:  //
1590      5:  PROCEDURE ACT0{prgcnt}
1591      6:  //
1592      7:  // display the appropriate menu type on the comment line
1593      8:  //
1594      9:  *-- Begin {Menu_Name}: \
1595     10:  { case Menu_Type of}
1596     11:  {popup:}POPUP \
1597     12:  {f_pick:}FILES \
1598     13:  {s_pick:}STRUCTURE \
1599     14:  {v_pick:}VALUES \
1600     15:  {bar:}BAR \
1601     16:  {btch:}BATCH \
1602     17:  { endcase}
1603     18:  Menu Actions.
1604     19:  *-- (before item, action, and after item)
1605     20:  *
1606     21:  //
1607     22:  // if the menu type is not a file, structure, value or batch
1608     23:  // include the dBASE case structure in the code.
1609     24:  //
1610     25:  PRIVATE lc_new, lc_dbf
1611     26:  lc_new=' '
1612     27:  lc_dbf=' '
1613     28:  {if not AT(mtype,"3459") then}
1614     29:  DO CASE
1615     30:  {else}
1616     31:  {  if Menu_Type != s_pick then}
1617     32:  listval=PROMPT()
1618     33:  {  endif}
1619     34:  {endif}
1620     35:  {cnt=0;
1621     36:    count=1;
1622     37:    windowvar=1;
1623     38:  }
1624     39:  { foreach FLD_ELEMENT k}
1625     40:  //
1626     41:  // increment the choice number
1627     42:  //
1628     43:  {   ++cnt;}
1629     44:  //
1630     45:  // Initialize to multi user flags to false.
1631     46:  //
1632     47:  {muser=0;}
1633     48:  {exclflg=0;}
```

(continued)

```
1634   49:  //
1635   50:  // NOT a line of text in the menu OR NOT an action (Text no act.),
                 skip it
1636   51:  //
1637   52:  {   if (not AT(mtype,"3459")) && (!Fld_Pictur || !Menu_Act) goto
                 newact endif}
1638   53:  //
1639   54:  // if the menu type is not a file, structure, value or batch,
1640   55:  // include the dBASE case statement in the code.
1641   56:  //
1642   57:  {     if not AT(mtype,"3459") then}
1643   58:  {        LMARG(1);}
1644   59:  //
1645   60:  {        if Menu_Type == bar then}
1646   61:  CASE PAD() = "PAD_{cnt}"
1647   62:  {        else}
1648   63:  CASE BAR() = {Row_Positn}
1649   64:  {        endif}
1650   65:  //
1651   66:  // if the menu is a popup associated with a pulldown set the
                 margin.
1652   67:  //
1653   68:  {        LMARG(4);}
1654   69:  {     else}
1655   70:  //
1656   71:  // if the menu is a batch object comment the action number
1657   72:  //
1658   73:  {        if Menu_Type == btch then}
1659   74:  {           replicate("*",20)} Action #{cnt} {replicate("*",20)}
1660   75:  {        endif}
1661   76:  {     endif}
1662   77:  //
1663   78:  // This section covers multi user actions
1664   79:  //
1665   80:  // Set the the muser variable to 1 for true.
1666   81:  //
1667   82:  {case Menu_Act of}
1668   83:  {appd:}
1669   84:  {  muser=1;}
1670   85:  {rcopy:}
1671   86:  {  muser=1;}
1672   87:  {repl:}
1673   88:  {  if Scope || While_Exp || For_Expr then}
1674   89:  {     muser=1;}
1675   90:  {  endif}
1676   91:  {dele:}
1677   92:  {  if Scope || While_Exp || For_Expr then}
1678   93:  {     muser=1;}
1679   94:  {  else}
1680   95:  {     muser=2;}
1681   96:  {  endif}
1682   97:  {reca:}
```

(continued)

```
1683    98:  {  muser=1;}
1684    99:  {pack:}
1685   100:  {  exclflg=1;}
1686   101:  {indx:}
1687   102:  {  muser=1;}
1688   103:  {rndx:}
1689   104:  {  exclflg=1;}
1690   105:  {sort:}
1691   106:  {  muser=1;}
1692   107:  {impt:}
1693   108:  {  muser=1;}
1694   109:  {expt:}
1695   110:  {  muser=1;}
1696   111:  {endcase}
1697   112:  //
1698   113:  // if the action requires exclusive use of the database
1699   114:  //
1700   115:  {if exclflg then}
1701   116:  SET EXCLUSIVE ON
1702   117:  {endif}
1703   118:  //
1704   119:  // Open item level view/database, if there is one.
1705   120:  //
1706   121:  {        if Item_View or Item_NDX or Item_Order then}
1707   122:  //
1708   123:  // capture the item level database/view
1709   124:  //
1710   125:  {if (not Item_Ovride) or (not Item_View) or (gc_view == Item_View)
                  then
1711   126:     lc_view = gc_view;
1712   127:  //
1713   128:  // capture the menu level index(es)
1714   129:  //
1715   130:     if (not Item_Ovride) or (not Item_NDX) or (gc_ndx == Item_NDX)
                  then
1716   131:       lc_ndx = gc_ndx;
1717   132:     else
1718   133:       lc_ndx = Item_NDX;
1719   134:     endif
1720   135:  //
1721   136:  // capture the menu level index order(s)
1722   137:  //
1723   138:     if (not Item_Ovride) or (not Item_Order) or (gc_ord ==
                  Item_Order) then
1724   139:       lc_ord = gc_ord;
1725   140:     else
1726   141:       lc_ord = Item_Order;
1727   142:     endif
1728   143:   else
1729   144:     lc_view = Item_View;
1730   145:     lc_ndx  = Item_NDX;
1731   146:     lc_ord  = Item_Order;
```

(continued)

```
1732   147:   endif
1733   148:   }
1734   149:   {if Item_Ovride != 2 then}
1735   150:   *-- Open Item level view/database and indexes
1736   151:   CLOSE DATABASES
1737   152:   lc_dbf='Y'
1738   153:   {          dbfOpen(lc_view,lc_ndx,lc_ord,0);}
1739   154:   {          itemdbf=1;}
1740   155:   {else}
1741   156:   {  if exclflg then}
1742   157:   CREATE VIEW Current FROM ENVIRONMENT
1743   158:   SET VIEW TO Current
1744   159:   {  endif}
1745   160:   {endif}
1746   161:   {        else}
1747   162:   {if Item_Ovride != 2 then}
1748   163:   //
1749   164:   // if the menu type is batch or exclusive use is required
1750   165:   // reopen the menu level database.
1751   166:   //
1752   167:   {          if (Menu_Type == btch && itemdbf) or exclflg then}
1753   168:   {            dbfOpen(gc_view,gc_ndx,gc_ord,0);}
1754   169:   {             itemdbf=0;}
1755   170:   {          endif}
1756   171:   {else}
1757   172:   {  if exclflg then}
1758   173:   CREATE VIEW Current FROM ENVIRONMENT
1759   174:   SET VIEW TO Current
1760   175:   {  endif}
1761   176:   {endif}
1762   177:   {        endif}
1763   178:   //
1764   179:   {     if muser then}
1765   180:   *-- Multi user file lock
1766   181:   DO Lockit WITH "{muser}"
1767   182:   IF gn_error <> 0
1768   183:     gn_error=0
1769   184:     RETURN
1770   185:   ENDIF
1771   186:   {     endif}
1772   187:   //
1773   188:   // if the exclusive flag is set turn exclusive usage off
1774   189:   //
1775   190:   {    if exclflg then}
1776   191:   SET EXCLUSIVE OFF
1777   192:   {    endif}
1778   193:   //
1779   194:   {if postn_menu then}
1780   195:   ON KEY LABEL F1 DO Postnhlp
1781   196:   ACTIVATE WINDOW Savescr
1782   197:   {endif}
1783   198:   {include "AS_TPOST.COD";}
```

(continued)

```
1784      1:  // $Header: /a/CCS/apgentc/cod/as_tpost.cod,v 1.2 88/02/17
                 18:07:44 dough Dev $
1785      2:  // Module Name: AS_TPOST.COD
1786      3:  // Current incident (atomname):
1787      4:  // Atoms used : Postn_Menu, Seek_Cond, Goto_Reco, Locate_for,
                 Locate_whl
1788      5:  // Date        : April 7, 1987
1789      6:  // Description: Record positioning (Ask at runtime)
1790      7:  // Notes      :
1791      8:  // Syntax     :
1792      9:  //
1793     10:  // Module Change Log
1794     11:  //    Date       Initials      Short Change Description
1795     12:  //  04/07/87       DCH           Created Module
1796     13:  //  07/28/87       KJN           Changed to New Atom Names
1797     14:  //
1798     15:  //
1799     16:  // No positioning menu
1800     17:  {if Postn_Menu == 0}
1801     18:  { if Seek_Cond}
1802     19:  SEEK {Seek_Cond}
1803     20:  { endif}
1804     21:  { if Goto_Reco}
1805     22:  GOTO {Goto_Reco}
1806     23:  { endif}
1807     24:  { if Locate_Scp || Locate_for || Locate_whl then}
1808     25:  LOCATE\
1809     26:  {   if Locate_Scp} {Locate_Scp}{endif}\
1810     27:  {   if Locate_for} FOR {Locate_for}{endif}\
1811     28:  {   if Locate_whl} WHILE {Locate_whl}{endif}\
1812     29:
1813     30:  { endif}
1814     31:  {endif}
1815     32:  // DO positioning menu
1816     33:  {if Postn_Menu == 1}
1817     34:  Do Position
1818     35:  {endif}
1819     36:  // EOP AS_TPOST.COD
1820    199:  {if postn_menu then}
1821    200:  DEACTIVATE WINDOW Savescr
1822    201:  ON KEY LABEL F1 DO 1HELP1
1823    202:  {endif}
1824    203:  //
1825    204:  // item before actions
1826    205:  //
1827    206:  {     foreach Item_Befor m in k
1828    207:          if Item_Befor then
1829    208:             print(rtrim(Item_Befor)+CHR(10));
1830    209:          endif
1831    210:        next m;
1832    211:  }
1833    212:  //
```

(continued)

```
1834   213:   // define window if specified
1835   214:   //
1836   215:   {if Wndow_Name}
1837   216:   {if Wndow_Char && Wndow_Bord != 3 then}
1838   217:   SET BORDER TO \
1839   218:   {case Wndow_Bord of}
1840   219:   {1:} DOUBLE\
1841   220:   {2:} PANEL\
1842   221:   {4:} NONE\
1843   222:   {endcase}
1844   223:
1845   224:   SET BORDER TO {Wndow_Char}
1846   225:   {endif}
1847   226:   DEFINE WINDOW {Wndow_Name} FROM
                 {nul2zero(Wndow_X1)},{nul2zero(Wndow_Y1)} TO\
1848   227:   {nul2zero(Wndow_X2)},{nul2zero(Wndow_Y2)}\
1849   228:   {case Wndow_Bord of}
1850   229:   {1:} DOUBLE\
1851   230:   {2:} PANEL\
1852   231:   {3:} {Wndow_Char}\
1853   232:   {4:} NONE\
1854   233:   {endcase}
1855   234:   {if Wndow_Clrs then}
1856   235:    COLOR {Wndow_Clrs}
1857   236:
1858   237:   {else}
1859   238:
1860   239:   {endif}
1861   240:   {if Wndow_Char && Wndow_Bord != 3 then}
1862   241:   SET BORDER TO
1863   242:   {endif}
1864   243:   ACTIVATE WINDOW {Wndow_Name}
1865   244:   {if windowvar then}
1866   245:   PRIVATE lc_window
1867   246:   {  windowvar=0;
1868   247:    endif}
1869   248:   lc_window="{Wndow_Name}"
1870   249:   {else}
1871   250:   {  if Menu_Type != btch && Menu_Act && Menu_Act != open &&
1872   251:     Menu_Act != retu && Menu_Act != quit && Menu_Act != batch then}
1873   252:   {    if Menu_Act == brow || Menu_Act == edit then}
1874   253:   ACTIVATE WINDOW Browscr
1875   254:   {    else}
1876   255:   ACTIVATE WINDOW Savescr
1877   256:   {    endif}
1878   257:   {  endif}
1879   258:   {endif}
1880   259:   {if AT(STR(Menu_Act)+",","2,3,7,19,20,") then}
1881   260:   SET SCOREBOARD ON
1882   261:   {endif}
1883   262:   //
1884   263:   // This is a comment which can be placed in
```

(continued)

```
1885   264:   // the code to reveal the the action number
1886   265:   // of a particular action. (refer to the
1887   266:   // enum statement in AS_MENU.COD)
1888   267:   //
1889   268:   //*-- ApGen Menu action number {Menu_Act}
1890   269:   //
1891   270:   {  if Item_Prmpt && Menu_Act && Menu_Act != open &&
1892   271:      Menu_Act != retu && Menu_Act != quit then}
1893   272:   SET MESSAGE TO "{alltrim(Item_Prmpt)}"
1894   273:   {endif}
1895   274:   {case Menu_Act of}
1896   275:   {case textno:}
1897   276:   {case open:}
1898   277:   {if Menu_Type != btch then   // not equal to batch process}
1899   278:   lc_new='Y'
1900   279:   {endif}
1901   280:   DO {Open_Menu} WITH "{if Open_Type == bar then}B{else}
                {endif}0{prgcnt}"
1902   281:   {case brow: include "ad_brow.cod";}
1903     1:   // $Header: /a/CCS/apgentc/cod/ad_brow.cod,v 1.17 88/08/16
                20:37:58 dough Dev $
1904     2:   // Module Name: AD_BROW.COD - Menu_Act = 2
1905     3:   // Selectors  : Brow_Frez, Brow_Lock, Brow_Width, Brow_Follw,
                Brow_Dele
1906     4:   //            : Brow_Appd, Brow_Menu, Brow_Init, Brow_Edit,
                Brow_Compr
1907     5:   //            : Brow_FMT, Brow_Clear, Flter_Cond, Item_View,
                Field_List
1908     6:   // Description: This module is included to issue the dBASE BROWSE
                command
1909     7:   // Syntax     : BROWSE [FIELDS <field name list>] [LOCK <expN>]
1910     8:   //                    [WIDTH <expN>] [FREEZE <field name>]
1911     9:   //                    [NOFOLLOW] [NOAPPEND] [NOMENU] [NOCLEAR]
1912    10:   //                    [NOINIT] [NODELETE] [NOEDIT] [COMPRESS]
1913    11:   //                    [WINDOW <window name>] [FORMAT]
1914    12:   //
1915    13:   {if Flter_Cond then}
1916    14:   SET FILTER TO {Flter_Cond}
1917    15:   GOTO TOP
1918    16:   {endif}
1919    17:   { if Brow_FMT then}
1920    18:   SET FORMAT TO {lower(Brow_FMT)}
1921    19:   {endif}
1922    20:   //
1923    21:   *-- Desc: Browse file - {Item_View}
1924    22:   BROWSE \
1925    23:   { if Field_list}FIELDS {lower(Field_list)} {endif}\
1926    24:   { if Brow_Lock}LOCK {Brow_Lock} {endif}\
1927    25:   { if Brow_Width}WIDTH {Brow_Width} {endif}\
1928    26:   { if Brow_Frez}FREEZE {Brow_Frez} {endif}\
1929    27:   { if Brow_Follw == 1}NOFOLLOW {endif}\
1930    28:   { if Brow_Init == 1}NOINIT {endif}\
```

(continued)

```
1931   29:  { if Brow_Menu == 1}NOMENU {endif}\
1932   30:  { if Brow_Appd == 1}NOAPPEND {endif}\
1933   31:  { if Brow_Dele == 1}NODELETE {endif}\
1934   32:  { if Brow_Edit == 1}NOEDIT {endif}\
1935   33:  { if Brow_Compr == 1}COMPRESS {endif}\
1936   34:  { if Brow_Clear == 1}NOCLEAR {endif}\
1937   35:  { if Brow_FMT}FORMAT {endif}\
1938   36:
1939   37:  {if Filter_Cond then}
1940   38:  SET FILTER TO
1941   39:  {endif}
1942   40:  { if Brow_FMT}
1943   41:  SET FORMAT TO
1944   42:  {endif}
1945   43:  //
1946   44:  // EOP AD_BROW.COD
1947  282:  {case edit: include "ad_edit.cod";}
1948    1:  // $Header: /a/CCS/apgentc/cod/ad_edit.cod,v 1.21 88/08/16
                20:38:17 dough Dev $
1949    2:  // Module Name: AD_EDIT.COD - Menu_Act = 3
1950    3:  // Selectors  : Edit_Frez, Edit_Lock, Edit_Width, Edit_Follw,
                            Edit_Dele
1951    4:  //           : Edit_Appd, Edit_Menu, Edit_Init, Edit_Edit,
                            Edit_Compr
1952    5:  //           : Edit_FMT, Brow_Clear Flter_Cond,Item_View,
                            Field_List
1953    6:  //           : For_Expr, While_Exp, Scope
1954    7:  // Description: to issue the dBASE EDIT/APPEND command
1955    8:  // Syntax    : EDIT [<scope>] [FIELDS <field name list>]
1956    9:  //                  [WHILE <expL>] [FOR <expL>]
1957   10:  //                  [NOFOLLOW] [NOAPPEND] [NOMENU] [NOCLEAR]
1958   11:  //                  [NOINIT] [NODELETE] [NOEDIT] [<expN>]
1959   12:  //
1960   13:  {if Flter_Cond then}
1961   14:  SET FILTER TO {Flter_Cond}
1962   15:  GOTO TOP
1963   16:  {endif}
1964   17:  //
1965   18:  SET STATUS ON
1966   19:  {if Edit_FMT}
1967   20:  *-- Desc: attach format file {Edit_FMT}.fmt.
1968   21:  SET FORMAT TO {Edit_FMT}
1969   22:  {endif}
1970   23.  {if Edit_Mode == 0}
1971   24:  APPEND
1972   25:  {else}
1973   26:  EDIT \
1974   27:  {if Scope}{upper(Scope)} {endif}\
1975   28:  {if Field_list}FIELDS {lower(Field_list)} {endif}\
1976   29:  {if While_Exp}WHILE {While_Exp} {endif}\
1977   30:  {if For_Expr}FOR {For_Expr} {endif}\
1978   31:  { if Edit_Follw == 1}NOFOLLOW {endif}\
```

(continued)

```
1979    32:   { if Edit_Appd == 1}NOAPPEND {endif}\
1980    33:   { if Edit_Menu == 1}NOMENU {endif}\
1981    34:   { if Edit_Init == 1}NOINIT {endif}\
1982    35:   { if Edit_Dele == 1}NODELETE {endif}\
1983    36:   { if Edit_Edit == 1}NOEDIT {endif}\
1984    37:   { if Edit_Clear == 1}NOCLEAR {endif}\
1985    38:   {endif // if Edit_Mode == 0}
1986    39:
1987    40:   SET STATUS OFF
1988    41:   //
1989    42:   {if Flter_Cond then}
1990    43:   SET FILTER TO
1991    44:   {endif}
1992    45:   {if Edit_FMT}
1993    46:   *-- close format file so as not to affect READ's
1994    47:   SET FORMAT TO
1995    48:   {endif}
1996    49:   //
1997    50:   // EOP AD_EDIT.COD
1998   283:   {case rept: include "ad_rept.cod";}
1999     1:   // $Header: /a/CCS/apgentc/cod/ad_rept.cod,v 1.19 88/08/16
                  20:39:15 dough Dev $
2000      2:   // Module Name: AD_REPT.COD - Menu_Act = 4
2001      3:   // Selectors  : FRM_Dest, FRM_File, FRM_Headng, FRM_Plain,
                  FRM_Eject,
2002      4:   //           : FRM_Summry, Flter_Cond, Scope, For_Expr, While_Exp
2003      5:   // Description: Call to REPORT
2004      6:   // Syntax    : REPORT FORM <report form file>/?
2005      7:   //                [PLAIN] [SUMMARY] [NOEJECT] [HEADING <expC>]
2006      8:   //                [<scope>] [FOR <expL>] [WHILE <expL>]
2007      9:   //                [TO [PRINT]/[FILE <expFN>]]
2008     10:   //
2009     11:   *-- Desc: Report
2010     12:   //
2011     13:   {if Flter_Cond then}
2012     14:   SET FILTER TO {Flter_Cond}
2013     15:   GOTO TOP
2014     16:   {endif}
2015     17:   //
2016     18:   {case FRM_Dest of}
2017     19:   {0: // Printer}
2018     20:   SET PRINT ON
2019     21:   {1: // File}
2020     22:   SET ALTERNATE TO {FRM_File}.prt
2021     23:   SET ALTERNATE ON
2022     24:   {3: // Ask at runtime}
2023     25:   gn_pkey = 0
2024     26:   DO PrintSet
2025     27:   IF gn_pkey <> 27  && esc
2026     28:      \
2027     29:   {endcase}
2028     30:   REPORT FORM {FRM_File}\
```

(continued)

```
2029    31:   {if not FRM_Plain} PLAIN {endif}\
2030    32:   {if FRM_Headng} HEADING "{FRM_Headng}"{endif}\
2031    33:   {if FRM_Eject} NOEJECT {endif}\
2032    34:   {if FRM_Summry} SUMMARY {endif}\
2033    35:   {if Scope} {upper(Scope)} {endif}\
2034    36:   {if For_Expr} FOR {For_Expr}{endif}\
2035    37:   {if While_Exp} WHILE {While_Exp}{endif}\
2036    38:
2037    39:   {case FRM_Dest of}
2038    40:   {0:}
2039    41:   SET PRINT OFF
2040    42:   {1:}
2041    43:   CLOSE ALTERNATE
2042    44:   {2:}
2043    45:   WAIT
2044    46:   {3:}
2045    47:     DO Cleanup
2046    48:   ENDIF
2047    49:   {endcase}
2048    50:   //
2049    51:   {if Flter_Cond then}
2050    52:   SET FILTER TO
2051    53:   {endif}
2052    54:   //
2053    55:   // EOP AD_REPT.COD
2054   284:   {case labl: include "ad_labl.cod";}
2055     1:   // $Header: /a/CCS/apgentc/cod/ad_labl.cod,v 1.17 88/08/16
              20:38:41 dough Dev $
2056     2:   // Module Name: AD_LABL.COD - Menu_Act = 5
2057     3:   // Selectors  : LBL_File, Scope, For_Expr, While_Exp, LBL_Sample,
2058     4:   //           : LBL_Dest, Flter_Cond
2059     5:   // Description: Call LABEL FORM
2060     6:   // Syntax     : LABEL FORM <expFN>/? [<scope>] [SAMPLE]
2061     7:   //                    [FOR <expL>] [WHILE <expL>]
2062     8:   //                    [TO PRINTER] [TO FILE <expFN>]
2063     9:   //
2064    10:   *--  Desc: LABEL command to call {LBL_File}.lbl
2065    11:   //
2066    12:   {if Flter_Cond then}
2067    13:   SET FILTER TO {Flter_Cond}
2068    14:   GOTO TOP
2069    15:   {endif}
2070    16:   //
2071    17:   {case LBL_Dest of}
2072    18:   {0: // Printer}
2073    19:   SET PRINT ON
2074    20:   {1: // File}
2075    21:   SET ALTERNATE TO {LBL_File}.prt
2076    22:   SET ALTERNATE ON
2077    23:   {3: // Ask at runtime}
2078    24:   gn_pkey = 0
2079    25:   DO PrintSet
```

(continued)

```
2080    26:  IF gn_pkey <> 27  && esc
2081    27:     \
2082    28:  {endcase}
2083    29:  //
2084    30:  LABEL FORM {LBL_File}\
2085    31:  { if Scope} {upper(Scope)} {endif}\
2086    32:  { if For_Expr} FOR {For_Expr}{endif}\
2087    33:  { if While_Exp} WHILE {While_Exp}{endif}\
2088    34:  { if !LBL_Sample} SAMPLE {endif}\
2089    35:
2090    36:  {case LBL_Dest of}
2091    37:  {0:}
2092    38:  SET PRINT OFF
2093    39:  {1:}
2094    40:  CLOSE ALTERNATE
2095    41:  {2:}
2096    42:  WAIT
2097    43:  {3:}
2098    44:     DO Cleanup
2099    45:  ENDIF
2100    46:  {endcase}
2101    47:  //
2102    48:  {if Filter_Cond then}
2103    49:  SET FILTER TO
2104    50:  {endif}
2105    51:  //
2106    52:  // EOP AD_LABL.COD
2107   285:  {case disp: include "ad_list.cod";}
2108     1:  // $Header: /a/CCS/apgentc/cod/ad_list.cod,v 1.19 88/08/16
                 20:38:46 dough Dev $
2109     2:  // Module Name: AD_LIST.COD - Menu_Act = 6
2110     3:  // Selectors  : Disp_Pause, Field_list, Flter_Cond, Scope,
                 For_Expr, While_Exp
2111     4:  // Description: List [<parameters>]
2112     5:  // Syntax     : LIST [OFF] [<scope>] [FIELDS <field name list>]
2113     6:  //                   [<exp list>]
2114     7:  //                   [FOR <expL>] [WHILE <expL>]
2115     8:  //           *:=      [TO [PRINTER]/[FILE <expFN>]]
2116     9:  //
2117    10:  //            LIST FILES [[LIKE] [<path>] <skeleton>] *
2118    11:  //
2119    12:  //            LIST HISTORY [LAST <expN>] *
2120    13:  //
2121    14:  //            LIST MEMORY *
2122    15:  //
2123    16:  //            LIST STATUS *
2124    17:  //
2125    18:  //            LIST STRUCTURE [IN <expWA>] *
2126    19:  //
2127    20:  *-- Desc: List [<parameters>]
2128    21:  CLEAR
2129    22:  //
```

(continued)

```
2130    23:   //
2131    24:   {if Field_list then}
2132    25:   SET FIELDS TO {lower(Field_list)}
2133    26:   {endif}
2134    27:   {if Flter_Cond then}
2135    28:   SET FILTER TO {Flter_Cond}
2136    29:   GOTO TOP
2137    30:   {endif}
2138    31:   //
2139    32:   {case Disp_Dest of}
2140    33:   {0: // Printer}
2141    34:   SET PRINT ON
2142    35:   {1: // File}
2143    36:   SET ALTERNATE TO list.prt
2144    37:   SET ALTERNATE ON
2145    38:   {3: // Ask at runtime}
2146    39:   gn_pkey = 0
2147    40:   DO PrintSet
2148    41:   IF gn_pkey <> 27  && esc
2149    42:     \
2150    43:   {endcase}
2151    44:   //
2152    45:   {if Disp_Pause then}
2153    46:   LIST\
2154    47:   {else}
2155    48:   DISPLAY ALL\
2156    49:   {endif}
2157    50:   {if Disp_Off then}
2158    51:    OFF\
2159    52:   {endif}
2160    53:   {if Scope} {upper(Scope)} {endif}\
2161    54:   {if For_Expr} FOR {For_Expr}{endif}\
2162    55:   {if While_Exp} WHILE {While_Exp}{endif}\
2163    56:
2164    57:   {case Disp_Dest of}
2165    58:   {0:}
2166    59:   SET PRINT OFF
2167    60:   {1:}
2168    61:   CLOSE ALTERNATE
2169    62:   {2:}
2170    63:   {  if not Disp_Pause then}
2171    64:   WAIT
2172    65:   {  endif}
2173    66:   {3:}
2174    67:    DO Cleanup
2175    68:   ENDIF
2176    69:   {endcase}
2177    70:   //
2178    71:   {if Field_list then}
2179    72:   SET FIELDS TO
2180    73:   {endif}
2181    74:   {if Flter_Cond then}
```

(continued)

```
2182    75:  SET FILTER TO
2183    76:  {endif}
2184    77:  //
2185    78:  // EOP AD_LIST.COD
2186   286:  {case appd: include "ad_apnd.cod";}
2187     1:  // $Header: /a/CCS/apgentc/cod/ad_apnd.cod,v 1.13 88/08/16
                   20:37:53 dough Dev $
2188     2:  // Module Name: AD_APND.COD - Menu_Act = 7
2189     3:  // Selectors  : Appnd_from, Appnd_type, For_Expr
2190     4:  // Description: to issue the dBASE APPEND command
2191     5:  // Syntax     : APPEND FROM <expFN>/?/ARRAY <array name>
2192     6:  //                  [FOR <expL>]
2193     7:  //                  [ [TYPE] DBASEII / DIF / FW2 / RPD / SDF /
                                  SYLK / WKS
2194     8:  //                       [DELIMITED [WITH BLANK/<delimiter>]] ]
2195     9:  //
2196    10:  lc_say='Appending records from file {if Appnd_type == 5}ARRAY
                   {endif}{Appnd_from}'
2197    11:  DO info_box WITH lc_say
2198    12:  //
2199    13:  SET TALK ON
2200    14:  APPEND FROM {if Appnd_type == 5}ARRAY {endif}{Appnd_from} \
2201    15:  {if For_Expr} FOR {For_Expr}{endif}\
2202    16:  {if Appnd_type && Appnd_type != 5 then} TYPE {endif}\
2203    17:  { case Appnd_type of}
2204    18:  { 0: // insert carriage return for DBF}
2205    19:
2206    20:  { 1:}dBASEII
2207    21:  { 2:}FW2
2208    22:  { 3:}RPD
2209    23:  { 4:}DELIMITED {if Appl_Delim}WITH {Appl_Delim}{endif}
2210    24:  { 5: // insert carriage return for ARRAY}
2211    25:
2212    26:  { 6:}SDF
2213    27:  { 7:}DIF
2214    28:  { 8:}SYLK
2215    29:  { 9:}WKS
2216    30:  { endcase}
2217    31:  // end of if Appnd_type
2218    32:  SET TALK OFF
2219    33:  //
2220    34:  // EOP AD_APND.COD
2221   287:  {case rcopy: include "ad_copy.cod";}
2222     1:  // $Header: /a/CCS/apgentc/cod/ad_copy.cod,v 1.14 88/08/16
                   20:38:08 dough Dev $
2223     2:  // Module Name: AD_COPY.COD - Menu_Act = 8
2224     3:  // Selectors  : Copy_Recrd, Copy_type, Scope, Field_list,
                   For_Expr, While_Exp
2225     4:  // Description: to issue the dBASE COPY command
2226     5:  // Syntax     : COPY TO <expFN>/ARRAY <array name>
2227     6:  //                       [<scope>] [FIELDS <field name list>]
2228     7:  //                       [FOR <expL>] [WHILE <expL>]
```

(continued)

```
2229    8:  //                          [ [TYPE] DBASEII / DIF / FW2 / RPD / SDF /
                                         SYLK / WKS
2230    9:  //                             [DELIMITED [WITH BLANK/<delimiter>]] ]
2231   10:  //
2232   11:  lc_say='Copying records to {Copy_Recrd}'
2233   12:  DO info_box WITH lc_say
2234   13:  SET TALK ON
2235   14:  *--  Desc: Copy records to {if Copy_type == 5}ARRAY
                    {endif}{Copy_Recrd}
2236   15:  COPY\
2237   16:  {if Copy_Recrd} TO {if Copy_type == 5}ARRAY
                    {endif}{Copy_Recrd}{endif}\
2238   17:  {if Scope} {upper(Scope)} {endif}\
2239   18:  {if Field_list} FIELDS {lower(Field_list)}{endif}\
2240   19:  {if For_Expr} FOR {For_Expr}{endif}\
2241   20:  {if While_Exp} WHILE {While_Exp}{endif}\
2242   21:  {if Copy_type && Copy_type != 5 then} TYPE {endif}\
2243   22:  { case Copy_type of}
2244   23:  { 0: // insert carriage return for DBF}
2245   24:
2246   25:  { 1:}dBASEII
2247   26:  { 2:}FW2
2248   27:  { 3:}RPD
2249   28:  { 4:}DELIMITED {if Appl_Delim}WITH {Appl_Delim}{endif}
2250   29:  { 5: // insert carriage return for ARRAY}
2251   30:
2252   31:  { 6:}SDF
2253   32:  { 7:}DIF
2254   33:  { 8:}SYLK
2255   34:  { 9:}WKS
2256   35:  { endcase}
2257   36:  SET TALK OFF
2258   37:  //
2259   38:  // EOP AD_COPY.COD
2260  288:  {case repl: include "ad_repl.cod";}
2261    1:  // $Header: /a/CCS/apgentc/cod/ad_repl.cod,v 1.9 88/08/16 20:39:10
                    dough Dev $
2262    2:  // Module Name: AD_REPL.COD - Menu_Act = 9
2263    3:  // Selectors  : Scope, For_Expr, While_Exp, Repl_fld*, Repl_with*,
                    Repl_Addtv*
2264    4:  // Description: Substitute values into database record
2265    5:  // Syntax     : REPLACE <field name> WITH <exp> [ADDITIVE]
2266    6:  //                    [,<field2> WITH <exp>...]
2267    7:  //                    [<scope>] [FOR <expL>] [WHILE <expL>]
2268    8:  //
2269    9:  lc_say='Replacing records in file {Sort_File}'
2270   10:  DO info_box WITH lc_say
2271   11:  //
2272   12:  SET TALK ON
2273   13:  *--  Desc: REPLACE records in {Sort_File}.dbf
2274   14:  REPLACE \
```

(continued)

```
2275    15:   {if Repl_fld1} {Repl_fld1} {if Repl_with1} WITH
                    {Repl_with1}{endif}\
2276    16:   {if Repl_Addtv1} ADDITIVE {endif}\
2277    17:   {endif}
2278    18:   {if Repl_fld2}, {Repl_fld2} {if Repl_with2} WITH
                    {Repl_with2}{endif}\
2279    19:   {if Repl_Addtv2} ADDITIVE {endif}\
2280    20:   {endif}
2281    21:   {if Repl_fld3}, {Repl_fld3} {if Repl_with3} WITH
                    {Repl_with3}{endif}\
2282    22:   {if Repl_Addtv3} ADDITIVE {endif}\
2283    23:   {endif}
2284    24:   {if Repl_fld4}, {Repl_fld4} {if Repl_with4} WITH
                    {Repl_with4}{endif}\
2285    25:   {if Repl_Addtv4} ADDITIVE {endif}\
2286    26:   {endif}
2287    27:   {if Repl_fld5}, {Repl_fld5} {if Repl_with5} WITH
                    {Repl_with5}{endif}\
2288    28:   {if Repl_Addtv5} ADDITIVE {endif}\
2289    29:   {endif}
2290    30:   {if Scope} {upper(Scope)} {endif}\
2291    31:   {if While_Exp} WHILE {While_Exp}{endif}\
2292    32:   {if For_Expr} FOR {For_Expr}{endif}\
2293    33:
2294    34:   SET TALK OFF
2295    35:   //
2296    36:   // EOP AD_REPL.COD
2297   289:   {case dele: include "ad_dele.cod";}
2298    1:    // $Header: /a/CCS/apgentc/cod/ad_dele.cod,v 1.7 88/08/16
                    20:38:13 dough Dev $
2299    2:    // Module Name: AD_DELE.COD - Menu_Act = 10
2300    3:    // Selectors  : Scope, For_Expr, While_Exp
2301    4:    // Description: to issue dBASE DELETE command.
2302    5:    // Syntax     : DELETE [<scope>] [FOR <expL>] [WHILE <expL>]
2303    6:    //
2304    7:    lc_say='Marking Records for deletion...'
2305    8:    DO info_box WITH lc_say
2306    9:    SET TALK ON
2307    10:   //
2308    11:   DELETE\
2309    12:   {if Scope} {upper(Scope)} {endif}\
2310    13:   {if For_Expr} FOR {For_Expr}{endif}\
2311    14:   {if While_Exp} WHILE {While_Exp}{endif}\
2312    15:
2313    16:   SET TALK OFF
2314    17:   //
2315    18:   // EOP AD_DELE.COD
2316   290:   {case reca: include "ad_recl.cod";}
2317    1:    // $Header: /a/CCS/apgentc/cod/ad_recl.cod,v 1.6 88/08/16 20:39:06
                    dough Dev $
2318    2:    // Module Name: AD_RECL.COD - Menu_Act = 11
```

(continued)

```
2319     3:  // Selectors  : Scope, For_Expr, While_Exp
2320     4:  // Description: Recall Records marked for deletion.
2321     5:  // Syntax     : RECALL [<scope>] [FOR <expL>] [WHILE <expL>]
2322     6:  //
2323     7:  lc_say='Recalling Records Marked for Deletion...'
2324     8:  DO info_box WITH lc_say
2325     9:  SET TALK ON
2326    10:  //
2327    11:  RECALL\
2328    12:  {if Scope} {upper(Scope)} {endif}\
2329    13:  {if For_Expr} FOR {For_Expr}{endif}\
2330    14:  {if While_Exp} WHILE {While_Exp}{endif}\
2331    15:
2332    16:  SET TALK OFF
2333    17:  //
2334    18:  // EOP AD_RECL.COD
2335   291:  {case pack: include "ad_pack.cod";}
2336     1:  // $Header: /a/CCS/apgentc/cod/ad_pack.cod,v 1.9 88/08/16 20:38:56
                 dough Dev $
2337     2:  // Module Name: AD_PACK.COD - Menu_Act = 12
2338     3:  // Description: Delete and pack
2339     4:  // Syntax     : PACK
2340     5:  //
2341     6:  lc_say='Looking for DELETED Records...'
2342     7:  DO info_box WITH lc_say
2343     8:  //
2344     9:  LOCATE FOR DELETED()
2345    10:  IF .NOT. EOF()
2346    11:     lc_say='Purging DELETED Records...'
2347    12:     DO info_box WITH lc_say
2348    13:     SET TALK ON
2349    14:     PACK
2350    15:     SET TALK OFF
2351    16:     GO TOP
2352    17:  ENDIF
2353    18:  //
2354    19:  // EOP AD_PACK.COD
2355   292:  {case indx: include "ad_ndx.cod";}
2356     1:  // $Header: /a/CCS/apgentc/cod/ad_ndx.cod,v 1.7 88/08/16 20:38:52
                 dough Dev $
2357     2:  // Module Name: AD_NDX.COD - Menu_Act = 13
2358     3:  // Selectors  : NDX_KEY, NDX_File, NDX_Unique, NDX_Descnd,
                 NDX_Tag, NDX_TagIn
2359     4:  // Description: Create a new index file.
2360     5:  // Syntax     : INDEX ON <expKEY> TO <expFN>
2361     6:  //               / [[TAG <expTN>] [OF <expFN>]]
2362     7:  //                 [UNIQUE] [DISTINCT] [DESCENDING]
2363     8:  //
2364     9:  lc_say = 'Indexing '+dbf()+'.dbf on {NDX_KEY}'
2365    10:  DO info_box WITH lc_say
2366    11:  SET TALK ON
2367    12:  //
```

(continued)

```
2368   13:   INDEX ON {NDX_KEY} \
2369   14:   {if NDX_Tag}
2370   15:   TAG {NDX_Tag} OF {NDX_TagIn} \
2371   16:   {else}
2372   17:   TO {NDX_File} \
2373   18:   {endif}
2374   19:   {if NDX_Unique}UNIQUE{endif} \
2375   20:   {if NDX_Descnd}DESCENDING{endif}
2376   21:
2377   22:   //
2378   23:   SET TALK OFF
2379   24:   //
2380   25:   // EOP AD_NDX.COD
2381  293:   {case rndx: include "ad_rndx.cod";}
2382    1:   // $Header: /a/CCS/apgentc/cod/ad_rndx.cod,v 1.4 88/08/16 20:39:20
                dough Dev $
2383    2:   // Module Name: AD_RNDX.COD - Menu_Act = 14
2384    3:   // Description: to issue the dBASE REINDEX command
2385    4:   // Syntax      : REINDEX
2386    5:   //
2387    6:   lc_say='Reindexing Database...'
2388    7:   DO info_box WITH lc_say
2389    8:   SET TALK ON
2390    9:   //
2391   10:   REINDEX
2392   11:   //
2393   12:   SET TALK OFF
2394   13:   //
2395   14:   // EOP AD_RNDX.COD
2396   15:
2397  294:   {case sort: include "ad_sort.cod";}
2398    1:   // $Header: /a/CCS/apgentc/cod/ad_sort.cod,v 1.7 88/08/16 20:39:24
                dough Dev $
2399    2:   // Module Name: AD_SORT.COD - Menu_Act = 15
2400    3:   // Selectors  : Sort_File, SortField*, Sort_Ord*, Sort_Case*
2401    4:   //             : Scope, For_Expr, While_Exp
2402    5:   // Description: to issue the dBASE SORT command
2403    6:   // Syntax      : SORT TO <expFN> ON <field name> [/A] [/C] [/D]
2404    7:   //                     [,<field name> [/A] [/C] [/D]...]
2405    8:   //                     [<scope>] [FOR <expL>] [WHILE <expL>]
2406    9:   //
2407   10:   *--  Desc: SORT records to {Sort_File}.dbf
2408   11:   lc_say='Sorting records to {Sort_File}'
2409   12:   DO info_box WITH lc_say
2410   13:   SET TALK ON
2411   14:   {if Sort_File}
2412   15:   SORT TO {Sort_File} \
2413   16:   { if SortField1}
2414   17:   ON {SortField1}{SUBSTR("/A/D",(Sort_Ord1*2)+1,2)}
                {if Sort_Case1 == 0}C{endif}\
2415   18:   { endif}
2416   19:   { if SortField2}
```

(continued)

```
2417   20:      , {SortField2}{SUBSTR("/A/D",(Sort_Ord2*2)+1,2)}
                 {if Sort_Case2 == 0}C{endif}\
2418   21:   { endif}
2419   22:   { if SortField3}
2420   23:      , {SortField3}{SUBSTR("/A/D",(Sort_Ord3*2)+1,2)}
                 {if Sort_Case3 == 0}C{endif}\
2421   24:   { endif}
2422   25:   { if SortField4}
2423   26:      , {SortField4}{SUBSTR("/A/D",(Sort_Ord4*2)+1,2)}
                 {if Sort_Case4 == 0}C{endif}\
2424   27:   { endif}
2425   28:   { if SortField5}
2426   29:      , {SortField5}{SUBSTR("/A/D",(Sort_Ord5*2)+1,2)}
                 {if Sort_Case5 == 0}C{endif}\
2427   30:   { endif}
2428   31:   {if Scope} {upper(Scope)} {endif}\
2429   32:   {if For_Expr} FOR {For_Expr}{endif}\
2430   33:   {if While_Exp} WHILE {While_Exp}{endif}\
2431   34:
2432   35:   {endif}
2433   36:   //
2434   37:   SET TALK OFF
2435   38:   //
2436   39:   // EOP AD_SORT.COD
2437  295:   {case impt: include "ad_imp.cod";}
2438    1:   // $Header: /a/CCS/apgentc/cod/ad_imp.cod,v 1.12 88/08/16 20:38:32
                 dough Dev $
2439    2:   // Module Name: AD_IMP.COD - Menu_Act = 16
2440    3:   // Selectors  : Imprt_File, Imprt_Type
2441    4:   // Description: to issue the dBASE IMPORT command
2442    5:   // Syntax     : IMPORT FROM <expFN> [TYPE]
2443    6:   //                   DBASEII / DIF / FW2 / PFS / RPD / SYLK / WKS
2444    7:   //
2445    8:   lc_say='Importing records from file {Imprt_file}'
2446    9:   DO info_box WITH lc_say
2447   10:   SET TALK ON
2448   11:   //
2449   12:   IMPORT FROM {Imprt_File} TYPE \
2450   13:   { case Imprt_type of}
2451   14:   { 0:}PFS
2452   15:   { 1:}DBASEII
2453   16:   { 2:}RPD
2454   17:   { 3:}FW2
2455   18:   { 4:}WK1
2456   19:   { endcase}
2457   20:   SET TALK OFF
2458   21:   //
2459   22:   // EOP AD_IMP.COD
2460  296:   {case expt: include "ad_exp.cod";}
2461    1:   // $Header: /a/CCS/apgentc/cod/ad_exp.cod,v 1.11 88/08/16 20:38:22
                 dough Dev $
2462    2:   // Module Name: AD_EXP.COD - Menu_Act = 17
```

(continued)

```
2463     3:  // Selectors  : Exprt_file, Exprt_Type, Scope, For_Expr, While_Exp
2464     4:  // Description: to issue the dBASE EXPORT command
2465     5:  // Syntax     : EXPORT [<scope>] TO <expFN> [FOR <expL>]
                [WHILE <expL>]
2466     6:  //                   [TYPE] DBASEII / FW2 / RPD / PFS
2467     7:  //                   [ FIELD <field name list> ]
2468     8:  //
2469     9:  lc_say='Exporting records to file {Exprt_file}'
2470    10:  DO info_box WITH lc_say
2471    11:  //
2472    12:  SET TALK ON
2473    13:  EXPORT TO {Exprt_file}\
2474    14:  { if Field_List} FIELDS {Field_List}{endif}\
2475    15:  { if Scope} {upper(Scope)} {endif}\
2476    16:  { if For_Expr} FOR {For_Expr}{endif}\
2477    17:  { if While_Exp} WHILE {While_Exp}{endif}\
2478    18:   TYPE \
2479    19:  { case Exprt_type of}
2480    20:  { 0:}PFS
2481    21:  { 1:}dBASEII
2482    22:  { 2:}FW2
2483    23:  { 3:}RPD
2484    24:  { endcase}
2485    25:  SET TALK OFF
2486    26:  //
2487    27:  // EOP AD_EXP.COD
2488    28:
2489   297:  {case fcopy: include "ad_fcopy.cod";}
2490     1:  // $Header: /a/CCS/apgentc/cod/ad_fcopy.cod,v 1.7 88/08/16 20:38:28
                dough Dev $
2491     2:  // Module Name: AD_FCOPY.COD - Menu_Act = 18
2492     3:  // Selectors  : File_from, File_To
2493     4:  // Description: to issue the dBASE COPY FILE command
2494     5:  // Syntax     : COPY FILE <expFN> TO <expFN>
2495     6:  //
2496     7:  lc_say='Copying file {File_from} to {File_To}'
2497     8:  DO info_box WITH lc_say
2498     9:  SET TALK ON
2499    10:  //
2500    11:  COPY FILE \
2501    12:  {if File_from then}{File_from} TO {endif}\
2502    13:  {if File_To then File_To}{endif}\
2503    14:
2504    15:  SET TALK OFF
2505    16:  //
2506    17:  // EOP AD_COPY.COD
2507   298:  {case dodB: include "ad_prog.cod";}
2508     1:  // $Header: /a/CCS/apgentc/cod/ad_prog.cod,v 1.7 88/08/16 20:39:02
                dough Dev $
2509     2:  // Module Name: AD_PROG.COD - Menu_Act = 19
2510     3:  // Selectors  : PRG_File, PRG_Parms
2511     4:  // Description: DO program, optional WITH parameters.
```

(continued)

```
2512    5:  // Syntax     : DO <program filename>/<procedure name>
2513    6:  //                  [WITH <exp list>]
2514    7:  //
2515    8:  DO {PRG_File}{if PRG_Parms} WITH {PRG_Parms}{endif}
2516    9:  //
2517   10:  // EOP AD_PROG.COD
2518  299:  {case indB: include "ad_inln.cod";}
2519    1:  // $Header: /a/CCS/apgentc/cod/ad_inln.cod,v 1.9 88/08/16 20:38:37
                 dough Dev $
2520    2:  // Module Name: AD_INLN.COD - Menu_Act = 20
2521    3:  // Selectors  : Inline_Do
2522    4:  // Description: Embed dBASE code
2523    5:  //
2524    6:  *-- Desc: Inline DO dBASE commands
2525    7:  {foreach Inline_Do j in k}
2526    8:  {  Inline_Do}
2527    9:
2528   10:  {next j;}
2529   11:  //
2530   12:  // EOP AD_INLN.COD
2531  300:  {case xdos: include "ad_xdos.cod";}
2532    1:  // $Header: /a/CCS/apgentc/cod/ad_xdos.cod,v 1.5 88/08/16 20:39:30
                 dough Dev $
2533    2:  // Module Name: AD_XDOS.COD - Menu_Act = 21
2534    3:  // Selectors  : DOS_File, DOS_Parm
2535    4:  // Description: to issue the dBASE RUN command
2536    5:  // Syntax     : RUN <DOS command> [<parameters>]
2537    6:  //
2538    7:  RUN {DOS_File}{if DOS_Parm} {DOS_Parm}{endif}
2539    8:  //
2540    9:  // EOP AD_XDOS.COD
2541  301:  {case call: include "ad_call.cod";}
2542    1:  // $Header: /a/CCS/apgentc/cod/ad_call.cod,v 1.8 88/08/16 20:38:03
                 dough Dev $
2543    2:  // Module Name: AD_CALL.COD - Menu_Act = 22
2544    3:  // Selectors  : Bin_File, Bin_Parms
2545    4:  // Description: to issue the dBASE CALL command
2546    5:  // Syntax     : CALL <module name> [WITH <expc>/<memvar>]
2547    6:  //
2548    7:  *-- Desc:  Load/Call program - {Bin_File}
2549    8:  LOAD {Bin_File}
2550    9:  CALL {Bin_File}{if Bin_Parms} WITH "{Bin_Parms}"{endif}
2551   10:  //
2552   11:  // EOP AD_CALL.COD
2553  302:  {case retu:}
2554  303:  *-- Return to caller
2555  304:  {case quit:}
2556  305:  *-- Quit dBASE
2557  306:  {case batch:}
2558  307:  *-- Batch process
2559  308:  DO {Batch_Name} WITH " "
2560  309:  {case plmac:}
```

(continued)

```
2561   310:   *-- Keyboard macro
2562   311:   PLAY MACRO {Macro_Name}
2563   312:   {otherwise:}
2564   313:   *-- What? ({Fld_Pictur}, action = {Menu_Act})
2565   314:   // end of menu actions
2566   315:   //
2567   316:   {   endcase}
2568   317:   // end of case Menu_Act
2569   318:   //
2570   319:   //
2571   320:   // if window specified deactivate and release it.
2572   321:   //
2573   322:   {if Wndow_Name}
2574   323:   DEACTIVATE WINDOW {Wndow_Name}
2575   324:   RELEASE WINDOW {Wndow_Name}
2576   325:   {else}
2577   326:   {   if Menu_Type != btch && Menu_Act && Menu_Act != open &&
2578   327:       Menu_Act != retu && Menu_Act != quit && Menu_Act != batch then}
2579   328:   {     if Menu_Act == brow || Menu_Act == edit then}
2580   329:   DEACTIVATE WINDOW Browscr
2581   330:   {     else}
2582   331:   DEACTIVATE WINDOW Savescr
2583   332:   {     endif}
2584   333:   {   endif}
2585   334:   {endif}
2586   335:   {if AT(STR(Menu_Act)+",","2,3,7,19,20,") then}
2587   336:   SET SCOREBOARD OFF
2588   337:   {endif}
2589   338:   //
2590   339:   // item after action
2591   340:   //
2592   341:   {   foreach Item_After m in k
2593   342:         if Item_After then
2594   343:            print(rtrim(Item_After)+CHR(10));
2595   344:         endif
2596   345:      next m;}
2597   346:   //
2598   347:   // if the multi user flag is set unlock the database
2599   348:   //
2600   349:   {   if muser then}
2601   350:   IF NETWORK()
2602   351:      UNLOCK
2603   352:   ENDIF
2604   353:   {   endif}
2605   354:   {case Menu_Act of}
2606   355:   {case retu:}
2607   356:   gc_quit='Q'
2608   357:   {   if Menu_Type != btch then}
2609   358:   {     if Menu_Type == popup then}
2610   359:   IF LEFT(entryflg,1) <> "B"
2611   360:      \
2612   361:   {     endif}
```

(continued)

```
2613   362:   DEACTIVATE {if Menu_Type == bar then}MENU {else}POPUP {endif}
                  && {mnuname}
2614   363:   {     if Menu_Type == popup then}
2615   364:   ELSE
2616   365:      DEACTIVATE MENU
2617   366:   ENDIF
2618   367:   {   endif}
2619   368:   { endif}
2620   369:   { if not AT(mtype,"3459") then}
2621   370:   RETURN
2622   371:   { else}
2623   372:   IF .T.
2624   373:      RETURN
2625   374:   ENDIF
2626   375:   { endif}
2627   376:   {case quit:}
2628   377:   CLOSE DATABASES
2629   378:   QUIT
2630   379:   {   endcase}
2631   380:   {   newact:  // get a new action}
2632   381:   { next k;}
2633   382:   // end of loop field
2634   383:   //
2635   384:   //
2636   385:   // if the menu is not a file, structure, value or batch,
2637   386:   // include the dBASE ENDCASE statment and set the choice to none.
2638   387:   //
2639   388:   {if not AT(mtype,"3459") then}
2640   389:   {   LMARG(1);}
2641   390:   {   if Menu_Type == bar then}
2642   391:   OTHERWISE
2643   392:      @ {scrn_size+3},00
2644   393:      @ {scrn_size+3},21 SAY "This item has no action. Press a key."
2645   394:      x=INKEY(0)
2646   395:      @ {scrn_size+3},00
2647   396:   { endif}
2648   397:   ENDCASE
2649   398:   {else}
2650   399:   //
2651   400:   // if the menu is a batch object draw a line of 40 asterisks
2652   401:   //
2653   402:   { if Menu_Type == btch then}
2654   403:   {    replicate("*",10)}
2655   404:
2656   405:   { endif}
2657   406:   {endif}
2658   407:   SET MESSAGE TO
2659   408:   IF SET("STATUS")="ON"
2660   409:      SET STATUS OFF
2661   410:   ENDIF
2662   411:   { if Menu_Type != btch then}
2663   412:   IF gc_quit='Q'
```

(continued)

```
2664   413:    DEACTIVATE {if Menu_Type == bar then}MENU {else}POPUP {endif}
                  && {mnuname}
2665   414:  ENDIF
2666   415:  {  endif}
2667   416:  //
2668   417:  {if Menu_Type != btch then  // not equal to batch process}
2669   418:  IF lc_new='Y'
2670   419:     lc_file="SET"+gc_prognum
2671   420:     DO &lc_file.
2672   421:  ENDIF
2673   422:  {  if Menu_Ovride != 2 then}
2674   423:  {    if itemview+itemndx+itemord then}
2675   424:  IF lc_dbf='Y' .AND. .NOT. lc_new='Y'
2676   425:     lc_file="DBF"+gc_prognum
2677   426:     DO &lc_file.
2678   427:  ENDIF
2679   428:  {    endif}
2680   429:  {  endif}
2681   430:  {endif}
2682   431:  RETURN
2683   432:
2684   695:  //
2685   696:  // Help procedure
2686   697:  //
2687   698:  {include "AS_HELP.COD"}
2688     1:  // $Header: /a/CCS/apgentc/cod/as_help.cod,v 1.22 88/08/17
                  19:55:37 dough Dev $
2689     2:  // Module Name: AS_HELP.COD
2690     3:  // Description: Help procedure file
2691     4:  //
2692     5:  {APPEND("0HLP$$$");}
2693     6:  {count=0;}
2694     7:  {menucnt=0;}
2695     8:  {rowpoint=0;}
2696     9:  *-- help for menu {mnuname}
2697    10:  {foreach FLD_ELEMENT k}
2698    11:  {  count=count+1;}
2699    12:  {  if !Fld_Pictur goto nexthlp;}
2700    13:  {  if !Pldwn_Menu && Menu_Type == bar && Menu_Act == open
                  && Open_Type then}
2701    14:  {    goto nexthlp}
2702    15:  {  endif}
2703    16:  {  if item_help then}
2704    17:  CASE "0{prgcnt}"=gc_prognum .AND. \
2705    18:  {    if Menu_Type == bar then}
2706    19:  PAD() = "PAD_{count}"
2707    20:  {    else}
2708    21:  BAR() \
2709    22:  {      if Menu_Type == popup then}
2710    23:  = {Row_Positn}
2711    24:  {      else}
2712    25:  <> 0
```

(continued)

```
2713    26:  {        endif}
2714    27:  {      endif}
2715    28:  {     rowpoint=itmhlp();}
2716    29:     ln_row=INKEY(0)
2717    30:  {  endif}
2718    31:  {  nexthlp:}
2719    32:  {next k;}
2720    33:  CASE "0{prgcnt}"=gc_prognum
2721    34:  {help_proc();}
2722    35:  {if !menucnt then}
2723    36:     @ 2,2 SAY "No Help defined."
2724    37:     ln_row=INKEY(0)
2725    38:  {else}
2726    39:     ln_row=INKEY(0)
2727    40:  {endif}
2728    41:  // EOP AS_HELP.COD
2729    699:
2730    700: {next mtree;}
2731    701: //
2732    702: // End of fortree loop
2733    703: //
2734    704: {APPEND(appl_name+".PRG");}
2735    705: @ {scrn_size+2},00 CLEAR
2736    706: RETURN
2737    707: *-- EOP: MPDEF.PRG
2738    708:
2739    709: {COPY("0HLP$$$");}
2740    710: //
2741    711: // Bottom half of help
2742    712: //
2743    713: ENDCASE
2744    714: SET ESCAPE {IF set_escape}OFF{ELSE}ON{ENDIF}
2745    715: @ {scrn_size+3},00
2746    716: DEACTIVATE WINDOW Helpscr
2747    717: RETURN
2748    718: {fileerase("0HLP$$$");}
2749    719: *-- EOP: 1HELP1
2750    720: {pause("Generation is complete -- press any key to continue");}
2751    721: //
2752    722: {NoGen:}
2753    723: //
2754    724: {return 0;}
2755    725: //----------------------------------
2756    726: // User defined function include file.
2757    727: //----------------------------------
2758    728: {include "as_udf.cod";}
2759    1:   // $Header: /a/CCS/apgentc/cod/as_udf.cod,v 1.44 88/08/17 19:58:42
                  dough Dev $
2760    2:   // Module name: as_udf.cod
2761    3:   // Description: Apgen User defined functions
2762    4:   //
2763    5:   {define dbfOpen(mdbf,mndx,mord,actflag)
```

(continued)

```
2764     6:    var tempext, // temporary extension
2765     7:          filestr  // file string
2766     8:  ;
2767     9:   tempext="";
2768    10:   filestr="";
2769    11:  //
2770    12:   if mdbf and (filetype(mdbf) == "DBF" || !filetype(mdbf)) then
2771    13:     tempext=".DBF";
2772    14:   else
2773    15:     if mdbf then
2774    16:        tempext="."+filetype(mdbf);
2775    17:     endif
2776    18:   endif
2777    19:  //
2778    20:   filestr="Error opening ";
2779    21:   if mdbf then
2780    22:     filestr=filestr+fileroot(mdbf)+tempext;
2781    23:   endif
2782    24:   if mndx then
2783    25:     if mdbf then
2784    26:        filestr=filestr+" or ";
2785    27:     endif
2786    28:     filestr=filestr+"index(es) "+upper(mndx);
2787    29:   endif}
2788    30:  lc_message="0"
2789    31:  ON ERROR lc_message=LTRIM(STR(ERROR()))+" "+MESSAGE()
2790    32:  {if tempext == ".VUE" || tempext == ".QBE" || tempext == ".QBO"
                then}
2791    33:  SET VIEW TO {mdbf}
2792    34:  {else}
2793    35:  {  if tempext == ".UPD" then}
2794    36:  DO {mdbf}
2795    37:  {  else}
2796    38:  USE {mdbf}
2797    39:  {  endif}
2798    40:  {endif}
2799    41:  {if mndx then}
2800    42:  IF "" <> DBF()
2801    43:     SET INDEX TO {mndx}
2802    44:  ENDIF
2803    45:  {endif}
2804    46:  {if mord then}
2805    47:  SET ORDER TO {mord}
2806    48:  {endif}
2807    49:  ON ERROR
2808    50:  gn_error=VAL(lc_message)
2809    51:  IF gn_error > 0
2810    52:     DO Pause WITH ;
2811    53:     "{filestr}"
2812    54:  {case actflag of}
2813    55:  {0:}
2814    56:     gn_error=0
```

(continued)

```
2815   57:     lc_file="SET"+gc_prognum
2816   58:     DO &lc_file.
2817   59:     RETURN
2818   60:   {1:}
2819   61:     lc_new='Y'
2820   62:     RETURN
2821   63:   {endcase}
2822   64:   ENDIF
2823   65:   lc_new='Y'
2824   66:   RELEASE lc_message
2825   67:   {return;
2826   68:    enddef;
2827   69:   }
2828   70:   //
2829   71:   // UDF to handle item level help.
2830   72:   //
2831   73:   {define itmhlp();}
2832   74:   {var hlprcnt;}
2833   75:   {hlprcnt=1;  // line counter}
2834   76:   {foreach Item_Help m in k}
2835   77:   {   if ALLTRIM(Item_Help) then}
2836   78:      @ {hlprcnt+1},1 SAY "{Item_Help}"
2837   79:   {   endif}
2838   80:   {   ++hlprcnt;}
2839   81:   {   if hlprcnt > 19 then}
2840   82:   {      hlprcnt=1;}
2841   83:   {   endif}
2842   84:   {next m;}
2843   85:   {return hlprcnt;}
2844   86:   {enddef;}
2845   87:   //
2846   88:   // UDF to handle Text in Before and After code embeds and Menu
                 help.
2847   89:   //
2848   90:   {define help_proc();}
2849   91:   {var hlprcnt;}
2850   92:   {hlprcnt=0;  // line counter}
2851   93:   {foreach Menu_Help}
2852   94:   {   if not hlprcnt then hlprcnt=1 endif;}
2853   95:   {   if ALLTRIM(Menu_Help) then}
2854   96:      @ {hlprcnt+1},1 SAY "{Menu_Help}"
2855   97:   {   endif}
2856   98:   {   ++hlprcnt;}
2857   99:   {   if hlprcnt > 19 then}
2858  100:   {      hlprcnt=1;}
2859  101:   {   endif}
2860  102:   {next k;}
2861  103:   {menucnt=hlprcnt;}
2862  104:   {return;}
2863  105:   {enddef;}
2864  106:   //
2865  107:   {
```

(continued)

```
2866   108:   define color(getcolor);
2867   109:   var blink, forground, background, enhanced, incolor;
2868   110:   //
2869   111:   forground = background = enhanced = 0;
2870   112:   //
2871   113:   if getcolor != 255 then                    // black on black?
2872   114:     blink = getcolor >> 7;                    // high order bit
                                                             set?
2873   115:     if blink then
2874   116:       getcolor = getcolor - 128;              // set high order
                                                             bit to zero
2875   117:     endif
2876   118:     background = getcolor >> 4;               // getcolor divided
                                                             by 16
2877   119:     forground  = getcolor - (background << 4); // (background times
                                                             16)
2878   120:     if forground > 7 then                     // high intensity?
2879   121:       enhanced = 1;
2880   122:       forground = forground - 8;
2881   123:     endif
2882   124:   endif
2883   125:   case forground of
2884   126:   0: incolor = "N";
2885   127:   1: incolor = "B";
2886   128:   2: incolor = "G";
2887   129:   3: incolor = "BG";
2888   130:   4: incolor = "R";
2889   131:   5: incolor = "RB";
2890   132:   6: incolor = "GR";
2891   133:   7: incolor = "W";
2892   134:   endcase
2893   135:   if blink then incolor = incolor + "*"; endif
2894   136:   if enhanced then
2895   137:     incolor = incolor + "+/";
2896   138:   else
2897   139:     incolor = incolor + "/";
2898   140:   endif
2899   141:   case background of
2900   142:   0: incolor = incolor + "N";
2901   143:   1: incolor = incolor + "B";
2902   144:   2: incolor = incolor + "G";
2903   145:   3: incolor = incolor + "BG";
2904   146:   4: incolor = incolor + "R";
2905   147:   5: incolor = incolor + "RB";
2906   148:   6: incolor = incolor + "GR";
2907   149:   7: incolor = incolor + "W";
2908   150:   endcase
2909   151:   return incolor;
2910   152:   enddef;
2911   153:   }
2912   154:   {define itemover(cursor);
2913   155:   //
```

(continued)

```
2914    156:  // these routines set a flag variable to indicate whether
2915    157:  // an item in the menu has an overide to the menu database.
2916    158:  // -------------------------------------------------------
2917    159:  // item database/view
2918    160:  //
2919    161:      if (not itemview) then
2920    162:          if cursor.Item_View and (cursor.Item_View != Menu_View) then
2921    163:             itemview=1;
2922    164:          endif
2923    165:        endif
2924    166:  //
2925    167:  // item index
2926    168:  //
2927    169:      if (not itemndx) then
2928    170:          if cursor.Item_NDX and (cursor.Item_NDX != Menu_NDX) then
2929    171:             itemndx=1;
2930    172:          endif
2931    173:        endif
2932    174:  //
2933    175:  // item index order
2934    176:  //
2935    177:      if (not itemord) then
2936    178:          if cursor.Item_Order and (cursor.Item_Order != Menu_Order)
                        then
2937    179:             itemord=1;
2938    180:          endif
2939    181:        endif
2940    182:  // -------------------------------------------------------
2941    183:  //
2942    184:   return;
2943    185:  enddef
2944    186:  }
2945    187:  {define nul2zero(number);
2946    188:   if !number then
2947    189:      number=0;
2948    190:   endif
2949    191:   return number;
2950    192:   enddef
2951    193:  }
2952    194:  // EOP AS_UDF.COD
2953    729:  //Eop As_menu.cod
2954 Compilation complete (no errors).
2955
```

Chapter 9

Documenting Your Applications

dBASE IV includes a reasonably good template for documenting your applications. It works with objects from the applications generator to produce reasonably good documentation. Although not as elegant as CLEAR (CLEAR Software, Brookline, MA), which prints flow charts, or as voluminous as The Documentor (Wallsoft Systems, New York, NY), or as tightly integrated as Symmetry IV (Symmetry Software, Chestnut Hill, MA), the dBASE IV documentation template is nevertheless much better than nothing at all. And it's specifically designed to work with the applications generator, making it a lot more efficient than general purpose documentation programs that must read all the code to figure out how it fits together.

This chapter will focus on using the documentation template DOCU-MENT.GEN. Those interested in a detailed analysis should look at Chapter 2 of the dBASE IV template language manual. The documentation program is used for the tutorial.

The documentation template includes a number of programs. The main program is DS_DOC.COD. Any source code file that starts with DS_ or DD_ is used to produce DOCUMENT.GEN.

I strongly recommend that you compile a new DOCUMENT.GEN and send the results to an output file. Just give the following command:

```
dtc -i ds_doc.cod -o \dbase\document.gen -1 document.out
```

Next, print the file DOCUMENT.OUT using the MODIFY COMMAND editor with line numbering turned on. You'll probably want to do this in compressed print mode, as some of the lines in the file are much longer than 80 characters.

The line numbers referenced to in this chapter should be pretty close to those you're looking at in your listed file.

Of far more interest is the appendix, which is the documentation for CUSTAPP, the customer application developed in the previous chapter. We'll look at this in some detail to see the kinds of information you can get from DOCUMENT.GEN.

Using the Documentation Template

Using DOCUMENT.GEN is about as simple as anything you'll ever do. First, load your application into the applications generator either by highlighting it in the Control Center and pressing Shift-F2 or by typing "MODIFY APPLICATION <application name>" from the dot prompt. Don't make any changes! This is important because if you change the application, your documentation won't match the program itself. Instead, press Alt-G to select "Generate." Turn "Display during generation" off (select NO), then move the bar to "Select template." Type in "DOCUMENT.GEN" and press Enter. Finally, select "Begin generation."

Warning! Danger!
The applications generator will remember the last GEN file you specified in the Generate/Select template menu. This happens even if you QUIT dBASE IV and shut off the computer. Be sure to set the file name back to MENU.GEN before you leave the applications generator. Otherwise, you may find yourself generating documentation when you wanted program code!

If a documentation file with the same name already exists, you'll be asked if you want to overwrite it. Of far more interest is the next question: Do you have an IBM graphics compatible printer? If you answer Y, the output file will contain all boxes and other IBM-extended graphics characters the way IBM defines the top half of the ASCII table. If you answer N, your output will look like that shown in the appendix to this chapter. Boxes, lines, and other characters will be approximated with regular nongraphics characters.

The documentation will be written to a file named "<application name>.DOC" in the same directory as the application. For example, the documentation file in the appendix was stored as "CUSTAPP.DOC." Line numbers are not included. Add them using the MODIFY COMMAND editor print-option to turn line numbers on before printing.

Before you exit the applications generator, be sure to reset the template to MENU.GEN. dBASE IV remembers the last template you used and will use it as the default the next time, so it's a good idea to reset the default yourself. Otherwise you'll find yourself producing documentation when you really wanted program code!

Handling Screens

One of the most interesting aspects of DS_DOC.COD is its ability to dump screen displays to an output file. Let's look at how this is handled.

Consider the first screen in CUSTAPP.DOC: the sign-on banner.

```
13 Screen Image:
14    0         10        20        30        40        50        60        70
15    >.....+....|....+....|....+....|....+....|....+....|....+....|....+....|....+.
16 00:
17 01:
18 02:
19 03:
20 04:
21 05:        #==========================================================#
22 06:        "                                                          "
23 07:        "                                                          "
24 08:        "                  Customer Application                    "
25 09:        "                                                          "
26 10:        "  Copyright, 1989, Pacific System Design Workshop, Inc.   "
27 11:        "                                                          "
28 12:        "                                                          "
29 13:        "                                                          "
30 14:        "                                                          "
31 15:        "                                                          "
32 16:        #==========================================================#
```

This and other screens are written to the file using the appropriately named template user defined function SCRNDUMP(), contained on lines 1145–1286.

Actually, SCRNDUMP() is the first UDF in the file DS_UDF.COD, included in DS_DOC.COD starting at line 1139:

```
1139    438:    include "ds_udf.cod";
1140      1:    // $Header: /a/CCS/apgentc/cod/ds_udf.cod,v 1.21 88/08/02 10:11:55
                   kirkn Dev $:
1141      2:    // Module Name: DS_UDF.COD
1142      3:    // Description: UDF's used in the system
1143      4:    //
1144      5:    {
1145      6:      define scrndump();
```

After initializing three variables, the phrase "Screen Image:" is output to the file on line 1152. This is followed by a ruler line on the next two lines. After that, SCRNDUMP() INCLUDEs the file DS_BOX.COD, which handles IBM graphics characters. The variable graph_prt, referenced on line 1155, is set to 1 if you answered YES to the question of having an IBM graphics compatible printer, 0 if NO. If you don't have an IBM printer or just don't care about IBM graphics characters, I recommend removing the question (lines 282–290) and the INCLUDE statement on line 1156. However, be sure you set graph_prt to 0 on line 290.

```
1146      7:
1147      8:    // This udf dumps the object image to the output stream with a
                   ruler line.
1148      9:
1149     10:    cnt = 0;
1150     11:    forflag = barflag = 1; // same as .T.
1151     12:    }
1152     13:    Screen Image:
1153     14:        0         10        20        30        40        50        60        70
1154     15:    >.....+....|....+....|....+....|....+....|....+....|....+....|....+....|....+....|
1155     16:    {if graph_prt then
1156     17:      // call graphics screen dump.
1157     18:      include "ds_box.cod";
1158      1:    // $Header: /a/CCS/apgentc/cod/ds_box.cod,v 1.13 88/08/02 10:11:22
                   kirkn Dev $:
1159      2:    // Module Name: DS_BOX.COD
1160      3:    // Description: Used to build graphics boxes for IBM compatible
                   printers
```

```
1161    4:  //
1162    5:  {//  This is a template language verison of SCREEN() - so that we
            can output
1163    6:  //  graphics characters around boxes.
1164    7:
```

The next two lines determine where to place the box on the screen. The function COL1() used in line 1166 returns the number of the first column of an object frame. If there is no frame on the screen, it returns a 0. Similarly, the function COL2() returns the number of the last column of a frame, returning a value of 79 if there is no frame. Thus, with no frame on screen, the full screen coordinates are used.

Lines 1168–1174 add a leading 0 to the variable linecnt if it is less than 10, thus preserving string length at two.

```
1165    8:      do while cnt < scrn_size
1166    9:        line = space(col1());
1167    10:
1168    11:       if cnt < 10 and barflag then
1169    12:           linecnt = "0"+str(cnt);
1170    13:        else
1171    14:          if barflag then // bar flag test for processing a bar menu
1172    15:              linecnt = str(cnt);
1173    16:          endif
1174    17:       endif
1175    18:
```

Similarly, the ROW1() and ROW2() functions return the top and bottom row numbers of a frame. Values of 0 and 24 are returned if there is no frame on screen. If you routinely use 43-line EGA screens, you may want to substitute your own default value for that of the ROW2() function.

The selector Mnu_border contains the following values:

0:    Single line
1:    Double line
2:    Panel
3:    No border

The CHR() function returns extended ASCII characters in the same way the CHR() function does in dBASE IV.

```
1176   19:       if cnt == row1() then  // START OF BOX
1177   20:         case Mnu_Border of
1178   21:            0: line=line+chr(219)+replicate(chr(219),
                          (col2()-col1())-1)+chr(219);
1179   22:            1: line=line+chr(218)+replicate(chr(196),
                          (col2()-col1())-1)+chr(191);
1180   23:            2: line=line+chr(201)+replicate(chr(205),
                          (col2()-col1())-1)+chr(187);
1181   24:            3: line=line+" "+replicate(" ",(col2()-col1())-1)+" ";
1182   25:         endcase
1183   26:       endif
1184   27:
1185   28:       if cnt == row2() then // END OF BOX
1186   29:         case Mnu_Border of
1187   30:            0: line=line+chr(219)+replicate(chr(219),
                          (col2()-col1())-1)+chr(219);
1188   31:            1: line=line+chr(192)+replicate(chr(196),
                          (col2()-col1())-1)+chr(217);
1189   32:            2: line=line+chr(200)+replicate(chr(205),
                          (col2()-col1())-1)+chr(188);
1190   33:            3: line=line+" "+replicate(" ",(col2()-col1())-1)+" ";
1191   34:         endcase
1192   35:       endif
1193   36:
```

Next, the lines between the two box rows have to be processes. The
GET_BOX_TEXT() UDF on line 1203 returns any text on the line in question. Line 1217 outputs a line number, a colon, and the line contents assem-
bled previously.

```
1194   37:       if cnt > row1() and cnt < row2() then   // Lines between box
1195   38:
1196   39:         // Test to see if we processed fields or lines of text yet
1197   40.         if forflag then
1198   41:
1199   42:           if Menu_Type == app then // if app process text lines
1200   43:               foreach Text_Element tline
1201   44:                 skipline:
1202   45:                 if row1()+Row_Positn == cnt then // on a line of text
1203   46:                    get_box_text(line,linecnt,text_item,col_positn);
1204   47:                 else // this is a blank line in object
```

```
1205   48:              line = space(col1());
1206   49:              case Mnu_Border of
1207   50:                  0: line=line+chr(219)+replicate(" ",
                              (col2()-col1())-1)+chr(219);
1208   51:                  1: line=line+chr(179)+replicate(" ",
                              (col2()-col1())-1)+chr(179);
1209   52:                  2: line=line+chr(186)+replicate(" ",
                              (col2()-col1())-1)+chr(186);
1210   53:                  3: line=line+" "+replicate(" ",
                              (col2()-col1())-1)+" ";
1211   54:              endcase
1212   55:              if cnt < 10 then
1213   56:                  linecnt = "0"+str(cnt);
1214   57:              else
1215   58:                  linecnt = str(cnt);
1216   59:              endif
1217   60:              print(substr(linecnt+":"+line,1,80)+crlf);
1218   61:              ++cnt;
1219   62:              goto skipline;
1220   63:            endif
1221   64:          next tline;
1222   65:
```

If this is not a text object, the program must process fields. The Fld_pictur selector returns the picture for the field.

```
1223   66:          else // Process fields in object
1224   67:              foreach Fld_Element flds
1225   68:                  get_box_text(line,linecnt,Fld_Pictur,col_positn);
1226   69:              next flds;
1227   70:          endif
1228   71:
```

Next, the program goes through the same procedure for bar menus. On line 1239, if it isn't a bar menu or text menu, it must be a pop-up of some sort. Other than that, the processing is straightforward.

```
1229   72:          if Menu_Type == bar then
1230   73:              mspace2 = space((col2()-len(line)));
1231   74:              case Mnu_Border of
1232   75:                  0: line = line + mspace2 + chr(219);
```

```
1233  76:                1: line = line + mspace2 + chr(179);
1234  77:                2: line = line + mspace2 + chr(186);
1235  78:                3: line = line + mspace2 + " ";
1236  79:             endcase
1237  80:             print(substr(linecnt+":"+line,1,80)+crlf);
1238  81:          endif
1239  82:       else
1240  83:          if Menu_Type != bar then
1241  84:             case Mnu_Border of
1242  85:                0: line=line+chr(219)+replicate(" ",
                           (col2()-col1())-1)+chr(219);
1243  86:                1: line=line+chr(179)+replicate(" ",
                           (col2()-col1())-1)+chr(179);
1244  87:                2: line=line+chr(186)+replicate(" ",
                           (col2()-col1())-1)+chr(186);
1245  88:                3: line=line+" "+replicate(" ",(col2()-col1())-1)+" ";
1246  89:             endcase
1247  90:             print(substr(linecnt+":"+line,1,80)+crlf);
1248  91:          endif
1249  92:          ++cnt;
1250  93:       endif // forflag
1251  94:
1252  95:       forflag=0;
1253  96:       loop;
1254  97:    endif // cnt > row1() and cnt < row2() then
1255  98:
1256  99:    if line > row2() then
1257 100:       line = "";
1258 101:    endif
1259 102:
1260 103:    if cnt < 10 then
1261 104:       linecnt = "0"+str(cnt);
1262 105:    else
1263 106:       linecnt = str(cnt);
1264 107:    endif
1265 108:
1266 109:    print(substr(linecnt+":"+line,1,80)+crlf);
1267 110:    ++cnt;
1268 111:    enddo
1269 112: }
1270 113: // EOP DS_BOX.COD
```

On the other hand, if we aren't using an IBM compatible printer, the program has to use straight ASCII characters. The built-in function SCREEN(<expN>) returns the ASCII string for screen line number <expN>. Thus, this code is straightforward when compared to the code to handle IBM graphics characters. For complex applications, processing will be considerably faster if you're willing to forego those graphics characters in the output file.

```
1271   19:   else
1272   20:     // call ascii screen dump.
1273   21:     do while cnt < scrn_size
1274   22:        line = SCREEN(cnt);
1275   23:        if cnt < 10 then
1276   24:           linecnt = "0"+str(cnt);
1277   25:        else
1278   26:           linecnt = str(cnt);
1279   27:        endif
1280   28:        print(substr(linecnt+":"+line,1,80)+crlf);
1281   29:        ++cnt;
1282   30:     enddo
1283   31:   endif // if graph_prt
1284   32:   print("   >.....+....|....+....|....+....|....+....|....+....|
                ....+....|....+....|....+."+crlf);
1285   33:   return;
1286   34: enddef;
1287   35: }
```

Conclusion

DOCUMENT.GEN is really pretty simple, but extremely useful. Even if you never change a line of the template code, it's still very useful to remind you what screens look like, which menus fit with which, and what actions go with each menu. Read Appendix A to see what kind of information you get from this template.

Appendix

CUSTAPP.DOC

```
 1 Page: 1  Date: 4-26-89
 2
 3
 4 Application Documentation for System: CUSTAPP.PRG
 5
 6 Application Author: Tony Lima
 7 Copyright Notice..: Copyright, 1989, Pacific System Design Workshop, Inc.
 8 dBASE Version.....: 1.0
 9
10
11 Display Application Sign-On Banner: Yes
12
13 Screen Image:
14     0         10        20        30        40        50        60        70
15   >.....+....|....+....|....+....|....+....|....+....|....+....|....+....|....+.
16 00:
17 01:
18 02:
19 03:
20 04:
21 05:        #==============================================================#
22 06:        "                                                              "
23 07:        "                                                              "
24 08:        "                     Customer Application                     "
25 09:        "                                                              "
26 10:        "    Copyright, 1989, Pacific System Design Workshop, Inc.     "
27 11:        "                                                              "
28 12:        "                                                              "
29 13:        "                                                              "
30 14:        "                                                              "
31 15:        "                                                              "
32 16:        #==============================================================#
33 17:
34 18:
35 19:
36 20:
37 21:
38 22:
39 23:
40 24:
41   >.....+....|....+....|....+....|....+....|....+....|....+....|....+....|....+.
42
43 Main Menu to Open after Sign-On: CUSTABAR.BAR
44
45 Sets for Application:
```

(continued)

```
46  --------------------
47   Bell          ON    Frequency 220 Duration 2
48   Carry         OFF
49   Centry        OFF
50   Confirm       OFF
51   Delimiters    OFF
52   Display Size 25 lines
53   Drive
54   Escape        ON
55   Path
56   Safety        OFF
57
58  Starting Colors for Application:
59  -------------------------------
60   Color Settings:
61     Text          : W+/B
62     Heading       : GR+/B
63     Highlight     : B+/W
64
65
66  Page: 2  Date: 4-26-89  6:38a
67
68     Box           : R/W
69     Messages      : R/B
70     Information   : RB/W
71     Fields        : N/W
72
73  Database/View: CUSTOMER
74  Index Order: CUSTCODE
75
76  =============================================================================
77
78  Menu/Picklist definitions follow:
79  ---------------------------------
80
81
82  Page: 3  Date: 4-26-89
83
84  Layout Report for Horizontal Bar Menu: CUSTABAR
85  -----------------------------------------------
86
87  Screen Image:
88    0          10        20        30        40        50        60        70
89    >.....+....|....+....|....+....|....+....|....+....|....+....|....+....|....+.
90  00:#=========================================================================
91  01:"Add      Browse    Move pointer    Set new key    Reports   Backup    Exit
92  02:#=========================================================================
93  03:
94  04:
95  05:
96  06:
97  07:
```

(continued)

```
 98 08:
 99 09:
100 10:
101 11:
102 12:
103 13:
104 14:
105 15:
106 16:
107 17:
108 18:
109 19:
110 20:
111 21:
112 22:
113 23:
114 24:
115   >.....+....|....+....|....+....|....+....|....+....|....+....|....+....|....+.
116
117 Setup for CUSTABAR follows:
118 --------------------------
119
120  Description: Customer Application Main Menu
121  Message Line Prompt for Menu: Select the activity you wish to perform
122
123 Colors for Menu/Picklist:
124 ------------------------
125  Color Settings:
126    Text         : W+/B
127    Heading      : GR+/B
128    Highlight    : B+/W
129    Box          : R/W
130    Messages     : R/B
131    Information   : RB/W
132    Fields       : N/W
133
134
135 Bar actions for Menu CUSTABAR follow:
136 ------------------------------------
137 Bar: 1
138  Prompt: Add
139  Action: APPEND
140  Format File: cust2pg2.fmt
141
142
143  Page: 4  Date: 4-26-89  6:39a
144
145  Message Line Prompt for Item: Add records to the Customer file.
146 ----------------------------------------------------------------------------
147
148 Bar: 2
149  Prompt: Browse
```

(continued)

```
150  Action: Browse File
151  Command Options:
152   NOAPPEND  NOFOLLOW  NODELETE  NOEDIT
153
154  Message Line Prompt for Item: Browse Customer Records
155  --------------------------------------------------------------------------
156
157 Bar: 3
158  Prompt: Move pointer
159  Action: EDIT
160  Command Options:
161   NOFOLLOW  NOAPPEND  NODELETE
162  Format File: cust2pg2.fmt
163  Position Record Pointer by: Do Procedure - Position
164  Message Line Prompt for Item: Locate and display a record.  (You may want
     to Select new key first.)
165  --------------------------------------------------------------------------
166
167 Bar: 4
168  Prompt: Set new key
169  Action: Run dBASE Program: DO KEYSET.PRG
170  Message Line Prompt for Item: Select a new index key.  A menu of available
     indexes will be displayed.
171  --------------------------------------------------------------------------
172
173 Bar: 5
174  Prompt: Reports
175  Action: Open a Popup Menu Named: CUSTPREP
176  --------------------------------------------------------------------------
177
178 Bar: 6
179  Prompt: Backup
180  Action: Copy Records to File backup
181  Command Options:
182   SCOPE NEXT 100
183  Message Line Prompt for Item: Copy Customer database to BACKUP.DBF.
184  --------------------------------------------------------------------------
185
186 Bar: 7
187  Prompt: Exit
188  Action: Return to calling program
189  Message Line Prompt for Item: Return to dBASE IV
190  --------------------------------------------------------------------------
191
192
193
194 Page: 5  Date: 4-26-89
195
196 Layout Report for Popup Menu: CUSTPREP
197  ------------------------------------
198
199 Screen Image:
```

(continued)

```
200     0         10        20        30        40        50        60        70
201   >.....+....|....+....|....+....|....+....|....+....|....+....|....+....|....+.
202 00:
203 01:
204 02:                                                        #====================#
205 03:                                                        "Customer Balances    "
206 04:                                                        "Customer Information"
207 05:                                                        #====================#
208 06:
209 07:
210 08:
211 09:
212 10:
213 11:
214 12:
215 13:
216 14:
217 15:
218 16:
219 17:
220 18:
221 19:
222 20:
223 21:
224 22:
225 23:
226 24:
227   >.....+....|....+....|....+....|....+....|....+....|....+....|....+....|....+.
228
229 Setup for CUSTPREP follows:
230 -------------------------
231
232   Description: Customer Reports Menu
233   Message Line Prompt for Menu: Select a Report
234
235 Colors for Menu/Picklist:
236 ------------------------
237   Color Settings:
238     Text          : W+/B
239     Heading       : GR+/B
240     Highlight     : B+/W
241     Box           : R/W
242     Messages      : R/B
243     Information   : RB/W
244     Fields        : N/W
245
246
247 Bar actions for Menu CUSTPREP follow:
248 ------------------------------------
249 Bar: 1
250   Prompt: Customer Balances
251   Action: Run Report Form CUST4FLD.frm
```

(continued)

```
252  Command Options:
253   PLAIN
254
255
256  Page: 6  Date: 4-26-89  6:40a
257
258   NOEJECT
259  Print Mode: Send to Default Printer
260  Set Order To BALANCE
261  Message Line Prompt for Item: Report on Customer Balances
262  ---------------------------------------------------------------------------
263
264 Bar: 2
265  Prompt: Customer Information
266  Action: Run Report Form CUSTOMER.frm
267  Command Options:
268   PLAIN
269
270  Print Mode: Send to Default Printer
271  Set Order To CUSTCODE
272  Message Line Prompt for Item: Customer Name, Address, Phone
273  ---------------------------------------------------------------------------
274
275
276 End of Application Documentation
277
```

Part III

Special Template Language Features

There are several template language features that do not fit into either objects or applications but need to be discussed. The first is a special template not really documented anywhere, FORMBROW.GEN. This template allows you to browse multiple tables on the same screen. It will give you some idea of the true power of the template language.

Second, the template language includes a compiler and interpreter/debugger. Chapter 11 will discuss how to use them both and how to insert debugging commands into template programs.

Chapter 10

A Special Template: FORMBROW.GEN

The template FORMBROW.GEN and its source code file is included with the sample data disk (installed in the SAMPLES subdirectory under the directory where you installed dBASE IV). FORMBROW is interesting because it allows you to develop multitable screen forms, a feature that has been highly touted for Paradox 3.0 and DataEase 4.0.

In this chapter, we'll see how to use FORMBROW to build a multitable form. We'll use three databases: CUSTOMER, INVOICE, and INVNTORY. CUSTOMER is related to INVOICE via the CUSTCODE field. This is a one-to-many relation. INVOICE is related to INVNTORY via the ITEMCODE field. Our objective is to display and edit item descriptions for each invoice for each customer.

Appendix A is a listing of CUSTINV.SCX, a special program file generated by FORMBROW. Appendix B contains the source code for the query required by the template. Appendix C is the source code listing for the main program, CUSTINV.PRG. We'll refer to parts of these programs but won't discuss them in great detail, focusing instead on how to use FORMBROW and modifications you might want to make. Be sure to print a copy of FORMBROW.COD with line numbers for reference use.

One final note: There is a limited amount of documentation of FORMBROW in the file INVOICE2.DOC included with the samples disk. If you want to see how FORMBROW works, use it with the sample data as suggested in the documentation. We'll concentrate on building a new form instead.

451

Using FORMBROW

The strategy is simple. First, set up a query relating the first two databases (CUSTOMER and INVOICE). Then, with this query as the open file, create a new screen form. Include fields from both files as you wish, then draw a box on the screen. Put the word "BROWSETABLE" on the first empty line of the box, save the form, and answer the questions the template asks during generation.

This is not too difficult, but all the same there are some tricks along the way that will save you some grief.

The first thing is to trick dBASE IV into using FORMBROW.GEN instead of FORM.GEN. Do this the easy way. In your dBASE IV directory, create a batch file called DFB.BAT. It has two commands:

```
SET DTL_FORM=FORMBROW.GEN
DBASE/T
```

The SET command substitutes FORMBROW.GEN for FORM.GEN. Note that this is a DOS SET command, not a dBASE SET.

If you don't want to put FORMBROW.GEN in your dBASE IV main directory, change the first line of the batch file to read

```
SET DTL_FORM=<DOS path>\FORMBROW.GEN
```

To start dBASE IV with FORMBROW.GEN active, just type DFB from the directory containing your data.

Second, FORMBROW generates code that loads the keyboard macro file INVOICE2.KEY. Be sure this file is in the directory with the data and screen form files. We'll see how these macros are used later in this chapter.

Design the Query

Next, we're going to design the query. It should have the same name as the form since the two names are used somewhat interchangeably. Figure 10-1 shows a query linking INVOICE and CUSTOMER. Although you can't see them, there are fields included from both databases. (Take a look at the SET FIELDS command in Appendix B for the complete list.)

The query can be one-to-one or one-to-many. This query is set up so each invoice will be displayed in numerical order. INVOICE is the parent database and CUSTOMER is the child.

```
 Layout    Fields    Condition    Update    Exit              11:29:54 am
┌──────────┬────────────────────────┬────────────────┬─────────────────────┐
│Invoice.dbf│ CUSTCODE               │↓INVOICENO      │↓ITEMCODE            │
├──────────┤└────────────────────────┴────────────────┴─────────────────────┤
│          │ EVERY LINK1            │                │                     │
├──────────┼────────────────────────┼────────────────┼─────────────────────┤
│Customer.dbf│↓CUSTCODE              │↓NAME           │↓ADDRESS1            │
├──────────┤│                        │                │                     │
│          │ LINK1                 │                │                     │
└──────────┴────────────────────────┴────────────────┴─────────────────────┘

 ┌View─────────┬──────────┬──────────┬──────────┬──────────┐
 │<NEW>        │Invoice─> │Invoice─> │Invoice─> │Invoice─> │
 │             │ITEMCODE  │PRICE     │QUANTITY  │EXTPRICE  │
 └─────────────┴──────────┴──────────┴──────────┴──────────┘

 Query    C:\db4\data\<NEW>        File 2/2                        CapsIns
   Next field:Tab  Add/Remove all fields:F5  Zoom:F9  Prev/Next skeleton:F3/F4
```

Figure 10-1   CUSTINV.QBE Query

If you wanted to simply see all invoices for a single customer and not include a third table, a simple modification to FORMBROW.COD will handle this.

Design the Form

The next step is to design a screen form. With the query active, create a screen form. Add fields from both databases in the top half of the screen. Then draw a box in the bottom part of the screen. Put the word "BROWSETABLE" in this box as shown in Figure 10-2.

When the screen is the way you want it, select "Exit/Save." You should see the word "FORMBROW.GEN" appear on the status bar. Then, after a few seconds, you'll see the questions shown in Figures 10-3 through 10-6. The database name in Figure 10-3 should be INVNTORY, although it isn't filled in there.

Note that only one field (DESCRIPT) is listed in Figure 10-4. If you want more fields, separate their names with commas. And make sure you have the structure of the database on hand, since no help is available at this point!

```
  Layout    Fields    Words    Go To    Exit              11:56:54 am
  [····▼·1····▼·2·▼····3·▼·········▼····▼·5····▼···6··▼····7·▼·····]

  Cust ID  XXXXXXXXXX   Name  XXXXXXXXXXXXXXXXXXXXXXXXXXXX
  Contact  XXXXXXXXXXXXXXXXXXXX       Telephone  XXXXXXXXXXXXXXXXXX
  Invoice #  XXXXX   Item Code  XXXXX
  Price    999.99  x  Quantity  999.999  =  Ext.Price  999999999.99



        BROWSETABLE




  Form    C:\db4\data\CUSTINV      Row:8 Col:17      View:CUSTINV      CapsIns
            Add field:F5  Select:F6  Move:F7  Copy:F8  Size:Shift-F7
```

Figure 10-2   CUSTINV Screen Form

```
                                                          11:57:42 am




  Please define your Browse table by answering the following questions.
  If you make an error, you will have a chance to correct your responses.


    Enter line item table name for browse (.dbf assumed) (required)






  CodeGen   C:\db4\FORMBROW.GEN      Lines: 0        CUSTINV
```

Figure 10-3   Line Item Database Name

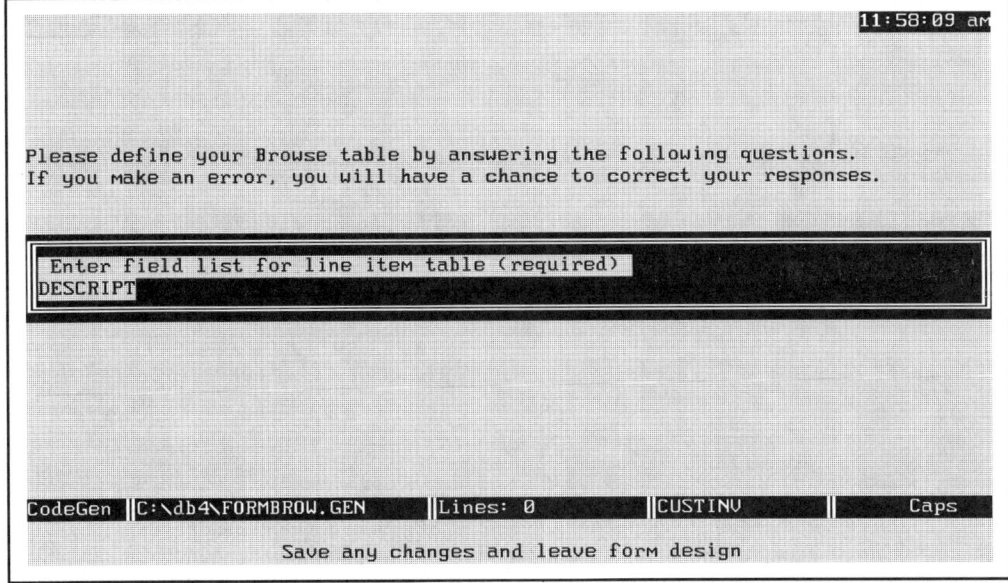

Figure 10-4   Field List for Line Item Table

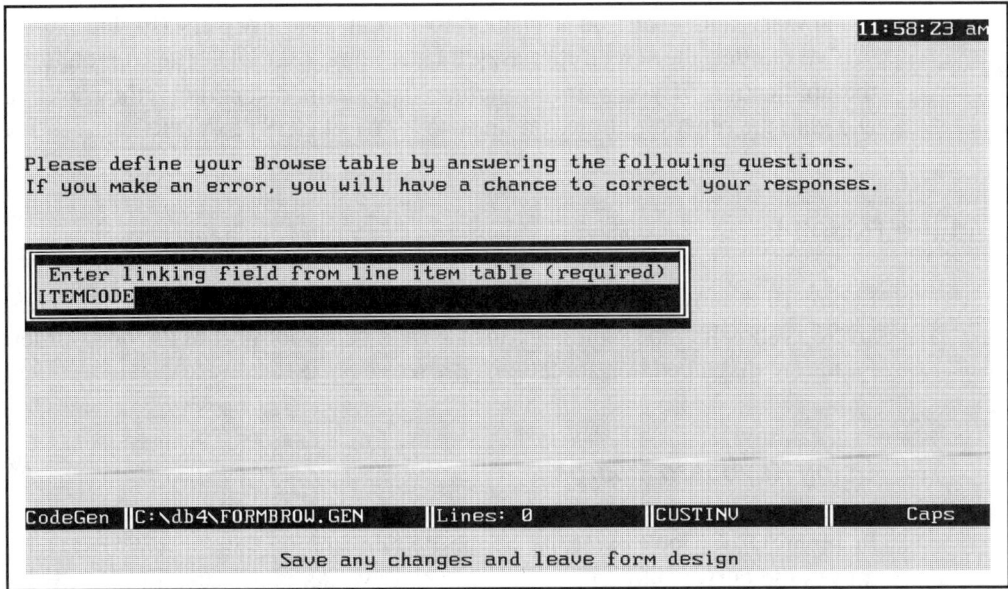

Figure 10-5   Linking Field from Line Item (Child) Table

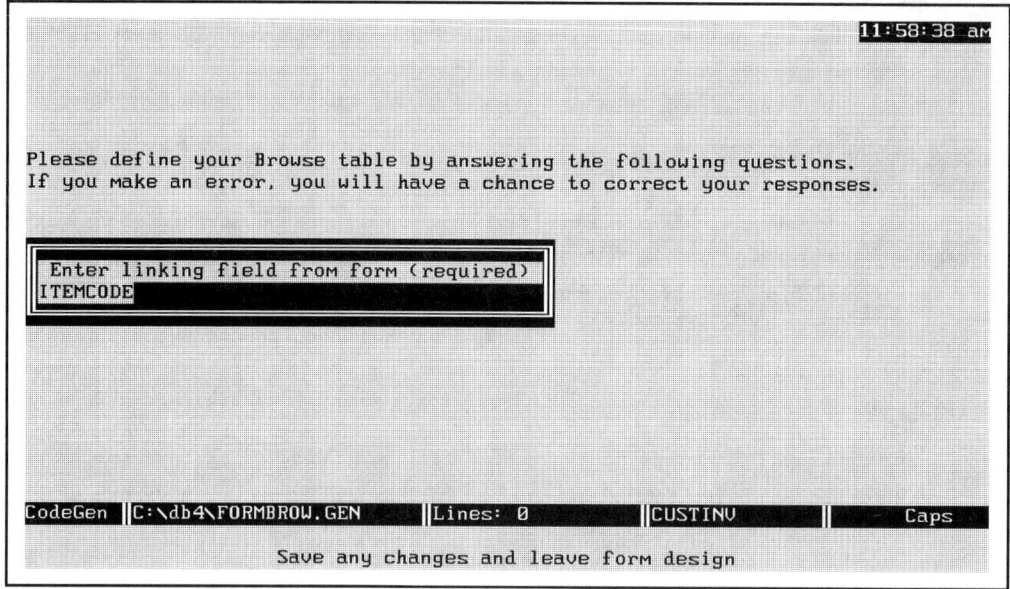

Figure 10-6   Linking Field from Screen Form (Parent) Table

When you've answered these four questions, FORMBROW will show you a summary and give you a chance to repeat your answers (Figure 10-7). We've omitted the screen that asks for the name of a UDF file to include in the application. If you want to include user-defined functions, they will be added to the function library on lines 457–467 of CUSTINV.PRG.

And the Result Is . . .

Figure 10-8 shows the result of this process. The description for item code GPSS is shown in the window with the field name above it in the box border. Fields are displayed horizontally in Browse format.

Using Keyboard Macros

In Figure 10-8, look carefully at the bottom line of the form. Pressing F9 moves the cursor into and out of the window. As is the case in dBASE IV itself, pressing F10 gives access to the menu bar. However, these seemingly simple activities are a little more complicated than they appear on the surface.

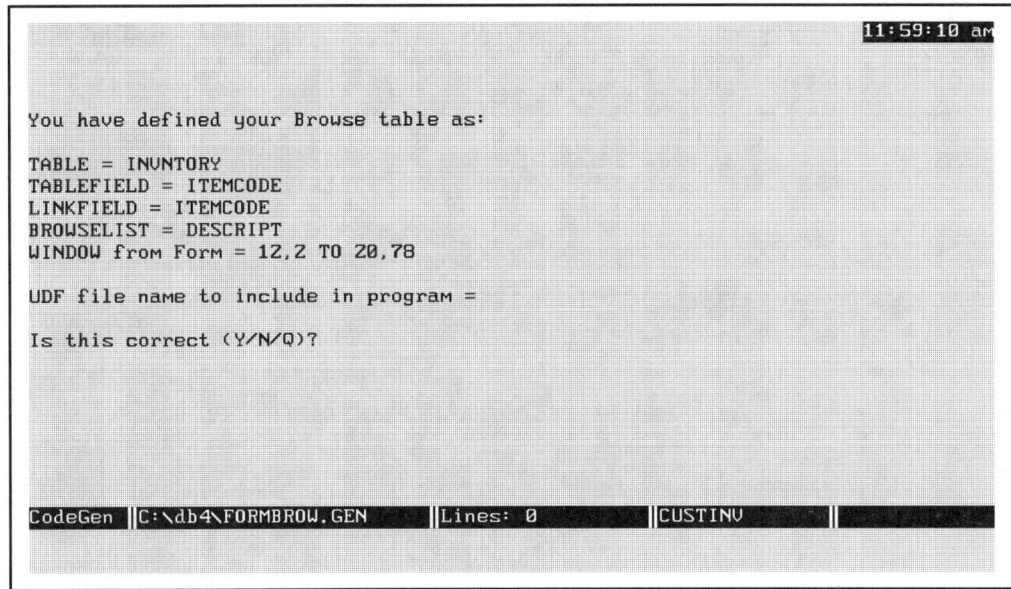

Figure 10-7   Line Item Table Summary Information

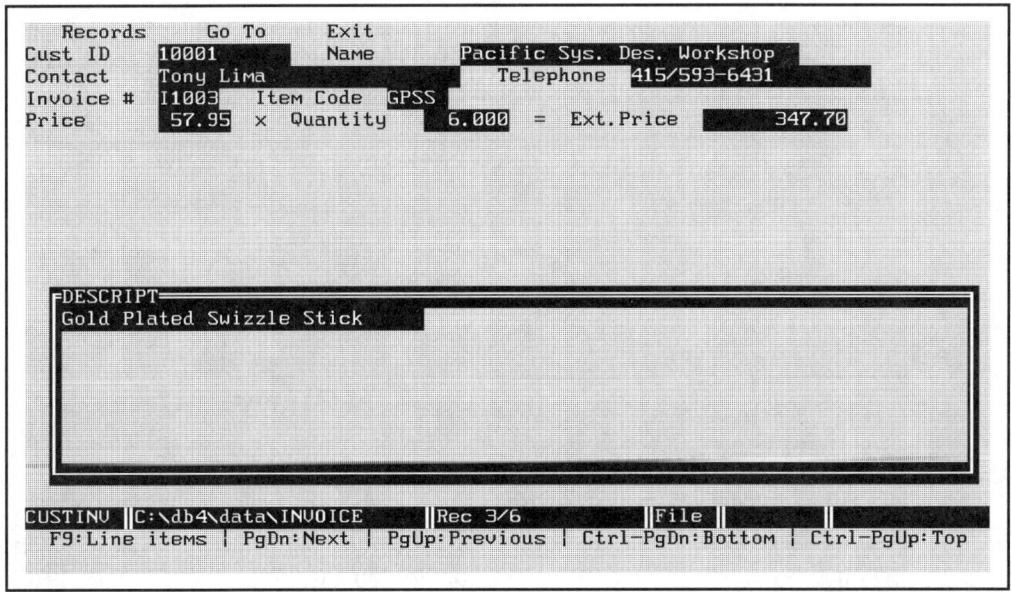

Figure 10-8   Screen Form with Browse Table

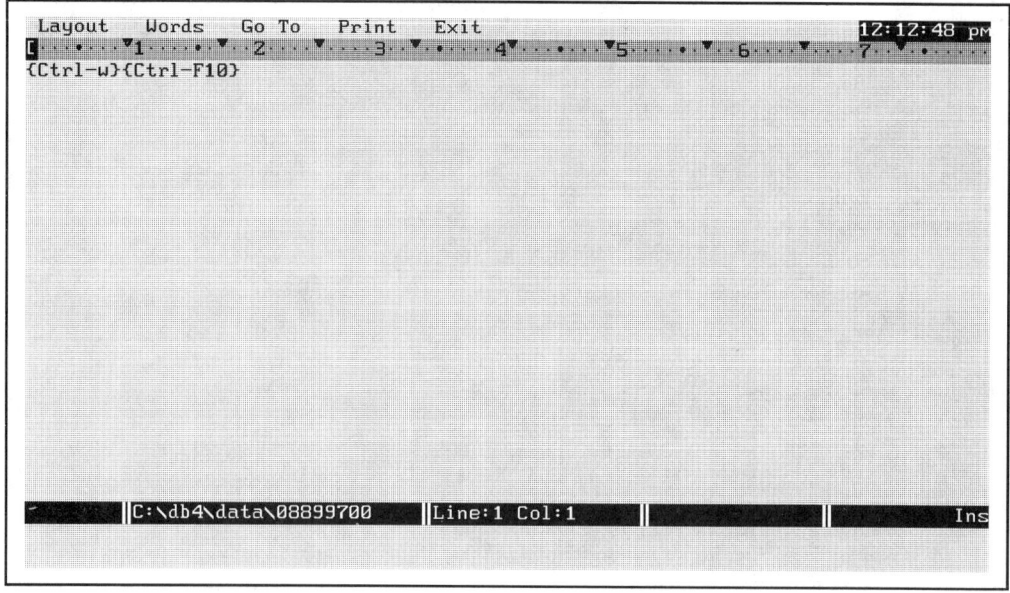

Figure 10-9   MENU Macro

Figure 10-9 shows the keyboard macro named MENU, while 10-10 shows
LINEITEM. (A third macro, EXIT_BROW, emulates pressing the Escape
key, but it is never used. If you want, you can assign it to a function key as
shown here.)

Lines 17 and 58–59 in CUSTINV.PRG show how the macros are used.

```
17 RESTORE MACROS FROM Invoice2

         .

         .

         .

58 ON KEY LABEL F9 PLAY MACRO Lineitem
60 ON KEY LABEL F10 PLAY MACRO Menu
```

When the user presses F10, dBASE IV treats this as Ctrl-W, Ctrl-F10. This
saves the current record and brings up an emulation of the menu bar created
with the procedure Defnmenu that begins on line 506 of CUSTINV.PRG
(Appendix C). Pressing F9 is the same as pressing Ctrl-W, Ctrl-F8, which
moves into the Browse window.

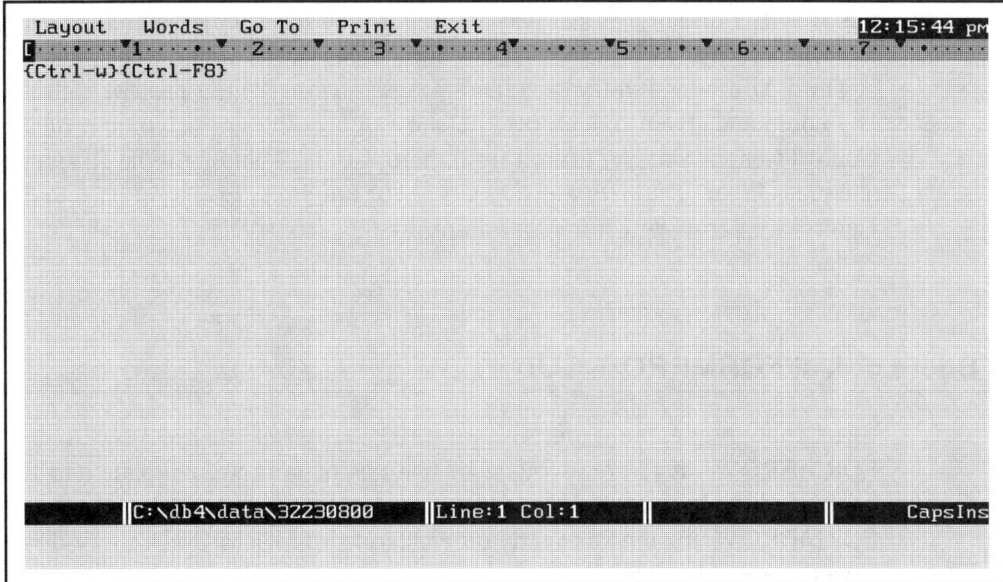

Figure 10-10   LINEITEM Macro

Minor Fixes

There are a couple of minor fixes that should be made to FORMBROW.COD, although it works fairly well already.

First, consider lines 69–73 of CUSTINV.PRG. Clearly, the syntax in line 71 is redundant. "USE INVNTORY ORDER ITEMCODE" will to the job as well. This code is generated from line 408 of FORMBROW.COD. Change it.

```
69 gn_sele = IIF(SELE()=10, SELE()-1, SELE())
70 SELE (gn_sele)
71 USE INVNTORY ORDER TAG ITEMCODE
72 SET FIELDS TO ITEMCODE, DESCRIPT
73 SET CARRY TO INVNTORY->ITEMCODE
```

Second, what about that file CUSTINV.SCX? It is processed (or produced) in lines 181–238 of FORMBROW.COD. Take a look at that code and you'll quickly see that if the SCX file already exists, the questions that set it up are bypassed. This means that if you want to change the list of fields in the browse window, for example, you have two choices. First, you can delete the SCX file and answer the questions during code generation. Or (better) you can edit the SCX file directly. Either way, however, you have to do something with this file before any changes will be written to the output program.

Third, you must run the generated program from the dot prompt with the DO command. Even though the file shows up in the Forms column of the Control Center, you can't run it from there. Try it — highlight the file name and press Enter. The error message is kind of fun. Press Esc to get back to the Control Center when you're done admiring the error screen.

A Brief Look at FORMBROW.COD

Even though the main purpose of this chapter is to see how to use FORMBROW, there are a couple of features of both the template and the generated code that bear more examination. The first 118 lines of FORMBROW are almost exactly duplicated from FORM.COD, so we don't have to look at them at all.

The BROWSETABLE Box

From line 119 to 141 the program searches for the BROWSETABLE box and builds variables for the box to be output in the FMT file.Once the BROWSETABLE box has been found (line 124), the if statement builds the other box variables.

```
119  // Look for Box with BROWSETABLE on it
120  foreach box_element b;
121    if row_positn-line_cnt  scrn_size then   exit   endif
122    boxrow = nul2zero(box_top)-line_cnt;
123    foreach text_element t;
124      if boxrow == row_positn and upper(alltrim(text_item)) ==
           "BROWSETABLE" then
125        table_wndeep = box_height - 3;
126        table_window = str(nul2zero(box_top)-line_cnt) + "," +
127           str(nul2zero(box_left)) + " TO " +
128           str(nul2zero(box_top)+box_height-line_cnt-1) +"," +
129           str(nul2zero(box_left)+box_width-1);
130      case box_type of
131        0: table_window = table_window + " ";
```

```
132                  1: table_window = table_window + " DOUBLE";
133                  2: table_window = table_window + " CHR(" +
                          BOX_SPECIAL_CHAR + ")";
134          endcase
135 //           color = getcolor(b.fld_display, b.fld_editable);
136 //           if LEN(color)  0 then
137 //             table_window = table_window + " COLOR " + color
                      +","+color;
138 //           endif
139        endif
140    next t;
141  next b;
```

Define the SCX File

Next, the program checks for the presence of an SCX file. This file defines the
Browse table relations and fields. If the SCX file isn't there, the questions to
define the file are presented to the user one at a time.

```
142  // Browse table design file open
143  open = Textopen(fmt_name+".SCX");
144  if not open then
145     do while (input_flg != "Y") or !table or
146        !table_field or !link_field or !browse_fields
147        input_flg="Z";
148        cls();
149        cursor_pos(6,0);
150        cput("Please define your Browse table by answering the
                 following questions.");
151        cursor_pos(7,0);
152        cput("If you make an error, you will have a chance to
                 correct your responses.");
153        table = askuser(" Enter line item table name for browse
                 (.dbf assumed) (required) ",table,8);
154        browse_fields = askuser(" Enter field list for line
                 item table (required) ",browse_fields,78);
155        table_field = askuser(" Enter linking field from line
                 item table (required) ",table_field,10);
156        link_field = askuser(" Enter linking field from form
                 (required) ",link_field,10);
```

```
157        udf_file = askuser(" Enter UDF file name to include in
              this program (optional) ",udf_file,78);
158        cls();
159        cursor_pos(4,0);  cput("You have defined your Browse
              table as:");
160        cursor_pos(6,0);  cput("TABLE = "+table);
161        cursor_pos(7,0);  cput("TABLEFIELD = "+table_field);
162        cursor_pos(8,0);  cput("LINKFIELD = "+link_field);
163        cursor_pos(9,0);  cput("BROWSELIST = "+browse_fields);
164        cursor_pos(10,0); cput("WINDOW from Form = "+
              table_window);
165        cursor_pos(12,0); cput("UDF file name to include in
              program = "+udf_file);
166        cursor_pos(14,0); cput("Is this correct (Y/N/Q)?");
167        cursor_pos(14,25);
168        do while at(input_flg,"YNQ") == 0
169            input_flg=upper(chr(cget()));
170        enddo
```

After this, there is a straightforward block of code that builds the SCX file. I recommend a simple modification to FORMBROW allows you to modify the SCX file at runtime. Lines 209–238 handle the situation when an SCX file already exists.

```
209  else
210     // There was a .SCX file for this form so read it
211     do
212      temp = textgetl();
213     while temp != eof
214        temp = ltrim(upper(temp));
215        if at("BROWSETABLE",temp) == 1 then
216          table = alltrim(substr(temp,at("=",temp)+1,len(temp)));
217        endif
218        if at("TABLEFIELD",temp) == 1 then
219          table_field = alltrim(substr(temp,at("=",temp)+1,
                len(temp)));
220        endif
221        if at("LINKFIELD",temp) == 1 then
222          link_field = alltrim(substr(temp,at("=",temp)+1,
                len(temp)));
223        endif
```

```
224        if at("FIELDLIST",temp) == 1 then
225          table_fields = alltrim(substr(temp,at("=",temp)+1,
               len(temp)));
226        endif
227        if at("BROWSELIST",temp) == 1 then
228          browse_fields = alltrim(substr(temp,at("=",temp)+1,
               len(temp)));
229        endif
230        if at("FNKEY",temp) == 1 then
231          func_key = alltrim(substr(temp,at("=",temp)+1,
               len(temp)));
232        endif
233        if at("UDF_FILE",temp) == 1 then
234          udf_file = alltrim(substr(temp,at("=",temp)+1,
               len(temp)));
235        endif
236      enddo
237    endif
238    textclose();
```

The function TEXTGETl() reads the SCX file in one line at a time. The series of IF statements after that process each line, assigning the table, field, and other names to variables. Note that the order in which the different objects are assigned in the SCX file doesn't matter, since they are processed by name. That is, if you reverse the order of the BROWSETABLE= and TABLEFIELD= commands in the SCX file, it won't make any difference to FORMBROW.

I recommend adding a question and some code between lines 143 and 144. The code should look like this:

```
{if open then;
VAR tlscx;
tlscx=ASKUSER("Do you want to use the existing SCX file (Y/N)?",
            "Y",1);
if tlscx != "Y" then;
  open = 0;
endif;
endif;}
```

This will, of course, require the user to enter all the information again without reference to existing data in the SCX file. A more elaborate approach is to add some code between lines 237 and 238 that allows the user to modify existing values of the five variables. This is not difficult. Here's an example using TABLEFIELD:

```
{VAR tltblfld;
 tltblfld=ASKUSER("Enter new fields list: ",table_field,254);
 table_field=tltblfld;}
```

Be sure to use different variable names for each field element. Note that we don't have to use the TABLEFIELD keyword since lines 215–217 have stripped it from the fields list.

The File Headers

As usual, you'll want to change the file headers. Lines 243–270 define these. In doing so, change the message on line 243 so it doesn't refer to invoices specifically. One solution is to replace it with the variable table created from the SCX file.

```
243  nmsg("Generating invoice program "+fileroot(fmt_name)+ " with
         line items");
244  print(replicate("*",80)+crlf);
245 }
246 *-- Name....: Stub {fileroot(fmt_name)}.FMT for
         {fileroot(fmt_name)}.prg
247 *-- Date....: {ltrim(SUBSTR(date(),1,8))}
248 *-- Version.: dBASE IV, Format {Frame_ver}.0
249 *-- Notes...: Format files use "" as delimiters!
250 {print(replicate("*",80)+crlf);}
251 @ 1,0 TO 21,79
252 @ 3,3 TO 19,76
253 @ 5,6 TO 17,73
254 @ 7,9 TO 15,70
255 @ 9,24 SAY "Stub format file for {fileroot(fmt_name)}.PRG"
256 @ 11,20 SAY "Type DO {fileroot(fmt_name)}.PRG from the dot
         prompt"
257 @ 12,20 SAY "to run this Multi File form program"
258 SET FORMAT TO
259 {
260  if not create(fmt_name+".PRG") then
```

```
261      pause(fileroot(fmt_name) +".PRG" + read_only + any_key);
262      goto nogen;
263  endif
264  print(replicate("*",80)+crlf);}
265 *-- Name....: {fileroot(fmt_name)}.PRG
266 *-- Date....: {ltrim(substr(date(),1,8))}
267 *-- Version.: dBASE IV, Format {Frame_ver}.0
268 *-- Notes...: Format files use "" as delimiters!
269 {print(replicate("*",80)+crlf);}
270 //
```

As usual, change the two file headers to reflect your personal programming style.

Keyboard Macros

You'll probably want to use your own keyboard macro file. Line 286 outputs the code to load the existing file INVOICE2.KEY. If you use your own macros, start by copying this file to a new file, with the name you want, so existing macros used by the program aren't lost!

```
286 RESTORE MACROS FROM Invoice2
```

GETQBE()

There's a user defined function called GETQBE(). It is used to read the QBE file that links the first two data tables. Line 306 contains the call to this UDF:

```
306    getqbe(); // APGEN UDF to read dBASE IV .qbe file
```

The UDF itself is contained in lines 1205–1244 of FORMBROW.COD. (It's the last UDF if your line numbers don't match.) Let's take a quick look at GETQBE(). Basically, it reads the QBE file one line at a time with the TEXTGETl() function, storing the results in the variable temp (line 1208).

```
1205  define getqbe();
1206    print("*-- Imported code from " + fmt_name + ".QBE" + crlf);
1207    do
1208        temp = textgetl();
```

Line 1210 checks for the end of a file condition to terminate the UDF processing loop. Line 1211 uses ALLTRIM() and UPPER() to remove all leading and trailing blanks from temp and convert it to upper case.

```
1209          // Need textgetl() by itself so WHILE comparsion works
              ok
1210              while temp != eof
1211                  temp = alltrim( upper( temp));
```

The rest of the UDF is a series of IF statements that check for the presence of various keywords in the line of QBE code being read. Lines 1212–1215 check for a SELECT, SET RELATION, or DBASE command. (My best guess is that the clause that checks for DBASE is looking for ! DBASE.)

```
1212          if at("SELECT",temp) == 1 or at("DBASE",temp) == 3 or
1213                              at("RELATION",temp) == 5  then
1214                              print(temp + crlf);
1215          endif
```

Lines 1216–1230 check for a USE command, then look for ORDER, IN, and AGAIN clauses. Part of the purpose of this exercise is to strip out the keyword AGAIN if it's there. (In version 1.0 of dBASE IV, the AGAIN clause sometimes caused the error message "File is already open" even if all files were closed — certainly a good reason to remove AGAIN from the output file!)

```
1216          if at("USE",temp) == 1 then
1217              if at("ORDER",temp) == 0 and at(" IN ",temp) == 0
                  then
1218                print(substr( temp, 1,
                      at("AGAIN",temp)-1)+crlf);
1219              else if at("ORDER",temp) > 0 and at(" IN ",temp)
                  > 0 then
1220                temp = substr( temp, 1, at("AGAIN",temp)-1) +
1221                    substr( temp, at(" IN ",temp)+1);
1222                    print(temp + crlf);
1223                            else if
                              at("ORDER",temp) <> 0 and
                              at(" IN ",temp) == 0 then
1224                temp = substr( temp, 1, at("AGAIN",temp)-1) +
```

```
1225                              substr( temp, at("ORDER",temp));
1226                         print(temp + crlf);
1227                                     endif
1228                                     endif
1229             endif
1230        endif
```

Lines 1231–1239 check for the SET FIELDS command and check for a semicolon continuation character, outputting the appropriate line(s) of text.

```
1231           if at("FIELDS",temp) == 5 then
1232             if at(";", temp)   0 then
1233                do while at(";", temp)   0
1234                     print(temp+crlf);
1235                   temp = upper(alltrim(textgetl()));
1236                enddo
1237             endif
1238             print(temp+crlf);
1239          endif
1240   enddo
1241 textclose();
1242 return;
1243 enddef
1244 }
```

That's all there is to GETQBE(). It's purpose is to convert a QBE file into straight program code. You can probably use a similar UDF in many of your applications.

Lines 311–335 are straight out of FORM.COD, defining the screen type and STATUS. Line 337 defines a menu bar for the program to use and outputs it to the file.

```
337 gc_messg = "{func_key}:Line items | PgDn:Next | PgUp:Previous
       | Ctrl-PgDn:Bottom | Ctrl-PgUp:Top"
```

Keyboard Macros Redux

Having opened the macro file, the program has to tell dBASE what to do with those keys.

```
365 ON KEY LABEL F1 DO {helpproc}
366 ON KEY LABEL {func_key} PLAY MACRO Lineitem
367 ON KEY LABEL F10 PLAY MACRO Menu
```

Fix the CARRY Bug

Lines 379–380 reproduce the minor bug we saw earlier in FORM.COD.

```
379             carry_len = carry_len + len(fld_fieldname + ",");
380             carry_lent = carry_lent + carry_len;
```

Change line 380 to read:

```
carry_lent = carry_lent + len(fld_fieldname + ",");
```

SELECT, SET FIELDS and SET CARRY

Line 406 uses the SELECT() function to check to see whether work area 10 has an open file in it.

```
406 gn_sele = IIF(SELE()=10, SELE()-1, SELE())
407 SELE (gn_sele)
408 USE {table} ORDER TAG {table_field}
```

If work area 10 is the currently selected area, work area 9 is opened instead. This is directly derived from QBE, which occasionally opens work area 10 but never uses area 9. If you're incorporating FORMBROW into a larger system, you'll want to use a more general test to find an unused work area. Try this dBASE IV code to find the first available work area:

```
gn_sele=1
SELECT (gn_sele)
lc_dbf=DBF()
DO WHILE LEN(lc_dbf) > 0
  gn_sele = gn_sele + 1
  SELECT (gn_sele)
  lc_dbf=DBF()
ENDDO
```

At the end of this loop, gn_sele will contain the number of the first available work area. Also, note that line 408 contains the phrase ORDER TAG, a holdover from pre-release versions of dBASE IV. Remove the word TAG.

The SET FIELDS command generated here is interesting. If you leave TABLEFIELDS blank, then all fields are included in the browse table.

```
409 SET FIELDS TO \
410 {if table_fields then}
411 {table_field}, {table_fields}
412 {else}
413 ALL EXCEPT {table_field}
414 {endif}
415 SET CARRY TO {table}->{table_field}
```

The interesting syntax is SET FIELDS TO ALL EXCEPT <field name>, new to dBASE IV.

BEGIN TRANSACTION

Line 434 adds transaction processing to the program:

```
434 BEGIN TRANSACTION
```

Lines 508–520 check to see if the user selected ROLLBACK from the menu. If so, a rollback is attempted to reverse all changes made to the current record. The ROLLBACK() function checks to see if the attempt was successful, sending a message to the screen if it didn't take.

```
508 IF gl_rollbck              && If user picked ROLLBACK option
                                  from menu
509    gl_rollbck = .F.        && Reset rollback variable
510    ROLLBACK
511 ENDIF
512 {lmarg(4);}
513 ENDDO
514 *
515 END TRANSACTION
516 *
```

```
517 IF .NOT. ROLLBACK()
518    DO Pause WITH "Undo not successful"
519    ACTIVATE SCREEN
520 ENDIF
```

Transactions rollback is a convenient way to manage an undo. You could modify this slightly to allow the user to make changes permanent or undo all changes made to date quite easily. Just move the BEGIN TRANSACTION command so it comes before any record processing. Add an item to the Records menu (defined starting at line 1038) to "Make all changes permanent". If the user selects that option, just have the program execute the command END TRANSACTION. Note that lines 1040–1041 define the menu option in the records menu to perform the rollback.

```
1039    DEFINE POPUP records FROM 1,0
1040      DEFINE BAR 1 OF records PROMPT "   Undo change
            to record";
1041      MESSAGE "Undo Change to current record"
```

SAYing, GETting, and BROWSEing

The three procedures that are the key to this are Show_get, Edit_get, and Showbrow. The first two are straightforward implementations borrowed from FORM.COD. Show_get is created on lines 563–666, while Edit_get is defined in lines 668–737. Showbrow (lines 743–763) is far more interesting:

```
743 PROCEDURE Showbrow
744 {lmarg(4);}
745 SELE {table}
746 SET FILTER TO
747 SEEK &GC_ALIAS.-{link_field}
748 IF EOF()
749    APPEND BLANK
750    REPLACE {table}-{table_field} WITH &GC_ALIAS.-{link_field}
751 ENDIF
752 SET FILTER TO &GC_ALIAS.-{link_field} = {table}-{table_field}
753 GO TOP
754 PLAY MACRO exit_brow
755 BROWSE;
756 {if browse_fields then}
```

```
757   FIELDS {browse_fields};
758 {endif}
759   WINDOW table COMPRESS NOMENU NOCLEAR
760 SELE &gc_alias.
761 ACTIVATE SCREEN
762 {lmarg(0);}
763 RETURN
```

The most absorbing part of this code is line 759. Using the NOCLEAR clause leaves the browse table on the screen after the user moves back to the master part of the form. NOMENU is interesting because the BROWSE menu appears at the top of the screen when the cursor is moved into the browse window. This menu is actually emulated by the menu system that starts on line 1030. The master light bar menu is editmenu. The popups include records, go_to, and exit. Thus, the user has access to a restricted form of the BROWSE menu.

Also note the command ACTIVATE SCREEN, which restores full-screen operations regardless of the number of currently open windows.

Procedure Keykill

An interesting set of procedures is used to turn off the function key operations. Line 768 calls the procedure:

```
768 DO Keykill
```

Keykill, and the procedure it calls, Nothing, are defined on lines 798–806. The procedure Nothing simply grabs a keystroke via INKEY() and stores it into a memory variable, which it then ignores. Use this setup the next time you want to turn off keys you have defined with ON KEY.

```
798 PROCEDURE Keykill
799    ON KEY LABEL F1 DO Nothing
800    ON KEY LABEL {func_key} DO Nothing
801    ON KEY LABEL F10 DO Nothing
802 RETURN
803
804 PROCEDURE Nothing
805    ln_key=INKEY()
806 RETURN
```

There is also a procedure called Keyset that turns the function key operations back on:

```
792 PROCEDURE Keyset
793    ON KEY LABEL F1 DO {helpproc}
794    ON KEY LABEL {func_key} PLAY MACRO Lineitem
795    ON KEY LABEL F10 PLAY MACRO Menu
796 RETURN
```

Summary

The real key to the operation of FORMBROW is the availability of keyboard macros that can be used to move the cursor around the screen without user intervention. Transaction rollback is used cleverly to emulate a super-undo. As we saw, we could even give the user the option to undo all changes made up to the previous "save changes" operation. FORMBROW should give you plenty of interesting ideas for your own templates. Study its structure and see how the pieces fit together.

Conclusion

This chapter has illustrated the use of FORMBROW, a multitable screen form generator. I recommend reading the code carefully to see exactly how it works. Many useful templates can be easily created with simple changes to this program.

Appendix A

CUSTINV.SCX

```
 1 **************************************************************************
 2 *-- Name: C:\DB4\DATA\CUSTINV.SCX - dBASE IV Line Item data file
 3 *-- Date:   4-26-89 11:59a
 4 *-- Created from: C:\DB4\DATA\CUSTINV.SCR
 5 *-- Used as extended design information for: C:\DB4\DATA\CUSTINV.PRG
 6 **************************************************************************
 7 BROWSETABLE=invntory
 8 TABLEFIELD=itemcode
 9 LINKFIELD=itemcode
10 BROWSELIST=descript
11 FNKEY=F9
12 UDF_FILE=
13 FIELDLIST=DESCRIPT
14
```

Appendix B

CUSTINV.QBE

```
 1 * dBASE IV .QBE file
 2 SET FIELDS TO
 3 SELECT 1
 4 USE INVOICE.DBF AGAIN NOUPDATE
 5 USE CUSTOMER.DBF AGAIN NOUPDATE IN 2 ORDER CUSTCODE
 6 SET EXACT ON
 7 SET FILTER TO
 8 SET RELATION TO A->CUSTCODE INTO B
 9 SET SKIP TO B
10 GO TOP
11 SET FIELDS TO B->CUSTCODE,B->NAME,B->CONTACT,B->TELEPHONE,A->INVOICENO,A;
12 ->ITEMCODE,A->PRICE,A->QUANTITY,A->EXTPRICE,B->ADDRESS1,B->ADDRESS2,B->;
13 CITY,B->STATE,B->ZIP,B->SALES,B->TERMS,B->BALANCE,B->CRLIMIT
14 SET FIELDS TO B->COUNTRY,B->EXEMPT,B->COMMENTS
15
```

Appendix C

CUSTINV.PRG

```
1 ************************************************************************
2 *-- Name....: CUSTINV.PRG
3 *-- Date....: 4-26-89
4 *-- Version.: dBASE IV, Format 1.0
5 *-- Notes...: Format files use "" as delimiters!
6 ************************************************************************
7
8 CLEAR WIND
9 CLOSE DATABASE
10 SAVE SCREEN TO custinv
11 CLEAR
12
13 DEFINE WINDOW Pause FROM 15,00 TO 19,79 DOUBLE
14 DEFINE WINDOW Cust_hlp FROM 3,00 TO 21,79 DOUBLE
15 ON ERROR DO Pause WITH "Line number in program "+Program()+":
    "+LTRIM(STR(LINE()))
16
17 RESTORE MACROS FROM Invoice2
18
19 IF EOF()
20    SKIP -1
21 ENDIF
22
23 IF SET("TALK")="ON"
24    SET TALK OFF
25    lc_talk = "ON"
26 ELSE
27    lc_talk = "OFF"
28 ENDIF
29 lc_escape = SET("ESCAPE")
30
31 *-- Imported code from C:\DB4\DATA\CUSTINV.QBE
32 * DBASE IV .QBE FILE
33 SET FIELDS TO
34 SELECT 1
35 USE INVOICE.DBF
36 USE CUSTOMER.DBF IN 2 ORDER CUSTCODE
37 SET RELATION TO A->CUSTCODE INTO B
38 SET FIELDS TO B->CUSTCODE,B->NAME,B->CONTACT,B->TELEPHONE,A->INVOICENO,A;
39 ->ITEMCODE,A->PRICE,A->QUANTITY,A->EXTPRICE,B->ADDRESS1,B >ADDRESS2,B->;
40 CITY,B->STATE,B->ZIP,B->SALES,B->TERMS,B->BALANCE,B->CRLIMIT
41 SET FIELDS TO B->COUNTRY,B->EXEMPT,B->COMMENTS
42 *------------------------------------------------------------------------
43 GO TOP
44
```

(continued)

```
45 *-- This form was created in EGA25 mode
46 SET DISPLAY TO EGA25
47
48 lc_status = SET("STATUS")
49 *-- SET STATUS was ON when you went into the Forms Designer.
50 IF lc_status = "OFF"
51    SET STATUS ON
52 ENDIF
53
54 gc_messg = "F9:Line items | PgDn:Next | PgUp:Previous | Ctrl-PgDn:Bottom |
      Ctrl-PgUp:Top"
55
56 DEFINE WINDOW Table FROM 12,2 TO 20,78
57
58 ON KEY LABEL F1 DO Cust_hlp
59 ON KEY LABEL F9 PLAY MACRO Lineitem
60 ON KEY LABEL F10 PLAY MACRO Menu
61
62 DO Defnmenu
63
64 gc_mdx = MDX(1)
65 gc_alias = ALIAS()
66
67 *-- Set up lineitem (BROWSE) workarea----------------------------------------
68
69 gn_sele = IIF(SELE()=10, SELE()-1, SELE())
70 SELE (gn_sele)
71 USE INVNTORY ORDER TAG ITEMCODE
72 SET FIELDS TO ITEMCODE, DESCRIPT
73 SET CARRY TO INVNTORY->ITEMCODE
74
75 *---------------------------------------------------------------------------
76
77 SELE &gc_alias.
78 gn_gorec = 0                        && Var for goto record option
79 gc_search = SPACE(200)              && Var for forward and backward search
80 gc_seek = SPACE( LEN( ITEMCODE))    && Var for seeking records
81 gl_newrec = .f.                     && Var for appended record
82 gl_chgrec = .t.                     && Var for testing if record position
                                          changed
83 gl_extloop = .f.
84 gl_rollbck = .f.
85 @ 23,0
86 @ 23,CENTER(gc_messg,00) SAY gc_messg
87
88 DO WHILE .NOT. gl_extloop
89    gn_recno = RECNO()
90    gl_lineitm = .T.
91    BEGIN TRANSACTION
92
93    DO WHILE gl_lineitm
94       IF gl_chgrec
```

(continued)

```
 95                *-- Paint Say's & Get's on screen
 96                DO Show_get
 97            ENDIF
 98
 99            *-- Show matching Browse Table data
100            DO Showbrow
101            *-- Back to suddo edit
102
103            *-- Edit Get's
104            DO Edit_get
105
106            READ
107
108            gn_inkey = INKEY()
109            gn_readkey = READKEY()
110            gc_readvar = VARREAD()
111            gl_lineitm = .F.
112
113            ACTIVATE SCREEN
114            DO CASE
115              CASE gn_inkey = -17
116                *-- CTRL-F8
117                DO Lineitem
118                gl_lineitm = .T.
119              CASE gn_inkey = -19
120                *-- CTRL-F10
121                ACTIVATE MENU Editmenu
122              CASE gn_readkey = 6 .OR. gn_readkey = 262 .OR. gn_readkey = 260 ;
123                   .OR. gn_readkey = 4
124                *-- Pgup or Up arrow
125                IF .NOT. BOF()
126                   SKIP -1
127                ENDIF
128              CASE gn_readkey = 7 .OR. gn_readkey = 263 .OR. gn_readkey = 5 ;
129                   .OR. gn_readkey = 261
130                *-- PgDn or Dwn arrow
131                SKIP
132                IF EOF() .AND. .NOT. gl_newrec
133                   CLEAR GETS
134                   SET DELI OFF
135                   @ 23,0
136                   @ 23,25 SAY "===> Add new records (Y/N)?" GET gl_newrec
                        PICT "Y"
137                   READ
138                   SET DELI ON
139                   CLEAR GETS
140                   @ 23,0
141                   @ 23,CENTER( gc_messg, 80) SAY gc_messg
142                ENDIF
143                IF gl_newrec
144                   DO Recappnd
145                ELSE
```

(continued)

```
146                IF EOF()
147                    SKIP -1
148                ENDIF
149            ENDIF
150          CASE gn_readkey = 34 .OR. gn_readkey = 290
151            *-- Ctrl-PgUp
152            GO TOP
153          CASE gn_readkey = 35 .OR. gn_readkey = 291
154            *-- Ctrl-PgDn
155            GO BOTTOM
156          CASE gn_readkey = 12  .or. gn_readkey = 270
157            *-- Esc
158            gl_extloop = .T.
159            EXIT
160        ENDCASE
161        *
162        gl_chgrec = IIF(gn_recno = RECNO(), .F., .T.)  && See if record #
                                                           changed
163        *
164        IF gl_rollbck           && If user picked ROLLBACK option from
                                      menu
165            gl_rollbck = .F.       && Reset rollback variable
166            ROLLBACK
167        ENDIF
168     ENDDO
169     *
170     END TRANSACTION
171     *
172     IF .NOT. ROLLBACK()
173        DO Pause WITH "Undo not successful"
174        ACTIVATE SCREEN
175     ENDIF
176     DO Chkdele
177 ENDDO
178
179 *-- Clean-up exit
180 *-- SET STATUS was ON when you went into the Forms Designer.
181 IF lc_status = "OFF"   && Entered form with status off
182    SET STATUS OFF      && Turn STATUS "OFF" on the way out
183 ENDIF
184 SET TALK &lc_talk
185
186 ON KEY
187 ON ERROR
188
189 SELE 1
190 CLOSE DATABASE
191
192 RELEASE MENU Editmenu
193 RELEASE POPUPS records, go_to, exit
194 RELEASE WINDOWS table,pause,seek,search,bsearch,Cust_hlp
195 RESTORE SCREEN FROM custinv
```

(continued)

```
196 RELEASE lc_talk,lc_fields,lc_status,lc_escape
197 RELEASE SCREEN custinv
198 RETURN
199
200 PROCEDURE Show_get
201    @ 1,0 SAY "Cust ID"
202    @ 1,11 GET customer->custcode PICTURE "XXXXXXXXXXX"
203    @ 1,25 SAY "Name"
204    @ 1,36 GET customer->name PICTURE "XXXXXXXXXXXXXXXXXXXXXXXXXXXX"
205    @ 2,0 SAY "Contact"
206    @ 2,11 GET customer->contact PICTURE "XXXXXXXXXXXXXXXXXXXXXXXXXX"
207    @ 2,39 SAY "Telephone"
208    @ 2,50 GET customer->telephone PICTURE "XXXXXXXXXXXXXXXXXXXXX"
209    @ 3,0 SAY "Invoice #"
210    @ 3,11 GET invoice->invoiceno PICTURE "XXXXX"
211    @ 3,19 SAY "Item Code"
212    @ 3,30 GET invoice->itemcode PICTURE "XXXXX"
213    @ 4,0 SAY "Price"
214    @ 4,11 GET invoice->price PICTURE "999.99"
215    @ 4,19 SAY "x"
216    @ 4,22 SAY "Quantity"
217    @ 4,33 GET invoice->quantity PICTURE "999.999"
218    @ 4,42 SAY "="
219    @ 4,45 SAY "Ext.Price"
220    @ 4,56 GET invoice->extprice PICTURE "999999999.99"
221    CLEAR GETS
222 RETURN
223
224 PROCEDURE Edit_get
225    @ 1,11 GET customer->custcode PICTURE "XXXXXXXXXXX"
226    @ 1,36 GET customer->name PICTURE "XXXXXXXXXXXXXXXXXXXXXXXXXXXX"
227    @ 2,11 GET customer->contact PICTURE "XXXXXXXXXXXXXXXXXXXXXXXXXX"
228    @ 2,50 GET customer->telephone PICTURE "XXXXXXXXXXXXXXXXXXXXX"
229    @ 3,11 GET invoice->invoiceno PICTURE "XXXXX"
230    @ 3,30 GET invoice->itemcode PICTURE "XXXXX"
231    @ 4,11 GET invoice->price PICTURE "999.99"
232    @ 4,33 GET invoice->quantity PICTURE "999.999"
233    @ 4,56 GET invoice->extprice PICTURE "999999999.99"
234 RETURN
235
236 PROCEDURE Showbrow
237    SELE INVNTORY
238    SET FILTER TO
239    SEEK &GC_ALIAS.->ITEMCODE
240    IF EOF()
241       APPEND BLANK
242       REPLACE INVNTORY->ITEMCODE WITH &GC_ALIAS.->ITEMCODE
243    ENDIF
244    SET FILTER TO &GC_ALIAS.->ITEMCODE = INVNTORY->ITEMCODE
245    GO TOP
246    PLAY MACRO exit_brow
247    BROWSE;
```

(continued)

```
248        FIELDS DESCRIPT;
249        WINDOW table COMPRESS NOMENU NOCLEAR
250      SELE &gc_alias.
251      ACTIVATE SCREEN
252 RETURN
253
254 PROCEDURE Lineitem
255    ln_key = INKEY()
256    DO Keykill
257    SELE INVNTORY
258       APPEND BLANK
259       REPLACE INVNTORY->ITEMCODE WITH &GC_ALIAS.->ITEMCODE
260    GO TOP
261    BROWSE;
262       FIELDS DESCRIPT;
263       WINDOW table COMPRESS NOMENU NOCLEAR
264    ACTIVATE SCREEN
265    DO Keyset
266    *-------------------------------------------------------------------
267    *-- Could put code here to SUM the order balance and replace in a total
           field
268    *-- Example:
269    *-- SUM ALL extended TO m->extended
270    *-- REPLACE &gc_alias.->Total_bill WITH m->extended
271    *-------------------------------------------------------------------
272    SELE &gc_alias.
273 RETURN
274
275 PROCEDURE Keyset
276    ON KEY LABEL F1 DO Cust_hlp
277    ON KEY LABEL F9 PLAY MACRO Lineitem
278    ON KEY LABEL F10 PLAY MACRO Menu
279 RETURN
280
281 PROCEDURE Keykill
282    ON KEY LABEL F1 DO Nothing
283    ON KEY LABEL F9 DO Nothing
284    ON KEY LABEL F10 DO Nothing
285 RETURN
286
287 PROCEDURE Nothing
288    ln_key=INKEY()
289 RETURN
290
291 PROCEDURE Chkdele
292    IF DELETED()
293       DEFINE BAR 4 OF records PROMPT "   Clear deletion mark";
294       MESSAGE "Mark/unmark this record for deletion"
295    ELSE
296       DEFINE BAR 4 OF records PROMPT "   Mark record for deletion";
297       MESSAGE "Mark/unmark this record for deletion"
298    ENDIF
```

(continued)

```
299 RETURN
300
301 PROCEDURE Recappnd
302    *----------------------------------------------------------------------
303    *-- Could put code here to advance the invoice number, etc.
304    GO BOTT
305    morder = ORDER_ID
306    APPEND BLANK
307    REPLACE order_id WITH SUBSTR(morder,1,3) +
          LTRIM(STR(VAL(SUBSTR(morder,4))+1))
308    *----------------------------------------------------------------------
309 RETURN
310
311 *-- The following procedures handle the selections of the edit menu --------
312 PROCEDURE Get_recs
313    *-- Get the user selection & store BAR into variable
314    gn_pick = BAR()   && Variable for bar testing
315    DO CASE
316       CASE gn_pick = 1
317          *-- Prepare variable for rollback operation on return
318          gl_rollbck = .T.
319       CASE gn_pick = 3
320           DO Recappnd
321       CASE gn_pick = 4
322          *-- Delete/recall record
323          IF DELETE()
324             RECALL
325             SELE INVNTORY
326             RECALL ALL
327          ELSE
328             DELETE
329             SELE INVNTORY
330             DELETE ALL
331          ENDIF
332          SELE (gc_alias)
333       CASE gn_pick = 5
334          *-- Blank record
335    ENDCASE
336    DO Chkdele
337    DEACTIVATE MENU
338 RETURN
339
340 PROCEDURE Get_goto
341    *-- Get the user selection & store BAR into variable
342    gn_pick = BAR()   && Variable for bar testing
343    mpict = REPLICATE("9", LEN( LTRIM( STR( RECCOUNT()))))
344    gc_search = gc_search + SPACE( 200 - LEN(gc_search))
345    gc_seek = gc_seek + SPACE(LEN( ITEMCODE) - LEN(gc_seek))
346    DO CASE
347       CASE gn_pick = 1
348          *-- Go to top of file
349          GO TOP
```

(continued)

```
350         CASE gn_pick = 2
351            *-- Go to bottom of file
352            GO BOTTOM
353         CASE gn_pick = 3
354            *-- Go to a specfic record
355            @ 4,39 GET gn_gorec RANGE 1, RECCOUNT() PICTURE mpict
356            READ
357            gn_gorec = IIF( gn_gorec=0, RECNO(), gn_gorec)
358            GO gn_gorec
359         CASE gn_pick = 4
360            *-- Skip a certain number of records
361            skiprec = IIF( RECCOUNT() > 9, 10, 5)
362            SET DELI OFF
363            @ 5,39 GET skiprec PICTURE mpict
364            READ
365            SET DELI ON
366            SKIP skiprec
367            IF EOF()
368               SKIP -1
369            ENDIF
370         CASE gn_pick = 6
371            ACTIVATE WINDOW seek
372            *-- Seek on key field
373            IF "" = ORDER()
374                tempmdx = TAG(1)
375                SET ORDER TO TAG &tempmdx.
376            ENDIF
377            @ 0,1 SAY "Enter search string for"
378            @ 1,1 SAY TAG(1)+":" GET gc_seek PICT "@S20";
379               MESSAGE "Cancel: Esc";
380               VALID LEN( TRIM( gc_seek)) > 0;
381               ERROR "No search condition entered"
382            READ
383            IF READKEY() <> 12
384               gc_seek = LTRIM( TRIM(gc_seek))
385               mrec = RECNO()
386               SEEK gc_seek
387               IF .NOT. FOUND()
388                  GO mrec
389               ENDIF
390            ENDIF
391            DEACTIVATE WINDOW seek
392            ACTIVATE SCREEN
393         CASE gn_pick = 7
394            *-- Forward search
395            ACTIVATE WINDOW search
396            @ 0,1 SAY "Enter search string:" GET gc_search PICT "@S21";
397               MESSAGE "Cancel: Esc";
398               VALID LEN( TRIM( gc_search)) > 0;
399               ERROR "No search condition entered"
400            READ
401            DEACTIVATE WINDOW search
```

(continued)

```
402            ACTIVATE SCREEN
403            IF READKEY() <> 12
404               gc_search = LTRIM( RTRIM( gc_search))
405               mrec = RECNO()
406               LOCATE REST FOR &gc_search.
407               IF .NOT. FOUND()
408                  GO mrec
409               ENDIF
410            ENDIF
411         CASE gn_pick = 8
412            *-- Backward search
413            ACTIVATE WINDOW bsearch
414            @ 0,1 SAY "Enter search string:" GET gc_search PICT "@S21";
415               MESSAGE "Cancel: Esc";
416               VALID len(trim(gc_search)) > 0;
417               ERROR "No search condition entered"
418            READ
419            DEACTIVATE WINDOW bsearch
420            ACTIVATE SCREEN
421            IF READKEY() <> 12
422               gc_search = LTRIM( RTRIM( gc_search))
423               mrec = RECNO()
424               DO WHILE .NOT. (BOF() .OR. &gc_search.)
425                  SKIP -1
426               ENDDO
427               IF BOF()
428                  GO mrec
429               ENDIF
430            ENDIF
431      ENDCASE
432      DEACTIVATE MENU
433 RETURN
434
435 PROCEDURE Get_exit
436      CLEAR GETS
437      *-- Prepare variable to exit loop
438      gl_extloop = .T.
439      DEACTIVATE MENU
440 RETURN
441
442 PROCEDURE Pause
443 PARAMETER lc_msg
444 *-- Parameters : lc_msg = message line
445 IF TYPE("lc_message")="U"
446      gn_error=ERROR()
447 ENDIF
448 lc_msg = lc_msg
449 lc_option='0'
450 ACTIVATE WINDOW Pause
451 IF gn_error > 0
452      IF TYPE("lc_message")="U"
453         @ 0,1 SAY [An error has occurred !! - Error message: ]+MESSAGE()
```

(continued)

```
454    ELSE
455       @ 0,1 SAY [Error # ]+lc_message
456    ENDIF
457 ENDIF
458 @ 1,1 SAY lc_msg
459 WAIT " Press any key to continue..."
460 DEACTIVATE WINDOW Pause
461 RETURN
462
463 *-- UDF library -----------------------------------------------------------
464 FUNCTION Center
465 *-- UDF to center a string.
466 *-- lc_string = String to center
467 *-- ln_width = Width of screen to center in
468 *--
469 *-- Ex. @ 15,center(string,80) say string
470 *-- Will center the <string> withing 80 columns
471 PARAMETER lc_string, ln_width
472 RETURN ((ln_width/2)-(LEN(lc_string)/2))
473 *-- End UDF library --------------------------------------------------------
474
475 PROCEDURE Cust_hlp
476 gc_readvar = VARREAD()                    && Could do context sensitive help
477 ACTIVATE WINDOW Cust_hlp
478 CLEAR
479 TEXT
480    Navigation HELP:
481    ----------------
482    F1: Displays this message
483    F9: Takes you from the top of your invoice to the line items
484    F10: Takes you to the menu system at the top of the invoice
485
486    PgDn: Takes you to the next invoice
487    PgUp: Takes you to the previous invoice
488    Ctrl-PgDn: Takes you to the last invoice in your database
489    Ctrl-PgUp: Takes you to the first invoice in your database
490    Esc: Exits the invoice
491 ENDTEXT
492 @ 16,5 say "Press any key..."
493 x = INKEY(0)
494 CLEAR
495 TEXT
496    Lino item HELP:
497    ---------------
498    F1: Displays this message
499
500    PgDn: Displays next screen of line items
501    PgUp: Displays previous screen of line items
502    Ctrl-PgDn: Takes you to the last screen of line items
503    Ctrl-PgUp: Takes you to the first screen of line items
504    Esc: Returns to header information part of invoice
```

(continued)

```
505 ENDTEXT
506 @ 16,5 say "Press any key..."
507 x = INKEY(0)
508 DEACTIVATE WINDOW Cust_hlp
509 ACTIVATE SCREEN
510 RETURN
511
512 PROCEDURE Defnmenu
513    *-- This menu simulates the F10 menu for edit for this edit program
514    *-- Not all of the actions will be able to be duplicated though.
515
516    SET BORDER TO DOUBLE
517
518    DEFINE MENU editmenu
519      DEFINE PAD records OF editmenu PROMPT "Records" AT 0,2
520        ON PAD records OF editmenu ACTIVATE POPUP records
521      DEFINE PAD go_to OF editmenu PROMPT "Go To" AT 0,14
522            ON PAD go_to OF editmenu ACTIVATE POPUP go_to
523      DEFINE PAD exit OF editmenu PROMPT "Exit" AT 0,24
524        ON PAD exit OF editmenu ACTIVATE POPUP exit
525
526    * -- Define popup menu
527    DEFINE POPUP records FROM 1,0
528      DEFINE BAR 1 OF records PROMPT " Undo change to record";
529      MESSAGE "Undo Change to current record"
530      DEFINE BAR 2 OF records PROMPT "-------------------------------" SKIP
531      DEFINE BAR 3 OF records PROMPT " Add new records";
532      MESSAGE "Add records to the end of the database file"
533      *-- Bar 4 is determined on the record being deleted or not
534      DO Chkdele  && Define bar 4 done in procedure
535      DEFINE BAR 5 OF records PROMPT " Blank record" SKIP ;
536      MESSAGE "Erase the contents of all the fields in this record"
537      DEFINE BAR 6 OF records PROMPT " Lock record";
538      MESSAGE " "
539      DEFINE BAR 7 OF records PROMPT " Follow record to new position  YES"
             SKIP
540      DEFINE POPUP go_to FROM 1,12
541      DEFINE BAR 1 OF go_to PROMPT " Top record";
542      MESSAGE "Move to the first record in this database file"
543      DEFINE BAR 2 OF go_to PROMPT " Last record";
544      MESSAGE "Move to the last record in this database file"
545      DEFINE BAR 3 OF go_to PROMPT " Record number";
546      MESSAGE "Move to the specified record number"
547      DEFINE BAR 4 OF go_to PROMPT " Skip";
548      MESSAGE "Move by skipping the specified number of records (minus for
             backwards)"
549      DEFINE BAR 5 OF go_to PROMPT "-------------------------------" SKIP
550      DEFINE BAR 6 OF go_to PROMPT " Index key search" SKIP FOR "" =
             gc_mdx;
551      MESSAGE "Use the index file to search for the specfied string"
552      DEFINE BAR 7 OF go_to PROMPT " Forward search         ";
```

(continued)

```
553     MESSAGE "Search a field for the specified string from the
            current record forward"
554     DEFINE BAR 8 OF go_to PROMPT "   Backward search       ";
555     MESSAGE "Search a field for the specified string from the
            current record backward"
556     DEFINE BAR 9 OF go_to PROMPT "   Match capitalization  NO" SKIP
557
558   DEFINE POPUP exit FROM 1,22
559     DEFINE BAR 1 OF exit PROMPT "   Exit";
560     MESSAGE "Save changes to current record and exit"
561     DEFINE BAR 2 OF exit PROMPT "   Transfer to Query Design  " SKIP
562
563   ON SELECTION POPUP records DO Get_recs
564   ON SELECTION POPUP go_to DO Get_goto
565   ON SELECTION POPUP exit DO Get_exit
566
567   DEFINE WINDOW seek FROM 8,15 TO 11,44
568   DEFINE WINDOW search FROM 9,15 TO 11,60
569   DEFINE WINDOW bsearch FROM 10,15 TO 12,60
570
571   SHOW MENU Editmenu
572 RETURN
573 *--------------------------------------------------------------------------
574 *-- EOP: CUSTINV.PRG
575
```

Chapter 11

The Template Compiler and Debugger

We've already used the template compiler to create new GEN files for virtually all of the source code files included with dBASE IV. Every language needs some sort of debugging tool. The template language is no exception.

This chapter will show you how to use the template debugger/interpreter DGEN.EXE. In particular, there are two debugging commands available in the compiler that must be added to a source code file. These commands can be used to give certain information, including the current values of selectors, information about the dBASE IV program code being produced, and so on.

However, this is a tedious process at best. There is no debugging tool for the template language nearly as good as the dBASE IV windowing debugger. Fortunately, the template language is a good deal more primitive than dBASE IV; its more primitive debugger works pretty well.

Debugging Strategy

Debugging template programs involves several steps. The first and most important is compiling your template program. This will catch mistakes such as missing {ENDIF} and {NEXT} statements as well as basic syntax errors.

The second step is to add debugging commands to your template source code files. We'll see how to use these commands later in this chapter. Once the debugging commands are in place, recompile the template source code, then use the interpreter DGEN.EXE to generate the dBASE IV source code for the program. DGEN recognizes the debugging commands and uses them to give you information. DGEN also produces the dBASE IV source code without having to actually run dBASE IV itself. This can be a shortcut if you don't need to compile and run the dBASE IV program but just want to look at the generated program.

On the other hand, you may want to use dBASE IV to compile the generated code. The compiler will catch syntax errors in the generated code and similar errors.

Finally, after you've looked at the debugging messages, go back and fix your template source code, removing the debugging commands if you think you've caught all your mistakes.

The debugging cycle can be long and tedious. Remember, you're changing source code that will be used to generate other source code. A fast computer with a fast hard disk is highly recommended to reduce the time for the debugging cycle.

Step 1: Compile Your Program

The first rule of debugging is to always use the -l <file name> option in your compile command. For example, here's the batch file DM.BAT. It compiles the applications generator:

```
dtc -i as_menu.cod -o c:\db4\menu.gen -l menu.out
```

The file MENU.OUT will contain a complete source listing of all files included with AS_MENU.COD. More important, it will contain any syntax or other error messages. If these messages exist, MENU.GEN will not be saved to disk. Therefore, you might want to add one command to DM.BAT:

```
erase c:\db4\menu.gen
```

Put this command the line before the DTC command. Then all you have to do is check to see whether MENU.GEN is in the c:\db4 directory. If it's there, you know there were no compile errors. If it's not there, use your editor on the file MENU.OUT. Do a search for the word "ERROR." Remember, files that are INCLUDEd have all their source code in the file, so you'll want to check to see the file name where the error occurred. It's a good idea to keep track of which files you have changed as well. That way, you'll have a better idea of where to look for errors.

Step 2: Using the Debugger

Compile-time errors are pretty simple to fix because they usually involve syntax errors or omitted statements. Far more complex are run-time errors. Often, you'll find these errors simply involve using the incorrect selector to perform a particular task. For example, consider the code we added to AS_REPT.COD in Chapter 9:

```
{
// Following block added by Tony Lima, April 25, 1989
}
{if ndx_file or ndx_order then;
  if ndx_file then
}
SET INDEX TO {ndx_file}
GOTO TOP
{   else
}
SET ORDER TO {ndx_order}
GOTO TOP
{  endif;
 endif
}
```

The problem is how to figure out the correct selector to use for the currently active index file or tag. The file APPLCTN.DEF contains several candidates:

```
APPL_NDX     0057, // Index file to use with application
                   // Menu Path: AMV  - Value: String
APPL_ORDER   0177, // Index order for dbf or view at Application
                       level
                   // Menu Path: AMV  - Value: String
MENU_NDX     0043, // Index file to use with menu
                   // Menu Path: MO,LO,BO - Value: String
MENU_ORDER   0088, // Index order for dbf or view at menu level
                   // Menu Path: MO,LO,BO - Value: String
QUICK_NDX    0057, // Quick application index file
                   // Menu Path: AG  - Value: String
QUICK_ORDR   0177, // Index order for dbf or view for Quick App.
                   // Menu Path: AG  - Value: String
```

```
ITEM_NDX      0132, // Index file to use with view or database
                    // Menu Path: IO   - Value: String
ITEM_ORDER    0178, // Index order for dbf or view at item level
                    // Menu Path: IO   - Value: String
NDX_FILE      0136, // INDEX file for generat index
                    // Menu Path: ICPG - Value: String
NDX_KEY       0137, // KEY expression for generate index
                    // Menu Path: ICPG - Value: String
NDX_ORDER     0229, // Index file for set sequence
                    // Menu Path: IR   - Value: String
NDX_TAG       0218, // TAG for generat index
                    // Menu Path: ICPG - Value: String
NDX_TAGIN     0219, // MDX file name for TAG (generate index)
                    // Menu Path: ICPG - Value: String
```

Some of these, such as QUICK_NDX and QUICK_ORDR can be eliminated fairly quickly because they obviously only apply to the quick application. However, there is really no good documentation of which of the others to use. You could solve this problem by trial and error, but that would involve several repetitions of the debugging cycle, something to be avoided at nearly any cost. Here's what to do instead.

```
{
// Following block added by Tony Lima, April 25, 1989
}
{DEBUG(4);
BREAKPOINT("Ndx_file is "+ndx_file+" and ndx_order is "+ndx_order);
BREAKPOINT("Appl_ndx is "+appl_ndx+" and appl_order is "
  +appl_order);
BREAKPOINT("Menu_ndx is "+menu_ndx+" and menu_order is "
  +menu_order)
}
{if ndx_file or ndx_order then;
  if ndx_file then
}
SET INDEX TO {ndx_file}
GOTO TOP
{   else
}
SET ORDER TO {ndx_order}
```

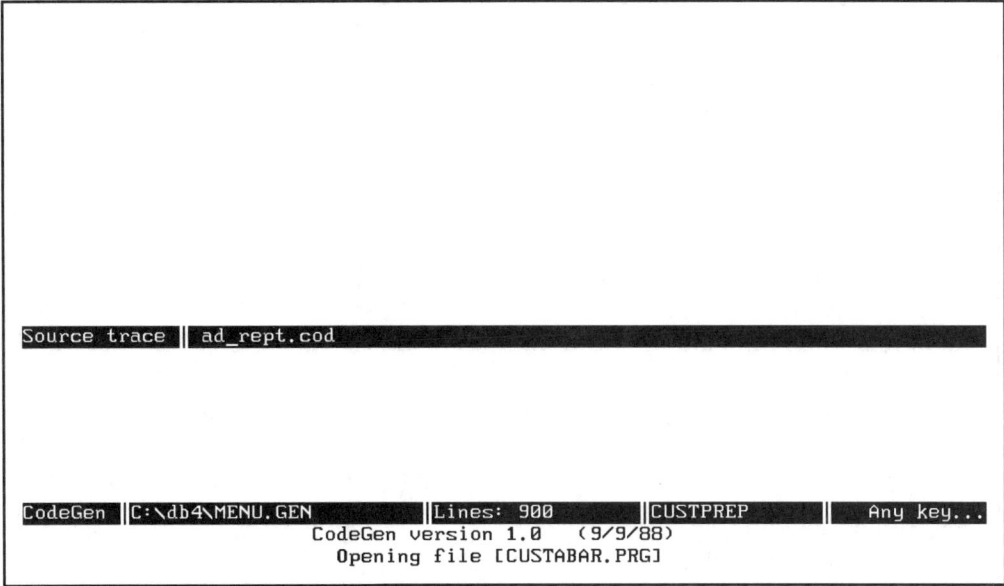

```
Source trace ║ ad_rept.cod




CodeGen ║C:\db4\MENU.GEN        ║Lines: 900      ║CUSTPREP     ║  Any key...
                CodeGen version 1.0   (9/9/88)
                Opening file [CUSTABAR.PRG]
```

Figure 11-1   DGEN.EXE Debugger

```
GOTO TOP
{  endif;
 endif
}
```

You can add as many breakpoint variables as you want. We'll discuss the DEBUG() function in a minute. First, let's see how BREAKPOINT() works.

Remember, the first thing to do is recompile AS_MENU.COD. Then use DGEN.EXE to generate the program code. The syntax is:

```
dgen -i custapp.app -t c:\db4\menu.gen -l menu.log
```

The options are straightforward. The -i option is the input file produced by the applications generator. Contrary to what is implied in the template language manual, only the main applications file need be included. The -t option is the name (and path) of the template to use. The -l option is the output file, similar to the output file produced by the template compiler.

When DGEN encounters the DEBUG() function, it will pause and wait for you to press a key as shown in Figure 11-1.

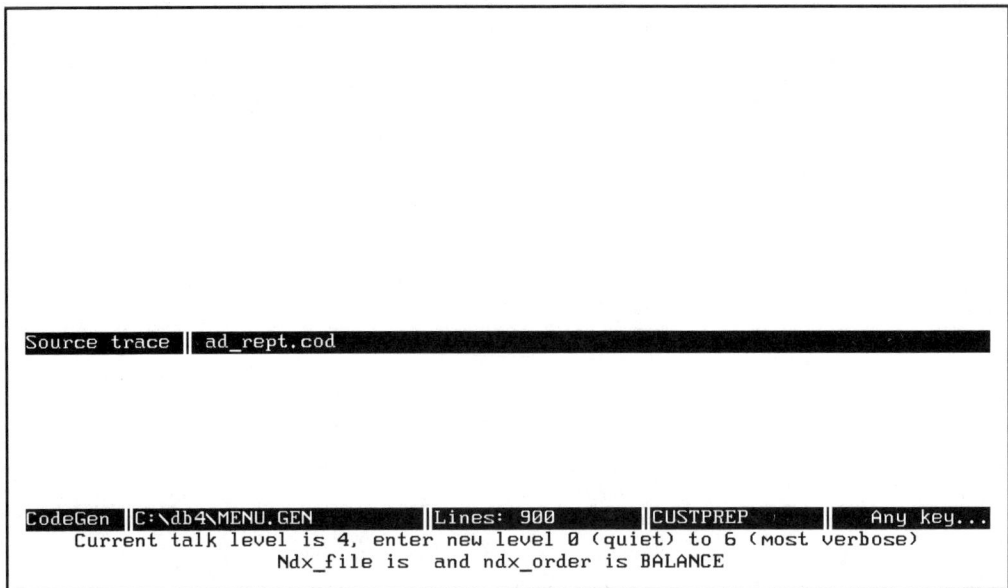

Figure 11-2   BREAKPOINT() Message

The thing to look for is the phrase "Any key . . ." at the right side of the status bar. Hit the space bar and you'll see Figure 11-2. Note the message at the bottom of the screen. (Actually, only the first BREAKPOINT() function was included for this run.)

DEBUG() with a level of 4 will let you step through the generation process one line at a time. It will also let you reset the DEBUG() level on the fly by pressing a number instead of the space bar or some other key. Press 0 to run until the value of one of the selectors changes. At that point, the BREAK-POINT() message will be displayed with the new value of the selector (Figure 11-3). The value of ndx_order is CUSTCODE instead of BALANCE.

Use BREAKPOINT() to display the values of expressions as well as selectors. Be sure you've included all those you're interested in and don't hesitate to use Shift-PrtSc to dump the screen to the printer. Or use a screen capture program to save it to a screen file. Believe me, the debugging cycle is slow enough that you're not going to want to go through it more than is absolutely necessary.

The output file contains the breakpoint messages. For example, here's MENU.LOG as produced from our example:

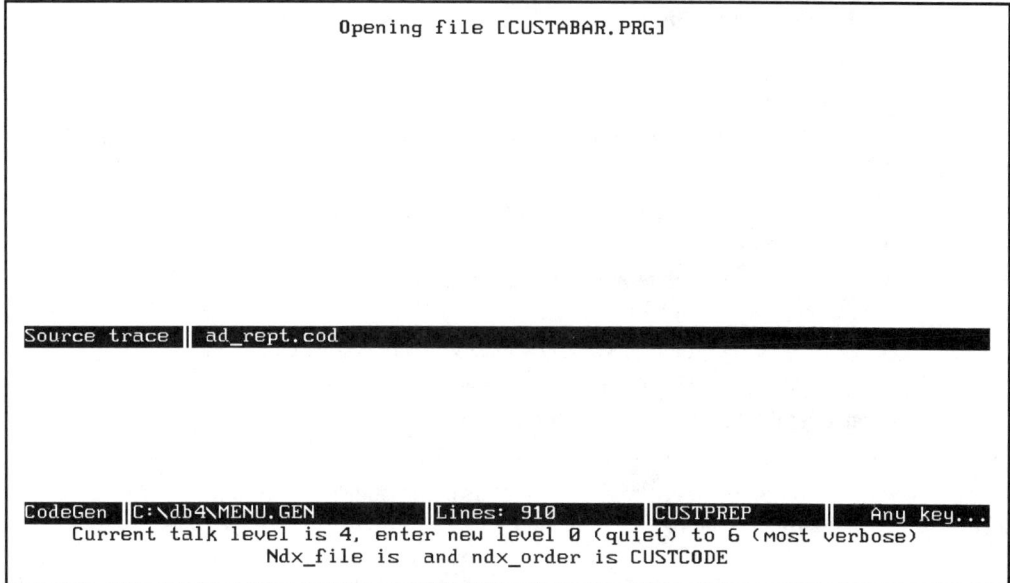

```
                    Opening file [CUSTABAR.PRG]




Source trace ‖ ad_rept.cod

CodeGen ‖C:\db4\MENU.GEN        ‖Lines: 910    ‖CUSTPREP    ‖  Any key...
    Current talk level is 4, enter new level 0 (quiet) to 6 (most verbose)
              Ndx_file is  and ndx_order is CUSTCODE
```

Figure 11-3　BREAKPOINT() Message

```
Application Template
--------------------
Version 1.96
Ashton-Tate (c) 1987, 1988
Ndx_file is  and ndx_order is BALANCE
Ndx_file is  and ndx_order is CUSTCODE
Generation run is complete
Template: C:\DB4\menu.gen
Total warnings: 0
Total errors: 0
Total lines: 967
```

Using DEBUG()

The BREAKPOINT() function is useful for displaying information. It will only be activated when DEBUG() is active as well. However, you can get a lot more than that by using different DEBUG() parameters. Table 11-1 shows a complete list of these parameters along with their functions.

Table 11-1   DEBUG(<expN>) Parameters

0:   DEBUG() off

1:   Display generated text from BREAKPOINT() on screen

2:   Display generated text and monitor keyboard for input of new DEBUG() level from 0–6.

3:   Display generated text and the operated-on template commands and monitor the keyboard.

4:   The same as 3 except that template commands are not displayed and the generation process is stepped through one line at a time.

5:   The same as 3 except that the stack and assembly code are also traced.

6:   The same as 4 except that the stack and assembly code are also traced. Also step is done on assembly instructions rather than generated code.

Note: At levels 3 through 6, the operated-on template commands are sent to the list file specified by the -l switch in the dgen command line.

Source: *Template Language* dBASE IV manual, (Ashton-Tate, Torrance, CA, 1988), pp. 6-3–6-4. Copyright © 1988, Ashton-Tate Corporation. All rights reserved. Reprinted by permission.

Using a Batch File

For complex debugging operations, it's convenient to make a couple of changes. First, move all the application object files used by your application into a new directory. Be sure you include all APP, BAR, and POP files. If you plan on running the application from this directory, add all data files as well as generated code from screen, report, and label objects. Then copy DGEN.EXE into that directory as well.

For example, suppose the application object is CUSTAPP.APP. It is copied into the subdirectory CAPP along with CUSTABAR.BAR and CUSTPREP.POP. The batch file shown in Example 11-1 will be useful for the debugging cycle.

Example 11-1   Batch File for Debugging Templates

```
:  (dmd.bat)
echo OFF
cls
echo  Phase 1 of CUSTAPP.APP generation:   compile
```

(continued)

•

```
:step1 -----------------------------------------------------
echo  Step 1
cd \db4\cod
dtc -i as_menu.cod -o c:\db4\menu.gen -l menu.out
if errorlevel == 1 goto err1
goto step2
:err1
echo  Compile error
PAUSE
goto done
:step2 ----------------------------------------------------
echo  Step 2
cd \db4\capp
dgen -i custapp.app -t c:\db4\menu.gen -l menu.log
if errorlevel == 1 goto err2
type menu.log
PAUSE
goto step3
:err2
echo  Generation error
PAUSE
goto done
:step3 --------------------------------------------------
echo  Step 3
:done
```

Source: Adapted from Chapter 15 of Dan Aspenwall and Gary Carter, *The Template Programming Language*, (Torrance, CA: Tate Publishing, Ashton-Tate, 1989).

Note that DTC.EXE and DGEN.EXE return DOS errorlevel values of 1 if there are errors that prevent the GEN file or the PRG file(s) from being produced.

Generally, after a pass through this file, you'll want to modify the template source code. You may want to add the editing command to the bottom of this file, add a label to the first line, and a GOTO <first line label> as the last line in the file. This creates an infinite loop, of course, but you can interrupt at any of the PAUSE statements by pressing Ctrl-Break.

Whatever modifications you make to the batch file (which I've named DMD.BAT), you'll find it much easier to debug templates this way. Go get a cup of coffee while the template is compiling and code is generating.

Using the Debugger with Non-Application Objects

DGEN.EXE is designed to be used with application generator objects. In order to use it with screen form (SCR), report (FRM), and/or label (LBL) objects, a special file with the extension NPI must be created at compile time. Unfortunately, there is no compiler switch to handle this. Instead, a DOS environmental variable must be set. From the DOS prompt, give the command:

```
SET DTL_TRANSLATE = ON
```

The compiler will then produce an additional source file with the extension NPI when the screen form, report, and/or label generators are used. Use this NPI file with the -i option of DGEN.EXE.

Example 11-2 shows a revised batch file to work with the screen form CUST2PG2.SCR.

Example 11-2   Batch File for Debugging Non-Application Templates

```
: (dfd.bat)
echo OFF
cls
SET DTL_TRANSLATE = ON
SET DTL_NOGEN = ON
echo  Phase 1 of CUST2PG2.SCR generation:  compile
:step1 ----------------------------------------------------
echo  Step 1
cd \db4\cod
dtc -i form.cod -o c:\db4\form.gen -l form.out
if errorlevel == 1 goto err1
goto step2
:err1
echo  Compile error
PAUSE
goto done
:step2 -------------------------------------------------
echo  Step 2
cd \db4\capp
dgen -i cust2pg2.npi -t c:\db4\form.gen -l form.log
```

(continued)

```
if errorlevel == 1 goto err2
type form.log
PAUSE
goto step3
:err2
echo  Generation error
PAUSE
goto done
:step3  --------------------------------------------
echo  Step 3
:done
```

Source: Adapted from Chapter 15 of Dan Aspenwall and Gary Carter, *The Template Programming Language*, (Torrance, CA: Tate Publishing, Ashton-Tate, 1989).

Other Environmental Variables

There are two other DOS environmental variables used by the debugger. SET DTL_NOGEN = ON suppresses actual generation of the dBASE IV code. This option should be used with DTL_TRANSLATE to produce an NPI file for debugging without generating source code, speeding up the debugging cycle considerably.

SET DTL_TRACE = ON will display all elements and attributes of the design object. The exception is frame level selectors as defined in the DEF files. I recommend using this only as a last resort.

Compiler and Debugger Option Switches

There are a number of option switches not commonly used but available should you need them. Compiler option switches are listed in Table 11-2.

Use the -a switch if you want to include pseudo-assembly code in the compiler listing. (For more information on template assembly code, see Chapter 13 of Aspenwall and Carter.)

The -z switch produces slightly smaller and faster GEN files. Other than that, it has no effect.

Table 11-2   Template Compiler Option Switches

-i <COD file name>:   name of source code (COD) file
-l <OUT file name>:   name of output file for compilation listing
-o <GEN file name>:   name of compiled output file
-a: include assembly language code in output listing
-z: suppress source code position markers in compiled output file.

Source: Adapted from Chapter 13 of Dan Aspenwall and Gary Carter, *The Template Programming Language*, (Torrance, CA: Tate Publishing, Ashton-Tate, 1989).

Compiler Listing Directives

There are two pairs of directives that can be placed anywhere in template COD and/or DEF files.

#lstoff and #lston respectively disable and enable output of compiler listings to the file specified with the -l switch for the compiler. This allows you to selectively include and exclude parts of files from the output file, which is very helpful for debugging as it produces a shorter, more manageable file. The default is #lston.

#codon and #codoff respectively enable and disable output of pseudo-assembly language code in the output file. They are used with the -a switch.

Interpreter Switches

Table 11-3 shows the interpreter switches.

Table 11-3   Switches for DGEN.EXE

-t <GEN file>:   compiled template file to process.
-i <obj file>:   object (APP, BAR, POP, or NPI) file name
-l <OUT file>:   name of file to store diagnostic listing]
-n: echo command line arguments to screen at start of execution.

Source: Adapted from Chapter 14 of Dan Aspenwall and Gary Carter, *The Template Programming Language*, (Torrance, CA: Tate Publishing, Ashton-Tate, 1989).

Conclusion

The compiler and debugger are adequate tools for handling template programs. What is missing are tools to produce flow charts, variable and selector listings, and similar output such as that created by CLEAR or The Documentor. Undoubtedly these will appear in the next year or two as the power of the template language becomes more understood.

The Future

The dBASE IV template language is a remarkably powerful and flexible tool. In the next few years we will see a number of templates developed for a variety of situations. This chapter looks at a few interesting possibilities.

Vertical Market Applications

There are a number of vertical market applications, such as accounting systems and industry-specific management programs, that could be easily produced with appropriate templates. This would allow customized vertical market packages. For example, an end user might want a report produced with subtotals on different fields or different groupings. If industry-wide variables can be identified, the flexibility to handle them can be programmed into a template. Changes that once took months to program can be done by answering a few simple questions.

Computer-assisted Instruction

Currently, producing computer-assisted-instruction (CAI) software is a real art, often involving knowledge of arcane programming languages such as LISP or SNOBOL. It's easy to imaging a series of CAI templates where the programmer would simply set up the tree structure of the CAI questions and feedback responses. The template would ask for questions, program transfers for user responses and feedback, and then produce a program automatically.

Although it would be efficient to use dBASE IV databases to store this information, it would not be required. (In fact, as we'll see in the next section, it wouldn't even be necessary to use dBASE at all, although it would certainly be convenient.)

Translating dBASE IV into Other Languages

Consider the possibility of producing Paradox code from dBASE IV objects. For example, you could use the dBASE IV screen form generator to produce a SCR file, then write a template to turn the SCR file into Paradox code. This would allow organizations that are restricted to using a single database manager to use the power of the dBASE IV screen, report, label, and applications generators to produce code in a completely different language.

Conclusion

None of this is particularly easy. However, once the templates are programmed, they can reduce development time so much that the initial investment is easily worth the time. The question is not what the template language is good for; it's what the creativity of programmers will do with it. The power is there. It's up to us to use it.

Template Language Operators, Commands, and Functions

Delimiters

Delimiter	*Description*
{ }	Command delimiters (outside comments).
\	Removes carriage return–line feed when placed at end of line. Anywhere else, means ignore special meaning of next character.
;	Separates template statements within braces. Prevents output of value of preceding expression to file.
( )	Enclose function arguments and nested expressions.
//	Treated as a comment when at beginning of line or within braces and not in double quotes.
Blank space	Before {<command>} causes new line to be output.
"	String delimiters (reserved).

Operators

Assignment Operators

Operator	Description
=	Equals
+=	x+=1 is the same as x=x+1
-=	x-=1 is the same as x=x-1
++	Increment by 1. ++x is the same as x=x+1
- -	Decrement by 1. - -x is the same as x=x-1

Note: ++ and - - cannot be used with string variables.

Unary Operators

+	Numeric positive
-	Numeric negative
!	Numeric logical *not*
not	Null=1, non-null=0
( )	Grouping
@	Return integer value for a selector

Note: @ must be followed by a selector.

Binary Operators

+	Numeric addition, string concatenation
-	Numeric subtraction

(continued)

*	Numeric multiplication
/	Numeric division
%	Numeric modulo
&	Bitwise numeric *and*
|	Bitwise numeric *or*
^	Bitwise numeric *xor* (x or y) *and not* (x and y)
<	Numeric or string *less than*
<=	Numeric or string *less than or equal*
>	Numeric or string *greater than*
>=	Numeric or string *greater than or equal*
==	Numeric or string *compare*
!=	Numeric or string *not equal*
&&	Logical *and*
||	Logical *or*
and	Logical *and*
or	Logical *or*
.	Dot operator

Note: The dot operator treats the expression on the left as a cursor and the expression on the right as a selector or integer. The value of the attribute of the indicated selector or integer is retrieved.

Bitwise Logical Operators

|	Inclusive OR
&	Inclusive AND
^	Exclusive OR (XOR)
~	1's complement unary operator

Shift Operators

<< <expN>	Shift <expN> left, throw away leading bits, add trailing zeroes.
>> <expN>	Shift <expN> right, throw away trailing bits, add leading zeroes.

Note: Numeric variables are stored internally as 32-bit integers. Therefore numbers may be shifted.

Precedence of Operators

Operators are evaluated in the following order:

```
. (dot operator)
!, not, ~, @, unary -
*, /, %
+, -
<<, >>
<, <=, >, >=
==, !=
&
|, ^
and, &&
or, | |
```

Note: Operations within nested parentheses are evaluated from the innermost to the outermost.

Commands

Symbols and Conventions

Items enclosed in angle brackets (< >) must be entered by the programmer. Do not type the angle brackets.

Example: FOREACH <loop selector>. Type in a loop selector such as FOREACH Fld_element.

Items enclosed in square brackets ([ ]) are optional. Do not type the square brackets.

Example: FOREACH <loop selector> [<cursor variable>]. The cursor variable is optional and can be omitted.

Limitations

File names are limited to eight characters with a three-character extension. Often the extension will be supplied by the template. Names must begin with a letter, cannot include embedded blanks, and can only contain letters, numbers, and the underscore character (_).
The following file extensions are reserved by the template language.

Extension	*File type*
APP	Application object
BAR	Bar menu
POP	Pop-up menu
STR	Structure list (pop-up)
FIL	Files list (pop-up)
VAL	Values list (pop-up)
BCH	Batch (pop-up)
SCR	Screen form
LBL	Label form
FRM	Report form
NPI	Source for DGEN.EXE

Compiler Commands

Command	Description
INCLUDE <file>	Include named file.
#CODON	Include assembler statements in listing.
#CODOFF	Omit assembler statements in listing (default).
#LSTON	Turns list output on if -l included in command line that invoked compiler (default).
#LSTOFF	If list output is on, # turns it off.

Definition Commands

These commands define variables and user-defined functions.

DEFINE	Declares the beginning of a template language user-defined function. Syntax: `DEFINE <function name> ([<variable name 1>][,<variable name 2>...]) ... RETURN ENDDEF` Rules: UDFs must begin with DEFINE and end with ENDDEF. DEFINEs may not be nested. Anything declared within a DEFINE is local to that UDF. If there is a pending value when RETURN/ENDDEF is reached, that pending value is the value returned.

ENUM	Substitutes a numeric or string constant value for a symbolic name at compile time. Syntax: `ENUM <symbol name> = <exp> [,,<symbol name> = <exp>] ... ]` Rules: After the first numeric assignment to a symbol, subsequent symbols are assigned values in increasing sequence. A new assignment starts a new sequence. Spaces can be used instead of commas. Sequential values are 0–*n*, A–Z. The entire ASCII standard set is available. Values greater than 255 are not output.
VAR	Declares variable names for later use within the template. Syntax: `VAR <variable name 1> [,<variable name 2>]...` Rules: <variable name *n*> must begin with a letter or underscore. Successive characters may be letters, underscores, or digits. A variable name can be up to 200 characters long. Variables declared within a DEFINE are local. Variables declared outside a DEFINE are global to the template. Local variables take precedence over global ones.

Program Flow Commands

CASE ... ENDCASE	Selects one action from a list.
	Syntax:
	`CASE <exp> OF [CASE] <n:> <commands>`
	`[ ... OTHERWISE] ... ENDCASE`
	Rules:
	CASE selectors (n:) must be numeric unless the ENUM command is used before the CASE statement.

GOTO	Transfers flow of control to a labeled statement. Syntax: `GOTO <label>` Rules: The specified label name follows the same rules as a variable name, must appear on a command line by itself, and must have a colon (:) as the last character.

IF ... THEN ... ENDIF

Tests for true/false and executes separate commands depending on the result.
Syntax:
```
IF <logical condition> [THEN] <commands>
[ELSE <commands>] ENDIF
```
Rules:
Nesting rules same as dBASE IF ... ENDIF

RETURN

Inside UDF, exits to calling routine and returns pending value if any. Outside UDF, terminates template run.
Syntax:
```
RETURN [<exp>]
```
Rules:
Command is optional inside UDFs. If not included, the RETURN value will be the pending value.
Outside UDFs RETURN terminates the template run. If any error condition exists at the end of the run, RETURN will send a value other than 0. Always specify RETURN 0 at the end of any template.
If using the template from within dBASE IV, error messages will be displayed. If using DGEN.EXE, check the DOS errorlevel variable.

Loop Commands

FOREACH ... NEXT

Processes repeated occurrences of DOS files, design object files, elements, or attributes.
Syntax:
```
FOREACH <loop selector> [<cursor variable>]
[IN <cursor variable>] ...
NEXT [<cursor variable>]
```
Rules:
Each construct declares a cursor variable that moves through some repeated data until it reaches the end of the data.
The FOREACH loop syntax always ends with the NEXT [<cursor variable>] command.
Loop selectors are found in the DEF files. For a complete list, see page 4–8 of the dBASE IV *Template Language* manual.

DO WHILE/UNTIL ... ENDDO — Similar to the same command in dBASE.

Syntax:

```
DO [<commands>] WHILE/UNTIL [<logical
condition>] ... ENDDO
```

Rules:

Statements that appear between the DO and the WHILE will be executed at least once.

Statements between the WHILE and the ENDDO are executed after the WHILE test. If the test returns logical false, the statements will not be executed.

If UNTIL is used in place of WHILE, the test is reversed. Statements between the UNTIL and the ENDDO will be executed before the test. Even if the test returns false, the statements will have been executed once.

Both WHILE and UNTIL may be used to conditionally exit from the FOR and FOREACH loops.

FOR ... NEXT — Used for incremental looping

Syntax:

```
FOR <variable name> = <expN1> TO <expN2>
[STEP <constant>] ... NEXT [<variable name>]
```

Rules:

The counter <variable name> is declared by the FOR statement. It is initialized to <expN1>.

The test FOR <variable name> = <expN2> is performed at the start of the loop. If <variable name> <= <expN2>, the commands within the loop are executed. NEXT increments <variable name> by <constant>. The loop may be executed from zero to many times depending on the results of this test. If STEP is not included, NEXT increments by 1.

You may use the ENUM command to assign a readable symbol to <constant>.

EXIT — Transfers control to the first statement following a loop construct.

Syntax:

```
Beginning of loop ... [EXIT] ... End of loop
```

Rules:

This command can be used in any of the loop constructs: DO WHILE, FOREACH, and FOR.

Control is passed to the command following the NEXT or ENDDO statement.

LOOP   Transfers control to the beginning of the current loop.
                                     Syntax:
                                     `Beginning of loop ... [LOOP] ... End of loop`
                                     Rules:
                                     Inside a FOREACH or FOR loop, control advances to the
                                     next WHILE or UNTIL test.
                                     If there is no WHILE or UNTIL test, the current cursor or
                                     counter is incremented and control is passed to the starting
                                     FOREACH or FOR.
                                     Inside a DO WHILE, control advances to the next WHILE or
                                     UNTIL test. If there is no test, control passes to the top of the
                                     DO loop.

Functions

Function	*Description*
ALLTRIM(<expC>)	Trims all leading and trailing blanks.
APPEND(<filename>)	Adds text to the end of an existing text file. If the named file does not exist, it will be created.
ASC(<expC>)	Returns the ASCII decimal value of the first character of <expC>.
ASKUSER(<expC1>,<expC2>,<expN>)	Opens a dialog box, displays the prompt string <expC1>, a default answer string <expC2>, and assigns a maximum length for input <expN>. The maximum value for <expN> is 78. The response is captured to a previously defined variable, viz., <variable name> = ASKUSER().
AT(<expC1>,<expC2>)	Returns the starting location of <expC1> in <expC2>. Returns 0 if not found.
ATALPHA(<expC>)	Returns the location of the first nonblank alphanumeric character in the expression.
ATOMC(<cursor>,<expN>)	Returns the attribute value of the selector referenced by the cursor variable and the IID given by <expN>. Allows the programmer to reference selectors by number rather than name.

BACKSLASH()	Inserts a \ into the output text file. Used to reference path names.
BREAKPOINT(<expC>)	Displays the current value of <expC> and requests the level of debugging action. If the -1 option has been used with DGEN.EXE, <expC> is written to the output file.
CGET()	Waits for any key to be pressed and captures the keystroke.
CHR(<expN>)	Returns the character corresponding to ASCII decimal value <expN>.
CLS()	Clears the screen and positions the cursor at 0,0.
COL1()	Returns the number of the first column of an object frame. If there is no frame, returns 0.
COL2()	Returns the number of the last column of an object frame. If there is no frame, returns 0.
COPY(<filename>)	Copies the contents of the named text file into the current output file.
CPUT(<expC>)	Writes the specified string to the current location of the screen cursor. Used to place messages on the screen.
CREATE(<filename>)	Creates and opens the named text file. Any text output before a CREATE() or APPEND() is placed in a file called <object name>.OUT.
CURLINE()	Returns the current line number being output. Reset to 0 when PAGEJECT() is executed.
CURSOR_POS(<expN1>,<expN2>)	Places the cursor at screen row <expN1> and column <expN2>. Coordinates measured as in dBASE IV.
DATE()	Returns the system date and time in the format mm-dd-yy h:mmx. where x. is a. or p.
DEBUG(<expN>)	Determines the amount and type of information output during code generation. For more information, see Chapter 11.
EOC(<cursor variable>)	Tests whether the cursor variable has reached the end of the set. If there are more elements to process, returns a 0. Returns a 1 otherwise.

EXEC(<filename>)	Runs the external program contained in <filename>. Can be used only with DGEN.EXE.
FILEDATE(<filename>)	Returns the DOS date and time stamp on <filename> in the form yyyy-mm-dd hh:mm:ss. A 24-hour clock is used.
FILEDRIVE(<filename>)	Returns the drive letter from a filename. See FILEPATH().
FILEERASE(<filename>)	Erases the file <filename>. May include a drive and path.
FILEEXIST(<filename>)	Tests for the existence of <filename>. May include a drive and path.
FILENAME(<filename>)	Extracts the filename and extension from a fully specified path.
FILEOK(<filename>)	Checks for a valid DOS file name.
FILEPATH(<filename>)	Returns the path portion of a fully specified file name.
FILEROOT(<filename>)	Returns the root of a file name (up to eight characters).
FILESIZE(<filename>)	Returns the size of the specified file.
FILETYPE(<filename>)	Returns the three-character extension of a file name.
GETENV(<expC>)	Returns the value of the DOS environmental variable specified by <expC>. For example, GETENV("PATH") will return the current DOS path as a character string.
IIDC(<cursor>)	Returns the integer selector value of the attribute pointed to by the cursor as a numeric value.
LEN(<expC>)	Returns the length of the specified string.
LMARG(<expN>)	Sets the left margin for subsequent text output. Any argument less than or equal to 1 will reset the left margin to 0. Use this function to indent commands.
LTRIM(<expC>)	Trims leading blanks from a string.

MAKEC(<expN>[,<cursor>] Creates a cursor using the internal selector number. Use the construct @<selector> for <expN>. Use <cursor> only if creating a DOS file cursor.

MAX(<expN1>,<expN2>) Returns the maximum of the two numeric expressions.

MIN(<expN1>,<expN2>) Returns the minimum of the two numeric expressions.

NEWFRAME(<expC>) Allows you to change the current object being processed. Returns a 0 if the change was successful, 1 if not. Used in the applications generator to process multiple applications elements.

NEXTC(<cursor>) Advances the cursor by one position. No return value.

NMSG(<expC>) Displays <expC> centered on the navigation line (23 or 41 if in 43-line EGA mode).

NUMSET(<expN>) Returns the internal numeric setting of dBASE indicators defined and documented in BUILTIN.DEF. In DGEN.EXE, always returns 0.

PAGEJECT() Outputs a CHR(12) and resets the CURLINE() function to 0.

PAGEL(<expN>) Sets a constant page length for output. Set <expN> to 0 or a negative number for no page breaks.

PATHEXIST(<expC>) Returns a 1 if the path exists, 0 otherwise.

PAUSE(<expC>) Stops template interpretation and displays a message to the user on the message line (24 or 42 in 43-line EGA mode). Waits for any keystroke before continuing.

PMSG(<expC>) Displays <expC> on the prompt line (24 or 42).

POKE(<expC>[,<expC ...]) Inserts the specified character expression into the text without any formatting. For example, {POKE(CHR(10))} will insert a line feed without the carriage return added by the PRINT() function.

PRINT(<expC>)

Outputs <expC> to the text file. A carriage return is automatically added to line feed characters. CURLINE() and LMARG() settings are maintained at their current values.

REPLICATE(<expC>,<expN>)

Repeats <expC> <expN> times.

ROW1()

Returns the number of the first row of an object frame. Returns a 0 if there is no frame.

ROW2()

Returns the number of the last row of an object frame. Returns a 0 if there is no frame.

RTRIM(<expC>)

Removes trailing blanks.

SCREEN(<expN>)

Extracts line <expN> from a screen object.

SETC(<cursor>,<expN>)

Moves the specified cursor to a new relative position. The cursor is advanced by <expN> positions. Within a FOREACH loop, the default is 1. SETC() does not have to be used in that case, as the cursor is automatically advanced by one position each time through the loop.

SPACE(<expN>)

Inserts the specified number of blank spaces into the text output file.

STR(<expN>)

Converts a numeric-type variable into a string-type variable.

STRSET(<expN>)

Allows the programmer to determine the internal character setting of dBASE IV indicators. These are defined and documented in BUILTIN.DEF. For example, {STRSET(_DEFDRIVE)} will return a C if the dBASE default drive was set to C.

SUBSTR(<expC>,<expN1>[,<expN2>])

Extracts a substring from <expC> starting at position <expN1> and continuing for <expN2> characters. If <expN2> is not specified, the remainder of <expC> is returned.

TABTO(<expN>)

Moves <expN> columns to the right in the output text file. Tabs are expanded; that is, blank spaces are output rather than the ASCII tab character.

TEXTCLOSE()	Closes a file opened by TEXTOPEN(). Files are automatically closed at the end of a template.
TEXTGETC()	Returns the character at the current position of the open text output file.
TEXTGETL()	Returns the line from the current position of the open text output file. The line may be up to 254 characters long. Line end characters and carriage return–line feeds are removed. If the line is longer than 254 characters, only the first 254 characters are returned, and the position is set to the next character in the line.
TEXTGPOS()	Returns the current file position of the open text output file.
TEXTOPEN()	Opens and initializes a text file for input. The file position is set to the start of the file. Returns a 1 if the file was successfully opened, 0 otherwise.
TEXTSPOS(<expN>)	Sets the file position in the text file to the number specified. The position specified should be a nonnegative number.

TYPEC(<cursor>)	Returns a number indicating the type of the value of the attribute currently pointed to by the cursor:
	    1: numeric
	    2: string
	    3: element
	    4: object
	    5: dosfile

UPPER(<expC>)	Converts <expC> to all uppercase.
VAL(<expC>)	Converts <expC> to its numeric equivalent.
VALC(<cursor>)	Returns the actual value of the attribute pointed to by the cursor. May be a number or a string. The value must be printable and an attribute, not an element or object.
VERSION()	Returns the generator version number. Useful for documenting text output files to keep track of which version of the applications generator was used.

Index

A

; , 97–98, 155, 503
{ }, 55, 503
( ), 503
\, 503
//, 55, 84, 503
" , 503
!=, 79
\\, 84
({,}), 138
'{ // }', 138
{"{ // }"}, 209
@S, 95
@...SAY...GETs processing

    FORM.COD
        boxes, handling of, 91–92
        for calculated fields, 91
        GETs, 95–96
        for memory variables, 91
        MESSAGEs, 97–98
        PICTUREs, 94–95
        RANGE processing, 96
        SAYs, handling of, 92–94
        VALID, 96–97
        WHENs and DEFAULTs, 97

Abort printing, REPORT.COD, 208
ACTIVATE SCREEN, 471
AD_, applications generator, 319
AGAIN, 466
ALLTRIM( ), 466

APPEND, 338
Append query, 47–49
APPLCTN.DEF, 56
Application definition file, 10
Application menu, 334–335
Application program, Query By
    Example (QBE), 21
Applications Definition screen,
    333–334
Applications generator, 7
    Application menu, 334–335
    Applications Definition screen,
        333–334
    backup, 350, 352
    Browse pad, 340
    COD files used, 319
        AD_ and AS_, 319
    exit pad, 343
    generating code, 354
    initial set-up, 333
    main menu, 335–338
    main program, 320
    menu bars
        for adding data to database,
        338–340
        assigning actions to, 338
    multiuser code, 331
    pop-up menu, adding, 345–350
    programs
        Applications generator
        template, listing of code,
        377–432

customer oriented programs
(CUSTAPP.PRG), listing
of code, 355–368,
371–376
KEYSET.PRG, listing of
code, 369–370
recommendations for improvement
index order, 325–328
omitting code not needed,
328–332
positioning of pointer,
320–325
record pointer, moving, 343
set new key pad, 341
splash screen, 334
usefulness of, 333
windows, defining, 352
AS_, applications generator, 319
ASCII characters, 93, 437, 441
ASCII sorts, 37
ASKUSER( ), 89
AS_MENU.COD, 273
AS_POSIT.COD, 272
Assembly language output, 77
Assignment operators, listing of, 504
AT( ), 94
AUTOEXEC.BAT, 37, 104

B

Backup
applications generator, 350, 352
COD files, 75
Barcnt, 264
Batch file, debugging, 494–497
Batch process, menu for, 13
BEGIN TRANSACTION, 470
BELL ON, 335
Binary operators, listing of, 504–505
Bitwise logical operators, listing of,
505
Blank lines
handling of, 120, 122
processing, 146–147

Blank space, 503
Body of report, 198–200
Boxes, creation of, FORM.COD,
91–92
BREAKPOINT( ), 491, 492, 493
Browse pad, applications generator,
340
BROWSETABLE=, 463
BROWSETABLE BOX,
FORMBROW.GEN, 452, 460–461
BUILTIN.DEF, 82, 190
templates, 55, 56, 60, 64

C

CALCFLDS( ), 140, 142
CALCULATE, 36, 37
Calculated fields
in FORM.COD, 91
printing code, LABEL.COD,
137–138
Query By Example (QBE), 30–34
usefulness of, 30, 34
with Views, 34
CARRY, ON setting, 85
CARRY bug, FORMBROW.GEN, 468
CASE, 149
CASE tools, 5
CHK4NUL, LABEL.COD, 157
CHR( ), 92, 437
COD files
backup, 75
insertion into DTL subdirectory,
75
COL1( ), 437
COL2( ), 437
Columns, printing, LABEL.COD,
139–140
Compiler, 4
commands, 508
interpreter switches, 498, 499
listing directives, 498
option switches, 497
template, 4

CONFIG.DB, 83
Constants
  defining, 78–79
  FORM.COD, 78–79
  listing of constants file, 115–118
CONTINUE, 142
COUNTC( ), 129
CREATE( ), 61, 82
CREATE APPLICATION, 333
CTOD( ), 138, 209
CTOD(SPACE(8)), 138
Cursor variable ecursor, 129

D

Data array, set-up, LABEL.COD,
  140–144
Data entry screen, 66–67, 71
Data typing, constants, defining, 78–79
Dates (DD), 94
dBASE IV
  files and extensions, 9
  future uses, 501–502
  special format files, 3, 8
  versions of files produced, 8, 10
  video modes, 66
dBASE ORDER( ), 269
DBFOPEN( ), 263
Debugging
  avoiding repetitions of, 490
  batch file, 494–497
  and compiling program, 487, 488
  DEBUG, use of, 491–494
  non-application objects, 496
  SET DTL_NOGEN=ON, 497
  SET DTL_TRACE=ON, 497
  steps in process, 490–493
DEFAULT, processing of, 97
DEFINE, 63, 80
DEFINE BAR, 346
DEFINE MENU, 346
DEFINE WINDOW, 84
Definition commands, listing of,
  508–509

Delimiters
  listing of, 503
  output to file and, 138
Design objects, 8, 9
  interaction of, 14
Detail lines, REPORT.COD, 205
DGEN.EXE, 487, 491, 494, 495, 496
DIFFERENCE( ), 27, 44, 46, 47
Display
  setting mode, 71
  values, testing, 81
DO, 202, 203
DO CASE, 83, 203, 264
Documentation template
  creating documentation file,
    434–435
  program code, listing of, 442–447
  programs in, 433
  resetting default, 435
  screen displays, dumping to
    output file, 435–441
DOCUMENT.GEN, 7
DOS, GEN files, setting defaults, 104
DO WHILE, 129, 131, 138, 208
DTC command, 77–78
DTL subdirectory, insertion of COD
  files, 75

E

EDIT, 338
ENDDEF, 63
ENDDO, 129, 131
ENDIF, 146
ENDPRINTJOB, 208
END TRANSACTION, 470
ENUM, 78–79, 81
EOC( ), 129
EOC(k), 144
ERROR, 332
Error messages, string constants
  defined for, 190
Error trapping, FORM.COD, 79–80
Exit pad, applications generator, 343

F

FIELDS, 338
File closing section, templates, 62–63
File extensions
    caution about, 12
    dBASE IV files and extensions, 9
    extensions/file types in template
      language, 507
FILEOK( ), 82
File pick list, 10
FILEROOT, 82
FILTER, 338
FIRST, 42
First occurrences, 42
Footers, REPORT.COD, group
    footers, 197, 209
FOR, 338
FOREACH, 85, 86, 93, 129, 131, 138,
    144, 147, 149, 155, 200, 209
FOREACH BAND_ELEMENT, 194
FOREACHNEXT, 84
Form Template
    @...SAY...GETs processing,
      90–99
        boxes, handling of, 91–92
        for calculated fields, 91
        GETs, 95–96
        for memory variables, 91
        MESSAGEs, 97–98
        PICTUREs, 94–95
        RANGE processing, 96
        SAYs, handling of, 92–94
        VALID, 96–97
        WHENs and DEFAULTs, 97
    COD files, backup, 75
    compiling template, 77–78
    constants, defining, 78–79
    constants file, listing of, 115–118
    display values, testing, 81
    error trapping, 79–80
    format file
        creation of, 82–89
        fields, processing, 84–85

        initialization code, 83–84
        new file, 99–103
        SET CARRY, 87–88
        Window, 85–86
    header, personalizing, 76–77, 78
    multiuser code, 89–90
    program code, listing of, 105–115
    user-defined functions, set-up, 80
    variables
        defining, 80
        initializing, 80
    writing to dBASE directory, 78
Format file
    FORM.COD
        fields, processing, 84–85
        initialization code, 83–84
        SET CARRY, 87–88
        Window, 85–86
FORMBROW.GEN, 7
    BROWSETABLE BOX, 452,
      460–461
    dBASE IV differentiation from
      FORM.GEN, 452
    documentation limitations, 451
    GETQBE( ), 465–467
    headers, 464–465
    keykill, 471–472
    macros, use of, 456–458, 465,
      467–468, 472
    programs
        CUSTINV.PRG, listing of
          code, 475–486
        CUSTINV.QBE, listing of
          code, 474
        CUSTINV.SCX, listing of
          code, 473
    query, design of, 452–453
    recommendations for
      improvement, 459–460
        CARRY bug, 468
    SAYing/GETing/BROWSEing,
      470–471
    screen form, design of, 453–456
    SCX file, defining, 461–464

SELECT( ), 468–469
SET FIELDS, 469
transaction processing, 469–470
FORM.DEF, 56
FOUND( ), 27
FRM file, REPORT.COD
check for, 192
scanning for band types, 194–196
FUNCTION, 146, 206
Functions, listing of, 512–517

G

GEN files, setting defaults, 104
GET, 89, 269
GETCOLOR( ), 86
GETQBE( ), FORMBROW.GEN,
465–467
GETs, processing of, 95–96
GETSTYLE( ), 154
GO TO, 77
GOTO TOP, 320, 321
GROUP, 194, 195
Group bands, REPORT.COD
handling of, 203–205
height of, 206–208
Group break variables,
REPORT.COD, reset of, 208
Group by, 37, 38

H

Headers
FORMBROW.GEN, 464–465
FORM.COD, personalizing,
76–77, 78
LABEL.COD, 132, 133
REPORT.COD, 191–192, 203
group headers, 209
templates, 53–55, 61
Hours (HH), 94

I

ID FOUND ..AND. .NOT. EOF( ), 142
if!Fld_editable, 93
IIF( ), 96–97, 180, 181
INCLUDEd files, 488
Include section, templates, 55–56
Indexes
include indexes option, 42–43
index order, applications
generator, recommendations for
improvement, 325–328
index swaps, quick applications,
269–271
Initialization
FORM.COD, 83–84
LABEL.COD, 128
REPORT.COD, 190–191, 193
variables, 80
INKEY( ), 471
Inner join, 21–25, 27–29
Introduction, REPORT.COD, 202–203
ISFOUND[ ], 139, 142, 147
Iteration, LABEL.COD, 155

J

Joins
inner join, 21–25, 27–29
outer join, 25
self-join, 20

K

Keykill, FORMBROW.GEN, 471–472
KEYLIST[ ], 269

L

Label Template, 54
blank lines, handling of, 120, 122
CHK4NUL, 157
complexities related to, 119–120

file names, creating and checking, 132

header, 132, 133

initialization, 128

input of initial code, 132–136

label code, 122–127

lines, calculation of, 129–131

multiuser code, 136–137

printing code
    calculated fields, 137–138
    columns, 139–140
    data array, set-up, 140–144
    multiple copies, 138–139

program code, listing of, 159–177

selectors, 132–133

setup for label, 120

user-defined functions
    blank lines, processing, 146–147
    iteration, 155
    looping, 155–157
    non-blank lines, 147–149
    print width, 149–154
    STYLE, 154

LABEL.DEF, 56

LASTKEY( ), 135

LEN( ), 149

LIKE( ), 27, 43–44

Lines
    labels
        blank lines, 120, 122, 146–147
        calculation of, 129–131
        non-blank lines, 147–149
    reports, blank lines, 180–181

LKSYS(0), 137

LKSYS(1), 137

LKSYS(2), 89

LMARG(4), 138–139

LOCATE, 27, 142

Looping
    LABEL.COD, 155–157
    loop commands, listing of, 510–512

LOWER( ), 86

M

m->, 94

Macros, FORMBROW.GEN, 456–458, 465, 467–468, 472

Mailing labels, 6–7 *See also* LABEL.COD

Main menu, applications generator, 335–338

MAKEC( ), 85

Many-to-many relations, Query By Example (QBE), 25–27

Mark query, 47

Matching operators, 45–47
    DIFFERENCE( ), 44, 46, 47
    LIKE, 43–44
    SOUNDEX( ), 46–47
    SOUNDS LIKE, 44

Memory variables, in FORM.COD, 91, 94

Menu bars
    for adding data to database, 338–340
    assigning actions to, 338

Menu Template, 273

MENU.GEN, 273

MENU.OUT, 488

Menus, type of system, 10

MESSAGE, processing of, 97–98

Minutes (MM), 94

MLINE( ), 141

MODIFY APPLICATION, 333

MODIFY COMMAND, 77, 253, 435

Multiple copies, labels, 138–139

Multitable forms. *See* FORMBROW.GEN

Multiuser code
    applications generator, 331
    FORM.COD, 89–90
    LABEL.COD, 136–137
    quick applications, 262
    REPORT.COD, 193–194

N

NOCLEAR, 471
NOMENU, 471
NOSAVE, 37
NOUPDATE, 37
NUL2ZERO( ), 86, 91
NUMSET( ), 81, 82

O

ON KEY, 471
ON PAGE, 202
ON PAGE AT, 198
OPEN WINDOW, 95
Operators
    assignment operators, 504
    binary operators, 504–505
    bitwise logical operators, 505
    precedence of, 506
    shift operators, 506
    unary operators, 504
ORDER TAG, 469
OUTBOX( ), 86, 93
OUTCOLOR( ), 93, 98
Outer join, 25

P

Page eject, REPORT.COD, 197
Page length, REPORT.COD
    calculation of, 198
    check of, 196
Page offset, columns, 147
PARAMETERS, 135, 206
PAUSE, 79
Pick list
    file pick list, 10
    queries, 29–30
    structure pick list, 12
    value pick list, 12
PICOUT( ), 96
Picture functions, 94
    adding to template, 152–154

picture template holder, 94–95
Pointer, application generator
    moving, 343
    positioning, 320–325
Pop-up menu
    adding, applications generator,
        345–350
    set-up of, 264
Printing code, labels, 137–144
PRINTJOB, 135, 198
Print-system memory variables, 263
Print width, LABEL.COD, 149–154
PRIVATE, 133, 192
PRNTRTRY, 332
PROCEDURE, 208, 210
PROCEDURE Setstore, 262
Processing section, templates, 58–61
Program code, listing of
    applications generator
        customer oriented programs
            (CUSTAPP.PRG),
            355–368, 371–376
            KEYSET.PRG, 377–432
        FORMBROW.GEN
            CUSTINV.PRG, 475–486
            CUSTINV.QBE, 474
            CUSTINV.SCX, 473
        FORM.COD, 105–115
        LABEL.COD, 159–177
        quick applications, 274–291
        REPORT.COD, 211–252
Program flow commands, 509–510
Programmable program generator. *See*
    Template language
PUTFLD( ), 150

Q

Queries
    functions of, 18
    ordinary queries, 17
    update queries, 17, 47–51
        view as result, 18

Query By Example (QBE)
  in application program, 21
  calculated fields with, 30–34
  inner and outer joints, 21–25
  many-to-many relations, 25–27
  matching operators, 45–47
  omissions, 8
  pick list, 29–30
  select and project operations,
    18–21
  selection/projection/inner join,
    27–29
  summary operators, 34–37
QUICKAPP.DEF, 56
Quick applications
  basic setup, 258–261
  changes to QUICKAPP.COD
    source code, 261–262
  customer oriented programs
    (CUSTOMER.PRG), listing of
    code, 292–317
  disk space used, 257
  listing of code, 292–317
  multiuser code, 262
  program code, listing of, 274–291
  recommendations for
    improvements
      clean up of code, 262–264
      index swaps, 269–271
      reports and labels, 264–269
      set data type for SEEK,
        271–273
  usefulness of, 257
QUIT, 343

R

RAND( ), 36–37
Random numbers, generation of, 36–37
RANGE, processing of, 96
Replace query, 49–51
Report Template, 54
  abort printing, 208
  blank lines, 180–181

  body of report, 198–200
  close of print job, 205
  complexities of, 179–180
  detail lines, 205
  footers, group footers, 197, 209
  FRM file
    check for, 192
    scanning for band types,
      194–196
  generated code, 181–190
  group bands
    handling of, 203–205
    height of, 206–208
  group break variables, reset of, 208
  header, 191–192, 203
  headers, group headers, 209
  initialization, 190–191, 193
  introduction, 202–203
  multiuser code, 193–194
  page eject, 197
  page length
    calculation of, 198
    check of, 196
  plain reports processing, 210
  program code, listing of, 211–252
  reset system, 210
  serial procedure generation, 210
  summary variables
    initialization, 200–204
    reset of, 197–198, 209
  variables, update of, 208
REPORT.COD, 54
  See Report Template
REPORT.DEF, 56
Reports, 7 *See also* REPORT.COD
RETURN, 343
ROLLBACK( ), 469
ROW1( ), 437
ROW2( ), 437

S

SAMPLE, 157
SAY, processing of, 92–94

SCAN ... ENDSCAN, 49, 51
SCOPE, 338
SCREEN(<expN>), 441
Screen forms, 6
    See also Form Template
SCRNDUMP( ), 435–436
SCX file, defining,
    FORMBROW.GEN, 461–464
Seconds (SS), 94
SEEK, set data type, for reports and
    labels, 271–273
SELECT( ), FORMBROW.GEN,
    468–469
Select and project operations, Query
    By Example (QBE), 18–21
Selection/projection/inner join, Query
    By Example (QBE), 27–29
Selectors
    classes of, 56
    dBASE IV files, 56
    LABEL.COD, 132–133
    in template language, 4
Self-join, 20
SEPARATE( ), 150, 153
Serial procedure generation,
    REPORT.COD, 210
SET( ), 36, 134, 197, 262, 321, 343
SET CARRY, 84
    output in FORM.COD, 87–88
SET CATALOG, 36
SET DISPLAY TO, 83
SET DTL_NOGEN=ON, debugging,
    497
SET DTL_TRACE=ON, debugging,
    497
SET FIELDS, 18, 467, 469
SET FIELDS TO, 20, 27, 34
SET FIELDS TO ALL EXCEPT, 469
SET FILTER, 18
SET FILTER TO, 21, 27, 34
SET FILTER TO FOUND(2), 27
SET INDEX TO, 320, 325
SET NEAR ON, 27
SET OFF, 36

SET ORDER TO, 320, 325, 327
SET PRINT ON/OFF, 322
SET RELATION, 18
SET RELATION FROM, 25
SET RELATION TO, 25, 27
SET SAFETY, 36
SET SKIP TO, 27
SET SPACE ON/OFF, 134
Setstore procedure, 262
SET TALK, 83, 133
SET TMP =, 37
Shift operators, listing of, 506
Sorting, 37–38, 41–42
    options for, 37–38
SOUNDEX( ), 46–47
SOUNDS LIKE, 44
Splash screen, 10, 11, 258
    applications generator, 334
STATUS, 84
STD( ), 208
STRSET, 82
Structure pick list, 12
STYLE, LABEL.COD, 154
Summaries, by group, 37, 38
Summary operators
    first occurrences, 42
    Query By Example (QBE), 34–37
Summary variables, REPORT.COD
    initialization, 200–204
    reset of, 197–198, 209
Symbols and conventions, template
    language, 507

T

TABLEFIELD, 463, 464, 469
TAGLIST[ ], 269
TAGs, 341
Template language
    compiler commands, 508
    data types, 78–79
    definition commands, 508–509
    delimiters, 503
    file extensions/file types, 507

functions, 512–517
loop commands, 510–512
operators
    assignment operators, 504
    binary operators, 504–505
    bitwise logical operators,
      505
    precedence of, 506
    shift operators, 506
    unary operators, 504
program flow commands, 509–510
selectors, 4, 56
symbols and conventions, 507
use of, 3, 5
Template objects, 8, 9
Templates. *See also* FORM.COD;
  LABEL.COD; REPORT.COD
  BUILTIN.DEF, 55, 56, 60, 64
  data entry screen, 66–67, 71
  file closing section, 62–63
  function of program, 66
  header, 53–55, 61
  include section, 55–56
  processing section, 58–61
  updates and, 54
  user-defined functions, 63
  variable initialization section,
    56–58
TEXTGET1( ), 463, 465
TMP4LBL[ ], 140
TO PRINT, 264
TRACE, 332
Transaction processing,
  FORMBROW.GEN, 469–470
TRANSFORM( ), 148
TYPE( ), 269

U

Unary operators, listing of, 504
UNIQUE, 42
Unmark query, 47
Update queries
  Append query, 47–49

Mark query, 47
Replace query, 49–51
Unmark query, 47
UPPER( ), 82, 466
USE, 263, 466
User-defined functions
  FORM.COD, 80
  LABEL.COD, non-blank lines,
    147–149
  templates, 63

V

VALID, processing of, 96–97
Value pick list, 12
VAR( ), 80, 208
Variables
  defining, 80
  initialization section of templates,
    56–58
  initializing, 80
  REPORT.COD, update of, 208
Video modes, 66
Views
  adding fields to, 18
  Calculated fields with, 34
  creation of, 18
  order of fields, 18
  removing field from, 18
  writing to disk file, 18

W

WHEN, processing of, 97
WHILE, 338
Windows
  creation in FORM.COD, 85–86
  defining, applications generator,
    352
WITH, 341